IRELAND

GUIDE

BE A TRAVELER - NOT A TOURIST!

AMAZON.COM REVIEWERS LOVE
OPEN ROAD'S IRELAND GUIDE!

• *"When your time is valuable don't waste it. A must read for anyone planning to visit Ireland."*

• *"The thing that most impressed me were the extensive write-ups on the places to visit, hotels, and restaurants -- they were far more in-depth than any other guidebook I looked at on Ireland."*

• *"This is a terrific book for the traveler returning to Ireland."*

• *"This book is a must have if you want to see Ireland in all of its glory!"*

CRITICAL ACCLAIM FOR
OPEN ROAD TRAVEL GUIDES

*Whether you're going abroad or planning a trip in the United States, take Open Road along on your journey. Our books have been praised by **Travel & Leisure**, **The Los Angeles Times**, **Newsday**, **Booklist**, **US News & World Report**, **Endless Vacation**, **American Bookseller**, **Coast to Coast**, and many other magazines and newspapers!*

Don't just see the world – experience it with Open Road!

ABOUT THE AUTHOR

Dan McQuillan is a professional writer specializing in travel and technical subjects. He is a direct descendant of Niall the First, who ruled Ireland from 380 to 405 AD. Dan makes his home in Denver, Colorado, with his wife and six children. If you'd like to contact Dan about anything in this book, his e-mail address is *danielmcq@juno.com*.

BE A TRAVELER, NOT A TOURIST - WITH OPEN ROAD TRAVEL GUIDES!

Open Road Publishing has guide books to exciting, fun destinations on four continents. As veteran travelers, our goal is to bring you the best travel guides available anywhere!

No small task, but here's what we offer:

• All Open Road travel guides are written by authors with a distinct, opinionated point of view – not some sterile committee or team of writers. Our authors are experts in the areas covered and are polished writers.

• Our guides are geared to people who want to make their own travel choices. We'll show you how to discover the real destination – not just see some place from a tour bus window.

• We're strong on the basics, but we also provide terrific choices for those looking to get off the beaten path and experience the country or city – not just see it or pass through it.

• We give you the best, but we also tell you about the worst and what to avoid. Nobody should waste their time and money on their hard-earned vacation because of bad or inadequate travel advice.

• Our guides assume nothing. We tell you everything you need to know to have the trip of a lifetime – presented in a fun, literate, no-nonsense style.

• And, above all, we welcome your input, ideas, and suggestions to help us put out the best travel guides possible.

IRELAND GUIDE

BE A TRAVELER - NOT A TOURIST!

Dan McQuillan

OPEN ROAD PUBLISHING

This book is dedicated to Teague McQuillan, who courageously left his beloved Ulster in 1617 for the liberty America offered.

3rd Edition

Text Copyright ©2001 by Dan McQuillan
Maps Copyright ©2001 by Open Road Publishing
- All Rights Reserved -

Library of Congress Control No. 00-134134
ISBN 1-892975-42-4

Front and back cover photos courtesy of Bord Failte (Irish Tourist Board), New York. Maps by Rob Perry.

The author has made every effort to be as accurate as possible, but neither the author nor the publisher assume responsibility for the services provided by any business listed in this guide; for any errors or omissions; or any loss, damage, or disruptions in your travels for any reason.

TABLE OF CONTENTS

19. SEARCHING FOR YOUR IRISH ROOTS   548

INDEX   560

MAPS

SIDEBARS

1. INTRODUCTION

I have traveled to many beautiful and exciting parts of the world, but I am always enchanted when I return to Ireland. And you'll be enchanted too. From the Cliffs of Moher to Dublin and Dunluce, from the Book of Kells to the Creevykeel Court Tomb, you'll experience some of the best and most beautiful sights this world has to offer.

On many of your previous travels you have probably sent postcards home to family and friends. Well, Ireland *is* a postcard. Grandeur and simplicity, mirth and meditation are all found in abundance on this beautiful green island.

And I'll help you experience it all. I have made every effort to ferret out each interesting nook and engaging cranny in Ireland.

But there's more to see than the scenery. Ireland is a place you must experience. Talk to the locals. Watch the buskers (street performers) ply their trade. Talk to the school children who want to have their pictures taken. Relax as your car or bicycle is engulfed by a sea of sheep or cattle headed nowhere in particular and in no hurry.

Ireland is a mystical, magical, mirthful land where leprechauns and shamrocks, miracles and massacres are woven together as tightly as the knit of an Aran sweater. I guarantee that you will have a rich and rewarding experience as you tour the Emerald Isle. An anonymous Irish poet wrote: "If you're lucky enough to be Irish...you're lucky enough." Even if your descendants do not come from the Emerald Isle (most unfortunate), you'll feel like an adopted member of the family during and after your visit.

So come along and prowl through the ruins of an ancient race. Drink their beer and listen to their tales. Learn of their past and appreciate their future. And maybe even envy their wee green corner of the world.

If this is your first trip to the Emerald Isle, it's a good bet it won't be your last. Ireland's many charms have a way of enticing you to return again and again.

2. OVERVIEW

If you've never been to Ireland, you are in for a treat. If you have been before, you're still in for a treat. Follow the pages of this book and you'll see some of the most popular Irish tourist attractions: the Blarney Stone and the Book of Kells, Waterford Crystal Factory, the Cliffs of Moher and the Rock of Cashel. But you'll also see much more: I'll lead you through 5,000 year old passage graves in Newgrange, help you prowl the brooding ruins of Dunluce Castle, and direct you to the ancient remains of a ritual murder victim in the National Museum. In addition, you'll contemplate the fate of a million people as you visit the overgrown famine graveyard in Dungarvan, or, on the lighter side, share a banquet with the lord of a medieval castle.

Ireland is divided into four provinces: Leinster, Munster, Connacht, and Ulster. I have used these natural divisions as the primary destination chapters in this guide. I have also provided a chapter on Northern Ireland, should you decide to visit that part of the Emerald Isle. The last chapter addresses genealogy, since there is a seven-in-ten chance that you are Irish — 70% of American and Canadian tourists who venture to the Emerald Isle have at least one Irish ancestor.

The following is a short synopsis of the high points of each of the destination chapters:

DUBLIN

Dublin is Ireland's capital city, and also one of the Emerald Isle's oldest cities. It is rich in wonderful hotels and inns, fine restaurants and fun pubs, and more than a few impressive sights. **Christchurch** and **St. Patrick's Cathedral** dominate Dublin's skyline, and are perhaps its most recognizable buildings. Find out which was known as the Church of the People, and which was known as the Church of the Government, and why.

At St. Patrick's, you'll be awed by the immense beauty of the cathedral. Considered the National Cathedral of the Church of Ireland, St. Patrick's was founded in 1191, but its history goes back much farther.

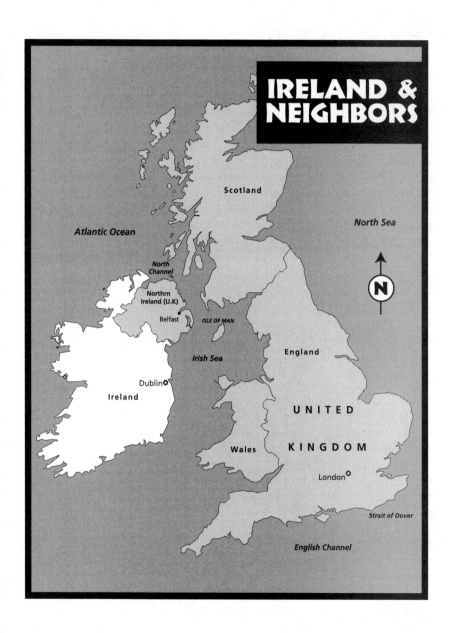

IRELAND & NEIGHBORS

Scotland

Atlantic Ocean

North Sea

North Channel

Northrn Ireland (U.K)

Belfast

ISLE OF MAN

Irish Sea

England

Dublin

Ireland

UNITED

KINGDOM

Wales

London

Strait of Dover

English Channel

N

Historians firmly believe St. Patrick's is perhaps the oldest Christian site in Dublin. It was on this spot that St. Patrick himself performed baptisms over 1,500 years ago. Physically, St. Patrick's Cathedral is impressive. The largest church in Ireland, its west clock tower rises 141 feet above Patrick Street, and the spire atop the tower rises another 101 feet, making the tip of the spire nearly 250 feet high.

The **Book of Kells** is one of the cultural sights you shouldn't miss in Dublin. Without a doubt, this is one of the most celebrated attractions in Ireland: four volumes worth of illustrations of the four Gospels painstakingly drawn by 9th-century monks. The elaborate artwork that graces the pages of the Latin text is truly a sight to behold, and a sight to be sure you see while you're in Dublin.

The **National Gallery of Ireland** is one of the gems in Dublin's tiara. Established by an Act of Parliament in 1854, it has grown to an impressive gallery of some of the finest art on display in western Europe. The great Irish playwright **George Bernard Shaw** claimed he owed half his education to the National Gallery of Ireland, where he spent hours upon hours within its walls as a youth. There are over 2,400 paintings, 300 sculptures, and a wide assortment of other forms of artwork located here. Feast on the works of impressive Irish artists as well as the fruit of such legendary artists as Degas, Rembrandt, Monet, and Van Dyck, to name a few.

A visit to Dublin isn't complete without a visit to the **National Museum of Ireland**. Sort of Ireland's Smithsonian Institute, this museum just celebrated its 100th birthday, and its second 100 years promise to be as great as its first 100. A fabulous collection of Irish antiquities is highlighted by items in the National Treasury, including the Ardagh Chalice, Cross of Cong, and the Tara Brooch. Their collection of gold artifacts is considered by many to be the finest collection in Europe. And if that's not enough to pique your interest, you can view the partially mummified remains of a ritual murder victim.

While Dublin is a delightful place to visit, it has had its share of dark days throughout history. **Dublin Castle** was the seat of government for the hated English conquerors, and **Kilmainham Jail** is the site of numerous executions and many more incarcerations. The **General Post Office**, fondly known as the GPO, is where Irish patriots defiantly declared Ireland's independence from Britain. In Irish history, it is comparable to Lexington Green. Eventually the revolution that started here resulted in independence for Ireland.

In recent years, there has been a bit of a food renaissance in Dublin. A number of Dublin restaurants have stepped to the fore in the preparation and presentation of quality cuisine. Follow my recommendations and your palate will be delighted.

Dublin's central location on the eastern seaboard of Ireland makes it an ideal place from which to tour **Leinster**, the Irish province that covers Ireland's east coast. Leinster extends from County Louth north of Dublin to the southeastern tip of the island in County Wexford, and as far west as County Offaly in central Ireland. Historically, much of northern Leinster was under control of the English, conquerors and occupiers of Ireland. Today, Leinster offers a variety of great sights and attractions not far from Dublin. Due to Dublin's central location in the center of the province of Leinster, Leinster serves as a Day Trips & Excursions chapter for Dublin. Here are a few of the Leinster highlights:

The southern half of Leinster is rich in natural beauty. The **Wicklow Mountains**, south of Dublin, are tall (by Irish standards, anyway!) and grand, and served in earlier times as hideouts for those not in favor with the English rulers. Immediately south of Dublin is County Wicklow, referred to as the **Garden of Ireland**. It offers a number of beautiful vistas and fascinating ancient ruins.

Foremost among the latter is **Glendalough**, site of an extensive monastic settlement and hermitage dating back to the 6th century. At the west end of the valley, Glenealo stream cascades in a waterfall into the valley, which is encompassed by heavily forested mountains. Add to all this natural beauty some exquisite and ancient ruins, and this is a wonderful place to visit.

Not far from Glendalough is fabulous **Powerscourt Gardens**. You've probably seen pictures of Powerscourt Gardens before – they are popular scenes used to depict the beauty of Ireland. The gardens were originally laid out beginning in 1745, and were revised to their present grand design in the mid-1800s. They cascade in a series of terraces down a slope from an ancient mansion house. The gardens are filled with greenery: sculpted shrubs, trees, and many varieties of flowering plants, along with an array of statues, fountains, and walkways. From the top of the terraces, the views sweep across the panoramic **Dargle Valley**, culminating in outstanding views of **Great Sugar Loaf Mountain** and **Kippure Mountain**. Nearby you can visit the **Powerscourt Waterfall**, the highest waterfall in Ireland, with water dropping more than 400 feet off the edge of Djouce Mountain. It is a favorite picnic area for tourists and locals alike.

County Wexford is found at the southeastern tip of Ireland and offers a number of scenic white sand beaches and port towns that are interesting to poke around in. **Rosslare** is a favorite seaside vacation spot for Dubliners. A host of leisure activities are available, including bird watching, golfing, windsurfing, fishing, and sunbathing.

The central-western part of Leinster consists of the wide flat plain called **The Curragh**, and is the Kentucky of Ireland. It is here that a number of national horseraces are held, as well as the location of a number of stud farms, including the internationally famous **National Stud** in Tully.

An hour's drive north of Dublin is the **Boyne River Valley**. For hundreds of years, this valley has played an important role in the history of Ireland. In ancient times, it was the gathering place of the kings of Ireland. It also served as the burial place for these same kings. Several well-preserved burial mounds dating back five millennia are found here, most notably **Newgrange**, where you can tour one of the finest cross-shaped ancient passage graves in existence. Inside Newgrange, visitors are led down a passage lined with massive stones and into the central burial chamber. The Newgrange mound is a well-preserved grave dating back to nearly 3,000 BC. During the winter solstice (December 21), rays from the sun glide down the narrow passageway gradually lighting the burial chamber.

The Boyne River Valley also represents a somber note in Irish history. This peaceful verdant vale is to Ireland what the sleepy crossroads town of Gettysburg was to the Confederacy. It was here that the armies of Protestant **William of Orange** routed the forces of Catholic **James II**, the King of England. James fled Ireland and died three years later while in exile in France. The resulting shift of power in England (and thus in Ireland) meant that an oppressed Irish Catholic populace would not receive their deliverance for another century (more on that in the history chapter).

MUNSTER

Munster comprises six counties in the southwestern quarter of the island. Much of Munster is rural, and the scenic views in this province are a match for any in the rest of the country. Breathtaking seascapes, rugged offshore islands, and country roads wending through green fields are typical of the scenery here.

If you know of only one place in Ireland, it is probably the **Blarney Stone**. Many folks are unaware that the Blarney Stone is part of **Blarney Castle**. The famous stone is located atop an ancient keep (castle stronghold) underneath its battlements. To kiss the stone – which legend says grants the kisser the gift of *blarney* (flattering eloquence) – you lay on your back and slide down and under the battlements. Locals are positioned to give you a hand. The verdant setting and the obligatory kiss of the Blarney Stone will be memorable parts of your visit to the Emerald Isle.

Waterford City is the location of the **Waterford Crystal Factory**, the world-renowned lead crystal manufacturer. Through the years, kings and queens, presidents and prime ministers have been presented gifts of this famous crystal in solemn ceremonies. Several years ago, the Super Bowl trophy was a large Waterford Crystal football on a pedestal (they have a replica of it in their showroom). The factory has a nice gallery, and their one-hour tour takes you within a few feet of the artisans who blow and cut the glass – much as it has been done for several hundred years at this site. I guarantee you'll never look at a piece of hand-blown crystal again without greater appreciation.

One of the most impressive ruins in Ireland is the **Rock of Cashel**, found in County Tipperary. You'll want to save plenty of film for one of the most awe-inspiring sites in Ireland. The setting for this chapel/round tower/Cathedral is on a mound towering some 200 feet above the surrounding plains. In addition to the ruins themselves, incredible views of the surrounding Tipperary plains await you from this lovely ecclesiastical site.

On the western edge of Ireland, rising dramatically and abruptly from the foaming sea, are the **Cliffs of Moher**. These incredible cliffs feature sheer 700-foot drops to the crashing ocean. They make for an impressive photo opportunity regardless of the weather. When it's clear and bright, the cliffs are regal and majestic; when it's gloomy and rainy, they sulk silently, like giant brows gathered in a menacing frown.

And of course, little **Killarney**, nestled as it is in the heart of some of the prettiest scenery in the country, is a place you simply must see. The natural beauty of the area will leave you in awe as you wander through the woods, take a fun jaunting car ride through the grounds of **Muckross House** or over the **Gap of Dunloe**, or just climb the cool green paths to **Torc Waterfall**.

CONNACHT

Connacht is located in the western part of the country. Much of this province consists of wide-open spaces embellished by beautiful heather enhancements. It also has a couple of energetic seaports in Galway and Westport counties. The **Connemara** district of **County Galway** is rugged and beautiful. Connemara is home of the **Twelve Bens**, twelve peaks that rise out of the solitude of Connemara – an area that many Irish will tell you is the real heart and soul of Ireland.

Off the western coast of Ireland, a trip to the **Aran Islands** is a trip into Ireland's past. Winding rock walls, ancient ruins, prehistoric forts, and megalithic tombs greet visitors with stony silence. Contrast that silence with the warmth of thatch-roofed cottages, amiable inhabitants, and the friendly pubs you'll find dotting the islands.

Known as Ireland's Holy Mountain, **Croagh Patrick** sits regally on the south side of **Clew Bay** and holds an important position in Irish history and legend. This is where St. Patrick enticed all of the snakes in Ireland to gather. After they had all assembled, St. Patrick rang his bell, and the snakes cast themselves to their deaths over a cliff! It must be true, because there are no snakes in Ireland! Croagh Patrick is an impressive mountain, and the site of yearly pilgrimages by many Catholic faithful. Whether you hike to the top as part of a pilgrimage or whether you just want to see the views, you won't be disappointed for your efforts.

ULSTER

Ulster is a politically divided province. It consists of nine counties, six of which constitute **Northern Ireland**, which is a part of the United Kingdom. The three remaining counties are part of the Republic of Ireland. Despite this political segregation, scene for scene, vista for vista, Ulster may have the most spectacular scenery on the island. Unfortunately, due to the troubles of recent years, most American and Canadian visitors have chosen not to visit Ulster in general, and Northern Ireland in particular. Even during the most tumultuous times in Northern Ireland, however, visitors to Ulster have encountered very few problems.

In recent years, there has been a fragile peace between the Irish Republican Army (the IRA) and Great Britain, and it has really turned North Americans on to Northern Ireland. Those who live in the North have warmly opened their arms to travelers, especially those from America and Canada.

What is there to see here? For starters, one of the most romantic ruins on the island is **Dunluce Castle**, on the northern coast of Northern Ireland. It is also one of the most photographed castles anywhere. It sits majestically atop an outcropping that juts abruptly out of the Atlantic Ocean. In ancient times, it made an impregnable fortress, and today it makes for superb photos.

Giant's Causeway, just up the coast from Dunluce Castle, is one of the most amazing geologic sites on the Emerald Isle. The Causeway consists of more than 40,000 hexagonal basalt pillars of varying heights. The symmetry is astounding, and well worth a visit. If you are the adventurous type, then perhaps **Carrick-a-Rede** is the place for you – a rope bridge that stretches across an 80-foot span from the mainland to an island. As you walk across it, the undulating bridge will convince you that someone behind you is jumping up and down on the bridge; a peek over your shoulder and you'll discover it is only the bridge's natural reaction to your passing. Hint: Hold on, and go slowly.

Along the eastern coast of Northern Ireland are the **Glens of Antrim**, and the Queen of the Glens, **Glenariff Forest Park**. You have a choice of numerous walking paths that allow you to stroll through lush green hills. Cascading waterfalls, beautiful wild flowers, and dense undergrowth add to the cool, quiet splendor of your walk. Not to be outdone by the sights of Northern Ireland, **County Donegal** on the northwest coast of Ireland is simply beautiful. Every turn of the road, every hill you top seems to reveal another beautiful lake or seascape. Donegal is one of the three counties in Ulster that is part of the Irish Republic.

GENEALOGY

I've included a chapter on genealogy in Ireland to help you find long-lost relatives. There is a good chance that if you are traveling from the United States or Canada, you have Irish ancestry because 70% of North Americans who visit Ireland have Irish roots. So you're a Murphy? Then be sure and visit Counties Cork, Donegal and Mayo, since those are the ancestral counties of the Murphy clan. If you're a Ryan, then be sure to include Counties Limerick and Tipperary in your itinerary.

Are you hoping your family in the "ould country" is having a clan reunion? In Chapter 19, *Searching For Your Irish Roots*, I've included information on how to find out if, when, and where your family is having that reunion. Or, if you'd simply like to visit long-lost cousins, I've provided a suggestion or two on how to make that happen.

So, whether you are coming to Ireland to search out your roots, see splendid scenery, mosey through museums, gaze at galleries, or prowl ancient ruins, Ireland offers it all to you. And you can use this book to guide your journey throughout the country.

3. SUGGESTED ITINERARIES

Here are a few suggested itineraries for varying lengths of stay in Ireland. I've outlined itineraries of three, four, seven, and fourteen days. Remember, these are just suggestions. If you are enjoying prowling around an old ruin longer than I suggest, by all means stay there as long as you wish. Remember: this is your vacation; go at your own speed. Conversely, if you find yourself a little ahead of schedule, stop at a Tourist Information Centre (TI) and ask for suggestions of things to see and do in the surrounding area. Or better yet, just follow your nose.

Whether you're in the city, the country, or somewhere in between, you should find something that will interest you, and it might even prove to be the highlight of your trip. Several of my most interesting pictures and best memories are of abandoned ruins on back roads I had taken on a whim.

Dublin is very different from the rest of Ireland. While it's a delightful city, many people's idea of Ireland runs more to romantic ruins, rolling fields of green, and stone walls wending their way through the verdant landscape. Nevertheless, Dublin is a wonderful city to visit. Museums, art galleries, and historical sights are plentiful.

If you visit Dublin, don't bother renting a car while you are there. Traffic is horrendous almost any time of day. Bicyclists, motorcyclists, and pedestrians will drive you batty, and it can be dangerous for you and those around you. If you do rent a car, it's probably easiest to park it several blocks from the city center and walk. In the past, I have been lucky and found parking around St. Stephen's Green. Most of the Dublin City sights are within easy walking distance from a central point like St. Stephen's Green.

There are a number of sights that are better as a part of a longer trip. The Skelligs, the Dingle Peninsula, the Ring of Kerry, and the Aran Islands are great places to visit, but they take the better part of a day to see. If your time is limited, I suggest you concentrate on the sights outlined on the following pages and save other areas for future visits (you *will* be back!).

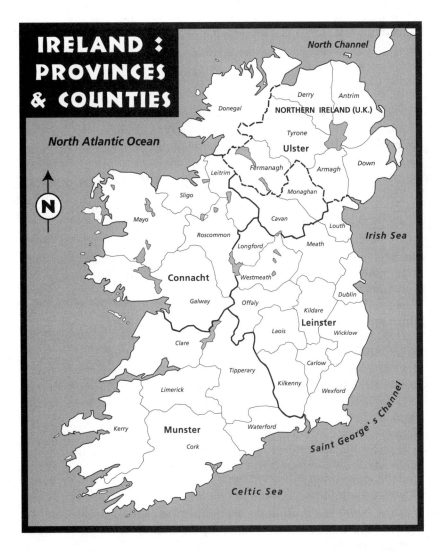

IRELAND :
PROVINCES
& COUNTIES

North Channel

North Atlantic Ocean

N

Donegal

Derry   Antrim

NORTHERN IRELAND (U.K.)

Tyrone

Ulster

Leitrim   Fermanagh   Armagh   Down

Sligo   Monaghan

Mayo   Cavan

Roscommon   Louth   Irish Sea

Longford   Meath

Connacht   Westmeath

Galway   Offaly   Dublin

Kildare

Leinster

Clare   Laois   Wicklow

Tipperary   Carlow

Limerick   Kilkenny   Wexford

Kerry   Waterford

Munster   Saint George's Channel

Cork

Celtic Sea

Most sights close between 5:30pm and 7:00pm during the summer months, earlier other times of the year. One way to maximize your touring is to see all you can in an area during the day, and use the evening to drive to your next destination. During the summer, it stays light until well after 9:00pm, and you can still see the beautiful countryside while you travel. This tactic makes B&B owners especially nervous, so be sure and call ahead to confirm your reservations and let them know you'll be late. Call in the afternoon if you can, but certainly no later than 6:00pm.

In the following itineraries, I recommend staying in the last town you're touring because it makes for a more leisurely schedule.

ITINERARY 1 - THREE DAYS IN DUBLIN

Day 1

Breakfast at Number 10

Trinity College: see multimedia show *The Dublin Experience* and Book of
    Kells

Visit the Bank of Ireland and the House of Lords

Grafton Street for window shopping and busker-watching

Lunch at Latchford's

Tour the National Museum

Tour the National Gallery

Stroll through St. Stephen's Green

Dinner at La Stampa or Patrick Guilbaud's (make reservations)

Spend the night at the Shelbourne Hotel

Day 2

Tour Dublin Castle and the Church of the Most Holy Trinity

Tour Christchurch Cathedral (watch the traffic!)

Tour St. Michan's Church

Lunch at Gallagher's Boxty House or Elephant and Castle

Tour St. Patrick's Cathedral

Francis Street for antique shopping/people watching

Visit Oliver St. John Gogarty's Pub for Irish music and some pub grub

Spend the night at the Russell Court Hotel

Day 3

Tour the Guinness Brewery

Tour the Dublinia exhibit (multimedia presentation on medieval Dublin)

Lunch at Cibo Restaurant

Tour Kilmainham Jail

Visit Phoenix Park

Take the DART to Howth for a stroll along the quay

Dine in Howth at Abbey Tavern; enjoy an evening of traditional Irish
    entertainment

ITINERARY 2 - THREE DAYS IN DUBLIN
& SURROUNDING AREAS

Day 1

Visit Monasterboice

Tour Mellifont Abbey

Tour Newgrange burial mound

Lunch at An Sos Cafe in Castlebellingham

Visit Malahide Castle and Fry Model Railway Museum

Howth Harbor for a stroll along the Quays
Dine at the Abbey Tavern and enjoy their Irish music show

Day 2
Visit Trinity College and the Book of Kells
Grafton Street
Tour the National Museum
Lunch
Tour St. Patrick's and Christchurch Cathedrals
Tour Kilmainham Jail
Phoenix Park
Drive to Rathnew to stay at Tinakilly Country House
Dinner at either Tinakilly Country House or Hunter's Hotel

Day 3
Visit Mt. Usher Gardens
Drive through the Vale of Avoca, stop and walk a bit
Visit Glendalough
Lunch
Visit Powerscourt Gardens and Waterfall
Tour Russborough House
Dine and spend the night at Mount Juliet

ITINERARY 3 - FOUR DAYS IN THE WEST

You can reach the west coast of Ireland from Dublin in about three or four hours driving, depending on your route and final destination. However, if you are going to spend your entire time in the west, then fly into Shannon and begin your tour from there.

Day 1
Drive to Killarney
Visit the shops in Killarney
Tour Muckross House and Kerry Life Experience
Have lunch at the snack bar at the Muckross House
Drive the Ring of Kerry up to Ladies' View
Drive part of the Dingle Peninsula, from Castlemaine to Dingle and back
Walk around Dingle Town
Rent a skiff to take you into the harbor to see Fungi, the Dingle Dolphin
      (or drive a little further out on the peninsula)
Spend the night in Killarney at Hotel Dunloe Castle

Day 2
Drive to Adare, tour the shops and the ruins of several abbeys
On to Limerick
Visit King John's Castle
Tour the Hunt Collection
Lunch in Limerick
Visit the Craggaunowen Project
Visit Bunratty Folk Park
Dine at Bunratty Castle Medieval Banquet
Spend the night at Dromoland Castle

Day 3
Visit the Cliffs of Moher
Drive through the Burren; visit the Burren Display Center
Head for Galway City
Lunch at MacDonagh's Seafood Restaurant
See the sights in Galway, visit the shops
Spend the night at Cashel House Hotel or Ballynahinch Castle

Day 4
(Lots of driving today)
Head to Clifden, visit the shops
Tour Connemara National Park, including Kylemore Abbey
Lunch at Kylemore Abbey
On to Westport – visit the shops and sites to see in Westport
Head south toward Ballinrobe and Galway (inland route); swing by
    Ashford Castle to see the grounds in Cong
Spend the night in Galway (about 90 minutes from Shannon Airport)

ITINERARY 4 - SEVEN DAYS IN IRELAND

Seven days is a fairly short time in which to see Ireland. This itinerary begins in County Wicklow just south of Dublin, circles the country, and ends in Dublin.

If the following itinerary seems a little rushed, you can divide the fourteen-day itinerary in half and just see half of the island. Days one through six and fourteen provide a thorough tour of the southern half of the island. The itinerary for days seven through fourteen makes sense for the northern half of the island, and includes Northern Ireland. If you take the latter option, fly into Shannon and out of Dublin to maximize your time.

Depending on your rental car company, there may or may not be an extra charge to drop your car in Dublin if you rented it in Shannon. Most agencies don't charge extra, but it's always good to check first.

Day 1
Fly into Dublin
Head south for County Wicklow
Visit Mt. Usher Gardens
Drive through the Vale of Avoca, stop and walk a bit
Visit Glendalough
Lunch
Visit Powerscourt Gardens and Waterfall
Tour Russborough House
Dine and spend the night at Mount Juliet in Thomastown

Day 2
Visit Waterford City
Tour Waterford Crystal Factory
Head north for Cahir. Tour Cahir Castle
Lunch in Cashel
Visit the Rock of Cashel
Visit the Bru Boru Heritage Center
Head for Cork
Visit Blarney Castle and Blarney Stone
Spend the night at Claragh House B&B in Blarney

Day 3
Head for Killarney
Visit the shops in Killarney
Tour Muckross House and Kerry Life Experience
Drive the Ring of Kerry up to Ladies' View, then back
Drive around the Dingle Peninsula (this will take about four hours)
Have lunch in and walk around Dingle Town
Rent a skiff to take you into the harbor to see Fungi, the Dingle Dolphin
Spend the night at Hotel Dunloe Castle or Adare Manor

Day 4
Visit King John's Castle
Tour the Hunt Collection
Drive to Adare, tour the shops and the ruins of several abbeys
Lunch in Adare
Visit Bunratty Folk Park
Visit the Craggaunowen Project
Drive to the Cliffs of Moher
Spend the night at Gregan's Castle in Ballyvaughan

Day 5
Head for Galway
Tour the city, especially the shops
Drive to Clifden, visit the shops
Lunch in Destry's, or Quay House
Visit Kylemore Abbey
Drive to Westport
Tour Westport City, especially the shops
Spend the night at The Rock Barton Lodge outside Westport

Day 6
Drive cross-country to the Drogheda area (about three and a half hours)
Visit Monasterboice
Lunch at An Sos Cafe in Castlebellingham
Tour Mellifont Abbey
Tour Newgrange burial mound
Howth Harbor for a stroll along the Quays
Dine at the Abbey Tavern and enjoy their Irish music show
Spend the night at Ariel House in Dublin

Day 7
Visit Trinity College and the Book of Kells
Grafton Street
Tour Dublin Castle
Lunch at Cibo Restaurant
Tour the National Museum
Tour the National Art Gallery
Tour St. Patrick's and Christchurch Cathedrals
Spend the night in Skerries at The Reefs B&B (not far from the airport);
    enjoy sunset over the Irish Sea for your last evening in Ireland

ITINERARY 5 - FOURTEEN DAYS IN IRELAND

Fourteen days gives you plenty of time to tour Ireland. You won't see everything, but you'll see many of the major sights and have time for a few of the minor ones, too. This itinerary begins in County Wicklow, and encircles the island in a clockwise manner. It ends in Dublin, so you can return your rental car, see Dublin without it, and save a few dollars. If you fly into Shannon, just start the tour in the middle.

Day 1
Head south for County Wicklow
Visit Mt. Usher Gardens

Drive through the Vale of Avoca, stop and walk a bit
Visit Glendalough
Lunch
Visit Powerscourt Gardens and Waterfall
Tour Russborough House
Dine and spend the night at Mount Juliet

Day 2
Head for County Wexford
Rosslare: visit their shops, walk along their beautiful beach
Lunch
Visit Dunbrodey ruins in Ballyhack
Visit Waterford City
Tour Waterford Crystal Factory
Tour the Waterford Heritage Center
Spend the evening at Blenheim House

Day 3
Head for Ardmore
On the way, go through Dungarvan, visit the Famine Graveyard
Visit Ardmore. Walk around the town, visit the round tower, take the cliff-side walk
Head north for Cahir. Tour Cahir Castle
Lunch in Cashel
Visit the Rock of Cashel
Visit the Bru Boru Heritage Center
Head for Cork
Visit Blarney Castle and Blarney Stone
Spend the night at Claragh House B&B in Blarney

Day 4
Visit the sights that are of interest to you in Cork City (Shandon Steeple, Crawford Art Gallery, English Market)
Visit the Fota Wildlife Park
Lunch in Cobh
Visit Cobh (your ancestors may have bid farewell to Ireland from here)
Visit the Queenstown Project in Cobh
Head for Kinsale
Visit Charles Fort in Kinsale
Head for Bantry
Visit the Bantry 1796 French Armada Exhibition Center in Bantry
Enjoy Bantry Bay
Spend the night in Bantry

Day 5
Head for Killarney
Visit Muckross House and Kerry Life Experience
Walk up to Torc Waterfall
Lunch in Killarney at either Gaby's or Foley's Town House
Take a jaunting car ride up the Gap of Dunloe
Drive a portion of the Ring of Kerry to Kenmare. (Stop to take pictures)
If there's time, visit the shops in Kenmare
Dine at Park Hotel Kenmare or La Cascade Restaurant at Sheen Falls
    Lodge
Stay in the Park Hotel Kenmare, Sheen Falls Lodge, or Sallyport House

Day 6
Head for Waterville on the Iveragh Peninsula
In Waterville, catch a boat to the Skelligs
Lunch in Waterville
Finish driving the Ring of Kerry along the northern side of the Iveragh
    Peninsula
Spend the night in Killarney at Hotel Dunloe Castle

Day 7
Spend this entire day on the Dingle Peninsula
Visit Dingle, walk around the shops
Rent a skiff to take you into the harbor to see Fungi, the Dingle Dolphin
Gallarus Oratory
Slea Head
Visit the Blasket Center
Visit Dunquin Pottery
Take O'Connor Pass to Kilcummin, then into Tralee
Spend the night in Tralee

Day 8
Head north toward Limerick
Visit Adare, tour the shops and the ruins of several abbeys
On to Limerick
Visit King John's Castle
Visit the Hunt Collection
Lunch in Limerick
Visit the Craggaunowen Project
Visit Bunratty Folk Park
Dine at Bunratty Castle Medieval Banquet
Spend the night in a B&B near Bunratty Castle

Day 9
Head northwest to see the Cliffs of Moher
Visit the Burren and the Burren Display Center
Visit Ailwee Cave
Drive to Galway
Visit the shops of Galway
Find Lynch's Memorial Window
Look for Salmon off the Salmon Weir Bridge
Visit Spanish Arch
Visit the Galway City Museum
Spend the night at the Sea Breeze B&B in Galway

Day 10
Visit the Aran Islands today

Day 11
Get out early – lots of driving today!
Head to Clifden, visit the shops
Tour Connemara National Park, including Kylemore Abbey
Lunch at Kylemore Abbey
On to Westport – visit the shops and sights
Spend the night at the Rock Barton Lodge B&B just outside Westport

Day 12
Get out early – head north to Donegal (long drive). Along the way, stop
    at Creevykeel Court Tomb, Drumcliffe and W. B. Yeats' grave
Visit the shops in Donegal Town.
Lunch in the Blueberry Tea Room.
Drive north and visit Glenveagh National Park
Skirt Derry (Londonderry)
Spend the night at Whitepark Country House in Ballintoy

Day 13
Visit Dunluce Castle, Giant's Causeway, and Carrick-a-Rede
Lunch in Ballycastle
Visit Bonamargy Friary. Find Julia McQuillan's gravestone
Take the Torr Head Drive out of Ballycastle to Cushendun
Take the inland route to Belfast
Visit sites in Belfast: Botanical Gardens, Ulster Museum, Crown Pub
Drive to Dundalk or Drogheda to spend the night

Day 14
Drive to Dublin
Visit Trinity College and the Book of Kells
Grafton Street
Lunch at Cafe En Seine
Tour the National Museum
Tour St. Patrick's and Christchurch Cathedrals
Tour Kilmainham Jail
Spend the night in Skerries at The Reefs B&B (not far from the airport);
    enjoy the sunset over the Irish Sea on your last evening in Ireland.

4. LAND & PEOPLE

THE LAND

The Emerald Isle is often said to be the size of Virginia or Kentucky (actually, it's a little smaller than both). In other words, it's not very large. The island is about 300 miles long from its northern beaches to its southern coves, and 170 miles from the Atlantic Ocean on the west to the Irish Sea on the east. No matter where you travel on this island paradise, you are never more than about 70 miles from the sea.

Ireland is divided into two political entities. The majority of the island (all but the northeastern portion) is called the Republic of Ireland. It is referred to as either the Republic or alternately as "the South." There are approximately 3.5 million people living in the Republic, which is about the size of Maine or Indiana.

Northern Ireland consists of six counties in the northeastern portion of the island and is a part of the United Kingdom. Northern Ireland, or "the North," is about the size of Connecticut, and is home to approximately 1.5 million people.

When I thought to ask the question, I was a little surprised to find that many who live in Northern Ireland consider themselves British living in Ireland, as opposed to being Irish living in Britain. There are, of course, those in the North and the South who feel Ireland is still occupied by invaders – the British – and who will not be happy until Northern Ireland is reunited politically with the Republic. This is the crux of "the Troubles" that are ongoing in the North.

Geologists estimate that Ireland has been an island for 8,500 years, having separated from the European continent during the thawing of the last Ice Age. The central portion of Ireland is a relatively level limestone plain. Rolling hills, rich foliage, and occasional peaks jutting up are typical of this area. The outer edge of the island is mountainous and blocks the interior from the sea. On the western shore of Ireland these mountains tend to drop off sharply to the sea, resulting in some dramatic seascapes. Indeed, some of the precipices are 700 feet high. Elsewhere on the island, the slope to the sea is more gradual, allowing for wide sandy beaches fit

FACTS ON IRELAND

Highest mountain: Carrantuohill in County Kerry (3,414 feet)
Longest River: Shannon River (230 miles)
Total ocean shoreline: 3,497 miles
Largest city: Dublin, nearly 500,000 (within the city limits)
Largest lake: Lough Neagh (153 miles of shoreline)
Total population:
Republic: 3.52 million (over 40% live within 60 miles of Dublin)
Northern Ireland: 1.66 million
Religious affiliation:
Republic: 93% Catholic, 4% Anglican, 3% other
Northern Ireland: 54% Protestant, 43% Catholic, 3% other
Unemployment:
Republic: 4.5%
Northern Ireland: 6.3%
Birth Rates:
Republic: 14.6 per 1,000
Northern Ireland: 14.8 per 1,000
Land use: 90% undeveloped or rural, 10% other
Total Area:
Republic: 32,595 square miles
Northern Ireland: 5,462 square miles
Form of Government:
Republic: constitutional democracy
Northern Ireland: will now be governed by the Northern Ireland Assembly

for frolicking and romantic strolls along their soft walkways. The beaches of Northern Ireland and of southwestern Ireland are especially inviting.

The mountains of Ireland are more rounded mounds than towering peaks. The **Mountains of Mourne** in the northeast are perhaps the best known, as they are mentioned in a number of poems and songs. "Sweeping down to the sea," as famed Irish poet and balladeer Percy French put it more than 100 years ago, the Mournes are a great granite range that have rounded with age, and are silent guardians of the North. South of Dublin in County Wicklow are more granite hills known as the **Wicklow Mountains**. Inland, the granite is replaced by red sandstone and quartzite that form the **Galtee, Knockmealdown, Slieve Aughty**, and **Slieve Bloom mountains**.

In the southwest, especially in southwest Counties Cork and Kerry, the same red sandstone crumbles into a series of finger-like peninsulas reaching into the sea. This makes for some marvelous harbors and harbor towns, seascapes and landscapes.

Central County Kerry boasts the highest red sandstone peak in Ireland at **Carrantuohill**. A steep and craggy peak, it lunges abruptly heavenward over 3,400 feet.

Up the western coastline to Galway, you come to the **Maamturk** and **Partry** ranges, quartzite mountains that provide wonderful jutting mounds. The most impressive and significant is **Croagh Patrick** near Westport, a peak surrounded by many legends and a place of pilgrimage for thousands each year. Farther north, you encounter the quartzite peaks of the

Nephin Mountains, in County Mayo. Still farther north, you arrive at the **Bluestack Mountains**, the predominant feature of County Donegal. Donegal is very mountainous by Irish standards, and the Bluestacks are the main range in Donegal. On the west coast of Donegal are the **Slieve League Mountains**, which feature an impressive drop to the sea.

Finishing a clockwise loop of the island, you'll find the softly rounded mounds of the **Sperrin Mountains** in Counties Derry and Tyrone. At the eastern edge of Northern Ireland you find the **Antrim Mountains**, whose wind-swept, rounded peaks drop off into the lovely Glens of Antrim, home to an incredible number of wildflowers, and, some say, leprechauns.

Several Irish landscape characteristics seem like anomalies. First, the climate supports plant life that ranges from arctic tundra to sub-tropical plants, often growing side by side. Second, on the central-western edge of the island is the **Burren**, a vast area of gray limestone hills and plains. At first glance, it seems as though it should be called the *Barren* instead of the *Burren*. This lunar-looking area continues to draw naturalists from all over the world to study its amazing qualities. Thousands of tiny plants, including some rare species of orchids, grow in the seemingly inhospitable environment. Countless underground caves, turloughs (lakes that appear during the rainy seasons, then disappear as the weather gets drier), and fissures criss-cross the face of the Burren. The contrast of the Burren to the rest of Ireland is awesome.

It may seem to you that Ireland has a quilt-like quality: seams run across the width and breadth of the island. Those seams are in reality rock walls. In some parts of the country, that is obvious; in other parts, it looks like the fields are separated by massive, straight hedgerows. They are hedgerows, but those hedgerows cover ancient stone fences. How ancient? Well, some have been there for thousands of years, but most likely the walls you are seeing have been in place for no more than several hundred years.

Prior to the widespread appearance of landlords in the late 1600s, Ireland was relatively devoid of stone fences. Oh, there were plenty of stone forts from the Celtic period – over 30,000 of them are still found in the country. But these were small and were not the stone walls you see today. When landlords came in, they began fencing "their" property with stone walls, marking it off in five- and ten-acre parcels, to be sold to other Protestants. Over time, even the native Irish adopted the practice of building stone walls, and soon stone walls covered the country and became indelibly Irish.

TURF FIRES

*If you are driving along in the lovely Irish countryside and see individuals laboring in fields relatively devoid of vegetation, stop and witness a tradition that has gone on in Ireland for hundreds, if not thousands, of years. In many areas of Ireland, there are huge expanses of peat bogs – wet areas that contain the carbonized remains of peat moss. Some ingenious (or desperate) soul long ago discovered that if chunks of this wet earth were dried, they could be burnt in a fireplace. These **turf fires**, as they're called, provided cooking fires, warmth, and light for otherwise cold, drab cottages. Turf fires provide a low-flame, long-burning, aromatic fire.*

Back to the people you saw laboring in the bog. They are probably doing one of two things: either they are cutting the wet bog into brick-size pieces, and turning them over so they will dry out, or they are collecting turf bricks that have already been cut and dried. The government passed a law allowing anyone in the country to go to a bog, free of charge, and "harvest" turf to be used in their own personal turf fires. You'll often see a car pulled over to the side of the road near a bog, with its trunk open. Not too far away you'll see individuals – often entire families – picking up turf bricks to put in the car.

Once, turf fires were the primary heating method in Ireland. Today, the tradition has been largely abandoned in the big cities, but in the rural areas it is still very common. Many pubs, restaurants, and hotels in Ireland still burn turf fires to give their establishment that homey, Irish feel and smell. As you drive through small rural villages, if you'll roll down your window and sniff the air, I guarantee you'll catch a whiff of turf fires – they smell like burning grass. It works best in the mornings or evenings, but you'll be able to smell it during the day, too. It's one of my most memorable (olfactory) memories of Ireland, and it may prove to be one of yours, too.

The Irish discovered the stone walls were practical and useful. In addition to marking land ownership, they kept certain animals in, and certain animals out. They served as a place to meet and chat and everyone leaned on the sturdy walls. During the days of the Penal Laws, they served as protection for **hedge schools**, places where Catholics were educated since it was illegal for them to receive a formal education. And I suppose countless generations of children climbed on them, ran along them, hid behind them, and used them in any way their imaginations could come up with.

THE PEOPLE

There are many beautiful sights in Ireland: sandy beaches, scenic sunsets, verdant valleys, and towering cliffs. But by far, the best part of Ireland is the people. They are among the most gracious and friendly people on the planet. From several people jumping up to give their seat to an elderly person or woman on a bus to the warm welcomes you receive in B&Bs to meeting your long-lost cousins, you'll find Irish hospitality wherever you go.

Here are a few interesting tidbits about the Irish:

• Ireland has gone from a country where it was illegal for Catholics to receive a formal education to a 98% adult literacy rate today.

• It has produced more than its fair share of literary giants. From the early days of the Celts, poets and minstrels have been among the most honored and respected members of Irish society. That reverence has spawned generations of internationally renowned poets, writers, and playwrights over the years: Jonathan Swift, George Bernard Shaw, W. B. Yeats, Oscar Wilde, Oliver Goldsmith, and James Joyce. Irish writers through the years have earned no fewer than three Nobel Prizes for Literature.

• Christianity first came to Ireland in approximately the late 4th century. One of its earliest missionaries was St. Patrick, who is credited with establishing over 60 churches in Ireland. By the early 1500s, Ireland was predominantly Roman Catholic. Today, about 93% of the citizens in the Republic of Ireland are Roman Catholic, as are 43% of the people in Northern Ireland.

Irish Language

Irish is the official language of the Republic of Ireland, with English recognized as a second language under the Constitution. **Gaelic** and **Irish** are generally interchangeable terms, although today the language is almost always referred to as Irish. Gaelic is most often used to refer to the language of the ancient inhabitants of Ireland, the Celts.

During the past century, English was becoming the daily language of the majority of the Irish people, and Irish was becoming a dead language. In an effort to combat this, the Gaelic League was formed in 1893. When the Irish state was formed in 1921, the government made the restoration and preservation of the Irish language one of its priorities. To this end, areas where Irish was still the daily language were designated as *Gaeltacht*, and special financial grants were made available to encourage individuals to remain in the largely rural areas. Large parts of counties Donegal, Galway, and Kerry, as well as parts of counties Mayo, Cork, Waterford, and Meath all qualified.

Today, linguists estimate only 5% of the Irish people speak Irish as their primary language. There is a very real concern that the Irish language will die out entirely.

Regional accents abound in Ireland. Around Dublin, the accents tend to have a strong English flavor. In County Cork in the southwest, accents have a more sing-songy quality. In the extreme west – Galway and Donegal in particular – accents are more what Americans expect – quite frankly, the accent you hear on the "Irish Spring" soap commercials! In Northern Ireland, accents have a strong resemblance to a thick Scottish brogue, most likely due to the predominance of Scottish settlers who settled there over the centuries.

SEPARATED BY A COMMON LANGUAGE

When my wife and I visited long-lost cousins in Northern Ireland, we had a delightful time. As we were leaving, one of the cousins took my wife's hand, and shaking it vigorously, said, "We're so glad you came. You are so plain and homely." For a moment we were both stunned by this seemingly insulting comment. But the broad smile on her face and the enthusiastic nods of agreement from the other Irish cousins present made us realize that in American English she was saying: "We're so glad you came. You are so down-to-earth and comfortable to be with."

That experience reinforced for us the fact that while we share a similar language with the Irish, there are some distinct differences. Another difference is that there are still many vestiges of Gaelic in their vocabulary. Many towns and villages retain their ancient Irish names and children are given seemingly unpronounceable Irish names, for example: Aoife, Oísin, and Niamh to name a few.

Below are some of the more common Irish words you are certain to encounter during your visit. Many of them are anglicized versions of Irish words – for example, Bally is the anglicized *Baile*, which means "town." Many small towns in Ireland carry the prefix Bally: Ballymena, Ballyconnell, Ballydonegan, Ballydoyle, etc.

ard	a high place
ath	ford
bally	town
ben	large hill or mountain
bord	office or board
burren	stone
cahir	stone fort

carrig	rock
cashel	stone fort
cavan	cave
ceile	dance
croagh	hill (especially a cone-shaped hill)
derry	oak
drum	low ridge or mound
dun fort	
êireann	Ireland
ennis	island
feile	festival or celebration
feis	feast or celebration
gal	river
grianan	palace
kil	church
knock	hill
lis	earthen fort
lough	lake
mac	son
mor	great
oughter	upper
quay	pier
rath earthen ring fort	
skerry	sea rocks
slieve	mountain
tully	small hill

Here are a few common English words that will be helpful to know in conversation, since the meanings are sometimes different in Ireland:

call	visit
hire	rent
homely	homey
on holiday	on vacation
pram	baby stroller
plain	down-to-earth
queue	line
ring	call on the phone
tariff	rate (as in the rate for a hotel room)

One last lesson: *Celtic* is pronounced differently than the way we pronounce the name of the NBA team from Boston. The Celtic you see in Ireland is pronounced Keltic, with a hard K, and it was spoken by Kelts. (Not *Seltic* spoken by *Selts!*)

OH, THOSE IRISH NAMES!

Sure, and I'm certain you are familiar with Irish names like Danny, Patrick, Darby, Mary, Molly, and maybe even Sean. But here are a few you might see that you may have problems pronouncing. Here's a little help:

Name	Pronounced
Aine	OWN-ya
Aishling	Ashling
Aoife	EE' fa
Caitriona	KA-trina
Ciaran	KEER-un
Colm	CALL-um
Donough	DUN-uh
Dymphna	DIM-pna (female)
Eamon	AY-mon
Eoin	Owen
Fiacha	Fee-AH-ka
Fionnala	Fi-nula
Kathleen	KAT-leen
Liam	LEE-um
Maeve	Mayve
Malachi	MAL-a-key
Moire	MOY-ra (Mary)
Niall	Neel or Nile
Niamh	Neev (female)
Oisin	O-SHEEN
Patrick	often Paddy (diminutive of Patrick)
Sean	Shawn
Seamus	SHAY-mus
Sinead	Shi-NAY-ud
Siobhan	SHI-vawn (female)

Irish Music

The written histories of Ireland are liberally sprinkled with references to music in the lives of the Irish people. Indeed, even today music is an important part of Irish celebrations, whether those celebrations are festivals, sporting events, parades, weddings, or even funerals.

What are the instruments most common in Irish culture? The **harp** was one of the most important musical instruments in ancient Ireland. Its place in Irish society was so revered that it has earned the honor of being the national emblem, and is stamped on all modern Irish coins. The harp was the main instrument of the Celtic minstrels, and references to harps and harpists can be found in contemporary accounts of Irish life as early as the 11th century.

Over the centuries, other instruments crept onto the Irish stage with the harp. New settlers brought the instruments of their cultures, and the Irish adopted many of those instruments. The Scottish brought **bagpipes**, which evolved to the Irish *uillean*, also known as union pipes. Union pipes are similar to bagpipes in design and sound, but they differ fundamentally in the way they fill the bag with air. Instead of using your breath to fill the bag, a bellows-like device held under the arm is used to fill it.

The **concertina**, a small accordion-like instrument, was introduced into Ireland by their English conquerors in the mid-1800s. Other important musical instruments include the fiddle, flute, tin whistle, and the *bodhran* (pronounced BOW-rawn), which is a small, goatskin-covered drum or tamborine that is played with a stick. It has a mesmerizing effect, as it sets the tempo for many an Irish song.

5. A SHORT HISTORY

Ireland is one of the most tranquil places you will ever visit. Unfortunately, her peaceful repose belies her rocky history. Oppression and domination have played a major role in Ireland's history for over 1,000 years. From subtle politics to bloody uprisings, Ireland's past is checkered with intrigue, drama, and pathos that rivals today's fictional best sellers.

And yet natives of this incredible island are resilient. Time and again they have broken the chains of their oppressors through the centuries to become the free people you find today – although there are those who feel the tyrant's grasp is still on that part of the Emerald Isle known as Northern Ireland.

ANCIENT HISTORY

The earliest signs we have of mankind in Ireland are signs of his death. Ireland is littered with stone tombs from five millennia ago – it is estimated some of them were built as long ago as 3,000 BC. Who were these people, and where did they come from? Why did they go to the trouble to build immense passage graves? How did they lift 50-ton stones onto pedestals to serve as tombs for their deceased? And why? Unfortunately, we can only speculate about what compelled these people to do all this.

The earliest Irish residents were probably **Mesolithic** hunters. It is widely believed that these ancient nomads arrived in the middle of the Stone Age, as people on the European continent expanded their fishing and hunting grounds to the western edge of the continent and on to what is now Ireland. They probably came on foot since some believe that Ireland was part of continental Europe at that time. Whether on foot or in skin coracles, they came, were seduced – by its beauty, abundance, or isolation – and stayed.

Little is known of these Mesolithic people. They left few traces of their passing. Ancient sites at the mouth of rivers and along the shores of lakes were taken over by succeeding generations, each making the settlement a little larger and a little better fortified against marauders.

The beginning of the New Stone Age was the first of many renaissances on the Emerald Isle, when **Neolithic** man appeared in Ireland. Perhaps the race multiplied beyond the rivers' abilities to support it, but it was during this time that these ancient groups moved into the interior of Ireland. Crude stone farm implements attest to their new occupation as tillers of the soil. As time went on, the crudeness of their tools softened to a unique sophistication. Stone axes were sharp and plentiful enough to make massive timbering projects possible on the island – as well as to provide protection if necessary. Remnants of their civilization indicate they mastered the arts of pottery and weaving.

It was these advanced Stone Age men that began the practice of building massive tombs for their dead. Thousands of these tombs can be found dotting the fields and hills of Ireland to this day. They include passage graves (so-called because of the presence of a central passage into the tomb), dolmens, stone circles along the same lines as Stonehenge, and a variety of other monuments, all apparently to honor their dead. Many of them also reflect a knowledge of astronomy, as they show some solar orientation. Some of the finest examples of these today include **Newgrange**, **Dowth**, **Knowth**, **Creevykeel**, and **Browne's Dolmen**.

The Bronze Age in Ireland lasted from about 2,000 BC to 500 BC, as evidenced by a significant and eclectic collection of relics such as fine jewelry, weapons, and tools that have been unearthed in recent years. Many of the finer examples are on display in museums such as the **National Museum** in Dublin.

The Bronze Age gave way slowly to the Iron Age as wandering bands of iron-users made their way to this small island. These new settlers came to be known by today's historians as **Celts**, although it's doubtful that's what they called themselves.

The Celts had a long and event-filled history on this tiny island. Their religious leaders were called **Druids**, and their gods became the gods of the Irish people for many hundreds of years. The Druids worshipped a number of deities, and presided over the human sacrifices that were often an important part of some of their ceremonies.

The language of the Celts is of Indo-Germanic origin, and soon became the predominant language of the island, eclipsing whatever form of communication had gone on before. **Gaelic**, still spoken in many parts of the country, evolved from the language spoken by the Celts.

By the time the seventh century BC rolled around, Ireland was known to the world beyond the Irish Sea as **Hibernia**. Maps of the period bear the name Hibernia for Ireland and Albion for Britain. They also show a number of towns – probably more like settlements than towns – around the country, primarily situated at the mouths of the rivers that emptied into the sea.

The next several hundred years saw the migration of various and sundry peoples to the Emerald Isle. Never coming in numbers large enough to alarm, much less subjugate the native Irish, these peoples were quickly absorbed into the culture, adding their own influences.

The Celtic culture was one regulated by a litany of laws and edicts. The law was passed on orally from jurist to jurist. Celtic law, which today is known as **Brehon Law**, covered everything from land and cattle ownership to the granting of kingships to divorce to control of "peeping Toms." During the English conquest, Queen Elizabeth is said to have found the laws "lewd, unreasonable, and barbarous."

THE BREHON LAWS

These and similar laws were in place in Ireland for nearly 1,700 years, from the first century BC to the early 17th century. The quotes below are taken from **Irish Laws**, *published by Appletree Press, Belfast, and are used with their gracious permission.*

Peeping Toms: *The fine for peering into your neighbor's house without permission is one cow.*

Debt: *If your neighbor does not repay the debt he owes you, you may prevent him from going about his daily business.*

Kindness: *If a pregnant woman craves a morsel of food and her husband withholds it through stinginess or neglect, he must pay a fine.*

Divorce: *February the first is the day on which a husband or wife may decide to walk away from a marriage.*

Doctor's responsibilities: *If the doctor heals your wound, but it breaks out anew because of his carelessness, he must return the fee you paid. He also must pay you damages as if he himself had wounded you.*

Hospitality: *Whoever comes to your door, you must feed him or care for him, with no questions asked.*

Health laws: *It is illegal to give someone food in which has been found a dead mouse or weasel.*

Intoxication: *The layman may drink six pints of ale with his dinner. But a monk may drink only three pints. This is so he will not be intoxicated when prayer-time comes.*

Liability: *If a chip of wood from the carpenter's ax hits a bystander, the carpenter is exempt from liability, unless he deliberately aimed the chip at the bystander.*

Neighbor's Dog: *If a dog commits a nuisance on a neighbor's land, the dog's ordure must be removed as far as its juice is found. The ground must be pressed and stamped upon by the heel, and fine clay put there to cover it. Compensation shall be paid in butter, dough or curds amounting to three times the size of the ordure.*

Celtic society was divided into various castes. At the top of the caste structure was a professional class of people consisting or jurists, poets, historians, nobility, Druids, smiths, artists, and musicians. Members of the professional caste were free to move among the people. The rest of the populace was relegated to the lower echelons of the caste system. Its grip was strong enough to last well into the era of Christianity.

During this period, it is highly unlikely that there were many formal towns, much less cities. The populace was scattered helter-skelter across the width and breadth of the country, tied to their level in the caste system and whichever noble to whom they owed their fealty.

During this period, nearly 150 kings ruled the 500,000 inhabitants of the Emerald Isle. (For you math majors out there, that's one king for every 20 square miles!) Perhaps "king" is too strong a word; they were more appropriately chieftains, perhaps patriarchs, of their own extended families. Over time, this system gave way to four or five kingdoms, precursors to today's four provinces of Leinster, Munster, Connacht, and Ulster.

CHRISTIANITY & THE EMERALD ISLE

Celtic society embraced an institution that eventually caused the weakening and eventual loss of their power. The institution? Slavery. In the late 4th century, a youngster was captured by slave traders in Britain and brought back to Ireland to serve as a sheep tender. That young man's name was Patrick – he later came to be known as **St. Patrick**. When he was finally able to throw off the chains of bondage, he escaped to the continent where he studied for the ministry. Later, he returned to the land of his captivity to begin his legendary missionary work.

St. Patrick was not the first Christian missionary in Ireland, but he was one of the earliest, and was perhaps the most indefatigable. Among other things, he is credited with establishing churches in over 60 locations in Ireland. His work to spread the Gospel in Ireland is mixed with so many legends that it seems nearly impossible to know what he did and what he didn't do. For example, did he or didn't he cleanse Ireland of snakes? Legend says he did. (By the way, there are no snakes in Ireland.) One thing is certain: during his ministry, Christianity grew by leaps and bounds. While it would be several hundred years before Christianity eclipsed the paganism practiced by the majority of the Celts, St. Patrick established a firm foundation for those who followed to build upon.

In addition to bringing the *religion* of Christianity, St. Patrick, his predecessors, contemporaries, and successors brought the *education* of Christianity. While the rest of Europe sunk into the depths of the Dark Ages, Ireland actually enjoyed its own mini-renaissance, led by learned and scholarly priests. Lacking extensive towns during this period, monasteries became the centers to which the population migrated.

Over several hundred years, Christianity continued to gain acceptance from the inhabitants until close to the end of the 8th century when things changed drastically.

VIKING INVADERS

Some historians mark the date as 795, others as 800, and still others as late as 807, but the exact date of the first **Viking** invasion is immaterial. What does matter is that the Vikings made their appearance on the Irish scene with a large dose of brutality and destruction. Wooden monastic settlements all across the island made easy and flammable targets for these marauders from the north. The Vikings torched the settlements and plundered them of their precious treasures. Fortunately, the Vikings left behind some of the greatest treasures: books and manuscripts. Many ancient books perished in the fires started by the Vikings, but those that didn't perish were often ignored by the non-reading Vikings who saw no value in them. The richly illustrated Books of Kells, Durrow, and Armagh (all on display at Trinity College) are examples of these unappreciated literary treasures that were left behind.

Like so many other visitors to the Emerald Isle, the Vikings liked what they found and decided to stay. They are responsible for a number of settlements that became seaports around Ireland, including Dublin, Limerick, Wexford, and Waterford. During this period, the Irish were noted for their clannishness, and their unwillingness to unite against a common foe. For several hundred years, the Vikings took advantage of these divisions and used these and other towns as their base for plundering the rest of the country.

It was these Viking raiders that we have to thank for the distinctive round towers that dot the Irish countryside. Prior to the Viking invasion, the monastic settlements consisted primarily of wooden structures. The need for additional protection prompted the Irish to construct stone round towers to serve as repositories of manuscripts and documents, as well as other treasures. They also served as watchtowers and places of refuge. An interesting aspect of the round towers is that their doors are often off the ground – some as high as 12 feet above the ground. Portable ladders provided access to the towers; once all were safely inside, the ladders were then retrieved inside the towers, and invaders found the fortresses impregnable.

As mentioned earlier, the Vikings were able to plunder Ireland by taking advantage of the clannishness and lack of unity among the Irish. During most of the 200-plus years the Vikings maintained their foothold in Ireland, there was no single king to unite Irish forces against these northern pests. In the year 1002, a prince of the ruling family in Munster, **Brian Boru**, came to power as the undisputed High King of Ireland. Brian Boru united the armies of the other Irish kings and drove the Vikings forever from the shores of the Emerald Isle. The decisive conflict was the Battle of Clontarf, where the Vikings were finally defeated. Unfortunately, Brian Boru was killed during the fighting: some legends say it was while he was praying for victory. Regardless, his forces were victorious, and the Vikings were no longer a power nor menace in Ireland.

Three of the four Irish kings supported the ouster of the Vikings from Ireland. The fourth was less than supportive; in fact, he joined with the Vikings and fought against his countrymen. Nearly 150 years later another Leinster king chose to oppose his royal peers. **Dermot MacMurrough** was viewed by some as a traitor. Others viewed him as an opportunist. Whatever his motivation, we now know that his actions resulted in over 750 years of occupation and subjugation of the Irish by the British.

ENGLISH INVADERS

The MacMurrough-O'Rourke Feud

In 1152, **Tiernan O'Rourke**, an Irish chieftain, and his wife Dervorguilla lived in relative happiness in their castle not far from what is today Innisfree. O'Rourke suddenly found himself under attack by the forces of Dermot MacMurrough, the king of Leinster. MacMurrough had convinced the lovely Dervorguilla to flee with him and his armies. Actually, the story is a little muddled: some accounts say she was kidnapped, others say she ran off with MacMurrough. Whatever the case, O'Rourke marshaled his forces, formed an alliance with other Irish chieftains, and was able to retrieve his sweetheart.

Dermot MacMurrough was censured by the other Irish kings for conduct unbecoming a king. **Rory O'Connell**, High King of Ireland, announced the united decision of the kings: banishment from Ireland for MacMurrough.

Not one to take banishment sitting down, MacMurrough sought and was granted an audience with **King Henry II** of England, during which he discussed the "injustice" he had suffered in Ireland at the hands of his fellow monarchs. Whether MacMurrough knew that King Henry already had designs on Ireland is unclear. However, years prior to the feud, Henry had applied for and been granted a "bull of legitimation" from **Pope Adrian IV**, which allowed him to begin his conquest of Ireland. Henry had merely been biding his time before his tempestuous neighbors provided him with the opportunity to begin his conquest. Henry saw MacMurrough's plight as just such an opportunity, and capitalized on it to expand his kingdom and assure additional kingdoms for his sons.

King Henry agreed to support MacMurrough in his efforts to regain his crown in Ireland by suggesting that he enlist the assistance of power-hungry barons in England and Wales. Many of them responded favorably, including the famous Earl of Pembroke, more commonly known as **Strongbow**. Over the next generation and a half, Ireland was under siege from warlords based across the Irish Sea. To secure his allegiance, MacMurrough proposed a wedding between Strongbow and Dermot's daughter. It must have worked: the wedding was consummated and the incursions into Ireland began.

Anglo-Norman success was initially along the eastern coast of Ireland, where their armored and well-coordinated attacks on settlements, towns, and villages were met with ineffective resistance. In 1170, Strongbow and his soldiers defeated the Irish Forces. The English established their foothold for future conquests of Ireland along a 30-mile by 20-mile strip of land in northern Leinster referred to as **the Pale**. It was over 750 years before the British could be persuaded to leave.

CENTURIES OF BATTLES

The warfare that took place in Ireland during this period affected primarily the Irish rulers and their armies. The common class – the laborers who worked the fields and tended the sheep – were not directly involved, and their lives continued relatively unaffected, except that they often found themselves serving new landlords.

As time went on and the Irish continued to lose battles because of overwhelming odds, they finally decided it was necessary to unite their forces to fight the Anglo-Norman onslaught. They united under a series of kings – generals or warlords, really – and imported mercenaries from Scotland. These professional fighting men were called *galloglasses*, from the Irish word for "foreign soldiers." Their entry into the fray helped check further significant incursions into the Irish countryside, and kept the majority of the English influence and occupation within the Pale.

In the middle of the 14th century, the fighting took a respite while both sides struggled to survive the onslaught of another, deadlier invader – the Black Death. The plague took its toll among all castes and nationalities. Irish chieftains, galloglasses, and Anglo-Norman citizens were not exempt.

As time progressed, the Anglo-Norman invaders became more and more Irish and less and less English. They intermarried, adopted the dress and customs of native Irish, and even began to speak their language. In 1366, in an unsuccessful attempt to stem the tide that was pulling powerful new rulers in Ireland away from the crown, the **Statutes of**

Kilkenny were drafted and approved. The statutes made intermarriage a treasonable offense, made it illegal for an Irishman to live within a walled town, and laid heavy penalties on those who spoke the Irish language or adopted their ways of dress or any of their customs. Alas, it was too late, as many of the very practices that were outlawed were already a normal way of life for the invaders.

Over time, the land settled into a relatively peaceful acceptance and toleration of the two peoples. Fighting became less common, and a sort of peace settled across the land. The Irish chieftains were allowed to roam the lands as they had been accustomed to doing, and the Anglo-Norman invaders were allowed to stay within their walled cities. Occasional skirmishes arose, mostly along the outlying edges of the Pale, but these were usually isolated affairs that lasted for short periods of time.

The schism between **Henry VIII** and the Roman Catholic Church further distanced native Irish from their occupiers. By now, Ireland was predominantly Catholic, and Henry's departure from the church would have dire consequences for the Irish in coming years. Gradually, the religion that was once embraced by the English was rejected, tolerated, and then disdained. It was this grand disdain for Catholicism that made the Irish more devout and the English more intolerant.

During the late 16th and early 17th centuries, the Irish engaged in a series of rebellions, and experienced crushing defeats at the hands of Elizabethan soldiers that were ever more prevalent throughout the country. This was known as the **Plantation Period**, during which soldiers were granted large tracts of land for their service to **Queen Elizabeth**. Elizabeth, in turn, felt she was protecting the "back door" to England.

QUEEN ELIZABETH OUTLAWS IRISH MUSIC

Poets and musicians have always played an important role in Irish society. From the days of the Celts, these cynical minstrels were honored, respected, and even a little feared. For political leaders their favor was paramount because a poet could turn the people for or against a particular king or chieftain.

They were such a critical cog in the machinery of the Irish culture that they were allowed to go about their business of music making and satire with little retribution for biting words and great honor for complimentary words and songs.

As you might imagine, the English conquerors did not fare well at the hands (or voices!) of the minstrels. Queen Elizabeth understood the power these men wielded in Ireland. She outlawed all traditional Irish music, and proclaimed, "Hang all the harpers where found, and burn the instruments."

There were fears in London that if Catholicism continued in Ireland, Spain might use that site to launch attacks on the shores of England. In 1580, the Spanish sent an expedition of 600 men to Ireland; their purpose was to assist in the defense of the Catholic cause in Ireland. This hapless army surrendered to a better-armed English army, and was summarily executed. But their efforts were viewed as an example of the very activity Queen Elizabeth feared. Her response was to flood Ireland with soldiers in an attempt to "pacify" the rebellious Irish; unfortunately, this pacification took the form of brutal repression and slaughter.

The Spanish continued to assist the Irish in their fray with England. Ammunition, money, and soldiers were sent periodically. In late 1601, an army of 4,000 men was sent to assist the Irish cause. They arrived too late to assist the beleaguered Irish army, and they themselves were besieged and defeated by **Lord Mountjoy** on Christmas Day, 1601. The leading rulers of the Irish fled Ireland at this time, and their departure was referred to as the **Flight of the Earls**.

After the Flight of the Earls, Ireland entered a period when the enmity between the Catholic Church and the English government grew more deeply. The church fanned the discontent of the Irish people; they told them they were being ruled by a queen whose birth was illegitimate in the eyes of God, and whose religion was heresy, the result of Henry VIII's lust. They told the Irish that rebellion against the crown was lawful, and indeed it was their holy duty to throw off the yoke of bondage.

Meanwhile, the Flight of the Earls opened up Ireland for settlement. Ulster was the targeted area, and the Crown moved to settle the area with loyal Protestants from England, Scotland, and Wales. Partially due to the numbers who were sent there, and partially due to the remoteness of Ulster, the settlement took hold, and many of its inhabitants today trace their ancestry to those settlers.

Between 1610 and 1640, Irish Catholics watched as their land was usurped by settling Protestants. The enmity and distrust between the conquerors and conquered grew, but seldom erupted in violence. It was a time when the conqueror needed the conquered to work his fields, and the conquered could not survive without working the fields of the conqueror. Despite the relative peace, vehemence was boiling beneath the surface, a boil in need of lancing, an explosion waiting to happen.

In an effort to introduce education and the reformed faith to Ireland, Queen Elizabeth founded **Trinity College** in Dublin in 1592. The college was located on the grounds of a priory (a monastery) suppressed by her father a generation earlier. But the Irish refused to attend; in fact, the Catholic Church specifically barred them from doing so. So, in a matter of several decades, we find a relatively educated Protestant populace and a relatively uneducated Catholic populace. The result of this educational inequity was a British contempt for the Irish and a corresponding resentment of the British.

In 1641, the Irish Catholics in Ulster revolted. Led by **Phelim O'Neill**, Protestants were massacred by the thousands. Men, women and children were caught in the maelstrom. While the wrath of the Irish was probably no worse than anything the English inflicted on the Irish, the results were widely reported in London, and great indignation followed.

In 1649, **Oliver Cromwell** was dispatched to Ireland. His hatred for and intolerance of Catholicism was legendary even at that time. Within four years, Cromwell laid waste to almost every square inch of Ireland. You can scarcely drive through the countryside in Ireland without finding a castle, monastery, or town that was sacked by Cromwell and his armies.

As armies were defeated and lands claimed for the crown, they were immediately granted to loyal Protestants. Irish rebels forfeited their lands to those who could prove that they had not been involved in the rebellion. If they couldn't prove they did not participate, rebels (and suspected rebels) lost their lands outright. It is estimated that at the time of the 1641 Uprising, 60% of the land in Ireland belonged to Irish Catholics; after Cromwell's efforts, less than 20% of the land was held by the Irish, and most of that in the inhospitable and relatively barren lands of Connacht.

In 1685, a glimmer of hope lighted the lives of the oppressed Catholic populace. **James II** of Scotland, who was also called Catholic James because of his religious affiliation, ascended to the throne of England. His reign lasted only a short time: Catholics were apparently as hated on the throne of England as they were in Ireland. The "Glorious Revolution" of 1688 chased James II from the throne and he sought and won the support of Irish Catholics. In fact, the Irish people accepted James II as a savior of sorts.

Unfortunately, due to the interplay of religious and political complexities, Catholic James did not enjoy the favor of **Pope Alexander VIII**, the very pope for whom his support had resulted in his ouster from England. James had hoped to flee to Ireland, gather troops there, and with the help of the French, reclaim his throne. Unfortunately, **Louis XIV** was too busy fighting his own battles within his own country, as well as with the Dutch and the English, to provide anything more than token assistance to James.

When James arrived in Ireland, most of the country was under the control of the Irish army. One notable exception was Derry, where English troops were under siege. They held out for nearly four months, and were on the verge of surrender when reinforcements arrived by sea, and caused James' forces to abandon their designs.

Enter on the scene one **William of Orange**. William, a Protestant and James' son-in-law, landed in Ireland near Carrickfergus Castle on June 14,

1690. Two weeks later, on July 1, his troops engaged James' troops in a massive battle on the banks of the River Boyne. The **Battle of the Boyne**, as it came to be called, signaled the end of any opportunity for James to be restored to the throne. James fled to Waterford, boarded a ship and left for France, where he died in exile three years later.

Ireland was still full of Irish troops. One by one, these armies lost a series of skirmishes with William's better-armed and better-led forces. Finally, one year later, 10,000 Irish troops surrendered after the **Siege of Limerick**, and they were allowed to leave the country. The sailing of these rebels from the shores of Ireland to the Continent was referred to by the bards as the "**flight of the wild geese**."

Undefended and leaderless, Ireland now faced some of its stiffest challenges – perhaps even greater than the trying times Oliver Cromwell brought. At the urging of Protestants in Ireland as well as those in England, William allowed Parliament to pass the infamous **Penal Laws**. These laws essentially disenfranchised the Catholics within the boundaries of their own country. They were not allowed to vote nor run for election to Parliament, they were excluded from military service and the legal profession, and they were not allowed to receive formal education. They could not possess arms, and they were not even allowed to own a horse worth more than five pounds. In short, they were rendered a nonentity in their own country. The practice of Catholicism was strictly controlled, and was only in the hands of a few licensed priests; ecclesiastical leaders at the level of bishop and above were banned from the country, and a death sentence was pronounced upon those who dared return. Catholic lands were forfeited to Protestants, and they were relegated to the status of tenant farmers.

The Penal Laws were a vicious retribution on what the British felt were a troublesome people. The laws were designed to keep the Irish down socially, economically, religiously, and politically. The laws were strictly enforced, and created a new caste system in Ireland. While there was some softening of its enforcement at times, Catholic emancipation was not completely won for another century and a half.

"Catholic emancipation" became the rallying cry for two generations of Irish patriots – or rebels, if viewed from the English side of the issue. It was during the early 18th century that **Jonathan Swift** (of *Gulliver's Travels* fame) penned the following sentiment that found its way across the ocean to bolster the cause of another English colony in rebellion: "All government without the consent of the governed is the very essence of slavery."

There were two primary classes in Ireland: the disenfranchised Catholics and the landed Protestants. Parliament and the Crown continued to meddle with the economy and lifestyle of the Irish, and found themselves alienating both the Irish natives and the "Old English," who by now had become quite Irish in most aspects except religion. Control of the lucrative Irish woolen trade, coining of Irish money by an individual investor in England, and other repressive actions on the part of the English led to the formation of an alliance between the rebellious Irish and the hitherto supportive Protestant landlords of Ireland.

The American Revolution provided some relief for the Catholics in Ireland. Fighting one major war on one front necessitated the attention of Parliament; they didn't want and could ill afford an active rebellion in another of their colonies. The American Revolution was strongly supported by Irish Catholics and the Protestant landlords. Indeed, the Irish in particular probably felt a certain kinship to these fellow colonists struggling for independence from the powerful crown. During this time, Ireland won important concessions from Parliament in the areas surrounding the Irish woolen market, relative legislative independence, and a lessening of some of the harsher aspects of the Penal Laws. But Catholics were still unable to vote, and they were still unable to stand for seats in Parliament.

Near the end of the 18th century another movement called the **United Irishmen** gained prominence. Led by **Theobald Wolfe Tone**, the United Irishmen were encouraged by both the American and French Revolutions. They hoped to wrest control of Ireland from the English and to establish an independent Irish republic. To mollify the rebels, additional modifications were made to the Penal Laws, the most important of which extended voting privileges to Catholics, the first time in a century.

Despite this major surge forward toward full emancipation, the United Irishmen were not satisfied. In 1798, active rebellion broke out in the northeast and southeast sections of the country, and English troops put them down with the ferocity of the former Cromwellian armies. French troops arrived too late to assist, and they, too, were defeated by the British army. Wolfe Tone was captured, and perished in prison. (Some say he was executed, others claim he committed suicide.)

During this period, individuals on both sides of the religious fence were working hard to unite the kingdom. Catholics saw this move as a positive step that would assure them total emancipation; Protestants saw it as a means of greater stability and strength for the Irish economy. Their support and the efforts of men such as **Edmund Burke** and **William Pitt** finally led to the establishment of the **United Kingdom of Great Britain and Ireland** on New Year's Day, 1801.

Despite the Union, full emancipation still did not see the light of day. For the next 25 years a number of movements arose – and were crushed – without realizing their dream of Catholic emancipation. These movements again fomented for the establishment of a Republic of Ireland.

Home Rule, or *Sinn Fein* (Irish for "Us Alone") became the rallying cry for this generation of Irish patriots.

The stage was now set for two of Ireland's most influential and revered men to step forward. **Daniel O'Connell** and **Charles Stewart Parnell** are the men credited with achieving complete Catholic emancipation. Parnell was a Protestant member of Parliament who lobbied hard for Catholic franchise. O'Connell was a Catholic from County Clare who won a seat in Parliament in 1828, but was refused the opportunity to take that seat because of his religious beliefs. He was a tireless supporter of the cause, and considered one of the greatest orators of his day. His impassioned speeches, coupled with large mass meetings and an avid Catholic following, swayed Parliament, and in 1829 the final vestiges of the Penal Laws were repealed.

The political scene was relatively quiet for the next several decades, although there were a series of aborted efforts to establish Ireland as an independent republic. But Ireland was moving quickly toward an event that was to devastate, demoralize, and decimate her population. Mother Nature accomplished what centuries of military campaigns, plans, and schemes of an antagonistic crown could not do. From 1845 to 1847, a scourge of epic proportion hit Ireland: the **Great Potato Famine**.

GREAT POTATO FAMINE

Ireland of the mid-1840s was primarily an agricultural nation. The vast majority of Ireland's eight million inhabitants relied on the hearty potato as the mainstay of their diet. It was natural for potatoes to take the lead in the Irish diet: great quantities could be grown on relatively little land, and it seemed to flourish whether planted in rich, loamy soil or in less arable land. With so little of Ireland in Irish hands, this combination made potatoes the ideal crop. But it was also akin to putting all their eggs in one basket.

The potato crop of 1845 was meager, and then a blight hit the plants, rotting potatoes in the ground before they could be harvested. Successive potato crop failures in 1845, 1846, and 1847 hit the nation, and the populace was devastated. It is estimated that between 1845 and 1848, one million Irish perished in the famine, and another million immigrated, mostly to America. One quarter of the population was gone from Ireland in a little over three years. Any talk of rebellion, independence, or an Irish Republic must have seemed like gossamer as the struggle to merely stay alive gripped the nation.

Much has been written on the famine over the years. At the beginning of the famine, the British government did little to assist the Irish, feeling that it wasn't the government's place to do so. When the 1846 potato crop failed, and the famine worsened, the British government relented, and began pumping vast sums of money into Ireland to provide public works employment, soup kitchens, and a variety of other efforts aimed at reducing the hardships encountered by over two-thirds of the population. Some applaud their humanitarian efforts; others judge them as too little, too late. In 1845, the pre-famine population of Ireland was 8,000,000; in 1848 the population stood at just over 6,000,000.

THE IRISH COME TO AMERICA

As devastating as the famine was, it may have been the beginning of the end for the United Kingdom of England and Ireland. A million Irish left famine-devastated Ireland during the famine years, and hundreds of thousands followed in the decades thereafter. As financially humble as their new lives were in America, these Irish immigrants were far better off economically than they would have been in Ireland. They also continued their clannishness, living in the same Irish neighborhoods, voting for the same politicians. Before long, the Irish vote became a much sought-after prize among politicians in the Irish strongholds of Boston and New York in particular.

And these Irish did not forget their roots. Dreams of Irish independence once again rekindled in the hearts of Irishmen, but now some of those Irishmen lived in America and could support their dreams with more than a voice and a body: money began to pour into any movement that supported Irish independence. At the same time, politicians understood that a large percentage of their constituency favored Irish independence. Indeed, at that time English newspapers and members of Parliament commented on the difficulty in keeping the Irish down, since such a strong group of (American) Irishmen was now out of their direct control.

MORE UPRISINGS

In an effort to help bring the famine to an end, the English government forced landlords to pay higher taxes in order to support relief projects under way. The landlords in turn put pressure on their Irish tenants to pay their rents. When they were unable to pay, landlords began evicting them in hopes of finding tenants who could – and would – pay the increased rents. These evictions became another hardship, and another reason to hate the English. Perhaps most important, it drove many who had previously been neutral on the idea of Irish independence to support it whole-heartedly.

As soon as the famine was over, the business of independence began again with renewed vigor and grimmer tenacity. Groups committed to Irish independence sprung up seemingly overnight in America as well as in Ireland. Some of the groups sought independence through political means, others through more militaristic methods. The **Fenians**, the **Irish Republican Brotherhood**, **Fenian Brotherhood** (in America), and other groups vowed independence for Ireland.

One by one the military efforts of each of these groups was met and put down. Occasionally, their leaders were executed; more often they were imprisoned for their efforts. But the Fenians finally hit upon a tactic that moved the purpose of independence a giant step forward: it was called the **Land League**, and it was highly effective.

The strategy of the Land League was simple: choose landlords who had been particularly aggressive in their evictions, and apply all means of non-military pressure available in order to make them more reasonable. Two of their tactics proved exceptionally effective. The first was the practice of withholding services. Landlords saw acres and acres of crops either go unplanted or rot in the ground because of their inability to find willing laborers to do the work. The second tactic was the social ostracism of individuals who either rented the homes of those who had been evicted, or who continued to work the landlord's lands despite the Land League's sanctions.

One of the first landlords targeted with this strategy was one **Captain Charles Boycott**. The sanctions against Captain Boycott were so effective in establishing negotiations that the hapless landlord forever lent his name to the practice of withholding labor and ostracizing workers who cross a picket line. Incidentally, the Land League and its members could not have implemented this strategy for any effective length of time without the monetary support of Irish-Americans.

Simultaneously, **Charles Stewart Parnell** had transitioned from a powerful ally to the chairman of the Irish parliamentary party. Mr. Parnell had a strong conviction for the Catholic cause in Ireland, despite his own Protestant beliefs. Both the Irish and the English considered him a leader of the Irish people.

As a result of Parnell's influence, sweeping changes in Ireland came about. In 1881, the **Land Act** was passed. This historic act brought much-needed protection in the areas of rent control and provided protection against arbitrary eviction. This victory, coupled with a short imprisonment at Kilmainham Jail, secured Parnell's leadership among the Irish.

This immense following enabled Parnell's party to seat 85 members of Parliament – a group who held the balance of power in the House of Commons. Their efforts, coupled with those of several English legislators, nearly bought independence for Ireland through political means. A **Home Rule** bill was proposed and nearly passed. However, the political stage was set: English opinion was beginning to swing toward the Irish, and it seemed that with a little patience, Irish Home Rule was imminent.

Unfortunately, the Irish party suffered a major setback when Charles Parnell was named in divorce proceedings as the paramour of **Kitty O'Shea**, the wife of another member of Parliament. The Victorian moral code of the day proved the undoing of Home Rule for a season. Parnell was deposed as the chairman of the party. Powerful support was lost from other members of Parliament, from within the Irish party itself, and from the Catholic church. The party was in disarray, and subsequent elections saw them lose the significant gains they had so recently made. Charles Stewart Parnell died a little over one year later at the age of 46, an Irish political enigma who had come so close to gaining independence for Ireland, but whose actions cost them – at least for awhile – the elusive prize.

INDEPENDENCE AT LAST

Despite this latest setback, Irish independence was not to be fore-stalled much longer. The flame of hope for independence burned too brightly to allow it to die out completely. Although Parnell's contemporaries abandoned him, the rising generation adored him. He became somewhat of a martyr for the cause among the youth, and gave them the strength to press forward in the cause he had embraced.

While Home Rule bill after Home Rule bill failed in Parliament, the first two decades of the twentieth century saw the rise of men who were learning the tactics that would eventually win the fight.

Simultaneously, as it appeared evident that Ireland was heading for Home Rule eventually, strong resistance in Ulster arose. Protestants objected strongly to an independent Ireland on religious grounds (their slogan was "Home Rule is Rome Rule"). They fought the battle on two grounds: first to avert Irish independence altogether, and second, if Irish independence were to be gained, that Ulster should be exempt and remain a part of the United Kingdom. So strong was the Ulster resistance that they firmly declared they would wage civil war – and they prepared to do so – if Ireland was granted its independence.

This demand to leave Ulster out of Irish independence was opposed by the majority of the Irish voters. But in the section of Ireland it most directly affected – Ulster – the majority of the residents there favored "partition," as the plan was called.

In November 1913, the **Irish Volunteers** were formed, a group of men bent on revolution. This small force of men – and a few women – eventually turned the tide and won independence for Ireland.

The Irish Volunteers chose Easter Sunday, 1916 to stage a country-wide uprising. The leadership was split on the issue, and orders canceling the rising were issued; those orders were repealed by yet another set of orders by other leaders. Confusion resulted, and only about 20% of the 10,000 members of the Irish Volunteers participated in the **Easter Rising**.

The leaders of the Irish Volunteers seized the General Post Office – the GPO – on O'Connell Street in Dublin. From its steps they proclaimed the free Republic of Ireland.

THE PROCLAMATION OF THE REPUBLIC OF IRELAND

Like the "Shot Heard Round the World," the following volley began the Irish War for Independence. Here are a few words from the Proclamation of the Republic, read Easter Sunday, 1916, from the steps of the GPO:

IRISHMEN AND IRISHWOMEN: In the name of God and of the dead generations from which she receives her old tradition of nationhood, Ireland, through us, summons her children to her flag and strikes for her freedom...

We declare the right of the people of Ireland to the ownership of Ireland and to unfettered control of Irish destinies, to be sovereign and indefeasible. The long usurpation of that right by a foreign people and government has not extinguished the right, nor can it ever be extinguished except by the destruction of the Irish people. In every generation, the Irish people have asserted their right to national freedom and sovereignty; six times during the last 300 years they have asserted it in arms. Standing on that fundamental right and again asserting it in arms in the face of the world, we hereby proclaim the Irish Republic as a Sovereign Independent State, and we pledge our lives and the lives of our comrades-in-arms to the cause of freedom, of its welfare, and of its exaltation among the nations.

The uprising lasted a week. During that time, nearly 500 people lost their lives in the fighting that ensued. Finally, out-manned and out-gunned, the rebels surrendered the GPO to the British. Fifteen men had signed the **Proclamation of the Republic**; after the smoke cleared, and the Easter Rising suppressed, all were executed at Kilmainham Gaol, and hundreds of participants were imprisoned. Their status in Ireland was immediately elevated to that of martyrs, and the cause of Ireland took a fierce and bloody step toward its goal: a free and independent nation.

As World War I ended, parliamentary elections were held in Ireland. *Sinn Fein* party members won 73 seats. Rather than journey to Westminster to claim their seats, these members of parliament instead established their own Irish Republican Parliament and called it *Dail Eireann* (literally meaning Meeting of Ireland). On January 19, 1921, they ratified the Proclamation of the Republic that was read five years earlier on the steps of the GPO, and another bold step toward independence was taken. It is interesting to note that 36 of the original members of the *Dail Eirann* were not present for their first meeting; they were still imprisoned for their role in the Easter Rising.

In addition to ratifying the Proclamation, they declared that the *Dail Eireann* was the only legislative body that could pass laws relative to the Irish people, and called for the evacuation of the English military machine from the country. They elected a government, headed by **Eamon de Valera**; they also set up their own judicial system.

The English government refused to bow to the wishes of the *Dail Eireann* and several years of guerrilla warfare ensued. Greatly outnumbered, the **Irish Republican Army** evolved from several former paramilitary organizations. Their goal was the disruption of the workings of the English government and military in Ireland through terrorist attacks. In response, the English retaliated swiftly and relied on "collective reprisals," openly admitting that some of those who were affected by the reprisals were not the perpetrators, but innocents that were in the wrong place at the wrong time.

This tactic was incredibly destructive to world public opinion. In England, America, Australia, and Canada, England was censured for their heavy-handedness. Ireland was increasingly becoming a political football where no matter what they did, England looked like the bad guy. And again, in this generation as in the last, funds from America kept the rebellion afloat and enabled the rebels to continue their cause.

The **1920 Government Act of Ireland** established separate parliaments for Northern and Southern Ireland. Elections that year returned *Sinn Fein* members for all seats except those representing the greater Dublin area. In the North, the seats were all won by Protestants, who favored remaining part of the United Kingdom. Once again, *Sinn Fein* members refused to take their seats in the Southern Ireland parliament, establishing the Second *Dail Eireann* instead.

It appeared there was to be no compromise: while Southern Ireland was closer to independence than it had ever been, Ulster was as far away as it had ever been. Those in Ulster had vowed to fight any attempts at secession from England. They saw themselves more closely aligned with England than with Ireland, and they simply did not wish to be governed by the wishes of the Catholic majority in the South.

In June 1922, Eamon de Valera was invited to participate in peace talks. During the talks, *Sinn Fein* representatives and representatives from the crown agreed to terms that essentially created two political entities: the **Irish Free State** in the south, and six counties in Ulster called **Northern Ireland**. Seven decades of hindsight help us see that representatives for the crown were the better negotiators. Through a series of

harangues, empty promises, and vague potentialities, the Irish represen-
tatives were encouraged to sign a treaty that recognized the South as the
Irish Free State, and recognized the *Dail Eireann* as the governing body
of that state.

However, in exchange, the Irish Free State was forced to swear
allegiance to the crown and allow her ports to be under English control
in times of war. Feeling perhaps that a bird in the hand was worth two in
the bush, on December 6, 1921, the **Anglo-Irish Treaty** was signed,
establishing southern Ireland as the Irish Free State.

These proceedings divided *Sinn Fein* into pro-treaty and anti-treaty
factions. Those who opposed the treaty did so on the grounds that once
Northern Ireland was separated, they felt no power could restore them to
the Republic (very prophetic); the idea of allegiance to the crown was also
repugnant to them. Those with these views were called **Republicans**. The
pro-treaty party – called the **Free Staters** – felt that something was better
than nothing, and that in the long run, Northern Ireland would come
around and want to be a part of the Republic. De Valera, a Republican,
was unable to win his seat in the Dail Eireann in the next election. The
ideological split caused a separation into two factions: the anti-treaty **Irish
Republican Army** (IRA) and the **Free State Army**. Both moved into
separate buildings in Dublin and continued their respective campaigns.

On June 22, 1922, an 11-month civil war broke out between the two
differing factions after **Sir Henry Wilson**, a military advisor to the
Northern Ireland government, was assassinated by members of the IRA.
During this time, many of the Republican leaders were either executed or
imprisoned. Eamon de Valera spent over a year in prison as a result of his
Republican leadership role.

Over the next two and a half decades, bits and pieces of the treaty were
rescinded. In 1949 the final ties of allegiance to the crown were severed
and Ireland, after over 750 years of British occupation, was now a free
republic in every way. (Except the North, of course!)

THE TROUBLES IN NORTHERN IRELAND

As outlined earlier, **the troubles** in Northern Ireland that exist today
had their beginnings many generations ago. Today, hostilities still wax
and wane, and as long as there are those who foment for one Republic,
and those who fight against it, there will be clashes between the two forces.

Over the years, the differences between the two ideological positions
have had a history of alternating between violence and peace. To
categorize the violence as a struggle between Catholicism and Protestant-
ism is inaccurate. It is true that in general those who want a united republic
tend to be Catholic and those that want Northern Ireland to remain with
Great Britain tend to be Protestant. But it is political opinion and who will

get and hold political and economic power – not religious affiliation – which causes the continuing troubles in Northern Ireland. The opposing religious beliefs of the political camps merely serve to galvanize the parties and, to some extent, muddy the issue. A street mural in a Protestant neighborhood of Belfast sums up the conflict succinctly: "Our message to the Irish is simple: The conflict is about NATIONALITY."

Bloody Sunday

As the press graphically reported in the late 1960s and 1970s, sometimes the clash of opinions erupted into violence and bloodshed. Sunday, January 30, 1972, was one of the darkest of many dark days in the recent history of Northern Ireland. Despite a ban on street demonstrations in Northern Ireland imposed by the British government, civil rights demonstrators planned and carried out a peaceful march on Derry. Their purpose was to protest the recent decision by the British government to jail suspected IRA terrorists without benefit of a trial.

An estimated 15,000 to 20,000 demonstrators marched into Derry carrying posters and chanting. As they entered the city, their intended route of march was interrupted as British army forces posted barricades across the roads. As the crowd began to turn away from the barricades, something went terribly wrong. Tear gas and rubber bullets were fired into the milling crowd of demonstrators. Within minutes, the tear gas and rubber bullets were replaced with real bullets, and panic swept through the demonstrators, many of them teenagers, as they fled from the withering fire of British army regulars.

The event was dubbed **Bloody Sunday**. When the gunsmoke cleared, 13 demonstrators were dead and one would die several months later from gunshot wounds. Six of the dead were 17-year-olds. The next two decades saw a series of bombings by Republican supporters and reprisals by the British government. There is no doubt that many innocent bystanders were injured and killed.

Northern Ireland Today

The last few years seem to have witnessed the dawn of a moderation of attitudes and extremist tactics. In the early 1990s, an armistice was agreed to between the Irish Republican Army and the British government. The armistice received worldwide attention and approval. When the IRA became impatient with the lack of progress in negotiations and resorted to several car bombings, international censure of their actions was quick in coming. At the time of this writing, that censure has kept extremist activities in check, and negotiations are continuing. In 1997 and 1998, the British government made further overtures to the IRA that have served to continue the peaceful, although tenuous, peace.

As a gesture of good faith, the British government removed all military checkpoints along the border between Northern Ireland and the Republic, and their presence is not so obvious in the historical flashpoints of Belfast, Derry, and Armagh. The longer the cease-fire is in place, the more peaceful Northern Ireland remains. As a result, tourism numbers in Northern Ireland are higher than they have ever been. The Irish are flocking to Northern Ireland as tourists, as are western European and North American tourists.

On May 22, 1998, voters flocked to the polls in Northern Ireland. They were expressing their opinion about the **Good Friday Agreement**, a peace accord that had been ironed out on April 10, 1998 by eight warring political factions on the Northern Ireland scene. Over 81% of Northern Ireland's registered voters turned out to vote, and over 71% of those voters approved the peace accord. Nearly 95% of the voters in the Republic of Ireland also approved the accord. (They were voting because the accord required a change in the Irish Constitution.)

The peace accord, crafted under the experienced hand of US negotiator **George Mitchell**, called for the establishment of a 108-member governing body called the **Northern Ireland Assembly**. While Northern Ireland will retain its political allegiance to England, the Northern Ireland Assembly will grant Northern Ireland a significant degree of local autonomy. The accord also called for the disarming of various Northern Ireland paramilitary groups and the release of hundreds of political prisoners currently in British and Irish prisons. (These are issues that still threaten to overturn the apple cart of peace in Northern Ireland, however.)

Will it work? Has peace finally come to this beautiful corner of the world? Even seasoned and cynical political observers are cautiously optimistic about the message sent by the voters. They admit that both the significant voter turnout and the resounding victory of the peace accord at the polls seem to bode well for a peaceful future in Northern Ireland. However, some of the more antagonistic factions in Northern Ireland have bowed their necks and refused to accept the obvious preference of the vast majority of Northern Ireland's citizens. This rebellion – and an associated return to violent means — jeopardizes the incredible progress that has been made.

However, I am hopeful that this most recent turn of events will indeed mean a peaceful future for the North. It certainly sets the stage for a season or two of peace. Let's hope it continues for many years to come.

While a return to violence cannot be ruled out, I have hope that differences will be ironed out peacefully in the future.

THE IRISH ECONOMY TODAY

Historically, Ireland's economy has been dependent on agriculture. In fact, even today 90% of the land in Ireland is undeveloped and considered agricultural. But the Irish government knew an agricultural economy would not meet the needs of their people in a global economy. As early as 1950, the Irish government became active in subsidizing and otherwise supporting industry, and one of their biggest pushes today is in the area of jobs creation. Their efforts have slowly transformed Ireland's economy into one centered on industry, which today accounts for 37% of gross domestic product, over 75% of exports, and is responsible for the employment of 29% of the work force.

As of this writing, the Irish economy is one of the hottest in the European Community. Wages increased by 44% from 1995 to 2000, and unemployment has plummeted from double digits in the mid-1990s to 4.5%. By far, most people work in the service sector, where 57% of the Irish population is employed.

IMPORTANT NAMES IN IRISH HISTORY

You'll see their names on street signs, parks, bridges, and railway stations. You'll hear ballads sung about them or disgust in the voices that utter them:

St. Patrick *(389–461?) – St. Patrick is probably as revered in Ireland as George Washington or Abraham Lincoln is in America. But the feelings for St. Patrick go beyond revere – almost to the point of adulation. While not the first Christian missionary to Ireland, St. Patrick was perhaps the most tireless, and certainly the most well known.*

St. Brigid *(5th century) – Saint Brigid founded an abbey during the 5th century.*

Brian Boru *(926–1014) – High King of Ireland whose armies defeated the Vikings in the Battle of Clontarf.*

Dermot MacMurrough *(1110–1171) – As it turns out, MacMurrough assumes the role of Benedict Arnold in Irish history. It was his anger at his censure and exile by the other Irish kings that sent him to London to plead for support from King Henry II. The ensuing invasion of land barons and their armies resulted in over 750 years of English rule in Ireland.*

Richard le Clare *(died 1176) – historians better know Richard le Clare as either the Earl of Pembroke, or simply as Strongbow. He was one of the first Englush noblemen to invade Ireland.*

Oliver Cromwell *(1599–1658) – The Darth Vader of Irish history. Probably the most powerful, ruthless, merciless, and efficient conqueror to invade Ireland. Many atrocities are attributed to him and his armies. Cromwell roared through Ireland leaving death, devastation, subjugation, and broken lives in his path.*

James II *– Called Catholic James, he fought William of Orange for the English crown at the Battle of the Boyne in 1690. He lost, ending all hopes of relief from oppression for Catholics.*

William of Orange *– Husband of Mary Stuart, Protestant daughter of James II. William defeated James, a Catholic king, for the crown of England. James' defeat signaled the end of a short period when Catholics in Ireland hoped for relief from Protestant occupation and conquest.*

Jonathan Swift *(1667–1745) – Swift was a writer and Dean of St. Patrick's Cathedral in Dublin. He is perhaps best known for his satirical Gulliver's Travels. He was also a tireless writer against the tyranny of the English Crown.*

Oliver Goldsmith *(1728–1774) – Goldsmith was an author, born in County Longford.*

Theobald Wolfe Tone *(1763–1798) – Leader of the United Irishmen who were fighting for Irish independence.*

Daniel O'Connell *(1775–1847) – Daniel O'Connell was known as "the Liberator." It was he who was responsible for the repeal of the Penal Laws, resulting in emancipation for Catholics.*

Charles Stewart Parnell *(1846–1891) – Considered the leader of the Home Rule campaign for Ireland and the leader of the Irish people. At one time in his career, he was called the uncrowned king of Ireland. A Protestant, he was a tireless fighter for Irish independence. He was the leader of the Irish parliamentary party. His affair with Kitty O'Shea split the Irish party and he lost support from his own party, the Catholic Church, and the Irish people in general.*

Oscar Wilde *(1854–1900) – Playwright and author. His works included Lady Windemere's Fan and The Importance of Being Earnest.*

George Bernard Shaw *(1856–1950) – Famous playwright born in Dublin. Some of his works include Arms and the Man, John Bull's Other Island, and Pygmalion. Shaw won the Nobel Prize for Literature.*

William Butler (W. B.) Yeats *(1865–1939) – A world-renowned poet, Yeats won the Nobel Prize for Literature. Yeats also served as a senator in the Irish Free State.*

James Joyce *(1882–1941) – Novelist, poet, and playwright born in Dublin. His works include Ulysses, A Portrait of the Artist as a Young Man, and Dubliners.*

6. PLANNING YOUR TRIP

WHEN TO GO - CLIMATE & WEATHER

Ireland enjoys a temperate climate year-round, thanks to the warm waters of the Gulf Stream. Most tourists find the weather pleasant and more than acceptable for vacationing from April through October, although I have been there in the winter months and found it to be delightful as well, although a wee bit chilly. During April and May, the temperatures are generally in the mid-50s during the days. During the summer months, you can expect the temperatures to be in the 60s, with even an occasional day or two in the 70s. Fall temperatures generally emulate those of the springtime, with daytime temperatures ranging from the high 40s to mid-50s most of the time. For the most part, winters on the Emerald Isle are also mild, with average temperatures in the mid-30s to low 40s.

But beware! There is a reason Ireland is known as the Emerald Isle. There are more shades of green than you can count, and they remain that way due to the frequency of rain, which can be anytime, anywhere throughout the year. (The average annual rainfall in Ireland is 43 inches.) However, despite frequent rain showers, it seldom rains hard enough to dampen the enjoyment of the many sights there are to see. I've found that a sweater (purchased in Ireland, of course), a lightweight raincoat, and (perhaps) an umbrella will make your touring pleasant.

On a recent flight to Ireland, as we neared Shannon, the captain announced to the passengers that there was a light skiff of snow on the ground. I had an inkling this was uncommon when many of the Irish passengers moved to the windows to see their island in white. While it does snow occasionally during the winter, it is generally warm enough to rain instead.

July and August are the peak tourist months, and it is during these months that you may find yourself waiting in line to see some of the more popular sights such as the **Blarney Stone** and the **Book of Kells**. During April, May, September and October, the numbers of tourists are noticeably less, and during the winter months you're liable to be downright lonely for the company of fellow travelers. There will be a few sights that aren't open until April or May, but I note those for you throughout the book.

As you might expect, rates in hotels and B&Bs are seasonal, and you'll pay slightly more during the high season (from June through August) than you will the rest of the year. Some hotels have another rate from March to May and during September–October that is less than the high season, but higher than the rate they charge from November to February.

Ireland has plenty of "dull days" – the Irish term for overcast or cloudy days. But other than providing an opaque backdrop for most of your photographs, there's really no harm done by the dull days. But oh – when the sky is a shimmering blue it is a sight to behold! Washed clean by the rains and ocean breezes, its brilliance accentuates the majesty of brooding ruins, augments the tranquil effect of verdant glens, and coaxes the true turquoise tint from the sea.

During most months of the year, there is an omnipresent breeze. A light sweater or sweatshirt is usually enough to combat its effects. As you visit some of the coastal sights you'll experience more wind – so hold on to your hat!

The Emerald Isle has Daylight Savings Time – called Summer Time. It begins the last Sunday of March, and reverts to Standard Time the last Sunday in October. This is a complimentary bonus of extra daylight hours with which to continue your walks on the beach, or an extra hour or two to prowl around deserted ruins.

AVERAGE DAYTIME TEMPERATURES
(FAHRENHEIT)

January	43°	July	60°
February	41°	August	61°
March	44°	September	56°
April	45°	October	49°
May	53°	November	44°
June	59°	December	41°

WHAT TO PACK

I've packed for Ireland two ways: heavy and light. On my first trip, I packed for every conceivable weather condition and social occasion. On my next trip, I packed lightly, going for versatile clothing. I'm here to tell you the latter method is far superior.

Here are the necessities for a week's trip: sweater, 3-4 shirts (usually long sleeve), a couple of pairs of casual-style pants, one skirt for women, comfortable shoes, several pair of underwear and socks. If you plan on eating in the finest restaurants in Ireland, of course you'll want to bring a suitable pair of slacks, a suit or sports jacket, and possibly a tie for men, and a nice dress, skirt and blouse, or pants suit and nylons and shoes for women. Children tend to go through their clothes faster, but I recommend you pack clothes comparable to what you pack for yourself, although they may need a few extra changes of clothes.

You should be prepared for rain. I prefer not to carry an umbrella, choosing instead to fend off the rain with a cap: on all of my trips to Ireland it has rarely rained hard enough to make me wish for an umbrella. I suggest taking one of those small retractable umbrellas, if a cap won't do the job for you. Since my first trip, I no longer take a raincoat either because I find that an Irish wool sweater does a fine job shedding the water and keeps me dry. You'll need to determine whether you think a raincoat is necessary.

You can get just about any toiletry you might need in Ireland: toothpaste, deodorant, shampoo, lotion, make-up and feminine care products. You'll have to decide how important your particular brand is to you, because it may not be sold in Ireland. If you require prescription drugs, I recommend you bring enough for your trip, but be sure you know exactly what you take, how often, and in what dose in case you lose your medication. Hair dryers are generally available in most hotels and many B&Bs and guesthouses. If you have to have a hair dryer, you should bring your own, but make sure you also bring a converter and plug adapter. Finally, there are places to have your clothes pressed; alternatively, you may want to purchase a small travel iron (with converter and adapter).

If you are traveling with kids, don't forget to bring books, crossword puzzles, magnetic games like chess, checkers, or backgammon, or a Gameboy (or whatever they like), to keep them entertained as you drive from town to town and in the evenings. Also, depending on their age, you should consider purchasing them their own disposable cameras so they can take pictures (it's their vacation too, after all), and they won't bug you to use your camera.

You will need good maps. If you are renting a car, the rental agency will give you one that is fairly general, but not too bad. Some of the smaller towns and more rural roads won't be on the maps you receive from them.

You may want to pick up regional maps in the areas you are traveling to; they are usually available at the tourist offices. If you plan on being in Ireland for more than one week, ask the car rental agency for an extra map. I usually wear a map out in a week.

You may want to supplement this guide with another B&B or hotel guide. The Irish Town and Country Homes Association produces a yearly book on Bed and Breakfasts for the Republic called *Guest Accommodation* (£2.50), which is updated yearly. The Irish Hotels Federation publishes a book called *Be Our Guest* (£2). Both books list hundreds of Bord Failte-approved B&Bs, guesthouses, and hotels throughout the country. Tourist offices will have them, and they are worth the money. Use this guide for personal insights into each accommodation; use these other two if you find you are out in the middle of nowhere and it's getting late, or if all the accommodations I have suggested are full.

ENTRY REQUIREMENTS

First and foremost, you must have a **current passport** to enter Ireland. If you have traveled internationally, you probably already have one; it's a good idea to check the expiration date well before you plan to travel. American passports are valid for five years for children and 10 years for adults. Canadian passports are valid for five years. All US citizens traveling to Ireland must have a valid passport. For Canadian citizens, children under 16 can be included on their parents' passports, but they must have their own passport if they are traveling alone.

If you are getting a new passport, you should apply six weeks before you plan to depart (four weeks in Canada). That should give you plenty of time to receive your passport. If you are inside the six-week window, don't fear – you can still get a passport, but it will be more expensive, as you will have to pay for overnight mail charges. About five days is the quickest you can get a passport, but I wouldn't cut it that short! Applications are available at US or Canadian passport offices as well as at some post offices. Some Canadian travel agencies also have passport applications.

Ireland requires only a passport for entry into their country. No visa is necessary if you are a citizen of the United States, Canada, Australia, or New Zealand and if your stay is less than 90 days (180 days in Northern Ireland). If you plan an extended stay that lasts longer than that, you must demonstrate that you have adequate funds to stay and already possess a return airline ticket.

If you are getting a new passport, here is what will be required:
• a notarized copy of your birth certificate. **A hospital copy won't work.** Naturalization papers or an old passport are acceptable.

- two identical passport photos taken within the last six months. I've found my local AAA agency to be the best place to get these.
- you'll need to bring a picture ID, such as a driver's license.
- if this is your first passport, you must apply in person.
- the cost is (currently) $65 if you are 18 or over, and $40 if you are younger than 18.
- if you are renewing a passport, and it was issued within the past 12 years, the cost is $55 (if you are over 18 and your last name is still the same.)

CUSTOMS REGULATIONS
American Citizens

Americans who have been out of the country for more than 48 hours may return to the US with up to $400 worth of goods without paying duty. In addition, you may return with up to 200 cigarettes and one liter of alcohol (you must be at least 21 years old to bring liquor back). If you are traveling as a family, the exemptions apply to each person, but can be pooled as a group.

If the total value of your purchases is greater than $400, you will be expected to pay additional duty. Currently, you must pay 10% duty on the next $1,000 worth of items you are returning with. Beyond the $1,400 threshold (the $400 duty free and the next $1,000 worth of goods), you will be assessed a fee based on the category your purchases fall into. If you need to pay additional duty, cash, checks, travelers checks, and (in some places) credit cards are acceptable.

Canadian Citizens

Once a year, Canadian citizens are allowed to bring C$300 worth of foreign goods back home without paying duty. That applies if you have been out of the country for at least seven days. If you have been gone less than seven days, but more than 48 hours, you can bring back C$100 duty-free each trip, and there is no limit to the number of times you can do this. Exemptions apply to all members of a family traveling with you, but the exemptions cannot be combined as a group.

You may also bring home, duty-free, 1.14 liters of wine or liquor or twenty-four 12-oz. bottles of beer or ale. If you are 16 years of age or older, you may bring home, also duty-free, 200 cigarettes, 50 cigars or cigarillos, and 400 tobacco sticks or 400 grams of manufactured tobacco.

Both American and Canadian citizens can mail gifts home duty-free if the gifts are valued at less than US$50 and C$60. You can only mail one package per day per addressee. Packages should be marked "Unsolicited gift." Packages should also be marked on the outside with the retail value. The value of these gifts is not part of your exemption, and they are duty-free.

During your return flight home, flight attendants will hand out Customs forms for you to complete. You are expected to declare the total value of all products you bring in with you.

IRISH REPRESENTATIVES ABROAD

Before you leave for Ireland, you may wish to contact some of the following organizations. They can be of great help in planning your vacation. Whether you are looking for brochures, travel information, advice, or just an Irish accent to listen to, they should be able to meet your needs.

United States
- **Irish Tourist Board**, *345 Park Avenue, New York, NY 10154. Tel. 212/371-9052, 800/223-6470.*
- **Irish Embassy**, *2234 Massachusetts Avenue NW, Washington DC 20008. Tel. 202/462-3939.*
- **Consulate General of Ireland**, *345 Park Avenue, New York, NY 10154. Tel. 212/319-2555.*
- **Consulate of Ireland**, *William McCarthy Building, 535 Boylston Street. Boston MA 02116. Tel. 617/267-9330.*
- **Consulate of Ireland**, *655 Montgomery Street, San Francisco, California 94111.*
- **Consulate of Ireland**, *Wrigley Building, 400 North Michigan Avenue. Chicago, Illinois 60611.*

Canada
- **Irish Tourist Board**, *160 Bloor Street East, Suite 1150, Toronto, Ontario M4W 1B9. Tel. 416/929-6783.*
- **Irish Embassy**, *170 Metcalfe Street, Ottawa, Ontario K2P 1P3. Tel. 613/233-6281.*

BORD FAILTE - THE IRISH TOURIST BOARD

The reception you receive as a tourist in Ireland will be warm and cheerful. The Irish take tourism in their country very seriously. Approximately one out of every 12 Irish citizens is employed in the tourism industry. Tourism in Ireland accounts for over 60% of all exports of services, and its growth rate is double that of the economy as a whole.

With that kind of impact on the Irish economy, you can be sure the **Irish Tourist Board** – *Bord Failte* (pronounced fall'-cha – which means "Welcome" in Irish) is anxious to see that you have a pleasant and enjoyable trip to their country. Several months prior to your trip, call or write to any of several Bord Failte locations, and they will provide you with an abundance of tourism material. You should request the specific types of information you are interested in: tourist attractions, Bed and Break-fasts, hotels, etc. Bord Failte also has an office in New York City *(Tel. 212-418-0800)*. Much of the material they send you is free. They'll also usually send you a price list for other materials you can purchase.

Bord Failte has a network of tourist offices throughout the width and breadth of Ireland. These local offices are a great source of information for points of interest in their respective areas. Following are the regional offices of Bord Failte:

- **Dublin City and County Regional Tourism Organization**, *1 Clarinda Park North, Dun Laoghaire. Tel. (01) 280-8571*
- **Northwest Regional Tourism Organization**, *Aras Reddan, Temple Street, Sligo. Tel. (051) 75823*
- **Southeast Tourism**, *41 The Quay, County Waterford. Tel. (071) 61201*
- **Ireland West Regional Tourism Organization**, *Aras Failte, Eyre Square, Galway. Tel. (091) 63081*
- **Midland-East Tourism Organization**, *Dublin Road, Mulingar, County Westmeath*
- **Southwest Regional Tourism Organization**, *Tourist House, Grand Parade, Cork. Tel. (021) 273251*
- **Shannon Development**, *Shannon Town Centre, County Clare. Tel. (061) 361555*
- **Northern Ireland Tourism Board**, *St. Anne's Court, 59 North Street, Belfast, Northern Ireland BT1 1ND. Tel. (028) 9023-1221*

GETTING TO IRELAND

You have several options for arranging your trip. If you are an experienced traveler, you may feel comfortable scouting for the best airfares around. Most of us, however, will benefit from the expertise of a qualified international travel agent.

Find an agent that specializes in international travel. Check with friends and relatives who have traveled abroad and get their recommendations. Interview several travel agencies until you find one with which you are comfortable. After you have decided on a travel agent, provide him or her with all the organizations you are affiliated with – AAA, AARP, your credit union, your company, etc. Sometimes these entities have negotiated special rates with the airlines, and your travel agent can find those rates for you. Also keep in mind that, depending on the season, airlines sometimes run discount fares that beat any affiliation-negotiated rates.

Every year, **Aer Lingus**, *Tel. 800/474-7424*, and **Delta,** *1
4141,* come up with attractive travel packages that include
rental, and lodging. Bear in mind that packages are typically
travel from the cities on the East Coast from which Aer Lingus or Delta
fly directly to Ireland. Getting to one of those cities may drive up your
costs considerably.

Transatlantic flights enter Ireland in one of two airports: Dublin or
Shannon. At the time of this writing, Aer Lingus and Delta are the only
airlines that fly directly to Ireland from North America. Delta flies from
Atlanta to Shannon, and from New York City (JFK) to Shannon or Dublin.
Aer Lingus flies from New York City (JFK), Boston, and Chicago directly
to Dublin and Shannon. Neither Delta nor Aer Lingus has direct flights
from Canada.

Other major airlines occasionally announce new service to Ireland
direct from the US, but as yet none of them have lasted. Other airlines fly
to Ireland via London where you then transfer to one of their interna-
tional partners: British Airways, British Midland, SAS, and a handful of
others. One advantage of connecting in London is that you can get a flight
to some of Ireland's minor airports: Cork, Galway, Kerry, Sligo, Knock,
and Belfast. If your eventual destination involves one of these locations,
you may want your travel agent to check on costs, times, etc.

GETTING AROUND IRELAND

There are many ways to get around Ireland, and the mode depends
entirely on your purpose, destinations, adventuresome spirit and desires.
Bicycle, bus, rental car, hitchhiking, and train – or a combination of any
of them – are the major options.

BY BICYCLE

If you choose to see the Emerald Isle on two wheels, congratulations.
This is one of the most popular modes of transportation for tourists from
May through October. Most cities of any size have bicycle rental shops
with bicycles for hire on a daily, weekly, and monthly basis. Expect to pay
about £7 per day, £30 per week, or £115 per month. Most bicycles for hire
are the currently popular 18- or 21-speed mountain bikes.

Many of the bicycle shops close down during the off-season, so if
you're going to Ireland from about November through March or April,
you may want to call the Tourist Office in the city where you want to begin
your cycling and get the names of companies that are open that time of
year.

BY BUS

Bus Eireann is the state-run organization that runs the bus (and train) lines. They run all the long-distance buses, as well as most of the local and sightseeing buses. If you choose to travel in Ireland by bus, you should purchase a **Provincial Bus Schedule** at any bus terminal, or at the many Newsagents scattered across the country (typically in small grocery stores).

There are several types of passes available. The rates are current as of this writing:

• **Irish Explorer Rail/Bus** – Valid for any eight days of travel within a 15-day window. The cost is £115 for adults and £58 for children ages 5-15. For travel in the Republic of Ireland only.

• **Emerald Card Rail/Bus** – Valid for any eight days of travel within a 15-day window. Similar to the Irish Explorer Rail/Bus pass listed above, except this allows you to go to Belfast and elsewhere in Northern Ireland. The cost is £115 for adults and £58 for children ages 5–15. There is also a pass for travel on any 15 days out of a 30-day window. The rates are £200 for adults, and £100 for children ages 5-15.

Children under age five travel free. If you'd feel more comfortable purchasing your passes before you leave, you can write to: **CIE Tours**, *108 Ridgedale Avenue, PO Box 2355, Morristown, New Jersey 07962.*

BY CAR

"Left is right and right is wrong" when it comes to driving in Ireland. That's right – the Irish drive on the left, as do the English.

Surprisingly, driving on the left is not difficult to get used to. However, if you rent a car with a manual transmission, you should have reasonable coordination since you'll be shifting with your left hand instead of your right. If you can't pat your head and rub your stomach at the same time, you may want to consider paying extra for an automatic transmission – but it will cost you from £8 to £15 extra per day, depending on the time of year, the agency, and the class of car you rent. That's a little pricey, and you have to make the decision, but it will be just one less thing to worry about. And one less thing to worry about is exactly what you'll need as you encounter your first "round-about."

ROUND-ABOUTS

Round-abouts can be intimidating the first few times you enter one. The following will help you navigate your way in and out:
- *traffic in round-abouts moves clock-wise;*
- *traffic already in the round-about has the right-of-way and cars in the round-about and those behind you will expect you to stop if the road is not clear;*
- *round-abouts are generally well-signed going into and within them;*
- *round-abouts that handle lots of traffic are often augmented by traffic signals.*

If you live in the eastern United States, you are probably familiar with traffic circles – the US name for round-abouts. But if you are from west of the original 13 colonies, they may be a mystery. Round-abouts are a traffic control system found at the intersection of two or more roads. Generally, no stop signs or traffic lights are employed – drivers merely enter the circle continuing on their journey until they reach the outlet that takes them in the direction they want to go (got that?). Initially a skeptic, I came to admire the smooth and efficient way they manage traffic.

There are several types of roads in the Republic and in Northern Ireland. In Northern Ireland, roads are categorized as *A*- or *B*-roads. *A*-roads are the main roads, and *B*-roads are the local roads.

In the Republic, there are three primary types of roads: *M*-, *N*- and *R*-roads.

M-roads are about the same as interstate highways in the United States. The speed limit on these roads is 70 mph. There are not many of these roads in Ireland.

N-roads (national roads) are similar to two-lane highways in the United States. The speed limit on N-roads is 60 mph. Occasionally you'll see signs for a "dual carriageway" and you'll come to love them. They are similar to divided highways and are a welcome sight after the narrow roads you primarily drive in Ireland.

R-roads (regional roads) make up the majority of the roads and are extremely narrow. They are well maintained and the speed limit on these roads is also 60 mph, unless otherwise posted. However, as a practical matter, I found 40 mph to be the speed at which I was most comfortable most of the time.

WATCH OUT FOR THOSE IRISH DRIVERS!

Many of the N-roads are two-lane highways with wide, flat, paved shoulders called hard margins. Even with oncoming traffic, cars behind you will pass you. You are expected to move over (to your left) and drive on the hard margin until they pass. Likewise, oncoming traffic will expect both the car they are passing and oncoming traffic – you – to move over, onto the hard margin. It's bizarre, but it works very well. Irish drivers faithfully use their turn signals before participating in this maneuver, and you should too. Watch carefully for a day or two before you try this maneuver.

Bear in Mind...

• Drivers and front seat passengers are required to wear seat belts.
• It is unlawful for children under age 12 to ride in the front seat.
• Motorcyclists and their passengers are required to wear helmets.
• Ireland has very aggressive laws when it comes to driving under the influence of alcohol.
• A solid white line serves the same purpose in Ireland as the solid yellow line does here – it means no passing.
• Gasoline is more expensive in Ireland than in the US, but on a par with the rest of Europe. The last time I was there, the cost averaged about 70 pence per liter. That works out to about £2.65 per gallon, or roughly $3.32 per gallon. The cost will vary, of course, depending on the exchange rate when you are traveling.
• Unless you are traveling on M-roads, remember travel times will be much slower than in the states due to narrow winding roads, frequent villages, tractors, sheep, cattle, etc. I found 40 miles an hour is a fairly aggressive estimate for most roads.
• In general, locals tend to drive at much higher speeds than I am comfortable with. In those cases, I simply look for an opportunity to pull over and let them pass, then continue my driving and sightseeing at a leisurely pace.

Driving in Cities

Driving in the cities requires special attention. Bicyclists, motorcyclists, and pedestrians are more plentiful and far more aggressive than in most American cities. Motorcyclists in particular can be maddening: passing on your left or right, darting in and out of traffic, and making a general nuisance of themselves! Traffic lights are on the corners – not hanging in the air over the intersections. I never did get accustomed to this, and had to consciously remind myself to watch closely. In the larger cities, (Dublin, Cork, Galway) it is virtually impossible, and dangerous, to sightsee while you are driving. Find a place to park, and walk around the cities, seeing all that you wish in relative safety.

I say relative safety, because as a pedestrian in Ireland you need to concern yourself with the different traffic patterns. Rather than looking left for traffic as you would in the US, you must look to the right! During World War II, Winston Churchill had an accident that underscores the importance of this. On a trip to New York City, he looked to the right for traffic – as he would in London – and stepped into the path of an oncoming taxi – coming from his left. Fortunately, he sustained only minor injuries. So remember: look to the right!

Parking

If you are driving in Ireland, you will assuredly be parking. Parking rules are a little different than in the United States, and sometimes the rules are not intuitively obvious. Here are a few pointers.

It is illegal to park:
• within five meters of an intersection
• at a taxi stand or bus stop
• where there is a continuous white line, unless the roadway has at least three traffic lanes
• in such a manner as to cause an obstruction
• within 15 meters of the approach side of a crosswalk, or within five meters on the other side of a crosswalk
• when double yellow lines are present; if a single yellow line is present, it is illegal to park from 8:30am to 6:30pm, Monday through Friday

Some of the larger towns and cities (e.g., Cork, Galway, Sligo, Drogheda, etc.) have a parking system called **Disk Parking** in their city centers. This fact is generally prominently displayed throughout the parts of the city where disk parking is required. **Do not ignore these signs**; if you do, you may find yourself the proud owner of a £15 parking ticket. (Do I sound as though I am speaking from experience?) Parking disks can be purchased at any Newsagent for the princely sum of 20p to 25p, and are very wise investments. These cards have a series of months, days, and years, as well as hours and minutes on them. When you find a parking place in a disk zone, park your car. Before you leave, scratch off the correct day, month, and year, as well as the correct hour and minute. Place the completed parking disk on the inside of the curb-side window.

Check the signs near your parking place for the maximum amount of time you can park with a parking disk —it is usually an hour or two. If the maximum period is two hours, you must complete two parking disks and have both displayed in your window. Once the maximum time has expired, you must move your car from that street for at least one hour. Each parking disk generally has instructions for its use on the back of the disk.

While Ireland is very tuned into tourists and tourism, there seems to be no hesitation to ticket rental cars for failing to follow the parking rules of the city!

Road Signs

Both Ireland and Northern Ireland have great road signs. The US could take a lesson from these tourist-conscious countries.

Irish signposts have a unique design: a single pole with any number of horizontal arrows with the name of towns and distances written on them. Each arrow is fastened to a pole with a circular clamp, much like those used on radiator hoses. It is a popular schoolboy prank to twist the signs around slightly, giving the unwary traveler a more...scenic...view of Ireland. If this happens, don't fret; enjoy the ride and the unplanned adventure – you'll find your way eventually!

SIGNPOSTS & ROAD NUMBERS

Once you get off the M- and N-roads, road numbers are pretty much just found on maps; there may be a sign with the road number on it out in the country at an intersection, but more than likely it won't be there (I'd guess 80% of the time it's not), and it's never posted on the road as you're driving along. The Irish are a little nonchalant about street addresses, and they're the same way about road numbers being marked anywhere on the roads themselves. The country is well-signposted with the names of towns, but not the road numbers.

Rental Cars

While airfares are usually fairly price-competitive, you will need to shop around for the best car rental rates. You can do this through your travel agent, or you can do it yourself. Rates on rental cars seem to change on a daily basis, and car rental agencies also have a series of discounts based on negotiated rates with affiliated companies and organizations. I recently checked the major rental car agencies – Avis, Budget, Hertz, National – and found a surprisingly wide range of prices. For a two-week rental, I was quoted prices from $425 to over $975 for the same class of car and the same coverages!

When comparing rental car rates, be certain you are shopping "apples to apples," such as length of time, type of insurance, size of car, mileage charges, service charges and taxes. When I checked, I asked the companies to include Collision Damage Waiver (CDW), theft insurance, and Value Added Tax. All the agencies I checked with included unlimited mileage in their rates, but ask just to make sure. Also, be sure you compare dollars to dollars, or pounds to pounds. Most agencies will quote their rates in dollars as well as pounds.

Regarding gasoline, some rental agencies give you a full tank of gas and require you to leave a £25 or £30 deposit. If you return the car with a full tank, they refund the deposit. Other agencies give you a full tank of gas and expect you to return it empty; they do not give you credit for any gas left in the tank, even if you filled it at the airport. Be sure and check which policy is in effect when you rent your car.

You'll need a valid US or Canadian driver's license and a major credit card to drive in Ireland, but you do not need an International Drivers license unless you are staying for more than one year.

One more caution: If you are renting a car in some of the smaller cities (Galway, Waterford, Killarney, etc.) expect to pay from two to three times more than if you rented one in Cork, Shannon, or Dublin. While cars are available in these smaller cities, the fleets are relatively small, and the costs are quite a bit higher. You might consider either flying into one of the main cities and renting your car there, or if you do fly into Galway (for instance), you might consider seeing Galway on foot, then take the bus to Shannon airport to pick up your rental car. (Note: You will only be flying into one of these smaller cities if you are coming from England. All international flights from the US land in either Shannon or Dublin.)

Most car rental agencies in Ireland will only rent to drivers who are at least 23 years old and younger than 75 years old. Some rental agencies require you to be at least 25.

Car Insurance: To Buy or Not To Buy

If you are accustomed to renting cars in the United States, you know your own car insurance usually covers you while you are driving a rental car in the US. *Such is not the case in Ireland.* Your domestic car insurance will *not* cover you while you are driving a rental car in Ireland. However, some credit card companies will cover your car rental insurance, so you can forgo the **Collision Damage Waiver** (CDW) charge. That amounts to about £8 or more per day.

However, before you accept or forgo the CDW, check with your credit card company because you may or may not be covered if you rent a car with your credit card. For example, my credit card company covers collisions, rollovers, vandalism, theft, tire blowout or damage, and windshield damage. Also check what restrictions, deductibles, or requirements apply. My credit card company has the following restrictions: covers rental car for a maximum of 31 days; all drivers must be listed on the rental agreement; all claims must be submitted to the credit card company within 20 days; the entire car rental must be charged to the credit card.

Many major credit card companies offer a similar service, but please don't assume yours does. Recently, several of the credit card companies chose to stop covering rentals in a few countries, including Ireland, presumably due to high accident rates. Regardless, check first: programs change, services expire, or new stipulations may be put in place. Before you go, check to be sure.

As you might expect, there are several dozen car rental agencies in Ireland. Following are a few of the more notable agencies. The 800 numbers can be called from the US prior to your departure. If you are in Ireland and want to make a reservation, dial the local number listed.

Car Rentals in Dublin

Alamo-Treaty Rent-a-Car, *Tel. 800/522-9696, (01) 844-4086*

Argus Rent-a-Car, *Argus House, 59 Terenure Road East, Dublin. Tel. (01) 490-4444, Fax (01) 490-6328*

Atlas Car Rentals Ltd., *Desk 1, Arrivals Hall, Dublin Airport. Tel. (01) 844-4859, Fax (01) 844-0732*

Auto-Europe, *US toll free 800/223-5555, in Ireland 800/558-892*

Avis Rent-a-Car, *Dublin Airport, Arrivals Hall, US toll-free 800/331-1084, (01) 605-7500*

IRISH DRIVING TERMS

bonnet	*hood*
boot	*trunk*
caravan	*trailer (like a travel trailer)*
car park	*parking lot*
dip	*dim (as in: dim your lights)*
diversion	*detour*
dual carriageway	*divided highway*
Garda	*police*
give way	*yield*
lay by	*rest area*
margin	*shoulder*
M_, Motorway	*interstate highway*
N_, National road	*two-lane highway*
Overtaking	*passing*
petrol	*gasoline*
way out	*exit*

Budget Rent-a-Car, *Dublin Airport, Arrivals Hall, US toll-free 800/472-3325, (01) 844-5150*

Casey's/Flannelly Car Rentals, *Tel. 212/935-0606*

Hertz Rent-a-Car, *Dublin Airport, Arrivals Hall, US toll-free 800/654-3001, (01) 844-5466*

Holiday Autos, *US toll free 800/422-7737*

Kemwell Rent-a-Car, *US toll-free 800/678-0678*

Long's Travel, *96 Ridgedale Avenue, Cedar Knolls NJ 07927, US toll free 800/524-0555*

Tom Mannion Self Drive, *US toll-free 800/666-4066*

Murray's EuropCar Car Rental, *Baggot Street Bridge, Dublin 4. Tel. (01) 668-1777, Fax (01) 660-2958; or toll-free 800/227-3876*

South County Car Rentals, *Rochestown Avenue, Dun Laoghaire, County Dublin. Tel. (01) 280-6005 Fax (01) 285-7016; or toll-free 800/521-0643*

Windsor Car Rentals, *South Circular Road, Rialto, Dublin 8. Tel. (01) 454-0800, Fax (01) 454-0122*

Car Rentals in Limerick

• **Cara Rent-a-Car Ltd.**, *Coonagh Cross, Ennis Road, Limerick. Tel. (061) 55811, Fax (061) 55369*

• **Dan Dooley/Kenning Rent-a-Car**, *Knocklong, County Limerick. Tel. (062) 53103, Fax (062) 53392; or toll-free 800/331-9301*

• **Payless/Bunratty Car Rentals**, *Coonagh Cross, Ennis Road, Limerick. Tel (061) 52781, Fax (061) 52516; or toll-free 800/524-0555*

• **Thrifty Irish Car Rentals**, *Maxol Station, Ennis Road, Limerick. Tel. (061) 53049, Fax (061) 53433; or toll-free 800/367-2277*

• **Treaty Rent-a-Car**, *37 William Street, Limerick. Tel. (061) 24211, Fax (061) 412266*

BY HITCHHIKING

Hitchhiking is legal in Ireland, and in former years it was a wildly exciting and romantic way to see the country. More recently, however, several highly publicized murders of hitchhikers have put a damper on it. However, having said that, you'll see far more people hitchhiking in Ireland than you do in the US. If you're going to hitchhike, use caution, go in pairs, and if you feel the least bit uncomfortable about a car or truck that stops to pick you up, wait for the next one.

BY TRAIN

The railways in Ireland literally criss-cross the country and you'll be able to get within striking distance of just about any place in Ireland you'd like to go. From Sligo in the northwest to Wexford in the southeast, from

Dublin to Killarney, the trains will get you to where you want to go. Train service is a little sparse in the province of Connacht, however.

Bus Eireann is the state-run organization that runs the train (and bus) lines. If you choose to travel in Ireland by train, you should purchase a **Train Timetable** at any train terminal, or at the many Newsagents scattered across the country (typically in small grocery stores).

There are several types of passes available. The rates are current as of this writing:

Irish Explorer Rail – Valid for any eight days of travel within a 15-day window – ideal if you want to stay a day or two and explore the surrounding areas before moving on to explore other cities or regions. The charge is £100 for adults and £50 for children ages 5–15. For travel in the Republic of Ireland only.

Irish Rover Rail – Valid for any eight days of travel within a 15-day window. Similar to the Irish Explorer Rail listed above, except this pass allows you to go to Northern Ireland. Rates are £115 for adults and £58 for youth ages 5-15.

Children under age five travel free. If you'd feel more comfortable purchasing your passes before you leave, you can write to: **CIE Tours**, *108 Ridgedale Avenue, PO Box 2355, Morristown, New Jersey 07962.*

HOTEL & INN TERMS

There is a broad spectrum of accommodations to choose from in Ireland – from low-budget hostels to exquisite five-star hotels. Many accommodation prices in Ireland are listed as *per person sharing* – in other words, each person staying in the room pays that price. Some of the hotels charge a flat rate for the first two people staying in the room, with a small supplement for additional guests. When you make your reservations, be sure and clarify whether the price is for the room or per person sharing.

Most Bed and Breakfasts and hotels charge a slight premium for renting a double room to a single traveler, since their rates usually are per person sharing. The "norm" and expectation is that two people will share a room. If a B&B lists its rate as £16 per person sharing, the cost for the room is £32 for two people. If only one person rents the room, instead of charging the full £32 for the double room, a "single supplement" is added to the per person rate, and is normally around £5. Therefore, if one person rents a double room, the cost is £21 (£16 + £5). If a B&B has a single room, they will generally list a single room charge (usually a few pounds less than a double room), with no single supplement added.

Given the above rates, if three people want to share a double room, the cost would be £48 (£16 per person sharing).

You'll also run across the term **ensuite**, which I use in this guide as well. If you get a room ensuite, this means you have a bathroom in your room or suite; otherwise, you'll have to use the bathroom out in the hall.

Many hotels in Ireland tack on a service charge to the cost of their rooms. These charges range from 10% to 15%. The proceeds from these charges are divided among the hotel staff – from the maids to the front desk personnel. I have made an effort to identify all the hotels that add a service charge, but it's still a good idea to check if there is a charge and how much it is when you make your reservations.

Most of the hotels have in-room dialing, bathrooms (referred to as ensuite), televisions, hair dryers, coffee and tea facilities, and trouser presses.

But beware! Guaranteeing a reservation at a hotel in Ireland with a credit card may mean just that – *guaranteeing* a reservation. At some of the upscale hotels in Ireland, if you cancel a reservation *within fourteen days* of your intended day of arrival, and you guaranteed the reservation with a credit card, you will still pay for one night's lodging whether you stay or not. With the rates at luxury hotels ranging from $200 per night to over $750 per night, that's a pretty expensive cancellation! So, when you make your reservation, be sure and ask about the hotel's cancellation policy.

RIDE IN A JAUNTING CAR!

A jaunting car is a small horse-drawn cart peculiar to Ireland. It generally holds the driver and from two to four passengers. If you saw the movie **The Quiet Man** *with John Wayne and Maureen O'Hara, they did their courting under the watchful eye of Barry Fitzgerald (as the driver) as they rode in his jaunting car.*

7. BASIC INFORMATION

BUSINESS HOURS

Businesses are generally open from 9:00am to 5:00pm, although in practice most stores open at 9:30am or 10:00am. In some of the larger cities, stores will stay open later one night of the week. In Dublin, that day is Thursday.

COSTS OF TRAVEL

Obviously, the mode of transportation you choose for your travels and the lifestyle you lead while in Ireland will have great bearing on your travel costs. Having said that, here's some general information about travel costs in Ireland.

Generally speaking, costs in Ireland are about what you'd expect to pay for things in the United States, if you ignore the dollar/pound conversion rate. In other words, if you'd expect to pay $4 for a sandwich, it will generally cost around £4 (which is really about $5.00). Or if you'd expect to pay $69 for a room, it will probably cost around £69 (which is really about $86). One notable exception is the cost of gasoline. For years, gasoline in Europe has been far more expensive than it is in the US. On my most recent trips, petrol was running about $3.32 per gallon.

Rates for Bed and Breakfasts (B&Bs) around the country generally range from about £16 to £24 per person sharing, guesthouses run from £29 to £75 per person sharing, and hotels run from £45 to £105 per room, and luxury hotels run much higher. If you choose to stay in youth hostels, where the accommodations are usually clean but very basic, expect to pay from £7 to £11. Rooms in Dublin, Belfast, and Cork as well as the tourist centers of Killarney, Westport, and Galway will generally be at the higher end of the spectrum and rooms in rural areas at the lower end.

Youth hostels are typically Spartan places to lay your head, get a shower, eat some basic food, and that's about it. Accommodations range from singles to dormitory-style (10 to 18 beds). Costs are low, ranging from £7 to £12 for the dormitories to the equivalent of B&B rates for a single room (£20+). These days, you'll see "youth" from ages 18 to 70 (literally), so don't let the label "youth hostel" stop you from considering it if you are looking for inexpensive lodging. Most hostels provide a small cafe or self-catering kitchen (for cooking your own food). Some charge extra for sheets and towels, and some include them in the price. Most take credit cards, some do not. Most do not include breakfast in their prices. All in all, hostels are an excellent way to lower your costs while in Ireland.

The rate for rental cars varies widely, so it pays to shop diligently. Generally speaking, the big international rental car companies are significantly more expensive than the smaller local companies, sometimes as much as three times the smaller companies' rates. A weekly rental should run you in the neighborhood of $300, depending on the car size, time of the year, etc. Occasionally the big international companies run specials that are attractive, but they still tend to be too expensive.

Train and bus travel is viable in Ireland. Both are under the control of a state-run agency. Again, rates will depend on how long you wish to stay and travel in Ireland. For example, you can purchase a pass for train and bus travel for any eight days of travel within a 15-day window. The cost is $120 for adults and $60 for children ages 5-15. This ticket is available for travel only within the Republic; for a few pounds more, you can have the same travel privileges extended to Belfast and all of Northern Ireland.

Bicycling across Ireland has become fashionable in recent years. The mild climate and beautiful country lends itself to this mode of transportation, even though the narrow roads do not. Bicycle shops are plentiful around the country, especially in areas such as Dublin, Killarney, Galway, Westport, Dingle, etc. Expect to pay around £7 per day, £30 per week, or £115 per month for a bicycle.

Shop owners usually require something of value for a deposit to be left behind, like your passport or a major credit card. Bicycling is an excellent way to augment motorized travel in Ireland, whether you've chosen car, bus, train, or hitchhiking. If you do rent a bicycle, please be careful. The roads are painfully narrow, with lots of curves. Bicycle riders are expected to ride with traffic, not against it.

ELECTRICITY

Electricity in Ireland is 220 volts (50 cycles) and an adapter is required. Most discount stores like Target, K-Mart, and Wal-Mart, as well as Sears and J.C. Penny's carry inexpensive adapters that will do the job nicely. Remember, if you expect to use your hair dryer, curling iron, or electric razor, you'll need an adapter. Oh yes – and unless you're going to bring lots of very expensive (and heavy) batteries, you'll want that adapter to recharge the batteries for your camcorder (common oversight).

EMBASSIES & CONSULATES IN IRELAND

American Embassy, *42 Elgin Road, Dublin 4. Tel. (01) 668-8777.* They are open Monday through Friday from 8:30am to 5:00pm. If you have cause to visit there, look for what is probably the ugliest building in Dublin. Set in the splendor of a beautiful Georgian residential neighborhood, its unfortunate modernistic, gray concrete and glass architecture sticks out like a sore thumb. It is really an eyesore.

• **Canadian Embassy**, *65 St. Stephen's Green. Tel. (01) 478-1988.* They are open Monday through Wednesday from 8:30am to 12:30pm, and from 2:00pm to 4:00pm, and Thursday and Friday from 8:30am to 12:30pm.

• **American Consulate in Northern Ireland**, *14 Queen Street, Belfast. Tel. (028) 9032-8239.* They are open Monday through Friday from 9:00am to 5:00pm.

• **Canadian Embassy for Northern Ireland**, *Lesley House, Shaftesbury Square, Belfast 2. Tel. (028) 9033-1532.* They are open Monday through Wednesday from 8:30am to 12:30pm, and from 2:00pm to 4:00pm, and Thursday and Friday from 8:30am to 12:30pm.

HEALTH & SAFETY

Before you leave for your holiday in Ireland, check with your health insurance company to see if you will be covered in the event of an emergency, illness, or injury during your travels in Ireland. If you are covered, find out the procedure they require you to follow before seeking treatment. As you may know, both Ireland and Northern Ireland have national health care systems, and unless you have insurance, you will only be treated in the event of an emergency. As of this writing, Medicare doesn't cover overseas medical expenses, but some of their supplemental plans do. Check before going.

Safety? If you use common sense in your travels you will be fine. Ireland is far from crime-free, although it is still one of the safest countries in which to travel.

I think the biggest concern I have in the area of safety is driving. Roads are narrow, speeds are fast, and there are a lot of Americans on the roads! Don't try to keep up with the locals until you have logged a few miles on these narrow roads. And on the exceptionally narrow roads of Counties Cork, Connemara, and Donegal, give way to those who are driving faster than you, and enjoy the scenery.

LAUNDRY

If you are staying for more than a week, you probably will need to do your wash. That is easier said than done. But, if you are diligent, (and in a city) you should be able to find a place.

You have several options. Most major hotels have valet laundry services. If you are staying in a B&B, many of the hostesses will allow you to use their washing facilities. The cost is usually minimal, roughly equivalent to what you'd expect to pay in a laundromat. But don't assume the B&B will allow you to use its facilities. When you call to make or confirm your reservation, ask about the policy.

You can also ask your host to direct you to the laundromat, or you can use the local "yellow" pages or inquire at the local tourist office. Laundromats are called *washeterias* or *launderettes*, and are self-serve. A *laundry shop* is what we call a dry cleaners.

MONEY & BANKING

The currency is officially known as a **punt** (pronounced *poont*), but is generally referred to as pounds. As with all foreign currencies, the exchange rate fluctuates. The past several years the conversion rate has been in the neighborhood of US$1.20 to $1.30 and CD $1.60 to $1.90 for each Irish pound (£1). To find out what the conversion rate is, call any sizable bank, AAA, currency exchange office or check the *Foreign Exchange* box in the business section of your local newspaper. Since Irish money is not quite as common as other foreign currencies, your bank may need a few day's notice to obtain the currency.

Ireland is part of the European Community, and as such has embraced the new monetary unit, the Euro. Beginning in the year 2001, Irish businesses will accept either Euros or Irish pounds, with full conversion to the Euro expected to be complete by 2002. The conversion rate is £1 = .787564 Euro.

If you forget or can't get to a bank or currency exchange office to exchange your money before you leave, don't worry. There are currency exchange kiosks in most gateway city airports (Chicago, Boston, New York, and Atlanta), as well as at the Shannon and Dublin airports. You'll have to pay a minimal service charge, usually around $5.00.

In the Republic, businesses will accept either Irish or British pounds (UK£). However, in Northern Ireland, most shops won't accept the Irish pound – only British Sterling. During most of my trips to Ireland the exchange rate for British Sterling was a few pennies more than the Irish pound. The shops in the South charge a small fee – about 10p per pound - when you use British pounds.

Banks in Ireland are open...well...they're open banker's hours. Traditionally, banks in the Republic are open Monday through Wednesday and Friday from 10:00am to 12:30pm, and from 1:30pm to 3:00pm. On Thursdays their *extended* hours are from 10:00am to 12:30pm and 1:30pm to 5:00pm. Banks in Northern Ireland are open from 9:30am to 4:30pm and closed from 12:30pm to 1:30pm. In the larger cities (Belfast and

Derry), they don't close for lunch. The banks in the Shannon, Dublin, and Belfast airports, however, are open every day to service incoming international flights.

Post offices in the main cities in Ireland will also exchange money for you. Be aware, however, that most post offices will not accept $100 bills. Some larger hotels will also change money for you.

Automatic Teller Machines (ATMs) have started making their appearance in Ireland. Although they are nowhere near as ubiquitous as in America, they can usually be found on the outside wall of banks. **Cirrus** and **Plus** are the international networks most of these ATMs are part of. Most of the banks that provide ATMs charge a small transaction fee for withdrawals (about $1.50). Check with the bank that issued your ATM card to see if your current Personal Identification Number (PIN) will work overseas. Many of the ATMs overseas only accept four-digit PINs.

EXCHANGE RATES

US$1 = £1.25 Irish Pounds

Irish Pound	£1	£10	£100	£500	£1000
Euro	1.27	12.73	127	636	1270
US Dollars	$1.25	$12.50	$125	$625	$1250

C$1 = £1.85 Irish Pounds

Irish Pound	£1	£10	£100	£500	£1000
Canadian Dollars	$1.85	$18.50	$185	$925	$1850

In recent months, the dollar has been very strong against the Irish pound and the Euro. World conditions could cause changes in the exchange rates, but these are representative as of the time of printing.

NEWSPAPERS

There are two main newspapers in Ireland: the *Irish Independent* and the *Irish Times*. If it's a hometown newspaper you're looking for, you may be in luck if you're from New York or consider the *Wall Street Journal* your hometown newspaper. Copies of the *Journal* and the *New York Times* can usually be found at Newsagents in the bigger cities, although they are usually a few days old.

POSTAL SERVICE

Letters sent from the Republic of Ireland to the US and Canada cost 45 pence (written as "45p") and postcards cost 45p as well. If you have occasion to send them to Europe, letters and postcards cost 32p. Stamps are available from the post office, or from most Newsagents. Postcards from the North to the US cost 35p and letters cost 41p.

Most post offices in the country are open Monday through Saturday from 9:00am to 6:00pm. In the larger cities some of the post offices may have extended hours. For example, the General Post Office (GPO) in Dublin is open Monday - Saturday from 8:00am to 8:00pm.

If you're going to be in one place for a time, you can arrange to have your mail sent to a post office in your area. They will hold the mail for you free of charge for three months.

RADIO

You are almost always within distance of radio stations, the most common being several BBC stations out of England. There are two national radio stations in Ireland, **Radio 1** and **Radio 2**. Radio 1 is a conservative station that features talk shows. Gay Burne, who hosts the *Late, Late Show* on television also hosts a morning talk show on Radio 1. Radio 2 is geared much more toward the younger generation, and features rock music. There is also a national radio station called **Radio Gaeltachta**, which broadcasts in the Irish language.

In recent years, regional radio stations have emerged and become immensely popular. These small stations focus on regional news, covering regional athletic teams, local horseracing results, and obituaries for the area. In addition, livestock prices are also an important part of the broadcasts.

TAXES

Ireland has a **Value-Added Tax (VAT)** that is applied to all goods and services. It amounts to from 12.5% to 17.5% in both the Republic and Northern Ireland. All prices you are quoted and all prices you see posted in stores include VAT. Products classed as luxury items (crystal, jewelry, etc.) are taxed at the higher rate.

The good news is, if you are not from a country that is a member of the European Community (EC), you can get a refund on the VAT you pay. Whenever you make a purchase, ask the proprietor for a **CashBack** form. Take the time to fill out all the forms you collect. Find the CashBack booth at the airport and present your forms to them. It only takes a few minutes to do this, so be sure you leave time to do this at the airport.

VAT also applies to food, but you do not get "cash back" on the VAT paid for food, nor for VAT paid on rental cars, hotel rooms, etc. You only get VAT refunds for purchased items such as an Aran sweater, Waterford crystal, or a Donegal tweed sports coat.

If you made your purchases with a credit card, your VAT refund will usually be mailed to you, or credited to your credit card. The refund company charges a small handling fee, but it's still worth your time to fill out the forms.

TELEVISION

Ireland has two television stations run by **Radio Teilifis Eireann**. The stations are called **RTE 1** and **Network 2**. Two of the most popular shows in Ireland are talk shows, similar to a serious Jay Leno (is there such a thing?). Friday nights at 9:30pm (after the 9:00pm news) you can watch the *Late, Late Show* hosted by Gay Burne. On Saturday evenings you can tune into another talk show called *Kenny Live*, hosted by Pat Kenny. Both shows are immensely popular, although the format is more restrained than you might be accustomed to in America. Typical guests might include a politician, CEO, rock star, or local athlete. The most popular Irish soap opera/drama is *Fair City*, a show about the (fictional) people of Dublin and their lives. *Fair City* airs Tuesday and Thursday evenings at 7:00pm.

In addition to the two Irish television stations, cable or satellite will bring you numerous BBC stations from England. These stations carry English television shows, as well as American and Australian entertainment. *Coronation Street* (Monday, Wednesday, and Friday evenings at 7:30pm) is a popular English soap opera about the people who live on a street in Manchester, England. American shows that are popular in Ireland include *Dr. Quinn, Medicine Woman*; *The Fresh Prince of Belair*; *Seinfeld*; and reruns of *Dallas*.

TIPPING

Tipping is acceptable and expected in Ireland. But be warned that if you give your customary 15% to 20% tip for outstanding service, you may in reality be giving over 35%. Many hotels and restaurants in the Republic automatically tack on a service charge of 10% to 15% to your room or meal. You might be interested to know that service charges are a hot issue in the hotel and tourism circles in Ireland. This should be settled one way or another within the next couple of years. Ever in tune with their customers, Bord Failte is well aware that Americans in particular bristle at the idea of service charges on hotel rooms.

It's customary to tip cab drivers around 10% (they don't automatically add it to the fare), more if the driver acts as a tour guide, filling you in on interesting tidbits of trivia about the sites you're passing. Porters should be tipped £1 per bag.

TELEPHONE

Unless you are a hermit, in trouble with the law, or trying to lose yourself from the world, you will need to use Alexander Graham Bell's grand invention – the telephone. Be warned: you will not find the same consistent, user-friendly interface you are accustomed to in North America. Without a doubt you will experience uncooperative phones, occasional poor reception, and just plain frustration. It may take you two or three times dialing exactly the same numbers to get a call through, or you may need to deposit your coins two or three times before they'll register. But, with a little patience, you will be able to get your calls placed.

If you think you might need a phone soon, and you see one, use it! Public phones are not as prevalent as they are in the United States. The surest place to find them is in hotels, although this is not always the case in smaller hotels.

TELEPHONE CODES
International Direct Dialing 011
International Credit Card 01
Ireland 353
Northern Ireland 44
Dublin City 01

Calling Ireland

If you need to call Ireland or Northern Ireland prior to your trip, the country code for Northern Ireland is 44, and the country code for the Republic of Ireland is 353.

In Ireland, there is no set way to list telephone numbers. They used to be listed as a five- or six-digit string of numbers. However, several years ago it became necessary to add a seventh digit to Dublin phone numbers, and the Dubliners haven't decided how best to deal with that. Until they decide on a format, I have Americanized all the telephone numbers for Dublin – any published telephone number in Dublin with less than seven numbers is out of date.

If you're going to call Ireland from the United States to make hotel reservations, you must dial the country code (353 for Ireland; 44 for Northern Ireland), and the city code, then the telephone number. *Sort of.* In the case of Dublin telephone numbers, the city code is 01, but you drop the 0 when dialing. Therefore, if you were calling the Berkeley Court Hotel from the United States, you should dial 011-353-1-497-8275. (011 is the international long distance direct dialing code; 01 is the international code for credit card calls.)

AT&T, MCI and Sprint offer competitive direct dialing rates to and from the Emerald Isle. Check with them for their latest rates. They both routinely run special programs and rates.

Calling from Ireland

When calling home from the Republic of Ireland, dial *800/550-000* if you're using AT&T, or *800/551-001* if you are using MCI. If you are calling from Northern Ireland, dial *0500-890-011* if you're using AT&T, or *0800/890-222* if you're using MCI. You will be connected to an AT&T or MCI operator in the United States who will help you complete your calling card or collect call. See the chart below:

CALLING OPTIONS FROM IRELAND

You'd be surprised at how many options you have to call home. You would also be surprised at the variation in costs to place that call home. I priced a ten-minute call from Dublin to the United States using the following four options, and I think you'll find the information surprising. As you can see, it will pay you to establish an international calling card account before you leave, rather than use the international operator once you arrive in Ireland. Here is what I found:

Option	First Minute	Each additional Minute	Total for 10-minute call
AT&T Card	*$1.24*	*$.17*	*$2.77*
MCI Card	*$1.19*	*$.16*	*$ 2.63*
Sprint Card	*$1.85*	*$.92*	*$10.13*
International Operator	*$4.67*	*$4.67*	*$46.70*

AT&T and MCI charge a $3 monthly surcharge for the plans quoted above.

These rates were in effect at the time I called. They are surely different now, especially with the fierce competition between the long distance heavyweights. Be sure and check with the carriers to determine which is the best deal.

Some hotels only allow you to place international calls through the operator (111) from their rooms. If that's the case in your hotel, you may want to use the pay phone in the lobby or on the street. While not as convenient, it's a lot more reasonable. Also, some hotels levy a surcharge for in-room international calls that can equal what the long distance carriers charge, effectively doubling the cost of your call. If this matters to you, check with the front desk before you make calls from your room.

Another option, and one I have found nearly as inexpensive and trouble free as international dialing plans, is to purchase international phone cards. The cost for calls to the US range from $.10 to $.50 per minute. I found the range varied widely, and those sold at Irish post offices tended to be more expensive per minute than those you purchase at grocery stores of Newsagents. The only problem with them is that you usually must find a card phone to use them, although some of them now have a toll-free number to call for access, and these can be used from any phone.

USEFUL TELEPHONE NUMBERS

Emergency 999
Directory Assistance – National 1181
Directory Assistance – Great Britain 1197
Directory Assistance – International 114
Operator Assistance – National 10

Dublin Airport (01) 844-4900
Shannon Airport (061) 471-444
Aer Lingus (01) 705-6705
Delta (01) 844-4170

Irish Rail (passenger info) (01) 836-6222
DART information (01) 836-3333
Bus Eireann (Irish Bus) (01) 836-1111
Dublin Bus (01) 873-4222
Irish Ferries (01) 661-0511

General Post Office (01) 872-8888
Bord Failte (Tourist Board) (01) 602-4000

Calling within Ireland

Most of your calls within Ireland will be made from one of two types of public telephones: coin phones or phonecard phones.

Most **coin phones** are being updated and will accept only 20p and 50p coins – *Irish* in the Republic, and *British* in Northern Ireland! All calls are metered. A digital screen on the phone registers the amount of money you enter, and counts down to 0 as you talk. At 0, you receive three warning tones, and if you do not add additional coins within 10 seconds, your call will be cut off. If you have credits remaining at the end of your call, you can push a button that allows you to make another call without adding additional coins. Unused, whole amounts will be returned to you.

Phonecard phones are becoming increasingly popular in Ireland. Post Offices and Newsagents sell phonecards of varying denominations: £2, £3.50, £8, and £16. Like the coin phones, once the card is inserted, a digital readout on the phone displays remaining units. On local calls, one unit is roughly equal to three minutes; slightly less for long distance calls, depending on the distance involved. Some of the phone cards now feature a toll-free number to dial, after which you input a PIN associated with that card. These phone cards can be used with any telephones.

Emergency Telephoning

In both the North and the Republic, remember **911 = 999**. If you have an emergency requiring police, an ambulance, or a fireman, dial 999.

TIME

Ireland is on Greenwich Mean Time, and for most of the year that means they are five hours ahead of New York and Montreal, and eight hours ahead of Los Angeles and Vancouver.

Ireland has Daylight Savings Time (called Summer Time), but it doesn't coincide exactly with the beginning of Daylight Savings Time in North America. Summer Time begins one week earlier than Daylight Savings Time – the last Sunday of March. It reverts to Standard Time the last Sunday in October as it does here.

TROUBLE - AND HOW TO AVOID IT

Crime in Ireland is far from non-existent, but the majority of it has tended to be of the non-violent type. Murders in Ireland send shock waves through the country and are always accompanied by front-page headlines and are the lead stories in newscasts. The **Gardi** (police) do not carry weapons, but are all "armed" with radios.

Dublin, like big cities all over the world, seems to be the most susceptible to crime. The majority of the crime there is petty theft and burglaries, although more violent crimes of rape and murder do occur. Throughout Dublin you'll see signs warning you of pickpockets, who work high-traffic areas like the DART stations, and Grafton and Henry Streets. Rental cars are also easy targets, especially if you leave purses, cameras, or other items of value in plain sight. Take a few extra seconds and put those things in the trunk of your car.

The streets of downtown Dublin are relatively safe, but there are areas you will definitely want to stay away from. The docks are notorious for crime, as are large areas of apartments – flats – to the west and northeast of the center of Dublin. If you confine your activities to the areas outlined in this guide, you should have no problem. Notwithstanding the relatively low crime rate, don't be lulled into a false sense of security; there are malevolent people in every land who prey upon the innocent and unsuspecting. It would be a shame to spoil a delightful holiday by taking silly chances.

Of course, when traveling on your own you should take some precautions. Let someone back home know your tentative schedule and when you expect to be back, for example. Lone travelers tend to be more of a target than two or more people traveling together. Just be cautious, and use common sense.

Ireland has very aggressive laws when it comes to driving under the influence of alcohol, so be sure and use a designated driver if you plan to imbibe at one of those delightful Irish pubs.

If you do have trouble, remember that in Ireland **911 = 999**.

WEIGHTS & MEASURES

For the most part, Ireland uses the metric system. The main concern this has for you is that the petrol you purchase for your rental car will be measured in liters. If you're like me and have this fetish for knowing how many miles to the gallon your car is getting, there are 3.7854 liters in a gallon.

The few speed limits you will see in the country are posted in miles per hour, not kilometers per hour. However, distances to nearby towns are listed on road signs as kilometers in the south and in miles in the north.

8. SPORTS & RECREATION

When it comes to sports and recreation, there is a lot to do in Ireland, both as a spectator and as a participant. For the purposes of this chapter, activities under **Sports** involve professional athletes and your role as the spectator. Those activities under **Recreation** involve your participation. That isn't to say that golf is not a sport; indeed it is.

The Irish are sports fanatics. They love a good contest, and they are as avid as fans anywhere in the world. They are fiercely proud of their national teams, especially those that compete in international competition. For example, when Ireland has a team competing in the World Cup in soccer, it becomes an all-consuming issue in the country. Front-page headlines carry the result of their games, and the games are often the lead stories on the evening news.

PROFESSIONAL SPORTS

GAELIC FOOTBALL

Gaelic football is a rough and tumble (literally) game that is a cross between rugby and soccer. Having watched a few games, I'd say it reminds me of the Australian Football games I've seen on ESPN. Gaelic football aficionados claim the Aussies got it from the Irish; I suspect the Aussies have the reverse opinion. At any rate, each team consists of 15 players who pass the ball to one another in an effort to move it down field and across an "end-zone." The ball is a little smaller than a soccer ball and can be handed, passed, and kicked to move it. The sport is much faster than American or Canadian football.

The field is huge – usually 140 or 160 yards wide by 100 yards long. There is a goal at each end of the field that looks like the combination of a soccer goal and football goalposts. Kicking the ball into the net scores three points, and kicking it through the uprights scores one point.

Gaelic football is played in the spring and summer, and the All-Ireland finals are held in Dublin in September. If you find yourself in Dublin in September, treat yourself to a game – you'll love the fast action and excitement. In recent years, the team from Kerry has been nearly unstoppable in Gaelic football, and they have an avid following.

While little boys in America dream of hitting the winning home run in the seventh game of the World Series, young Irish lads grow up dreaming of leading their county's team to the **All-Ireland Title** (the equivalent of the World Series or the Super Bowl), and becoming instant national heroes. Gaelic football was particularly good to one fellow named Jack Lynch. Lynch was the gifted captain of Cork's Gaelic football and hurling teams that won six consecutive All-Ireland titles. His fans showed their appreciation for his athletic prowess by twice electing him Prime Minister!

Gaelic football can be watched throughout the season at **Croke Park** in Dublin (about 15 to 20 minute's walk north of O'Connell Bridge), or you can catch a bus at O'Connell Bridge that will take you there. Games are played every other Sunday (the same stadium is used for Gaelic football and hurling). Tickets will cost £6 and £12.

For ticket information and schedules, contact the **Gaelic Athletic Association**, *Tel. (01) 836-3222.*

HORSE RACING

Horse racing is followed as avidly as any other sport in the country. Results of races are broadcast hourly by many radio stations, and it is always part of the evening news sports section. At last count, races are held on 233 days of the year, at 27 different racetracks. (Remember – Ireland is about the size of Kentucky.)

Check the local newspapers or visit the local Bord Failte office for information on the location and times of the races closest to you. The **Jameson Irish Grand National** is run at **Punchestown Race Course** in County Kildare. Other popular racetracks are at **Leopardstown** (near Dublin), and in Galway, **Fairyhouse** in County Meath, Killarney, Tralee, and Listowel. Punchestown and Fairyhouse racetracks are the venue for the extremely popular steeplechase races.

HURLING

Hurling was a popular game in Ireland long before *Bill and Ted's Excellent Adventure* gave the term a different (and more disgusting) twist. Hurling is a high-speed game of ancient (probably Celtic) origin that is extremely popular with the Irish. Fifteen players per team use a short (approximately 3') stick – called a *caman* or *hurley* – that is curved on the end to bat, catch, and hurl a small leather ball down-field and into the opponent's goal. The ball, called a *sliotar*, is slightly smaller than a tennis ball. The game is incredibly fast-paced, and seems to combine elements of lacrosse, hockey, soccer, and rugby in its execution.

Along with Gaelic football, hurling is considered part of the "**National Games**," sponsored by the Irish Gaelic Athlete Association. Games are played throughout the summer, and the All-Ireland finals are held in Dublin in September. If you have the opportunity, stop and watch a game.

Hurling can be watched throughout the season at **Croke Park** in Dublin (about 15 to 20 minute's walk north of O'Connell Bridge), or you can catch a bus at O'Connell Bridge that will take you there. Games are played every other Sunday (the same stadium is used for Gaelic football and hurling). Tickets will cost £6 and £12.

For ticket information and schedules, contact the **Gaelic Athletic Association**, *Tel. (01) 836-3222.*

RUGBY

Rugby is also a wildly exciting game played in Ireland, and its followers are as avid here as they are anyplace else. If you've never seen rugby, it's sort of a non-stop football game where husky men try and ram an over-inflated football through the defense of their opponent. One interesting aspect of rugby in Ireland is that their international team consists of players from both the Republic and Northern Ireland – the only team sport on the Emerald Isle that ignores political differences and has one Irish team made up of players from both countries. Rugby is played at **Lansdowne Stadium** in Ballsbridge, right next to the DART station. If you want to attend a rugby match, you might try staying at Michael O'Brien's Ariel House (see *Where to Stay* in Dublin). In addition to being a wonderful place to stay, it's about a two-minute walk from Lansdowne Stadium.

For ticket information and schedules, contact the **Gaelic Athletic Association**, *Tel. (01) 836-3222.*

SOCCER

Ireland is considered a European nation, and as such, they play soccer. (I think this must be required to become a member of the European Economic Community!) But the Irish are not as obsessed as the rest of Europe with soccer – they save their obsession for Gaelic football and hurling.

Soccer is played primarily in and around Dublin (attesting to centuries of strong English presence there) and Belfast. Having said that, let Ireland's team compete in the **World Cup**, and soccer is followed avidly on the radio and television (yawn). Unlike Gaelic football and hurling, soccer has gone the way of many pro sports in America. Players play for whichever team pays the most, and many Irish players play on teams other than Ireland's team. In recent years, the English soccer team in Manchester has had significant Irish representation, and accordingly has a significant Irish following.

When Ireland's international soccer team plays in Dublin, they play at **Lansdowne Stadium** in Ballsbridge, right next to the DART station. Semi-professional soccer teams play at **Dalymount Park** in Phibsborough in north Dublin, at the corner of Phibsborough Road and Dalymount/ North Circular Roads. It's about two and a half miles northwest of the O'Connell Street Bridge.

According to the Irish Tourist Board, the number one outdoor activity among visitors to Ireland is hill walking, followed by golf and angling (fishing). But there are many other things to do as well - cycling, horseback riding and believe it or not, surfing and scuba diving.

While the Irish are great spectators, they are nowhere near as obsessed with fitness as Americans are. In all my trips to Ireland I have only seen a handful of joggers – and they were probably all Americans! The one healthy activity that is regularly practiced in Ireland is walking. But there is a difference. It's not like the power walking you see in America, but rather leisurely strolls along country lanes, or young mothers pushing their babies in prams.

ANGLING

Ireland has a lot to offer in the way of fishing. Salmon, sea trout, brown trout, pike, and a variety of other fish are plentiful in Ireland's lakes and streams, not to mention those available off the coast.

You are required to have a license and the laws are a little confusing; you usually need at least one license or permit, and sometimes you need a license, a permit, and a "day ticket." It's best to ask at the local angling shop for instructions. They'll be more than happy to help you out. A state license costs from £3 to £25, depending on how long you want it for, and whether it is for one particular angling district or multiple districts. The only fish requiring a state license are salmon and sea trout (you don't need a state license for brown trout). The other permits are available on an annual, weekly, or daily basis, and are relatively inexpensive.

The Irish angling industry uses two terms you may not be familiar with. They are **game angling** and **coarse angling**. Game angling refers to the pursuit of trout, salmon, and pike. Coarse angling refers to fishing for perch, tench, rudd, bream, etc. You need a state license for game fishing, but not for coarse fishing.

Don't worry about finding a good spot to fish. The proprietors of an angling shop in Dublin – **Patrick Cleere and Son** on Anglesea Street – told me that most Irish fishermen are happy to take a fellow fishing "for the company."

In addition to getting a license, another good place to learn about the local hot spots is in the local angling shop. They are all over the country, especially in towns near lakes and streams.

Here are a few you can pop into:

- **Patrick Cleere and Son**, *Anglesea Street, Dublin. Tel. (01) 677-7406*
- **O'Neill's Fishing Tackle**, *6 Plunkett Street, Killarney, County Kerry. Tel. (064) 31970*
- **Jim Robinson's Angling Center**, *43 Lower Gerald Griffin Street, Limerick, County Clare. Tel. (061) 414900*
- **Nestor Brothers Sports Store**, *28 O'Connell Street Limerick, County Clare. Tel. (061) 414096*
- **Dermot Killeen**, *Main Street, Shannonbridge, County Offally. Tel. (0905) 74112*
- **Erne Marine**, *Bellanaleck, Enniskillen, County Fermanagh. Tel. (028) 6638-7077*
- **Lakeland Marina**, *Muckross, Kesh, County Fermanagh. Tel. (028) 6632-3481*

Here are good spots to try for the following fish:

- **Salmon** – River Shannon (Co. Limerick and Clare), River Clare (Co. Galway), River Fergus (Co. Clare), River Feale (Co. Kerry), River Moy (Co. Mayo), Mulcair River (Co. Limerick), River Maigue (Co. Limerick), and the Brosna River (Co. Offaly). Loughs Conn (Co. Mayo), Eske (Co. Donegal), Corrib (Co. Galway), Leane (Co. Kerry), and Melvin (Co. Leitrim). There are two primary seasons for salmon: from March to May and the end of May through September.
- **Sea trout** – River Feale (Co. Limerick), River Bandon (Co. Cork), Lough Eske (Co. Donegal), River Slaney (Co. Wexford), and Lough Glencar (Co. Leitrim and Sligo).
- **Brown trout** – the Shannon (Co. Galway), Blackwater (Munster), Clare (Co. Galway), Barrow (Co. Carlow/Kilkenny), Fergus (Co. Clare), Nore (Co. Laois), Laune (Co. Kerry) rivers and the following loughs: Derg (Co. Clare), Conn (Co. Mayo), Inchiquin (Co. Clare), Melvin (Co. Leitrim), Mask (Co. Mayo), and Leane (Co. Kerry).

• **Pike** – Lough Derg (Co. Clare), and the lakes of the River Fergus (Co. Clare).

BIRD WATCHING

Ireland is noted for many fine locations for bird watching. Whether it's off **Bull Island** north of Dublin, or the **Skelligs**, or many of the loughs (lakes) in Northern Ireland, you'll have a great selection of sites to visit and birds to see.

In the southeast, the best place for bird watching is off the coast at the village of **Kilmore Quay**. Just offshore are the **Saltee Islands**, and they have the distinction of being the largest bird sanctuary in Ireland. Ornithologists claim there are over three million birds representing 47 species located on and around the Saltee Islands. The most predominant birds are cormorants, guillemots, kittiwakes, petrels, puffins, and sea gulls. Boats in the harbor will take you out to the islands for a closer look.

Off the southwestern coast of Ireland lies little **Clear Island**, where another colony of birds has taken up residence. Though the numbers aren't quite as extensive as at the Saltee Islands, there are plenty to see. In addition to the species that can be spied at the Saltees, add the much rarer black-bowed albatross. As with the Saltees, boats can be hired in **Baltimore** (County Cork) to take you out for a closer look.

Further up the west coast of Ireland you come to the Skelligs, a small cluster of islands off the **Iveragh Peninsula**. In addition to the fine ruins of an ancient monastic site on the largest of the islands, there are two islands that have significant colonies of sea birds. **Little Skellig** serves as the breeding ground for more than 20,000 pairs of gannets, and **Puffin Island** hosts thousands of petrel, shearwaters, and puffins. Boats can be hired in Waterville to take you out to the Skelligs.

On to **Northern Ireland** for your bird-watching pleasure. Ireland is the first stop for many autumn-migrating birds, and Northern Ireland is their first chance to rest their weary wings after many miles. Northern Ireland is one of the few places left where ornithologists can see species such as chough and corncrake.

At the northwest point of Northern Ireland is **Lough Foyle**, a large lake that draws a great number of species to its mud flats and saltwater marshes. Species that can be seen here include curlew, bar-tailed godwits, Greenland white-fronted geese, and whooper swans. In addition, there are large numbers of buzzards, gyrfalcon, finches, kestrel, larks, merlins, peregrine falcons, petrel, and sparrowhawks.

Lough Neagh is the largest freshwater lake in the British Isles. It is a wonderful place to see many different species of birds, including golden-eye, crested grebe, pochard, scaup, whooper and Bewick's swans.

In County Down, Belfast, Carlingford, and Strangford Loughs are havens for a number species of birds, including dark- and pale-bellied brant geese, cormorants, curlews, dunlin, gadwall, godwits, golden plover, greenshank, knot, lapwings, oystercatchers, red-breasted mergansers, redshank, sandwich terns, shelduck, and whooper swans.

CYCLING

If you have the time, desire, and endurance, cycling is probably the all-around best way to see Ireland (if the roads just weren't so darned narrow!). When it comes to cycling around this beautiful green oasis, you have several options. First, you can rent a bike at one of the many bicycle shops in Ireland, and roll out of the shop on your way to great adventures. Or, you can engage a company that provides excursions for bikers. You'll see the vans and buses of these companies all over Ireland. For a reasonable fee, they'll rent you a bicycle and helmet, shuttle your personal belongings to the location where you'll be spending the night, and they'll even pack lunch for you if you wish. They also provide maps and details about the routes you'll be taking.

These companies usually provide package deals that include meals, bike rental, maps, itinerary, luggage transport, roadside maintenance, and accommodations (usually at B&Bs) for a set price. The prices vary according to your requirements, but figure on paying around £300 for a week and £575 for two weeks. When you figure what a week's bicycle rental (about £30) and one week's B&B accommodations (about £140) would run you, that's not really too bad a deal. Most of the companies listed here will also arrange to pick you up at the airport and return you there at the end of your journey as part of the package.

CYCLING TOUR OPERATORS

Celtic Cycling Ltd.	*Tel. (0503) 75282*
Cycle Ireland	*Tel. (064) 32536*
Irish Cycle Hire	*Tel. (041) 41067*
Irish Cycling Safaris	*Tel. (01) 260-0749*
Shannon Cycle Center	*Tel. (061) 361280*

GOLF

It's hard to get an accurate count of how many golf courses there are in Ireland. Sources that should be "in the know" vary in their information; I've seen numbers quoted from 200 to over 300. As a golfer, I prefer to think of the number as over 300. That means there is one golf course about every 100 square miles in Ireland, so theoretically, you should never have to travel more than 10 miles to find a golf course.

Golf courses in Ireland are among some of the most beautiful and challenging in the world. Some are verdant, lush, and about everything you've ever dreamed of for a game of golf. Others are links courses, with their dunes and deep bunkers, and fairways that have cliff hazards along the edge of the fairway – don't slice, or you'll watch your golf ball sail over the edge to the ocean 200 feet below (great distance, but...). Others have the pins set on the far side of tall drumlins (mounds) that have a stick at the top to tell you where to hit your nine iron.

Green fees vary, of course, but you can expect to pay between £15 and £30 for 18 holes. Green fees are slightly more on the weekends. Most courses have clubs available for rent (the term in Ireland is "club hire"), as well as golf carts and caddies, but you should ask to be sure when you make your tee-time.

Many of Ireland's golf courses are actually part of a golf club. But unlike America and other countries around the world, these courses welcome players who do not belong to their club. The only restriction is that weekends are sometimes reserved for club members (as are some other weekdays at some courses).

While it's not practical to list all 300 golf courses in Ireland, here's a sampling of some of the better courses, with a bit of information about each. Green fees are given in weekday/weekend format. I have sprinkled more information about these and other courses throughout the various chapters in the book.

In The Republic of Ireland
• **Adare Manor Golf Club**, *Adare, County Limerick. Tel. (061) 396566,* £30 (resident)/£35 (nonresident). Visitors are welcome weekdays. Par 72, 7,138 yards.
• **Ballybunion**, *Ballybunion, County Kerry. Tel. (068) 27146,* £25/£35. Visitors are welcome weekdays. Par 72, 6,216 yards.
• **Connemara Golf Club**, *Clifden, County Galway. Tel. (095) 23502,* £18/£18. Visitors are welcome every day except Sunday. Par 72, 7,174 yards.
• **County Tipperary Golf Club**, *Dundrum, County Tipperary. Tel. (062) 71116,* £15/£20. Visitors are welcome any time. Par 72.
• **Deer Park Golf Course**, *Howth, County Dublin. Tel. (01) 832-2624,* £11/£12. Visitors are welcome any time. Par 72.
• **Donegal Golf Club**, *Murvagh, County Donegal. Tel. (073) 34054,* £15/£18. Visitors are welcome any time. Par 73, 7,153 yards.
• **Dooks Golf Club**, *Glenbeigh, County Kerry. Tel. (066) 68205,* £15/£16. Visitors are welcome on weekdays. Par 70, 6,010 yards.

- **Dromoland Castle,** *Newmarket-on-Fergus, County Clare. Tel. (061) 368144,* £20/£25. Visitors are welcome weekdays. Par 71.
- **Lahinch Golf Club,** *Lahinch, County Clare. Tel. (065) 81003, £40.* Visitors are welcome daily. Par 72, 6,613 yards.
- **Mt. Juliet Golf Club,** *near Thomastown, County Kilkenny. Tel. (056) 24725,* £65/£75. Visitors are welcome daily. Par 72, 7,172 yards.
- **Portmarnock,** *Portmarnock, County Dublin. Tel. (01) 846-2968,* £40/£50. Visitors are welcome Monday, Tuesday, and Friday. Par 72, 7,051 yards.
- **Royal Dublin Golf Club,** *Bull Island, County Dublin. Tel. (01) 833-6346,* £35/£45 Visitors are welcome Monday and Tuesday, Thursday and Friday. Par 73, 6,763 yards.
- **Shannon Golf Club,** *Shannon, County Clare. Tel. (061) 471849,* £20/£25. Visitors are welcome anytime. Par 73.

In Northern Ireland
- **Ballycastle Golf Club,** *Ballycastle, County Antrim. Tel. (028) 2076-2536,* UK£13/UK£18. Visitors are welcome any time. Par 68, 5,692 yards.
- **Malone Golf Club,** *Dunmurry, Belfast, County Antrim. Tel. (028) 9061-2758,* UK£25/UK£30. Visitors are welcome Monday, Thursday, and Friday. Par 71, 6,642 yards.
- **Portstewart Golf Club,** *Portstewart, County Derry. Tel. (028) 7083-2015,* UK£22/UK£27. Visitors are welcome Monday, Tuesday, and Friday. Par 72, 6,784 yards.
- **Royal County Down,** *Newcastle, County Down. Tel. (028) 4472-2419,* UK£50. Visitors are welcome Tuesday, Thursday, and Friday. There are two separate championship courses: Par 71, 6,991 yards and Par 71, 6,087 yards.
- **Royal Portrush Golf Course,** *Portrush, County Derry. Tel. (028) 7082-2311,* Dunluce course: UK£37.50/UK£45, Valley Course: UK£15/UK£20. Visitors are welcome weekdays except Wednesday and Friday afternoons. Dunluce course: Par 72, 6,772 yards; Valley course: Par 72, 6,273 yards.

HORSEBACK RIDING

You knew horseback riding would be available in Ireland, didn't you? There are hundreds of equestrian centers in Ireland where you can arrange to see Ireland from a slightly different perspective. While Leinster is the heart of Ireland's horse country, you can find riding stables all across the Emerald Isle. Expect to pay anywhere from £8 to £25 per hour, depending on where you are and the extent of the experience you want.

Whether you are interested in riding trails, jumping, or even hunting, you can find it in Ireland. Here are a few riding stables that would love to acquaint you with Ireland from horseback:

In Connacht
- **Ashford Equestrian Center,** *Cong, County Mayo. Tel. (092) 46507*
- **Broadfield Stables,** *Turloughmore, County Galway. Tel. (091) 797075*
- **Errislannan Manor,** *Connemara, County Galway. Tel. (095) 21134*
- **Munsboro Riding Holidays,** *Sligo, County Sligo. Tel. (0903) 26449*
- **Sligo Equestrian Center,** *Carramore, County Sligo. Tel. (071) 61353*

In Leinster
- **Auburn Riding School,** *Auburn Moate Road, Athlone, County Westmeath. Tel. (0902) 74460*
- **Brennanstown Riding School, Ltd.,** *Kilmacanogue, County Wicklow. Tel. (01) 286-3778, Fax (01) 282-9590*
- **Castle Hill Equestrian Center,** *Julianstown, County Meath. Tel. (041) 29430*
- **Devil's Glen Equestrian Center,** *Ashford, County Wicklow. Tel. (040) 440013*
- **Kill International Equestrian Center,** *Kill, County Kildare. Tel. (045) 877208, Fax (045) 877704*
- **Mt. Juliet Riding Stables,** *Thomastown, County Kilkenny. Tel. (056) 24455*

In Munster
- **Ballmee Equestrian Center,** *Doneraile, County Cork. Tel. (022) 24135*
- **Clarina Riding Center,** *Clarina, County Limerick. Tel. (061) 353087*
- **Killarney Riding Stables,** *Ballydowney, County Kerry. Tel. (064) 31686*
- **Knocknamanna Stables,** *Minane Bridge, County Cork. Tel. (021) 887111*
- **Maynooth Equestrian Center,** *Bannockstown, Maynooth, County Kildare. Tel. (01) 628-9048*
- **Melody's Horse Riding and Pony Trekking,** *Ballymacarbry, County Waterford. Tel. (052) 36147*
- **Rocklands Riding Stables,** *Rockfield, Tralee, County Kerry. Tel. (064) 32592*
- **Skevanish Riding Center,** *Innishannon, County Cork. Tel. (021) 775476.*
- **Kilotteran Equestrian Center,** *Kilotteran, County Waterford. Tel. (051) 384158*

In Ulster
- **Ashleigh Riding School,** *Rosslongan, County Donegal. Tel. (073) 22386*
- **Carrigart Riding Stables,** *Carrigart, County Donegal. Tel. (074) 55114*
- **Drumhoney Stables,** *Lisnarick, County Fermanagh. Tel. (028) 6862-1892*

• **Lagan Valley Equestrian Center,** *172 Upper Malone Road, Belfast. Tel. (028) 9061-4853*
• **Lenamore Stables,** *Muff, County Donegal. Tel. (077) 84022*
• **Stracomer Riding School,** *County Donegal. Tel. (072) 41787*

If you'd like a complete listing of equestrian centers in Ireland, write to:
• **The Association of Irish Riding Establishments,** *Daffodil Lodge, Eadestown, Naas, County Dublin, Ireland, Tel. (01) 495-5990*
• **British Horse Society of Northern Ireland,** *House of Sport, Upper Malone Road, Belfast, Northern Ireland BT9 5LA, Tel. (028) 9038-1222*

Cashel House Hotel on Cashel Bay and **Hotel Castle Dunloe** in Killarney have riding stables for their guests and the hotels are reviewed in the *Where to Stay* sections of the Connacht and Munster chapters.

SAILING & WINDSURFING
There are two things Ireland has plenty of: water and wind. With such a combination of the two, it is only natural that windsurfing and sailing are popular sports. (Heck, sailing was a popular sport in Ireland before sailing was even considered a sport!) Today, there are a number of sailing and windsurfing centers around the Emerald Isle. Here are a few:

In Connacht
• **Galway Sailing Center,** *Renvyle, Oranmore, County Galway. Tel. (091) 794527*
• **Little Killary Adventure Center,** *Salruck, Renvyle, County Galway. Tel. (095) 43411*
• **Sligo Yacht Club,** *Rosses Point, County Sligo. Tel. (071) 77168*
• **Sunset Sails and Windsurfing,** *Adelaide Street, Sligo, County Sligo. Tel. (071) 62792*

In Leinster
• **BIC Sport Windsurfing and Canoe Center,** *872 Santry Avenue, Dublin 9. Tel. (01) 842-6577*
• **Fingall Sailing School,** *Malahide, County Dublin. Tel. (01) 845-1979*
• **Rosslare Sailboard Center,** *Rosslare, County Wexford. Tel. (053) 32101*

In Munster
• **Cappanalea Outdoor Education Center,** *Killorglin, County Kerry. Tel. (066) 69244*
• **Derrynane Sea Sports,** *Derrynane, Caherdaniel, County Kerry. Tel. (066) 947-5266*

- **Jamie Knox Windsurfing and Surfing**, *Castlegregory, County Kerry. Tel. (066) 713-9411*
- **International Sailing Center**, *5 E. Beach, Cobh, County Cork. Tel. (021) 811237*
- **Kenmare Bay Sea Sports**, *Dromquinna Manor, Kenmare, County Kerry. Tel. (064) 42255*
- **Kinsale Outdoor Education Center**, *Kinsale, County Cork. Tel. (021) 772896*
- **Oysterhaven Holiday and Activity Center**, *Oysterhaven, County Cork. Tel. (021) 770738*
- **Rathcoursey Water Sports Center**, *Earl Ferry, County Cork. Tel. (021) 631634*

In Ulster
- **Marble Hill Windsurfing**, *Dunfanaghy, County Donegal. Tel. (074) 36231*
  You can get more information on your sailing options in Ireland by getting in touch with:
- **Irish Sailing Association**, *3 Park Road, Dun Laoghaire, County Dublin, Ireland, Tel. (01) 280-0239, Fax (091) 280-7558*
- **Royal Yachting Association of Northern Ireland**, *House of Sport, Upper Malone Road, Belfast, Northern Ireland BT9 5LA, Tel. (028) 9038-1222*

SCUBA DIVING

It might surprise you to learn that scuba diving is available in Ireland. It's not widespread, but it is gaining in popularity. Some of the towns where scuba diving is offered are Bantry, Dalkey, Donegal, Kilkee, Killybeg, Kinsale, Tralee, Waterford, and Westport. Check with the local angling shop or Tourist Office in the city you're going to be in for more information. Conditions in the water are generally good, especially on the west coast of Ireland. Visibility is usually at least 45 feet, and often exceeds 100 feet. Here are a few places to get you started:

In Connacht
- **Atlantic Dive Center**, *Georges Street, Killalla, County Mayo. Tel. (096) 32797*
- **Kilkee Diving and Underwater Center**, *Georges Head, Kilkee, County Clare Tel. (065) 56707*
- **Scubadive West**, *Renvyle, County Galway. Tel. (095) 43922*

In Leinster
- **Oceantec Adventures**, *10/11 Marine Terrace, Dun Laoghaire. Tel. (01) 280-1083*
- **Scubadive Diving School**, *Coliemore Harbour, Dalkey. Tel. (01) 850357*

In Munster
- **Baltimore Diving and Watersports Center,** *Baltimore, West Cork. Tel. (028) 20300*
- **Cork Sub-Aqua Club,** *Cork, County Cork. Tel. (021) 271224*
- **Derrynane Diving School,** *Derrynane Harbor, County Kerry. Tel. (066) 75119*
- **Kinsale Dive Center,** *Folk House, Guardwell, County Cork. Tel. (021) 772382*
- **Waterworld,** *Tralee, County Kerry. Tel. (066) 712-5803*

In Ulster
- **Donegal Surf Center,** *Donegal, County Donegal. Tel. (073) 21179*

If you'd like a complete listing of dive shops in Ireland, write to:
- **Irish Underwater Council**, *Maritime Museum, Haigh Terrace, Dun Laoghaire, County Dublin, Ireland, Tel. (01) 280-0969*
- **Diving Association of Northern Ireland**, *House of Sport, Upper Malone Road, Belfast, Northern Ireland BT9 5LA, Tel. (028) 9038-1222*

SURFING

There are a several beaches along the south and west coasts of Ireland that are gaining reputations as great surfing beaches. In fact, just outside **Waterville** (near Rossknowlagh) in County Donegal, the **Irish Surfing National Championships** are held every year. Other popular areas for surfing include Caherdaniel (County Kerry), Carlingford (County Louth), Kinsale (County Cork), Rosslare (County Wexford), and Schull (County Cork).

Here are a few shops and surfing clubs that will be happy to introduce you to the joys of surfing in Ireland:

In Leinster
- **BIC Windsurf / Surf and Canoe Center**, *872 Santry Avenue, Dublin 9. Tel. (01) 842-6577*

In Munster
- **Cork County Surf Beaches**, *Garrettstown, Courtmacsherry, Barley Cove*
- **Jamie Knox Windsurfing and Surfing**, *Castlegregory, County Kerry. Tel. (066) 713-9411*
- **Kinsale Outdoor Education Center**, *Kinsale, County Cork. Tel. (021) 772896*

In Ulster
- **Atlantic Drive and Surf**, *102 Main Street, Portrush. Tel. (028) 7082-3272*

For more information on surfing in Ireland, write or call:
- **Irish Surfing Association**, *Tigh na Mara, Rossknowlagh, County Donegal, Ireland, Tel. (073) 21053*
- **Irish Surfing Association**, *Murray House, Easkey, County Sligo, Ireland, Tel. (096) 49020*
- **Surfing Association of Northern Ireland**, *House of Sport, Upper Malone Road, Belfast, Northern Ireland BT9 5LA, Tel. (028) 9038-1222*

WALKING

Ireland is a haven for walkers and hikers the world over; according to statistics kept by the Irish Tourist Board, hill-walking is the number one tourist activity. The terrain and climate lend themselves to walking. The terrain is seldom arduous, and more often than not your walking will consist of treks up pleasant rolling hills or across flat plains. For those of a more adventurous nature, there are also a number of strenuous walking trails that conquer the peaks of numerous Irish mountain ranges. The weather is almost always pleasant, and seldom too cold. With summer hiking temperatures rarely above the low- to mid-60s, it's ideal weather for walking. Rain, of course, is a threat at any time, but is seldom of the heavy downpour variety.

Trails criss-cross the country. Some are very popular and well marked; others are more obscure, and not sign-posted well, if at all. Some of the more popular walking trails are the **Wicklow Way** (82 miles), the **Ulster Way** (500 miles), and the **Dingle Way** (50 miles). The Wicklow Way was established in 1982, and was the first sign-posted walking trail in Ireland. Since that time, 19 additional trails have been established and sign-posted. These 20 paths are called **Waymarked Ways**, and have been developed and are maintained under the joint direction of Bord Failte and the Irish Forestry Board. There are over 1,100 miles of paths included in the Waymarked Ways hiking trails – plenty for you to explore!

These Waymarked Ways have been developed to provide walkers with a good day's hike, not a marathon. In general, the longest leg of a walk is 14 to 18 miles, although some of the very rural walks are a little longer. Generally speaking, B&Bs, hotels, and youth hostels are conveniently located along the Waymarked Ways, and cater to walkers. Many of them provide drying facilities (for your damp clothes), pack storage, and even sack lunch preparation if you wish.

There is no charge for walking these paths, unless you employ a guide to take you to show the way, comment on the topography, flora, and fauna, etc. But these trails were generally designed for freelance walkers.

If you think this sounds like an ideal activity, there are several books that will be helpful to you. The first is published by Bord Failte, and is called *Walking Ireland – The Waymarked Ways*. It gives you an overview of each walking way and is available at most Tourist Offices. Another book that is available in bookstores in Ireland is called *Irish Long Distance Walks – A Guide to the Waymarked Trails* by Michael Fewer. It covers 10 of the trails in detail. One other book I have found helpful and informative is by Paddy Dillon. Called *The Trail Walker Guide*, it covers six of the trails in detail. Between the latter two books, 12 of the 20 trails are covered (four of Paddy Dillon's trails are also covered in Michael Fewer's book).

Maps of the Waymarked Ways can be obtained in most bookstores in Ireland, as well as from **An Oige**, the Irish youth hostel organization, and may be obtained by writing or calling them. Contact them at: *61 Mountjoy Street, Dublin 7, Tel. (01) 830-4555*. Remember, the Waymarked Ways are walking trails. You are requested not to ride mountain bikes or horses on the trails. Also, since many of the trails traverse pastures where sheep and cattle graze, dogs are not welcome on the trails.

If you want to be a little more adventurous, or if you would feel more comfortable having a guide along to show you the way and teach you a little of the history of the area, there is an entire industry that has grown up around this activity. Most of these organizations offer a wide variety of tours, beginning with city tours for as little as £4 up to and including two-week excursions that include room and board along the way for £200 or more per person. Virtually all these groups have set excursions, but are quite willing and adept at tailoring a program to fit your interest and pocket book.

WALKING TOUR OPERATORS

Ballyhoura Country Holidays	*Tel. (063) 91300*
Ballyknocken House	*Tel. (0404) 44614*
Burren Walking Holidays	*Tel. (065) 74411*
Connemara Walking Center	*Tel. (095) 21379*
Croagh Patrick Walking Holidays	*Tel. (095) 26090*
Crutchs Hillville House Hotel	*Tel. (066) 38118*
Hidden Ireland Tours	*Tel. (066) 51868*
Irish Walking Way Holidays	*Tel. (055) 27479*
Mourne Country (N.I.)	*Tel. (028) 4372-4059*
Nature Reserves of Fermanagh	*Tel. (01356) 21588*
Southwest Walks Ireland	*Tel. (061) 419477*
Western Trekking	*Tel. (091) 25806*

9. SHOPPING

Ireland is a wonderful place to purchase all those things that remind you of Ireland: sweaters, Irish linen, Irish whiskey, wools and tweeds, and crystal, to name a few. There are a number of traditional "shopping towns" in Ireland, including Clifden, Donegal, Galway, Killarney, and Westport. Each of these towns has an energy and vibrancy that makes the shopping experience as memorable as the purchases you make. I was pleasantly surprised to find that merchandise prices varied little across the width and breadth of the country. The cost of items seemed driven more by the variations in their design than by the area of the country where they were purchased. Remember, it is a small country, smaller than the majority of the states in the United States, so it makes sense that there is little variation in price across the country.

The following table will give you an idea of what you can expect to pay for a variety of items:
• **Sweaters**, £35 – £100+
• **Tweed jackets**, £80 – £150
• **Tweed skirts**, £40 – £60
• **Irish linen tablecloths**
     54"x90", £ 55
     72"x108", £100
• **Irish lace handkerchief**, £100+
• **Crystal wine goblet**, £25 – £50
• **Claddagh Ring** (gold), £39 and up
• **Claddagh Ring** (silver), £7 and up

Both the Dublin and Shannon airports have large "Duty-Free" shops. Not only are they duty-free, but they are also free of the dreaded VAT. And their prices are actually quite good. I recently saw a television special that compared Duty-Free shops in airports all over the world. While some of them are horrendous rip-offs, the Dublin and Shannon shops were named as two of the best. The only problem I have with these shops is that

CLOTHING SIZES IN IRELAND

Clothing sizes in Ireland do not strictly follow the American, Canadian, or European sizing formats. Below is a chart comparing Irish sizes to sizes in the United States, Canada, and Europe. Your best bet, however, is to try on any article before buying it.

Men's suits

Irish/US/Can.	36	38	40	42	44	46
European	46	48	50	52	54	56

Shirts

Irish/US/Can.	14	15	16	17	18
European	36	38	41	43	46

Women's dresses

Irish	32	34	36	38	40	42	44
US	8	10	12	14	16	18	20
Canadian	10	12	14	16	18	20	22
European	38	40	42	44	46	48	50

Men's shoes

Irish	6	7	8	9	10	11
US/Can.	6 1/2	7 1/2	8 1/2	9 1/2	10 1/2	11 1/2
European	40	41	42	43	44	45

Women's shoes

Irish	2	3	4	5	6	7
US	3 1/2	4 1/2	5 1/2	6 1/2	7 1/2	8 1/2
Canadian	4	5	6	7	8	9
European	34 1/2	35 1/2	36 1/2	37 1/2	38 1/2	39 1/2

the selection may not be as broad as you would like it to be. This seems to be especially true when it comes to sweaters, linen, and tweeds. They do a fine job of stocking a good selection of other items, such as Waterford and Tipperary Crystal.

Shopping hours in Dublin are slowly beginning to expand, but the rest of the country still doggedly clings to the hours they have had for at least a generation. Typically, stores are open from 9:00am to 5:30pm Monday through Saturday, and closed on Sunday. Some Dublin stores (primarily on Grafton Street and several new downtown malls) are open late on Thursday evenings (6:30pm or 7:00pm), and some are even beginning to stay open on Sunday. But this latest venture is the exception rather than the rule. When you're in the rural parts of Ireland, expect Sunday to be a very slow day for shopping.

Newsagents in the towns tend to open a little earlier than most stores – around 7:00am, as do bakeries. Newsagents have sort of a country-store feel, even in the city. They are typically small, with cribs full of fresh produce, and a little bit of everything.

CRYSTAL

The name **Waterford** is synonymous with lead crystal in Ireland, although there are several other glass manufacturers that make lead crystal on the Emerald Isle. Waterford Crystal products have become world-renowned, and with good reason. These handcrafted items, from Superbowl trophies to chandeliers, from goblets to vases, are exquisite in every detail. (A tour of their factory gives you an idea how incredible the human effort is.)

Waterford and **Tipperary** (a nearby competitor) crystal both consist of 33% lead oxide. The resulting works of art are heavy, to say the least. The products from other competitors around the country generally only have 22% lead content. Both Waterford and Tipperary crystal are blown and hand-etched. The results are exquisite. Both brands are proudly sold throughout the country.

The prices vary little from store to store, and buying in the town of Waterford is no guarantee of lower price. The lowest prices I have found are in the Duty-Free shops in the Dublin and Shannon Airports, and you don't have to pay VAT for these items. They carry a good selection of goblets, wine and water glasses, vases, and the like.

If you buy lead crystal because of the prestige of the name, Waterford Crystal is for you. But it you buy because of the sheer beauty and craftsmanship, Tipperary Crystal might be your choice. In recent years, many have recognized the quality craftsmanship of Tipperary, as well as the price tag that is substantially lower than for Waterford. I recently purchased eight Tipperary Crystal water glasses for about two-thirds the cost of similar glasses from Waterford.

ARAN SWEATERS

Aran sweaters have become extremely popular with tourists the last several years. As a consequence, the prices for these woolen works of art have risen significantly.

These heavy sweaters were originally knitted for the men and boys who earned their way in life by fishing in the inhospitable Atlantic waters off the west coast of Ireland. The sweaters served a dual purpose: they were heavy and dense and so afforded maximum protection from the omnipresent wind and rain. A slightly grimmer and equally practical purpose was to identify the bodies of drowned fishermen. These original sweaters featured a combination of stitches unique to each fishing village; drowned sailors could then be returned to their village of origin by those who found them.

Many Aran sweaters today are machine-made of lighter wools than that used for hand-made sweaters. The hand-made sweaters are heavier and a little more expensive than those made by knitting machines. If you want a hand-knit masterpiece, check the tag, ask the store owner, or simply feel the difference in weight. If it's the pattern, stitch, and functionality you seek, the machine-made sweaters will be a little less expensive. **Hehirs Woolens** *(Clifden, Tel. 095 21282, Market Street)*, **Padraic O'Maille's** *(Galway, Tel. 091 562696, 35 Eyre Square)*, and **Standun's Irish Heritage Store** *(Spiddal, Tel. 091 553108)* have good selections of Aran sweaters.

IRISH LACE

Hand-made Irish lace is a great gift and an elegant adornment to any table. The art of tatting lace is liable to be a lost one in the coming generations: fewer and fewer women have the patience or time to continue the time-intensive practice of tatting Irish lace. Today, the majority of Irish lace comes from convents, where the art is kept (barely) alive through the fingers of these religious tatters. Occasionally, the Duty-Free shops in the Dublin and Shannon airports have some Irish lace, but when they do, their selection is limited.

CLADDAGH RINGS

Claddagh rings are incredibly popular with the Irish as well as tourists. In fact, as I boarded the plane to return home on my last trip, I noticed that about half of the women were wearing either a Claddagh ring or a Claddagh necklace. These symbolic rings that are oh-so-Irish feature a heart with a crown on it. On either side of the heart are hands holding onto the heart. The heart represents love, the crown represents loyalty, and the hands represent friendship. With its symbolism, you can appreciate how popular the ring is as an engagement or wedding ring.

But beware –there is a right and a wrong way to wear a Claddagh ring! If your heart is taken (by a sweetheart, fiancee, or spouse), then the bottom of the heart should be worn facing toward your wrist. If, however, your heart is available, you wear the ring with the bottom of the heart facing out – toward the end of your finger. That lets prospective suitors know your availability, or lack thereof.

Claddagh rings are available in every jewelry store in Ireland, as well as in most souvenir and craft shops. They are available in gold as well as silver. One of the most extensive selections in the country is at **Faller's Jewelers** *(Galway, Tel. 091 561226, Williamsgate Street)*, but you'll have no trouble finding them elsewhere in the country.

TWEEDS

Ireland's northwest coast is known for its Irish tweeds, in particular Donegal tweeds from the county of the same name. These woven woolens are made into coats, capes, scarves, and skirts. If you're in Donegal, most clothing shops will carry Donegal tweeds, including **Magee's** *(Donegal Town, Tel. 073 22660, The Diamond)*.

You can also pick up some fine tweeds from the **Avoca Handweavers** *(Avoca, Tel. 0402 35105)* south of Dublin in County Wicklow.

10. TAKING THE KIDS

If you are thinking about sharing your vacation with your children, Ireland is definitely the place to do it. Ireland is a young country; over 45% of Irish citizens are under age 25 and large families are typical.

Most tourist attractions have discounted fares for children, as do most Bed and Breakfasts and many of the hotels in the country. The discount for attractions and activities is generally about 50% off the adult fare, and many attractions offer family fares, typically discounted rates covering the admission charge for two adults and up to four children.

There are a number of activities around the country targeted specifically for families with children. As the father of six children, I know well how quickly children tire of a steady diet of museums, cathedrals, and art galleries. If you can find diversions to break up the day for your children, you (and your children) will have a pleasant visit to Ireland.

Don't forget to bring books, crossword puzzles, magnetic games like chess, checkers or backgammon, or a Gameboy (or whatever they like), to keep them entertained as you drive from town to town and in the evenings. Also, depending on their age, you should consider purchasing them their own throw-away cameras so they can take pictures (it's their vacation too, after all), and they won't bug you to use your camera.

SUGGESTED KID'S ITINERARY FOR DUBLIN

To have a successful family vacation in Ireland, you should intersperse "kid-activities" between those things you want to see. For example, here's a sample itinerary for a day in Dublin with children:

I recommend spending the morning at the **National Museum of Ireland** while the kids are still fresh. When you leave the museum, let the kids lead you through **Grafton Street**. Let *them* decide how long to look at which buskers (street entertainers), which stores to stop at, which side lanes to explore, etc. They'll get a kick out of it and feel that the vacation is theirs as well. Give them a time limit, perhaps an hour, or you may end up there all day.

From Grafton Street, head to **Trinity College** for a look at the **Book of Kells,** and maybe even watch the audiovisual presentation called **The Dublin Experience** if they're not too fidgety. That might be pushing it, but it will give everyone a chance to sit down and rest and hopefully learn something.

From Trinity College, head back up Grafton Street, stop along the way (at **Bewley's**, maybe?) and pick up a little something to eat. Get it "take away", and head for **St. Stephen's Green** at the top of Grafton Street for a picnic. Be sure and buy some rolls or bread because there will be plenty of ducks to feed when you get there.

After lunch, while you're still in St. Stephen's Green, have your kids close their eyes (unless you carry a blindfold with you), and take them on a tour of the Braille gardens. These gardens have signs written in Braille for the blind, and the flora in the garden is resilient enough to be handled by those who "see" with their hands. It is a fun and educational activity for your children (you, too!).

If you are fortunate, there will be an afternoon concert serenading you from the Victorian bandstand in St. Stephen's Green. You can just listen as you go about your planned activities, or if your kids like music you can sit and listen for awhile.

After lunch, with rested children, head for **Kilmainham Gaol** (Jail). This is a tough call, not all kids will be interested in Kilmainham Gaol, it really depends on the age of your children.

Following your journey into Kilmainham, head over to **Phoenix Park**. There are a host of activities here, and what you should do again depends on the ages and interests of your children. There's a zoo (the number one tourist attraction in Ireland every year), polo fields (they may really enjoy watching the horses), cricket fields, rose gardens, and of course, the obligatory ducks to feed.

To complete your first day of touring with the kids, ride the **DART** out to **Howth** and **Abbey Tavern** for an evening of Irish entertainment. Unless your children are very, very young, they'll enjoy the action and merriment. If you arrive early for dinner and the show, walk along the quay, or over to see the fishing boats up close.

OTHER FUN ACTIVITIES

There are a number of other things to do in addition to those mentioned in the suggested itinerary. Ireland is made for outdoor activities, and since the weather rarely runs to extremes, outdoor activities are especially enjoyable in Ireland.

Take a ride in a jaunting car around the grounds of Muckross House, or ride a steam train through the countryside in Tralee. Delve into one of

Ireland's numerous caves and see stalagmites and stalactites, have a fisherman row you out into Dingle Harbor in search for Fungi, the Dingle Dolphin, or take a ferry out to Aran Islands or the Skelligs.

These are just a few of the many activities that await you and your children. Put yourself in their shoes and look for activities that will enrich as well as entertain your children. But above all, have a good time with them in Ireland.

Farms & Zoos

There are perhaps 40 or 50 farms throughout Ireland that allow children to handle, pet, and hold farm animals. **Newbridge House** north of Dublin is an example of one of those farms. Most children love animals, and enjoy seeing them up close and personal. Some farmers will let the kids bottle-feed a baby lamb or milk a cow.

There are a number of good zoos around Ireland, including **Phoenix Park** and the zoo at **Westport House**, as well as the fascinating **Fota Wildlife Park** in Cork.

Folk Villages

Dotting the Irish countryside are Irish Folk Villages that recreate the past for you and your children. Watch your daughter's eyes as she learns the art of candle making, pottering, or weaving; see how your son responds to the arduous work of a blacksmith (or vice-versa). Help them learn perspective as they realize families of eight or ten people shared entire houses no larger than the room they complain about having to share with their little brother or sister.

Some of the better examples of these folk villages include the one at the **Ulster Folk and Transport Museum** in Bangor (near Belfast), the **Bunratty Castle and Folk Park** in County Limerick, the **Kerry Country Life Experience** in Killarney, County Kerry (next to Muckross House), and the **Folk Village** at Glencolmkille in County Donegal.

Hiking

Hiking is one of the most popular tourist activities in Ireland. And kids love to hike (run, skip, jump). Whether you are a family that's into serious hiking and want to hike 15 miles a day, or whether you just need a mile or two of trail to work off some energy, Ireland has it all. There are thousands of miles of walking trails throughout Ireland and you'll easily find a few trails to suit your family.

Lakes & Rivers

Ireland is blessed with a considerable number of lakes and rivers. There are nearly 9,000 miles worth of rivers, and over 4,000 loughs (lakes) in this small country. The lakes are all beautiful, and perfect places for shoreline picnics, inexpensive boat rides out to islands lush with greenery and guarded by ancient ruins, and fishing (angling equipment can be rented).

As you can imagine, there is a great selection of lakes and rivers to choose from for your children to explore. Start with the **Grand Canal** that runs along the south side of Dublin near the Ballsbridge area. Nice walking paths are available for enjoying the canal. The **Shannon River** is a peaceful river that wends its way through a large portion of the country, and offers lots of opportunities for exploration. You might also try the **River Suir** at Carrick on Suir – it's very picturesque.

When it comes to lakes, one of my favorite is island-studded **Lough Corrib** in County Galway. **Lough Derg** also has some islands to explore, including some impressive ruins. **Lough Dan** and **Lough Tay** in the Wicklow Mountains are smaller than Loughs Corrib and Derg, but equally as inviting. **Glencar Lough** in County Leitrim features a few waterfalls to explore at the north end of the lake. And, of course, any of the lakes around Killarney are beautiful and worth taking the time to explore.

Ocean & Sea

There is no place in Ireland that is more than 70 miles from the ocean, and there are many shores that children in particular would enjoy. Whether they want to swim, skip along the shore, build sand castles, or just throw rocks in the water, the ocean is always near-by. The Irish do swim in the Atlantic Ocean and the Irish Sea. Their swimming season usually doesn't begin until around mid- to late-June, and extends into September. The water never gets really warm, but (apparently) warm enough for hardy swimmers.

The beaches to watch for are those that have been designated as **Blue Flag** beaches. These beaches have been judged safe for swimming, and they will have a tall flagpole with a blue flag flying. Many of them also have lifeguards on duty throughout the day. Some popular blue flag beaches around the country are in **Rosslare** (County Wexford), **Brittas Bay** and **Jack's Hole** (County Wicklow), **Waterville** (County Kerry), **Rossknowlagh** and **Downings** (County Donegal), and **Portrush** (County Derry).

If you are in Ireland when the water is too cold to swim, don't automatically discount the beaches. If your kids are like mine, they will still enjoy the sand between their toes, the jetsam and flotsam that washes up on the shores, and the thrill of being at the ocean.

Ruins

There are ruins all over Ireland, castles, abbeys, friarys, houses, stables, and burial grounds. If your kids need to burn off some energy, look for a deserted ruin, (you'll only have to look a short time), and let the kids explore them and give flight to their fantasies. Let them pretend they are defending or attacking a castle, or let them imagine what it would have been like to be a monk looking desperately for a place to hide the literary treasures of his monastery from an approaching army.

Ruins that offer an opportunity for young imaginations to run wild include **Dunbrodey Abbey** (County Wexford), **Bonamargy Friary** (County Antrim), **Mellifont Abbey** (County Meath), and about 10,000 unnamed ruins across the countryside.

11. FOOD & DRINK

FOOD

In recent years, prepared food in Ireland has undergone somewhat of a renaissance. In the past, food critics the world over described the food in Irish restaurants as unimaginative, bland, and relatively unexciting. (Supporters of Irish food call it "simple.") The Irish food industry took the criticism to heart. Chefs trained in Europe were brought in, and the food took on a decidedly European flavor. In Dublin, "French-Irish" or "Irish with Continental influences" are rapidly becoming popular specialties, and there is now a wide selection of ethnic restaurants.

Throughout the rest of Ireland, much of the food can still be described as unimaginative (simple), since the culinary changes sweeping Dublin have not spread to the rest of the country. There are exceptions, of course, as marvelous chefs have been hired to whip up delicacies that rival meals any of the Dublin restaurants produce. The province of Munster, for example, has a number of top-flight restaurants.

As an island nation, Ireland is particularly proud of their seafood. Salmon, scallops, prawns, lobster, sea trout, mussels, and oysters are generally plentiful, especially in Ireland's seaport towns such as Galway, Kinsale, Westport, Dublin, Wexford, and Waterford.

What can you expect from a traditional Irish meal? Well, potatoes are a good start. Potatoes have been a mainstay in the Irish diet for many years. Potato scones are a specialty in the northern part of the island.

SOME IRISH DINING PHRASES

creamed potatoes	*mashed potatoes*
gammon	*thickly cut grilled ham*
jacket potatoes	*baked potatoes*
take away	*take-out (as in: take-out food)*

Spread with butter or honey, these are mouth-wateringly delicious. Potato cakes are also eaten, primarily for breakfast with bacon and eggs, as are baked and boiled potatoes. Irish stew contains healthy portions of potatoes. And of course, a plain baked potato (called a jacket potato) with butter is always available and filling.

An Irish specialty that should not be missed is Irish soda bread. This flavorful brown bread is made from stone-ground wheat flour. Its crust is, well, crusty, and covers soft and succulent dough on the inside. It is used to accompany just about any meal, but more particularly it is served with seafood platters of salmon, mussels, or scallops.

A RECIPE FOR IRISH STEW

*Ireland's national dish is **Irish Stew**. There are probably as many recipes for Irish Stew as there are Irish cooks. Here's one for you to try:*
- *5 pounds of lamb shoulder chops*
- *20 baby red-skinned potatoes*
- *6 large carrots, peeled and sliced*
- *3 medium onions*
- *2 medium leeks*
- *1/3 cup chopped fresh parsley*
- *1 1/2 tablespoons chopped fresh thyme*
- *2 cups water*

Trim the fat and bones from the lamb shoulder chops, and cut the remaining meat into 1" to 2" square chunks. Put the fat in a large pot and cook on medium high temperature until about 3 tablespoons of drippings are present (5 to 7 minutes). Remove large pieces of fat from the pot.

Salt and pepper the chunks of lamb, add them to the pot and sauté until brown (you'll probably have to do this a little at a time until all the lamb is browned). Remove lamb, add the bones to the pot with the drippings and cook for about 5 minutes. Remove the bones.

Add the carrots, onions (peeled and quartered), leeks (slice only the white and pale green parts into 1/2" pieces), parsley, and thyme into the pot and stir regularly so nothing burns.

Return the meat and the bones to the pot, along with 2 cups of water. Bring to a boil, then reduce to medium-low heat. Cover pot tightly, simmer and stir occasionally until the lamb is tender and the vegetables are soft (about an hour and a half).

Remove approximately one cup of the vegetables, puree, and return to the stew. Season to taste with salt and pepper. Serves six.

The stew can be made one day ahead of time.

Most restaurants, and especially those in the country, boast that they use only the freshest ingredients. It is not an idle boast. Many of the country restaurants use herbs and vegetables from their own kitchen gardens, and they are assuredly some of the freshest and most flavorful meals you'll ever have. And the freshest ingredients are not limited to herbs and vegetables. You can also be served eggs from free-range hens, seafood from the ocean your table overlooks, or venison from the local farmer's fields.

In recent years, Irish farmhouse cheeses have become quite popular. Once you taste them you'll understand why. These hand-made delicacies are considered among the finest in the world. As often as not, you'll be asked to choose from a selection the restaurant presents on a cheese trolley, similar to the dessert trolleys you might be more familiar with. Several favorites to keep your eye out for include *Knockalara* (made with sheep's milk), *Cahills, Round tower*, and smoked *Gubbeen*. There are others, certainly – over 40 kinds at last count.

IRELAND'S BEST RESTAURANTS

My criteria for the best restaurants in Ireland include quality, presentation, selection, service and ambiance.

DOYLE'S SEAFOOD BAR, *4 John Street, Dingle, County Kerry, Province of Munster. Tel. (066) 51174. Set dinner menu for £13.50. Diners Club, Mastercard, and Visa accepted. 10% service charge.*

Doyle's gets my vote for the best seafood restaurant in Ireland. The setting isn't bad either, out on Dingle Peninsula. John and Stella Doyle have been cooking seafood for the local populace and tourists since the 1970s, and they do a good job of it. Doyle's combines a homey atmosphere with fresh and exceptionally well-prepared seafood to the delight of all their guests. One of their specialty dishes is millefeuille of warm oysters with Guinness sauce, a dish that has received international attention. Other dishes include baked lemon sole, mussels in herb and garlic sauce, and fried scallops.

KEE'S RESTAURANT, *Stranolar, Ballybofey, County Donegal, Province of Ulster. Tel. (074) 31018. £10.95 to £17. All major credit cards accepted.*

The Kee family has a right to be proud of their restaurant that serves both their guests (this is a part of their hotel) and the general public. In fact, I think so highly of this restaurant that I made a special effort to find it again. Several years ago during a trip to Ireland, my wife and I stumbled across this restaurant. We were delighted with what we found: *wonderful* service (even by Irish standards), a sumptuous meal, and exquisite presentation, almost too magnificent to eat! But, I forgot where it was.

Though I wasn't exactly certain, I thought it was somewhere in County Donegal. So on my next trip to Ireland, I retraced the route my wife and I had taken through County Donegal. Just as I was ready to give up, to my delight I stumbled across it again.

Of course I had to eat there again, and it was as delicious as the first time I visited. Chef Frederic Souty is the master behind the fare, and he doesn't disappoint you with his expertise. The menu is well represented by beef, lamb, seafood, and other wonderful concoctions. Try the roast rack of Donegal spring lamb or the grilled fillet steak with wild mushroom essence. Add one of the finest wine lists in the country, and you have a combination that's difficult to beat. By the way – since my first visit, Frederic married the Kee's daughter, so he will probably be a permanent fixture at Kee's Restaurant for many years to come!

The restaurant's dark wood enhances the quiet, private atmosphere of the room. The framed tapestries around the walls are the work of past owners of the hotel and restaurant.

NUMBER 10, *10 Fitzwilliam Street Lower, Dublin. Tel. (01) 676-1367. £13.95 to £24.95. All major credit cards accepted.*

If exquisite dining is what you are looking for in Dublin, look no further. Number 10, the restaurant that also serves Longfield's Hotel, is arguably one of the finest dining establishments in Dublin. As you descend white and black tile steps below street level, you enter into a small but engaging restaurant. The open fire, accentuated by the crystal and linen on the tables immediately lets you know you've come to some place special. But that is only the beginning. The service, the meal, and the ambiance all combine to provide an elegant and graceful dining experience.

Number 10's internationally trained chef whips up meals fit for a king. His presentation is as tasteful and exquisite as is the food itself. The staff is attentive and you can be assured of top-notch service. The manager describes the fare a Number 10 as "light French cuisine with Irish influences." The chef from Ireland's only two-star restaurant occasionally frequents Number 10 on his days off. Need I say more? Number 10 seats only 35 or so, and it fills up quickly. Reservations are strongly recommended; you'll probably not get in without them on the weekends.

ARBUTUS LODGE RESTAURANT, *Montenotte, Cork City, Province of Munster. Tel. (021) 501237. Set dinner menus for £22.95 and £27.75. All major credit cards accepted.*

The restaurant for Arbutus Lodge is considered one of the 10 finest in Ireland by most food critics. Traditional Irish food prepared with care and presented with an artistic flair all topped by outstanding service are hallmarks of the restaurant. From seafood to steak, lobster to lamb, all the meals are cooked with fresh ingredients, many of them from Arbutus Lodge's own kitchen garden.

Hungry for seafood? Try their pan-fried mussels with a walnut and garlic dip, or perhaps you prefer Irish beef. If that's the case, try their spiced beef with chutney or fillet of steak. If it's wild game you like, there's always the roast venison with raspberry coulis, or the chartreuse of pigeon and rabbit with fresh chanterelle sauce. As a bonus that you don't get in many upscale restaurants in Ireland, the portions are large.

LONGUEVILLE HOUSE PRESIDENTS' RESTAURANT, *Mallow, County Cork, Province of Munster. Tel. (022) 47156. Set dinner menu for £28. All major credit cards accepted.*

This elegant country restaurant is something special. On the walls surrounding the dining area are the somber portraits of former Irish Presidents overseeing the service and food in the dining room.

They needn't be concerned: the food is exquisite, the service impeccable, and the experience memorable. The freshness, ingenuity, and interesting combinations of delicious edibles all combine to make your dining an event rather than just another meal.

Part of the success of the restaurant is Chef William O'Callaghan's insistence on the freshest of ingredients; indeed, many of the vegetables, fruit, herbs, lamb, and salmon are from within a few hundred yards of the house. The others come from nearby farms or waters.

Mr. O'Callaghan tempts his guests with a variety of exceptional offerings, including an ever-popular *Surprise Taste Menu*, which is a seven-course treat. Other tempting specialties include such favorites as roast of Longueville lamb with a gratin of turnips, pan-fried medallions of monkfish, or Kilbrack pork. Desserts will leave you dreaming of the ones you didn't order – you may decide to come back just for a new dessert! Longueville House is renowned for their pyramid of chocolate with an enchanting orange sauce.

ASSOLAS COUNTRY HOUSE RESTAURANT, *Kanturk, County Cork, Province of Munster. Tel. (029) 50015. Set dinner menu for £28. All major credit cards accepted. No service charge.*

The restaurant at Assolas Country House is as elegant and delightful as you'd expect it to be. The fruits, the vegetables, and the herbs impart such magnificent subtleties of taste to the food and all are grown in Assolas Country House's kitchen garden. The menu changes daily, but the quality is always the same. Typical offerings include fillet of brill oven-baked in a basil butter sauce, Kenmare mussels, sautéed oysters with shallots and cream in brioche, or confit of duck. If wild game is your preference, several options are usually available, including venison, pheasant and quail.

CASHEL HOUSE RESTAURANT, *Cashel, County Galway, Province of Connacht. Tel. (095) 31001. Set dinner menu for £29. All major credit cards accepted. 12.5% service charge.*

Cashel House the restaurant is as impressive as Cashel House the accommodation. For starters, the dining room overlooks the impressive floral-strewn grounds. Heads of state have eaten here, and you should to. If you do stop by for dinner, you'll be treated as royally as any head of state who has dined here. The menu is simple, yet offers plenty of options, such as sautéed monkfish with a shrimp sauce, roast rack of spring lamb, filo chicken in a tarragon sauce, and even guinea fowl with grapes and Madeira. Vegetarian dishes are also available.

EARL OF THOMOND ROOM, *Newmarket-on-Fergus, County Clare, Province of Munster. Tel. (061) 368144. Set lunch menu for £18, set dinner menu for £35 and £45. All major credit cards accepted. 15% service charge.*

I was totally captivated by the restaurant in Dromoland Castle. High ceilings, rich dark wood, gorgeous crystal chandeliers, crisp starched linen tablecloths, gleaming china, and an Irish harpist, singer or fiddler all contribute to an elegant and opulent dining experience. As you dine, the watchful eyes of the former Lords and Ladies of the castle gaze down at you from larger-than-life-size portraits spread around the room.

The menu is beyond exquisite, and the food exceeds all expectations. Typical offerings include picatta of milk-fed veal, in classic "Nicoise" style, pan-fried fillet of John Dory set upon a nage of leeks and mushrooms, and terrine of Dromoland estate venison with fig chutney. All are tastefully presented, and the service is impeccable and personalized, but not overbearing.

RESTAURANT PATRICK GUILBAUD, *21 Merrion Street. Tel. (01) 676-4192. £15 to £46. Reservations are a must all year. All major credit cards accepted.*

If you want to eat in *the* restaurant in Ireland, this would be the place. Restaurant Patrick Guilbaud is the first restaurant in Ireland to be awarded a second Michelin star, and when you dine here, you'll agree that it is well deserved.

The restaurant is housed in an old Georgian home that has been exquisitely renovated. The moment you enter, you'll feel the richness of the environment. But there's no stuffiness – pleasant conversation is encouraged by the well-lit surroundings. Lovely furnishings are designed to complement the fare that you'll soon be enjoying. Take a moment to notice the paintings that adorn the walls. Each painting is by an Irish artist who lived and painted in France. Mr. Guilbaud is proud to have acquired these paintings in his home country and returned them to their native Ireland.

The food is marvelous. From the roast quail to the poached Connemara lobster, it is as tasteful to the eye as it is to the palate. Set menus are available for £18.50 for lunch and £30 for dinner. There is even a *Menu Surprise* for £46 for those wishing a dining adventure! The dress is casual but nice – most diners will be dressed in coat and tie and dresses. During your dining experience, you are likely to meet Mr. Guilbaud, as he is active in serving, greeting and conversing with his dinner guests.

DRINK

People all over the world associate **pubs** with Ireland – and rightfully so. There are an unbelievable number of pubs in Ireland. By some estimates, there are over 10,000 pubs in Ireland - one for every 500 inhabitants. Indeed, if you come to a spot in the road with two buildings, one of them is sure to be a pub! Dublin alone is reported to have nearly 1,000 pubs, giving rise to the nickname *Publin*.

Liquor is big business in Ireland. There is a wide range of ales, beers, and lagers, although Ireland is probably best known for the bitter dark stout **Guinness** exports all around the world. Whether you've tried Guinness before or not, you must try it in Dublin. All Irish agree that it tastes better when sipped within the Dublin city limits. Beer experts (to be found in pubs all over Ireland) claim there are a number of factors that add to the flavor of Guinness. These include esoterica such as a constant temperature from the brewery to the cellar to the tap, frequency of flow, and just the right pressure from the tap. Throw in a healthy dose of pub atmosphere, and you've got all the makings of a velvety smooth drink.

Ireland also produces a variety of other liquors, including gin, vodka, and whiskey. They are proud to be the nation that brought the world whiskey. None other than monks introduced whiskey into Ireland in the sixth century. In fact, the word whiskey comes from the anglicized Irish words *uisce beatha* (pronounced ISK-kee-BAH-hah), which means the "water of life." By the time Anglo-Norman invaders hit the shores of Ireland, whiskey was well established in the Irish culture. Unable to pronounce *uisce beatha*, the English soldiers shortened it to *uisce*, which they eventually anglicized to whiskey.

John Jameson established the **Jameson Distillery** in Dublin in 1780, and over the centuries his successors have perfected the recipe and process to give us the most recognizable of Irish whiskies. Irish whiskey is made from malted and unmalted barley and other native grains such as wheat, oats, and a little rye. The whiskey is matured in wooden casks from three to twelve years. Connoisseurs of whiskey will immediately notice the difference between Irish whiskey and Scotch whisky (other than the fact that one uses an "e" in its spelling, and the other does not). The difference is attributed to the malt: Irish malt is dried in a closed kiln, as opposed to being dried over open peat fires as is the malt in Scotland. The latter method imparts a distinct smoky flavor to Scotch whisky that is absent in Irish whiskey. Irish whiskey is also distilled three times, while Scotch is distilled only twice.

Jameson is perhaps the best-known Irish whiskey, but the local favorite is **Power's Gold Label**. Running a close third is the whiskey distilled in the **Bushmills Distillery** in Northern Ireland. You should try all three to determine which is your personal favorite. But don't bother trying it before you come to Ireland. Irish whiskey, like Guinness, is reputed to be best when taken within the shadow of its distillery.

As quaint and fun as pubs are, they are also of great concern for Ireland. Alcoholism is higher here than in just about any other European nation. That statistic, coupled with an unemployment rate consistently over 15%, poses a staggering challenge for the country. Put another way by one who hosted me at a pub, "Aye, lad," said he, " 'tis a real difficulty for us here."

As you wind down your Irish holiday, and you lift your glass to toast Ireland, think of this famous Irish toast: *May the road rise to meet you, May the wind be always at your back, May the sun shine warm upon your face, And the rain fall soft upon your fields. And until we meet again, May God hold you in the hollow of His hand.*

HOW TO MAKE AN IRISH WHISKEY PUNCH!

Irish Whiskey Punch is a favorite holiday treat, or a favorite treat for any other occasion you can think of! They say it's good for what ails you.
- *1 3/4 cups Irish (of course!) whiskey*
- *1/4 cup golden brown sugar*
- *1 large (or 2 small) lemons sliced into six wedges*
- *24 whole cloves*
- *3 cups hot water*

Put the whiskey and brown sugar into a pitcher and mix thoroughly (until the sugar is dissolved). Place in six cups. Put four cloves into each lemon slice, and place in each cup. Pour 1/2 cup of hot water into each, stir; drink; enjoy.

12. IRELAND'S BEST PLACES TO STAY

While most of the accommodations I've stayed in over the many years I've been going to Ireland have been quite good, there are a few that still linger in my memory. These were the ones I couldn't wait to tell my family and friends about when I got home.

Some of these hotels and B&Bs you'll remember for their history and beauty; others for their genuine warmth and the people you meet there. For each selection – other than those for Dublin, which simply list the Dublin street address – I've included the province as part of the address, so you'll have an easier time finding it in this guide and in your travels around Ireland.

THE ARCHES COUNTRY HOUSE, *Lough Eske, Barnesmore, Donegal. Tel. (073) 22029. 6 rooms. Rates for singles: £27.50, doubles: £20 per person sharing. Rates include breakfast. No credit cards accepted. No service charge.*

Nestled snuggly amid the rolling hills of the verdant Blue Stack Mountains, the Arches Country House awaits to welcome you with traditional Irish charm and elegance.

Of all the B&Bs I've visited and stayed in, this one earns my vote as the *Best Irish Bed and Breakfast*, and the main reason the Arches gets the nod over many other fine B&Bs is its proprietor, Mrs. Noreen McGinty. She is a lovely and gracious hostess, certain to offer you a positive experience to enhance your Irish holiday.

The B&B itself is also wonderful. Its six rooms are all large, and by B&B standards they border on being spacious. They are tastefully decorated with lovely furnishings and light colors. Each of the rooms is individually decorated, all with light floral accents. As a special bonus, each room has large windows, which offer stunning views of peaceful Lough Eske, just down the hill from the Arches Country House. The bathrooms in each of the rooms have been recently refurbished with new tile and fixtures. You'll appreciate the quality used in the construction of The Arches – the beautiful dark wood throughout gives the B&B a sense of elegance.

The newly added dining room, complete with knotty-pine open-beam ceiling and large windows, offers a marvelous setting in which to enjoy your Irish breakfast. And what a breakfast! Mrs. McGinty offers you a wide variety of breakfast dishes to choose from, and the results are delicious.

The grounds surrounding The Arches provide another bonus to your stay. They include a lovely fountain, walking paths, and chairs and benches for sitting and enjoying the peaceful green Irish countryside. Lots of grassy areas, sculpted trees and an ample car park all attest to the care taken by Mrs. McGinty (and *Mr.* McGinty, too!).

About two kilometers down the road from their B&B, the McGintys have purchased some lakefront property. They have a rowboat for their guests to use to explore Lough Eske and enjoy the peaceful beauty of this quiet corner of Ireland.

All in all, from top to bottom and from side to side, you can't beat The Arches Country House. If you stay here, I guarantee you'll be glad you did! And when you stay here, please tell Mrs. McGinty "Hello" for me.

ARIEL HOUSE, *50 - 52 Lansdowne Road, Dublin 4. Tel. (01) 668-5512, Fax (01) 668-5845. 40 rooms. Rates for doubles: £25 to £79 per person sharing, superior doubles: £112 per person sharing, suites: £169 per person sharing. Call for special rates that are offered from time to time, especially during the winter months. Rates do not include breakfast. Mastercard and Visa accepted. 10% service charge.*

Without a doubt, one of the warmest welcomes and most pleasant stays you can have in Ireland is at the Ariel House. Three Victorian (not Georgian) townhouses, built in the 1850s, have been converted into the award winning "Best Small Hotel in Ireland" for 1995. Michael O'Brien, who has been the proprietor of Ariel House since 1960, is your gracious host. Referred to by some as "The grandfather of the Bed and Breakfast industry in Ireland," Mr. O'Brien is a pleasure to visit with. The front sitting room is equally as wonderful, furnished with comfortable leather chairs surrounded by antiques all situated before a lovely fireplace.

Twenty of the thirty rooms are furnished almost exclusively with furniture from the Victorian era. (Ask Mr. O'Brien why Victorian furniture is so much better suited to B&Bs than Georgian furniture.) The rooms range from lovely to elegant. Ask to see the junior and senior honeymoon suites, also called the presidential suites (depending on the occasion). They are nothing short of spectacular. The large four-poster bed, the seven-foot tall armoire, and the crystal chandelier complement one another nicely and combine for a marvelous effect. All the rooms have upgraded bathrooms, televisions, ironing boards and hair dryers.

There are an additional 10 rooms added onto the back of Ariel House that are strictly functional. Their style and feel are more like small hotel rooms, and are a bit of a let-down after seeing the rest of the house. But they are less expensive than the other rooms, and are a nice clean place to stay.

Breakfast is served each morning in a lovely alcove at the back of one of the original townhouses that overlooks the gardens and back yard of Ariel House. The breakfast is delicious, and there is a nice selection of entrees to choose from.

While Ariel House is several miles from downtown Dublin, it is 100 yards from the Lansdowne DART station, about a three-minute ride to downtown.

THE RUSSELL COURT HOTEL, *Harcourt Street, Dublin 2. Tel. (01) 478-4066, Fax (01) 478-1576. 48 rooms. Rates for singles: £80, doubles: £100, suites: £105. Rates include continental breakfast. One restaurant, a pub and several lounges. All major credit cards accepted. 12.5% service charge.*

What a find! The Russell Court Hotel is one of the best-kept secrets in Dublin. The Hotel does not advertise because they have a loyal clientele – mostly business people – that keeps them full all year long.

From the moment you walk into this hotel – three converted Georgian townhouses – you'll feel comfortable and at home. No two rooms are alike, except for the fact that they are all large, with high ceilings, and are beautifully decorated. Rich wood molding, solid wood doors, and attention to detail makes this a beautiful hotel. Combine all that with its close proximity to Grafton Street and St. Stephen's Green, and this is the perfect place to stay.

On-site is Dicey Reilly's Pub, with a beer garden that's very popular in the spring and summer, and four nights a week of live music, from traditional Irish to jazz to contemporary.

If you want to stay here, you'd better make your reservations several months in advance.

BALLYNAHINCH CASTLE HOTEL, *Recess, Connemara. Tel. (095) 31006, Fax (095) 31085; E-mail: bhinch@iol.ie; Website: www.commerce.ie/ ballynahinch. 28 rooms. Rates for singles: £72 to £95, doubles: £52 to £75 per person sharing, suites: £110 to £125 per person sharing. Rates include breakfast. Restaurant, gardens, croquet, riding, shooting, walking trails. All major credit cards accepted. 10% service charge.*

Ballynahinch Castle is a lovely hotel, with a real red fox that often greets tourists at the front door. Ancestral home of the Martin Clan of

Connemara, Ballynahinch Castle has been converted into a four-star hotel. The rooms – all individually decorated – are spacious and offer beautiful views of either the mountains or the lake. The service is impeccable.

During the 1930s, the eccentric (and wealthy) Maharajah Ranjitsinji purchased Ballynahinch Castle as a winter get-away to relax and entertain his friends. Pictures of the Maharajah grace some of the walls and help put a name with the face.

In recent years, Ballynahinch Castle Hotel has earned the reputation as a shooting center, where sporting folk come from all over the world to participate in five annual woodcock bird hunts sponsored by the hotel.

In addition to the exceptional service and the warmth of Ballynahinch Castle, the restaurant is also impressive. Looking out over the Owenmore River as it quietly fills Ballynahinch Lake, the floodlit shores add a peaceful touch to your dining experience. The food is delicious, the service efficient, and the atmosphere tranquil.

Ballynahinch Castle Hotel is rightfully proud of their designation as Ireland's Hotel of the Year in 1994.

CASHEL HOUSE HOTEL, *Cashel, Connemara. Tel. (095) 31001, (095) 31077, US toll free 800/223-6510; E-mail: info@cashel-house-hotel.com; Website: www.cashel-house-hotel.com. 32 rooms. Rates for singles: £55 to £85, doubles: £54 to £80 per person sharing, suites: £74 to £100 per person sharing. Rates include breakfast. Restaurant, gardens, riding, walking trails. All major credit cards accepted. 12.5% service charge.*

This is a very impressive hotel. The owners, Dermot and Kay McEvilly, have been in the hotel business since 1968 and are responsible for Cashel House emanating the feel and personality of a B&B, but having the facilities and amenities of a hotel. Built in the 19th century, Cashel House has been magnificently renovated. Antiques, old (*old!*) oil paintings, and plush hand-made Connemara rugs grace the floors throughout the hotel.

Each room is lavish and unique from one another. Each is tastefully wallpapered and carpeted, and flowers from the extensive gardens are found daily in your room – just the right touch to make you feel all that much more welcome. And if that's not enough, their restaurant is considered one of the best in Ireland. Located at the front and side of the house, the dining room has large windows that look out onto the grounds of Cashel House. Dermot McEvilly and his crew of cooks are excellent chefs; their specialty is seafood.

Riding stables on-site are constantly in use by the guests, and in keeping with their thoughtful manner, the owners provide boots and riding helmets for their guests to ensure safe and enjoyable rides. And their luxurious gardens assure either a quiet beginning or a romantic end to your day. Pound for pound, pence for pence, this is probably the be lodging for the money in western Ireland.

TINAKILLY COUNTRY HOUSE, *Rathnew. Tel. (0404) 69274, Fax (0404) 67806; E-mail: reservations@tinakilly.ie; Website: www.tinakilly.ie/ pages/oldindex. 52 rooms. Rates for singles: £116 to £124, doubles: £68 to £76 per person sharing, suites: £85 to £130 per person sharing. One restaurant, putting green, croquet. All major credit cards accepted. No service charge.*

Tinakilly feels more like being at home – well, a very expensive home, than staying in a hotel. Antiques abound, from the sitting room with its blazing fire to the spacious rooms, most with lovely views of the Irish Sea. They also have a marvelous restaurant. This old Victorian mansion was built in the 1870s as a token of appreciation for Captain Robert Halpin, who commanded the *Great Eastern*, from which was laid the first telegraph cable that linked Europe and America.

PARK HOTEL KENMARE, *Kenmare. Tel. (064) 41200, Fax (064) 41402; E-mail: phkenmre@iol.ie; Website: www.parkkenmare.com. 50 rooms. Rates for singles: £132 to £152, doubles: £122 to £175 per person sharing, suites: £205 to £242 per person sharing. One restaurant, croquet, tennis. All major credit cards accepted. No service charge. Only open from mid-April through mid-November.*

I must admit, I was probably more curious to meet the owner of the Park Hotel in Kenmare than I was to actually stay at his hotel. It seemed that nearly every hotelier to whom I mentioned my upcoming stay at the Park Hotel asked me to say "Hello" to Francis Brennan for him or her. Several of them, general managers at some of Ireland's most prestigious hotels, had learned their craft at Francis' hand. I wasn't disappointed, either in Mr. Brennan, his staff, or in the hotel.

The hotel was built in 1897 to serve as the hotel for the railroad that dead-ended there. Since that time, it has been renovated and expanded, and the results are marvelous. From the turned-down beds to the bathrobes and slippers, to the clean windshield in the morning "...to get a clear view of our Emerald Isle," you'll be delighted you stayed. The rooms are nice-sized, and the ones in the back are the nicest, offering views of Kenmare Bay and most of the 11 acres of gardens. The halls are filled with antiques and portraits.

On-site is an award-winning restaurant that overlooks Kenmare Bay. The menu offers a good selection, but on my last visit I finally settled on the grilled fillet of beef studded with truffles and a fricassee of wild mushrooms. It was, without a doubt, one of the most delicious meals I had while I was in Ireland. The beef was tender and practically dissolved in my mouth, and the flavor was as exceptional as I have ever experienced.

k Hotel Kenmare is only open from mid-April through
after their season is over, Mr. Brennan takes his entire
pense paid international vacation as a reward for their
ve me, they deserve it.

SHELBOURNE MERIDIEN HOTEL, *27 St. Stephen's Green, Dublin
2. Tel. (01) 676-6471, Fax (01) 661-6006; E-mail:
shelbourneinfo@fortehotels.com; Website: www.shelbourne.ie. 190 rooms. Rates
for singles: £165 to £185, doubles: £195 to £255, and suites: £380 to £950. One
restaurant and two bars. All major credit cards accepted. 15% service charge.*

The Shelbourne Hotel receives my vote for the nicest of the nice in
Dublin. From the rich dark wood to the lovely antique Waterford crystal
chandelier in the Lord Mayor's lounge, to the flawless service, you'll be
delighted with every aspect of your stay at the Shelbourne.

The Shelbourne isn't as flamboyant as some of the other brass and
crystal hotels you'll find in Dublin. Instead, it is all grace and grandeur,
refinement and splendor. No impressive lobby awaits your arrival, but a
rather understated journey from the front door to the reception desk. But
that's all that is understated. The rooms and the furnishings, the fine
equestrian art, and the ambiance are as rich and lovely as you'll find in
Dublin.

The Shelbourne, like so many other hotels in Dublin, is three
Georgian townhouses that were converted in 1824. The rooms are large
and spacious, and no two are alike in their layout, size, or decor. All the
rooms are lavishly furnished and very comfortable. Ask for a room
overlooking St. Stephen's Green – the views are among the best in Dublin.

For a treat, ask to see the Presidential Suite – more fondly referred
to as the Princess Grace Room in honor of that grand lady's stay here
several years prior to her death. It is a large, attractive, multi-roomed suite
overlooking St. Stephen's Green. Near one of the windows is a picture of
Princess Grace, and it adds a touch of, well...*grace*...to the room! If the
room is not occupied, the front desk staff assures me it is possible to have
a short tour.

History buffs will be interested to know that the Irish Constitution
was drafted in the Shelbourne in 1922. The Shelbourne boasts many
heads of state, actors, and actresses, and many of the world's *glitterati* as
their honored guests. And you will feel equally honored during your stay
here.

DROMOLAND CASTLE, *Newmarket-on-Fergus, County Clare. Tel.
(061) 368144, Fax (061) 363355, US toll free 800/346-7007; E-mail:
dromoland@dromoland.ie; Website: www.commerce.ie/dromoland. 100 rooms.
Rates for standard rooms: £140 to £254 per room, deluxe rooms: £216 to £312*

per room, state rooms and suites: £231 to £675; children under age 12 stay free with parents. One restaurant, indoor swimming pool, spa, sauna, fitness center, beauty salon, tennis, snooker, golf, riding, fishing, shooting, bicycles. All major credit cards accepted. No service charge.

"A fantasy come true," "A piece of heaven," "Exceeded every expectation I had" – these were the last three entries in the guest book on the morning after I stayed at Dromoland Castle, and they accurately represent my own feelings. Dromoland Castle is the sister castle to Ashford Castle, and you can certainly see the family resemblance. But if Ashford is the elegant, classic beauty, Dromoland is the sister with the personality. Dromoland exudes grace and charm.

Dromoland Castle was once the estate of the powerful O'Brien Clan, descendants of Brian Boru, High King of Ireland. Chock full of antiques and portraits of the previous inhabitants, it retains its regal feeling without being stuffy. Adding to the fairytale feeling, Dromoland Castle is set amid 370 acres of woodlands, parks, and golf fairways and greens.

The rooms are spacious and tastefully decorated. The rooms in front have lovely views of a small lake and the golf course. All rooms come with nightly turndown service, warm robes, and chocolates on your pillow.

On-site is an outstanding restaurant – the Earl of Thomond Room – that provides one of the most delectable dining experiences in the country. I'm not sure whether it was the exceptional food, or the Irish harpist and singer softly serenading the diners, or the beautiful views out the dining room windows, or the feeling that I was dining where kings and queens would feel comfortable, but meals at Dromoland Castle are superb in all respects. For a full review of the restaurant, see Chapter 11, *Food & Drink*.

ASHFORD CASTLE, *Cong. Tel. (092) 46003, Fax (092) 46260, US toll free 800/346-1001; E-mail: ashford@ashford.ie; Website: www.commerce.ie/ ashford. 83 rooms. Rates for standard rooms: £140 to £254, deluxe rooms: £216 to £312, state rooms: £370 to £467, suites: £545 to £642. Restaurant, gardens, tennis, grounds, fishing, walking trails, golf. All major credit cards accepted. No service charge.*

What an exquisite hotel this is! Ashford Castle is far better experienced than described (although I'll try). Just to give you a point of reference, Ashford Castle has been highlighted repeatedly on television, and was one of the hotels President Ronald Reagan stayed in during his visit to Ireland.

Resting regally amid 350 acres of luscious parkland, this 13th-century Norman castle is a sight to behold. Inside, the scores of high quality antiques and old portraits combined with rich paneled walls and luxurious carpets give you the feeling you've stumbled into the private chambers of an ancient ruler. The public rooms are elegant, filled with rich leather chairs, dark paneling, and views of the verdant grounds. The bedrooms are all different, and are probably the largest you'll find in Ireland for each class of room. All have antiques aplenty, plush carpets, and marvelous bathrooms. Thick robes, slippers, mineral water, and a bowl of fruit greet you upon arrival.

If you are romanced by the hotel, you will be positively seduced by the dining experience here. The Connaught Room is a small, intimate restaurant overlooking the grounds of the estate. Rich, dark paneling, an exquisite Waterford crystal chandelier and an open fireplace are the perfect touches to put you in the mood for a wonderful dinner. The specialty is French cuisine, and typical offerings include Cleggan lobster tail in a ginger fish consomme with tomato and leeks, or whole duckling carved at your table.

But wait – you've only learned about one of the restaurants in Ashford Castle. In addition to the Connaught Room, there is the equally lovely George V Room. With an open fire, gorgeous chandeliers, and beautiful light oak paneling that gives the room less of a regal feel and more of a traditional Irish feel, which is the perfect complement to the traditional Irish cuisine featured here. Whether you prefer fish or beef, either is prepared to perfection and served with elegant efficiency.

Ashford Castle has been featured twice on *Lifestyles of the Rich and Famous*, is repeatedly listed among the top hotels in the world in travel magazines and industry publications, and is quite simply a wonderful place to visit. It has hosted kings and queens, princesses and presidents – so why not you? If you can fit Ashford Castle into your travel plans, I predict it will be one of your most memorable experiences in Ireland.

13. DUBLIN

With slightly over one million people in its greater metropolitan area, **Dublin** is the largest city on the Emerald Isle. Its original Irish name, *Baile Atha Cliath*, means "Town of the Hurdle Ford." However, British conquerors renamed it Dublin after a nearby trading area called *Dubh Linn*, which means "Black Pool." Located on the eastern coast of Ireland, Dublin has been an important seaport for nearly a millennium. The **River Liffey** is the major waterway in Dublin, and it bisects the city from east to west.

Dublin is the ideal place to both begin and end your journey to the Emerald Isle. Cultural, architectural, and historical sights and sounds are present on nearly every corner and around every bend in Dublin. Museums, art galleries, historic sites, marvelous shopping, and quiet sunsets all vie for your time and attention.

Dublin's history begins with the Viking settlement of *Dyflin*, founded in 841. Sailing up into the mouth of the River Liffey, these intrepid Norsemen founded a small community that would one day become the most important seaport in Ireland. The native Irish were not pleased with their presence, and the next 150 years saw a series of battles between the Irish and these northern interlopers. But it wasn't until 988 (some historians say 989) that the town was permanently wrested from foreign hands. Despite its initial founding in 841, Dubliners consider 988 as the founding date for their hometown.

In 1170, English and Norman mercenaries under the **Earl of Pembroke**, also known as **Strongbow**, came to the aid of Dermot MacMurrough, the King of Leinster in his dispute with other Irish kings. These Anglo-Norman invaders overwhelmed the walled town's defenses and established a firm stronghold in Dublin. It was the beginning of over 750 years of English domination over Dublin and Ireland. Shortly after the invasion, Dublin swelled with the arrival of immigrants from England. This was the beginning of a number of waves of English settlement. Even today the accents of native Dubliners have a strong British flavor.

This began a period of renaissance, maturing, and building for the small seaport town. Some of Dublin's existing attractions came into being during this period. Small churches were rebuilt on a grand scale during this time: **Christchurch Cathedral** (1173), **St. Audoen's Church of Ireland** (1190), and **St. Patrick's Cathedral** (1190 and 1220). In addition, **Dublin Castle** was built in 1204, although the structure in place today has been rebuilt numerous times. The **Record Tower** is the only remaining part of the original castle.

As the center of English rule and power in Ireland, Dublin found itself ostracized from the rest of Ireland. Over the ensuing years, Anglo-Norman control over Ireland was exercised from within the walled city of Dublin and their influence and domination became firmly implanted along the eastern coastline, centered in Dublin. This area came to be known as **The Pale**.

DUBLIN'S MUST-SEE SIGHTS

BOOK OF KELLS – *Housed at Trinity College. Ancient monks hand-illustrated the four gospels over 1,100 years ago.*

CHESTER BEATTY LIBRARY AND GALLERY OF ORIENTAL ART – *This is a very impressive museum. Located behind Dublin Castle, it's definitely worth spending a few minutes to visit.*

CHRISTCHURCH CATHEDRAL – *The two finest cathedrals in Ireland are located in Dublin. St. Patrick's is one, Christchurch is the other.*

GENERAL POST OFFICE (GPO) – *There aren't many cities where I'd suggest going to see the main post office. But the GPO has played such an important part in Irish history, it's a must.*

GRAFTON STREET – *This pedestrian shopping street provides ample opportunity for shopping and people watching.*

GUINNESS BREWERY – *Visit the brewery that made Dublin famous. The tour no longer takes you back into the brewery itself, but provides a video tour.*

HUGH LANE MUNICIPAL GALLERY OF MODERN ART – *Another fine art gallery in Dublin. This one focuses on contemporary art.*

NATIONAL GALLERY OF IRELAND – *The National Gallery is the best art gallery in Ireland, and is well worth a visit.*

NATIONAL MUSEUM – *If you see only one museum in Ireland, let this be the one.*

PHOENIX PARK – *Phoenix Park has a lot to offer if you are interested in lots of greenery, cricket games or polo matches, ducks and ponds, a fabulous zoo, or people watching.*

ST. PATRICK'S CATHEDRAL – *So indelibly associated with the history of Ireland you have to visit.*

Dublin served as the launching point for various and sundry military campaigns against the native Irish during the 16th through 19th centuries. It enjoyed a resurgence of prominence during the mid-17th century as a result of the successes of Oliver Cromwell.

During the 19th century, massive efforts to revitalize and restore Dublin were undertaken. As a lasting tribute to the Georgian period in Dublin's history, streets were laid out and widened and beautiful townhouses were erected.

ARRIVALS & DEPARTURES

Dublin can be reached by air, train, or car. It can also be reached by ferry if you are coming from France, England, or Wales.

By Air From The United States

Dublin International Airport, *Tel. (01) 705-2222*, is about six miles north of Dublin's city center. It is the principal airport for flights from Europe, England, Scotland, and the United States. The airport code is DUB.

Transatlantic flights to Ireland from the US land in Dublin (some flights land in Shannon first, then continue on to Dublin). **Aer Lingus** and **Delta** are the only two carriers (at this time) that fly directly to Ireland from the United States. Canadian passengers flying to Dublin or Shannon must connect in Chicago, Boston, New York, or London.

Dublin Airport is a small but modern airport. The fact that it has only one terminal also makes it easy to navigate. Signs are plentiful, and if you're the least bit confused or lost, there are plenty of helpful airport employees willing to lend a hand.

Don't be alarmed if you see military personnel leisurely patrolling the halls with Uzi machine guns slung casually over their shoulders. This is a common sight in most European airports, and Europeans pay as little heed to their presence as Americans pay to pistol-toting police officers in America.

From the airport to Dublin's city center you can choose a taxi, bus, express bus, or rental car.

By Air From England

Since many international carriers do not fly directly into Ireland but connect in London, many tourists visiting Ireland first spend a few days in England. If that's the case with you, it's relatively easy to get to Ireland from England, and you have several choices.

Nearly two dozen flights a day arrive from London's Heathrow and Gatwick airports. In addition, daily flights arrive from Edinburgh and

Glasgow as well as from a number of England's regional airports, including Birmingham, Bristol, Liverpool, Luton, Manchester, and Newcastle.

Airlines flying to Dublin from London and England's regional airports include Aer Lingus, British Airways, British Midland Airways, and Ryanair. Flights from Ireland's regional airports (Cork, Galway, Knock, Sligo, and Waterford) also land at Dublin Airport.

If you do spend a few days in England prior to coming to Ireland, and your fare doesn't yet include a stop in Ireland, the fares from London to Ireland are quite reasonable. Depending on the time of year, and your days of travel (weekdays are more expensive than weekends), you can expect to pay £85 to £140 for round-trip airfare to Shannon or Dublin from London.

Getting to Town By Taxi

The taxi stand is just outside the doors of the Arrivals Hall. If you hire a taxi, the 25-minute ride from the airport will cost you around £15 including tip, and is certainly the quickest way to get into town.

Getting to Town By Bus

You have two choices for a bus ride into the city: express or regular bus. The **express bus** gets you into town nearly as quickly as does a taxi, but at a considerably lower cost. The 35-minute ride costs £3.00. It can take about 15 minutes longer during rush hour. The express bus takes you into the heart of Dublin, stopping at **Busaras Station** *(Tel. 01 836-6111, Store Street)* in the O'Connell Street District north of the River Liffey. The service runs daily every half hour from 7:30am to 11:00pm. To catch the express bus, turn left coming out of the Arrivals Hall, and walk about 100 feet to bus stop #1.

To catch the **regular bus** into the city, go about 50 feet further than the express bus stop to bus stop #2. This bus stops all along the way into downtown Dublin, but it only costs £1.55. It takes a bit longer – about 45 minutes without heavy traffic. This bus takes you to any number of places in downtown Dublin, but not to Busaras, the main bus station.

Renting a Car at the Airport

If you are renting a car when you arrive, your path through Customs will deliver you into a large hall where Avis, Budget, Hertz, Murray's EuropCar and National are located. If you are using one of the other, lesser-known car rental agencies, they are tucked around the corner at the far end of the hall (the opposite end from where you enter after Customs). If you don't find them right away, ask for directions from any of the uniformed airport employees.

You can get rental cars at the following agencies in Dublin:
- **Alamo-Treaty Rent-a-Car**, *Tel. 800/522-9696*
- **Argus Rent-a-Car**, *Argus House, 59 Terenure Road East, Dublin. Tel. (01) 490-4444, Fax (01) 490-6328*
- **Atlas Car Rentals Ltd.**, *Desk 1, Arrivals Hall, Dublin Airport. Tel. (01) 844-4859, Fax (01) 844-0732*
- **Auto-Europe**, *800/223-5555*
- **Avis Rent-a-Car**, *Dublin Airport, Arrivals Hall, Tel. 800/331-1084*
- **Budget Rent-a-Car**, *Dublin Airport, Arrivals Hall, Tel. 800/472-3325*
- **Casey's/Flannelly Car Rentals**, *Tel. 212/935-0606*
- **Hertz Rent-a-Car**, *Dublin Airport, Arrivals Hall, Tel. 800/654-3001*
- **Holiday Autos**, *Tel. 800/422-7737*
- **Kemwell Rent-a-Car**, *Tel. 800/678-0678*
- **Long's Travel**, *96 Ridgedale Avenue, Cedar Knolls NJ 07927, 800/524-0555*
- **Tom Mannion Self Drive**, *Tel. 800/666-4066*
- **Murray's EuropCar Car Rental**, *Baggot Street Bridge, Dublin 4. Tel. (01) 668-1777, Fax (01) 660-2958; or toll-free 800/227-3876*
- **South County Car Rentals**, *Rochestown Avenue, Dun Laoghaire, County Dublin. Tel. (01) 280-6005 Fax (01) 285-7016; or toll-free 800/521-0643*
- **Windsor Car Rentals**, *South Circular Road, Rialto, Dublin 8. Tel. (01) 454-0800, Fax (01) 454-0122*

Sample trip lengths from Dublin around the country (on the main roads):
- Belfast: 3 hours
- Cork: 4 hours
- Donegal: 3 hours
- Dundalk: 1 hour
- Galway: 3 hours
- Kilkenny: 2 hours
- Killarney: 5 hours
- Limerick: 3 hours
- Wexford: 3 hours

By Bus

If you are arriving in Dublin on a bus from elsewhere in Ireland, you will arrive at **Busaras Station** on Store Street. You'll be about four blocks west of O'Connell Street, and two blocks north of the River Liffey. The neighborhood is marginal – not too bad, but I wouldn't advise walking too far west or northwest of there. The closer you get to O'Connell Street, the better the neighborhood gets.

By Ferry From England

If you want to continue to use the rental car you rented in England, drive to Holyhead or Fishguard in Wales. From there, ferries depart for Ireland on a regular basis. The **B&I Line** *(Tel. 0171 491-8682 in England)* runs ferries from Holyhead to Dublin, and **Stena Sealink** *(toll free in the US and Canada: 800/677-8585 or 01233 647047 in England)* runs ferries from Holyhead to Dun Laoghaire.

Ferries may sound romantic and fun, and that may be. But they are no bargain compared to airfares. Expect to pay about £200 one way, or £350 round-trip for your car, yourself, and three passengers. You'll pay less if it is just you, or just you and a companion, but it is still roughly equivalent to airfare. Ferries run three to five times daily, depending on the time of year. The trip across the Irish Sea takes about an hour and 45 minutes.

By Train

Ireland has a well-regulated and much-used rail system, with stations in many towns and cities across the country. If you are coming to Dublin by train from elsewhere in Ireland, you will either arrive at Heuston Station or Connolly Station.

If you are coming from (or going to) Belfast, Rosslare, or Sligo Town, you will use **Connolly Station**, *Amiens Street, Tel. 01 836-6222*. From there it is a 10-minute walk to Dublin's city center, or a short and inexpensive (£3) taxi ride.

If you are coming from (or going to) anywhere else in Ireland, your train will be at **Heuston Station**, *King's Bridge, Tel. 01 836-6222*, about a 20-minute walk to Dublin's city center, a £5 cab ride, or a 10-minute, 60p bus ride to O'Connell Bridge. Buses depart frequently from Heuston Station headed for O'Connell Bridge.

Like the neighborhood around Busaras Station, the closer you get to O'Connell Bridge, the better the neighborhoods become. Nothing too scary around Heuston or Connolly Stations, but the areas are marginal.

ORIENTATION

Dublin is a relatively easy town to get around in, once you get used to the way the streets change names every other block or so (really!). While that sounds strange, it is really incredibly efficient for finding places. For example, rather than having to know where the 2500 block of Elm Street is, all you need to know is what names a given thoroughfare has over a distance. For example, the street on the north side of **St. Stephen's Green** is called (interestingly) St. Stephen's Green North. If you walk east on that street for six blocks, the name changes to Merrion Street, Baggot Street Lower, Baggot Street Upper, and then Pembroke Street. At first I found it frustrating, but I soon figured out how easy it is to follow. Probably 60% of the restaurant and hotel owners I spoke with didn't even know the addresses of their own businesses, they just knew the street name!

Most of the major streets in Dublin are wide and easy to negotiate, and many of them are one-way. When the streets are not one-way, remember to drive on the left, not the right. They have come up with a unique way to protect people who come from countries where they drive on the right-hand side of the road. As you step off the curb at cross-walks, written on the road in big bold letters are the words LOOK TO THE RIGHT - > or < - LOOK TO THE LEFT, depending on which side of the street you're on and whether you are on a one-way or two-way street.

Traffic in Dublin is a good reason to leave your rental car parked or wait until you are ready leave Dublin before you rent one. Drivers in Dublin are maniacal. Add to their craziness aggressive motorcyclists and daring pedestrians, and you'll be tempted to turn in your AAA card and international driver's license if you try to drive in Dublin!

The principal sights in Dublin are located in a four by three-mile rectangle covering the heart of Dublin city. From the Dublin Area Rapid Transit (DART) rails on the east to **Phoenix Park** on the west, and from Parnell Square on the north to the Ballsbridge area on the south, you'll have lots to see and do, as well as plenty of places to stay and eat.

There is a **Bord Failte** tourist office in the Dublin airport that can assist you when you arrive in Dublin. If you have left the airport, the main Bord Failte office in Dublin is located at the corner of Lower Baggot Street and Wilson Terrace, *Tel. (01) 676-5871,* just inside the Grand Canal. There are two other locations: Upper O'Connell Street, *Tel. (01) 674-7733,* and in the heart of Dublin on Suffolk Street, *Tel. (01) 605-7777.*

GETTING AROUND TOWN
By Bicycle

Bicycling is an excellent way to see Dublin, and there are many bicycle rental shops in the city from which to rent a bicycle. Rates average about £7 per day and £30 per week, and most bike shops require a deposit, usually £30 to £40. In fact, there is a bike rental shop, called **Rent-a-Bike**, right around the corner from the Busaras station, at the corner of Lower Gardener Street and French Lane. If you do rent a bicycle to see Dublin, please use caution. The main thoroughfares in the city are often congested with traffic, especially at rush hour. However, once you get out of the heart of the city, bicycling is quite pleasant.

Here are a few other shops where you can rent a bicycle:
• **C. Harding's**, *30 Bachelor's Walk, Dublin. Tel. (01) 873-3622*
• **McDonald's Bikes**, *38 Wexford Street, Dublin. Tel. (01) 475-2586*

• **Little Sport**, *3 Merville Avenue, Dublin. Tel. (01) 833-2405*
• **Raleigh Rent-A-Bike**, *Kylemore Road, Dublin 10. Tel. (01) 626-1333*
• **Rent-A-Bike**, *58 Lower Gardiner Street, Dublin. Tel. (01) 872-5931*

By Bus

Buses crisscross the city on a regular basis, and are relatively inexpensive. Fares are charged based on distance to your destination, from 50p to £1.10. They run regularly from 6:30am (9:30am on Sundays) until 11:30pm each night. You can catch the bus at any number of stops in the city. Most routes begin at or near O'Connell Bridge and bus starters at O'Connell bridge will be more than happy to point you to the correct bus stop. (Bus-starters are bus company employees at the O'Connell Street station whose job it is to make sure individuals – especially tourists – get on the right bus.)

If you are planning to use the bus, get a map since O'Connell Bridge may not be convenient. If you are on the outskirts of the city, just look for the bus destination signs that say *An Lar*, Irish for "the center."

By Foot

I believe you can comfortably see most of Dublin's sights on foot. **Dublin** is a very easy city to get around. Most of the interesting sights are within a relatively compact area, and well within walking distance.

By Taxi

There are several **taxi stands** throughout the city: the airport, the Busaras station, Connolly, Pearse, and Heuston train stations, on O'Connell Street, College Green (in front of the Bank of Ireland), and St. Stephen's Green North. You can also call a cab company and have a taxi pick you up, although there is usually an additional charge (£2 to £4) to have them do so. In the past you couldn't hail a taxi in Dublin, but that is changing. While I have witnessed numerous unsuccessful attempts to hail empty on-duty taxis when I was last in Dublin, I also saw a few stop and pick up passengers who hailed them.

Taxi service in Dublin is efficient and relatively inexpensive. However, unless you are going outside of the immediate downtown area, you're just as well off walking. However, in the event you do decide to take a cab, here are the numbers of several taxi companies in Dublin:
• **A1 Taxis**. *Tel. (01) 285-9333*
• **Blue Cabs**. *Tel. (01) 676-1111*
• **Capital Cabs**. *Tel. (01) 490-8888*
• **Central Cabs**. *Tel. (01) 836-5555*
• **City Group**. *Tel. (01) 872-7272*
• **Metro Cabs**. *Tel. (01) 668-3333*

By Train

The **Dublin Area Rapid Transit** (**DART**) is an electrified train that reaches from Dublin's city center to outlying communities as far north as Howth and as far south as Bray. It runs every 15 minutes (every five minutes during rush hours) from 6:30am until 11:30pm. If you are heading north on the DART, you need to be on the west platform, and if you are headed south, you should be on the east platform. These green trains are models of efficiency that zip their passengers to their destinations swiftly and relatively quietly. DART has a well-deserved reputation for timeliness, and you can practically set your watch by it. Fares are reasonable and distance-dependent. You can purchase an all-day DART pass for £3.20 if you plan to ride it for more than just a few trips. There is no smoking on DART and the fine for doing so is £400!

At some stations you may feel a moment's disorientation due to the use of a common word in an uncommon manner. Watch for signs directing you to the "subway". This is not an underground train with which you may be familiar, but rather a "subterranean walkway" that takes you under the tracks to the exit. If you are really confused, just follow the crowds, or ask someone.

WHERE TO STAY

In Dublin, you have the full spectrum of lodging from which to choose: from austere youth hostels to luxurious five-star hotels, and everything in between. I've tried to give you plenty of selections in each price category.

The rates listed are "rack" rates. Chances are if you work for a major corporation, or belong to an organization like AAA, you can get a reduced rate, especially in the major hotels. In the hotel listings, "All major credit cards accepted," means Access, American Express, EuroCard, Mastercard, and Visa. If any one of these is not accepted, I have specifically listed those that are accepted. I have listed a range of rates if the rates vary throughout the year. The lower rates are typically only valid during the off or low seasons, and the higher rates are valid from about June through September. Hotels are numbered to correspond with the hotel map on page 145.

NORTH DUBLIN
At or Near the Airport

1. **FORTE CREST HOTEL**, *Dublin Airport, Dublin 9. Tel. (01) 844-4211, Fax (01) 842-5874. 188 rooms. Rates for singles: £99, doubles: £89 to £99. One restaurant and one bistro. All major credit cards accepted. 15% service charge.*

The only hotel located at the airport, the Forte Crest serves business travelers well. The rooms are about average size, but nicely furnished and

DUBLIN'S TOP HOTELS

The following hotels are listed from least to most expensive. You can get more information on each selection below. I've left the numbers at the front of each selection for easy reference in the reviews and on the hotel map.

6. OLIVER ST. JOHN GOGARTY'S YOUTH HOSTEL, 18-21 Anglesea Street, Dublin 2. Tel. (01) 671-1822, Fax (01) 671-7637. 27 rooms, 130 beds. Rates for twins: £19 to £21 per person sharing, three beds: £14 to £18 per person sharing, four beds: £15 to £20 per person sharing, dormitory: £14 to £17 per person sharing. One of the nicest and most comfortable hostels in Ireland.

22. ARIEL HOUSE, 50 - 52 Lansdowne Road, Dublin 4. Tel. (01) 668-5512, Fax (01) 668-5845. 40 rooms. Rates for doubles: £25 to £79 per person sharing, superior doubles: £112 per person sharing, suites: £169 per person sharing. Probably the best guesthouse in Ireland, with a proprietor in the same category!

14. THE RUSSELL COURT HOTEL, Harcourt Street, Dublin 2. Tel. (01) 478-4066, Fax (01) 478-1576. 48 rooms. Rates for singles: £80, doubles: £100, suites: £105. A gem of a hotel. Mid-range in price, top-flight in ambiance. One of the best-kept secrets in Dublin (but not any more!).

28. BURLINGTON HOTEL, Upper Leesom Street, Ballsbridge, Dublin 4. Tel. (01) 660-5222, Fax (01) 660-5064, US toll free 800/448-8355. 503 rooms. Rates for singles: £180, doubles: £133 to £210, suites: £360. 15% service charge. If the Shelbourne exemplifies "old money" grace, the Burlington symbolizes "new money". Plenty of marble, brass and dark wood await you here.

17. SHELBOURNE MERIDIEN HOTEL, 27 St. Stephen's Green, Dublin 2. Tel. (01) 676-6471, Fax (01) 661-6006; E-mail: shelbourneinfo@fortehotels.com; Website: www.shelbourne.ie. 190 rooms. Rates for singles: £165 to £185, doubles: £195 to £255, and suites: £380 to £950. 15% service charge. The best "old money" elegance in Dublin. The best of the upper-class hotels.

very comfortable. They offer a business center with secretarial services and conference facilities that can accommodate up to 150 people. There is a shuttle bus that runs from the hotel to the airport on demand.

2. THE DOYLE SKYLON HOTEL, *Drumcondra Road, Dublin 9. Tel. (01) 837-9121, Fax (01) 837-2778, US toll free 800/448-8355. 90 rooms. Rates for singles: £65, doubles: £95. One restaurant and one bar. All major credit cards accepted. 15% service charge.*

This is probably the most basic of the Doyle Hotel Group properties. On the main road into Dublin from the airport, the Doyle Skylon is a

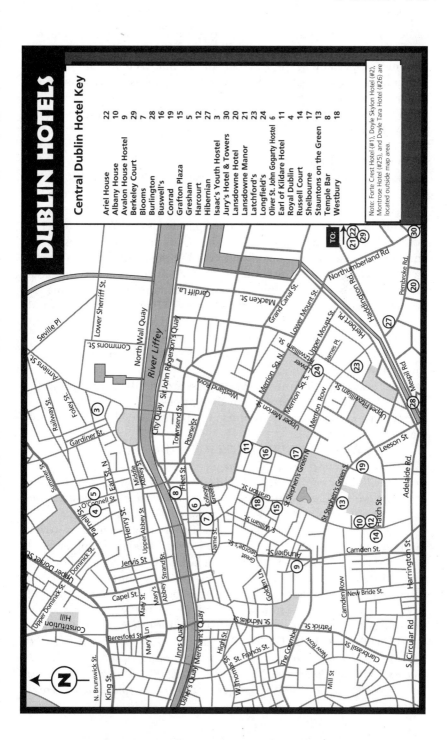

DUBLIN HOTELS

Central Dublin Hotel Key

Ariel House	22
Albany House	10
Avalon House Hostel	9
Berkeley Court	29
Blooms	7
Burlington	28
Buswell's	16
Conrad	19
Grafton Plaza	15
Gresham	5
Harcourt	12
Hibernian	27
Isaac's Youth Hostel	3
Jury's Hotel & Towers	30
Lansdowne Hotel	20
Lansdowne Manor	21
Latchford's	23
Longfield's	24
Oliver St. John Gogarty Hostel	6
Earl of Kildare Hotel	11
Royal Dublin	4
Russell Court	14
Shelbourne	17
Stauntons on the Green	13
Temple Bar	8
Westbury	18

Note: Forte Crest Hotel (#1), Doyle Skylon Hotel (#2), Montrose Hotel (#25), and Doyle Tara Hotel (#26) are located outside map area.

rather uninspiring building from the outside, and mostly functional on the inside. The main floor was recently remodeled, and the results are very nice, especially in the new bar and Rendezvous Restaurant. The rooms are a nice size, but they are not as extravagant as the rooms at some of the other Doyle properties.

The Doyle Skylon is a convenient place for conducting business if that is what brings you to Dublin.

O'Connell Street District

3. ISAACS YOUTH HOSTEL, *2 French Lane, Dublin 1. Tel. (01) 836-3877. 200 beds. Rates for singles: £18, six bed dorms: £7.75, 12 bed dorms: £6.25. No credit cards accepted – cash only! No service charge.*

One of the most Spartan of the Spartan, Isaacs Youth Hostel is nonetheless clean and inexpensive. The rooms are generally just large enough to house the number of beds they are made for. There are large lockers in each of the dorm rooms. They are not large enough to hold a standard suitcase, but certainly large enough to store any objects you may be uncomfortable leaving out, such as cameras. Common bathrooms and showers serve each of the dorm room floors and men and women do not stay on the same floors.

There is no restaurant or cafe, but there is a self-catering kitchen on the premises.

The Isaacs Youth Hostel is located just around the corner from the Busaras bus station. Ask around for the hostel – the employees all know where it is. I wasn't overly impressed with the neighborhood; it was marginal at best.

4. THE ROYAL DUBLIN HOTEL, *O'Connell Street, Dublin 1. Tel. (01) 873-3666, Fax (01) 873-3120; E-mail: enq@royaldublin.com; Website: www.fitzwilliamh.com/royal/welcome. 120 rooms. Rates for singles: £82 to £99, doubles: £100 to £126, and suites: £150 to £180. Rates include breakfast. One restaurant. All major credit cards accepted. No service charge.*

Don't be fooled by the name. The Royal Dublin isn't very royal. Perhaps a better name would be The *Functional* Dublin. This older hotel is located right on O'Connell Street, but lacks the elegance and finery of some of the other hotels in the area. It is certainly not a dump, but the rooms are small and uninspiring, and are in bad need of fresh paint and new carpeting. But it is functional, and if you really want to stay on O'Connell Street, it's a decent choice, if not a little pricey for what you get.

5. THE GRESHAM HOTEL, *23 Upper O'Connell Street, Dublin 1. Tel. (01) 874-6881, Fax (01) 878-7175. 206 rooms. Rates for singles: £ 135 to £150, doubles: £160 to £180, suites: £200, £250, £400, £500. One restaurant and two pubs. Free parking for guests. All major credit cards accepted. 12.5% service charge.*

The Gresham Hotel was built 1817 and was probably something to behold back then. Now, the marble in the lobby is a little older and the chandelier doesn't gleam quite as brightly as it once did. But it is still a fine hotel, and speaks more of elegance, grace, and refinement than the many new hotels with their gleaming brass and Italian marble. Old it may be, but run-down it is not. Freshly painted walls in cream and light yellow give it a bright and cheery feeling.

The Gresham has served as the host for many important and famous people in the world, including Ronald Reagan, Dwight Eisenhower, Richard Burton and Elizabeth Taylor, Bob Hope, and other luminaries.

The rooms are nice and large, and are tastefully furnished. Those at the front of the hotel overlook busy O'Connell Street with all its comings and goings. These rooms are a little noisier (though not too bad). If you like quieter surroundings, ask for a room away from the front. They also have a range of nice suites, although a little smaller than you'd expect from a four-star hotel.

For those who are traveling on business, there is a 24-hour business center equipped with secretarial assistance, PCs with standard software, and a laser printer. Their on-site travel agency is also helpful in the event you need to adjust flight arrangements.

Close to a number of museums, the theater district, and shopping on Henry Street, The Gresham is also an easy five- to ten-minute walk to Trinity College and Grafton Street.

SOUTH DUBLIN
Temple Bar District
6. OLIVER ST. JOHN GOGARTY'S YOUTH HOSTEL, *18-21 Anglesea Street, Dublin 2. Tel. (01) 671-1822, Fax (01) 671-7637. 27 rooms, 130 beds. Rates for twins: £19 to £21 per person sharing, three beds: £14 to £18 per person sharing, four beds: £15 to £20 per person sharing, dormitory: £14 to £17 per person sharing. One cafe. American Express, Mastercard, and Visa accepted. No service charge.*

This is the newest and one of the nicest youth hostels in Ireland. Opened in October 1995, it is in very good condition, with new plumbing, comfortable (albeit bunk) beds, and clean linens. The small cafe provides a continental breakfast for £1.10 or a full breakfast for £2.95. There is a television room if you need to rest your tired feet after a long day trekking around Dublin. Often, youth hostels are not in the best parts of town, but this is not the case with Gogarty's – it is located in the trendy, up-and-coming Temple Bar District, Dublin's answer to Paris's Left Bank. If you are looking for budget accommodations in Dublin, this is the place to stay. As it gets better known, you may find it difficult to just drop in and get a room. I was there recently in the winter, and they were already taking reservations for the summer months. So make your reservations in advance.

7. THE BLOOMS HOTEL, *6 Anglesea Street, Dublin 2. Tel. (01) 671-5622, Fax (01) 671-5997; E-mail: blooms@eirecom.net; Website: homepage.tinet.ie/~blooms. 86 rooms. Rates for singles: £61 to £73, doubles: £75 to £84. One restaurant, one cafe and one pub/nightclub. All major credit cards accepted. 15% service charge.*

The Blooms Hotel is located in the heart of the Temple Bar District, and is a relatively inexpensive hotel in this fashionable jazz section of Dublin. Many of their rooms have been recently refurbished with new paint, upgraded bathrooms, new furniture, etc. Typical of Irish hotels, the rooms are on the small side, although they are comfortable. Several of the rooms have balconies, which are nice in the spring and summer, although the views are mostly of the tops of Dublin buildings.

Their nightclub plays live music seven nights a week, and the music can be dimly heard throughout most of the hotel. If you are accustomed to turning in early, or are bothered by a little noise, you may want to look elsewhere.

8. TEMPLE BAR HOTEL, *Fleet Street, Dublin 2. Tel. (01) 677-3333, Fax (01) 677-3088. 108 rooms. Rates for singles: £95, doubles: £120. Rates include breakfast. One restaurant and one disco bar. All major credit cards accepted. No service charge.*

Don't let the unconvincing exterior dissuade you from staying at the Temple Bar Hotel (although the rates might). The hotel itself is very nice and comfortable. The rooms are good sized and comfortably if not lavishly decorated. The bathrooms are upgraded and modern. The Terrace restaurant serves Temple Bar Hotel patrons as well as the public. It's a pleasant, light and airy restaurant.

This hotel does a lot of travel package business, so they are relatively full most of the year. They are little pricey for my taste, especially compared to some of the other hotels in the area.

Grafton Street District

9. AVALON HOUSE YOUTH HOSTEL, *55 Aungier Street, Dublin 2. Tel. (01) 475-0001, Fax (01) 475-0303; E-mail: info@avalon-house.ie; Website: www.avalon-house.ie. 185 beds. Rates for singles: £18 to £25 per person sharing, twins: £16 to £18 per person sharing, four beds: £13 to £15 per person sharing, dormitory: £10 to £12 per person sharing (rates include light continental breakfast). One cafe. American Express, Mastercard, and Visa accepted. Cafe on site. No service charge.*

The Avalon House Youth Hostel is probably the busiest and offers the most amenities of any of the hostels in Dublin. There is a small cafe in the Avalon House, as well as a Bureau de Change, self-catering kitchen facilities, laundry service, TV room, luggage storage, and secure bicycle storage. Linens are provided in the rate. The cafe has a wonderful bohemian feel and always seems to be busy.

All twin and single rooms are ensuite (have bathrooms), but the larger rooms and the dormitory rooms share community bathrooms. None of the rooms are huge, but you'll marvel at the way they utilize every available square foot. Men and women share the same shower facilities, but don't worry – each shower has its own locking stall.

The only real drawback to the Avalon House is that the neighborhood didn't "feel" as good as most of the others in this guide. I am a little uneasy walking some of the dark side streets around the Avalon House at night.

10. ALBANY HOUSE BED AND BREAKFAST, *84 Harcourt Street, Dublin 2. Tel. (01) 475-1092, Fax (01) 475-1093. 33 rooms. Rates for singles: £60, doubles: £50 per person sharing. All major credit cards accepted. No restaurant. No service charge.*

Albany House is one of the finest examples of many fine examples of Georgian architecture in Dublin. Built in the late 18th century, Albany House was once part of the estate of the Earl of Clonmel.

From the moment you enter Albany House, you'll be impressed with about everything you see and experience. The lobby/sitting room is dominated by a large and inviting fireplace, the furnishings and objet d'art are elegant, and the feeling is one of quiet dignity. Soft colors and appropriate use of lighting helps add to the regal feeling.

Moving to the bedrooms, you'll find spacious rooms comfortably and expensively furnished. The high ceilings accentuate the spaciousness of the rooms, and the tall windows let plenty of light into each room. All rooms have satellite television, telephones, hairdryers, and tea- and coffee-making facilities.

Albany House is located a block southwest of St. Stephen's Green on Harcourt Street, just minutes away from most of the principal sights in Dublin. It would be an excellent place to base your explorations of Ireland's capitol.

11. THE EARL OF KILDARE HOTEL, *42-47 Kildare Street, Dublin 2. Tel. (01) 679-4388, Fax (01) 679-4914. 32 rooms. Rates for singles: £45, doubles: £65. Rates include breakfast. One restaurant. All major credit cards accepted. No service charge.*

The Earl of Kildare Hotel, formerly known as The Powers Hotel, has recently completed a top-to-bottom extensive renovation, and the results are marvelous. It is a converted Georgian home, and sports those typical large rooms and lovely tall ceilings common to these lovely old homes. It is a wonderful hotel and one that you will feel quite comfortable in. It is within easy walking distance to Grafton Street, Trinity College, and St. Stephen's Green, so it is a great place to base your Dublin explorations.

There is no elevator, so if you're not into climbing stairs, this will present a problem.

12. THE HARCOURT HOTEL, *60 Harcourt Street, Dublin 2. Tel. (01) 478-3677, Fax (01) 475-2013; Website: www.harcourthotel.com. 46 rooms. Rates for singles: £70 to £80, doubles: £85 to £95, and suites: £120. Rates include breakfast. One pub and nightclub. All major credit cards accepted. No service charge.*

The Harcourt Hotel is located just up the street from St. Stephen's Green and Grafton Street. Like so many of the hotels and guesthouses in Dublin, the Harcourt Hotel is a conversion of three old Georgian townhouses. Prior to its conversion into a hotel, George Bernard Shaw rented a room in one of the town homes from 1874 to 1876. His portrait hangs in the lobby, and his stern visage stares down at guests. Unfortunately, the rooms and furnishings in the hotel are unremarkable, and the hotel has a bit of a tired feeling.

The rooms feel small and cramped, even though most have high ceilings that usually offset the smallness of the room. About half the rooms have their own bath and shower, and there are shared bathrooms for the rest. The pub and nightclub on the premises provide live music seven nights a week, from traditional Irish to jazz to New Age.

13. STAUNTONS ON THE GREEN, *83 St. Stephen's Green South, Dublin 2. Tel. (01) 478-2300, Fax (01) 478-2263; Website: www.stauntons.com. 38 rooms. Rates for singles: £70 to £80, doubles: £60 to £70 per person sharing, suites: £105 to £130. Rates include breakfast. No service charge.*

On the south side of St. Stephen's Green, Stauntons is a series of converted Georgian townhouses. From the moment you enter her grand and dignified lobby, you will be delighted when you see how wonderfully the owners have restored the rooms.

The bedrooms are large and individually decorated with taste and elegance. The high ceilings common to these old Georgian homes just make the rooms seem...well...roomy and spacious. The rooms at the front of the house overlook St. Stephen's Green and those at the back of the hotel overlook flower gardens. If you are overly sensitive to traffic noise, forego the views of the Green and opt for the views of the garden. The rooms are all exceptionally decorated in soft colors and floral accents. All the rooms offer in-room telephones, televisions, tea- and coffee-making facilities, and hairdryers.

Stauntons has had the pleasure of hosting several celebrities, including film star Woody Allen and international musician Jools Holland.

Stauntons on the Green is an ideal place to base your exploration of Dublin. Across the street from St. Stephen's Green, you are within easy walking distance of the major sights, restaurants, and activities Dublin has to offer.

14. THE RUSSELL COURT HOTEL, *Harcourt Street, Dublin 2. Tel. (01) 478-4066, Fax (01) 478-1576. 48 rooms. Rates for singles: £80, doubles: £100, suites: £105. Rates include continental breakfast. One restaurant, a pub and several lounges. All major credit cards accepted. 12.5% service charge.*

What a find! The Russell Court Hotel is one of the best-kept secrets in Dublin. They do not advertise because they have a loyal clientele – mostly business people – that keeps them full all year long.

From the moment you walk into this hotel – three converted Georgian townhouses – you'll feel comfortable and at home. No two rooms are alike, except for the fact that they are all large, with high ceilings and beautifully decorated. Rich wood molding, solid wood doors, and attention to detail in every respect makes this a beautiful hotel. Combine all that with its close proximity to Grafton Street and St. Stephen's Green, and you've got a great place to stay. On-site is Dicey Reilly's Pub, with a beer garden that's very popular in the spring and summer, and four nights a week of live music, from traditional Irish to jazz to contemporary.

If you want to stay here, you'd better make your reservations several months in advance, because the Russell Court Hotel is a favorite and it may be difficult to get á room if you don't.

15. GRAFTON PLAZA HOTEL, *2 Johnson's Place, Dublin 2. Tel. (01) 475-0888, Fax (01) 475-0908. 75 rooms. Rates for singles: £90, doubles: £105, suites: £125. Restaurant and pub/nightclub. All major credit cards accepted. No service charge.*

The Grafton Plaza is located just around the corner from Grafton Street and all the activities that abound there. The rooms at the Grafton Plaza are not big, but light, cheery and nicely furnished. They reminded me of a standard Marriott room in the US, just a little smaller.

The Grafton Plaza sports an interesting pub and disco. The pub is quite large with a large square serving island. Plenty of room for talking, drinking, and enjoying the atmosphere.

16. BUSWELL'S HOTEL, *25 Molesworth Street, Dublin 2. Tel. (01) 676-4013, Fax (01) 676-2090. 60 rooms. Rates for singles: £90, doubles: £146, triples: £160. Rates include breakfast. One restaurant and bar. All major credit cards accepted. No service charge.*

This nice older hotel is just a few steps from the Leinster House and the National Museum. The hotel has recently undergone extensive renovation, and the results are marvelous. As you walk into the lobby, you'll be impressed with the deep blue carpet that complements the rich dark wood reception desk. The rooms are decent size, although there are a few that are a bit small.

The restaurant is Truman's, and it is known locally as a restaurant of quiet elegance. The silver, crystal, and linen tablecloths make for a nice dining experience.

Perhaps a little on the expensive side for what you get, Buswell's is still a nice place to stay. It is close to Grafton Street but far enough away that it has a less harried feel.

17. SHELBOURNE MERIDIEN HOTEL, *27 St. Stephen's Green, Dublin 2. Tel. (01) 676-6471, Fax (01) 661-6006; E-mail: shelbourneinfo@fortehotels.com; Website: www.shelbourne.ie. 190 rooms. Rates for singles: £165 to £185, doubles: £195 to £255, and suites: £380 to £950. One restaurant and two bars. All major credit cards accepted. 15% service charge.*

The Shelbourne Hotel receives my vote for the nicest of the nice in Dublin. From the rich dark wood to the lovely antique Waterford crystal chandelier in the Lord Mayor's lounge, to the flawless service, you'll be delighted with every aspect of your stay at the Shelbourne.

The Shelbourne isn't as flashy and flamboyant as some of the other brass and crystal hotels you'll find in Dublin. Instead, it is all grace and grandeur, refinement and splendor. No impressive lobby awaits your arrival, but a rather understated journey from the front door to the reception desk. But that's all that is understated. The rooms and the furnishings, the fine equestrian art that graces the hallway walls, and the ambiance are as rich and lovely as you'll find in Dublin.

The Shelbourne is three Georgian townhouses that were converted into a hotel in 1824. But I doubt the former inhabitants lived anywhere near as exquisitely as you will while staying here. The rooms are large and spacious, and no two are alike in their layout, size, or decor. These old Georgian homes had so many odd and assorted corners, nooks, and crannies that when converted into a hotel, they add a certain element of personality to each room. All the rooms are lavishly furnished, and they are all very comfortable. Ask for a room overlooking St. Stephen's Green – the views are among the best in Dublin.

For a treat, ask to see the Presidential Suite – more fondly referred to as the Princess Grace Room in honor of that grand lady's stay here. It is a large, attractive, multi-roomed suite overlooking St. Stephen's Green. Near one of the windows is a picture of Princess Grace, and it ads a touch of, well...*grace*...to the room! If the room is not occupied, the front desk staff assures me it is possible to have a short tour.

History buffs will be interested to learn that the Irish Constitution was drafted in the Shelbourne in 1922. The Shelbourne boasts many heads of state, actors and actresses, and many of the world's *glitterati* as their honored guests. And you will feel equally honored during your stay here.

18. WESTBURY HOTEL, *Grafton Street, Dublin 2. Tel. (01) 679-1122, Fax (01) 679-7078, US toll free 800/423-6953. 156 rooms. Rates for singles: £264 to £289, doubles: £280 to £330, suites: £285 to £600. Two restaurants and one bar, fitness center. All major credit cards accepted. 15% service charge.*

Your first view of the Westbury Hotel will help you understand why this is one of the brightest gems in the Doyle Hotel Group tiara. The contemporary lobby, decorated in cream and red marble with brass and crystal aplenty, lets you know you've made a grand selection. Comfortable sofas and chairs are placed throughout the lobby where guests can visit quietly, take afternoon tea, or simply enjoy the serene splendor of the hotel. The grand piano tinkling in the background adds to the quiet ambiance that is the Westbury Hotel.

The rooms are smallish by American standards, although they are lavishly decorated. The modern furniture is almost plush. The junior and senior suites were much nicer. Cherry wood desks and tables add to the rich and extravagant setting.

The Russell Room is their elegant and graceful restaurant, and downstairs is the Sandbank Seafood Bar with its rich wood and brass furnishings. A small fitness center with rowing machine, stair stepper, and treadmill are available to help you work off some of those calories you are sure to consume during your stay.

Another plus for the Westbury Hotel is its location: just a half block off Grafton Street (even though their address is given as Grafton Street), it is in the hub of activity in Dublin. Free parking for guests is included.

19. CONRAD HOTEL, *Earlsfort Terrace, Dublin 2. Tel. (01) 676-5555, Fax (01) 676-5424, US toll free 800/Hilton. 191 rooms. Rates for singles: £190, doubles: £225, suites: £425 to £900. Two restaurants and one pub. All credit cards accepted. 15% service charge.*

If it feels as though you have walked into a Hilton when you enter the lobby of the Conrad, it is because the Conrad is a part of the Hilton Hotels group. From its glimmering marble and brass lobby to its ultra-luxurious Presidential Suite, everything is top quality.

The rooms are ample size, and very nicely decorated with quality furnishings and soft salmon-colored decor. The Conrad is also one of the few hotels in Ireland that is air conditioned. Most of the rooms have relatively boring views, but the rooms in the front of the hotel overlook the National Concert Hall across the street. When there is a concert (most nights), the Concert Hall is lit up and makes for a stunning view out your bedroom window. The suites are spacious and lavish, and are among the nicest in all of Ireland.

The Conrad hotel enjoys a wider variety of guests, from vacationing tourists to international business people.

There are two restaurants at the Conrad. The Alexandra Restaurant is their formal dining facility and it offers elegant dining in a gracious and pleasant setting. There is also a more informal cafe-style dining facility, the Plurabelle, which offers a more relaxed atmosphere and a little less expensive meal.

Ballsbridge District

20. LANSDOWNE HOTEL, *27 Pembroke Road, Dublin 4. Tel. (01) 668-2522, Fax (01) 668-2309, US toll free 800/527-3460; Website: www.lansdownehotel.com. 40 rooms. Rates for singles: £50 to £65, doubles: £80 to £95. One restaurant and one pub. Mastercard and Visa accepted. No service charge.*

This converted Georgian townhouse is in a very quiet residential neighborhood in Georgian Dublin. Set back off the street a little further than most of the hotels in this area, you will be assured of a quiet and pleasant stay. The rooms are large and plainly decorated. While the furnishings are functional and comfortable, they are not particularly memorable.

The Green Blazer Bar is the pub located in the basement of the hotel, and it is a pleasant place to quaff your thirst and meet some of the locals, who always seem willing to chat with you.

21. LANSDOWNE MANOR GUESTHOUSE, *46 - 48 Lansdowne Road, Dublin 4. Tel. (01) 668-8848, Fax (01) 668-8873; Website: lansdownemanor.com. 22 rooms. Rates for singles: £45 to £55, doubles: £65 to £95, suites: £80 to £130. Rates include breakfast. All major credit cards accepted. No service charge.*

This four-star guesthouse is a lovely converted Victorian house. The rooms, typical of these converted town homes, are large and the light paint makes each room feel expansive. They are tastefully decorated. Lansdowne Manor is located in the upscale, low-crime Ballsbridge area. Many of the overflow guests from the nearby five-star Berkeley Court Hotel are referred to Lansdowne Manor.

22. ARIEL HOUSE, *50 - 52 Lansdowne Road, Dublin 4. Tel. (01) 668-5512, Fax (01) 668-5845. 40 rooms. Rates for doubles: £25 to £79 per person sharing, superior doubles: £112 per person sharing, suites: £169 per person sharing. Call for special rates that are offered from time to time, especially during the winter months. Rates do not include breakfast. Mastercard and Visa accepted. 10% service charge.*

Without a doubt, one of the warmest welcomes and most pleasant stays you can have in Ireland is at the Ariel House. Three Victorian (not Georgian) townhouses, built in the 1850s, have been converted into this award-winning, "Best Small Hotel in Ireland" for 1995. Michael O'Brien, who has been the proprietor of Ariel House since 1960, is your gracious host. Referred to by some as the "grandfather" of the Bed and Breakfast industry in Ireland, Mr. O'Brien is a pure delight to visit with.

The front sitting room is furnished with comfortable leather chairs surrounded by antiques all situated before a lovely fireplace. Twenty of the 30 rooms are furnished almost exclusively with furniture from the Victorian era. Ask Mr. O'Brien why Victorian furniture is so much better suited as B&B furniture than Georgian furniture. (Hint: it has to do with the relative size of Queen Victoria and King George!) The rooms range from lovely to elegant. Ask to see the junior and senior honeymoon suites, also called the presidential suites (depending on the occasion). They are nothing short of spectacular. The large four-poster bed, the seven-foot tall armoire, and the crystal chandelier complement one another nicely and combine for a marvelous effect.

There are an additional 10 rooms added onto the back of Ariel House that are strictly functional. Their style and feel are more like small hotel rooms, and are a disappointment after seeing the rest of the house. But they are less expensive than the other rooms, and are a nice clean place to stay. All rooms in the hotel have upgraded bathrooms, televisions, ironing boards and hair dryers.

Breakfast is served each morning in a lovely alcove at the back of one of the original townhouses that overlooks the gardens and back yard of Ariel House. The breakfast is delicious, and there is a nice selection of entrees to choose from.

While Ariel House is several miles from downtown Dublin, it is only 100 yards from the Lansdowne DART station, only about a three-minute ride to downtown.

23. LATCHFORDS OF BAGGOT STREET, *99 - 100 Lower Baggot Street. Tel. (01) 676-0784, Fax (01) 662-2764. 22 rooms. Rates for studios: £55 to £75, superior studios: £75 to £90, one bedroom: £60 to £90, two bedroom: £70 to £109. One restaurant. All major credit cards accepted. No service charge.*

Latchfords offers self-catering for those who want to cut corners by cooking their own food while on vacation. Each room is furnished with an efficiency refrigerator, microwave oven (some have hot plates), and a sink. The rooms in this converted Georgian townhouse are large and high-ceilinged and brightly decorated. There is a separate entrance to the facility which guests are given a key to, so that they can come and go as they please without the need of a night manager.

If you tire of eating your own cooking, next door is Latchfords, one of the most affordable restaurants in the area. (See *Where to Eat*.)

24. LONGFIELD'S HOTEL, *10 Fitzwilliam Street Lower. Tel. (01) 676-1367, Fax (01) 676-1542; Website: www.dublinhotels.com/hotels/longfields. 28 rooms. Rates for singles: £85, doubles: £105, superior doubles: £125. One restaurant. All major credit cards accepted. No service charge.*

Longfield's Hotel has all the ingredients that make for a nice stay: lovely comfortable rooms, a safe neighborhood, a great location close to shopping and sights, and personable, outgoing staff. This is one of the nicest small hotels in Dublin.

Located just a few blocks east of St. Stephen's Green, Longfield's is a converted Georgian townhouse. The rooms are nice size – although not huge – with tall ceilings and light colors. All the rooms are ensuite, although some have a shower with no bathtub, so if that matters to you, be sure and specify that you want a tub. The rooms that overlook Fitzwilliam Street are a little noisy due to traffic, so you may want to request a room at the back of the hotel. There is an elevator, by the way.

Number 10 Restaurant is in the basement of Longfield's, and it is one of the best restaurants in Dublin. And their lunch menu is every bit as exquisite as their dinner menu at half the price. (See *Where to Eat* section.)

25. MONTROSE HOTEL, *Stillorgan Road, Dublin 4. Tel. (01) 269-3311, Fax (01) 269-1164, US toll free 800/448-8355. 179 rooms. Rates for singles: £95, doubles: £95. One restaurant and one pub. All major credit cards accepted. 15% service charge.*

The Montrose Hotel on the southern outskirts of Dublin is another outstanding hotel belonging to the Doyle Hotel Group. It recently received an extensive (and expensive) facelift – inside as well as outside. The results are a great success.

The bedrooms fared particularly well in the renovation. Fresh paint, new wall paper, furnishings, and carpet make these rooms pleasant and luxurious. Mahogany furniture and marbled bathrooms give the Montrose a plush feeling. The suites are equally as spacious and luxurious, and you'll be impressed not only with their size, but also with the lavishness of the furnishings. Belfield Bar is a good pub located on the premises, with an open fireplace welcoming weary travelers as well as locals. The restaurant – the Belfield Room – provides elegant dining in a bright atmosphere.

Unlike most of the hotels in this guide, the Montrose is a little removed from the action. It is about a 15-minute cab ride from the city center, and is too far to walk. Still, it is a lovely hotel, and if your plans include trips to the south of Ireland, this is a good jumping-off point.

26. DOYLE TARA HOTEL, *Merrion Road, Dublin 4. Tel. (01) 269-4666, Fax (01) 269-1027, US toll free 800/448-8355. 114 rooms. Rates for singles: £83, doubles: £103. One restaurant and one pub. All major credit cards accepted. 15% service charge.*

Perhaps the most prominent feature in the Doyle Hotel Group's Tara Hotel is its view of Dublin Bay. Located only a quarter mile from the bay, the views are outstanding. As with all of the Doyle properties, the lobby is elegant and well-appointed. The feeling carries throughout the facility, from the Joycean Bar and its finely carved dark wood and period furnishings to the contemporary airiness of the Conservatory Restaurant. Despite its loveliness, the Doyle Tara is a little more relaxed than its glitzy sister hotels. The rooms are all large and comfortable, with bright floral patterns on many of the bedspreads and window coverings that complement the cherry wood furnishings. Ask for a room on the Dublin Bay side of the hotel for the views.

The hotel is about four miles from St. Stephen's Green, so it's a bit far to walk. It is about a half mile from the Booterstown DART station, or a short cab ride from the city center.

27. THE HIBERNIAN HOTEL, *Eastmoreland Place, Dublin 4. Tel. (01) 668-7666, Fax (01) 660-2655; E-mail: info@hibernianhotel.com. 40 rooms. Rates for singles: £120 to £135, doubles: £150 to £160, suites: £185 to £205. Rates include breakfast. One restaurant. All major credit cards accepted. No service charge.*

Built originally as a home for nurses, this unpretentious red brick building has been recently converted into a very comfortable hotel. Just off Baggot Street between Ballsbridge and St. Stephen's Green, this hotel offers you both warmth and comfort. The rooms are not huge, but certainly more than ample for the nice cherry wood furnishings in each room. Most of the bathrooms need updating, but they are clean. There is a nice library and lounge for relaxing at the end of a day's sightseeing. The Patrick Kavanaugh Room is their restaurant and features a nice selection.

The Hibernian has won a number of awards through the years, and is included in a publication listing the best small hotels in the world. While the price is a little steep, it is a nice hotel and you'll be impressed with the personal service and genuine warmth of the staff.

28. BURLINGTON HOTEL, *Upper Leesom Street, Ballsbridge, Dublin 4. Tel. (01) 660-5222, Fax (01) 660-5064, US toll free 800/448-8355. 503 rooms. Rates for singles: £180, doubles: £133 to £210, suites: £360. Two restaurants, one lounge and one pub. All major credit cards accepted. 15% service charge.*

The Doyle Hotel Group certainly seems to know what it is doing when it comes to providing luxurious hotels, and the Burlington Hotel is no exception. Crystal chandeliers, marble and brass, dark wood and plush carpet all welcome you with surprising warmth and gaiety as you enter the lobby of the hotel. The only thing that compares is the warm reception you'll receive from the hotel staff. They seem genuinely glad to see you.

The rooms are large and bright, and the furnishings are top quality. The bathrooms are similarly luxurious. Together they combine to make your stay a pleasant one. The suites are expansive and lavish and filled with lovely comfortable furnishings.

The Burlington Hotel boasts two fine restaurants on their premises: the Sussex and the Diplomat. Both offer elegant surroundings and delicious meals. But my favorite place here is Buck Mulligan's Pub. The pub has the look and feel of being on an old sailing ship of days gone by. (Buck Mulligan is the "Huck Finn-esque" character from James Joyce's epic novel *Ulysses*.) For nearly 20 years, the Burlington Hotel hosts a traditional Irish dinner and cabaret that provides a fun and rollicking evening. The evening will cost you £33 for the dinner and show, or £23 for the show only. The cabaret runs from early May through October.

29. BERKELEY COURT HOTEL, *Lansdowne Road, Ballsbridge, Dublin 4. Tel. (01) 660-1711, Fax: (01) 497-8275, US toll free 800/423-6953. 200 rooms. Rates for singles: £165, doubles: £185, suites: £240 to £600; Penthouse Suite: £1,600. Two restaurants and a lounge. All major credit cards accepted. 15% service charge.*

If you want plush, elegant, and a wee bit of the extraordinary, the Berkeley Court Hotel is the place to stay. Another hotel in Dublin belonging to the Doyle Hotel Group, this five-star hotel is about as far as you'll get from the stereotypical one-room-cottage-warmed-by-a-turf-fire abode that many picture Ireland to be. Beautiful furnishings and appointments abound throughout the hotel.

From the moment you enter the magnificent lobby with its deep blue and gold carpet you'll be transported into a world of luxury that only a handful of hotels in Ireland can offer. There is rich dark paneling in the Royal Court Bar and a serene elegance in the Berkeley Room restaurant. The bedrooms are large and equally as inviting and luxurious as the public rooms. Decorated in soft pastels, the rooms are light and airy, with comfortable, classic furniture.

The Berkeley Court is located in the quiet residential area of Ballsbridge on Lansdowne Street. Its grounds were once the site of the Botanical Gardens of University College Dublin, and much of that beauty has been retained for guests to enjoy. If you have business with the American Embassy, this is a convenient hotel, as the embassy is within a 10-minute walk from the hotel.

30. JURY'S HOTEL AND TOWERS, *Pembroke and Lansdowne Roads, Ballsbridge, Dublin 4. Tel. (01) 660-5000, Fax (01) 660-5540; Website: www.jurys.com. 300 rooms. Rates at Jury's Hotel for singles: £140, doubles: £180, suites: £300. Rates at The Towers for singles: £160, doubles: £180, and suites: £350 to £450. Two restaurants, a coffee bar, and a pub. Indoor and outdoor swimming pools, spa, sauna, beauty salon, and masseuse. All major credit cards accepted. 12.5% service charge.*

Jury's Hotel and Towers is two separate hotels – Jury's Hotel and a connected exclusive wing called The Towers. Guests at The Towers share the common facilities of Jury's Hotel: pool, sauna, whirlpool, as well as two restaurants, a coffee bar, and the Dubliner Bar. But separate entrances and electronic locks into The Towers lets you know it's exclusive.

You'll be impressed when you walk into the lobby – modern, lavish, and very busy. Unfortunately for the Jury's Hotel, that's the most impressive part of your visit there. The rooms are a little cramped, and the furnishings are underwhelming but functional – far less than you'd expect from a luxury hotel.

The rooms at The Towers, on the other hand, are much larger and more elegantly and tastefully decorated, more befitting the price of the rooms. Their suites are particularly inviting – spacious, elegant, and comfortable. My favorite feature is the television built into a ledge at eye-level with the bathtub! Room rates include a continental breakfast for guests at The Towers. The Towers is air conditioned; Jury's is not.

There are two restaurants associated with the hotel. Raglan's Restaurant specializes in seafood, and the Embassy Garden Restaurant features international cuisine. Locals as well as hotel guests frequent both restaurants.

One of the most popular aspects of the Jury's complex is their internationally famous Irish Cabaret. It runs from early May through October, and makes for a wonderfully enjoyable evening. Irish dancers, Gaelic storytellers, and a lot of fun are present during the evening.

Jury's Hotel and Towers is located near the American Embassy and a short walk from the business district along Baggot Street. If you're looking for an exclusive lodging experience, The Towers is a good choice. Pay the extra few pounds for a room there rather than in the main part of the hotel.

NORTH OF DUBLIN

31. THE REEFS BED AND BREAKFAST, *Balbriggan Coast Road, Skerries, Co. Dublin. Tel. (01) 849-1574. 4 rooms. Rates for singles: £16 to £24, doubles: £16 to £19 per person sharing. Rates include breakfast. No service charge. Open from April 1 through October 31.*

About half an hour north of Dublin lies the small harbor town of Skerries, and less than a mile up the road from Skerries is The Reefs Bed and Breakfast, run by Mrs. Violet Clinton. Views of the sea as well as the Mourne Mountains add spice to this pleasant B&B. Sitting just across the road from the Irish Sea, this relatively new B&B is an enjoyable and relaxing place to stay. (If you want relaxation, just walk across the road and sit on the shoreline of the Irish Sea and enjoy the sunrise, or at the end of the day, the sunset over that lovely body of water.)

Although there is no DART station nearby, you can catch a train from Dublin's Connolly Station that stops in Skerries. You can also catch bus #33 in Dublin at Eden Quay – it passes right by The Reefs. The Reefs is a convenient place to base your exploration of a number of the sights north of Dublin. Malahide Castle and Newgrange are about 30 minutes down the road, and Newbridge House is just a few minutes down the road in Donabate. If you are a golfer, there are about 10 courses within just a few minutes' drive from here. I have used The Reefs as the B&B for my last evening in Ireland. It provides lovely, serene seascapes, a pleasant "last remembrance" of Ireland, and is only 20 minutes from the airport.

32. THE VILLA BED AND BREAKFAST, *150 Howth Road, Clontarf, Dublin 3. Tel. (01) 833-2377, Fax (01) 833-2377 (manual). 5 bedrooms. Rates for singles: £30, Doubles: £22.50 per person sharing. Rates include breakfast. No service charge.*

The Villa, run by Mrs. Nuala Beston, is a pleasant older Victorian home set on nice grounds. Inside, the home is comfortable, although a little cramped. But the rooms are nice size, very clean, and comfortable. Four of the five rooms are ensuite, and each room has tea- and coffee-making facilities and a television.

The grounds at the Villa are pleasant and tranquil, with a variety of flowering and non-flowering plants to catch you eye and relax your soul.

The Villa is in the north-side suburb of Clontarf, and its location makes for an ideal place to either begin or end your Irish holiday.

33. SHASTON BED AND BREAKFAST, *20 Mount Prospect Avenue, Clontarf, Dublin 3. Tel. (01) 833-6336. 3 rooms. Rates for singles: £28, doubles: £20 per person sharing. Breakfast included in rates. No service charge. Open March 1 through October.*

Mrs. Ann O'Dolan runs a nice B&B. This beautiful home is tastefully and richly decorated, and is a pleasant place to stay. While the bedrooms are not particularly large, they are furnished comfortably. Each room has tea- and coffee-making facilities. Since the Shasta B&B is in Clontarf, you're within easy reach of the airport as well as the city center.

34. AISHLING HOUSE BED AND BREAKFAST, *19/20 St. Lawrence Road, Clontarf, Dublin 3. Tel. (01) 833-9097, Fax (01) 833-8400. 6 rooms. Rates for singles: £30 to £40, doubles: £22.50 to £25 per person sharing. Discounts for children range from 20% to 50%, depending on the age of the children. Rates include breakfast.*

Your hosts at Aishling House are Robert and Frances English. A lovely Victorian residence, you'll not be disappointed in either the furnishings or the welcome you'll receive here.

Aishling House is actually the combination of two elegant Victorian town houses. Resting on a half acre of manicured grounds and fruit trees, the setting is one of peace and tranquillity in the heart of the Victorian village of Clontarf (now a suburb of Dublin).

The bedrooms have recently undergone extensive renovation, and the results are delightful. Some maintain the traditional Victorian style of floral prints while others offer a more modern feel of green, pink, and cream pastels. Even though each room is individually decorated, they have one thing in common: they are all large and spacious. Especially spacious are three "family rooms." These high-ceilinged rooms, converted from six smaller rooms into three larger ones, are expansive and specially designed to host families. A couple of the rooms have a double bed and three single beds.

If you've had a busy day sightseeing, you can relax with a stroll through the lovely rose garden at the front of the house, or you can visit the orchard out back. If you've brought young children, they can get the wiggles out by playing on the swing-set or in the sandbox on the property.

Throughout Aishling House, you'll discover an impressive collection of antiques, as well as a lovely Waterford crystal chandelier. In addition, the large dining room features crystal and crisp starched Irish linen to complement your breakfast. And what a breakfast it is! Mrs. English does a wonderful job of whipping up a tasty Irish breakfast of eggs, bacon, brown bread, and coffee.

All-in-all, this is a lovely place to stay while in Dublin. It has the feel of a country home, but it is located in the heart of the city.

35. DEER PARK HOTEL, *Howth, Co. Dublin. Tel. (01) 832-2624, Fax (01) 839-2405. 49 rooms. Rates for singles: £65, doubles: £96. Rates include breakfast. One restaurant. All major credit cards accepted. No service charge.*

The setting for the Deer Park Hotel is probably as green and serene as any in Ireland. The hotel is surrounded by five golf courses and a 30-acre rhododendron patch, with a view of the Irish Sea that prompted H.G. Wells to describe it as "the finest view west of Naples."

With all that beauty, the hotel itself pales in comparison. With fresh paint and wallpaper, as well as an interior decorator's touch, the hotel could be spectacular. Instead, it feels much like a 1960s era hotel. The rooms are large, and the furnishings adequate.

If you don't drive from Dublin, the best way to get to the hotel is to call a cab. The hotel is about a mile from the DART station, but the last half mile or so is uphill, and would be a bear if you were carrying luggage. However, if you have little or no luggage and the weather is nice, it is a beautiful 20-minute walk from the DART station. Turn right as you leave the Howth DART Station, and the entrance to Deer Park Hotel is about one half mile down the road on your left. From there, you have another half-mile walk (slightly uphill) to reach the hotel. They have no shuttle bus.

36. HOWTH LODGE HOTEL, *Howth, Co. Dublin. Tel. (01) 832-1010, Fax (01) 832-2268. 46 rooms. Rates for singles: £55 to £65, doubles: £75 to £98. Rates include breakfast. One restaurant, one bistro and one pub. All major credit cards accepted. No service charge.*

Nestled comfortably beside the sea, Howth Lodge Hotel offers beautiful scenery and fresh sea breezes. Family owned and operated by the Hanratty family, you'll feel more like a guest in their home than a patron at their hotel. Many of the rooms have views of the sea and the impressive "Ireland's Eye" – a quartzite island that sits just offshore. Once the site of a 7th-century monastery, the island is now a bird sanctuary.

Back to Howth Lodge – the views *are* distracting! The rooms themselves are large and bright and cheery. They are furnished comfortably and tastefully. The hotel recently added a nice leisure center with a swimming pool, gym and weight room, Jacuzzi, steam room/sauna, and a beauty salon. They even have a tanning room (available for a small additional fee). Their restaurant is a popular place for Dubliners. Specialties are seafood, caught fresh each day by local fishermen, and steak, for which they are deservedly proud.

If you take the DART to Howth, your two options to get to the hotel are to catch a taxi or walk. The walk is very pleasant, only about 10 minutes from the Howth DART station, which is about a 20-minute ride from downtown Dublin. Turn right as you leave the DART station, and Howth Lodge is about one half mile down the road on your right.

SOUTH OF DUBLIN

37. HARKIN HOUSE BED AND BREAKFAST, *7 Claremont Villas, Glenageary, Dun Laoghaire, County Dublin. Tel. (01) 280-5346. 5 rooms. Rates for singles: £24.50 to £26.50, doubles: £18 to £20 per person sharing. Breakfast included in the rate. No service charge.*

If you like well-kept Victorian homes, try this Bed and Breakfast run by Mrs. Ann Harkin. This 122-year-old spacious home has been lovingly restored to its former grandeur, and the results are wonderful. Located in a quiet upscale residential area, you'll enjoy the neighborhood as much as the home.

There are five bedrooms, four of which are ensuite. The rooms are nice sized, and each has tea-making facilities. Mrs. Harkin also provides you with the opportunity to use her laundry facilities if you should have that need. Mrs. Harkin is intimately familiar with the sights to see in and around Dun Laoghaire, Dublin, and County Wicklow, and will be an immense help in planning your day.

38. ANNESGROVE BED AND BREAKFAST, *28 Rosmeen Gardens, Dun Laoghaire, Co. Dublin. Tel. (01) 280-9801. 4 rooms. Rates for singles: £25, doubles: £18 to £22 per person sharing. Breakfast included in the rate. No service charge.*

Mrs. Anne d'Alton runs the lovely Annesgrove B&B, located in a quiet neighborhood in the Dublin suburb of Dun Laoghaire. Annesgrove is relatively close to the Sandycove DART Station (about two minutes' walk), the ferry terminal, and the bus lines.

As you arrive at Annesgrove in the afternoon or evening, you'll be welcomed first by Mr. or Mrs. d'Alton along with a steaming cup of coffee or tea. Annesgrove B&B offers guests a choice of four rooms. Two of the rooms are ensuite and two are standard rooms (that is – they share a common bathroom). The bedrooms are simply but tastefully decorated.

Mrs. D'Alton and her husband are both intimately familiar with Dun Laoghaire and the surrounding areas and are delighted to help you plan your trips into Dublin or south into County Wicklow. They'll make certain you see all that you would like to see.

39. CILL DARA BED AND BREAKFAST, *5 Tivoli Road, Dun Laoghaire, Co. Dublin. Tel. (01) 280-7355. 3 rooms, 2 ensuite and 1 standard. Rates for singles: £27 to £33, doubles: £18 to £20 per person sharing. Breakfast included in the rate. No service charge.*

Mrs. Mary Lehane is your hostess, Dun Laoghaire is the location, and Cill Dara is the B&B that many a weary traveler has put his feet up at. Located 25 minutes from downtown Dublin, Cill Dara is a comfortable home directly across from the Dun Laoghaire Golf Club. Mrs. Lehane is a member there and can provide you with all the information you need about golfing there, as well as information about golfing at other nearby courses. The bedrooms are comfortable and simply but pleasantly decorated. Even though one of the rooms is standard (no bathroom in the bedroom), there is a bathroom that is reserved for the use of that room's guests.

Mary's husband Chris is the expert on the area sights to see, and he is most willing to share his expertise to ensure that you see all you have an interest in. He and Mary will help you plan your day, with helpful suggestions on sights to see, time to get to and from each sight, and how much time you can expect to spend at each. Cill Dara is located within a short distance of the DART station and ferry terminal, as well as being near to a host of interesting pubs and restaurants.

40. CHESTNUT LODGE, *2 Vesey Place, Monkstown. Tel. (01) 280-7860, Fax (01) 280-1466. 5 rooms. Rates for singles: £32 to £40, doubles: £25 to £30 per person sharing. Rates include breakfast. Mastercard and Visa accepted. No service charge.*

Mrs. Nancy Malone's welcome to her mid-19th-century Georgian home is as warm as the croissants she prepares for breakfast. The rooms are large and spacious, and the ones at the front of the house have views of chestnut trees and an occasional glimpse of the sea beyond.

41. COURT HOTEL, *Killiney, Co. Dublin. Tel. (01) 285-1622, Fax (01) 285-2085. 86 rooms. Rates for singles: £60 to £80, doubles: £82 to £89. Breakfast included in the rates. One restaurant and grill. All major credit cards accepted. 12.5% service charge.*

Killiney Bay provides magnificent views for guests at the Court Hotel. About 10 miles south of Dublin, the hotel can be reached either by car or DART. The Killiney DART Station is about 100 yards from the hotel. In fact, the hotel employees are fond of saying they have their own DART station. The hotel was formerly a seven-room mansion built about 180 years ago. It has since been renovated and expanded. The rooms are smallish, and many of the back rooms have a rather close-up view of the hillside the hotel is built up against. The front rooms, especially those on the third floor, have beautiful views of Killiney Bay. For the most part, the rooms are not especially memorable, but they are clean and adequate.

42. ROYAL MARINE HOTEL, *Marine Road, Dun Laoghaire. Tel. (01) 280-1911, Fax (01) 280-1089. 104 rooms. Rates for singles: £70 to £90, doubles: £90 to £100. Restaurant, pub. All major credit cards accepted. 10% service charge.*

Located in Dun Laoghaire overlooking Dublin Bay, the Royal Marine Hotel was probably a very nice hotel when built in the 1960s. Today, the original rooms are in need of some good attention: upgraded furnishings, wall coverings, and bathroom facilities. The newer addition is much nicer, and the rooms have more comfortable furnishings and more acceptable decor.

43. FITZPATRICK CASTLE HOTEL, *Killiney Hill Road, Killiney, Co. Dublin. Tel. (01) 284-0700, Fax (01) 285-0207. 90 rooms. Rates for singles: £85 to £100, doubles: £96 to £124, suites: £180 to £214. Two restaurants, a pub and a nightclub. All major credit cards accepted. 15% service charge.*

The Fitzpatrick Hotel is located about 10 miles south of Dublin. Their literature says they are near the DART station, but don't make the mistake of walking there from the Killiney DART Station. It may only be a mile or two (depending on the DART station you get off at), but it is all uphill. They do have a shuttle bus, but they seem to be unable to find anyone to drive it on a consistent basis! Your best bet is to drive there yourself if you have a car.

Originally a castle built in 1741, in recent times it has been renovated by the Fitzpatrick family into a hotel. Before I arrived I had seen several pictures of the hotel, and it looked enchanting. In person, the exterior is old and dumpy, but indoors you'll see that it is enchanting, beginning with the suit of armor near the front desk. The rooms in the hotel are somewhat small, but the tall ceilings give the rooms a larger feel. The furnishings are comfortable and functional, but that's about it. Ask for a room in the front of the hotel. They all have small patios from which you can sit and enjoy the spectacular views of Dublin Bay. They have seven suites, and they are quite nice. Two of them are end rooms, and they have large windows overlooking the bay. Each suite has a Jacuzzi.

In addition to the two restaurants (the Truffles Restaurant is popular with Dubliners), the hotel offers other amenities, including a pool, sauna, small gym, aerobics classes, and a beauty salon.

WHERE TO EAT

The Irish are a lively people, insisting on good friends, good pubs, and good food – not necessarily in that order! Fortunately they are all easy to come by in Ireland, and in Dublin in particular. From small bistros to hotel dining rooms to top-notch restaurants, Dublin offers you a wide selection.

Over the past few years, Dublin has seen the introduction of a number of fine restaurants, the renovation of a number of older restaurants, and the rapid growth of good ethnic restaurants. French, Italian, Indian, Spanish, Greek, and Chinese restaurants, as well as just about any other ethnic restaurant you can think of, are now quite plentiful.

Since the majority of the sights in Dublin are south of the River Liffey and Trinity College, most of the restaurants I review are also south of the River Liffey, in the Temple Bar, Grafton Street, and Ballsbridge areas. I've also included several in the suburbs. The Temple Bar and Ballsbridge areas are about a five- or ten-minute walk from Grafton Street.

For each restaurant, I've included samples of what's on the menu and their price. Remember, however, that prices are subject to change, and restaurants tend to change their menus daily or seasonally. Unless specifically noted, all the prices listed here are for dinner (salad, entree, dessert, and coffee). Often the lunch menus are merely scaled-down versions of the dinner menus, at about half to two-thirds the cost of dinner.

I have also provided their hours of business. In most cases, the closing times listed are the last time they will accept orders, although for many it also depends on business. If business is really slow due to weather or some other reason, they might close a little early; if business is brisk at closing time, they might stay open longer. Most if not all of these restaurants are closed on Christmas and Easter.

"All major credit cards accepted," means Access, American Express, EuroCard, Mastercard, and Visa. If any one of these is not accepted, I have specifically listed those that are. As in the hotel section, I have Americanized the telephone numbers.

Dublin, and most of Ireland, is very casual, and restaurants are no exception. Every restaurant I've been to in Dublin except one (Number 27 the Green) says casual dress is fine – though a number of the more upscale restaurants request no blue jeans or grubbies. In practice, most of the clientele in the nicer restaurants wear suit and tie and dresses.

Dublin restaurants automatically tack a 10% to 15% gratuity onto your bill. If you feel the service was exceptional beyond that level, feel free to leave an additional tip. The legal drinking age is 18, although many restaurants (especially) and some pubs enforce a house minimum of 21 years. As in the hotel section above, the restaurants are numbered to correspond with the restaurant map (page 167).

SOUTH DUBLIN
Temple Bar District

The Temple Bar District is south of the River Liffey, and just a few minutes' walk west of Trinity College. Cafes dominate here, and as a rule are less expensive than the cafes and restaurants closer to Grafton Street.

1. THE ALAMO, *22 Temple Bar. Tel. (01) 677-6546. £3.95 to £7. Open 11:00am to midnight Sunday through Thursday, and 10:30am to 12:30am on Fridays and Saturdays. Mastercard and Visa accepted.*

For a little bit of Tex-Mex, Irish-style, try this little cafe. You'll smile at the "longhorn" skull and horns over the heating stove – it's really a water buffalo skull and horns! The food is typical Mexican fare, such as tacos and chimichangas and is just okay. It just seems strange to me to have Mexican food in Ireland (your call, though)! Very casual dress.

DUBLIN'S TOP RESTAURANTS

The following restaurants are listed from least to most expensive. You can get more information on each selection in the reviews that follow.

23. LA STAMPA, *35 Dawson Street. Tel. (01) 677-8611. £8.95 to £17.95. All major credit cards accepted. Despite bad art, the restaurant is considered one of the best in Ireland.*

24. THE IMPERIAL CHINESE RESTAURANT, *13 Wicklow Street. Tel. (01) 677-2580. £9 to £18. All major credit cards accepted. The Imperial Chinese Restaurant is probably the best Chinese restaurant in Dublin, if not the best in Ireland.*

34. NUMBER 10, *10 Fitzwilliam Street Lower. Tel. (01) 676-1367. £13.95 to £24.95. All major credit cards accepted. All things considered (price, service, presentation, flavor, etc.), this is my favorite restaurant in Dublin.*

41. ABBEY TAVERN RESTAURANT, *Abbey Street. Tel. (01) 839-0307. £19 to £24.95, American Express, Mastercard, and Visa accepted. You have to go here just to experience the traditional Irish Cabaret.*

37. LE COQ HARDI, *35 Pembroke Road. Tel. (01) 668-9070. £21.95 to £35. All major credit cards accepted. Quiet dining in an old Georgian mansion, Le Coq Hardi features French cuisine that is marvelous.*

28. THE COMMONS RESTAURANT, *85 - 86 St. Stephen's Green South. Tel. (01) 475-2597. £32 to £42. All major credit cards accepted. Downstairs on the south side of St. Stephen's Green, The Commons Restaurant features candlelight and crystal decor.*

38. RESTAURANT PATRICK GUILBAUD, *21 Merrion Street. Tel. (01) 676-4192. £10 to £46. Open Tuesday through Saturday for lunch from 12:30pm to 2:00pm, and for dinner from 7:30pm until 10:15pm. Reservations are a must all year. All major credit cards accepted.*

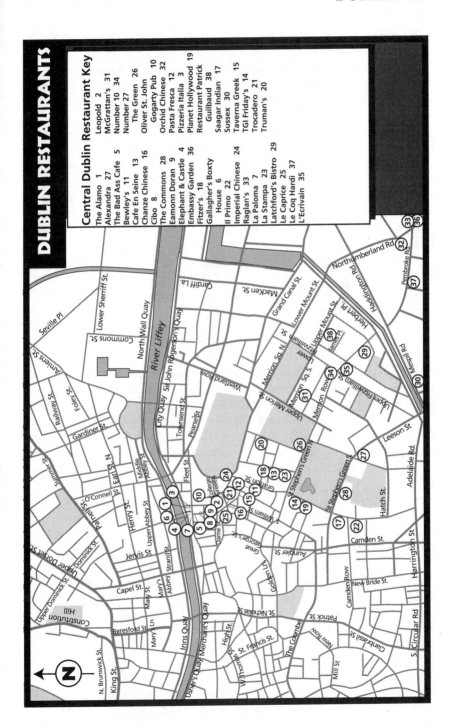

DUBLIN RESTAURANTS

Central Dublin Restaurant Key

The Alamo 1
Alexandra 27
The Bad Ass Cafe 5
Bewley's 11
Cafe En Seine 13
Chanze Chinese 16
Cibo 8
The Commons 28
Eamonn Doran 9
Elephant & Castle 4
Embassy Garden 36
Fitzer's 18
Gallagher's Boxty House 6
Il Primo 22
Imperial Chinese 24
Raglan's 33
La Paloma 7
La Stampa 23
Latchford's Bistro 29
Le Caprice 25
Le Coq Hardi 37
L'Ecrivain 35

Leopold 2
McGrattan's 31
Number 10 34
Number 27
The Green 26
Oliver St. John Gogarty Pub 10
Orchid Chinese 32
Pasta Fresca 12
Pizzeria Italia 3
Planet Hollywood 19
Restaurant Patrick Guilbaud 38
Saagar Indian 17
Sussex 30
Taverna Greek 15
TGI Friday's 14
Trocadero 21
Truman's 20

2. CAFE LEOPOLD, *6 Anglesea Street. Tel. (01) 671-5622. £4 to £10. Open every day 10:30am to 11:30pm. All major credit cards accepted.*

Located in Bloom's Hotel, this little cafe has a limited menu, but they serve decent food. It has a modern feel and a pleasant chatty atmosphere. Reservations are not required and the dress is casual. Examples of their fare include chicken Kiev and minute steak.

3. PIZZERIA ITALIA, *23 Temple Bar. Tel. (01) 677-8528. £4 to £10. Open every day 12:30pm to 11:00pm. No credit cards accepted.*

Nothing fancy here, but this is one of the best places in Dublin to get a pizza. They offer a surprisingly large selection of items in addition to pizza. There's not much in the way of atmosphere; this is just a small eatery with stools and counters around the windows and one long rectangular table with eight chairs. Examples of their selections are Napoli pizza, fettuccine Italia, and spaghetti carbonera. Very casual dress.

4. ELEPHANT & CASTLE, *18/19 Temple Bar. Tel. (01) 679-3121. £4.75 to £10.95. Open from 8:00am to 11:15pm Sunday through Thursday and 10:30am to 12:15am Friday and Saturday. No reservations taken. All major credit cards accepted.*

Kind of an "art deco in wood" style, this place is pleasant, coffee shop noisy, and very busy. During the spring and summer seasons you will probably have a bit of a wait during lunch and dinner. The music selection piped in is typically light jazz, and the black and white pictures on the walls are an interesting and eclectic assortment, ranging from scenes from the American old west to early Dublin. Casual dress.

5. BAD ASS CAFE, *2 Crown Alley. Tel. (01) 671-2596. £5 to £10. Open from 11:30am to 10:00pm Sunday through Thursday and 11:30am to 11:00am Friday and Saturday. All major credit cards accepted.*

To be honest, the reason this is in the book is because it is an incredibly popular place to go; why, I don't know. But it does have an almost cult following. It is in an old warehouse, where little has been done to decorate it. The food, like the decor, is underwhelming. They offer a variety of dishes, including pizza, chicken, steak, and burgers. Perhaps its biggest claim to fame is that Sinead O'Connor worked here prior to making it big. Perhaps that, their "Eeyore-like" logo, or the name contributes to its success. At any rate, it's always quite full during the tourist season. Casual dress.

6. GALLAGHER'S BOXTY HOUSE, *20-21 Temple Bar. Tel. (01) 677-2762. £5.45 to 12.95. Gallagher's is open from noon to 11:30pm Monday through Thursday, and until midnight on Fridays and Saturdays. No reservations. Mastercard and Visa accepted.*

A "boxty" is a potato, but Gallagher's Boxty House offers more than just potatoes. From the sweet smell of the turf fire in the fireplace (a turf fire is dried peat moss set ablaze, traditionally used as fuel in the countryside) to the antique pine tables to their Irish Stew, you'll get a very traditional Irish meal and atmosphere here. Menu selections include corned beef and cabbage, poached salmon steak, and Irish stew. They also have a set menu for £9.95, which includes an appetizer, entree, tea or coffee, and dessert.

7. LA PALOMA, *17B Asdylls Road. Tel. (01) 677-7392. Lunch from £3 to £5, dinner £8.95 to £10.95. Open from noon until midnight every evening. Mastercard and Visa accepted.*

This pleasant restaurant is around the corner from Elephant & Castle, and is easy to miss if you're not careful. Dining at this lovely Spanish restaurant is a great way to get away from the bustle, eat tapas and listen to Spanish music. Specialties include Milanesa de Ternera, pollo al chilindron, and their tapas platter, £8.95 each. The dress is casual, and on weekends during the tourist season you'll need reservations.

8. CIBO RESTAURANT, *15 - 16 Crown Alley. Tel. (01) 671-7288. £5.50 to £12.95. Open from noon to 10:00pm Sunday through Thursday and noon to 11:00pm Friday and Saturday. They do not take reservations. American Express, Mastercard, and Visa accepted.*

Just a few doors up from The Bad Ass Cafe, this two-story bistro features contemporary, light jazz, and blues music playing unobtrusively in the background. Modern and impressionistic artwork graces the walls. Ask for a table on the second floor – it's light and airy and very pleasant. If you are fortunate, a table by the window will be available, and you can do a little people watching as you eat your meal. The owners pride themselves on their use of fresh Irish ingredients, and they have their own butcher to ensure the best cuts of fresh meat. Their specialties are seafood and various meat dishes, including fresh salmon, T-bone steak, and a variety of burgers. Casual dress.

9. EAMONN DORAN, *3A Crown Alley. Tel. (01) 679-9773. £6.50 to £14.95. Open daily from 11:30am to 2:00am. Reservations are recommended during the tourist season, especially on weekends. All major credit cards accepted.*

This restaurant is sort of a cross between a pub, a cafe, and a restaurant. There are lots of interesting pictures on the wall to keep you entertained as you wait for your meal. Some of their specialties are *Gaeltacht* chicken, Irish salmon dijonaise, and New York sirloin steak (with Irish beef, of course). Casual dress.

10. OLIVER ST. JOHN GOGARTY, *58 - 59 Fleet Street. Tel. (01) 288-4707. £7.95 to £14.95. Open every day from 12:30pm until late. All major credit cards accepted.*

"Pub grub" is getting increasingly more popular in Ireland, and the traditional Irish food served at Oliver St. John Gogarty's pub is among the best. The crowded, noisy atmosphere doesn't detract a bit from the decent food.

Most nights they have traditional Irish music in a small bar upstairs, and there is often Irish music on the first floor also. Impromptu traditional music sessions have been known to occur at the drop of a hat here, so keep your eyes and ears open. Dress is very casual.

Grafton Street District

11. BEWLEY'S, *78 - 79 Grafton Street. Tel. (01) 677-6761. £4.95 to £8.95. Open daily from 7:30am to 12:30am. They do not take reservations, but tables turn over quickly. American Express, Mastercard and Visa are accepted.*

Bewley's is sort of a cross between McDonald's and a bistro. There is a very busy cafeteria on the first floor, and a slightly less busy mezzanine section as well as the James Joyce Room. All serve relatively inexpensive and decent fare. Located on Grafton Street, it's a convenient place to stop for a bite to eat while you're shopping. It's worth going to either the mezzanine or the James Joyce Room to look out on the Grafton Street crowd below. Be sure and ask for a table near the window. The fare is simple, consisting mainly of sandwiches. They have a few other dishes such as Chicken Creole and Irish oak smoked salmon. Dress is very casual (it's mostly shoppers).

12. PASTA FRESCA, *2 - 4 Chatham Street (near the Westbury Hotel off Grafton Street). Tel. (01) 475-2597. £3.75 to £9.95. Open Monday through Saturday from 7:30am to 11:30pm, and from noon until 8:00pm on Sundays. Mastercard and Visa accepted.*

The atmosphere in this Italian restaurant is light and cheerful (almost *fun*), and their pasta has delighted patrons for over a decade now. Their main claim to fame is that they make their own pasta fresh daily. There always seems to be people in here, especially at lunchtime and dinnertime. Examples of items on the menu include fettuccine pasta fresca and bistecca al Pepe. Dress is casual.

13. CAFE EN SEINE, *40 Dawson Street. Tel. (01) 667-4369. £3.95 to £10.95. Open Monday through Friday from 10:30am until 11:00pm, and on Sundays from noon until 11:30pm. All major credit cards accepted.*

This is a trendy cafe on Dawson Street, one block east of Grafton Street. This art deco, quasi-Parisian restaurant attracts all kinds – from the bohemian to the business person, from the avant-garde to the traditionalist. Contemporary jazz music greets you as you step into this long restaurant. They specialize in sandwiches and soups. It's worth a stop if only to stroll through and do a little people watching. Offerings include sandwich au poulet, le grand plateau, and fillet mignon.

14. T.G.I.FRIDAYS, *2 St. Stephen's Green. Tel. (01) 478-1233. £4.95 to £10.95. Open noon to 11:00pm Monday through Saturday, and 12:30pm to 10:30pm Sundays. All major credit cards accepted.*

This American-style restaurant is one of the newest on the Dublin dining scene, and has received a warm reception from locals and tourists alike.

This is a large, well-lit restaurant and bar with a fun and lively atmosphere. The food isn't gourmet, but it is filling. They have a nice assortment of burgers and sandwiches. Dress is casual.

15. TAVERNA GREEK RESTAURANT, *33 Wicklow Street. £6.95 to £12.95. Open Monday through Saturday from noon until midnight, and Sundays from 3:00pm until 11:30pm. Reservations are recommended during the tourist season. Diners Club, Mastercard, Visa accepted.*

Absolutely *the* best Greek restaurant in Ireland! Well, actually, according to the owner, it is the *only* Greek restaurant in Ireland. (I did find one other fine Greek restaurant in County Wicklow.) At any rate, this nice little restaurant about a half block off Grafton Street is a great place to visit. It has two rooms, both set with about a dozen small tables, all with red-checkered tablecloths. The Greek music adds to the pleasant atmosphere. If you're lucky, and usually toward the end of the evening, patrons may literally be dancing in the aisles – just enjoying one another's company, the food, and the moment.

It's always packed on the weekends and during the tourist season. Try the souvlakia, the lamb kleftiko or if you have the time and appetite, the house specialty: mezes – three courses of a variety of Greek dishes. The dress is casual.

16. CHANZE, *7 St. Andrew Street. Tel. (01) 679-9866. £6 to £12.95. Open 11:00am until midnight Monday through Saturday, and 5:00pm until midnight on Sundays. Reservations are recommended on weekends during the tourist season. All major credit cards.*

This is a nice, quiet Chinese restaurant not far from Grafton Street. While not as upscale as The Imperial Chinese Restaurant (just around the corner), it is roughly half the price. While the restaurant isn't particularly large, the décor is simple but pleasant and there are booths and several tables available. The food is also quite good. Try their Szechuan pork, the Cantonese roast duck, or the fillet of beef. Casual but nice dress.

17. SAAGAR INDIAN RESTAURANT, *16 Harcourt Street. Tel. (01) 475-5060. £7 to £12.95. Open 12:30pm to 3:00pm and 6:00pm to 11:30pm Monday through Friday and 6:00pm to 11:30pm Saturday and Sunday. Reservations are suggested. All major credit cards accepted.*

As I entered Saagar's one evening, I met a journalist friend of mine coming out of the restaurant. He is a food critic for one of the London newspapers, so I figured he'd be a good person to ask about the fare that Saagar's had to offer. He responded enthusiastically, "This is by far the best Indian food I have had in years, and certainly the best in Ireland." I took that as a well-informed and sound endorsement (especially because he was exceptionally caustic about other restaurants in the area – none of which are in this book).

The owner, Meera Kumar, is proud of his restaurant and likes to point out they are the only Indian restaurant in Ireland that is owned and run by people from India. The chefs, Yen Bhadhur Rawat and Vivek Sahni, are internationally trained and world famous. Examples of dishes they serve include lamb curry, murgh sufed korma, and kachche gosht ki biryani. Dress is casual.

18. FITZER'S CAFE, *51 Dawson Street. Tel. (01) 677-1155. £9.95 to £12.95. Open Monday through Saturday from 12:30pm until 11:30pm, and Sunday from noon to 3:00pm. All major credit cards accepted.*

This is a nice, inexpensive eatery located on Dawson Street, which runs parallel to Grafton Street. The atmosphere is relaxed and easy, and it is very casual. The lunch menu items include chicken breast and ricotta cheese (£7.50) and prawns and fried potatoes (£7.95). The dinner menu offers such treats as duck liver and sweet potatoes (£9.95) and roast duck stuffed with pistachio nuts (£12.95). The cafe has...interesting...artwork on the walls. Dress is casual.

19. PLANET HOLLYWOOD, *119 St. Stephen's Green West. Tel. (01) 478-7827. £3.95 to £12.95. Open Monday through Friday from noon to 10:30pm, and Saturday and Sunday from noon until 11:30pm. All major credit cards accepted.*

If you like other Planet Hollywood restaurants, you should like this one also. Lots of Hollywood memorabilia graces the walls and display cases, and most of them have an Irish connection. For example, you can see the parasol Sara Miles used in the 1970 *Ryan's Daughter*, which was filmed on Ireland's west coast on the Dingle peninsula. You can also see the bicycle Liam Neeson rode in the 1996 movie *Michael Collins*. The most ...present...feature is the Cyborg from the 1991 *Terminator II – Judgment Day* movie.

In addition to an intriguing environment, the food is pretty good here too. You'll fine soups, salads and sandwiches, along with more substantial offerings such as hickory roasted chicken, fajitas and New York strip steak.

20. TRUMAN'S, *23 Molesworth. Tel. (01) 614-6529. £7.95 to £14.95. Open Monday through Saturday from 6:30am to 9:45am for breakfast, 12:30pm to 2:30pm for lunch, and 6:00pm to 9:30pm for dinner. Reservations are recommended on the weekends during the tourist season. All major credit cards accepted.*

This is the restaurant for Buswell's Hotel. You'll find a quieter crowd here, several blocks away from both Grafton Street and Trinity College, which may be just what you are looking for after a bustling, long day.

Truman's is a place where you'll find a tranquil dining experience complemented by elegant table settings, linen tablecloths, and Wedgwood china. The service is efficient and friendly, and you'll feel very much the welcomed guest here.

The food is exceptional, and is presented in a manner that makes you think it is almost too pretty to eat. Examples of their menu items include fillet steak chasseur, chicken Kiev, and lamb cutlets. Casual but nice dress.

21. TROCADERO RESTAURANT, *3 St. Andrews Street. Tel. (01) 677-5545. £8 to £15. Open Monday through Friday from 12:30pm to 3:00pm and from 6:00pm until 11:00pm, and Saturday from 6:00pm to 11:00pm. Reservations are recommended throughout the year on the weekends. All major credit cards accepted.*

This restaurant, between Grafton and Trinity Streets, is popular with the theater crowd – those in front of the stage as well as on it. The restaurant is especially busy in the late evenings after the curtains have closed for the evening on the various theatrical productions around the city. The crowds that come to the Trocadero seem inordinately demonstrative and outgoing, and the feeling is generally one of frivolity spiced with devil-may-care attitudes. The walls in the various snugs and cubbies are graced with the photographs of film and stage stars.

The food at the Trocadero is excellent as well. Examples of their fare include chicken fromage, escalope of pork, and tagliatelle al pesto. They also do a good job with their steaks – priced around £12.95. Casual but nice dress.

22. IL PRIMO, *16 Montague Street. Tel. (01) 478-3373. £9 to £14.95. Open Monday through Saturday from noon to 3:00pm and 6:00pm to 11:00pm. Reservations recommended during the tourist season and on the weekends. All major credit cards accepted.*

It's a little difficult to find, but Il Primo Restaurant is worth the hunt. At the south end of Grafton Street, continue walking south on St. Stephen's Green West. At the corner, bear just slightly to your right on Harcourt Street. About a block down on your right will be an alley marked Montague Street. Turn right, and it's one of the first buildings on your left.

The outside is relatively unremarkable, as is the view when you enter from the street into their bar area. You ascend a steep, narrow staircase to reach the dining room, which is only slightly less narrow than the staircase. The dining room is probably no more than 12 feet wide and about 30 feet long, and seats about 30. While the dining area is compact, it provides for a homey kind of atmosphere. Guests generally enjoy quiet meals that are enhanced by the pleasant buzz of quiet conversation.

While there's not much fancy about the restaurant, the food is absolutely exquisite. It has been referred to by some as new-wave Italian, but the owner, William Frisby, says they serve Italian fare with special Irish variations, such as lasagna with chicken and mushrooms in a red wine sauce, ravioli Il Primo, cannelloni Il Primo, and insalata d'Anitra.

As you ascend the staircase to the dining room, take a moment to notice the paintings on the walls. They are all by local artists and are for sale if you are so inclined. Casual but nice dress.

23. LA STAMPA, *35 Dawson Street. Tel. (01) 677-8611. £8.95 to £17.95. Open Monday through Friday from 5:30pm to midnight, Saturday from 6:00pm to 12:30am and Sunday from 6:30pm to 11:30pm. Reservations are suggested on the weekends. All major credit cards accepted.*

This upscale award-winning restaurant features a variety of European dishes. As you move from the entrance into the dining room, you'll pass a number of bizarre paintings by Irish-born avant-garde artist Graham Kmuttel. The artwork features dark-countenanced, scowling people, distrustfully looking at one another (many have their hands in their coats as though they are preparing to draw a gun). Once you forget the art, the service as well as the food is great. The dining area has high ceilings, and is long and narrow with floor-to-ceiling mirrors. Examples of their varied offerings include char-grilled fillet of beef, buttered linguini with baby spinach, and confit lamb. The clientele is varied, and you'll see dress from chinos to tuxedos. (Maybe the management will replace the paintings before you dine here!)

24. THE IMPERIAL CHINESE RESTAURANT, *13 Wicklow Street. Tel. (01) 677-2580. £9 to £18. Open daily from noon until midnight. Reservations are strongly recommended every day during the tourist season, and on weekends throughout the year. All major credit cards accepted.*

Beautiful indigo carpets accentuate the light rose-colored walls at The Imperial Chinese Restaurant. As you enter the dining area, you'll pass a small fish pond and rock fountain. All this gives the restaurant a quiet, serene ambiance. One of the next things you'll notice is the number of Chinese patrons dining here – always a good sign in a Chinese restaurant. The Imperial Chinese Restaurant has become a popular dining spot for the Dublin Chinese community, and with good reason.

Although a little pricey, the food is excellent. They have several set menus, one of which is £16 per person (minimum of two), and another that is £18 per person (minimum of three). A la carte specialties include Peking duck, king prawns, and fried squid. While the dress is casual but nice, most of the diners dress in suits and ties and dresses.

25. LE CAPRICE, *12A St. Andrew Place. Tel. (01) 679-4050. £5.95 to £19.95. Open Tuesday, Thursday and Sunday from 6:00pm until 11:00pm and Friday and Saturday from 6:00pm to 11:30pm. Reservations are strongly recommended on weekends and during the tourist season. All major credit cards accepted.*

This is a nice, tidy little Italian restaurant a block and a half off Grafton Street. Dinner music by first-class pianists adds to the pleasant and lively atmosphere and is a special touch. Specialties of the house include fresh fish caught locally, as well as escalope of veal champignon, lasagna Caprice, and sole of grilled meuniere. Nice casual dress requested.

26. NUMBER 27 THE GREEN, *27 St. Stephen's Green. Tel. (01) 676-6471. £12.95 to £23. Open daily from 7:15am to 10:30am for breakfast, 12:30pm to 2:30pm for lunch, and 6:15pm to 10:30pm for dinner. Reservations are strongly recommended on the weekends during the tourist season. All major credit cards accepted.*

This is the main restaurant for the Shelbourne Hotel. The same impeccable service, pleasant ambiance, and beautiful surroundings that characterize the hotel extend to the restaurant. They have received numerous awards for their breakfast, and their dinners are excellent as well. They have a set dinner menu for £23, as well as á la carte items such as fillet of cod, grilled fillet of beef, and hickory fillet of salmon, all for £14.50 each. There's also an extensive wine list awaiting your selection. Jacket and tie are expected, and they will provide you a tie if you are without.

27. THE ALEXANDRA, *Earlsfort Terrace. Tel. (01) 676-5555. £15.95 to £33. Open Monday through Friday from 12:30pm to 2:30pm for lunch, and from 6:30pm until 10:30pm for dinner. Saturdays they are open only for dinner from 6:30pm until 10:30pm. Closed Sunday. Reservations are required. All major credit cards accepted.*

Located in the Conrad Hotel, the Alexandra Restaurant is elegant and courtly. The room is richly accented with dark wood, lovely paintings, and shimmering chandeliers. This marvelous, intimate restaurant serves a delicious variety of taste treats, including blackened sole, mignon of beef, and Chateaubriand. Jacket and tie are requested.

28. THE COMMONS RESTAURANT, *85 - 86 St. Stephen's Green South. Tel. (01) 475-2597. £32 to £42. Open Monday through Friday from 12:30pm to 2:30pm and from 7:15pm to 10:15pm. Closed weekends. Reservations are required for dinner, and recommended for lunch. All major credit cards accepted.*

The Commons is one of the nicest restaurants in Dublin. Located on the south side of St. Stephen's Green in about the middle of the block, it is easy to miss because it is below street-level, and is not particularly well marked. Unlike many of the restaurants in Dublin, tables are not too close together and allow you to converse quietly, enjoy your candlelit meal, and relax in the romantic glow created by the fire in the large fireplace. During the spring and summer they use their lovely garden patio for drinks and socializing. The walls are covered with artwork commissioned by the owners of the restaurant. Irish artists were asked to paint their impressions of the writer James Joyce, and their efforts grace the walls.

Their menu is primarily French with an Irish influence, and they have several set menus ranging in price from £32 to £42. Dress is jacket and tie.

Ballsbridge District

29. LATCHFORDS BISTRO, *99 - 100 Lower Baggot Street. Tel. (01) 676-0784. £10.95 to £14.95. Open Monday through Thursday for lunch from 6:00pm to 10:00pm, and Friday and Saturday from 6:00pm to 11:00pm for dinner. Closed Sunday. Reservations are recommended. All major credit cards accepted.*

This family-run bistro has a warm, comfortable atmosphere topped only by the excellent cuisine. It is very popular with the locals, and tourists haven't discovered it yet. They specialize in a sort of contemporary French/Italian menu ranging from roast pheasant in a lentil and orange sauce (outstanding) to noisettes of lamb to fillet of salmon, or you can choose their set dinner menu for £18.95. They also have an impressive wine list. The presentation of the dishes is nearly as impressive as the flavor. Save room for dessert – the sticky toffee gateau on a raspberry coulis is to die for! The lunch menu is comparable for about half the price. Dress is casual but nice, although most dress in suits.

30. SUSSEX RESTAURANT, *Upper Leeson Street. Tel. (01) 660-5222. £7 to £18. Open daily from 7:00am to 10:00am for breakfast, 12:30pm to 2:30pm for lunch, and 6:30pm to 10:30pm for dinner. Reservations are recommended most weekends, and every evening throughout the tourist season. All major credit cards accepted.*

The Sussex Restaurant is the formal restaurant associated with the Burlington Hotel. It is one of the few restaurants listed here that request at least a jacket, if not a tie. The atmosphere is pleasant and open. They have a set menu from £16.50, and á la carte items including medallions of beef au poivre and fillet of lemon sole.

31. MCGRATTAN'S RESTAURANT, *76 Fitzwilliam Lane. Tel. (01) 661-8808. £10.95 to £18.50. Open daily from 12:30pm to 4:30pm, and from 6:00pm until 10:30pm for dinner. Reservations are recommended on the weekends and during the tourist season. All major credit cards accepted.*

The atmosphere at McGrattan's is candlelight and crystal, fine china and Irish linen, accompanied by a crackling fire in the fireplace and live piano music to enhance your dining experience. (The pianist plays for guests Thursday through Sunday evenings.) And lest you are distracted by your surroundings, your meal from the first course to the last will be delicious. Their clam chowder is possibly the best I have ever had. While seafood is the specialty, McGrattan's offers a varied menu, from a set menu (£18.50) to á la carte items such as grilled swordfish, salmon, and chicken Kiev. The food is outstanding, and the portions served are large. Be sure and save room for dessert, especially the Bailey's mousse with fresh fruit coulis – it's light, tasty and superb! Dress is casual, but patrons tend to dress in jacket and tie and dresses.

32. THE ORCHID RESTAURANT, *120 Pembroke Road. Tel. (01) 660-0629. £8 to £20. Open Monday through Friday for lunch from 12:30pm to 2:00pm, and daily for dinner from 6:00pm until 11:30pm. Due to its close proximity to the Jury's Hotel and Towers, reservations are necessary on the weekends, especially so during the tourist season. All major credit cards accepted.*

As I stood outside this restaurant debating whether or not to eat here, a local Dubliner stopped and volunteered that it was a marvelous Chinese restaurant. With that unsolicited recommendation, I ventured in, and was not disappointed. The Orchid offers a set menu (£18 to £20) as well as á la carte selections. On the á la carte menu, you can select from such savory dishes as Cantonese roast duck, Szechuan spicy chicken, and sweet and sour pork. Dress is casual but nice.

33. RAGLAN'S RESTAURANT, *Pembroke Road. Tel. (01) 614-2666. £12.50 to £20.95. Open Monday through Saturday from 12:15pm to 2:30pm and Monday through Sunday from 6:30pm until 10:15pm (9:30pm on Sunday). Reservations are recommended, especially on the weekend. All major credit cards accepted.*

Associated with the Jury's Hotel, this seafood restaurant provides a nice selection of fresh fish. Scallops and prawn flambe, mussels á la mainiere, and sole walesha are samples of their offerings. Dress is casual but nice. Because of the popularity of the Jury's Hotel and Towers, the Kish Restaurant is usually very busy.

34. NUMBER 10, *10 Fitzwilliam Street Lower. Tel. (01) 676-1367. £13.95 to £24.95. Open Monday through Thursday from 12:30pm to 2:30pm and from 6:30pm to 10:00pm, Friday and Saturday from 12:30pm to 2:00pm and from 7:00pm to 11:00pm, and Sunday from 7:00pm to 9:00pm. Reservations are strongly recommended, and you'll probably not get in without them on the weekends. All major credit cards accepted.*

If exquisite dining is what you are looking for in Dublin, look no further. Number 10, the restaurant that also serves Longfield's Hotel, is arguably one of the finest dining establishments in Dublin. As you descend white and black tile steps below street level, you emerge into a small but engaging restaurant. The open fire accentuated by the crystal and linen on the tables, immediately signals you that you've come to a special place. The service, the food, and the ambiance all combine to provide an elegant and graceful dining experience.

Number 10's internationally trained chef whips up meals fit for a king. His presentation is both tasteful and exquisite. Adding to the wonderful dining experience, the staff is attentive and assure that top-notch service is a reality. According to the manager, the fare is light French cuisine with Irish influences. From confit of French duck to an outstanding ravioli stuffed with fresh crab, you'll enjoy this savory adventure. They offer a set dinner menu for £24.95 that includes appetizer, salad, soup, granite (like a sorbet, only with no sugar), entree and dessert. They offer an equally excellent award-winning breakfast menu for £8.50, and their lunch menu is as delectable as their dinner menu for about half the price.

The chef from Ireland's only two-star restaurant occasionally frequents Number 10 on his days off. Need I say more? The restaurant seats only 35 or so, and it fills up quickly. Dress is casual but nice, although diners are usually dressed in jacket and tie and dresses.

35. L'ECRIVAIN, *109 Lower Baggot Street. Tel. (01) 661-1919. £21.95 to £27.95. Open Monday through Friday for lunch from 12:30pm to 2:00pm, Monday through Saturday for dinner from 7:00pm to 11:00pm (open at 6:30pm on Saturdays). Reservations are a must. All major credit cards accepted.*

You'll think you missed a turn and ended up in Paris when you walk into L'Ecrivain. This lovely restaurant just south of St. Stephen's Green just looks and feels like a French restaurant should. For you French speakers out there, you know that L'Ecrivain means "the writer" in French, and the walls of this restaurant are decorated with paintings that pay homage to a number of Irish writers – present as well as past.

A traditional French restaurant, L'Ecrivain offers a set dinner menu for £27.50 with a surprisingly wide selection, including crisp confit of duck and rack of lamb. They also have an excellent four-course set lunch menu. Their extensive wine list is considered one of the best in Dublin, with nearly 150 selections. For dinner, a jacket is required and a tie is suggested.

36. EMBASSY GARDEN, *Pembroke Road. Tel. (01) 660-5000. £12.95 to £30. Open daily from 7:00am to 10:00am for breakfast, noon to 2:30pm for lunch, and 6:15pm to 10:15pm for dinner. Reservations are recommended on the weekends. All major credit cards accepted.*

Located in Jury's Hotel, just walk across the footbridge and over the stream into the relaxed, fine dining room. Ask for a table by the windows overlooking the hotel's garden and pool. This restaurant specializes in French food, including Chateaubriand, osso buco (veal), and a variety of beef, lamb, and veal dishes. Dress is casual but nice.

37. LE COQ HARDI, *35 Pembroke Road. Tel. (01) 668-4130. £21.95 to £35. Open Monday through Friday from 12:30pm until 3:30pm for lunch, and Monday through Saturday from 7:00pm until 11:00pm for dinner. Reservations are required for dinner. All major credit cards accepted.*

Located in a converted Georgian home, Le Coq Hardi is perhaps the best place in Ireland for French cuisine. The restaurant is expensively and elegantly decorated with rosewood and brass, and linen, fine china, and crystal make for elegant table settings.

Try the house special: coq hardi, baked chicken breast stuffed with potatoes, mushrooms and a variety of seasonings wrapped in bacon, and flamed at your table. If that doesn't strike your fancy, there's lobster, prawns, and turbot, rack of lamb, Gaelic steak, and roast goose to choose from. You can't go wrong with any choice here. Only the freshest ingredients are used, and the fish is as fresh as any you'll find on the Emerald Isle. Their wine list is extensive, with some of the finest French wines available. Dress is definitely jacket and tie – you'll feel uncomfortable and out of place in anything else.

38. RESTAURANT PATRICK GUILBAUD, *21 Merrion Street. Tel. (01) 676-4192. £15 to £46. Open Tuesday through Saturday for lunch from 12:30pm to 2:30pm, and for dinner from 7:30pm until 9:30pm. Reservations are a must all year. All major credit cards accepted.*

If you want to eat in *the* restaurant in Ireland, this would be the place. Restaurant Patrick Guilbaud is the first restaurant in Ireland to be awarded a second Michelin star, and when you dine here, you'll agree that it is well deserved.

The restaurant is housed in an old Georgian home that has been exquisitely renovated. The moment you enter, you'll feel the richness of the environment. But there's no stuffiness – pleasant conversation is encouraged by the well-lit surroundings. Lovely furnishings are designed to complement the fare that you'll soon be enjoying. Take a moment to notice the paintings that adorn the walls. Each painting is by an Irish artist who lived and painted in France. Mr. Guilbaud is proud to have acquired these paintings in his home country and returned them to their native Ireland.

The food is marvelous. From the roast quail to the poached Connemara lobster, it is as tasteful to the eye as it is to the palate. Set menus are available for £18.50 for lunch and £30 for dinner. There is even a *Menu Surprise* for £46 for those wishing a dining adventure! The dress is casual but nice – most diners will be dressed in coat and tie and dresses. During your dining experience, you are likely to meet Mr. Guilbaud, as he is active in serving, greeting and conversing with his dinner guests.

NORTH OF DUBLIN

There are many delightful and affordable restaurants north of Dublin. Many are on the DART system. Howth, Clontarf, Swords, and other small towns are all popular due to their close proximity to Dublin.

39. ADRIAN'S RESTAURANT, *3 Abbey Street, Howth. Tel. (01) 839-1696. £8 to £18.50. Open Monday through Thursday from 12:30 until 11:00pm, Friday and Saturday from 12:30pm until 3:30pm, and from 6:00pm until 11:30pm. They are open on Sundays from 1:00pm until 10:00pm. All major credit cards accepted.*

This small award-winning restaurant is reasonably priced. Fish caught daily by local fishermen are presented in an appealing manner. Dress is casual.

40. HOWTH LODGE RESTAURANT, *Howth Harbor. Tel. (01) 832-1010. £11.95 to £18.50. Open Monday through Saturday from 7:00pm until 9:30pm. Reservations are suggested for the weekends. All major credit cards accepted.*

You'll love the views of Howth Harbor when you dine at Howth Lodge Restaurant. Local fishermen supply the entrees each day. In addition to their excellent seafood, Howth Lodge Restaurant is known for its excellent Irish beef. Their fare includes medallions of Monkfish, sea trout, and layered salmon. The atmosphere is casual and comfortable.

Turn right as you leave the Howth DART station, and walk about a half mile down the road, the restaurant is on your right.

41. ABBEY TAVERN RESTAURANT, *Abbey Street, Howth. Tel. (01) 839-0307. £19 to £24.95. Open from 12:30pm to 3:30pm and from 7:00pm until 10:00pm Monday through Saturday. Reservations are a must during the tourist season. American Express, Mastercard, and Visa accepted.*

This is one of the most popular tourist and dining attractions in the Dublin area. The unmistakable smell of peat burning in the fireplace (turf fire) and the original 16th-century stone walls and gas lights give you a sense of having stepped back into time. Along with their fantastic traditional Irish music program, which runs Monday through Saturday from 8:30pm to 10:30pm, the folks at the Abbey Tavern serve remarkably good food, especially seafood. Try the sole of Abbey, a decadently prepared specialty. Dress is casual but neat, although many of the diners will have jackets.

As you leave the Howth DART station, turn left and head toward the quay. Several blocks down on your right is Abbey Street, and Abbey Tavern is up the hill about 100 yards on the right.

42. KING SITRIC, *East Pier, Howth Tel. (01) 832-5235. £17.50 to £30. Open Monday through Friday for lunch from 12:30pm to 2:15pm, and Monday through Saturday from 6:30pm to 10:15pm for dinner. Reservations are strongly suggested on the weekends and during the tourist season. All major credit cards accepted.*

The harbor master who formerly lived here never had as good a meal as you'll find at the King Sitric Restaurant. Located at the tip of Howth Harbor, the only thing separating you from the sea is the road and a retaining wall. Striking views of the sea complement the wonderful meals prepared here. This comfortable, yet elegant restaurant was named for the famous Norse King Sitric Silkenbeard. Surrounded by antiques, you'll enjoy just sitting back and taking it all in. As you would expect, seafood is the specialty, and it is excellent. From baked haddock to fillet of lemon sole, if you are a seafood lover you won't be disappointed. Dress is casual but nice, although most diners will be in jacket and tie.

The King Sitric is about a seven-minute walk from the Howth DART Station. As soon as you walk out of the station, turn left and walk up the street. The restaurant is at the end of the street just as you get to the quay.

SOUTH OF DUBLIN
These restaurants are well south of Dublin, and will require you to drive or take the DART.

43. DE SELBY'S, *17 Patrick Street, Dun Laoghaire. Tel. (01) 284-1761. £9 to £12.95. Open daily from 5:30pm to 11:00pm for dinner, and from noon until 10:00pm on Sunday. All major credit cards accepted.*

Near the shopping district and both the Dun Laoghaire and Sandycove DART stations, De Selby's is a nice family-run seafood restaurant with an acceptable selection available for beef-eaters and vegetarians. The wine list seems to go for quality rather than quantity. Try the prawn stir-fry – it's great.

44. LIBRARY GRILL, *Killiney Bay, Killiney. Tel. (01) 285-1622. £4 to £7. Open from 12:30pm to 10:30pm. Reservations are not taken. All major credit cards accepted.*

This nice little grill is located in the Court Hotel overlooking Killiney Bay. It has a pleasant atmosphere and adequate food. Menu items include burgers, fillet of plaice, and Chicken Marcus. If you have ventured south of Dublin to see the sights in and around Killiney Bay, this would be a good place to stop for refreshment. Dress is casual.

45. JOHNNIE FOX'S PUB, *Glencullen. Tel. (01) 295-5647. £7.95 to £17.95. Open Monday through Saturday from 10:30am to 11:30pm, and Sunday from 11:00am to 2:00pm and from 4:00pm to 11:00pm. All major credit cards accepted.*

Located in the mountains south of Dublin, Johnnie Fox's was recently awarded the "Bar Food of the Year" award by a major industry watcher. The atmosphere smacks of pure schtick – sawdust-strewn stone floors, old photographs on the walls along with a ton of knickknacks everywhere, and traditional Irish music. But it's fun, and the food is a real treat. In keeping with the setting, the menu is traditional Irish, but not boringly so. The selection is surprisingly wide, and ranges from wild oak-smoked salmon with prawns and salad, to hot crab claws in butter, to roast rack of spring lamb, and of course you can always get an excellent steak.

46. ISLAND RESTAURANT, *Killiney Bay, Killiney. Tel. (01) 285-1622. Set menu £19.95. Open from noon to 2:30pm for lunch, and 6:30pm to 11:00pm for dinner. Reservations during the tourist season and on the weekends. All major credit cards accepted.*

This is a very popular restaurant for Dubliners to come to for lunch and dinner. It is the main restaurant for the Court Hotel, and is right across the street from Killiney DART Station – a mere 20-minute ride from downtown Dublin. The restaurant looks out on Killiney Bay, and the views are frankly spectacular. The entry is the original to the old mansion and it is gorgeous. Much of the original dark woodwork has been preserved. The best part of this restaurant is the view. Jackets are recommended.

47. PJ'S RESTAURANT, *Killiney Hill Road, Killiney. Tel. (01) 284-0700. £15 to £23. Open daily from 7:00am to 10:00am for breakfast, 12:30pm to 2:30pm for lunch, and 6:00pm to 10:00pm for dinner. All major credit cards accepted.*

This nice restaurant is located in the Fitzpatrick Castle Hotel, about eight miles south of Dublin City. You'll have a nice, quiet dining experience here. The food is acceptable although not remarkable. The best part of the dining experience may well be the views of Dublin Bay you can enjoy during a walk before or after dinner, especially at night. If you decide to try this restaurant, you'll probably need a car. The Killiney DART Station is about a mile to a mile and a half from the hotel, but it's mostly uphill. They do have a shuttle, but they seem to have a hard time finding the driver just when you need a ride. Dress is casual but nice.

48. THE TREE OF IDLENESS, *on the waterfront, Bray, County Wicklow. Tel. (01) 286-3498. £15 to £21. Open Tuesday through Saturday from 7:30pm until 10:00pm. Closed Monday. All major credit cards accepted.*

This wonderful little Greek-Cypriot restaurant on the waterfront in Bray is a winner. The original Tree of Idleness was in Bellapais, Cyprus. Located in an old Victorian house, owner Susan Courtellas has managed a winning combination: fine Greek food, a marvelous wine list, stunning dessert selection, and a pleasant atmosphere. Your selection is wide and varied and ranges from spinach ravioli stuffed with crab mousse to fillet of Irish beef to pheasant with grapes and chestnuts. The roast lamb and feta cheese is also wonderful.

SEEING THE SIGHTS

Dublin is the most populous city in Ireland, and has many interesting and historical sights. There's plenty to do, from pub crawls to shopping malls, from castles to dungeons.

While you're in Dublin, I highly recommend that you *do not* rent a car. It would be counter-productive. The things to see in Dublin are for the most part within walking distance, and those things that are not are a short bus or DART ride away. If you rent a car, you'll spend all your time looking for a parking place, and then end up walking further than if you had walked from a centrally located hotel.

North Dublin

O'Connell Street runs north for two blocks from the River Liffey, but it is one of the most important streets in Dublin. It is not nearly as long as you'd expect it to be, given the important role it has played in Dublin's history. But it seems to have a mesmerizing affect on all those who visit. O'Connell Street hosts one of the finest hotels in Dublin (the Gresham), and one of Ireland's most important buildings (the General Post Office – the GPO) lists O'Connell Street as its address. It is the namesake of Daniel O'Connell, one of Ireland's most revered individuals. O'Connell Street was once a grand thoroughfare where the ladies and gentlemen of Dublin's High Society liked to be seen, and where others of Dublin's not-quite-so-High-Society went to see them.

Today it is not quite as impressive as it must have been in those bygone days. Many of the lovely old Victorian homes and buildings are gone and have given way to more modern structures. Still, the wide central island is punctuated with large green trees and statues of Irish greats: Daniel O'Connell (former Dublin mayor and winner of Catholic emancipation), William Smith O'Brien (leader of one of Ireland's many rebellions against British authority), Sir John Gay (newspaper editor), James Larkin (a historic union leader), Father Theobald Mathew (a revered priest known as "the apostle of temperance, and honored for his tireless efforts during a cholera epidemic in 1832), and Charles Stewart Parnell (key figure in the Home Rule campaign).

Included with all these impressive statues along O'Connell Street is the **Anna Livia Millennium Fountain** (in the center island across from the GPO). Unveiled as part of the festivities during Dublin's 1,000-year celebration (1988), Anna Livia represents the River Liffey. I stood in front of the fountain for half an hour and questioned Dubliners about the fountain. None of them knew anything about Anna Livia, but they all knew the site by the more common appellation *The Floozie in the Jacuzzi*.

Like the Grand Canal in the south, the **Royal Canal** begins at Dublin Bay. The Royal Canal makes a circular route around the north side of Dublin, then runs into the countryside until it joins the Shannon River in the middle of the country. Forty-seven locks along its route compensate for the rise in elevation as the canal runs into the countryside. Construction on the canal began in 1792, and was completed in 1817.

The Royal Canal was used to bring turf for fires and heating into Dublin. It was also used extensively by the Guinness Brewery. Grain was brought into Dublin on barges for use in the brewery, then kegs of Guinness were transported to the interior of the country. When the kegs were empty, they made the trip back to Dublin to be refilled. The canal was used for that purpose up until it closed in 1960. Now anglers and pleasure boaters are its most frequent users.

General Post Office (**GPO**), *O'Connell Street, open Monday through Saturday 8:00am until 8:00pm, Sundays from 10:30am to 6:30pm. Tel. (01) 872-8888.* This is probably the most talked-about building in Dublin. It is the main post office, and as such everyone is familiar with it. But its mark on history goes much beyond postal service: it was the flash point of the 1916 Easter Rising. It was from the seized GPO that Irish rebel leaders proclaimed their message of a new republic. The ensuing battle destroyed most of the area around O'Connell Street. Some of the GPO's massive stone columns still bear the scars of flying bullets. As a result of the fighting, the GPO was virtually gutted by fire and British artillery. Its renovation was completed in 1929 and faithfully restored the GPO to its former grandeur. The words of the proclamation read by the rebel leaders on that fateful Easter morning is inscribed in a green marble plaque in the GPO. All those who signed the proclamation also signed their death warrants. All were taken to Kilmainham Prison and executed.

Inside the GPO in a window looking out onto O'Connell Street is a magnificent statue of **Cuchulainn** (pronounced Koo-hoo'-lin). He was a legendary Irish warrior who has been immortalized by generations of Irish storytellers and idolized by generations of Irish children. He was the leader of the Red Branch Knights, an elite army charged with defending Ulster from her many enemies. As famous and colorful as Davey Crockett, Daniel Boone, and Paul Bunyan, Cuchulainn is a legendary Irish hero of epic proportion. While he was probably a real person, his actual exploits are now shrouded in so much myth and hero-worship that it is hard to differentiate between fact and fiction. The annals report that after a lifetime of warring, Cuchulainn fought in one last ferocious battle. Fearlessly facing a daunting number of foes, he bravely and single-handedly fought on and on, spilling the blood of many enemies.

Mortally wounded, he is said to have lashed himself to a stone so that he could face his enemies while remaining on his feet. His foes wouldn't

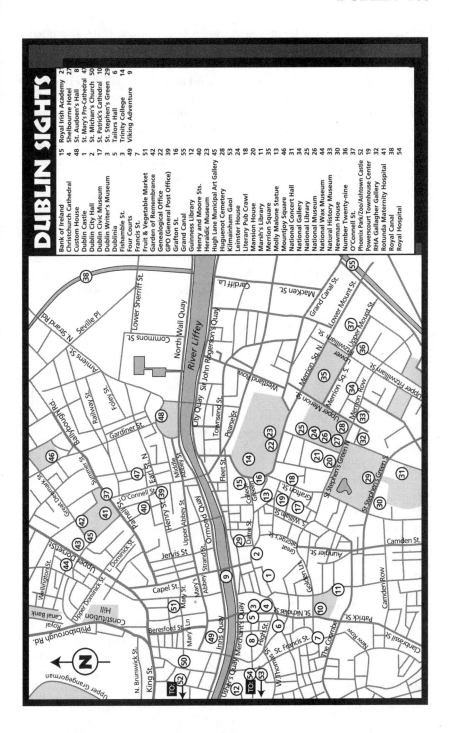

DUBLIN SIGHTS

Bank of Ireland 15
Christchurch Cathedral 4
Custom House 48
Dublin Castle 1
Dublin City Hall 2
Dublin Civic Museum 17
Dublin Writer's Museum 3
Dubiinia 5
Fishamble St. 3
Four Courts 49
Francis St. 7
Fruit & Vegetable Market 51
Garden of Remembrance 42
Genealogical Office 22
GPO (General Post Office) 39
Grafton St. 16
Grand Canal 55
Guinness Library 12
Henry and Moore Sts. 40
Heraldic Museum 23
Hugh Lane Municipal Art Gallery 45
Huguenot Cemetery 28
Kilmainham Gaol 53
Leinster House 24
Literary Pub Crawl 18
Mansion House 20
Marsh's Library 11
Merrion Square 35
Molly Malone Statue 13
Mountjoy Square 46
National Concert Hall 31
National Gallery 34
National Library 25
National Museum 26
National Wax Museum 44
Natural History Museum 33
Newman House 30
Number Twenty-nine 36
O'Connell St. 37
Phoenix Park/Zoo/Ashtown Castle 52
Powerscourt Townhouse Center 19
RHA Gallagher Gallery 32
Rotunda Maternity Hospital 41
Royal Canal 38
Royal Hospital 54

Royal Irish Academy 2
Shelbourne Hotel 27
St. Audoen's Hall 8
St. Mary's Pro-Cathedral 47
St. Michan's Church 50
St. Patrick's Cathedral 10
St. Stephen's Green 29
Tailors Hall 6
Trinity College 14
Viking Adventure 9

approach his body, the legend says, until a bird landed on the shoulder of the lifeless warrior. The statue depicts his last moments. It is an appropriate tribute to those few warriors who took on the British Empire almost single-handedly and wrested Ireland from her grasp. Out front of the GPO, there are three magnificent stone statues atop the portico representing three other legendary figures: **Mercury, Hibernia, Fidelity.**

The intersection in front of the GPO – Henry and North Earl Streets and O'Connell Street – was formerly the location of one of the city's most recognizable landmarks – the **Nelson Pillar**. A 135-foot pillar, complete with spiral staircase leading to the viewing platform at the top, was a tribute to British Admiral Nelson. On a March night in 1966, a tremendous blast reduced the pillar to rubble, an act of Irish loyalists who resented Admiral Nelson's lofty position in the city center. The demolition took place just prior to the 50th anniversary of the 1916 Easter Rising.

Henry Street bisects O'Connell Street one block north of the River Liffey. Like Grafton Street on the south of the river, Henry Street is a pedestrian shopping area. Grafton Street has largely replaced it as *the* shopping street in Dublin, but it is still crowded with shoppers most hours of the day and evening. The stores are a little older and the architecture a little more tired, but the atmosphere is similar to Grafton Street.

About a half block off O'Connell Street on the right is a large tile mosaic on the walkway that announces the entrance to **Moore Street**, which for generations has been the fruit, vegetable, and flower market of Dublin. You can hear the (mostly) women vendors shouting to call your attention to their produce. In days gone by, many of the shops lining Moore Street were butcher shops, but discount stores and other shops have slowly replaced them. It's a fun place to go, and it's especially colorful and cheery on a sunny day.

The **Rotunda Maternity Hospital**, *Parnell Street. Tel. (01) 873-0700.* Originally known as the Lying-in Hospital, this was the brainchild of **Dr. Bartholomew Mosse**, a Dublin who was a midwife 20 years before the American Revolution. His vision and mission in life was to provide a "modern" hospital for pregnant women and childbirth. As a fundraising project, Mosse and a group of investors purchased a set of adjoining gardens (now the site of the Garden of Remembrance), where a series of benefit concerts were held to raise money to fund the work Mosse was doing on the hospital.

Through much tribulation, Mosse saw the completion of the hospital in 1757, and immediately began work on a chapel. The chapel is at the top of the central staircase of the hospital, and its ornate ceiling – a tribute to motherhood – is internationally famous, the work of **Barthelemy Cramillion**. The mahogany pews, paneling and fluted columns are all some of the finest craftsmanship in Ireland. Unfortunately, Mosse never saw it: he died at the age of 47, three years prior to the chapel's completion.

Garden of Remembrance, *Parnell Square. Open daily from November through February from 11:00am to 4:00pm, from 11:00am to 7:00pm March and April, from 9:30am to 8:00pm from May through September, and from 11:00am to 7:00pm in October. Admission is free.* On the fiftieth anniversary of the Easter Rising of 1916, which eventually lead to Ireland's independence, the Garden of Remembrance was built to commemorate those who gave their lives that Ireland might be a free nation. (Think of it as the Minuteman statue in Lexington, Massachusetts.) This is a very peaceful and contemplative place where visitors can think about Irish patriots who gave their lives for a free Ireland.

The square features an ornamental pond in the form of a crucifix, and the setting is very serene and peaceful. Just beyond the small pond is a statue that looks like children chasing geese and making them fly away. It is in reality a statue of the children of Lir, who were turned into swans (according to legend).

THE CHILDREN OF LIR

Lir was an ancient Celtic chieftain who lived 900 years before Christianity came to the shores of Ireland. After the death of his wife, Lir married an enchantress named Aoife. Aoife was insanely jealous of Lir's four children by his first wife, and used her magic to change the poor children into swans (talk about a wicked stepmother).

Even though they were swans, the children retained their human capabilities, and used their voices to sing songs that brought great joy to the inhabitants of the surrounding countryside. The spell ended 900 years later when Christianity was introduced into Ireland. The children resumed their former personalities, and were said to have been converted to Christianity by St. Mochaomhog.

Dublin Writer's Museum, *18/19 Parnell Square, open October through March on Fridays and Saturdays from 10:00am to 5:00pm, and Sundays from 1:00pm to 5:00pm; from April, May and September it is open Tuesday through Saturday from 10:00am to 5:00pm, and Sundays from 11:00am to 6:00pm; June through August it is open Monday through Friday from 10:00am to 7:00pm. Admission is £3.00 for adults, £2.55 for students and children. There is a family ticket for £7.75. Tel. (01) 872-2077.* Ireland has always loved its writers and poets, and there has always been a special place for them in the heart of every Irish man and woman. Now there is a museum for them, too. The

Dublin Writer's Museum opened in 1991 and has quickly become one of Dublin's top attractions. It is one of the most elegant, tasteful and well thought-out museums in Ireland.

This exquisitely restored Georgian home houses the Gorham Library on the first floor. Be sure to take a look at its beautiful ceiling. Permanent exhibits in the museum feature famed Irish authors such as **Samuel Beckett, Brendan Behan, George Bernard Shaw, Jonathan Swift**, and **Oscar Wilde**. Paintings, photographs, letters, and memorabilia are all part of the various exhibits.

Adjacent to the museum is the Irish Writer's Centre, a gathering place for current writers to meet, talk, and host readings. If the exhibits spark an interest in the works of these writers, there is a bookstore that sells most of the works of the authors represented in the museum. If it's food you're thinking of, they also have a cafe on site.

National Wax Museum, *Granby Row, open Monday through Saturday from 10:00am to 5:30pm, and Sunday from noon to 5:30pm. Admission is £3 for adults, senior citizens and students £2.50, children £2. Tel. (01) 872-6340.* It's okay for a wax museum, but to be honest, I find most wax museums, well, sort of lifeless. You can see the Pope, along with Madonna's paraffin persona here, along with a host of Irish personalities.

Hugh Lane Municipal Gallery of Modern Art, *Parnell Square, open Tuesday through Friday, 9:00am to 6:00pm, Saturday from 9:30am to 5:00pm, Sunday from 11:00am to 5:00pm. Admission is free. Tel. (01) 874-1903.* Built in the mid-18th century, this former townhouse of Lord Charlemont has been restored and now houses a fine collection of modern art. Works by **Picasso, Monet, Renoir, Degas**, and **Manet** are all part of the collection of artworks owned at one time by Hugh Lane. Upon Mr. Lane's death on the *Lusitania* off the southwest coast of Ireland in 1915 (which some claim was the work of the English to bring America into the first world war, but that's another story), his collection of art was to go to the Dublin Corporation.

But several years prior to his death, Mr. Lane was angered when the Dublin Corporation decided not to build a special gallery to house his collection, so he stipulated that 39 of his paintings were to go to London instead. However, after his death, a contested (unwitnessed) codicil was discovered reversing his decision and bequeathing the paintings to the Dublin Corporation, his original preference. The collection was tied up in legal proceedings for nearly 50 years until London and Dublin decided on a compromise: the paintings would rotate every five years between the two cities. Included with Lane's collection are a number of other fine works by 19th and 20th-century artists, as well as a room devoted to stained glass artisan Harry Clarke.

Mountjoy Square, *Upper Gardiner Street*. A couple of blocks north and east of O'Connell Street is Mountjoy Square, a large greenbelt area the size of a city block. Once in the midst of one of the ritziest neighborhoods in Dublin, the area now borders on a section of the city that's been a bit neglected. Mountjoy Square is named after **Luke Gardiner**, the third Viscount Mountjoy, hence the name.

St. Mary's Pro-Cathedral, *Marlborough Street, open daily 8:00am to 6:00pm. Admission is free. Tel. (01) 874-5441*. Six columns support a massive portico at the front of St. Mary's Pro-Cathedral. If you've been to the Temple of Theseus in Athens, those six columns might make you think that the architect was trying to imitate it, and you'd be right. It was indeed patterned after the Athenian temple. Completed in 1825, the interior is done in Grecian-Doric architectural style, and seems a little out of place in the capitol city of the Emerald Isle.

This church (it was never endowed with cathedral status) has been the location of the funerals for key government officials for years. It is considered the main Catholic church in Ireland. The crypt is open irregular times, but is an interesting place to explore. Ask if it is open when you arrive, or call ahead for times when you can visit it.

The Custom House, *Custom House Quay, not open to the public (unfortunately)*. If you spend any time whatsoever in Dublin, you are certain to wonder what the large, obviously governmental-type building is that faces the River Liffey two blocks east of O'Connell Street. It is the Custom House, and it is a very impressive sight, especially at night when it is brightly lit.

The Custom House is a building that evokes strong feelings of pride in Dubliners – it really is a beautiful, stately building. But that wasn't always the case. When construction began in 1781, opponents hired ruffians on more than one occasion to attack the builders. Notwithstanding these efforts and numerous death threats to the builder, James Gandon, work on the building continued – but he felt the threats were serious enough that he began wearing his sword to the job site.

A suspicious fire broke out in a portion of the unfinished building in 1789, but the damage was repaired and the Custom House opened on schedule in 1791. But, unlike characters in fairy tales, the Custom House did not live happily ever after. Another fire struck in 1833, and then a fire of monumental proportions devastated the structure in 1921. Local fire crews were unsuccessful in putting out the fire, and it burned out of control for five days. The fire was so hot that it melted brass door fittings and cracked stonework.

Once again restoration and repair work put the building back in commission. In the early 1970's, it was determined that additional cracks in the stonework, probably caused by the fire in 1921, would need to be fixed. An aggressive restoration program was completed in the early 1990s. The Custom House has once again been restored to its prior grandeur. And you benefit from the work.

Four Courts, *Inns Quay, open Monday through Friday 10:00am to 4:00pm. Admission is free. Tel. (01) 872-5555.* The Four Courts is a landmark building. Its dome, sitting majestically above the River Liffey is a familiar site, and very impressive at night. Housing the Irish Law Courts, the Four Courts has been on the Dublin scene since its completion in 1802.

During the Irish Civil War in 1922, the Four Courts was nearly destroyed by fire and artillery shelling and the Public Records Office next to it was destroyed, along with generations of irreplaceable legal, land, and genealogical records, a most regrettable loss. Fortunately the building was not razed, and years of renovation have restored it to its previous glory.

The front portico is supported by six massive columns, and Moses, the Law Giver, stands tall at the center of the top of the portico and is flanked by the statues of Justice and Mercy. Behind and above the portico is an immense circular dome. If you have the time, be sure and visit the upper rotunda of the dome. It provides some nice views of Dublin.

St. Michan's Church, *Church Street, open March through October Monday through Friday from 10:00am to 12:45pm, and from 2:00pm to 4:45pm, and Saturdays from 10:00am until 1:00pm, and November through February Monday through Friday 12:30pm to 3:30pm, and Saturday 10:00am to 1:00pm. Admission to the vaults is £2.00 for adults, and 50p for children and senior citizens. Tel. (01) 872-4154.* Originally built in 1095 as a Viking parish church (the only one north of the River Liffey for over 500 years), St. Michan's was rebuilt to its current state in 1686, and has had several facelifts since then. Most of the renovations have been faithful to the original workmanship of the church. As you peruse the interior, be sure and notice the beautiful woodwork throughout the chapel.

Legend has it that **Handel** played St. Michan's magnificent 18th-century organ while composing *The Messiah*. (It's the Irish equivalent of "George Washington slept here.")

One of the oddities at St. Michan's is the "stool of repentance," where misbehaving parishioners did public penance. Perhaps the most unusual aspect of St. Michan's is the partially mummified remains of three 17th-century people in the vaults. The limestone in the ground of the vaults removed moisture from the air, preserving the bodies remarkably well. If the mummified cat and mouse at Christchurch made you queasy, you might want to pass on these fellows.

South Dublin – Temple Bar District

The **River Liffey** is the lifeblood, the main artery of Dublin. Dublin itself is here because of the inland access the river provided for its earliest and most intrepid settlers – the Vikings. With its beginnings in the Wicklow Mountains to the south, the river meanders its way through the Irish countryside. Poems have been written about The River, songs have been sung to it, and it is fondly regarded by the populace of Dublin, like a favorite uncle, or to some, like a mysterious mistress. Dark and musty, it is not a particularly resplendent river, but it is still special to Dubliners.

Two of the most beautiful evening sites in Dublin are along the banks of the River Liffey. The Custom House and the Four Courts offer gorgeous lighted views at night.

The River cuts through the center of Dublin, and most addresses are geographically described as either north or south of the River Liffey. Once it enters Dublin, a dozen bridges span its girth. The most familiar and popular are the **O'Connell Bridge** and the **Ha'penny Bridge**. The former has been in place for about 200 years. Originally called Carlisle Bridge, its name was changed to honor **Daniel O'Connell**, who fought long and hard for Catholic emancipation – the right of Catholics to be elected to parliament and to participate in the governance of Ireland. The bridge is nearly as wide as it is long and the large statue in the center island of O'Connell Street, as you pass from the south to the north side of Dublin, is a monument to Mr. O'Connell. Ha'penny (pronounced hay'-penny) Bridge, the only strictly pedestrian bridge in Dublin, derives its name from the toll charged to use the bridge in earlier days. Originally called Wellington Bridge, it's officially called the Liffey Bridge. However, most continue to call it the Ha'penny.

Dublin Castle, *Castle Street, open Monday through Friday 10:00am to 5:00pm, Saturdays, Sundays and bank holidays from 2:00pm until 5:00pm. Last admission is 15 minutes before closing. Admission is £3.00 for adults, £2.00 for seniors and students and £1 for children. Tel. (01) 677-7129.* Dublin Castle is symbolic of English rule over Ireland for 600 years, from the early 13th century until the independence of Ireland in 1922. As such, it is not exactly well liked by Dubliners.

However, it *is* a great place to visit. There is a guided tour around the grounds and through the State Apartments, which formerly served as the residences for the English Viceroys. These elaborate rooms are adorned with rich Donegal carpets and Waterford crystal chandeliers, and are truly luxurious. Today the State Apartments are used primarily for ceremonial affairs from time to time. The remainder of the castle has been converted into government offices.

Several of the rooms are exceptionally exquisite. You'll marvel at most of the rooms, but the ones that elicit the most "Oohs" and Ahs" are the Apollo Room (sometimes called the Music Room), the Round Drawing Room, and the Wedgwood Room. The highlight of the Castle is St. Patrick's Hall. This large room (82 feet by 40 feet) is graced with a hand-painted ceiling and beautiful gilded pillars. It is the venue for Irish presidential inaugurations and various state functions.

The oldest section of Dublin Castle is the Record Tower (the public is not allowed in), a part of the original structure dating from 1220. Over the years the Record Tower was also called at one time or another the Black Tower, Gunner's Tower, and Wardrobe Tower.

On the grounds of Dublin Castle is the **Royal Chapel**, also known as the **Church of the Holy Trinity**. This charming little (by cathedral standards) church has beautiful oak panels and lovely stained-glass windows. The exterior is embellished with the carved heads of all the kings and queens of England. The Royal Chapel was completed in 1814 based on the designs of Francis Johnston. It served the Anglican Church for over 125 years. However, beginning in 1943, the Catholic Church began using it for their services, and continues to do so today.

The Chester Beatty Library and Gallery of Oriental Art, *the Clocktower Building behind Dublin Castle, open Tuesday through Friday from 10:00am to 5:00pm, Saturday from 11:00am to 5:00pm and Sunday from 2:00pm to 5:00pm. Admission is free. Tel. (01) 407-0750.* In 1956, Sir Alfred Chester Beatty bequeathed his private collection of Oriental art to Ireland. This outstanding collection of Oriental art and antiquities contains over 22,000 items, including rare books and manuscripts, miniature paintings, over 270 ancient copies of the Koran, clay tablets from Babylon, and some of the earliest known Biblical papyri in existence. In fact, their extensive Biblical collection includes Armenian, Coptic, Ethiopian and Syriac texts.

Dublin City Hall, *Castle Street/Cork Hill, open Monday through Friday 9:00am to 5:00pm. Admission is free. Tel. (01) 679-6111.* City Hall is the home of the Dublin Corporation, the Dublin City government. The building was completed in 1769. The entry hall contains fluted columns that tend to cause your eyes to lift upward, where you'll see an impressive domed ceiling. Further on in the Muniment Room you'll find the Dublin City sword and mace. There are no public tours, but you can walk about in the public areas.

Fishamble Street is the location of historic Dublin. Look for a narrow street next to the relatively modern (great controversy in Dublin over that!) Civic Offices; this is Fishamble Street. The area between Christchurch Cathedral and Wood Quay is where the original Viking settlement of Dylfin was founded in 841. It was originally a fish market, bustling with activity. Excavations in this area during the 1970's unearthed a treasure-load of Viking artifacts, many of which are now housed in the National Museum.

An ironworks now stands on the site of a Music Hall that once stood on the corner of Fishamble Street. Next door, a house with a plaque marks the site of the first public performance of **Handel's** *The Messiah* on April

13, 1742. The event drew over 700 of Dublin's well-heeled aristocracy. The space was limited, and as large crowds were expected, ladies were asked to refrain from wearing hoop skirts and men were asked to leave their swords home!

Christchurch Cathedral, *Christchurch Place, open Monday through Saturday 10:00am until 5:00pm and Sundays between church services. Call for an appointment between November and April Admission is £2.00 for adults, £1.50 for seniors and children, and a family ticket is available for £5.00. Tel. (01) 677-8099.* Christchurch Cathedral was built in 1038 for the Norse King Sitric Silkenbeard. Originally a wooden structure, major renovation was undertaken between 1173 and 1220, and the wooden structure was replaced with stonework. In 1831, the cathedral received one final major facelift, and was redone in the Gothic style you see today.

This magnificent cathedral includes a self-guided tour through the ancient crypt below the cathedral. It's a little dusty, so if you suffer from asthma you may want to forego this part of the cathedral. Two of the more surprising sights in the crypt are the mummified bodies of a cat and rat that apparently participated in a deadly game of "cat and mouse" in days gone by. The rat raced into an organ pipe with the cat hot on his tail. The cat became lodged in the pipe, and both diner and dinner perished.

The tomb of **Strongbow**, the first Norman conqueror of Ireland, is located in the cathedral. Not to burst your enthusiastic bubble at seeing the image of the eight centuries-old great Norman conqueror of Ireland, but Strongbow's actual tomb was destroyed 400 years ago when part of the roof caved in. The tomb was replaced with the effigy of a long-forgotten knight. However, the heart (yes, the actual heart) of St. Lawrence O'Toole is preserved in a metal casket at the east end of the cathedral. He was the Archbishop of Dublin at the time of Strongbow's invasion.

The most noticeable aspects of the interior of Christchurch Cathedral are the elaborate stonework and elegant stained glass that grace the walls of the cathedral. Like St. Patrick's, Christchurch Cathedral belongs to the Church of Ireland.

Dublin Medieval Heritage Centre, *Christchurch Place, open daily from 10:00am until 5:00pm from April through September, and Monday through Saturday 11:00am to 4:00pm, Sundays and holidays from 10:00am to 4:30pm. Admission is £3.95 for adults, and £2.90 for students and senior citizens. There is a family pass available (2 adults and 2 children) for £10 (children under 5 are free). Tel. (01) 679-4611.* Located in Synod Hall across from Christchurch Cathedral, the Dublin Medieval Heritage Centre (more commonly called Dublinia) allows visitors to step back into 400 years of Dublin history. This is one of the best history learning centers in Dublin. You'll receive an audio headset that will guide you through the exhibit, beginning with the invasion of Strongbow in 1170, after which you'll be whisked through the sights and sounds of medieval Dublin up until the mid-1500's. Life-size models and rebuilt city scenes will help transport you back to days gone by. The tour is enlightening, educational, and entertaining – truly an enjoyable way to learn about Ireland's medieval times.

Tailors Hall, *Back Lane of Christchurch Place, open Monday through Friday from 9:00am to 5:00pm. Admission is free. Tel. 454-4794.* Tailors Hall is the last of what was once many guild halls in Dublin. Dating from 1706, this building has served as the guildhall of a number of trades, including saddlers, tanners, surgeons, and hosiers. Currently, it is the home of *An Taisce*, the Irish National Trust, whose charter is to preserve and restore the many ancient buildings in Ireland. Be sure to check out the carved musician's balcony.

Francis Street has become the de-facto antique section of Dublin. Although you'll find antique shops elsewhere in Dublin, nowhere is there the concentration as thick as you'll find here on Francis Street, just a block west of St. Patrick's Cathedral. Visitors will be enticed by many of the small shops, some of whose owners are as precious and delightful as the antiques they peddle.

Church of Ireland St. Audoen's, *High Street, open June through September daily from 10:00am until 4:30pm. Admission is £1.50 for adults, £1.00 for seniors and students, 60p for children and a family ticket is available for £4.00. Tel. (01) 677-0088.* St. Audoen's Church is the only existing medieval church in Dublin. It was originally called St. Ouen's, but has been altered through the years to its present name – St. Audoen's. The church is in a lovely park-like setting, surrounded by portions of the old city wall, and includes the only surviving gate to the city, **St. Audoen's Arch**. St. Audoen's boasts a set of bells that were made in 1423, and they are thought to be among Ireland's oldest. An extra treat is a good audiovisual presentation called *The Flame on the Hill*, which covers the history of Ireland before the arrival of the Vikings.

If you walk down the steps from the grounds of St. Audoen's to the Arch, you'll be on Cork Street, originally the location of most of Dublin's coffin-makers. Don't mistake this St. Audoen's for the nearby Catholic St. Audoen's. This one is a mere 700 or so years newer than the Catholic church of the same name.

The Dublin Viking Adventure, *Essex Quay, open Tuesday through Saturday from 10:00am until 4:30pm. Closed 1:00pm to 2:00pm from November through February. Tel. 679-6040.* The Dublin Viking Adventure does its best to transport its visitors back to the days when Vikings ruled this part of Ireland. You are escorted about the recreated Viking city, including houses and shops and other typical sights, — even the sounds and smells. If you can, stay into the evening and enjoy a Viking dinner banquet.

The adventure all takes place within the walls of the converted Saints Michael and John Church. This former Catholic church has also served as a playhouse, so the Viking actors are right at home there.

St. Patrick's Cathedral, *Patrick Street, open Monday through Friday 9:00am to 6:00pm, Saturdays 9:00am to 5:00pm, and Sundays 10:00am to 4:30pm (it closes at 4:00pm on weekends between November and March). Admission is £2.30 for adults, £1.60 for seniors and children, and a family ticket is available for £5.50. Tel. (01) 475-4817.* If you see only two cathedrals in Dublin, this should be one of them. Aside from the peaceful grounds, the immense beauty of the cathedral is truly a sight to behold.

Considered the National Cathedral of the Church of Ireland, St. Patrick's was founded in 1191. But its history goes back much farther. Local historians will tell you that this is perhaps the oldest Christian site in Dublin. It was on this spot that tradition says St. Patrick himself performed baptisms. Originally built outside the Dublin city walls, the location earned St. Patrick's the reputation of being the "church of the people," while Christchurch, which was built within the city walls, was considered by some to be the "church of the government."

Physically, St. Patrick's is impressive. The largest church in Ireland, its west clock tower rises 141 feet above Patrick Street, and the spire atop the tower rises another 101 feet, making the tip of the spire nearly 250 feet above your head. As you walk into St. Patrick's, if it feels like the front of the cathedral is about a football field's length away, you're exactly right: the interior of the cathedral is 300 feet long. As you might expect, St. Patrick's also boasts a number of stunning stained glass windows.

It's hard to believe that Oliver Cromwell showed his contempt for this magnificent structure by demanding that his horses be stabled inside the cathedral. This was a practice he replicated throughout the country at other churches, cathedrals, and town halls.

Jonathan Swift, the author of *Gulliver's Travels*, was Dean of St. Patrick's for over 30 years, from 1713 to 1745. His pulpit is still on display in the cathedral, along with sundry items belonging to him. At the west end of the nave you'll find Jonathan's bust, along with his pointed epitaph which he wrote: "Here he lies, where bitter indignation can no longer lacerate his heart. Go traveler and imitate if you can one who was, to the best of his powers, a defender of Liberty."

The organ, one of the more modern additions to the Cathedral, was installed in 1902, and is considered the most robust and powerful in all of Ireland.

The year Columbus set sail for America, two of Ireland's most powerful men, the Earl of Kildare and the Earl of Ormond, had been warring. The Earl of Ormond sought sanctuary in the Chapter House, and a standoff ensued. Tired of the war, the Earl of Kildare approached the

Chapter House and chopped a hole in the door. As an act of reconciliation, he thrust his arm through the hole and grasped the hand of his enemy, ending the war. The door – called the "Door of Reconciliation" – is on display in the northeast section of the cathedral.

Marsh's Library, *St. Patrick's Close, Patrick Street, open Monday and Wednesday through Friday from 10:00am to 12:45pm and from 2:00pm to 5:00pm, and Saturdays from 10:00am until 12:45pm. Admission is £2.00 for adults and £1 for seniors and children. Tel. (01) 454-3511.* If you are a book lover, this is a place you'll want to visit. Narcissus Marsh, the Archbishop of Dublin, established the first public library in Ireland, Marsh's Library in 1701. The brick exterior of the library is unpretentious, and doesn't prepare you for what you'll find inside.

The decor is magnificent and dark oak bookcases and wire cages house over 25,000 books and some 300 rare manuscripts. Most of the books are from the 16th through 18th centuries. Famed writers like Jonathan Swift and James Joyce used the library in their day. The Stillfleet Collection alone has over 10,000 books that date back to 1705. Books can no longer be checked out at Marsh's, but you can view some of the volumes in one of the wire cages. Marsh's Library is located behind St. Patrick's Cathedral.

Guinness Brewery, *Crane Street, open April through September Monday through Saturday 9:30am until 5:00pm, and Sunday from 10:30am to 4:30pm, October through March Monday through Saturday from 9:30am to 4:00pm and Sunday from noon to 4:00pm. Admission is £4 for adults, £3 for students, and senior citizens and £1 for children. (01) 453-8364 (information line). Tel. (01) 408-4800. (for reservations for large groups, or to talk to the Hop Store).* A trip to Ireland would not be complete unless you try their world famous Guinness beer. And there is no better place than the sprawling, 60-acre Guinness Brewery where Dubliners swear the beer tastes better! For the uninitiated, Guinness is a dark, heavy, bitter beer with a creamy head served at room temperature. For many, it is an acquired taste, but all beer lovers should try it at least once.

Arthur Guinness founded the brewery on the banks of the River Liffey in 1759, and his descendants have carried on his work. The brewery produces an amazing four million pints of Guinness beer *per day*. Tours of the brewery itself are no longer conducted, but a fine audiovisual presentation on the history of the brewery is available in the Hop Store. At the close of the presentation, a complimentary sample of Guinness is available to those who wish to sample the dark brew.

The four-story Hop Store has been converted into a museum, and the top floor serves as a venue for art shows.

South Dublin – Grafton Street District

Molly Malone Statue, *Suffolk and Grafton Streets*. O'Connell Street may have *The Floozie in the Jacuzzi*, but Grafton Street has the bronze statue of **Molly Malone**, *The Dish with the Fish!* Molly Malone, standing at the corner of Suffolk and Grafton Streets, is a featured character in an old Irish folk song. The song is taught to school children, sung in pubs, and bellowed at rugby, soccer, hurling, and Gaelic football games. The bodice on Molly's dress is so scandalously low (even for a statue!) that she has another name: *The Tart with the Cart*.

Trinity College, *College Street, open daily from 8:00am to 10:00pm. Admission is free. Tel. (01) 608-2320.* Stately Trinity College is always alive with activity, both inside and outside its grounds. Personally, one of the things I like best about Trinity College is its *presence*. During your stay in Dublin, you will see it in paintings and drawings that are hundreds of years old – it was such an important site in the 16th through 19th centuries. It still is, for that matter.

Trinity College was built during the reign of **Queen Elizabeth I** in 1592 on the grounds of confiscated Catholic property, the Augustinian Priory of All Hallows. Most of the buildings now date from the early 1700s to the mid-1800s. Its buildings and grounds cover some 40 acres in the heart of the city center.

Currently, Trinity College has about 8,000 full-time students. It was the first European university to allow women to earn degrees. However, for most of Trinity College's history, Catholics were barred from entering, not by the college, but rather by the Catholic Church. In the 1960s, this ban was lifted and Trinity College has become the renowned university it is today.

Statues of two of Trinity's most famous alumni — orator Edmund Burke and poet Oliver Goldsmith flank the front gate (known creatively as *The Front Gate!*). As you move beyond its huge wooden doors, check out the many announcement boards to see what's going on. Often, lunchtime concerts are scheduled, and everyone is welcome to attend.

Book of Kells, *Trinity College Colonnades, open Monday through Saturday 9:30am to 5:00pm, Sunday noon to 4:30pm. From June to September Sunday hours are 9:30am to 4:30pm (last tour begins half an hour before closing). Admission is £4.50 for adults, £4.00 for senior citizens, students and children (children under 12 are free), and there is a family ticket available for £9 (two adults and four children). Tel. (01) 677-2941.* Without a doubt, the most important holding at Trinity College is the Book of Kells, the ornately illustrated four Gospels written by the monks of the Kells monastery in County Meath. Written (drawn?) in the 9th century, the Book of Kells is four volumes of elaborate ornamental drawings of the four Gospels. The title pages of each Gospel are particularly elaborate. There are also gorgeous pictures depicting many scenes from Christ's life, including his temptation and arrest.

The Book of Kells is kept in a glass case in a room with muted lighting. Two Gospels are shown at a time, and the pages are turned each day. The pages are calfskin made from 185 calves! As you look at the incredible craftsmanship and stunning artwork of the books, it's hard to imagine that these lovely works were once hidden under a roll of sod to protect them from the ravages of invaders!

As you enter the room, there are also cases along the walls (which you walk past while in line), that contain other ancient books, including the **Book of Durrow**, which was written in 675, and is the earliest surviving decorated book of the Gospels. The **Book of Armagh** is another you'll see, and it was written in 807.

To see the Book of Kells, you'll probably have to stand in line, especially during the peak tourist season. But the line moves quickly thanks to college employees who gently encourage you to look and move along your way, a fact you appreciate more when the line moves than you do when you are finally the one who gets to look at the beautiful pages!

After you view of the Book of Kells, you are treated to a fascinating stroll through the lavish **Long Room of the Old Library** on your way out. This impressive room is over 200 feet long and 40 feet wide. For nearly 200 years, Trinity College has been receiving a copy of every book published in Ireland and England, and many of them are on display here in the Old Library. You'll also be in the midst of another of the library's prized possessions: tall oak bookcases filled with over 200,000 old volumes of books. You walk between busts of **Homer**, **Plato**, **Cicero**, **Newton**, **Demosthenes**, and many other scholars.

Included in the holdings of the library are first editions of some of Shakespeare's works, as well as copies of the original printing of the *Proclamation of 1916* (Ireland's equivalent of the Declaration of Independence). Watch for a copy of the *Proclamation of 1916* as soon as you enter the Long Hall. (It's usually displayed on your left.) In addition, there is a wonderful 15th-century harp on display. It is in remarkable condition, from its oak and willow woodwork to its 29 brass strings. Legend has it that the harp once belonged to the Irish warrior/poet/king Brian Boru; however, scholars point out that Brian was born some 500 years before the harp was made (spoilsports!).

The Dublin Experience, *Trinity College Davis Theater, Arts Building, open daily between 10:00am and 5:00pm from late May through the end of September. The shows run every hour on the hour. Admission is £3.00 for adults (£5 for the combined Book of Kells and the Dublin Experience), £2.50 for students and senior citizens (£4 combined ticket), £1.50 children. Tel. (01) 702-1688.* Trinity College has developed an excellent multimedia presentation on the first 1,000 years of Dublin history, although it covers much of the same ground other similar presentations in the city do. If you've seen any of them, pass on this one.

Bank of Ireland, *College Green, open Monday through Friday from 10:00am to 12:30pm and 1:30pm to 4:00pm. Admission is free. Tel. (01) 671-1671.* Across from Trinity College at the corner of College and Dame Streets is the semi-circular Bank of Ireland. When the edifice was completed in 1729, it housed both houses of Parliament – the House of Commons and the House of Lords, and was the first building ever built for the express purpose of housing Parliament.

In the House of Lords hangs two very old and very impressive tapestries: one portrays William of Orange's defeat of King James II at the Battle of the Boyne in 1690, and the other depicts the 15-week Siege of Derry in 1689. These were significant turning points in Ireland's history. Both tapestries have hung here since 1735 – over 250 years! Encased in glass at one end of the room is the ornate speaker's mace.

In 1800, the Irish Parliament did something no other Parliament had done or has since done – they voted themselves out of existence, handing over all governance to the good graces of London. The building was then sold to the Bank of Ireland, who has been its only tenant since then. When the Bank of Ireland purchased the building, they converted the House of Commons into a spacious lobby, but left the House of Lords intact. You can browse around the House of Lords (it's not very big), and nearby attendants will answer questions and tell you a little of the history of the room and building.

Across from Trinity College is **Grafton Street**, a long pedestrian open-air mall. Grafton Street is a fascinating blend of antique, jewelry, and upscale shops, with a generous mix of *buskers,* street entertainers, ranging from musicians to magicians, jugglers to Marionette masters, and a host of other talented individuals. Street peddlers also hawk their wares, ranging from silk ties and silver rings to cassettes and macramé.

To say that Grafton Street is an experience not to be missed would be an understatement. Give yourself plenty of time to stroll along the crowded sidewalks and sample a wee bit of this aspect of Irish culture. The naturally demonstrative nature of the buskers comes through delightfully as they sense an audience gathering around them. Watch for **Rocky Thompson**, my favorite busker, on Grafton Street sitting astride a small box and playing an old guitar retrofitted with half a dozen piano-like keys, and decorated with various Irish coins glued to the guitar's face. You'll be mesmerized as you listen to Rocky croon out a diverse assortment of tunes, from Irish ballads to Beatles and Bob Dylan songs, to a host of other artists. His unique voice, style and showmanship routinely win him large audiences.

DUBLIN LITERARY PUB CRAWL

The Literary Pub Crawl meets at The Duke Pub, Duke Street, May through September: Nightly at 7:30pm, Monday - Saturday 3:00pm, Sundays at noon. October through April: Sundays at noon, Friday and Saturday 7:30pm. Admission is £6.50. Tel. (01) 454-0228. As you walk south on Grafton Street from Trinity College, look for their temporary sign along the left side of the walk directing you onto Duke Street. The Duke Pub is about a half block down on your left. The admission charge doesn't cover the cost of any drinks you consume as you move from pub to pub.

Officially called the **Jameson Dublin Literary Pub Crawl**, *this trip around Dublin is well worth your time. Local actors (eight of them) take turns entertaining, informing, shocking, and delighting their guests with tales of Ireland's most noteworthy writers:* **Behan, Joyce, Yeats, Wilde, Goldsmith, Shaw,** *and others. Each session is conducted by a two-some (mine were Derrick and Donough).*

These very accomplished actors take your group on a tour of several pubs frequented by famous writers – usually four or five, as well as onto the grounds of Trinity College. Along the way they regale you with stories and anecdotes from the lives of these writers. You'll find out which journalist referred to himself as a "bicycle built for two" (and why) and learn which writer characterized himself as "A good drinker who had trouble with writing." Blended in is some of the history of Irish struggles against the English, but it's done without a lot of serious political rhetoric.

A rollicking good time, full of literary one-liners, a little irreverence, lots of laughs, (a little bawdy at times), and plenty of good, mostly clean fun.

Dublin Civic Museum, *58 South William Street, open Tuesday through Saturday 10:00am to 6:00pm, Sundays 11:00am to 2:00pm. Free admission. Tel. (01) 679-4260.* This small museum is a winner for history buffs. The museum's primary focus is the history of Dublin, its people, and its environs. The eclectic collection includes Stone Age implements to Viking tokens to the sculpted head of Admiral Horatio Nelson. Admiral Nelson's image once had a slightly more lofty and dignified position atop Nelson's Pillar beside the General Post Office. However, in 1966 on the fiftieth anniversary of the Easter Rising, Admiral Nelson lost his head, and pillar, to a bomb. Seems as though Irish loyalists resented the good Admiral's image presiding over the goings-on at the GPO!

Powerscourt Townhouse Centre, *Clarendon Street.* As you are walking south on Grafton Street, turn right onto narrow Johnston's Court and you'll find Powerscourt Townhouse – a converted Georgian townhouse chock full of a score of shops and cafes. It's one of the most charming "malls" you'll ever visit.

Mansion House, *Dawson Street.* The official residence for the Lord Mayor of Dublin, the Mansion House was built in 1710 for **John Dawson**. Five years later he sold it to the Dublin Corporation to serve as the Mayor's residence, which it has served as since that time. Several important events in modern Irish history happened within the four walls of the Mansion House: the first Irish Parliament met here in 1919; the Declaration of Independence from England in 1919 was adopted, and the truce that ended the fighting between England and Ireland in 1921 was signed here.

Unfortunately, the house is not generally open to the public, although it is often the site for various exhibits such as antique shows and book fairs. When special exhibits are showing, street placards will be out on the street at the entrance to the Mansion House, and information on the exhibit will generally appear in the local newspapers. Regardless of what the exhibit is, if you see one advertised it would be worth your time to take it in, as it will give you the opportunity to see the wonderful interior of the Mansion House.

The Royal Irish Academy, *19 Dawson Street, open Monday through Friday 10:30am to 5:00pm. Admission is free. Tel. (01) 676-2570.* The Royal Irish Academy was founded in 1752 and has been located here since 1852. The leading scholarly society in Dublin, the Royal Irish Academy takes great pride in its collection of ancient manuscripts. One of its most valuable is the Psalter of **Saint Columcille**, a partial copy of the Vulgate version of Psalms. Another is the *Book of the Dun Cow*, a 12th-century manuscript penned at Clonmacnoise. Each week the Academy presents an exhibition of an ancient manuscript.

Genealogical Office, *2 Kildare Street, open Monday through Friday from 9:30am to 5:30pm. Admission is free.* So your mother was an O'Kelly and your grandfather a Murphy, and you'd like to do a little genealogical research into the family tree? The Genealogical Office is a good place to begin. The employees here are helpful in assisting you to identify and locate those long-lost cousins.

Researching your genealogy in Ireland is like doing it anywhere in the world: the more information you have the better, and the more successful your search is likely to be. Pump Mom and Dad, your grandparents and anyone else in your family for as much information as you can: dates of birth (even an approximate year), county, town, parish, maiden names, parent's names, etc. See the *Genealogy* chapter in this book for more information.

Heraldic Museum, *2 Kildare Street, open Monday through Friday from 10:30am to 12:30pm and 2:00pm to 4:30pm. Admission is free. Tel. (01) 661-4877.* Co-located with the Genealogical Office, the Heraldic Museum has a fine display of coats of arms that extend back many centuries. Go in and see if you can find yours! In addition, they'll have maps that list the traditional ancestral homes of thousands of Irish surnames. So, if you cannot find yours family surname in the *Genealogy* chapter in this travel guide, the Heraldic Museum should be able to assist you in this area.

In addition to being a phenomenal resource for genealogical research, the Genealogical office / Heraldic Museum serves as a small museum, with over 500 ancient Irish artifacts on display.

Leinster House, *Kildare Street, open when Parliament is not in session. Admission is free. Tel. (01) 678-9911.* Built over 250 years ago (1725) for the Duke of Leinster, Leinster House serves as the meeting place for the Irish House of Representatives (*Dail Eireann*) and the Senate (*Seanad Eireann*).

Visitors are only admitted to the visitor's gallery upon invitation of a member of Parliament. Check with the Dublin Tourism Center, *Tel. (01) 605-7777,* to see if they can arrange a visit (they often can). The Irish sometimes view their elected officials with humor. As an example, Leinster House has sometimes been referred to as "The National Home for the Terminally Bewildered."

The National Library of Ireland, *Kildare Street, open Monday through Wednesday from 10:00am until 9:00pm, Thursday and Friday 10:00am until 5:00pm, and Saturdays 10:00am until 1:00pm. Admission is free. Tel. (01) 603-0200.* The National Library of Ireland is so much more than a library. First of all, it is a visual treasure. Architecturally stunning, the highlights of the library are the large rotunda and the domed reading room. In addition, exhibits are frequently available on Irish art and history. Many first editions are owned by the library, including the works of Ireland's most famous (writing) sons: James Joyce, George Bernard Shaw, Oscar Wilde, etc.

National Museum of Ireland, *Kildare Street, open Tuesday through Saturday 10:00am to 5:00pm and Sunday from 2:00pm to 5:00pm. Admission is free (except for special exhibits). Tel. (01) 677-7444.* The National Museum of Ireland recently celebrated its 100th anniversary (1890 – 1990) and is looking forward to another outstanding 100+ years. Located next to the Leinster House on Kildare Street, the National Museum of Ireland was originally the combination of several historical collections. It has a number of fascinating displays which take you through the history of Ireland from the Bronze Age (2200 BC to 700 BC) to the present.

The Treasury Exhibition (the only part of the museum requiring a modest admission fee) includes the lovely Tara Brooch (8th-century), the Ardagh Chalice (8th-century), and the silver and bronzed Cross of Cong (12th-century), and much more. One of the highlights of the museum is a replica of the Newgrange passage grave in County Meath. The actual cross-shaped tomb – about an hour north of Dublin – is nearly 5,000 years old and is wonderfully preserved. If you can't make the drive, be sure and see the replica at the museum. *Ar Thóir na Saoirse*, which means "The Road to Independence," is a permanent exhibit that deals with the major personalities and events that took place from 1916 to 1922 in the struggle for Ireland's independence.

Much like the Smithsonian, there are multiple locations for the National Museum of Ireland. This location contains the archaeology and history exhibits, the location on Merrion Street houses the natural history collection, and the site on Benburb Street houses the decorative arts collection. A shuttle bus runs between the various locations throughout the day.

Shelbourne Hotel, *27 St. Stephen's Green North. Tel. (01) 676-6471.* The Shelbourne Hotel bears mentioning here. Across the street from the north side of St. Stephen's Green, The Shelbourne is where the drafting of the Irish Constitution took place in 1922. The staff does not mind you coming in and looking around a bit. Better yet, stop in for a spot of tea or coffee in the superb Lord Mayor's lounge. As you walk into the Lord Mayor's lounge, you'll feel as though you have walked into a Victorian sitting room. The feeling is rich and warm – emanating both from the elegance of the room as well as the sincerity of the greeting and service you'll receive.

Huguenot Cemetery, *St. Stephen's Green North.* As you face the Shelbourne Hotel, several yards to the right of the hotel is the Huguenot Cemetery, final resting place of French Huguenots who left persecution in their native lands for Ireland. Alas, you cannot walk through the grounds, but you can view them from the wrought-iron gates. The sight of the well-maintained cemetery is one of quiet and peaceful tranquillity; something the Huguenots found little of during their stressful lives.

St. Stephen's Green, *at the south end of Grafton Street*, is a very peaceful, serene city park. In the 17th century this 22-acre area was an open common, but in the early 1800s it became a private garden for residents whose property circled it. An annual one guinea (about $1.75) maintenance fee was charged for upkeep and access to the gardens. In 1877, Sir Arthur Guinness (of brewery fame) was instrumental in passing an act of Parliament that opened the park to the public. Because of his magnanimous gesture, Dubliners allowed him to personally pay for many of the improvements to the park, including the lake, fountains, trees and many of the gardens.

There are a number of memorials in the park that are worthy of your attention. The Romanesque arch over the main entrance at the northwest corner of the park is called the Fusiliers Arch, and it is a memorial to the Dublin Fusiliers who fought and died during the Boer War. There is a memorial dedicated to the memory of **W. B. Yeats**. Don't miss the fountain and statue of the Three Fates, a statue given to the Irish by a grateful German government for the relief they provided to the needy at the close of World War II. Other individuals memorialized in St. Stephen's Green include **James Joyce**, **Wolfe Tone**, and those who perished in the potato famine.

There is a children's playground, lots of ducks for the children (and you) to feed, a Victorian bandstand (where free lunch time concerts are given throughout the summer), and a unique garden designed especially for the blind. The plants are labeled in Braille, and they are also resilient enough to be handled.

Newman House, *85/86 St. Stephen's Green South, open June through September Tuesday through Friday from 10:00am until 4:30pm, Saturdays 1:00pm until 3:30pm and Sundays from 11:00am until 1:00pm. Admission is £1 for adults, and 75p for children and senior citizens.* Across the street from the south side of St. Stephen's Green is Newman House. Newman House is named after **Cardinal John Henry Newman**, who founded the first Catholic University in Dublin at Number 86, St. Stephen's Green South. **James Joyce** was one of the more illustrious individuals to call the Catholic University his alma mater (he attended from 1899 to 1902). In fact, one of the rooms has been renovated to look as classroom would have looked at the turn of the century. The period furniture nicely accents the masterful plaster work in both houses. The small admission fee includes a guided tour of both buildings, as well as a short video presentation on the history of the building.

Don't forget to take a peek at **Iveagh Gardens** that run behind Newman House and **Iveagh House**. The entrance to the gardens is around the corner, left at Harcourt Street, then left on Clonmel Street to the garden gate.

National Concert Hall, *Earlsfort Terrace, prices range from £3 to £15. Tel. (01) 475-1666.* At the southeast corner of St. Stephen's Green and across the street from the Conrad Hotel is the National Concert Hall. Formerly the location of the University College of Dublin, the Concert Hall is the site of many events throughout the year. It is especially dazzling on performance nights, when it is lit with spotlights. Large posters in the DART stations and the local newspapers list the dates and times of the performances that are held at the National Concert Hall.

Royal Hibernian Academy (RHA) Gallagher Gallery, *Ely Place, open Monday through Wednesday and Friday through Saturday from 11:00am to 5:00pm; Thursday from 11:00am to 9:00pm, Sundays from 2:00pm until 5:00pm. Admission is free.* This small Gallery houses an eclectic collection of Irish and continental art. With several other more notable art museums close by, this one tends to get passed over by most visitors. I enjoyed it.

Natural History Museum, *Merrion Street, open Tuesday through Saturday from 10:00am to 5:00pm, Sunday from 2:00pm until 5:00pm. Admission is free. Tel. (01) 667-7444.* The Natural History Museum, founded in 1857, is part of the National Museum of Ireland. George Bernard Shaw reportedly said that he owed much of his education to the gallery and showed his gratitude by leaving one third of his estate to the museum.

The collection includes an outstanding exhibit of Irish fauna, including an especially impressive skeleton of a giant Irish deer, a distant cousin of the elk, African and Asian animals, and two large whale skeletons suspended from the ceiling. (The whales are former Irish residents *of sorts* – they washed up on Irish shores!) The museum is also internationally renowned for its extensive entomological collection. If you are vacationing with children, I'm sure they'd enjoy this museum.

National Gallery of Ireland, *Merrion Square West, open Monday through Saturday 10:00am to 5:30pm, (Thursday until 8:30pm), Sunday from 2:00pm until 5:00pm. Admission is free. Tel. (01) 661-5133.* Established by an Act of Parliament almost 150 years ago (1854), the National Gallery of Ireland spent 10 years collecting paintings, sculptures, and other pieces of art before opening in January 1864. The grand opening of the museum boasted over 100 paintings and numerous statues. Today there are over 2,400 paintings, 300 sculptures and an incredible assortment of various other pieces to catch your eye.

If you are hoping to see works of art by Irish painters, you won't be disappointed. I suppose every major Irish artist – and many not-so-major artists – are represented here. In addition, there is a fine European collection, including works by such notables as **Rembrandt, Degas, El Greco, Goya, Monet, Reynolds, Rubens, Titian, Van Dyck**, and others. One of the museum's most extraordinary aspects is a four story circular staircase lined with paintings of three centuries worth of notable personalities in Irish history, a kind of wall of fame.

Guided tours are offered on Saturday afternoons at 3:00pm and Sundays at 2:30pm, 3:15pm, and 4:00pm. If you find yourself here around lunchtime, there is an award-winning self-serve restaurant available to meet your gastronomical needs.

Laid out in the center of one of the most impressive displays of Georgian architecture in the city, **Merrion Square** is a place to get away from the omnipresent Dublin traffic. Merrion Square is about a half-block south and east of the Trinity College grounds. The park dates from 1762, and is a lovely assemblage of gardens, shrubs, and trees. Over the years, a number of Ireland's most important and esteemed citizens called the fine Georgian townhouses around Merrion Square home, including **Oscar Wilde's** parents *(Number 1)*, **Daniel O'Connell** *(Number 58)*, **W. B. Yeats** *(Numbers 52 and 82)* and the **Duke of Wellington** *(Number 24 Upper*

Merrion Street). Many of the homes have plaques identifying their famous inhabitants.

Number Twenty-Nine Fitzwilliam Street, *open Tuesday through Saturday from 10:00am to 5:00pm, Sunday from 2:00pm to 5:00pm. Admission is £2.50 for adults, £1.00 for seniors and students, children under 16 free. Tel. (01) 702-6165.* The National Museum of Ireland and the Electricity Supply Board have combined their talents and funds to restore Number Twenty-Nine as it likely was in the late 18th century – the home of a middle-class family. Great attention to detail has been given to everything from the woodwork to the furnishings, walls and ceilings. Take special note of the floor and window coverings, as well as the numerous paintings. Number Twenty-Nine is a little more subdued than a similar exhibit at the **Newman House**, but both are nice (and this one is free).

South Dublin – Ballsbridge District

The **Grand Canal** runs from Dublin Bay in a semi-circular route around the south side of Dublin and then it wends its way out into the Irish countryside all the way to the river Shannon in the center of the country. The Grand Canal was used to transport passengers as well as fragile cargo such as pottery and glass products (manufacturers preferred the smooth canal to the bumpy roads). Farmers also used the canal to bring produce to market.

Construction on the canal began in 1756 and was completed in 1804, and was formerly in constant use for commercial ventures, as small barges and canal boats navigated its waters through a series of locks. Today, the paths along the canal see the most use as Dubliners and others stroll along the banks.

Sandymount Strand is the closest beach to Dublin. It's about three miles long, and when the tide goes out, it extends about a mile out. A favorite beach of **James Joyce**, Sandymount Strand has a prominent role in Joyce's work *Ulysses.* This is a popular place to collect shellfish. The walk out to Poolbeg lighthouse is a pleasant one, and a favorite of locals and tourists alike. This isn't a particularly good beach for swimming, though, as the surf has a tendency to come in very rapidly. Walk along its shores, or search for shellfish, but be alert for the rapidly rising tides.

You can reach Sandymount Strand by taking the DART to Sandymount Station. Head east on Sandymount Avenue to Gilford, then you can turn left or right: either way will get you to Sandymount Strand. It's about a 300-yard walk.

Waterways Visitors Centre, *Ringsend Basin, open June to September every day from 9:30am to 5:30pm, and October through May Wednesday through Sunday from 12:30pm to 5:00pm. Call for appointment November through February. Admission is £2.00 for adults, £1.50 for seniors and students, £1.00* *for children and a family ticket is available for £5.00. Tel. (01) 677-7510.* This unique modern building sits on stilts in the Grand Canal Basin near the Pearse Street Bridge. It houses an interesting exhibit on the history and importance of the various waterways in Ireland, including a working model of a canal lock. There is also a section on the marine life – animal and plant – found throughout the canals.

West Dublin

Phoenix Park originally opened to the public over 250 years ago, is the largest city park in Europe at over 1,700 acres, and it is a delightful place to visit. If you enjoy parks and have the time, you could easily spend a half day here; a full day if you also go to the zoo, watch a polo match or a cricket game. With green fields punctuated by pools and ponds, the park serves as a relaxing contrast to the hustle and bustle of the city. Phoenix Park is about two miles from Dublin's city center.

As you enter the park from its main gate on the southeast side, the 195-foot monument honoring Arthur Wellesley, the first Duke of Wellington, greets you. You may ask yourself why this British general who defeated Napoleon at Waterloo rates a monument in Dublin? After all, a similar monument to the British **Admiral Nelson** – another victor over Napoleon – was so ill-received by Dubliners that it was blown to pieces by some unknown hand. The answer is simple — Wellington was a native Dubliner. Despite his choice of armies, his victory at Waterloo earned him fame and hero status in Ireland. An ironic tidbit of historical trivia is the fact that Arthur Wellesley detested his Irish roots. When queried about his Irish beginnings, he reportedly replied, "The fact that I was born in a stable does not make me a horse." Point well made!

Across the road from Wellington's monument is the **People's Garden**, a lovely set of banked gardens surrounding a small lake. Just ahead on your right is the **Phoenix Zoo**, which was founded in 1831. It has a wide variety of animals, and an area for the children to get "up close and personal" with a number of less exotic creatures like rabbits, chickens, and goats.

The **polo grounds** are just beyond the zoo, and practices or matches are fun to watch, whether you understand all the rules or not (I don't). The horses are magnificent, and to see them wheeling and charging is really a treat. The riders aren't bad either.

Just past the polo grounds is the home of the president of Ireland, called **Aras an Uachtarain**. In 1882, the British Chief Secretary to Ireland and his assistant were murdered outside the house by five extremists, members of a rebel band called "The Invincibles." One of the killers turned state's witness, and his four partners were executed at Kilmainham jail. Shortly afterwards, the pardoned killer tried to flee the country for

Cape Town, but was assassinated by another member of the Invincibles. The murderer of the murderer/informant was later convicted and executed.

On the far south side of the park is the former site of the **Dublin Dueling Grounds**, where the gentility of Dublin came to shoot at each other. Today the area hosts far more civilized hostility and competition in the form of hurling, cricket, and football. Matches/games are typically played around 3:00pm on Saturdays and Sundays from mid-May through September.

The beautiful park is not named after the mythological bird that rises from the ashes, but rather from the Irish words *fionn uisce* (clear water), which sounds like Phoenix in English. On nice days, old men and women in their Sunday best sit on many of the park benches, just enjoying the nice weather and watching the people go by. Families cavort on the grass, visit the zoo, and feed the omnipresent ducks. Lovers walk arm and arm oblivious to the beauty around them.

Dublin Zoo, *Phoenix Park, open Easter through September on Monday through Saturday from 9:30am until 6:00pm and Sunday from 10:30am to 9:00pm, October through March on Monday through Saturday from 9:30am until 5:00pm and Sunday from 10:30am to 5:00pm. Admission is £5.50 for adults, £4.00 for students and £3.00 for children under 16, 3 and younger are free. Family tickets available for £13 (two adults and two children), or £15.00 (two adults and four children). Tel. (01) 677-1425.* The zoo's main claim to fame is that lions breed here almost as well as they do in the wild. They are one of the few zoos in the world that can make that claim. And they do it in a big way – over 700 lions have been bred here since they began the program in 1851. The famous MGM lion claims the Dublin Zoo as his birthplace.

Ashtown Castle, *Phoenix Park, open daily from mid-March through May from 9:30am until 5:00pm, daily from June through September from 10:00am to 6:00pm, daily in October from 9:30am to 5:00pm, November and December on Saturday and Sunday from 9:30am to 4:30pm, and January through mid-March on Saturday and Sunday from 9:30am to 4:30pm. Admission is £2.00 for adults, £1.50 for seniors and students, £1.00 for children and a family ticket is available for £5.00. Tel. (01) 677-0095.* This unassuming medieval fortress was built in the 17th century. The small visitors center hosts presentations on the history of Phoenix Park and on the various plants and animals you'll find there. I was frankly underwhelmed, but you might find it interesting.

Kilmainham Gaol Historical Museum, *Inchicore Road, open April through September daily from 9:30am until 6:00pm, and October through March Monday through Friday from 9:30am until 5:00pm and Sunday from 10:00am until 6:00pm. The last tour begins one hour before closing. Admission is £3.00 for adults, £2.00 for seniors and £1.25 for students and children, and a family ticket is available for £7.50. Tel. (01) 677-6801.* Step into the darker side of

Ireland's past. This restored prison gives its guests a peek into the terrible conditions endured by Irish patriots awaiting execution or a one-way ticket to Australia. From its first political prisoners in 1796 until its last in 1924, Kilmainham Gaol meant nothing but misery for Irish patriots. Among the most infamous acts committed here was the execution of those who penned their names to the Proclamation of the Republic in 1916 (the Irish equivalent of the Declaration of Independence).

After the last prisoner was released in 1924 (it happened to be the former president of the rebel Irish Republic, Eamon de Valera) the prison fell into disrepair and seemed destined for the wrecking ball. It was through the efforts of a few who didn't wish for this chapter to be forgotten that the jail was restored. You'll chill as you view the Hanging Room and you'll cringe as you walk about the prison yard where executions took place. A short audiovisual presentation is included in the tour, and gives you the highlights of the Irish struggle for independence.

Royal Hospital Kilmainham/Irish Museum of Modern Art, *Kilmainham Lane, open Tuesday through Saturday 10:00am to 5:30pm, Sundays from noon until 5:30pm. Admission is free. Tel. (01) 612-9900.* This splendid building was formerly the Royal Hospital Kilmainham (RHK). It was built in 1684 after the manner of *Les Invalides* in Paris, and its original purpose was to house ill and infirm soldiers, a tribute to their service to Britain. After the establishment of the Irish Free State in 1922, the building was closed and fell into severe disrepair. A 15-year, $30,000,000 renovation project has paid handsome dividends – the building is once again a grand structure.

Now the RHK is home to the Irish Museum of Modern Art (IMMA): four galleries surrounding a large and lovely courtyard. An eclectic array of 20th-century art is exhibited throughout the museum, and there always seems to be a one-man show, or theme exhibit going on. The Banqueting Hall is now the site of frequent concerts and special activities. Perhaps the prettiest room is the chapel, which has rich wood paneling and a Baroque ceiling. This grand structure is worth a visit even if you have no interest in modern art.

OUTSIDE THE CITY LIMITS - NORTH OF DUBLIN
National Botanic Gardens

Glasnevin Road, Glasnevin, open during the summer months Monday through Saturday from 9:00am until 6:00pm, Sundays from 11:00am to 6:00pm; open during the winter months Monday through Saturday from 10:00am to 4:30pm, and Sundays from 11:00am to 4:30pm. Admission is free. Tel. (01) 837-7596 or (01) 837-4388. This is a real treat and worth the short drive (or bus – numbers 13, 19, or 34, or cab ride). Visitors have enjoyed these gardens for over 200 years.

The gardens boast over 20,000 plant species spread over 45 acres, but the oversized arboretum threatens to steal the show. Completed in 1869, it recently went through an extensive restoration. The greenhouses – over 400 feet of them – house an astounding variety of exotic plants and trees, such as orchids, banana trees, and palm trees. The Tolka River runs through the gardens. Cross over the wooden bridge into the extraordinary rose gardens for a special treat.

Two and a half miles north of Dublin along the seaside is the residential community of **Clontarf**. Running east of Clontarf is the **North Bull Wall**, a man-made wall built to prevent silt from building up in Dublin Harbor. Not only did it succeed in doing that, but it also added a new geological sight to Ireland, North Bull Island. Due to the gradual build-up of silt, North Bull Island is over three miles long and still growing. Other unforeseen benefits are new plant and animal life along the sand dunes and salt marshes. Tens of thousands of migrating birds, such as ducks and geese, can now be seen here during the winter months.

Howth

Lying about nine miles north of Dublin city center, Howth (pronounced Hoath) is a small, picturesque seaside fishing village. In recent years, Howth has spruced up its appearance, and the town is really quite nice to visit. A short 20-minute DART ride from Dublin, Howth offers several excellent restaurants, splendid views, and stunning sunsets. They have a nice quay that extends out into the harbor that is popular with Dubliners, locals, and tourists.

Howth Cliff Walk begins at the end of the main street in Howth, near King Sitric Restaurant. This one and a half mile cliff walk takes you along the edge of the cliff to the apex, where you'll find the Bailey Lighthouse, built in 1814 as a beacon for generations of incoming sailors.

Transport Museum, *Howth, open July to September Monday through Saturday from 10:00am to 5:30pm and Sunday from 2:00pm to 5:30pm, October through June on Saturday from 11:00am to 5:30pm and Sunday from noon until 5:30pm. Admission is £1 for adults and 50p for children. Tel. (01) 848-0831.* Near the Howth DART station is the Transport Museum. A variety of transport vehicles are on display from the horse and buggy days to the present time. Horse-drawn vehicles, old tractors, military vehicles, and double-decker buses are on display. The star of the show is the old Number 9 – the Hill of Howth tram. The tram ran to the top of Howth Hill and back for nearly 60 years before its retirement in 1960. In recent years volunteers have been working to restore it to its former condition.

Howth Castle Gardens, *Howth, open daily year-round from 8:00am to sundown. Admission is free.* Behind Deer Park Hotel, the Howth Castle Gardens offer a distinct treat: over 30 acres of rhododendron gardens.

They are best seen from April through June, when there are in full bloom. There are over 2,000 varieties of rhododendrons, including many rare species. Also located in the gardens is a large Neolithic dolmen.

Malahide

Just north of Dublin on the eastern coastline is the small village of Malahide. Aside from a bedroom community for commuters who work in Dublin, it also hosts a couple of sights that are worth taking a few minutes to drive up to see.

Marino Casino, *Malahide Road, Malahide, open May daily from 10:00am to 5:00pm, June through September daily from 10:00am to 6:00pm, October daily from 10:00am to 5:00pm, November on Sunday and Thursday from noon to 6:00pm, February and March on Sunday and Thursday from noon to 4:00pm, and April on Sunday and Thursday from noon to 5:00pm. Last admission is 45 minutes before closing. Admission is £2.00 for adults, £1.50 for seniors and students, £1.00 for children and a family ticket is available for £5.00. Tel. (01) 833-1618.* About two and a half or three miles north of the Dublin city center is Marino Casino. Don't worry about bringing lots of money to gamble with, because the term "Casino" in this case does not refer to a gambling hall at all. It takes its name from the Italian *cassino*, which means "small house." In other words, it merely identifies this smaller house that is associated with a larger house. In this case, Marino Casino was once associated with the much larger Charlemont Mansion, the residence of **James Caulfield**, the first Earl of Charlemont, which was destroyed in 1921.

Fortunately, the Casino, whose neo-classical architecture gives it a sense of classical prowess and grace, still stands proudly. Restored in 1984, the 16-room Casino has been refurbished with appropriate ornamentation, period furnishings, and antiques.

Look closely at the exterior of this fine building that dates from 1780. The urns at the top double as chimneys and the ultra-impressive columns are actually hollow, serving as drainage pipes for the frequent rains!

Malahide Castle, *Malahide, open April through October Monday through Saturday from 10:00am to 5:00pm and Sunday from 11:00am to 6:00pm, November through March Monday through Friday from 10:00am to 5:00pm and Saturday and Sunday from 2:00pm to 5:00pm. Closed from 12:45pm until 2:00pm for lunch. Admission for adults is £2.75, students (12 to 18 years) and senior citizens £2.15, and children (3 to 11 years) £1.40. There is a family ticket (two adults and four children) for £7.50. Combination tickets (with the Fry Railway Museum) are available for adults £4.35, students and seniors £3.35, children £2.25, and a family ticket for £10.95. Tel. (01) 846-2184.* Malahide Castle is located in the small town of Malahide just a few miles north of Dublin. This ancient fortress was built in 1174, and was lived in by members of the Talbot family until 1975, when the last Lord Talbot died. A jewel set in a crown of over 250 luscious acres of land, Malahide Castle is remarkably well preserved. Unlike many of the fortresses and castles in Ireland, it did not go through years of neglect and destruction, but enjoyed the continual habitation of owners who cared for and took care of it.

The Banqueting Hall, Oak Room, and Drawing Room are just a few of the rooms you'll see as you tour the castle. Each is furnished in exquisite period furniture, such as a side table decorated with a beautiful, detailed inlay of oak leaves. Many of the antiques here were originally used in the castle. On July 1, 1690, 14 members of the Talbot family breakfasted together at the long table that still exists in the Banqueting Hall. It was to be their last meal together; by nightfall, all had been killed in the Battle of the Boyne. Included on the grounds is a botanical garden containing over 5,000 varieties of plants, and the Fry Model Railway Museum (see the next entry). There is also a gift shop and restaurant on the castle premises if you get hungry or are looking for souvenirs.

A special treat is the National Portrait Collection of the National Gallery of Ireland. It just seems appropriate to have the portraits of some of Ireland's greatest individuals housed in this ancient castle.

You can reach Malahide Castle in a number of ways. If you are driving, take the N1 to Swords, then watch for the signs to Malahide. You can catch the #42 bus on Talbot Street in Dublin, or you can take the Drogheda-Dundalk train from **Connolly Station** in Dublin. As soon as you exit the railway station, you'll see signposts directing you to the castle.

The Fry Model Railway Museum, *Malahide Castle, open April, May and September Monday through Thursday and Saturday from 10:00am to 1:00pm and 2:00pm to 5:00pm, and Sunday from 2:00pm to 6:00pm, June through August Monday through Saturday from 10:00am to 1:00pm and 2:00pm to 5:00pm and Sunday from 2:00pm to 5:00pm, October through March Saturday, Sunday and bank holidays from 2:00pm to 5:00pm. Admission for adults is £2.35, students (12 to 18 years) and senior citizens £1.75, and children (to 11 years) £1.30. There is a family ticket available for £6.75 (two adults and four children). Combination tickets (with Malahide Castle) are available for adults £4.35, students and seniors £3.35, children £2.25, and a family ticket for £10.95. Tel. (01) 846-3779.* Located in the gardens of Malahide Castle, the railway museum is the result of the life-long work of a passionate railroad fan, Cyril Fry. Fry, a railroad engineer, spent years painstakingly working to build the trains and a miniature Dublin, complete with models of Connolly and Heuston stations, O'Connell and Ha'penny bridges, cars, boats, barges (on the River Liffey, of course!) and elevated tracks. The "city" and railway is laid out on a 72 feet by 32 feet display.

Mr. Fry began his work on the railway in the 1920s, and continued adding, reworking and retouching his masterpiece over the ensuing decades.

Donabate

Donabate is a sleepy little burg on the northern outskirts of Dublin. You can get there by taking the N1 from Dublin. Just beyond the Swords bypass, take the Donabate exit.

Newbridge House, *Donabate, open April through September, Tuesday through Saturday from 10:00am to 1:00pm and 2:00pm to 5:00pm and Sunday 2:00pm to 6:00pm, and October through March Saturday and Sunday from 2:00pm until 5:00pm. Admission is £2.50 for adults and £1.25 for children. Tel. (01) 843-6354.* This Georgian home set on 350 acres of land has been restored for your enjoyment. The main house was built in 1740, and an addition was added 15 years later. Not all of the house is open to the public, but there is a lovely Drawing Room, several reception rooms, and the original 18th-century kitchen and laundry, both purporting to have the actual original utensils used in both rooms, that you can see. Each room has been painstakingly restored with many original furnishings to represent what it might have looked like in the 1700s. Paintings, furniture, and a variety of knickknacks will make you feel as though you've walked into the parlor of the Archbishop of Dublin, for whom the house was built.

Tara's Palace, a miniature dollhouse, has over two dozen decorated rooms. There is also an antique doll collection that has over 150 dolls.

Outside in the courtyard you'll find the dairy, blacksmith's and carpenter's shops. There is even a mini-farm, where children can pet rabbits, sheep, goats, and other sundry farm animals.

Not as grand as some of the other Georgian homes that are open to the public in Dublin, the Newbridge House offers a little more, such as the doll collection and the mini-farm.

You can reach Newbridge House in a number of ways. If you are driving, you can take the N1 just past the Swords bypass, then take the signs to Donabate. You can catch the #33 bus on Eden Quay in Dublin, or you can take the Drogheda-Dundalk train from **Connolly Station** in Dublin.

OUTSIDE THE CITY LIMITS - WEST OF DUBLIN

Castletown House, *Celbridge. Open late April through October Monday through Friday from 10:00am until 6:00pm, Saturday 1:00pm to 6:00pm, and Sunday from 1:00pm until 6:00pm, October Monday through Friday from 10:00am to 5:00pm and Sunday from 1:00pm to 5:00pm, November Sunday from 1:00pm to 5:00pm. Last admission one hour before closing. Admission is £3.00 for adults, £2.50 for seniors and students, £1.25 for children, and a family* *ticket is available for £7.50. Tel. (01) 628-8252.* On the outskirts of Dublin in the community of Celbridge rests the luxurious Castletown House. Castletown House is another of Ireland's impressive Palladian-style mansions. Built in 1722 as the home of William Connolly, Speaker of the Irish House of Commons, the two wings are connected to the main house by colonnaded galleries.

The interior hallway features the handiwork of those talented Italian brothers Francini – they were considered to be among the best plaster workers on the continent and very much in demand in Ireland. The interior is exquisitely decorated with period furnishings, and makes for an awe-inspiring visit. The Long Gallery is especially impressive with its soft blue paint, Venetian chandeliers, and period furnishings.

Maynooth Castle, *Maynooth. Open from June through September daily from 3:00pm until 6:00pm. Other times by appointment. Admission is free.* Just off the N4 (watch for the signposts) lies the small village of Maynooth, and with it Maynooth Castle. Its ruins greet the Catholic seminarians who attend nearby St. Patrick's College. The keep is still in relatively good condition, as is the gate tower, although most of the rest of the castle was destroyed during the Cromwellian period.

Straffan Butterfly Farm, *Straffan. Open May through August daily from noon until 5:00pm. Admission is £1. Tel. (01) 627-1109.* Located in the tiny town of Straffan, just a ten-minute ride from Maynooth on the R408, the Straffan Butterfly Farm is a unique and interesting diversion from the ruins and cathedrals that abound in Ireland. The greenhouse features exotic and tropical plants, and a host of butterflies and moths.

Straffan Steam Museum, *Straffan. Open June through August Tuesday through Sunday from 2:00pm until 6:00pm, and April May and September on Sunday from 2:00pm to 6:00pm. Admission is £3 for adults and £2 for children and seniors. Tel. (01) 627-3155.* This museum is devoted to the history of steam power in Ireland. Over 20 steam locomotives are on display, in addition to steam engines (called Stationary Industrial Engines) that were used for more sedentary work, such as churning butter and threshing wheat. Some of the steam engines are activated on days called "live steam" days; call ahead to find out when the "live steam" days are going to be. You can end your visit with a stop in the adjacent Steaming Kettle Tea House and Gift shop.

Punchestown Racecourse, *Punchestown.* Punchestown Racecourse lies amid the verdant undulating foothills of the Wicklow Mountains. About three miles southeast of Naas, the racecourse is a popular place among horse racing fans, and perhaps is most famous for its steeplechase event that takes place every April.

Jigginstown House, *Naas.* Just south of Naas on the N7 is Jigginstown House, one of the most intriguing residential structures in this part of the country. The mansion is only partially finished – it was begun in 1633 as a residence by the Earl of Strafford. But it was never finished due to the premature death of the Earl in 1641 (he was executed). The front of the red brick mansion is over a football field's length – almost 375 feet long.

Take a few minutes and drive to the **Hill of Allen**, about five miles northwest of Newbridge. The hill rises 676 feet above the famous Curragh Plain. As one of the lone hills in the area, it offers sweeping panoramas of the surrounding countryside. As you might imagine, due to its wide views it was formerly the location of the residences of several royal palaces during medieval times. The hill was also reputed to be the home of the legendary Fionn MacCumhaill, warrior leader of the vaunted Fianna during the 3rd century.

St. Brigid's Cathedral, *Kildare. Open daily from 10:00am to 6:00pm. Admission is free, although a small donation is requested. To go to the top of the tower, the cost is £2.* St. Brigid's Cathedral is built on the original site chosen by St. Brigid in the 5th century. The cathedral was built in the early 13th century, and boasts several fine medieval tombs. The interior offers serenity and some lovely stained glass windows. In the churchyard a round tower rises over 100 feet, and offers fine views of the surrounding area for those who make the effort to climb to the top.

OUTSIDE THE CITY LIMITS - SOUTH OF DUBLIN

Dun Laoghaire, pronounced *Dun Leary* (no kidding!), is a favorite escape for Dublin city dwellers as well as tourists. In Irish the name means Leary's Fort. A short DART ride south of Dublin (about 7 miles), this pleasant, predominantly residential town is also where you can catch the ferry to Holyhead (and visa versa), three and a half to four hours away.

People come to relax, take in the salt air and walk out on the two fine piers that extend about a mile and a half into the Irish Sea. Sundays are the most popular days in Dun Laoghaire. Today, the town still proudly exhibits its Victorian homes along with many excellent pubs and restaurants. For nearly 100 years, from 1821 to 1920, Dun Laoghaire was called Kingstown in honor of a brief visit from England's King George IV. But the citizens decided to reclaim the original Irish name during the Civil War with England. To get here, take the subway to the Dun Laoghaire DART Station.

The National Maritime Museum, *Haigh Terrace, Dun Laoghaire, open May through September Tuesday through Sunday 1:00pm to 5:30pm. Admission is £1.50 for adults and 75p for children. Tel. (01) 280-0969.* The National Maritime Museum is housed in Mariner's Church, and is home to an eclectic collection of nautical novelties, including a captured French longboat and the Bailey Optic, which until 1972 illuminated the night for many seafarers from the old 1814 Bailey lighthouse at Howth Head.

People's Park, *Dun Laoghaire.* On the road from Dun Laoghaire to Sandycove, this small public park is a pleasant retreat with marvelous views, lovely landscaping, and a playground for active children.

James Joyce Tower, *Sandy Cove, Dun Laoghaire, open April through October Monday to Saturday from 10:00am to 5:00pm (closed from 1:00pm to 2:00pm for lunch) and Sunday from 2:00pm to 6:00pm. The rest of the year you need to call for an appointment. Admission fee is £2.50 for adults, students (12 to 18) and seniors are £2, and £1.30 for children (3 to 11 years). There is a family ticket for £7.50 (2 adults and 4 children). Tel. (01) 280-9265 or (01) 872-2077.* Strange as this may seem, we can thank Napoleon for this exhibit. From 1804 through 1815, strong stone structures called Martello Towers were built on strategic promontories on the south and east coasts of Ireland to give early warning of the feared approach of Napoleonic forces. Strongly fortified in the event of attack, these impressive structures are made of 40 feet high, eight feet thick granite, and offer a commanding view of the sea for miles around. In modern times, many of the Towers were converted into living quarters, and such is the case with the James Joyce Tower.

Internationally famed author and Irish son **James Joyce** lived here for a short time around the turn of the century as a guest of his friend **Oliver St. John Gogarty** (who had rented it from the Army for the princely sum of 67 pence a month). He was so impressed with the tower that it figures prominently in the opening pages of his famous book *Ulysses*. He was also impressed with his friend; Gogarty was to Buck Mulligan what Tom Blankenship was to Mark Twain's Huckleberry Finn. (For those of you who may not have read *Ulysses*, the main character is Buck Mulligan.)

A collection of Joycean artifacts are on view in the James Joyce Tower: his waistcoat, cigar case, a tie, numerous first editions of his book, a piano and guitar once belonging to him, and his death mask.

Forty-Foot Bathing Pool, *Dun Laoghaire.* Near the James Joyce Tower is a swimming area called the Forty-Foot Bathing Pool. It has been traditionally frequented by nude male swimmers. In recent years, however, women have made inroads into this male haven, but generally speaking, men are still the predominant bathers here.

NIGHTLIFE & ENTERTAINMENT

It is estimated that 50% of the populace of Dublin is under 25 years old, and on a Friday or Saturday night you can be sure a healthy percentage of those individuals are out and about on the town. There is a lot of fun nightlife in Dublin, and much of it is centered around pubs and nightclubs. Within each category of nightlife, the selections are listed in alphabetical order.

Traditional Irish Music

ABBEY TAVERN, *Howth. Tel. (01) 839-0307.*

As mentioned in the *Where to Eat* section, Abbey Tavern could be one of the best places in Ireland for an evening of traditional Irish music. Abbey Tavern has been serving up ale and frothy brew for nearly 200 years at this very sight. It is a bit touristy, so if you are looking for that atmosphere, you'll find plenty of it here. If, however, you are looking for something a little less touristy, you may want to try some of the other places listed below.

THE AULD DUBLINER, *Anglesea Street. Tel. (01) 677-0527.*

The Auld Dubliner Pub is a typical Irish pub, offering lively traditional Irish music several nights a week, and almost every night during the tourist season. Call to find out when, and who is performing, or better yet, just wander in during your strolls around the Temple Bar District. If you do (wander in), then you'll find character and personality that has changed little in the past few decades. You'll also find exposed brick walls, tables and booths, and plenty of "regulars" to visit with.

THE BAILEY, *2-3 Bridge Street. Tel. (01) 677-5711.*

The Bailey is a slice of living Irish history that blends three important aspects of Irish life: politics, literature, and Guinness. Built in 1837, The Bailey has been an important watering hole almost from its inception. It was here that many of the founders of the Irish Free State gathered to discuss their plans. It was frequented by Arthur Griffith, the founder of *Sinn Fein*, the political party responsible for the drive for independence. Mr. Griffith was also the owner of *The United Irishman*, a newspaper irrevocably pledged to fight for Irish Independence. Writers, including the Irish dignitaries such as W.B Yeats, Brendan Behan, and James Stephens were often found here tilting a glass of Guinness and observing the human existence that they wrote so eloquently about.

Michael Collins, the hard-as-nails, driving general of the Irish Republican Army, is said to have visited this haven when he was trying to dodge the British Army. Today, the pub is still a going concern, and you'll find the atmosphere pleasantly smoky and crowded, with a significant amount of philosophy, politics and good humor thrown in.

BRAZEN HEAD, *20 Lower Bridge Street. Tel. (01) 677-9549.*

One of the most famous venues for traditional Irish music in Dublin, the Brazen Head is reputed (and disputed) to be Dublin's oldest pub. It has served many a pint continually since 1688. Even though the Brazen Head was chartered as a pub in 1688, its beginnings are much older – records indicate a building on this site was used as a way station for weary travelers since the 12th century.

Like The Bailey, the Brazen Head served as a gathering place for Ireland's political powerhouses and literary legends (both groups frequented more than one pub!). Some of the most famous men in Ireland passed through the skewed doorway of The Brazen Head: Daniel O'Connell (The Liberator), Wolf Tone, Robert Emmett, James Joyce, and Brendan Behan were some of the more notable patrons of the Brazen Head. Not quite so notable was Mr. John Langan, whose literary merits are limited to the seven words he etched in a piece of glass still visible at The Brazen Head: "John Langan halted here 7th August, 1726."

When you walk into the Brazen Head, it feels like a pub ought to feel, and in no time at all you'll feel right at home in this oldest of Dublin's pubs. Particularly enjoyable are the Sunday evening sing-alongs for which they have become famous. Each night of the week is filled with toe-tappin', tune-humming music that will linger in your mind long after you've left the pub. (Thursday evenings are reserved for Jazz and Blues, but the other evenings traditional Irish music is played.)

BURLINGTON HOTEL, *Upper Leesom Street, Ballsbridge. Tel. (01) 660-5222.*

From early May through October, the Burlington runs one of the most enjoyable traditional Irish cabarets around, with lots of music and laughs. An evening here is an evening you won't want to miss, especially if you haven't had the opportunity to visit The Abbey Tavern in Howth or Johnnie Fox's Pub in Glencullen. Mirth and merriment, ballads and the steady beat of the bodhran will keep your feet tapping, and may even elicit a tear or two for one of those the balladeer wails for. It is really quite an enjoyable evening, and will be a favorite memory or your visit to Dublin.

THE CELLARS, *Merrion Square. Tel. (01) 661-6799.*

Located in the Mont Clare Hotel, The Cellars provides an enjoyable evening of traditional music. Not as rustic as others around town, they still put on a good show filled with music, singing, storytelling, and lots of laughs. Like the Abbey Tavern in Howth, The Cellars caters specifically to tourists and the atmosphere reflects that focus.

CISS MADDEN'S, *22 Donnybrook Road. Tel. (01) 283-0208.*

New but trying hard to have that ancient feel, Ciss Madden's offers traditional Irish evenings. Call to find out which evenings they are performing, as the schedule is not set. Ciss Madden's has also earned quite a positive reputation for its bar food, so whether you are hungry for food, drink, or just plain good company, you can't go wrong with Ciss Madden's.

DAVY BYRNE'S, *21 Duke Street.*

Davy Byrne's is one of those pubs you fall in love with the moment you enter. It was immortalized in James Joyce's *Ulysses* (he called it a "moral bar"), and continues to be a proper hangout for the proper and, on occasion, the not so proper! Davy Byrne's consists of three bars, any one of which can and will serve up some of the finest Guinness in the country. While there, take a moment to note the splendidly engraved mirror over the *Ulysses* bar. It is a portrait of Dublin Castle's upper yard around the turn of this century. It is quite intricate and fascinating in its detail.

DOHENY & NESBITT, *5 Lower Baggot Street. Tel. (01) 676-2945.*

The large polished brass sign at the front of the bar advertises Doheny and Nesbitt as a Tea and Wine Merchant. As you slide through the door, the warm vaporous air seems to draw you into its warmth and the camaraderie and friendliness that you'll find here. The atmosphere is accentuated with a wonderfully Victorian feel, with wonderful wooden walls that provide a little privacy if you wish, but not so private as to make it snobbish. The antique Victorian mirrors only add to the old-time feel of this bar, which is nearing its 140th birthday. Most evenings you'll be elbow-to-elbow with some of the greatest characters in Dublin.

JOHNNIE FOX'S PUB, *Glencullen, Co. Dublin. Tel. (01) 295-5647.*

About eight to 10 miles (depending on if you get lost, and for how long) from downtown Dublin, Johnnie Fox's caters specifically to tourists. Advertised as "The highest pub in Ireland" (I'm not so sure – others claim the same title), Fox's offers enjoyable evenings of traditional Irish song and dance. Its rustic interior, dusty antiques, lovely colleens, and lively atmosphere are a lot of fun. Be sure and call for directions before you go, unless you want to see more of the Wicklow Mountains than you plan.

Notwithstanding a fun and lively atmosphere that really appeals to tourists, there are a lot of locals that make the 45-minute drive from Dublin to enjoy the brew and the activity.

JURY'S HOTEL, *Pembroke and Lansdowne Roads, Ballsbridge. Tel. (01) 660-5000.*

If you're looking for a traditional Irish pub, this isn't the place. But if you are looking for an Irish cabaret with lots of singing and good times, Jury's will be able to accommodate you. They have been offering a traditional Irish cabaret for years, and they are very, very good at it. Irish ballads, captivating music, and storytellers that will weave their tales more tightly than an Aran sweater are just a few of the things you'll experience at Jury's Irish cabaret.

MOTHER REDCAP'S TAVERN, *Christchurch Back Lane. Tel. (01) 453-8306.*

The decorators have done a nice job here in their efforts to recreate the look, feel and atmosphere of a 17th-century pub. Traditional Irish evenings are held; call to find out which evenings.

O'DONOGHUE'S, *15 Merrion Row. Tel. (01) 676-2807.*

Lively is the adjective usually applied to O'Donoghue's, and the music is among the best in Dublin. O'Donoghue's offers a venue that is appreciated by all types of pub patrons: it is frequented by a young crowd, a goodly number of business people, and it always has a lot of tourists. One young Dubliner told me that the place is "mad and lunatic" (her actual words). I believe she meant it as a compliment of the highest order. It has become quite the trendy place to be if you are young and like the latest music. But don't come late on the weekends unless you want to spend the evening standing around, because all the seats will be long gone.

OLIVER ST. JOHN GOGARTY'S, *59 Fleet Street. Tel. (01) 671-1872.*

The *real* Oliver St. John Gogarty was an over-achiever of sorts. He was successful in many of the ventures he undertook, and the roles he played were many, including doctor (he was a surgeon), humorist, and writer. While there is nothing spectacularly different about this pub, it's typical of many of the pubs in Ireland. I found it to be quite pleasant and enjoyable to cruise in and just sit back and enjoy others enjoying themselves. The atmosphere is pleasant, and traditional Irish music is scheduled several evenings a week. Add to that the impromptu music sessions that sprout every now and again, and this is a great place to spend an evening.

THE STAG'S HEAD, *1 Dame Court. Tel. (01) 679-3701.*

At this location since before the American Revolution, the Stag's Head is an authentic, smoke-filled pub. Owing to its south central location, there is a good cross-section of people here: local Dubliners, students, and tourists. They tell me that the Guinness that is on tap here is some of the best in Dublin. Perhaps you should venture in and find out.

Trendy, Modern Pubs

While traditional Irish pubs are what many tourists look for when they go to Ireland, that's not all that is there. Here are a few pubs known more for their trendiness.

THE BARGE, *42 Charlemont Street. Tel. (01) 475-1869.*

This is a nice pub, decorated like (interestingly enough) an old Barge. It is really more interesting than perhaps that sounds, and you should check it out.

BREAK FOR THE BORDER, *2 Johnson's Place. Tel. (01) 475-0888.*

This nice, large pub and nightclub is associated with the Grafton Plaza Hotel. The pub features a disk jockey until 10:30pm, at which time the pub closes and patrons are invited (for £8) to continue their merriment in the downstairs nightclub, where a live band is featured.

BRUXELLE'S, *Harry Street. Tel. (01) 677-5362.*

If you want to practice your German, here's a good place to do so. For whatever reason, in recent years this seems to have become a haunt of German tourists (probably in some German guidebook!). The cost for drinks is a little higher here than some of the other places in town.

BUSKER'S, *Fleet Street. Tel. (01) 677-3333.*

This lively pub is primarily for the younger set who like loud music. It's a nice place if you like loud music! Seriously, this is the place where up-and-coming rock bands in the Dublin area come to strut their stuff. The crowds are generally enthusiastic, and while the quality of the bands varies, their volume is never in question.

THE HARCOURT HOTEL, *60 Harcourt Street. Tel. (01) 478-3677.*
The pub of the Harcourt Hotel features live music seven nights a week. It ranges from jazz (one of the best places in town), to New Age to traditional Irish. Call ahead to see what's playing.

THE PINK ELEPHANT, *South Frederick Street. Tel. (01) 677-5876.*
A favorite hangout of Trinity students, The Pink Elephant is a popular spot that brings rising European rock groups into their establishment.

Nightclubs

There aren't nearly as many nightclubs as there are pubs in Dublin. But there are a few here and there (some are both pubs and clubs, so I've included them here too). All have cover charges ranging from £5 to £8.

BAD BOB'S, *35 East Essex Street. Tel. (01) 677-5482.*
In the Temple Bar District you'll find Bad Bob's, a nightclub specializing in country music. I was surprised to find a lot of interest in country music in Ireland. In fact, you might say there's a bit of a cult following here. And Bad Bob's is where the young and the beautiful will probably be on any given weekend evening. If you wish to go, do so early or you'll find yourself visiting with lots of people – outside while you're standing in line!

GARDA CLUB, *Harrington Street*
This nightclub is more of a discotheque, catering to the mid-20s crowd. The music is mostly contemporary Top 40 stuff. Historically, you'll find large numbers of Trinity College students here, so if you're looking to meet some young college students, this would be a great place to make their acquaintance.

THE KITCHEN, *Temple Bar. Tel. (01) 677-6178.*
The Kitchen is a nightclub in the Clarence Hotel, and the rock group U2 owns both. You'll find the young and the restless, and the wild and wonderful crowds here. The Kitchen is another of those places in Dublin where you'll find the young and the beautiful as well as some pretty good music.

POD, *Harcourt Street. (01) 478-0166.*
The POD (which stands for *Place of Dance*), is the place to be for the upwardly mobile and socially conscious in Dublin. The artistic professionals (models, artists, advertising, etc.) seem to gravitate to the POD.

THE ROCK GARDEN, *Crown Alley. Tel. (01) 679-9114.*
Another of the nightclubs in the Temple Bar District, The Rock Garden caters almost exclusively to the younger college crowd. With Trinity College just around the corner, you can imagine the popularity of this bar.

Theaters

The Irish are generally a demonstrative people, outgoing, and gregarious by nature. They also seem to enjoy seeing their fellow countrymen and women display their talents on stage. The principal theaters in Dublin are the Gate, Abbey, Peacock, Gaiety, and Olympia. Buy a local paper at any Newsagent (located throughout the city, in bus depots, and train stations) to see what's playing. Most shows are reasonably priced, generally ranging between £5 to £15.

ABBEY THEATER, *Lower Abbey Street. Tel. (01) 878-7222.*

The Abbey theater has been the venue for many important dramatic plays in Ireland's history. It opened in 1904, and some of its most important patrons and benefactors included **W. B. Yeats** and one **Lady Gregory**, a member of the Dublin gentry who spent enormous amounts of time and money furthering the arts in Dublin. In addition, Lady Gregory wrote and directed dozens of plays that ran at the Abbey. Playwright **J. M. Synge** benefited from their interest in the arts and also presented a number of plays at the Abbey.

The original theater burned in 1951 in a fire many felt was arson, and it wasn't rebuilt until 1966.

GAIETY THEATER, *South King Street. Tel. (01) 677-1717.*

Since 1871, the Gaiety Theater has provided family-oriented entertainment. Its yellow facade is easy to spot, and it's worth the price of admission to simply see the wonderful ornately decorated interior.

GATE THEATER, *Cavendish Row. Tel. (01) 874-4045.*

The Gate Theater has a rich history, and has had the privilege of having such world-famous actors as Orson Welles and James Mason grace her stage. Today the Gate Theater features the contemporary efforts of young native dramatists.

OLYMPIA THEATER, *Dame Street. Tel. (01) 677-8962.*

Along with the Gaiety Theater, the Olympia provides the Dublin arts scene with a host of family-oriented entertainment.

PEACOCK THEATER, *Lower Abbey Street. Tel. (01) 478-7222.*

The Peacock Theater, in the same building as the Abbey Theater, might best be classed as an experimental theater. One man shows, novelty presentations, and plays in Gaelic are typical.

SPORTS & RECREATION

There are a number of activities that you can watch and participate in around the Dublin area. Here are a few of them.

Angling

To find the local fishing hot spots, purchase a license, or talk about the big one that got away, stop at **Patrick Cleere and Son**, *Anglesea Street,*

Dublin, Tel. (01) 677-7406. Patrick and his son (and his daughter, too!) are amicable characters that love to talk about fishing. I found them quite informative about fishing in and around Dublin. They were also quite conversant on other areas of the island, and more than willing to share their expertise and information.

Gaelic Football

Gaelic football can be watched throughout the season at **Croke Park** in Dublin (about 15 to 20 minute's walk north of O'Connell Bridge), or you can catch a bus at O'Connell Bridge that will take you there. Games are played every other Sunday (the same stadium is used for Gaelic football and hurling). Tickets will cost £6 and £12.

For ticket information and schedules, contact the **Gaelic Athletic Association,** *Tel. (01) 836-3222.*

Golf

Deer Park Golf Course, *Howth, County Dublin. Tel. (01) 832-2624, £11/£12.*

Deer Park Golf Course is actually a series of golf courses, from pitch-and-putt to several 18-hole courses. All the courses are wide-open, with gorgeous views of the Irish Sea. While the views can be distracting to your game, they'll be sure to provide some memorable golf memories for you. Visitors are welcome any time. Par 72.

The Island Golf Club, *Donabate, County Dublin. Tel. (01) 843-6205, £30/£35.*

As the name implies, this golf course is situated on an island. Once an exclusive club, the course is now open three days a week to the general public. If you venture here, you'll find a superb links-style course. If your iron game isn't tuned up, you'll have a tough time finding the smallish greens. Visitors are welcome on Monday, Tuesday, and Friday. Par 71, 6,625 yards.

Portmarnock Golf Club, *Portmarnock, County Dublin. Tel. (01) 846-2968, £40/£50.*

Considered one of the premier golf courses in Ireland, Portmarnock is world-renowned and its gorgeous greens and fairways are a treat for any golfer. Through the years, Portmarnock has earned quite a few feathers for her cap – she has hosted The Irish Open no fewer than 18 times, and has also been the venue for The World Cup, The British Amateur Open, and the Walker Cup.

The fifteenth hole has bedeviled several generations of golfers, and may prove to be your undoing also. It's not terribly long – only 183 yards, but it *is* wicked. The ocean runs the full length of the right side of the fairway, but there is a steep drop on the left side of the green. If you play it "safe" as far as the water is concerned, then you are apt to see your ball skidding down a rather nasty drop off on the left side of the green. Here's a tip on how to master this hole: Those in the know say that if the wind is blowing in from the ocean (almost always!), then you need to hit your shot out over the water and let the wind blow it back onto the course. Right! Visitors are welcome Monday, Tuesday, and Friday. Par 72, 7,051 yards.

Royal Dublin Golf Club, *Bull Island, County Dublin. Tel. (01) 833-6346, £35/£45.*

This is one of the oldest courses in Ireland. A links course alongside the ocean, you'll enjoy the challenge of this outstanding course. It is only about five miles from Dublin, so you can easily get in a few holes before or after your sightseeing. Three times the Irish Open has been played here, and you can play where the pros have played. Visitors are welcome every Monday and Tuesday, Thursday and Friday. Par 73, 6,590 yards.

St. Margaret's Golf Club, *County Dublin. Tel. (01) 864-0400, £25/£30.*

This is a new course by Ireland's standards, having just passed its 6th birthday. But it has earned a reputation as a pleasant, scenic, challenging course. Visitors are welcome any day of the week. Par 72, 6,965 yards.

Horse Racing

Horseracing is wildly popular in Ireland, and there are venues all over the country to stop and see a race or two. The closest main racetracks to Dublin are **Leopardstown**, *Tel. (01) 289-3607*, **The Curragh** in *Kildare, Tel. (045) 41205*, and **Fairyhouse** in *County Meath, Tel. (01) 825-6167*.

Horseback Riding

There are many horseback riding centers in the Dublin area. Here are a few you might try if you are interested in seeing Ireland from a slightly different perspective:
- **Brennanstown Riding School, Ltd.**, *Kilmacanogue, County Wicklow. Tel. (01) 286-3778, Fax (01) 282-9590*
- **Castleknock Riding Center**, *Castleknock. Tel. (01) 820-1104*
- **Devil's Glen Equestrian Center**, *Ashford, County Wicklow. Tel. (040) 440013*
- **Dundrum Riding and Driving Club**, *Willow Road, Dundrum. Tel. (01) 298-6112*

Hurling

Hurling can also be watched throughout the season at **Croke Park** in Dublin. Tickets will cost £6 and £12. For ticket information and schedules, contact the **Gaelic Athletic Association**, *Tel. (01) 836-3222.*

Rugby

You can watch professional rugby games at **Lansdowne Road Stadium**, *Lansdowne Road, Ballsbridge*. The stadium is right next to the DART tracks, about 100 yards from the Lansdowne Road DART station in the fashionable Georgian neighborhood of Ballsbridge in south Dublin.

You can get information on upcoming games and tickets through the **Irish Rugby Football Union**, *62 Lansdowne Road, Dublin, Tel. (01) 668-4601.*

Sailing & Windsurfing

- **BIC Sport Windsurfing and Canoe Center**, *872 Santry Avenue, Dublin 9. Tel. (01) 842-6577*
- **Fingall Sailing School**, *Malahide, County Dublin. Tel. (01) 845-1979*

Scuba Diving

- **Oceantec Adventures**, *10/11 Marine Terrace, Dun Laoghaire. Tel. (01) 280-1083*
- **Scubadive Diving School**, *Coliemore Harbour, Dalkey. Tel. (01) 850357*

Soccer

In addition to rugby, soccer games are also played at **Lansdowne Road Stadium**. You can get more information on schedules from the **Football Association of Ireland**, *80 Merrion Square S., Dublin, Tel. (01) 676-6864.*

SHOPPING

Dublin is a wonderful place to shop as well as sightsee. From antiques to woolens and linens to just about anything your heart desires, you are sure to have a lot of fun shopping in Dublin. Following are a few shops that might interest you:

Blarney Woolen Mills, *21 Nassau Street. Tel. (01) 671-0068.* Blarney Woolen Mills outlets are located all over Ireland and feature a wide variety of Irish goods, ranging from woolens and tweeds to Beleek china and Waterford crystal. The prices are a little higher than other places, but the selection is impressive.

Brown Thomas, *Grafton Street. Tel. (01) 679-5666.* Brown Thomas is considered Dublin's elite department store, and you'll find a nice range of expensive name-brand fashions on display here.

Celtic Note, *15 Nassau Street. Tel. (01) 670-4157.* Take a moment out of your sightseeing day and drop into the Celtic Note to pick up some traditional Irish music.

Claddagh Records, *2 Cecilia Street. Temple Bar. Tel. (01) 677-0262.* You'll find a nice selection of traditional Irish tunes in this small shop in the Temple Bar district.

Conlon Antiques, *21 Clanbrassil Street. Tel. (01) 453-7323.* Conlon's features a wide variety of interesting and intriguing items from days gone by.

Dunnes Department Stores, *St. Stephen's Green Centre. Tel. (01) 478-0188 and Henry Street, Tel. (01) 872-6833.* Dunnes is Ireland's best-known department store and it has several locations in Dublin. Sort of like a JC Penney and Walgreen's combined, you'll find clothing, household goods and even a selection of groceries available here.

Fleury Antiques, *57 Francis Street. Tel. (01) 473-0878.* Fleury's is one of the most recognizable names in Irish antiques, since they are one of the nation's largest dealers. I found them to be a little pricey, although it is more than worth a visit just to see the quantity and quality of furnishings and bric-a-brac they offer. It is sort of like visiting an exquisite museum where you can take pieces home if you are willing to pay the price.

Ha'penny Bridge Galleries, *15 Bachelor's Walk. Tel. (01) 872-3950.* You'll find a large variety of knick-knacks, statuary, silver and china at this gallery/store.

Hodges Figgis, *56 Dawson Street. Tel. (01) 677-4754.* If you like books, you'll want to wander into Hodges Figgis. They boast that they have over 1.5 million books displayed on the three floors of their store. Once here, you'll believe their boast.

Kilkenny Shop, *5 Nassau Street. Tel. (01) 677-7066.* The Kilkenny shop is the place to find a nice selection of Irish goods, from the ever-popular and beautiful Waterford crystal to the creamy satin glean of Beleek china.

McDowell's Jewelers, *3 Upper O'Connell Street. Tel. (01) 874-4961.* This outstanding jewelry store has been serving Dubliners (and tourists) for over 100 years.

O'Sullivan's Antiques, *43-44 Francis Street. Tel. (01) 454-1143.* If you want to be amazed and astounded, stop by O'Sullivan's and gaze admiringly on the variety of fine Edwardian, Victorian and Georgian furniture, gilt mirrors, chandeliers and paintings.

Patrick Cleere and Son, *Anglesea Street, Temple Bar. Tel. (01) 677-7406.* If you think you'll be doing any fishing (angling) while in Ireland, stop by Patrick's shop in the Temple Bar district to get outfitted. They'll also be more than willing to dispense a little angling advice and counsel along with whatever you purchase.

Powerscourt Townhouse Centre, *Clarendon Street.* As you are walking south on Grafton Street, turn right onto narrow Johnston's Court and you'll find Powerscourt Townhouse – a converted Georgian townhouse chock full of a score of shops and cafes. It's one of the most charming "malls" you'll ever visit.

St. Stephen's Green Centre, *St. Stephen's Green West*. At the south end of Grafton Street you'll find the relatively new St. Stephen's Green Centre, a newish mall filled with a variety of clothing, jewelry, boutiques and dozens of other stores and restaurants. Once inside, it frankly has the feel of an American mall. Its nouveau Victorian design does make it a little more pleasant to the eye, however.

Winding Stair, *40 Ormond Quay. Tel. (01) 873-3292*. This is a wonderful store to spend a few minutes in if you like books. You'll find a nice mix of new and used books here, along with a pleasant atmosphere.

PRACTICAL INFORMATION

American Express

American Express, *116 Grafton Street, Dublin 2. Tel. (01) 677-2874*, can be your best friend if you lose traveler's checks, need money exchanged, or need some travel agency assistance.

Automobile Association – AA

The **Automobile Association**, *23 Rockhill Street, Blackrock, Dublin. Tel. (01) 283-3555*, can help out if you run into problems getting your car to start, or if you need to be towed.

Buses, Planes, & Trains

• **Bus Eireann**, *Tel. (01) 836-6111*
• **Aer Lingus**, *Tel. (01) 844-4777*
• **Delta Airlines**, *Tel. (01) 844-4170*
• **DART information**, *Tel. (01) 836-6222*
• **Irish Rail**, *Tel. (01) 836-6222*

Business Hours

Businesses are generally open from 9:00am to 5:00pm in Dublin, although from a practical standpoint, most stores open at 9:30am or 10:00am. The exceptions to this rule are bakeries and Newsagents – they are usually open at 7:00am. There has been a tendency of late for some of the stores to stay open longer (until 7:00pm or 7:30pm) one day a week, usually on Thursday evening. This hasn't caught on entirely yet, so if you really want to do some shopping, try to get it completed before 5:00pm.

Embassies & Consulates

• **US Embassy**, *42 Elgin Road, Dublin 4. Tel. (01) 668-8777*
• **British Embassy**, *29 Merrion Street, Ballsbridge, Dublin 4. Tel. (01) 205-3700*. Open Monday through Friday 9:00am to 12:45pm and 2:00pm to 5:15pm (5:00pm on Fridays).
• **Canadian Embassy**, *65 St. Stephen's Green, Dublin 2. Tel. (01) 478-1988*

Laundry Service
As you might suspect in a city Dublin's size, there are a number of laundromats around the city. Here are a few:
• **All-American Launderette**, *Wicklow Street, Dublin. Tel. (01) 677-2779*
• **The Laundry Shop**, *Parnell Street, Dublin. Tel. (01) 872-3541*

Pharmacies
In Ireland, pharmacies are called "Chemists," and can be located through any of the Tourist Offices, or in the "Yellow Pages."

Post Offices
The **General Post Office** is located on O'Connell Street and is open Monday through Saturday from 8:00am to 8:00pm. Smaller branch offices are scattered around the city, and their hours are shorter, usually Monday through Saturday from 9:00am to 6:00pm.

Restrooms
Public restrooms are not prevalent in Ireland; your best bet is usually a hotel or a pub. (Most hotels have at least one pub, and the restrooms are usually located near the pub.)

Tourist Information
There are a number of tourist offices in Dublin:
• **Baggot Street Tourist Information Office**, *Baggot Street Bridge, Dublin 2. Tel. (01) 676-5871*
• **Dublin Airport Tourist Information Office**, *Arrivals Hall, Dublin Airport*
• **Dublin Tourist Information Office**, *Suffolk Street, Dublin 2. Tel. (01) 605-7777.* (This is the main tourist office. It has the most thorough selection of maps, brochures, and tidbits of interest to tourists.)

14. LEINSTER
- EXCURSIONS FROM DUBLIN

Virtually all of Ireland is reachable within a day from Dublin. (Remember – Ireland is only about 300 miles long and 170 miles wide.) However, there are a number of terrific, interesting excursions just outside of Dublin that are worthwhile day trips. I've planned a few jaunts into the countryside of **Leinster** province that will inform, delight, and enchant you.

In addition to these short trips, I have included a few longer trips into Leinster that you can take from Dublin. Depending on your mood and plans, you can either stay in or around these sights in north and south Leinster, or you can return to Dublin for your evening's lodging.

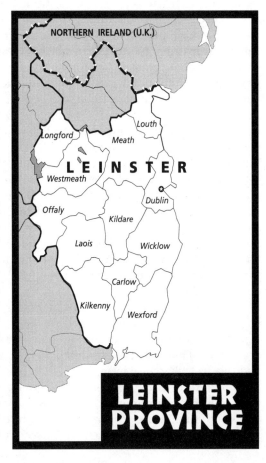

Many of these destinations don't offer much in the way of accommo-
dations and restaurants, which is why you won't sometimes see sections
on *Where to Stay, Where to Eat, Nightlife,* etc; these are really intended as day
trips from Dublin.

Here's a little overview about what awaits you on your day trips and
excursions:

North of Dublin lies the portion of Leinster that was occupied for
seven centuries by the English. Known as **The Pale**, much of this area was
fought and bled for many times over during the years of English
occupation. Scattered all along this part of Ireland are castles, walled
cities, and scores of ruined monasteries. Some of them make for wonder-
ful photo opportunities and great adventures.

Some of the most impressive sights in north Leinster are the ruins of
several monasteries. **Mellifont Abbey** and **Monasterboice** are two fine
sights you can visit to get a feel for the monastic life of those lonely monks
who labored for their Lord during lawless and sometimes merciless times.

And you simply cannot venture north of Dublin without visiting the
Boyne River Valley. Not to do so would be tantamount to visiting the town
of Boston without going to Concord, Lexington, or the old North Church,
or like going to Gettysburg and not visiting the nearby battlefield. While
you're visiting the Boyne River Valley, you will need to stop at the
magnificent passage grave of Newgrange – the grave of the former kings
of Ireland – and try to figure out its 5,000 year-history. (Don't feel bad if
you can't. Scholars who have worked their entire lives trying to figure it
out have only suppositions and guesstimates!)

Once you've seen all there is to see north of Dublin, turn your
attention further to the south. South of Dublin are several sites that are
definitely worth a day trip. **County Wicklow** is the county immediately
south of Dublin County, and is a popular place for both vacationing
Dubliners fleeing the big city and foreign tourists. In a country that has
an abundance of luscious flora, the fact that County Wicklow is referred
to as the **Garden of Ireland** gives you some indication of the beauty of this
part of the Emerald Isle.

The Wicklow Mountains run from the north end of the county to the
south, tapering gently into the Irish Sea on the east and dropping
smoothly down to the River Barrow plain on the west. These mountains
are a series of hills and dales, conical peaks and wooded glens. So secluded
and relatively inaccessible are parts of these mountains that they served
for hundreds of years as resorts of escape for feisty Irish chieftains and
their followers who thumbed their noses at the representatives of the
British crown. Even today there are only two passes through these
mountains that allow them to be traversed from east to west.

GREAT LEINSTER ACCOMMODATIONS

HUNTER'S HOTEL, Rathnew. Tel. (0404) 40106, Fax (0404) 40338; E-mail: reception@hunters.ie; Website: indigo.ie/~hunters. 16 rooms. Rates for singles: £60, doubles: £53 to £60 per person sharing. Don't let the outside fool you. This is a great place!

MOYGLARE MANOR, Maynooth. Tel. (01) 628-6351, (01) 628-5405; E-mail: moyglare@iol.ie; Website: www.iol.ie/moyglaremanor. 17 rooms. Rates for singles: £85, doubles: £65 per person sharing, suites: £350 night. Impressive mansion, bountiful antiques, a warm welcome, and fabulous service.

TINAKILLY COUNTRY HOUSE, Rathnew. Tel. (0404) 69274, Fax (0404) 67806; E-mail: reservations@tinakilly.ie; Website: www.tinakilly.ie/pages/oldindex. 52 rooms. Rates for singles: £116 to £124, doubles: £68 to £76 per person sharing, suites: £85 to £130 per person sharing. No service charge. This marvelous old mansion has been lovingly restored and offers large, comfortable rooms, antiques, and views of the Irish Sea.

RATHSALLAGH HOUSE, Dunlavin. Tel. (045) 403112, Fax (045) 403343. 17 rooms. Rates for singles: £110, doubles: £55 to £105 per person sharing. 18th-century converted horse stables have never been so comfortable!

MOUNT JULIET, Thomastown. Tel. (056) 24455, Fax (056) 24522; E-mail: info@mountjuliet.ie; Website: www.mountjuliet.ie. 54 rooms. Rates for singles in the main house and Hunter's Yard: £115 to £190, doubles: £135 to £245, suites: £210 to £432. Rates for singles in the Rose Garden Lodges: £285 to £495. One of the premier country houses in Ireland, Mount Juliet is set in 1,500 acres of park land. The rooms are nearly as spacious, and the views are incredible.

KILDARE HOTEL AND COUNTRY CLUB, Straffan. Tel. (01) 601-7200, Fax (01) 601-7299; Website: www.kclub.ie. 45 rooms. Rates for singles: £155, doubles: £310 to £360, suites: £550 to £1000. Kildare Hotel is an exquisite five-star hotel that will make you feel like you are a member of the privileged class.

These heavily wooded hills, some of which rise over 3,000 feet from the Irish Sea, conceal some of the prettiest spots in Ireland. **Powerscourt Gardens and Waterfall**, **Loughs Dan** and **Tay**, **Glendalough**, and **Devil's Glen** are just a few of the spectacular places to be visited throughout County Wicklow.

Further south in the province of Leinster, you'll find the lovely resort town of **Wexford**, at the southeastern tip of Ireland. This handsome seaside town is a great place to spend a day or two, enjoying their lovely sandy beaches, shopping in town, or touring any of the museums in the area.

As you go a little inland, you'll find a few jewels there, too. Kilkenny is a very busy market town with an important history and a wonderful castle to explore – **Kilkenny Castle**. The countryside around Kilkenny hosts a number of impressive ruins just waiting for you to explore them: **Jerpoint Abbey** and **Duiske Abbey** are two of the most intriguing. These ancient ruins are still impressive in their stony silence.

So, if you've seen what you want to see in Dublin and are looking to venture out a bit, here are a few options for you. We'll start by heading north out of Dublin, then we'll head to the southern part of Leinster, and then finish with some sights in the inland portion of Leinster.

Without a doubt, the majority of hotels in Leinster are located in Dublin and its environs. Still, there are a good number of hotels, manor houses, guesthouses, and B&Bs spread throughout the province.

DROGHEDA & THE BOYNE RIVER VALLEY

The **Boyne River** gushes into the Irish Sea at the small city of **Drogheda**. Drogheda (pronounced DRAW-hed-a) is one of the busiest towns in this part of Ireland. Its Irish name is *Droichead Atha*, which means

LEINSTER'S BEST RESTAURANTS

HUNTER'S HOTEL, Newrath Bridge, Rathnew. Tel. (0404) 40106. Set lunch is £14.00 and set dinner is £18.50. All major credit cards accepted. The award-winning restaurant is quietly elegant.

CROOKEDWOOD HOUSE, Crookedwood, Mullingar, Co. Westmeath. Tel. (044) 72165. £12.95 to £19.95. All major credit cards accepted. The Crookedwood House is best known for its exceptional beef dishes. Featured in a recent special edition of Bon Appetit magazine.

LACKEN HOUSE, Dublin Road. Tel. (056) 61085. Set dinner menu £23. All major credit cards accepted. The meals at this country house are legendary.

TINAKILLY COUNTRY HOUSE RESTAURANT, Rathnew. Tel. (0404) 69274. £15.95 to £36. All major credit cards accepted. The restaurant at Tinakilly Country House is recognized as one of the best in the country.

MOUNT JULIET HOTEL RESTAURANT (called Lady Helen McCalmont Dining Room). Tel. (056) 24455, Thomastown, set dinner menu for £33. All major credit cards accepted. The Franco-Irish fare at the Lady Helen McCalmont Dining Room is award winning and exceptional.

"The Bridge of the Ford." At one time, Drogheda was one of the most important cities in Ireland. Today it is a bustling and busy industrial town of some 30,000 or so. Its main industry is cement, which it provides to the entire country.

Spanning the River Boyne, Drogheda was formerly two towns – one on each side of the river. But the towns grew together, and it made sense to some medieval city fathers to combine the towns and call them one. Drogheda physically resides in two counties: Louth and Meath, since the River Boyne separates the two counties at this point.

Drogheda's history extends back to its founding as a permanent site by Vikings in the early 10th century. Prior to that, a small community lived here where the River Boyne empties into the Irish Sea. Considering the presence of Newgrange, Knowth, and Dowth just up the Boyne Valley from Drogheda, it is likely that this area was host to some of Ireland's earliest inhabitants. The passage graves at these three sites, for example, date to 3,000 BC.

LEINSTER'S PREMIER SIGHTS

GLENDALOUGH – *This ancient monastic site is remarkably peaceful and beautiful.*

JERPOINT ABBEY – *These impressive ruins contain intriguing stonework.*

MELLIFONT ABBEY – *Mellifont Abbey was once the most important religious center in Ireland. Not far from Monasterboice, you can see from the extent of the ruins what an impressive sight this must have been.*

MONASTERBOICE – *The ruins of this ancient monastery include a round tower and a number of well-preserved high crosses.*

MOUNT USHER GARDENS – *On an island that is considered a garden spot itself, in a county that is called "The Garden of Ireland," Mt. Usher Gardens are some of the prettiest anywhere.*

NATIONAL STUD – *The Irish love their horses, and the National Stud is, as the name suggests, the national stud farm, where Irish racehorses are bred. There is also an interesting museum here.*

NEWGRANGE – *Lots of questions still remain about this passage grave that is 5,000 years old. The site is well preserved and well worth the visit.*

POWERSCOURT GARDENS AND WATERFALL – *This impressive estate is well worth the time to stop and visit. The grounds are incredible, and the waterfall is pretty impressive, too.*

ARRIVALS & DEPARTURES

By Bus

Buses leave throughout the day and night for locations within Leinster (including Drogheda) from **Busaras Station**, *Store Street, Tel. (01) 836-6111* in the O'Connell Street district of Dublin. Buses arrive hourly after a 50-minute ride from Dublin at the **Drogheda Bus Station**, *John Street, Tel. (041) 35023.* The fare from Dublin is £5.

By Car

Drogheda lies about 35 miles north of Dublin on the N1. The drive on the N1 is usually quite congested, as this is the main thoroughfare to northern Leinster as well as to Northern Ireland. For a less rushed trip, you might consider taking the coastal road (the R166) to Drogheda.

By Train

Trains leave for Drogheda eight times daily from Dublin's **Heuston Station**, *Tel. 01 836-6222, King's Bridge*, and the fare is £9.50 for a round-trip ticket. Buses arrive and depart from **Drogheda Train Station**, *John Street, Tel. (041) 38749.*

WHERE TO STAY

There are a number of fine Bed and Breakfasts in north Leinster, from the outskirts of Dublin all the way up to the Northern Ireland border. Unfortunately, the selection of hotels is a little more limited. Here are a few of the best accommodations I found during my travels in north Leinster:

THE REEFS BED AND BREAKFAST, *Balbriggan Coast Road, Skerries, Co. Dublin. Tel. (01) 849-1574. 4 rooms. Rates for singles: £16 to £24, doubles: £16 to £19 per person sharing. Rates include breakfast. No service charge. Open from April 1 through October 31.*

About half an hour north of Dublin lies the small harbor town of Skerries, and less than a mile up the road from Skerries is The Reefs Bed and Breakfast, run by Mrs. Violet Clinton. Views of the sea as well as the Mourne Mountains add spice to this pleasant B&B. Sitting just across the road from the Irish Sea, this relatively new B&B is an enjoyable and relaxing place to stay. If you want relaxation, just walk across the road and sit on the shoreline of the Irish Sea and enjoy the sunrise, or at the end of the day, the sunset over that lovely body of water.

Although there is no DART station nearby, you can catch a train from Dublin's Connolly Station that stops in Skerries. You can also catch bus #33 in Dublin at Eden Quay – it passes right by The Reefs.

The Reefs is a convenient place to base your exploration of a number of the sights north of Dublin. Malahide Castle and Newgrange are about

30 minutes down the road, and Newbridge House is just a few minutes down the road in Donabate. If you are a golfer, there are about 10 courses within just a few minutes' drive from here.

I have used The Reefs as the B&B for my last evening in Ireland. It provides lovely, serene seascapes, a pleasant "last remembrance" of Ireland, and is only 20 minutes from the airport.

BOYNE VALLEY HOTEL, *Castlebellingham, Drogheda, County Louth. Tel. (041) 37737, Fax (041) 39188. 37 rooms. Rates for singles: £55, doubles: £45 per person sharing. Rates include breakfast. Restaurant, swimming pool, tennis courts, golf. All major credit cards accepted.*

The Boyne Valley Hotel is a lovely country house, set amid 16 acres of park land. Its gardens are serene, and make for a nice evening walk.

The rooms are nice sized, and pleasantly furnished. I was particularly impressed with the service I received here – I felt more like a dear friend of the family than merely a guest staying for the evening.

If you have an interest in golfing while on holiday here, you may take advantage of the hotel's 18-hole pitch-and-putt golf course.

The Boyle Valley Hotel makes a nice place to base your exploration of such sights as Newgrange, Mellifont Abbey, and Monasterboice. Trips into Drogheda can also be based here, as well as jaunts into nearby Counties Monaghan and Cavan.

HODSON BAY HOTEL, *Athlone, County Westmeath. Tel. (0902) 92444, Fax (0902) 92688; E-mail: info@hodsonbayhotel.com; Website: www.hodsonbayhotel.com. 100 rooms. Rates for singles: £55 to £100, doubles: £70 to £110, suites £165. One restaurant, pub, indoor swimming pool, fitness center, sauna. All major credit cards accepted. 10% service charge.*

As they say in the real estate business, the most important three words are "Location, location, location." And the Hodson Bay Hotel has certainly taken those instructions to heart. Poised magnificently on the shores of Lough Ree, the hotel offers scenic views of the lough and the surrounding countryside.

In addition to providing sleeping facilities for its guests, Hodson Bay Hotel provides a host of activities, from golf at the nearby Athlone 18-hole golf course to swimming, to a leisurely beach to play and/or relax on.

While the rooms aren't particularly large, they are pleasantly and comfortably furnished, and half of the rooms offer beach and lake views that are memorable. But the other half of the rooms don't have bad views either, as they overlook the emerald fairways and greens of nearby Athlone golf course. Several years ago they built a new addition to the hotel, and those rooms are the nicest.

If you've brought your children along, you'll find a host of activities available for them, including swimming, nearby horseback riding, and even baby-sitting services.

WHERE TO EAT

Not many exceptional restaurants to mention in this part of Leinster, but here's one I ran across that I just had to include:

AN SOS CAFE, *Castlebellingham. Tel. (042) 72149. £3 to £7. Open during the summer months Monday through Saturday from 8:00am to 6:00pm, and Sunday from 11:00am to 4:00pm. Winter hours vary, but are generally Monday through Friday 9:00am to 4:00pm, Saturday 9:30am to 2:30pm, and closed Sundays. Mastercard and Visa accepted.*

Flight attendants have a reputation for knowing where to eat, and an Aer Lingus flight attendant tipped me off to this outstanding little cafe that is easily missed if you're not looking for it. As you are zooming along the N1 between Drogheda and Dundalk, slow down as you go through the hamlet of Castebellingham and watch for the thatch-roofed cottage known as *An Sos* Cafe.

This charming cafe run by Julie McMahon specializes in breakfast and a warm welcome. You'll probably sit among locals, and the mornings in particular are quite busy. The menu is surprisingly varied, from a full traditional Irish breakfast for only £3, to smoked salmon, to Julie's special-recipe lasagna, which features garlic, spinach, and ricotta cheese.

SEEING THE SIGHTS

Several hundred years after the Vikings inhabited the site and established Drogheda as one of the most important trading centers on the island, the town – as with many others across the country – was taken by the Anglo-Norman **Hugh de Lacy**. Over the next several hundred years Drogheda's importance and its position on the borders of "the Pale" justified the heavily fortified city wall. Ten gates allowed access into the city, but only one remains for visitors to see today: **St. Lawrence's Gate**, *on St. Lawrence Street,* is freely accessible. Impressive towers and a vaulted arch overlook the low passageway.

In 1649, Drogheda was unable to withstand the onslaught of **Oliver Cromwell's** armies, and between 2,500 and 3,000 captured soldiers were executed. According to Cromwell, the executions were "...a righteous judgment of God upon those barbarous wretches...."

At the opposite end of St. Lawrence Street from St. Lawrence's Gate is the domed 18th-century *Tholsel,* or city hall. The building is no longer used as city hall and now houses a bank. Nearby, at the corner of St. Peter's and William Street, is the proud **St. Peter's Church**, a 19th-century Gothic structure. The church was built in memory of a Catholic martyr, **Oliver Plunkett**. At one time he was the Archbishop of Armagh. He was one of many to be martyred in London in 1681 (he was canonized by the church in 1975). Not only was the church erected in his honor, but he is

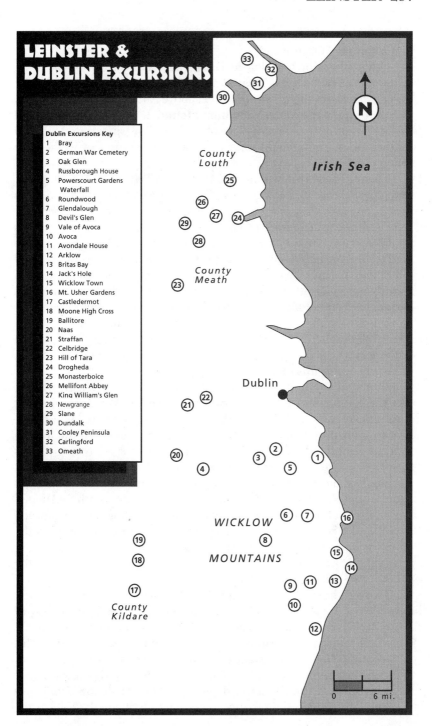

LEINSTER & DUBLIN EXCURSIONS

Dublin Excursions Key
1 Bray
2 German War Cemetery
3 Oak Glen
4 Russborough House
5 Powerscourt Gardens
  Waterfall
6 Roundwood
7 Glendalough
8 Devil's Glen
9 Vale of Avoca
10 Avoca
11 Avondale House
12 Arklow
13 Britas Bay
14 Jack's Hole
15 Wicklow Town
16 Mt. Usher Gardens
17 Castledermot
18 Moone High Cross
19 Ballitore
20 Naas
21 Straffan
22 Celbridge
23 Hill of Tara
24 Drogheda
25 Monasterboice
26 Mellifont Abbey
27 King William's Glen
28 Newgrange
29 Slane
30 Dundalk
31 Cooley Peninsula
32 Carlingford
33 Omeath

County Louth

Irish Sea

County Meath

Dublin

WICKLOW

MOUNTAINS

County Kildare

N

0   6 mi.

remembered today in a singular manner: his head is preserved in a shrine in the church. Macabre, at best.

Other sites worth seeing in Drogheda are the ruins of the 13th-century **St. Mary d'Urso Augustinian Abbey.** All that remains is the tower, which rises slightly over 100 feet above Abbey Lane. On the south side of town is a hill called **Millmount Mound.** It is said that the mound was built over the final resting place of the son of Milesius around the 11th century BC. Cromwellian forces took its 14th-century fort in the 17th century.

Today it houses the **Millmount Museum,** *Millmount Mound, Drogheda. Open April to October Tuesday through saturday from 10:00am and Sunday from 2:00pm to 6:00pm, and November through March on Wednesday, Saturday and Sunday from 2:00pm until 6:00pm. Admission is £1.50 for adults and 75p for children. Tel. (041) 33097. (The craft shops are open all year from 9:30am until 6:00pm Monday through Saturday.)* On Millmount Mound are a set of old English barracks, part of which have been converted into a museum featuring eight centuries of Droghedan history. Also included in the barracks are crafts shops and a picture gallery. The museum spends far more space on the domestic history of Drogheda than on its military history. A number of exhibits highlight Drogheda's progression from a settlement whose principle occupations were fishing and farming to the industrial center it is today.

After you've completed your exploration of the town of Drogheda, take the N1 north of Drogheda for about six miles. Watch for the first Dunleer exit north of Drogheda, then follow the signs to **Monasterboice.** It is not signed particularly well from the N1, but watch for the forlorn round tower off the west side of the N1 and make your way over to it. This site offers one of the premier exhibits of finely preserved high crosses in Ireland. It is the monastic settlement of Monasterboice, which takes its name from the Irish *Mainstir Buithe*, which means "St. Buithe's Abbey."

St. Buithe founded a monastery on this site during the 5th century. In 1097, the round tower suffered a devastating fire, destroying the monastic library that was stored there for safe keeping. The monastery was eventually abandoned in the 12th century. The site consists of the ruins of two churches, a round tower, and three high crosses.

Two of the high crosses at Monasterboice are among the best examples of high crosses in the world. One of them, the **Cross of Muiredach,** is remarkably well preserved. An inscription at the base of the cross says, "A prayer for Muiredach by whom this cross was made." This 10th-century High Cross stands almost 17 feet tall, and has scenes depicting Adam and Eve, Cain and Abel, Christ as the Judge, and Michael weighing souls. It also contains a depiction of the crucifixion. **Tall Cross** (21 feet high) depicts the sacrifice of Isaac by Abraham, the Vigil at the

Tomb, Judas' kiss of betrayal, and the crucifixion. One other cross, the **North Cross**, only partially survived the years. Scholars speculate that these crosses served more than an artistic outlet for some sculptor; they believe the crosses were used by monks to teach their non-reading followers about the scriptures.

The forlorn round tower that keeps a silent vigil over Monasterboice is nearly 110 feet tall, even without its peaked cap, which was lost many centuries ago. There is also a six-foot tall granite sundial enclosed with a railing that is interesting to see. In 1979, Monasterboice hosted a visit from Pope John Paul.

There is no charge to visit Monasterboice. Just park your car in the small carpark across the street, and let yourself in the gate.

Mellifont Abbey, *near Tullyallen. Tel. (041) 982-6459, open from May through mid-June daily from 10:00am to 5:00pm, and mid-June through mid-September daily from 9:30am until 6:30pm, mid-September through October from 10:00am to 5:00pm. Admission is free. A guided tour is available at £1.50 for adults, £1 for seniors, and 60p for children. A family ticket is available for £4.*

Located about three miles northwest of Drogheda just off the R168 is Mellifont Abbey, which was founded in 1142 by St. Malachy O'Morgair, and was the first Cisterian monastery in Ireland. A chapter house is the meeting place for a chapter (group) of monks. Only bits and pieces of the original buildings are still available to see, but the remains are enough to tell you it was an extensive site in its day. In fact, its Irish name *An Mhainistir Mhor,* means "The Big Monastery." Portions of the cloister still exist, along with parts of a chapter house built in the 12th century.

About seven miles west of Drogheda off the N51 is **King William's Glen**. This peaceful verdant vale is to Ireland what the sleepy crossroads town of Gettysburg was to the Confederacy. It was here that the armies of Protestant William of Orange routed the forces of Catholic James, the Stuart King of England. James fled Ireland and died three years later while in exile in France. The resulting shift of power in England (and thus in Ireland) meant that an oppressed Irish Catholic populace would not receive their deliverance for another century (more on that in the *Short History* chapter).

King William's Glen is the area where part of King William's army hid themselves just prior to the Battle of the Boyne. The site of their battle on July 1, 1690 is marked nearby.

Ledwidge Cottage and Museum, *Slane. Open April through September daily from 9:00am to 1:00pm and 2:00pm to 7:00pm, and October through March daily from 9:00am to 1:00pm and from 2:00pm to 4:30pm. Admission is £1. Tel. (041) 24285.* On the east side of Slane (about eight miles west of Drogheda) is a small stone cottage that once belonged to celebrated Irish poet Francis Ledwidge. He was an up-and-coming and very popular lyric poet who was killed during World War I. The home has been restored and stocked with period furnishings as a tribute to his short life.

About eight miles west of Drogheda on the N51 is the country village of Slane, and about a mile outside of town is Slane Castle, a 19th-century Gothic fortress. On the grounds of the castle is the 16th-century church called the **Hermitage of St. Erc**, the first bishop of Slane. In addition to the buildings, you can take peaceful strolls through the tree-filled estate.

Hill of Slane, *near Slane*. A mile north of Slane is Hill of Slane, one of the most famous hillocks in Ireland. It is revered as the place where **St. Patrick** lit a paschal fire in 433 AD, signifying the arrival in Ireland of Christianity and proclaiming the beginning of his ministry. The lighting of the Paschal fire defied a royal prohibition against such acts and served as a symbolic end for the Druidic religion in Ireland. Atop the hill are the remains of a 16th-century Franciscan friary, which were built on the ruins of the church St. Patrick built on that same spot.

Navan. The small city of Navan, population 3,500, is about a 45 minute drive from Dublin on the N3, or about 20 minutes from Drogheda on the N51. Navan serves as an important furniture manufacturing location for the country. Its Irish name is *An Uaimh*, which means "The Cave." It has ancient beginnings, but like so many other towns in this part of Ireland it saw its greatest growth and stature when Hugh de Lacy walled and fortified the city, as he did Drogheda, and secured it as one of the frontier towns of the English Pale.

The main street in Navan is Trimgate Street, and on it you'll come across **St. Mary's Church**, a 19th-century Catholic church. Its most striking feature is the 18th-century carving of the Crucifixion, one of the finest ever done by Irish wood carver and sculptor **Edward Smyth**.

Hill of Tara, *near Navan. Open early May through mid-June daily from 10:00am to 5:00pm, mid-June through mid-September daily from 9:30am to 6:30pm, and mid-September through October daily from 10:00am to 5:00pm. Admission is £1.50 for adults, £1.00 for seniors and students, 60p for children and a family ticket is available for £4.00.* Eight miles south of Navan just off the N3 (watch for the signpost) is the Hill of Tara, one of the most significant historic, religious, secular, and mythical sights in Ireland. It is the ancient site of the coronation of the Celtic kings of Ireland. Every three years a great *feis* (pronounced fesh) or large assembly was held to pass laws, regulate trade, settle disputes, and forge alliances among the kings of Ireland. It was revered through the centuries as a place of awe. With the lighting of **St. Patrick's** paschal fire not far away on Hill of Slane, the power and influence of the Hill of Tara began to wane. (A paschal fire is a fire used to celebrate the feast of the Passover.)

Atop this legendary hill is a statue of St. Patrick, and a small pillar called the *Lia Fial*, the stone believed to have been used as an ancient coronation stone. Legend has it that when the High King of Ireland (called the *Ard Ri*) was crowned at this sight, if the coronation was acceptable to the pagan gods, the Lia Fial roared mightily. The pagan Celtic kings would probably roll over in their graves if they knew the statue of this zealous Christian missionary had been erected on the hill of their ancient coronations.

Today, little else is on the Hill of Tara except grass-covered mounds and the occasional grazing sheep – the new kings of Tara.

Hill of Tara Interpretive Center, *near Navan. Open in May and September daily from 10:00am until 5:00pm, and June through August daily from 9:30am until 6:30pm. Admission is free. Tel. (041) 24824.* Located in a converted Church of Ireland building, a small interpretive center gives you the background of the Hill of Tara. The center features a short audio-visual presentation that helps you understand the historical significance of the Hill of Tara.

Trim. South of Navan on the R161 is the small market town of Trim. Sitting handsomely on the banks of the River Boyne, Trim's Irish name means "Town of the Elder-Tree Ford" (*Baile Atha Truim*). Religious and secular history swirled around this quiet crossroads town through the centuries. Like so many towns in Ireland, it was stormed and taken by Oliver Cromwell's armies, and like so many others, most of its inhabitants were put to the sword. Places to see in and around Trim include **Trim Castle, Yellow Steeple,** and **St. Patrick's Church.**

If you'd like to go to Trim directly from Dublin, it is about 25 miles northwest of Dublin via the N3, connecting to the R154 at Black Bull.

Trim Castle, *Trim. Open mid-June through mid-September daily from 10:00am to 6:00pm. Admission is £2.50 for adults, £1.75 for seniors and students, £1.00 for children, and a family ticket is available for £6.00.* Overlooking the River Boyne looms Trim Castle, a massive Anglo-Norman fortress said to be the largest in Ireland. The ruins of the castle cover more than two acres. Built by Hugh de Lacy, he seemed to be preparing for Armageddon – the huge fortress consists of a massive square keep with turrets soaring 70 feet, and towers in the middle of each wall. The walls themselves are a mere 11 feet thick! The fortress originally featured a drawbridge, which has long since disappeared. It spanned a moat which was filled from the River Boyne. The outer wall is over a quarter of a mile long, and originally its walks joined the town's walls. This was one impressive fortress in its day; the ruins are impressive today.

Yellow Steeple, *Trim.* The Yellow Steeple is what remains of a 13th-century Augustinian abbey (although the steeple is much newer – it was built in 1368!). Most of the tower was destroyed to prevent Cromwell's troops from taking it, and now only the 125-foot wall remains, a silent witness of the ugliness that dogged this quiet settlement through the centuries. The steeple gets its name from the soft amber glow it emits at sundown.

Newgrange. *Open March through April daily from 9:30am to 5:30pm, May daily from 9:00am to 6:30pm, June through mid-September from 9:00am to 7:00pm, mid-September to the end of September daily from 9:00am to 6:30pm, October daily from 9:30am to 5:00pm, and November through February daily from 9:30am to 5:00pm. Admission to the visitor centre only is £2.00 for adults, £1.50 for seniors and students, £1.00 for children and a family ticket is available for £5.00. Admission to the visitor centre and Newgrange is £4.00 for adults, £3.00 for senior citizens and students, £1.25 for children, and a family ticket is available for £10.00. Admission to the visitor centre, Newgrange and Knowth is £7.00 for adults, £5.00 for senior citizens and students, £3.25 for children, and a family ticket is available for £17.25.* Between the N2 and N1 north of Dublin is the Boyne River Valley in County Meath, where a number of important archaeological discoveries have been made in recent years. Newgrange, Dowth, and Knowth, within close proximity to one another, are the sites of three ancient burial mounds. Of the three, Newgrange's cross-shaped passage grave is the most impressive. Inside Newgrange, visitors will be led down a passage lined with massive stones and into the central burial chamber.

The Newgrange mound is a well-preserved grave dating back to nearly 3,000 BC. During the winter solstice (December 21), rays from the sun glide down the narrow passageway gradually lighting the burial chamber. For those unable to be at Newgrange during the winter solstice, modern technology recreates the effect. At 8:58am on December 21 of each year, the rising sun strikes an aperture in the roof of the passage grave. The sunlight is directed down into the passage grave, and as the sun rises its rays slowly move down the passage until they arrive in the main burial chamber, illuminating it. The rest of the year the effect is simulated by shining a light down the passage and into the burial chamber, as though it was really December 21, simulating the path the sun's rays take.

The burial mounds at Dowth and Knowth are also impressive, though neither has the dramatic winter solstice effect Newgrange offers. Dowth, in fact, has two chambers to its passage-tomb, and Knowth offers two main tombs surrounded by 18 others. Both Dowth and Knowth are in the process of excavation, and sometimes parts of them are open to visitors. When they are, the hours are the same as those listed above for Newgrange.

All three sites offer splendid examples of ancient artistic/ritualistic craftsmanship, as the tombs are all graced with wonderful stone carvings. These are impressive reminders of ancient man's devotion to his god or gods. These were the burial sites of the ancient kings of Ireland, and are well worth a visit.

Newtown. Less than a mile east of Trim, nestled along the banks of the River Boyne, are the ruins of what was at one time the largest cathedral in Ireland. Built in 1210 by Simon de Rochfort, all that remain of this magnificent building are the choir, crossing, and a portion of the nave. What a beautiful sight this must have been!

Kells. Near the intersection of the N3 and the N52 northwest of Dublin lies the monastic settlement of Kells. Its Irish name *Ceanannus Mor*, meaning "Great Residence." Built around the 6th century by **St. Columcille** (also called **St. Columba**), Kells survived repeated raids over several hundred years from their ill-mannered Viking neighbors. Their greatest claim to fame, however, is the 9th-century production of the richly illustrated *Book of Kells*, now on display in Dublin at Trinity College. But there is a modern reproduction of the book on display at St. Columba's Church in Kells.

St. Columba's also features a graveyard with five ancient high crosses. As with other high crosses, these are elaborately carved with scenes from the scriptures. See if you can identify any of the stories depicted (hint: look for Cain and Abel, Christ's Judgment, Daniel in the Lion's Den, Abraham's sacrifice of Isaac in the wilderness, and the miracle of the loaves and fishes). Four of the crosses are still in relatively good shape, but only a portion of the fifth survives. Sadly, in more troubled times, the fifth cross was used as a gallows during the 1798 uprising.

High Crosses first began to appear in Ireland in the 8th century. Theological experts have theorized that they served another purpose beyond merely representing the crucifixion. They speculate that the Biblical figures on the crosses may have helped the priests teach their non-reading parishioners stories from the scriptures. This theory may be true; or it may simply be that someone wanted to express his adulation and remembrance on a grand scale, and the idea caught on.

Nearby is **St. Columba's House**, an impressive example of the craft of building an entirely stone building, including the steeply pitched stone roof. St. Columba's House is similar in design to those found at Glendalough (St. Kevin's House) and at Cashel (Cormac's Chapel). The building itself measures 24 feet by 21 feet, is 40 feet tall at the ridge, and has walls that are more than four feet thick.

Near the church is a wonderfully erect round tower, dating from before the 12th century. The tower is nearly 100 feet tall, and there are five windows at the top, each providing a view of the various entrances to the ancient city. The tower no longer has its conical cap but is still an impressive sight.

SPORTS & RECREATION
Golf
> **County Louth Golf Club**, *Baltray, County Louth. Tel. (041) 22329, £35/ £40.* Visitors are welcome Monday, and Wednesday through Friday. Par 73, 6,783 yards.

Horse Racing
• **Fairyhouse Racetrack**, *County Meath, Tel. (01) 825-6167*

PRACTICAL INFORMATION
Post Offices
• **Drogheda Post Office**, *West Street. Tel. (041) 38157*

Tourist Offices
• **Drogheda Tourist Information Office**, *Donore Road, Drogheda. Tel. (041) 37070.* (Open June through September.)
• **Newgrange Tourist Information Office**, *Newgrange. Tel. (041) 24274.* (Open April through October.)
• **Trim Tourist Information Office**, *Mill Street, Trim. Tel. (046) 37111*

DUNDALK & THE COOLEY PENINSULA
Dundalk's Irish name, *Dun Dealgan* means Delga's Fort. The town has been here at the mouth of Dundalk Harbor since the 7th century, and has a history of attacks, sacks, and burnings. Dundalk is not far from the small town where death came to the legendary hero **Cuchulainn** of the Red Branch Knights. A statue commemorating his fearless stand and brave death graces the lobby of the GPO (General Post Office) in Dublin.

The town was walled in about 1185 by Bertram de Verdon. For nearly 300 years, Dundalk was considered a frontier town at the northern end of the English-controlled Pale. Because of this, it was frequently visited by native chieftains with murder and mayhem on their minds.

The Cooley Peninsula features some magnificent sights as you drive along the picturesque **Carlingford Lough**. Green hills, fascinating ruins, and an ancient burial sight are all part of the places worth visiting on the peninsula.

ARRIVALS & DEPARTURES
By Bus
Buses leave hourly from **Busaras Station** in Dublin headed for Dundalk. They arrive in Dundalk at the **Bus Eireann Station**, *Long Walk, Tel. (042) 34075.* The trip takes about two hours, and costs £8.

By Car

The harbor town of Dundalk is about 55 miles north of Dublin and 22 miles north of Drogheda on the N1. It takes about 90 minutes to get to Dundalk from Dublin (if you don't stop along the way to take pictures, visit sights, etc.). The Cooley Peninsula is a small peninsula that juts out into the Irish Sea northeast of the town of Dundalk.

By Train

Seven trains a day leave Dublin's Connolly Station and take a little over an hour to get to Dundalk. They arrive at **Dundalk Station**, *Carrickmacross Street, Tel. (042) 35521.* The fare for the train is about £10.

WHERE TO EAT

QUAGLINO'S, *88 Clanbrassil Street, Dundalk. Tel. (042) 71124. £17.50 to £26.95. Open Monday through Saturday from 6:30pm to 11:00pm (Saturday until 11:30pm). Visa, American Express, Access, and Diner's Club cards accepted.*

As the name signifies, Quaglino's is an Italian restaurant, but the menu is a little more diverse than most Italian restaurants have and allows for any number of dishes beyond the traditional Italian fare. If you are in the mood for seafood, you might find an appetizing morsel or two like smoked salmon, poached Dublin Bay prawns, or perhaps even baked oysters in a light garlic butter sauce. If it is traditional Italian fare you have an appetite for, you'll find outstanding Italian dishes, such as veal and eggplant parmagiana, and numerous pasta dishes. If you can't make up your mind between Italian and seafood, why not compromise, and try the seafood fettuccine?

The dress for Quaglino's is nice casual.

SEEING THE SIGHTS

Today, Dundalk is a bustling town of about 25,000 with a few interesting sights to see. One of the more interesting sights in Dundalk is **St. Patrick's Church** (1847) with its stone-carved high altar and pulpit. Its Newry-granite exterior is an imitation of King's College Chapel in Cambridge, England. On Clanbrassil Street is one of Dundalk's oldest surviving structures, **St. Nicholas' Church**, originally built in 1207. It was added to in the 1400s and renovated in 1707. In the adjoining graveyard, its most celebrated resident is Agnes Galt, the sister of Scottish poet Robert Burns, who is also commemorated by a pillar on the right side of the entrance to the church. On Castle Street stand the ruins of "The Castle," which really wasn't (and isn't) a castle at all. Rather, it is actually the bell-tower of a ruined 13th-century Franciscan friary.

Perhaps the most interesting sight in Dundalk isn't man-made. On the outskirts of the city are extensive salt flats and marshes, home to about a trillion different species of birds.

Tourism in Dundalk suffers from the plethora of more rustic ruins, scenic settings, and dazzling displays elsewhere in the country. Unless your family came from Dundalk, or lives here now, you may want to travel on to other locales. But there are a number of fine sights to see outside of Dundalk:

Cooley Peninsula Drive, *north of Dundalk*. Northeast of Dundalk on the N1, watch for the R173 and signposts to Carlingford and the Coast Road. Following these will take you around the peninsula. This scenic six-mile drive affords memorable views of the Irish Sea and the rolling green Irish countryside.

Proleek Dolmen, *Ballymascanlon*. In the hamlet of Ballymascanlon, behind the hotel of the same name, is the Proleek Dolmen, which has been here for roughly 5,000 years. A *dolmen* is a simple megalithic tomb that has three or more stones that serve as pillars or pedestals for a large stone (called a capstone) that is placed on top of them. Sometimes these capstones weigh up to 100 tons. The capstone for the Proleek Dolmen *only* weighs about 50 tons!

The medieval town of **Carlingford** sits on the north side of the Cooley Peninsula, nestled at the foot of Slieve Foye (1,935 feet) on the south shore of Carlingford Lough. There are a number of interesting medieval ruins in the town, although only one of them is available to the public. **King John's Castle** is a picturesque ruin still guarding the mouth of the harbor, as King John directed in the 13th century. It sits on the south end of town between the N1 and Carlingford Lough. Take a few minutes to explore the ruin, or take the half-mile or so walk on the quay that goes out into the lough. Other interesting ruins include the 15th-century **Mint House** and **Taafe's Castle**, an immense square keep off Newry Street and a contemporary of the Mint House.

A few miles southwest of Dundalk is the village of **Ratheddy**, a mile outside of **Knockbridge**. Ratheddy is home to *Clochafermor*, which means Cuchulainn's Stone. Cuchulainn (pronounced Koo-hoo'-lin) is a legendary hero, a member of the Red Branch Knights. As famous, colorful, and mighty as Davey Crockett, Daniel Boone, and Paul Bunyan, Cuchulainn is a legendary Irish hero of epic proportion. While he was probably a real person, his actual exploits are now shrouded in so much myth and hero-worship that it is hard to differentiate between fact and fiction. The annals report that after a lifetime of warring, Cuchulainn fought in one last ferocious battle. Fearlessly facing a daunting number of foes, he bravely and single-handedly fought on and on, spilling the blood of many enemies. Mortally wounded, he is said to have thrown his sword into a nearby lake and then lashed himself to a stone so that he could face his enemies standing. His foes wouldn't approach his body, the legend says, until a bird landed on the shoulder of the lifeless warrior.

Whether you believe the stories or not, Cuchulainn's Stone stands in Ratheddy. Interestingly, a nearby bog bears the Irish name *Lochan an Chlaiomh*, which means "The Lakelet of the Sword." Sometimes, truth really is stranger than fiction.

About four miles southwest of Dundalk on the R171 (after you go through Ratheddy) lies the hamlet of Louth. This serene hilltop town is traditionally given as the site of the first church built by St. Patrick in the 5th century. Nothing remains of that ancient house of worship. What remains is the 10th-century oratory named after the first bishop of Louth, now called **St. Mochta's House**. An excellent example of the Irish stone house, its tall stone roof is splendid.

PRACTICAL INFORMATION
Post Offices
• **Dundalk Post Office**, *3 Clanbrassil Street. Tel. (042) 34444*

Tourist Office
• **Dundalk Tourism Information Office**, *Jocelyn Street, Dundalk. Tel. (042) 35484*

BIRR
Without the popular **Birr Castle Demesne**, the town of Birr might be completely ignored by tourists. Its inland location and distance from main roads makes it easy to ignore. But the castle and its estate are worth a short detour to see. Birr has been called the *Navel of Ireland* as a result of its location in the center of the Emerald Isle.

ARRIVALS & DEPARTURES
By Bus
Three buses a day leave Dublin's **Busaras Station**, *Tel. (01) 836-6111, Store Street, Dublin* for Birr. The fare will cost you £9.

By Car
Birr is on the N62 north of Roscrea, about 85 miles from Dublin. Both towns are west and just a little south of Dublin. Take the N7 west out of Dublin to Roscrea, then north on the N62.

WHERE TO EAT

CROOKEDWOOD HOUSE, *Crookedwood, Mullingar. Tel. (044) 72165. £12.95 to £19.95. Open Monday through Saturday 6:30pm to 10:00pm for dinner, and for lunch on Sunday from 12:30pm to 2:30pm. All major credit cards accepted.*

Welcome to one of the top beef restaurants in Ireland! While there are a number of other items on the varied menu (roast pigeon, salmon and trout, roast duck, etc.), the Crookedwood House is best known for its exceptional meat dishes. Featured in a special edition of *Bon Appetit* magazine, owner/chef Noel Kenney is a master at his art. Try any of his beef plates, like his sirloin steak with colcannon and a mead/tarragon sauce that's exceptional. Wild meat specialties include medallions of venison with port and cranberries.

A little out of the way, the Crookedwood House is well worth the effort. Be sure and call for directions before you leave, but you can get in the general neighborhood by taking the N4 into Mullingar, and then north to Crookedwood town via the R394.

SEEING THE SIGHTS

Birr Castle Demesne, *Birr. Tel. (509) 20336, open daily from 9:00am to 6:00pm. Admission for adults is £4.00, £3.20 for students and seniors, and £2.50 for children.* In the small, quiet village of Birr, you'll find the Birr Castle, a romantic castle built in Gothic style in the early 1600s. Unfortunately, the castle isn't open to the public (it's still lived in by the Earls of Rosse), but the grounds are, and they are well worth the time it takes to see them.

The castle is set in a gorgeous 100-acre park-like setting. Spring is a particularly good time to visit, as the cherry trees, magnolias, and a host of other trees and flowers are in full bloom. Of particular interest are the 30-plus foot tall hedges.

Birr is a scant 10-minute drive from the inspiring **Slieve Bloom Mountains**. Hikers from all over the world come to sample the beauties found along numerous walking trails here. Stop at the Tourist Information Centre in Birr and ask for a map of *The Slieve Bloom Way*, which will help you find your way past towering peaks, wonderful waterfalls, and blooming bogs. The tallest peak is called *Ard Erin*, which means "Ireland's Highest," even though that honor really belongs to Carrantuohill in County Kerry.

Clonmacnoise, *Co. Offaly. Open mid-March through mid-May daily from 10:00am to 6:00pm, mid-May through mid-September daily from 9:00am to 7:00pm, mid-September to October from 10:00am to 6:00pm and November through mid-March daily from 10:00am to 5:30pm. Admission is £3.50 for adults, £2.50 for seniors and students, £1.50 for children, and a family ticket is* *available for £8.00. Tel. (0905) 74195.* About a 20-minute drive from Birr brings you to one of Ireland's most serene settings. On a ridge above the Shannon River rests the 6th-century monastic site of Clonmacnoise. Its Irish name means "Meadow of the son of Nos" (*Cluain Mic Nois*). Founded by St. Ciaran in 548, the goodly saint never realized how important the monastery would become – he died the year he founded it. It was once considered the most important religious center in Ireland.

Over the years, monks laboring within its walls produced several valuable manuscripts that are still in existence: *The Book of the Dun Cow* (currently on display at the Royal Irish Academy in Dublin) and the *Annals of Tighernach*. Alas, like so many other monastic sites around Ireland, Clonmacnoise suffered repeated attacks, plunderings, and burnings during its turbulent history. It seems every invading group conducted attacks against the community, from the Vikings to the Normans to the English under Oliver Cromwell.

The walled monastery is littered with ruins and crosses. Central to the ruins is the cathedral, which due to un-neighborly visits consists of various building and rebuilding (!) efforts, ranging from the 10th to the 15th centuries. Little is left except the walls. In addition to the cathedral, there are the ruins of eight churches and two round towers within or adjacent to the walls of the site.

One of the ruins is that of the 9th-century oratory called Temple Kieran. Tradition says that St. Ciaran's tomb is contained therein.

Scattered over the site are gravestones of varying ages. In addition, there are three high crosses, the most famous of which being the Cross of the Scriptures. It is said to mark the gravesite of **King Flann Sinna**, who died in 914. Like its counterparts in several other parts of Ireland (Glendalough and Monasterboice, to name two), this cross is richly carved with various scenes from the scriptures. Watch for the betrayal, arrest, and crucifixion of Christ, and the Judgment, all popular scenes for these crosses. In addition, this cross depicts King Dermot helping St. Ciaran laying the cornerstone of the church.

The Royal Irish Academy in Dublin, in addition to having *The Book of the Dun Cow*, also has in its possession the Crosier of Clonmacnoise, and it is considered to be one of the finest, best-preserved ancient Irish crosiers in existence. (A crosier is a staff with a crook in it, generally carried by or before a bishop or abbot. It is symbolic of his pastoral role as shepherd of the flock of God.)

You'll find Clonmacnoise by taking the N62 north out of Birr to the R357. Go west on the R357 to the wide spot in the road called Shannonbridge and watch for the signs directing you to Clonmacnoise. (You'll be turning north out of Shannonbridge.)

Clonmacnoise is definitely worth a few hours. It's a little off the beaten track, so you are more likely to have few tourists to battle, and may even be able to do a little personal meditation, as the sight certainly lends itself to that past-time.

Charleville Castle, *Tullamore. Open April and May Saturdays and Sundays from 2:00pm to 6:00pm, and from June through September Wednesday through Sunday from 11:00am until 5:00pm.* This grand mansion is set in an unspoiled park-like setting amid trees and gardens. Built while the War of 1812 was raging in America, this house is a splendid example of the way the wealthy Irish of the day lived.

Tullamore is located due west of Dublin. Take the M4/N4/N6 from Dublin toward Athlone. At Kilbeggan, watch for signs to Tullamore.

PRACTICAL INFORMATION

Tourist Office

Birr Tourist Information Office, *Rosse Row, Birr, Tel. (0509) 21110,* is open from May through September, and is located across from Birr Castle.

BRAY

The busy Victorian town of **Bray** lies south of Dublin along the southern sweep of Killiney Bay. Its beaches are of the sand and shingle variety, good for walking and feeling the sea breeze on your face. Worth seeing in Bray are the **Heritage Center** in the Old Courthouse, the **Bray Esplanade** with its aquarium, and **Bray Head**. It's also a popular get-away point for Dubliners.

ARRIVALS & DEPARTURES

By Bus

Several buses leave downtown Dublin for Bray, and you can catch them for the short ride there if you'd like. Bus # 84 leaves from Eden Quay, and bus #45 leaves from Burgh Quay.

By Car

Bray can be reached by taking the M11 south out of Dublin. It won't take you long to get there, so be on the alert. If you want a little more scenic route, watch for signs to Dalkey, Ballybrack, or Shankill. You can catch the R750 in those towns and travel along the coast down to Bray.

By Train

Bray is the last stop on the southern leg of the DART system. You can catch the DART at **Connolly Station**, *Amiens Street, Tel. 01 836-6222*, or at any of the other DART stations in town. The 45-minute ride is a memorable one, as parts of the track skirt the Irish coastline in County Wicklow.

WHERE TO EAT

THE TREE OF IDLENESS, *on the waterfront, Bray, County Wicklow. Tel. (01) 286-3498. £15 to £21. Open Sunday through Friday from 7:30pm until 11:00pm (10:00pm on Sunday). Closed Monday. All major credit cards accepted.*

This wonderful little Greek-Cypriot restaurant on the waterfront in Bray is a winner. The original Tree of Idleness was in Bellapais, Cyprus. Located in an old Victorian house, owner Susan Courtellas has managed a winning combination: fine Greek food (the result of chef Ismail Basran's expertise), a marvelous wine list, stunning dessert selection, and a pleasant atmosphere. Your selection is wide and varied and ranges from spinach ravioli stuffed with crab mousse to fillet of Irish beef to pheasant with grapes and chestnuts. The roast lamb and feta cheese is also wonderful.

SEEING THE SIGHTS

Bray Esplanade, *Bray*. A mile and a half-long esplanade that skirts the beach is extremely popular for strolling, feeling the sea breezes, and watching people, especially on nice summer evenings when the walkways can be fairly populated. There's also a new **National Aquarium** with over 700 different species of aquatic life on display that has proven quite popular.

South of the Bray Esplanade is a walking path that takes you to **Bray Head**, a promontory that rises 800 feet above the shores of the Irish Sea. Needless to say, views from here are beautiful on a clear day. The hike up and back takes a couple of hours.

Skirting the base of Bray Head is a pleasant trail called the **Cliff Walk**. It heads south from Bray Head to Greystones, four miles away. The walk is a pleasant one, requiring less effort than climbing Bray Head, but it also provides serene seascape views.

Kilruddery House and Gardens, *Bray. Open May, June, and September daily from 1:00pm until 5:00pm. It is possible to make an appointment in April, July, and August by calling ahead. Admission is £4.00 for adults, £2.50 for senior citizens and students, and £1.25 for children, and a family ticket is available for £10.*

On the Bray-Greystones Road is Kilruddery House and Gardens, a stately gray granite Elizabethan mansion that sits amid verdant trees and colorful gardens. The home was built in 1820. Kilruddery House is one of two County Wicklow sites for the annual **Festival of Music in Great Irish Houses** (the other location is Russborough House). Irish musicians come to Kilruddery House during the first or second week of June each year (it varies according to the musicians' schedules) and perform their musical magic. Violinists, cellists, or chamber orchestras are usually the featured performers.

For schedule and ticket information on the concerts – both at Kilruddery and Russborough Houses, as well as around the country – write to Mr. Crawford Tipping, *31 Beechwood Lawn, Dun Laoghaire, County Dublin, Ireland.*

ASHFORD

Ashford is known primarily for one thing: **Mount Usher Gardens**. The town itself isn't much more than a wide spot in the road, so watch closely for the gardens. They'll be on your left if you're on the N11 coming from Dublin.

ARRIVALS & DEPARTURES

By Car

Take the M11/N11 south out of Dublin to get to Ashford.

SEEING THE SIGHTS

Mount Usher Gardens, *Ashford. Open daily from mid-March through October 31 from 10:30am until 6:00pm. Admission is £3.50 for adults, £2.50 for seniors and students, £1.50 for children, and a family ticket is available for £8.00. Tel. (0404) 40205.* A little over four miles northwest of Wicklow Town is the small town of Ashford, and its main claim to fame: Mount Usher Gardens. In the 1860s, **Edward Walpole** planted a half-acre garden here, and it has expanded to the 20 acres you can see today. Located along the banks of the River Vartry, the verdant area is covered with a medley of trees, shrubs, flowers, and plants.

As you enter Mount Usher Gardens, you'll pass by a series of craft shops and a small restaurant. You are free to wander through the paths that wend their way through the gardens and over the river.

Devil's Glen, *north of Ashford.* Just north of Ashford, you'll come to spectacular Devil's Glen (watch for the road signs). This area is stunningly beautiful, and has a number of walking paths well laid out that provide some magnificent views. Devil's Glen is a deep gorge whose sides are graced with trees and shrubbery. The River Vartry tumbles nearly 100 feet into a pool called the Devil's Punchbowl.

WICKLOW TOWN

The county seat of County Wicklow is **Wicklow Town**, situated about 30 miles south of Dublin on the coast of the Irish Sea. County Wicklow is often called the Garden of Ireland, but Wicklow Town is a little less than a bed of roses. I found it to be congested and confusing, and not particularly user-friendly to get around. However, it does have an inspiring setting, overlooking a beautiful curved bay of the Irish Sea.

In the fifth century, a contemporary of St. Patrick's built a monastic settlement on the site and called it *Cill Mhantain* (St. Mantan's Church). However, in the 8th century, the Vikings saw the value of the area as a protected harbor, and moved in, calling the new settlement *Wykinglo*, which means "Viking Meadow." Over the years, the name was anglicized somewhat to the present day Wicklow.

ARRIVALS & DEPARTURES

By Bus

Buses leave from **Busaras Station**, *Tel. 01 836-6111, Store Street* in Dublin headed for Wicklow Town four times a day. You can catch the bus outside the **Grand Hotel**, *Main Street, Wicklow Town*. The round-trip fare is £3.50.

By Car

Continue south on the N11 to reach Wicklow Town, which is about 20 miles south of Dublin. Again, you can take the quick way by traveling on the M11/N11 out of Dublin, or you can maximize your viewing pleasure by taking the R750 along the coast.

By Train

Four trains a day run between **Wicklow Train Depot**, *Church Street*, and Dublin's **Connolly Station**, *Amiens Street, Tel. (01) 836-6222*. The round-trip is £4.

WHERE TO STAY

There are a number of classy places to stay in County Wicklow, and several of them are either in or close to Wicklow Town. Here are a few of them:

HUNTER'S HOTEL, *Rathnew. Tel. (0404) 40106, Fax (0404) 40338; E-mail: reception@hunters.ie; Website: indigo.ie/~hunters. 16 rooms. Rates for singles: £60, doubles: £53 to £60 per person sharing. One restaurant and pub. All major credit cards accepted. No service charge.*

You'll be surprised by this hotel, especially if you have the tendency to judge a book by its cover. Underwhelming on the outside, it nonetheless offers old-world charm and...creakiness...on the inside. Originally a coaching inn during the early 19th century, generations of the Gelletlie family have hosted, wined, and dined visitors here at Hunter's Hotel, and if you choose to stay here, you'll feel as though long lost relatives have welcomed you into their home.

Old – perhaps better classified as well-seasoned – but clean and warm, Hunter's Hotel oozes personality. Be sure to take the time to notice the variety of things that are hanging on the walls throughout the hotel, as there are a number of interesting and intriguing items. A sign in the garden emulates its owners' matter-of-fact opinion of the world: "Gentlemen and ladies will not, and others shall not, pick the flowers."

The rooms are all individually decorated and possess their own special character and personality. The rooms are filled with antiques to help convey a feeling of cordial personality.

The restaurant at Hunter's Hotel is considered one of the best south of Dublin (see *Where to Eat* section.). It has garnered a number of awards, and is gaining somewhat of an international reputation for its excellence.

THE OLD RECTORY, *Wicklow Town. Tel. (0404) 67048, Fax (0404) 69181; E-mail: mail@oldrectory.ie. 8 rooms. Rates for singles: £65, doubles: £52 per person sharing. Rates include breakfast. Dinner is available for £30.50. One restaurant. Fitness suite, sauna. All major credit cards accepted. No service charge.*

An excellent place to base your investigation of Wicklow Town and County Wicklow is The Old Rectory in Wicklow Town. This elegant old Victorian mansion has been around since 1875, and its renovation has provided a wonderful place to stay. Sitting at the edge of Wicklow Town amid lovely gardens, this courtly country home just seems to beckon you to come and stay for awhile.

The bedrooms at The Old Rectory are large and inviting with bright floral accents and comfortable furnishings, including some of the largest beds you'll experience in Ireland's B&B community. You'll find several nice touches in the rooms, including fresh-cut flowers from the gardens.

The owners are Paul and Linda Saunders, and they are rightfully proud of The Old Rectory. After fleeing the corporate world in London two decades ago, the Saunders seem to have found their niche in providing excellent accommodations and dining for guests.

To say that there is a restaurant on-sight is an understatement, as The Old Rectory Restaurant has gained international recognition for its excellence (see *Where to Eat* section following). So you can imagine the quality of the breakfast you'll sit down to during your stay.

TINAKILLY COUNTRY HOUSE, *Rathnew. Tel. (0404) 69274, Fax (0404) 67806; E-mail: reservations@tinakilly.ie; Website: www.tinakilly.ie/ pages/oldindex. 52 rooms. Rates for singles: £116 to £124, doubles: £68 to £76* *per person sharing, suites: £85 to £130 per person sharing. One restaurant, putting green, croquet. All major credit cards accepted. No service charge. One restaurant, putting green, croquet. All major credit cards accepted. No service charge.*

What a lovely hotel. It feels more like being at home (well – maybe at a very expensive home!) than like being at a hotel. Antiques abound, from the sitting room with its blazing fire to the splendid pieces in the rooms. This old Victorian mansion was built in the 1870s as a token of appreciation for Captain Robert Halpin, who commanded the *Great Eastern* as it laid the first telegraph cable that linked Europe and America. He must have been very pleased with the gift.

The rooms are wonderful – spacious, antique-laden, and most with lovely views of the Irish Sea. Many of the rooms have four-poster beds that seem to envelop you as you unwind after a day in the Wicklow Mountains. Tinakilly Country House is so impressive that it often overshadows the exquisite setting of the house – verdant green grounds overlooking the turquoise waters of the Irish Sea. Take a few minutes and stroll around the property and enjoy the beauty of a sunset (or sunrise!) on this portion of the Irish coast. Tinakilly Country House also sports a marvelous restaurant (see *Where to Eat*).

WHERE TO EAT

Perhaps because of its close proximity to Dublin, County Wicklow seems to have its fair share of excellent, award-winning restaurants. Several are associated with manor houses or guesthouses. The short drive from Dublin (roughly 45 minutes), the relaxed atmosphere, and extraordinary countryside all make the restaurants of County Wicklow a popular venue for Dubliners and tourists alike.

HUNTER'S HOTEL, *Newrath Bridge, Rathnew. Tel. (0404) 40106. Set lunch is £14 and set dinner is £18.50. Open daily for lunch from 1:00pm to 3:00pm and for dinner from 7:30pm to 9:00pm. All major credit cards accepted.*

Don't let the exterior of Hunter's Lodge put you off, as you'll miss a dining treat if you do. Mrs. Gilletlie is justifiably proud of the traditional meals prepared here for her hotel guests as well as those who journey here specifically for a meal. The menus vary day to day, but you'll always find quality, such as oak-smoked trout fillet, and Irish lamb and beef, all complemented with vegetables fresh from Hunter's Hotel's gardens.

ROUNDWOOD INN, *Roundwood. Tel. (01) 281-8107. £7.95 to £21.95. Open for lunch daily from 1:00pm to 2:15pm, and for dinner from 7:30pm to 9:30pm. If the restaurant is closed, the bar serves from a scaled-down menu from noon until 10:00pm. All major credit cards accepted.*

This German-style restaurant in the Wicklow Mountains is a real find. The German owners, Jargen and Aine Schwalm, have combined the best of German and Irish cuisine to come up with a distinctive and tasteful menu. There are numerous German dishes (wiener schnitzel, blueberry pancakes, veal) alongside traditional Irish dishes on the menu. Seafood, beef, and wild meat dishes are plentiful.

The Roundwood House is a cross between a pub and restaurant, and the ambiance is casual, from jacketed business people to hill-climbers in shorts and walking boots.

TINAKILLY COUNTRY HOUSE RESTAURANT, *Rathnew. Tel. (0404) 69274. £15.95 to £36. Open daily from 12:30pm to 2:00pm for lunch and from 7:30pm until 9:00pm for dinner. All major credit cards accepted.*

Set in the corner of the exquisite Victorian mansion once belonging to Captain Robert Halpin, Commander of the *Great Eastern,* and leader of the expedition to lay the first cross-Atlantic telegraph cable to America, the restaurant at Tinakilly House is a touch of elegance complemented by serenity and dining excellence.

The menu is wide-ranging, and main courses are augmented by fresh produce that is grown on the estate. They have gained some renown of late for their treatment of lamb. Other menu items include seafood (of course), Irish beef, and several vegetarian dishes. Aside from any of the lamb dishes, you might consider their excellent beef tenderloin with spring vegetables and champignon. Other specialties include baked tartlet of mushrooms, baked escalope of salmon, and roast breast of Barbary duck with fruit sauce. Their table d'hote menus are £18.50 for lunch and £30 for dinner.

OLD RECTORY, *Wicklow Town. Tel. (0404) 67048; E-mail: oldrec@indigo.ie. £18.95 to £30. Open daily 8:00pm to 9:30pm for dinner. All major credit cards accepted. 10% service charge.*

The Old Rectory restaurant is run by Linda Saunders, and blends the best of French and Irish cuisine to present an appetizing addition to your Irish holiday. The menu is extensive, and varies on a regular basis. Depending on when you are there, you may be treated to such specialties as fillet of black sole, roast quail with wild mushrooms, or sea trout and smoked salmon. The restaurant features a bright and floral-accentuated atmosphere, along with lively conversation among the guests. Linda and the restaurant have garnered a handful of awards, including such prestigious awards such as "Best Breakfast in Ireland," and "Inspector's Selected for Ireland."

In her spare time (ha!) Linda Saunders runs a cooking school in the spring and fall. Aspiring chefs can take advantage of half-day or full-day courses that are devoted to a variety of cooking topics such as wild mushrooms, vegetarian dishes, "wild food" sessions, and "sauces, soups, and salads." Class sizes are small – typically 12 or fewer students, and plenty of supervision is provided as you try your own hand at these things.

If you are interested in the cooking school, write, call, or e-mail Linda for dates and costs. The rates are really quite reasonable, especially when you consider the fine reputation Linda is gaining in the culinary world.

Reservations are essential during the spring and summer months. Dress is nice casual, although many of the guests will be dressed in suits and ties or dresses.

SEEING THE SIGHTS

Wicklow Town has a lovely main street lined with lovely, mature trees. At one edge of town are the ruins of a **Franciscan friary**, built in the 1200s. The ruins are not generally open to the public, but can be visited by arrangement with the priest who lives in a nearby home *(Tel. (0404) 67196)*.

On the north side of town is **Broad Lough**, a saltwater lake that receives the River Vartry before it empties into the Irish Sea. Walkways around the lake are popular for morning and evening strolls.

Black Castle, *Wicklow Town*. Black Castle, an Anglo-Norman stronghold built in 1176 by **Maurice Fitzgerald**, one of **Strongbow's** cronies, sits atop a rocky cliff just south of Wicklow harbor. Commanding views of much of the Wicklow coastline made this castle a valuable strategic position. Because of that, it was the site of many attacks from warring Irish chieftains through the years. The extensive ruins are accessible to the public.

Brittas Bay, *south of Wicklow Head*. This scenic sweep of sandy beach is a favorite among Dubliners and many of the Irish on holiday. Long (more than three miles) and unspoiled, it's a picturesque place to walk along the beach.

Jack's Hole, *south of Wicklow Head*. Six miles south of Wicklow Town are the spacious silky sands of Jack's Hole, a secluded seaside beach.

WICKLOW MOUNTAINS

The **Wicklow Mountains** run from the north end of County Wicklow to the south, tapering gently into the Irish Sea on the east and dropping smoothly down to the River Barrow plain on the west. These mountains are a series of hills and dales, conical peaks and wooded glens. So secluded and relatively inaccessible are parts of these mountains that they served for hundreds of years as resorts of escape for feisty Irish chieftains and their followers who thumbed their noses at the representatives of the British crown. Even today there are only two passes through these mountains that allow them to be traversed from east to west.

These heavily wooded hills, some of which rise over 3,000 feet from the Irish Sea, conceal some of the prettiest spots in Ireland. **Powerscourt**

Gardens and Waterfall, Loughs Dan and **Tay**, the **Vale of Avoca**, and **Glendalough** are just a few of the spectacular places to be visited in the Wicklow Mountains.

ARRIVALS & DEPARTURES

By Bus

The Wicklow Mountains are accessible via a number of bus routes that run from Dublin on a regular basis. Buses leave from **Busaras Station**, *Store Street, Tel. (01) 836-6111, Store Street* in Dublin as well as from some of the Dublin Quays, depending on your specific destination.

Special tour buses leave from Dublin on a regular basis. **St. Kevin's Bus Service** leaves for Glendalough daily from St. Stephen's Green West at 11:30am and 6:00pm (11:30am and 7:00pm Sundays). The round-trip fare is £8. **Bus Eirann** also runs tour buses to Glendalough April through September. Buses leave from **Busaras Station** daily at 10:30am.

By Car

You can reach the Wicklow Mountains by taking the M11/N11 south out of Dublin. Within a very short time you'll begin seeing signs for many of the sights the Wicklow Mountains have to offer.

If you're headed for Glendalough, take the M11/N11 south out of Dublin to Ashford, then take the R763 over to Glendalough.

WHERE TO STAY

RATHSALLAGH HOUSE, *Dunlavin. Tel. (045) 403112, Fax (045) 403343. 17 rooms. Rates for singles: £110, doubles: £55 to £105 per person sharing. Rates include breakfast. Restaurant, garden, croquet, indoor swimming pool, sauna, tennis, golf, snooker. All major credit cards accepted. No service charge.*

On this site in 1798, a lovely Queen Anne house burned down, leaving only the stables. Pity the house, but rejoice that the stables were spared, because they have been converted into a romantic hide-away that may well be one of your most pleasant memories of your stay in Ireland.

There are two types of rooms here – large and spacious, and smaller but warmer. The choice is yours, but either should serve your needs well.

Rathsallagh House is set in over 500 acres of emerald greenery, and the feeling is one of getting away from it all. You can golf on the 18-hole golf course, curl up with a book in the drawing room in front of the fire, or walk around the lovely grounds. And all this about 45 minutes from downtown Dublin.

SEEING THE SIGHTS

Powerscourt Gardens and Waterfall, *Enniskerry. Tel. (01) 204-6000. The gardens are open March through October daily from 9:30am until 5:30pm. Admission is £3.50 for adults, £3.20 for students and £2 for children under 12 (under 5 free). The waterfall is open all year from 9:30am until 7:00pm (in the winter from 9:30am until dusk). Admission to the waterfall area is £1 for adults and 50p for children.* If heaven is half as majestic as Powerscourt Gardens, I'll die a happy man! You've probably seen pictures of Powerscourt Gardens before – they are popular scenes used to depict the beauty of Ireland.

Powerscourt House was completed in 1740 for Sir Richard Wingfield, the first viscount of Powerscourt. The house is in the classical Roman Palladian style, and was designed by Richard Castle, who designed the Russborough House while overseeing the construction of Powerscourt House. Unfortunately, an accidental fire gutted the lovely home in 1974 and left it unfit and unavailable for touring. However, in the summer of 1997 an extensive renovation project was completed, and the home was restored to its original splendor.

The gardens were originally laid out beginning in 1745, and were revised to their present grand design in the mid-1800s. They cascade in a series of terraces down a slope from the house. The gardens are filled with verdant greenery: sculpted shrubs, trees, and many varieties of flowering plants, set among statues, fountains, and walkways. From the top of the terraces, the views sweep across the breathtaking Dargle Valley, culminating in outstanding views of Great Sugar Loaf Mountain and Kippure Mountain. In addition to the views, Powerscourt offers a tearoom, garden center and small shop.

Three miles south of the gardens is the **Powerscourt Waterfall**. The highest waterfall in Ireland, the water free-falls more than 400 feet off the edge of Djouce Mountain. It serves as a favorite picnic area for tourists and locals alike.

German War Cemetery, *Glencree.* West of Enniskerry is a secluded garden spot that represents a little sanity and humanity during a time of insanity and inhumanity. In the town of Glencree is a well-kept graveyard for German airmen who crash-landed in Ireland as a result of damage incurred in their bombing runs and air battles over England. Irish citizens donated a plot of land for the graves of these soldiers, and they have been lovingly kept through the years.

Oak Glen, *near Glencree.* On the road between Glencree and Enniskerry, closer to Glencree on the south side of the road, is Oak Glen, an experimental tree farm. Thousands of native oaks have been planted in an effort to re-vegetate the valley with the original flora that was here before being stripped for various building projects over the centuries. You can only access the lands by foot, but it makes for a serene stroll, not overrun by tourists.

Poulaphouca Reservoir, *near Blessington*. This reservoir supplies most of Dublin's drinking water. It was formed by flooding the King and Liffey Rivers. Now the reservoir is an important place of play for those who like water-sports such as boating, water-skiing, wind surfing, and the like.

Russborough House, *between Hollywood and Blessington. Open from June to August daily from 10:30am until 5:30pm, May and September Monday through Saturday from 10:30am to 2:30pm, and April and October on Sunday from 10:30am to 5:30pm. Admission is £3.00 for adults, £2.00 for students and seniors and £1.00. Tel. (045) 652329.* Wow! It only seems fitting that this Palladian mansion should be found near a town called Hollywood. It's actually closer to Blessington (two miles south), but its visage conjures up movie stars and the rich life. Built between 1740 and 1750, this impressive granite manor sits in the Wicklow Mountains, viewing them across an expanse of grass and a small lake. Its two wings on either side are connected to the main building by semi-circular colonnaded galleries.

Now owned by Sir Alfred Beit, the house features the current owner's inspiring art collection, consisting of a number of paintings by well-known artists (**Goya**, **Reynolds**, **Rubens**, and **Velasquez**, among others), as well as a variety of bronze sculptures. The collection was once much more extensive, but a series of criminal activities prompted the donation of a number of the more valuable works to the National Gallery of Ireland in Dublin. The house itself is an art treasure also; particularly the plaster work which was crafted by the **Francini** brothers, artisans of great fame in their day. If you like the wooded grounds that surround the house, they are available for strolls.

Tiny **Roundwood** has the distinguished honor of being the highest village in Ireland at about 900 feet above sea level. It's a small, relatively quiet town, but they have a lively market each Sunday afternoon where homemade wares such as jellies, jams, and baked goods are peddled. Perhaps the best product they have at the market, however, is the bustling congeniality of the event. Roundwood sits at the crossroads of the R763 (from Ashford), the R785 (from Newtownmountkennedy) and the R755 (from Enniskerry).

Not far (less than five miles) to the west of Roundwood you'll find two beautiful lakes, **Lough Dan** and **Lough Tay**. You can drive to Lough Dan and catch any of a number of walking trails that ascend the surrounding mountains and afford lovely views of the area. Watch for signposts in Roundwood directing you to Lough Dan. If you prefer walking to Lough Dan, you can catch the Wicklow Way about halfway between Roundwood and Sally Gap on the R759. It's a short walk to Lough Dan through the valley that lies between Lough Dan and Lough Tay. (You can see Lough Tay, but you cannot visit: it's on private land.)

Glendalough, *Co. Wicklow. Visitors Center open mid-March through May daily from 9:30am to 6:00pm, June through August daily from 9:30am to 6:30pm, September to mid-October daily from 9:30am to 6:00pm, and mid-October through March daily from 9:30am to 5:00pm. Admission is £2 for adults, £1.50 for seniors, and £1 for children. Tel. (0404) 45325.* "The glen of the two lakes" – *Glen Da Locha* – is perhaps one of the most serene places in the world. In the 6th century, **St. Kevin** sought refuge from the world, and founded a hermitage here. It is easy to see why. At the west end of the valley, Glenealo stream cascades in a waterfall into the valley. Two lakes grace the valley with their elegance and beauty – they are called simply Upper Lake and Lower Lake. Heavily forested mountains encompass the valley. Add to the natural beauty some exquisite and ancient ruins, and this is a wonderful place to visit. But don't rush your visit here – take your time and see all there is to see. A webwork of walking paths laces the woods all around Glendalough, and if you're interested in that aspect of touring, they offer wonderfully serene views.

The best place to begin your tour of Glendalough is at the visitor's center. Here they have a fine audio-visual presentation on Glendalough and its history.

In the 6th century when St. Kevin originally sought his solitude here, it is said he slept on a shelf above the Upper Lake. Tradition indicates that the place of Kevin's repose is a small hole in the rock of a cliff about 30 feet above the lake. It is called **St. Kevin's Bed**. After Kevin's death, the monastic settlement that he founded burgeoned. The settlement saw both its share of peace and serenity, as well as war and carnage. Repeated attacks by the Vikings in the ninth and tenth centuries took their toll, but it wasn't until English attacks in 1398 that the settlement was finally abandoned.

At the south end of Upper Lake is **Teampaill na Skellig** (Church of the Rock), a small (25 feet by 14 feet) granite church. This small church dates from the 6th century, as do the ruins of the **Reefert Church**, another small stone church of the same era. Tradition holds that Reefert Church is the burial place of local chieftains. Near Reefert Church are the ruins of a small beehive-shaped hut called **St. Kevin's Cell** that also served as home for the lonely St. Kevin. The south end of the lake is only accessible by a locally hired boat.

Moving from the Upper Lake to the Lower Lake, you encounter some of the finest religious ruins in Ireland.

To begin with, the gateway, next to the Royal Hotel, is the only surviving structure of its kind in Ireland. Inside the gateway is a graveyard with many intricately carved crosses. For what it's worth, I am not impressed with the placement of the hotel – it is a sensational setting for a hotel, but its presence mars the ancient mystery and beauty of the area for me!

Towering above the trees, the well-preserved 100-foot tall **Round Tower** stands as a mute witness of past oppressors and as a sentry against future invaders. Built in the 10th century, the only entrance is a doorway a mere 25 feet above the ground!

The **Cathedral** located at Glendalough is in relatively good shape, given its age (11th century) and the history of conquest this valley has had. The nave, chancel, and small sacristy are still intact.

St. Kevin's Kitchen is nearby, and this small church has a high-pitched stone roof. It is thought this structure was also built in the 11th century. And don't miss **St. Kevin's Cross**, (it would be hard to), an 11-foot granite cross 1,300 years old.

Other ruins of interest in Glendalough include **St. Savier's Church** (12th century), **Church of our Lady** (the oldest ruin in the lower valley), and the **Priest's House**, site of burials for priests. On the east end of Upper Lake you'll find an old fort (**Caher**) dating from the late Bronze or early Iron age. Look for the five crosses between the Reefert Church and Lower Lake. These crosses once marked the boundary of the monastic settlement.

From Glendalough, head south to Rathdrum, and watch for the signposts to Avoca. The trip takes you through the famous **Vale of Avoca**, a lush green valley immortalized by **Thomas Moore**. It was in this wooded valley, about a mile and a half north of Avoca at the point where the Avonbeg and Avonmore rivers mingle their waters and change their name to the Avoca River, that he penned the poem *The Meeting of the Waters*. Splendid nature trails wend through the heavy woods and provide a nice diversion. If you're fortunate to be here in early spring, the verdant green of the valley is punctuated with the snow-white cherry blossoms of wild cherry trees. The stretch of road between Woodenbridge and Rathdrum is all considered the Vale of Avoca.

On the R752 between Woodenbridge and Rathdrum lies the quiet little berg of **Avoca**. This diminutive village reposes amid wooded hills and the remains of an active copper industry that thrived until the early 1980s, when the industry closed down.

Avoca Handweavers, *Avoca. Tel. (0402) 35105. Open Monday through Friday from 9:30am to 5:30pm, and Saturday and Sunday from 10:00am to 6:00pm.* Next to the natural beauty of the area, the main attraction in Avoca is Avoca Handweavers, reportedly the oldest handweaving mill in Ireland. Take a few minutes and stop by the mill. They'll tell you that some of their weavers are second- and third-generation weavers. Their handweaving looms produce a colorful assortment of woven garments. Visitors can purchase items that catch their eye in a small shop, as well as snag a cup of coffee and a snack before continuing your trip. You can purchase a variety of items, from coats and scarves to bedspreads and caps.

Avondale Forest Park/Avondale House. *Open daily from 11:00am to 6:00pm. Admission is £2 for adults and £1 for children and senior citizens, and a family ticket is available for £5. Tel. (0404) 46111.* Avondale Forest Park is the setting for Avondale House, once birthplace and residence of **Charles Stewart Parnell** (1846-1891), one of the most famous and influential players in Ireland's drive for independence. Charles was a gifted and eloquent Parliamentary speaker and untiring advocate for the cause of home rule for Ireland. Unfortunately, his much-publicized affair with Kitty O'Shea *(Mrs.* Kitty O'Shea) scandalized the country and split his political allies. He died a year after the revelation, some say of a broken heart.

Parnell's home has been meticulously restored and is a pleasure to visit. Built in 1779, the original owner, Samuel Hayes, spent years planting a variety of trees around his estate, and the results are evident all around you when you visit. Parnell's great-grandfather John Parnell purchased the property in 1795.

SPORTS & RECREATION
Horseback Riding
- **Brennanstown Riding School, Ltd.**, *Kilmacanogue, County Wicklow. Tel. (01) 286-3778, Fax (01) 282-9590*
- **Devil's Glen Equestrian Center**, *Ashford, County Wicklow. Tel. (040) 440013*

PRACTICAL INFORMATION
Post Offices
- **Laragh Post Office**, *(near Glendalough), Main Street, Laragh. Tel. (0404) 45236*
- **Wicklow Town Post Office**, *Main Street, Wicklow. Tel. (0404) 68834*

Tourist Offices
- **Arklow Tourist Information Office**, *Main Street and St. Mary's Road, Arklow. Tel (0402) 31854*
- **Glendalough Tourist Information Office**, *Glendalough. Tel (0404) 45581. (Open June to September.)*
- **Wicklow Tourist Information Office**, *Fitzwilliam Street, Wicklow. Tel (0404) 69117*

WEXFORD

The southeastern tip of Ireland is chock full of things to see and do. At the end of the Emerald Isle sits **Wexford Town**. It rests alongside the Slaney River as it enters Wexford Harbor. The town is ancient, showing up on 2nd-century AD maps drawn by Ptolemy. Its Irish name, *Loch Garman*, means "Garman's Lake." However, like Wicklow, it takes its current name from an anglicized Viking word. The Viking name of the town was *Waesfjord*, which means "the harbor of the mud flats."

One of the first towns taken by the Anglo-Norman invaders during the 12th century, Wexford always seemed to be up for a fight. In 1649, Oliver Cromwell took the city and slaughtered its inhabitants. For a short period during the 1798 Uprising, the town was held by Irish rebels, who met ignominious defeat at **Vinegar Hill**. (Spears and courage didn't fare well in the face of artillery, swords, and cavalry!)

Today, Wexford is a fascinating place to visit. When in Wexford, just follow your nose, and it's sure to take you someplace interesting. There are so many things to see and do, you need to let your interests guide you. From the **Maritime Museum** to the **Irish National Heritage Park**, to gorgeous sandy beaches on the Irish and Celtic Seas, you can't go wrong.

In addition to Wexford Town, the Wexford Peninsula seems to be made for tourists of all ages and interests. Whether you're interested in fabulous seascapes, antique windmills, or sublime ruins of ancient origin, you are in for a real treat. Read on for some fun and interesting sights.

ARRIVALS & DEPARTURES

By Bus

Bus service runs between Dublin's **Busaras Station**, *Store Street, Tel. (01) 836-6111*, and Wexford's **O'Hanrahan Station**, *Redmond Square. Tel. (053) 22522*, five times a day. The two-hour ride will cost you £9 for a round-trip ticket, and £8 for a one-way ticket. O'Hanrahan Station is about a third of a mile from the town center, and the neighborhood is fine to walk through.

By Car

Wexford is about 90 miles south of Dublin on the N11. If you were to drive it straight through, it would probably take you three hours, but who wants to drive straight through such beautiful country with so many impressive sights to see in between?

Sample trip lengths on the main roads:
• Cork: 3 hours
• Donegal: 6 hours
• Dublin: 3 hours

- Galway: 4 hours
- Killarney: 4 hours
- Limerick: 3 hours

By Train

Train service from Dublin's **Heuston Station**, *Tel. (01) 836-6222*, to Wexford's **O'Hanrahan Station**, *Redmond Square, Tel. (053) 22522*, runs three times a day, and will cost you £12 for a round-trip ticket, £11 for a one-way ticket. The trip takes about three hours.

ORIENTATION

Wexford is at the southeastern tip of Ireland. A town built (primarily) along the south bank of the River Slaney as it empties into the Irish Sea, it is a pleasant place to take a walk around town. Wexford is by no means large, and can be traversed in minutes via automobile or bicycle. If you're walking, it will take you a little longer, but not too much longer.

GETTING AROUND TOWN

By Bicycle

The most efficient way to see Wexford Town is via bicycle. It is also perhaps the most pleasant. Beware, however, as some of the roads are quite narrow – scarcely a dozen feet wide in some parts of town.

By Car

Wexford is so small and compact that you'll probably spend more time looking for a parking place than you will if you park and see the town by foot.

By Foot

If you have the time, Wexford Town is quite nice to see on foot. The city is not large, and you can get from one end to the other quickly.

WHERE TO STAY

LEMONGROVE HOUSE, *Blackstoops, Enniscorthy. Tel. (054) 36115. 9 rooms. Rates for singles: £23 to £25, doubles: £18 to £25 per person sharing. Rates include breakfast. Credit cards not accepted. No service charge.*

This newer neo-Georgian B&B offers a pleasant place to stay and a warm Irish welcome from Colm and Ann McGibney. There are five ensuite and four standard rooms to choose from, and all are furnished smartly and are warm and comfortable. The rooms feature soft colors and views of the countryside. Each room offers a television and tea- and coffee-making facilities.

Located at the northern edge of Enniscorthy (north of Wexford), Lemongrove House would be an excellent place to base your discovery of the Wexford area. The McGibneys are well acquainted with the surrounding area, and will be happy to help you plan your adventures in southeastern Ireland. If you've brought your children along, you'll appreciate the 25% reduction the McGibneys will offer you.

HILLSIDE HOUSE B&B, *Tubberduff, Gorey. Tel. (055) 21726; Fax (055) 22567; E-mail: hsh@eircom.net. 8 rooms. Rates for singles: £25 to £30, doubles: £20 to £25 per person sharing. Rates include breakfast. Mastercard and Visa accepted. No service charge.*

If you are looking for a wonderful B&B, look no further. George and Ann Sunderland are your hosts, and Hillside House is the place you'll really enjoy. Built in the countryside of County Wexford, Hillside House offers you what you hope every Irish B&B will offer: peace, tranquillity, and a genuine warm Irish welcome. There is a sitting room for guests with a wonderful fireplace that sets just the right ambiance, television if you wish, and even a stereo to listen to some of those CDs of Irish music you picked up on your trip.

There are six ensuite rooms available at Hillside House. Each is large, individually decorated, and quite pleasant. Several of the rooms – those at the back of the house – have stunning views of the Irish countryside. All of the rooms have television, hairdryers and electric blankets (just in case it has been a cool or damp day out).

The Sunderland's are rightfully proud of the reputation they have earned as warm and friendly hosts. Their knowledge of the area is gladly shared, and they'll help you find the sights or activities that appeal most to you. If you're coming to this neck of the Irish woods, you can't go wrong staying at Hillside House.

NEWBAY COUNTRY HOUSE, *Newbay, near Wexford. Tel. (053) 42779, Fax (053) 46318; E-mail: newbay@newbayhouse.com; Website: www.newbayhouse.com. 6 rooms. Rates for singles: £45, doubles: £35 to £45 per person sharing. Rates include breakfast. Diners, Mastercard, and Visa accepted. No service charge.*

Located just a few miles outside Wexford in Newbay, the Newbay Country House offers a nice place from which to explore the Wexford peninsula. While the outside of the house is not particularly memorable, the interior will be more to your liking. A number of antiques combine with a warm welcome to make Newbay Country House a pleasant place to stay. The bedrooms are all spacious and nicely furnished. Four-poster beds are a treat, but don't expect to flop on the bed and catch CNN – there are no televisions in the rooms, helping to foster that rustic country feeling that pervades the rest of the house.

KELLY'S RESORT HOTEL, *Rosslare. Tel. (053) 32114, Fax (053) 32222; E-mail: info@kellys.ie; Website: www.kellys.ie. 99 rooms. Rates for singles: £80; doubles: £55 to £71 per person sharing. Two bars, one restaurant, tennis, swimming pools, squash, snooker, croquet, miniature golf, bicycling, children's playroom. All major credit cards accepted.*

Rosslare is a noted resort town, and Kelly's Resort Hotel does all they can to cater to those who come here looking for a resort vacation. Four generations of the Kelly family have put together a sound sleeping and resort package for their guests. The hotel sits right on a wide sandy beach, so you'll be just moments from the water. The rooms in this hotel are wonderful, bordering on elegant. All are tastefully furnished and spacious. Ask for a room overlooking the bay, or perhaps you'd like the rooms that open out into the hotel's gardens.

GREAT SOUTHERN HOTEL, *Rosslare Harbor. Tel. (053) 33233, Fax (053) 33543. 100 rooms. Rates for singles: £50; doubles: £80 to £102. Swimming pool, fitness room, sauna, snooker, hairdresser. All major credit cards accepted.*

The recently refurbished Great Southern Hotel overlooks Rosslare Harbor and is a pleasant and enjoyable place to stay. The rooms are of a nice size and comfortably furnished. Their remodeled lounge and reception area are light and airy, and give you a feeling of casual hospitality. But the service is anything but casual. You'll enjoy your stay here immensely.

WHERE TO EAT

GALLEY CRUISING RESTAURANT, *New Ross. Open Easter through October. Lunch is £11, afternoon tea is £5, and dinner is £20. Tel. (051) 21723.*

Recommended if you find yourself in New Ross and think you might enjoy a lunch cruise on the River Barrow. Fish caught locally is the specialty.

ARCHER'S PUB, *Redmond Square, Wexford. Tel. (053) 22316. £3.95 to £13.95. Open Monday through Saturday from 10:30am to 11:30pm, Sunday from 12:30pm to 2:00pm. Visa and Access cards accepted.*

While you are out and about in Wexford Town, look for Archer's Pub and pop in for a bite to eat. You'll have a choice of a substantial meal or a lighter snack, depending on the time of day and the mood you're in when you drop by. Pub grub is generally available from noon until 3:00pm Monday through Saturday, and the rest of the time you can choose from such entrees as cod or monkfish, prawns in garlic butter, or a variety of roasts (lamb or beef). They generally even offer at least one vegetarian dish most of the time. Dress is casual.

The atmosphere here is warm and comfortable, and you'll always find a pleasant welcome and a friend or two here are Archer's.

THE GRANARY RESTAURANT, *Westgate, Wexford. Tel. (053) 23935. £12.95 to £18.95. Open Monday through Saturday from 6:00pm to 10:00pm. All major credit cards accepted.*

The Granary is one of those restaurants you'll be anxious to tell your friends back home about. This warm and friendly place features a series of booths that enable you to quietly enjoy the pleasant atmosphere you'll find here, not to mention the food. It won't take much imagination on your part to figure out that the restaurant once served as a granary, as the heavy pillars and massive beams are still very evident.

The owners, Paddy and Mary Hatton, are serious about providing a wonderful dining experience blended with the Granary's pleasant surroundings. Since Wexford is on the sea, you would expect seafood to their specialty, and you won't be disappointed. For starters, you might sample the Kilmore crab claws in garlic butter with Cashel bleu cheese melted over fresh treacle bread. Follow that with a sumptuous serving of Kilmore scallops poached in white wine and you'll be delighted you stopped by. If you're in the mood for something other than seafood, the menu offers a wide selection of other entrees, including duck, lamb, pigeon, venison, and Irish steaks. If you prefer vegetarian meals, they also generally have at least one or two vegetarian entrees on the menu. Each dish is prepared and presented in marvelous manner. Dress is nice casual.

KELLY'S RESORT RESTAURANT, *Rosslare, County Wexford. Tel. (053) 32114. £18.95 to £24.95. Open Monday through Saturday from 6:00pm to 10:00pm. All major credit cards accepted.*

The restaurant for Kelly's Resort is large yet inviting, extravagant yet somehow appealing simple. You'll be impressed by any number of things the dining room has to offer, from top-tier service to elegant table settings to spectacular art on the walls. But don't stop there. The menu offers a wide variety of entrees that are designed to whet your appetite and please your palate. Sitting on the ocean as Kelly's Resort does, you'd expect to see a number of seafood offerings, and your expectations in this regard will be exceeded. Whether you prefer mussels, crab, shrimp, salmon, or lobster, you'll find the seafood dishes appetizing and delicious. But if your interests are more along the lines of beef or lamb, you won't be disappointed either. The restaurant is proud of their wide range of offerings in this area, from their rack of Rosslare lamb to their Irish steaks to their scallopini of venison and bacon.

Dress is nice casual, although you won't feel out of place with a suit and tie or dress for the evening meal.

MARLFIELD HOUSE RESTAURANT, *Gorey, County Wexford. Tel. (055) 21124. £30.95 to £45.95. Open daily from 12:30pm to 2:30pm and 7:00pm to 9:30pm. Visa, American Express, Access, and Diner's Club cards accepted. 10% service charged.*

*Visa, American Express, Access, and Diner's Club cards accepted. 10%
service charged.*

On your way to exploring Wexford, if you find yourself in or around
Gorey near the lunch or dinner hours, you may want to stop at Marlfield
House Restaurant. If you do, I guarantee you'll have a splendid dining
experience.

Marlfield House Restaurant is located in a fine old 19th century
country home owned by Ray and Mary Bowe. They have gained quite a
substantial reputation for the meals they serve in their restaurant. Part of
the reason is their insistence on only the freshest ingredients, from the
herbs and produce grown in their own garden to the fish or meat
harvested from the surrounding rivers, ocean, and countryside. Although
Gorey is not generally a destination point for tourists, Marlfield House
Restaurant has caught the eye (and palates) of a number of food critics –
they have won a number of industry awards for their fine fare.

Seafood is a specialty, and you are liable to find a wide variety on their
ever-changing menus. If you're lucky, one of the starters may be the crab
and salmon sausage with spring onions and a light mustard sauce. If not,
you won't be disappointed in such entrees as baked salmon stuffed with
asparagus or roast breast of Barbary duck with onions braised in a cream,
white wine, and wild mushroom sauce. Wexford mussels in an exquisite
sauce are a local favorite.

Either before or after dinner, take the time to stroll around the
grounds of Marlfield House. They are exquisite, from the lovely gardens
to the pond out back of the house. They make the perfect setting for your
dining experience.

If you find the price a little much for your pocketbook, consider
stopping for lunch instead of dinner. While the menu is a bit more limited
than the dinner menu, the same quality is available for about half the price
of dinner.

Dress is nice casual, although you'll feel more comfortable at dinner
with a suit and tie or dress.

SEEING THE SIGHTS

Wexford Waterfowl Preserve. There is a reason why the Vikings
called this town *Waesfjord*, "the harbor of the mud flats." As the River
Slaney empties into Wexford Harbor, its silt build-up was noticeable even
a 1,000 years ago. Perhaps it wasn't as bad then, but bad enough to call
it by that name. Today, the north bank of the River Slaney provides a
broad waterfowl preserve on those same silt mud flats. Walking across the
bridge that spans the River Slaney at the west end of town takes you to the
preserve. Over half of the year, Greenland white-fronted geese make this
their home.

If you are a veteran of the United States Navy, you may want to make your way to the large bronze statue of **Commodore John Barry**, considered the "Father of the American Navy." Born in the nearby village of Ballysampson in 1745, he immigrated to America and became one of her most brilliant naval officers during the War for Independence.

Church of the Immaculate Conception/Church of Assumption, *Rowe and Bride Streets.* These two churches are called "the Twin Churches," because these 19th-century Gothic churches are identical on the exterior, from the base of their corner stones laid on the same date to the tips of their lofty, 230-foot spires.

Tradition has it that **Selskar Abbey** is located on the oldest site of Christian worship in County Wexford. Built on the former site of a Viking temple to Odin, you'll find the ruins of Selskar Abbey just to the south of Westgate Tower Heritage Center.

Westgate Tower, *corner of Westgate and Slaney Streets. Open July and August Monday to Saturday from 9:30am to 1:00pm, and from 2:00pm to 5:30pm Sunday from 2:00pm to 5:00pm. March through June and September through Novembert it is also open from 11:00am to 1:00pm and 2:00pm to 5:00pm. Admission is £1.50 for adults and £1 for children. Tel. (053) 20733.* This gate tower, a red sandstone remnant of the old city wall, has been meticulously restored. It is the only one of five original gate towers that remains today. It serves now as the home of the Westgate Heritage Center, where you can see a short audio-visual presentation of the history of Wexford.

Franciscan Church, *School Street.* Built on the site of a former Franciscan abbey, the abbey features marvelous plaster work on its ceiling. A glass case enshrines the remains of St. Adjutor, a young man who is considered an early Christian martyr. The son of a pagan father and Christian mother, the lad was raised as a Christian by his mother, unbeknownst to his father. When the news reached his father, he was so incensed that he slew his son with an ax.

Wexford Bull Ring, *Quay Street.* Many of us look disapprovingly on sports that feature cruelty to animals. Such was the sport of bull baiting, for which the Wexford Bull Ring was used. Bull baiting was a popular sporting event for the Anglo-Norman rulers. Worse still, this ring was used by Cromwell's soldiers as the sight of execution for over 300 townspeople who had gathered there to pray for safety when the city was attacked by British forces.

Irish National Heritage Park, *Ferrycarrig. Open March to November from 10:00am to 7:00pm (last admittance at 5:00pm). Admission is £5 for adults, £5 for senior citizens and students, and £3 for children, and a family ticket is available for £12.50. Tel. (053) 20733.* At the northern edge of Wexford you'll find the small village of Ferrycarrig, and the Irish National Heritage

Park. This fun and educational park traces Ireland's heritage from the Stone Age through the conquest of the Anglo-Normans. Thirty acres are filled with a myriad of life-size structures – dwellings, forts, a monastery, Norman castle, etc., to give you an idea of how the ancient Irish lived, worked, and were buried. Actors in period dress answer questions and share their skills at weaving, pole lathing, and pottery through frequent demonstrations.

This is a lot of fun and very interesting. In about an hour and a half you'll get a good overview of about 4,000 years of Irish history.

Enniscorthy Castle & County Wexford Museum, *Enniscorthy. Open June through September, Monday through Saturday from 10:00am to 1:00pm and 2:00pm to 6:00pm, and Sunday from 2:00pm to 5:30pm, February through May, October and November Monday through Saturday from 2:00pm to 5:30pm. Admission is £3 for adults, £2 for students and children. Tel. (054) 35926.* About 14 miles north of Wexford on the N11 you'll find the town of Enniscorthy and Enniscorthy Castle and County Wexford Museum. This massive square keep is wonderfully preserved. Originally built in 1199 by one of the early Anglo-Norman invaders, the castle was rebuilt in 1586. It withstood the guns of Cromwell in 1649, and has served as a prison, residence (of the English poet Edmund Spenser), and now serves as the county museum. The museum has a number of interesting exhibits, including two that focus on the uprisings that occurred in 1798 and 1916. Don't miss the country "still" that was used for brewing Ireland's own brand of white lightning. It's called *poteen* (pronounced potcheen), and the Irish say a good batch will knock you for a loop.

Vinegar Hill, *Enniscorthy, guided tours of the site are available from mid-May through September for £3. Tel. (054) 36800.* Just outside of Enniscorthy, you come to Vinegar Hill, the site of a pivotal battle between the British and the Irish during the 1798 uprising. Over 18,000 Irish rebels made a valiant stand against the British army. Their only weapons were spears, and they took a frightful pounding from the constant artillery barrage leveled at them by the British. Today there's not much left except about half of the stone windmill that served as headquarters for the rebel leaders.

Following the battle, the rebel leader Bagenal Harvey fled to a cave on an island off the south Wexford coastline, where he was later captured.

Rosslare Beach, *Rosslare.* Rosslare and its fine beach are about 10 miles from downtown Wexford Town. Take the N25 south out of Wexford, and then take either the R736 or the R740 until you reach the beach.

This is one of the prettiest beaches along the eastern coast of Ireland (some would argue that it's the prettiest in the country). Long stretches of sandy beaches (about five miles' worth) and safe swimming areas make this a popular place for tourists as well as the Irish. Rosslare is a booming metropolis of 700 people; from May through October visitors outnumber locals by a significant number.

Follow the signposts from Wexford toward the beautiful fishing village of Kilmore Quay (the N25 to the R739), where you'll find thatched-roof cottages and pleasant villagers. Along the way, watch for the signposts directing you to Tacumshin; follow those signs to Tacumshin, and you'll be treated to a picturesque sight – the **Tacumshin Windmill**. This old thatched windmill, reminiscent of those Holland is famous for, was built in 1846 and used until 1936. Stop into the small store that is in front of the windmill, and the proprietor will unlock the door so you can go inside and view the inner workings of the windmill, most of which are the original wooden mechanisms. It makes for great photos! Note: as you near Tacumshin (it's very small) watch carefully for the windmill – it is behind a small store. You can park in the store's small (two or three car) carpark, or along the side of the road if the carpark is full. By the way — the proprietor is as delightful and picturesque as the windmill is!

The word for **Kilmore Quay** is picturesque. It is a radiant little village with thatched roofs and whitewashed cottages. Sitting on a small peninsula on the Celtic Sea, the sea views are fabulous, the air is fresh, and the local villagers are warm and cheerful.

The **Ring of Hook Drive** is undoubtedly as peaceful a drive through the Irish countryside as you are likely to take. From Wellington Bridge, take the R733 toward Fethard-on-the-Sea. From there, follow the signs for the Ring of Hook lighthouse and the Celtic Sea. It's a great place to take plenty of pictures.

Duncannon Fort, *Duncannon, open daily June through August from 10:00am to 6:00pm. Admission is £1.50 for adults, £1.00 for seniors and students, 50p for children and a family ticket is available for £4.00. Tel. (051) 325208.* The Ring of Hook ends at **Duncannon**, just across the harbor from Waterford. Duncannon's Irish name (*Dun Conan*) means "The Fort of Conan." At the edge of town you'll find that fort, and perhaps you'd like to visit it. As you do, just think of the terrible strife it has seen through the years. Ships of the Spanish Armada attacked it in 1588, Oliver Cromwell took a few whacks at it in 1649, William of Orange assaulted it during his tour of Ireland in 1690, and finally, the United Irishmen attacked it during the 1798 Uprising.

For many years Duncannon was a site of military importance, particularly as protection against marauding ships of (take your choice) Vikings, Anglo-Normans, Irish rebels, the Spanish Armada, Napoleon's navy, etc. No matter who controlled this site, they kept the three-acre fort fortified and ready to greet any foes that ventured her way.

Between Arthurstown and Wellington Bridge you'll find the ruins of **Tintern Abbey**. Tintern Abbey is a sister abbey to nearby Dunbrodey Abbey. A plaque on the site says, "Founded in 1200 by William Earl Marshall. This abbey was called 'Tintern de Voto' after Tintern Abbey in Wales, from where its monks came." The abbey is largely intact, and has recently undergone extensive renovation. The remains consist of a vaulted chapel, nave, tower, and chancel. Take a few moments to check it out, and consider what life at this peaceful sight may have been like. (However, it wasn't always peaceful – it was attacked numerous times during its history.)

Little **Ballyhack** sits at the mouth of Waterford Harbor on the R733. It has been an incredibly popular locale for artists and photographers from all over the world. This stereotypical fishing village offers plenty to paint, sketch, or photograph: fishing boats, old **Ballyhack Castle**, and the assorted local residents, full of character. Ballyhack Castle was originally part of the preceptory (a religious house) of the Knights Templar; today its ivy-covered and weathered rock walls keep watch over the harbor. A short car ferry ride that will set you back £5 across the harbor will take you to another picturesque Irish fishing village in County Waterford: **Passage East**, which competes with Ballyhack for its share of photographers and artists. It's nice competition – everybody wins.

Dunbrody Abbey and Castle, *near Campile, visitor center open April through September Monday through Friday from 10:00am to 6:00pm, Saturday and Sunday 10:00am to 8:00pm. Admission is free. Tel. (051) 88603.* Three miles north of Ballyhack on the R733 are the imposing ruins of Dunbrody Abbey and Dunbrody Castle. The Abbey was built in the late 12th century, and the castle (adjacent to the Abbey) is of similar vintage.

The ruins are set back from the main road about 150 yards, and on sunny days especially, it makes for marvelous pictures. The extensive ruins are approached via a dirt road that slips between green fields, and the ruins are a delight to explore. Sitting next to the peacefully flowing Barrow River, the Abbey must have been a wonderfully serene setting for its former inhabitants to do whatever it was they did at the Abbey.

Stop in at the small visitor's center across the street from the ruins. It encompasses a museum, tearoom, and gift shop.

John F. Kennedy Memorial Forest Park, *near Dunganstown. Open daily from 10:00am to dusk. Admission is £2 for adults and £1 for children. Tel. (051) 388171.* Located at Dunganstown is the small cottage that was the birthplace of John F. Kennedy's great-grandfather. Perhaps you have seen this cottage in old films of President Kennedy's visit here in the 1960s. Nearby is the 400-acre memorial park, wherein the Irish people pay homage to President Kennedy's life and works. Americans of Irish descent donated the cost of the park.

Ballylane Farm, *near New Ross. Open May through September daily from 10:00am to 8:00pm, March and April Saturday and Sunday from noon to 5:00pm, April to March from 10:00am to 6:30pm. Admission is £2.00 for adults, £1.50 for seniors and £1 for children. A family ticket is available for £7 (2 adults and 4 children). Tel. (051) 425666.* Two hundred acres of interesting sights, sounds, and smells await your visit to Ballylane Farm. This working farm presents a variety of things for you to see and experience, including activities on tillage, pheasant and deer raising, sheep and forestry. The hour tour is educational and interesting.

The village of **New Ross**, population 5,000, is due west of Wexford Town on the N25. Its Irish name is *Ros Mhic Treoin*, which means "The Wood of the Son of Tream." The town is built against and on a steep hill, which leads down to the River Barrow. An ancient town dating to the early 6th century (a monastery was founded here by St. Abban), its real importance emerged as an inland port during the 13th century. It was one of many towns in this part of the country that fell to the advancing Cromwellian armies.

Sinister intrigue swirled around New Ross during the 1798 uprising. Rebel forces fighting for Bagenal Harvey were attempting to negotiate peace with the British commander, **Lord Mountjoy**, who was garrisoned with his forces in New Ross. The rebels sent a peace envoy into the garrison; he was summarily shot. Realizing the magnitude of the error, Lord Mountjoy sought a meeting to placate the rebels. He was shot and killed in reprisal for the envoy's death, which in turn ignited fierce fighting for the town. The British forces finally gave way and vacated. But while the exhausted rebel forces were enjoying their hard-fought victory, fresh British reinforcements arrived and inflicted heavy casualties on the rebels before forcing them from the town.

New Ross is immensely quieter these days. Take a few minutes to stretch your legs here. If you do, you'll find a town with a medieval feel, with narrow winding streets, many of which are closed to vehicular traffic. If you're up for a river cruise dining experience, check out the Galley Cruising Restaurant (see *Where to Eat* above).

SPORTS & RECREATION
Golf
- **Courtown Golf Club**, *Kiltennel, County Wexford. Tel. (055) 25166.* Visitors are welcome daily. Par 71.
- **Enniscorthy Golf Club**, *Enniscorthy, County Wexford. Tel. (054) 34519*
- **Rosslare Golf Club**, *Rosslare Strand, County Wexford. Tel. (053) 32203.* Visitors are welcome daily. Par 72.

Horse Racing
· **Wexford Racecourse**, *Bettyville, County Wexford. Tel. (053) 42307*

Horseback Riding
· **Ballingale Farm**, *Taghmon, County Wexford. Tel. (053) 34387*
· **Blackstone Trekking Center**, *Blackstone, Duncormick, County Wexford. Tel. (051) 63126*
· **Borohill Equestrian Center**, *Clonroche, Enniscorthy, County Wexford. Tel. (054) 44117*
· **Horetown Equestrian Center**, *Horetown, County Wexford. Tel. (051) 565771*
· **Laraheen Pony Trekking**, *Gorey, County Wexford. Tel. (055) 28289*
· **Schmalier Riding Stables**, *Forth Mountain, Taghmon, County Wexford. Tel. (053) 39251*

Sailing and Windsurfing
· **Rosslare Sailboard Center**, *Rosslare, County Wexford. Tel (53) 32101*

Swimming
There are a number of safe, sandy beaches to enjoy around County Wexford. One of the most enjoyable is **Rosslare Beach**, but others include the beaches at **Curracloe**, **Duncannon**, and **Courtown**.

PRACTICAL INFORMATION
Laundry Service
· **My Beautiful Launderette**, *St. Peter's Square, Wexford. Tel. (053) 24317*

Post Offices
  Wexford Post Office, *Anne Street. Tel. (053) 22587*

Tourist Offices
· **Rosslare Terminal Tourist Information Office**, *Rosslare. Tel. (053) 33622*
· **Wexford Tourist Information Office**, *Crescent Quay, County Wexford. Tel. (053) 23111*

KILDARE
The Irish have a love affair with horses, and nowhere is it more apparent than in County **Kildare** in general, and Kildare Town specifically. This village in the heart of Ireland's horse country is a special place, and one you should plan on visiting. In and around Kildare you'll find

wonderful sights to entrance and entertain you. You'll find yourself in the center of the world-famous **Curragh**, birthplace and training center of some of the world's finest racehorses. I guarantee you'll see some beautiful animals in and around Kildare. While in Kildare, you'll want to be certain and stop by the **National Stud**, and the **Japanese Gardens** in Tully are exquisite beyond belief.

ARRIVALS & DEPARTURES

By Bus

Bus Eirann runs a number of buses daily between Kildare and Dublin's **Busaras Station**, *Tel.(01) 836-6111, Store Street.*

By Car

Kildare is about an hour's drive west of Dublin on the N7/M7.

By Train

Trains run between Dublin's **Heuston Station**, *King's Bridge, Tel. (01) 836-6222,* and the **Kildare Train Depot** every 40 minutes, so if you want to come to Kildare by train, you shouldn't have too many problems.

WHERE TO STAY

KILDARE HOTEL AND COUNTRY CLUB, *Straffan. Tel. (01) 601-7200, Fax (01) 601-7299; Website: www.kclub.ie. 45 rooms. Rates for singles: £155, doubles: £310 to £360, suites: £550 to £1000. Restaurant, tennis, croquet, golf, indoor swimming pool, fitness center, squash, sauna, shooting, horse-back riding, beauty salon. All major credit cards accepted. No service charge.*

The Kildare Hotel and Country Club (affectionately known as the K-Club), is a relatively new (1991) five-star hotel located just 17 miles from downtown Dublin in the peaceful town of Straffan. The cost, of course, is commensurate with the surroundings.

From outside, the structure suggests opulence. The grounds – including a mile-long stretch of the River Liffey and five lakes – are nothing short of spectacular, as are the gardens. Leaflets at the front desk provide you with details of walks you can take through the grounds. Inside, you'll not be disappointed in anything you encounter – the interior is as exquisite as the exterior. Antiques, including a fine collection of artwork complement lavish furnishings. The bedrooms? Large and tastefully (and expensively) outfitted. Luxurious bathrobes, slippers, hand-made chocolates, bowls of fruit and mineral water are nice touches in the rooms.

For those of you who have a passing interest in golf, the Kildare Country Club was the venue for the European Open for 1995, 1996, and 1997. It presides over the Arnold Palmer-designed course.

MOYGLARE MANOR, *Maynooth. Tel. (01) 628-6351, (01) 628-5405; E-mail: moyglare@iol.ie; Website: www.iol.ie/moyglaremanor. 17 rooms. Rates for singles: £85, doubles: £65 per person sharing, suites: £350 night. Restaurant, tennis, garden. All major credit cards accepted. 12.5% service charge.*

As you enter the grounds of Moyglare Manor, you'll feel lost in the midst of verdant beauty. Splendid gardens and sprawling lawns and park land serve as the backdrop for this imposing Georgian mansion.

However, the only thing imposing about Moyglare Manor is the manor house itself. Once you darken the doorway, you'll feel welcomed and warmed immediately. Your stay will be punctuated with friendly service and serenity – most of the rooms do not have television to ensure the tranquillity of the experience. The Lady of the house is Norah Devlin, and even in antique-crazy Ireland she is known for her eye for antiques – many of which are displayed throughout the width and breath of Moyglare Manor. The rooms are large and comfortable. Most have four-poster beds and tasteful decor. To preserve the peaceful nature at Moyglare Manor, you are respectfully requested not to bring children under age 12.

SEEING THE SIGHTS

National Stud and Iron Horse Museum, *Tully (near Kildare). Open February through November daily from 9:30am until 6:00pm, and Sunday from 2:00pm until 6:00pm.Admission for a combined ticket for the National Stud, Iron Horse Museum and the Japanese Gardens is £6 for adults and £4.00 for children. Tel. (045) 21617.* In case you didn't know it, Ireland loves horses, and that love is probably centered in Tully at the National Stud. This is where breeding stallions are kept and where horse groomers and trainers work their magic on the mares of Ireland.

Located with the National Stud is the Iron Horse Museum, a museum that traces equestrian history from the Bronze Age to the present. If you're really into horses and horse racing, you'll know the name of Arkle, probably the most famous (and winningest) Irish racehorse. His skeleton is on display at the museum. Visitors to the National Stud have fairly free access to the fine horses that are stabled here.

Japanese Gardens, *Tully (near Kildare). Open February through November daily from 9:30am until 6:00pm, and Sunday from 2:00pm until 6:00pm. Admission for a combined ticket for the National Stud, Iron Horse Museum and the Japanese Gardens is £6 for adults and £4.00 for children. Tel. (045) 21617.* A little over a mile south of Kildare is the village of Tully, with its famous Japanese Gardens. Early in this century, Lord Wavertree commissioned famous Japanese landscape designer Tassa Eida to design and lay out these gardens. The results of his work are exquisite. The design symbolizes man's passage through mortality and into eternity. This is really worth a visit.

Moone High Cross, *Moone (near Ballytore)*. About 15 miles south of Newbridge on the N9 and just south of Ballytore is the small hamlet of Moone with its famous high cross. Over 17 feet tall, the cross has a number of carvings depicting biblical scenes. My favorite is of Shadrach, Meshach and Abednego facing the fiery furnace. Can you identify any of the others?

Emo Court and Gardens, *near Portarlington, Gardens open mid-June through mid-September Tuesday through Sunday from 10:30am to 5:00pm. Admission is £2.00 for adults, £1.50 for seniors and students, £1.00 for children and a family ticket is available for £5.00. Tel. (0502) 26110.* Ten miles west of Kildare and about five miles outside of Portarlington is Emo Court and Gardens. James Gandon, who designed the Custom House and The Four Courts in Dublin, also designed the house. You'll note he seems to have been unable to do anything on a small scale. The house is exquisite, and is truly a sight. It has an impressive domed rotunda, and the lighting currently in use accentuates its grandeur.

The grounds are quiet and serene, and include numerous statues, shrubs, and walkways. This is a nice quiet diversion.

SPORTS & RECREATION
Golf
Kildare Country Club Golf Course, *Straffan, County Kildare. Tel. (01) 627-3333, £100.*

Wow! If you want to see how the other half plays golf, this is the course to do so. Arnold Palmer designed the course, some of the best golfers in the world have played here, and you can too. The course is a series of doglegs, sand and water hazards, and stunningly maintained fairways and greens. If you have the opportunity to play here, don't pass it up. Kildare has hosted a number of major championships, and you'll feel like a pampered champion if you play here.

Visitors are welcome daily except from 1:30pm to 2:30pm, and 9:00am to 1:00pm on Saturday. Par 72, 6,536 yards.

Horse Racing
• **The Curragh Racecourse**, *County Kildare. Tel. (045) 541205*

Horseback Riding
• **Kill International Equestrian Center**, *Kill, County Kildare. Tel. (045) 877208, Fax (045) 877704*
• **Maynooth Equestrian Center**, *Bannockstown, Maynooth, County Kildare. Tel. (01) 628-9048*

PRACTICAL INFORMATION

Tourist Office

• **Kildare Tourist Information Office**, *The Square, Kildare. Tel. (045) 522696. Open June through September.*

CARLOW

The county seat of County Carlow, **Carlow** is a busy burg of about 12,000 sitting quietly beside the River Barrow. Carlow has more industry than many of its neighboring towns, mostly centered on processing agricultural products such as sugar beets, wheat, and malt. Its Irish name is *Ceatharlach,* which means "Fourfold Lake."

Serving during much of Ireland's recent history as one of the southern borders of the English Pale, the area has a history rife with violence, as Irish chieftains often sought to throw off the chains of their oppressors. They fought and bled much in County Carlow. During the 1798 Uprising, 640 patriots perished here; their efforts are remembered by a Celtic high cross that was erected on the site of their graves on Church Street.

Today, things are a little quieter in Carlow. Located about 50 miles south of Dublin on the N9, it offers salmon and trout fishing (called angling here), golfing, and river cruising along the River Barrow. Sights in and around Carlow that are of interest include the **Cathedral of the Assumption, Carlow Castle, Carlow County Museum,** and **Browne's Dolmen**.

ARRIVALS & DEPARTURES

By Bus

Bus Eirann runs six buses daily between Carlow and Dublin's **Busaras Station**, *Store Street, Tel. 01 836-6111.*

By Car

Carlow is located about 50 miles southwest of Dublin on the N9.

By Train

Trains run between Dublin's **Heuston Station**, *King's Bridge, Tel. (01) 836-6222,* and Carlow four times per day. The one-hour trip costs £11.

SEEING THE SIGHTS

Cathedral of the Assumption, *Tullow Street, Carlow. Open daily from 10:00am until 8:00pm. Admission is £1 for adults and 50p for children. Tel. (0503) 31227.* Built in the shape of a cross, the late 19th-century Gothic

Cathedral of the Assumption is known for its lovely stained-glass windows. In addition, its lantern tower soars an impressive 151 feet above the street. You'll also be impressed with a fine marble monument to the builder of the cathedral, **Bishop James Doyle** (1786-1834). Bishop Doyle was a tireless agitator for Catholic emancipation at a time when it was exceptionally hazardous to do so. He was a prolific political writer, and his pen was continually busy for the Catholic cause.

Carlow Castle, *Castle Hill Street, Carlow.* Built in the 13th century to provide a modicum of defense against local raiders, Carlow Castle originally had a large rectangular keep with a round tower at each of its corners. Today, all that remains are one wall and the two towers that abut it. It still stands poised to defend Carlow at this point near the bridge that crosses the River Barrow.

Carlow Castle is one of the few fortresses that was able to repel the advances of Oliver Cromwell's armies, which it did in 1650. However, it fell to idiocy several hundred years later when its new owner accidentally destroyed most of the castle through the inauspicious use of explosives. (He was trying to alter the thickness of the walls.)

Today, access to the castle is through the grounds of Corcoran's Mineral Water Factory. Ask at the factory office for permission to enter. (Weekdays only.)

County Museum, *Centaur Street, Carlow. Open Tuesday through Saturday from 9:30am to 5:30pm, Sunday from 2:30pm to 5:30pm. Admission is £1 for adults and 50p for children. Tel. (0503) 31759.* The Town Hall is the venue for the small County Carlow Museum. The exhibits are interesting if not extensive. As you enter the building beneath the two-story portico upheld by massive columns, look for several exhibits depicting life in old Carlow. A blacksmith's forge and primitive kitchen will give you an appreciation for the life of some of Carlow's residents in the 19th century. In addition, there are several fine examples of carpentry and barrel-making tools, as well as a number of military items from the 18th and 19th centuries.

Dolmen on Browne's Hill, *Carlow.* About two miles east of Carlow on the R725 is the largest *dolmen* in Ireland. (A dolmen is a prehistoric tomb or monument, which consists of a large flat rock resting on a series of upright smaller stones.) Located in Browne's Hill demesne (estate), the large rock on top (the capstone) was once elevated by a number of smaller stones underneath. Its weight (102 tons!), the weather, and the elements have all combined to cause one end of the capstone to drop to the ground. It's impressive to contemplate how on earth prehistoric man possibly accomplished the feat of maneuvering that large stone into place with the few ancient tools he had.

The dolmen is approached in a circuitous 200-yard route around a farmer's field, and is protected by a few cows in a nearby (fenced) field that watch closely as you pass.

About three miles west of Carlow on the R430 are the ruins of **Killeshin Church**, an excellent example of Hiberno-Romanesque architecture. The arched doorway is particularly impressive. Killeshin Church is a 6th-century monastery founded by St. Diarmuid. There are several interesting and ancient tombstones in the vicinity of the church. This is one of those ruins you can let your kids' imaginations run wild in; or see which is the oldest date they can identify on one of the scores of ancient tombstones scattered about the churchyard. Chances are there won't be a lot of other tourists around, and you can explore to your heart's content here with few distractions.

Black Castle, *Leighlinbridge*. Seven miles south of Carlow on the N9 are the ruins of Black Castle. Sitting near the River Barrow, the castle dates from the Anglo-Norman conquest of Ireland in the late 12th century. Its peaceful demeanor belies the fact that it was a place of great violence in days gone by. As one of the first strongholds of the Anglo-Norman invaders, it was the scene of many sieges and attacks, and the surrounding grounds have been moistened with great quantities of blood over the centuries. Not much of the castle remains today other than a decrepit tower.

St. Laserian's Cathedral, *Old Leighlin*. A couple of miles west of Leighlinbridge on a minor road (watch for the signposts) is the hamlet of Old Leighlin, the site and ruins of St. Laserian's Cathedral. St. Laserian founded a monastic settlement on this site in the 7th century. In the 12th century a church was built to commemorate St. Laserian's work, and was expanded in the 16th century. This was the cathedral for the diocese of Leighlin, and it became one of the most important monastic sites in Ireland during the 14th century. There are several well-preserved relics here: an ancient Cross of St. Laserian and an 800 year old baptismal font. There are also several ancient tombs inside the cathedral.

PRACTICAL INFORMATION
Tourist Office
• **Carlow Tourist Information Office**, *College Street, Carlow. Tel. (0503) 31554*

KILKENNY TOWN

I strongly suggest you spend a little time in **Kilkenny Town**. Kilkenny's Irish name is *Cill Cainneach*, which means "Canice's Church" – and the town and county both owe their name to the 6th-century cleric called **St. Canice**. Kilkenny Town, straddling the River Nore, is home to nearly 10,000 people. It is an ancient and royal town. In former days, it was the capital of the Kingdom of Ossory. During the Anglo-Norman invasion, it was presided over by **William le Mareschal**, the son-in-law of the Irish archenemy **Strongbow**.

As peaceful as Kilkenny is today, it is associated with an incident or two of infamy. In an effort to segregate the Anglo-Norman conquerors from the "Irish rabble," the 1366 **Statutes of Kilkenny** were passed here. The statutes laid out strict punishment for Anglo-Normans who deliberately embraced Irish culture. For example, marriage by an Anglo-Norman to an Irish citizen was punishable by death; Irishmen were forbidden to live within walled cities; Anglo-Normans were banned from wearing Irish clothing, naming their children with Irish names, and from learning Gaelic. This segregation and separation widened the 200 year-old rift – physical as well as political – between the native Irish and the invaders from across the Irish Sea.

The two most popular sights in Kilkenny are **St. Canice's Cathedral** and **Kilkenny Castle** – be sure you don't miss them. There are also a number of interesting and intriguing shops on the narrow streets of Kilkenny for you to stroll into. The countryside around Kilkenny contains a great number of interesting sights to take in. **Jerpoint** and **Duiske Abbeys**, just a few miles south of Kilkenny, are marvelously preserved ruins that will tempt you to ask who these ancient clerics were and just what did they do with their time?

You may have heard about Kilkenny in your youth, but have forgotten about it. Check out this old limerick, and see if it brings back any memories:

There once were two cats from Kilkenny,
Each thought there was one cat too many.
So they fought and they fit,
And they scratched and they bit,
'Til excepting their nails and the tips of their tails,
Instead of two cats there weren't any.

No one quite remembers who wrote the limerick, or why, or when, but it is familiar to many. Now you can at least see the town of these cats' nativity!

ARRIVALS & DEPARTURES

By Bus

Bus service runs from **Busaras Station**, *Store Street, Tel. (01) 836-6111,* in Dublin to Kilkenny's **McDonagh Station**, *Castlecomer Road, Tel. (056)*

22024, five times a day. McDonagh Station is just off the center of town on Castlecomer Road, an easy walk to the sights and shopping Kilkenny has to offer. The area around McDonagh Station is a nice neighborhood. The bus ride from Dublin costs £7 for a one-way ticket, and £8 for a round-trip ticket.

By Car

Kilkenny is 75 miles southwest of Dublin. To arrive in Kilkenny, take the N7 west out of Dublin through Naas. Watch for the N9, as well as for signs directing you to Carlow and Kilkenny. Kilkenny is about 25 miles southwest of Carlow on the N9.

Sample trip lengths from Kilkenny around the country (on the main roads):

• Cork: 2 hours
• Donegal: 5 hours
• Galway: 3 hours
• Killarney: 3 hours
• Limerick: 2 hours
• Wexford: 1 hour

By Train

Train service runs from Dublin's **Heuston Station** to Kilkenny's **McDonagh Station**, *Castlecomer Road, Tel. (056) 22024*, four times a day. The 90-minute trip costs £12 for a round-trip ticket and £11 for a one-way ticket.

ORIENTATION

Kilkenny Town is home to nearly 10,000 individuals. As such, it is a little larger than most of the other country towns in this part of Leinster. Like so many other towns in Ireland, Kilkenny lies along a river. The River Nore flows through the town on a north-south route on its way to Waterford Harbor some 30 miles south of Kilkenny.

With narrow streets, 10,000 citizens, and lots of tourists, Kilkenny is far from small and it is not particularly easy to get around in. But the main sights are all located within a rectangle about 200 yards wide by a half-mile long. At the southeast end of the rectangle is Kilkenny Castle, sitting aristocratically above the River Nore. Heading north down the hill on Castle Road/The Parade and a short jaunt to the left on Rose Inn Street brings you to Patrick/High/Parliament Streets and the primary sights in town to see. At the northwest end of the rectangle (at the north end of Parliament Street) you'll come to St. Canice's Cathedral, which is about a 10-minute walk from Kilkenny Castle.

GETTING AROUND TOWN

By Bicycle

I am not a fan of bicycles in Kilkenny. The sights to see are all along the main street (Patrick/High/Parliament Streets) and that is a narrow, busy street. Since the majority of the sights are along this street and within a half mile of each other, I'd suggest walking. However, if you must bicycle, you can rent one at **J.J. Wall Bicycle Hire Shop**, *88 Maudlin Street, Tel. 056) 21236.* While the town is a bit cramped, there are a number of wonderful country lanes to explore in the countryside around of Kilkenny.

By Car

Don't do it. I wouldn't suggest trying to see Kilkenny by car, or you'll spend all your time looking for a parking spot. If you already have a car, park it on one of the side streets west of High/Parliament Street, or near Kilkenny Castle, and use your feet. It'll be quicker and allow you to see the sights as well as the wonderful shops that liberally dot the street.

On Foot

Well, if you haven't gotten the message by now, the sights in Kilkenny are made to be seen on foot. An especially nice walk is along the River Nore below Kilkenny Castle. Follow Rose Inn Street (below Kilkenny Castle) to the river, then head south along the river.

By Taxi

If you feel a need for a taxi, the most you'll pay is about £3 or £4.

WHERE TO STAY

LAUNARD HOUSE B&B, *2 Maidenhill, Kells Road, Kilkenny. Tel. (056) 51889, Fax (056) 71017; E-mail: launardhouse@email.com; Website: www.eiretech.com/launard. 5 rooms. Rates for singles: £25 to £30, doubles: £18 to £19.50 per person sharing. Rates include breakfast. Visa and Mastercard accepted. No service charge.*

This pleasant B&B in Kilkenny is four years young and provides a delightful place to stay as well as wonderful hosts, John and Sandra Cahill. Several years ago the Cahills retired from the corporate world in Dublin and decided to use their retirement years meeting people. And what better way to do so than to open and run a B&B?

Launard House is a newer, "purpose-built" B&B about one mile from downtown Kilkenny. It nestles comfortably amid well-maintained gardens and well-kept grounds. The bedrooms are nice sized, and have been decorated personally by Sandra. They feature heavy warm comforters, soft colors, light floral accents, and plush carpets. Each bedroom is equipped with tea- and coffee-making facilities, television, clock radio, and hairdryer. The bathrooms are equipped with special "power showers" that provide you with an invigorating experience to begin your day. (You'll wish more Irish B&Bs did!)

John and Sandra are very familiar with the sights and sounds of Kilkenny, and are happy to help you plan your exploration of them. If you are a golfer, you will find a soul-mate in John, and he'll be glad to point you to a few places that might interest you. If the weather doesn't cooperate, don't fear – there is a full-sized snooker table available in the B&B for you to try out. The Cahills are proud of their recent award for *Guest Care and Service*, which they received from the Kilkenny Chamber of Commerce. Once you experience their hospitality, you'll understand why they were recipients of such an award.

SHILLOGHER HOUSE, *Callan Road (N56), Kilkenny. Tel. (056) 63249, Fax (056) 64865, Mobile (087) 231-2103. 5 rooms, all ensuite. Rates for singles: £25, doubles: £18 to £20 per person sharing. Rates include breakfast. Visa and Mastercard accepted. No service charge.*

Wow! This is a modern, luxurious B&B located just minutes from Kilkenny Castle. Set in an emerald-green, sculpted park-like setting, Shillogher House is a wonderful place to base your explorations of Kilkenny. As you enter their drive, you'll be impressed with the elegance of this new B&B. And when you enter their front door, you will continue to be impressed. The B&B is tastefully and expensively decorated throughout. The dining room, where you'll have your breakfast, is a long rectangular room overlooking lovely gardens and is pleasantly decorated in mauve and white.

The bedrooms are large by B&B standards, and well appointed. The furnishings are all new and the rooms are decorated with light floral patterns and soft colors. Each room has a large window overlooking the lovely grounds. One of the rooms is a large "family room," specially designed for traveling families. If it's a dull or damp day out, each of the rooms is outfitted with central heating, and as an extra touch, electric blankets help chase the chill away.

Bill and Margaret are rightfully proud of Shillogher House, and feel they offer hotel amenities at a B&B price. While new to the B&B business, they have spent years in the service industry and know how to make guests feel welcome. I predict you'll enjoy the time you spend here.

SONORA B&B, *Drakelands, Kilkenny. Tel. (056) 22877, Fax (056) 21734; E-mail: jimhayes@iol.ie. 3 rooms. Rates for singles: £23 to £25, doubles: £20 per person sharing. Rates include breakfast. No credit cards accepted. No service charge.*

Mrs. Una Hayes runs a lovely B&B with beautiful gardens round about. There are three ensuite rooms, and all are light and pleasant and decorated with antiques. The conservatory offers serene views of the gardens. A small waterfall and series of pools are on the grounds, and provide a serene backdrop to this B&B.

Mrs. Hayes is delightful and is fluent in German, if you have that need (or maybe if you want to see how much of your high school German you remember!). She is rightfully proud of Sonora House. Her breakfasts are excellent, and the menu is extensive enough to please even the most finicky eaters. If you wish to stay here, you'll only find Sonora House open from April through September.

BLANCHVILLE HOUSE, *Dunbell, Maddoxtown. Tel. (056) 27197, Fax (056) 27636; E-mail: info@blanchville.ie; Website: www.blanchville.ie. 6 rooms. Rates for singles: £35 to £40, doubles: £30 to £35 per person sharing. Rates include breakfast. Dinner available for £22.50. American Express, Mastercard and Visa accepted. No service charge.*

Just a few miles east of Kilkenny you'll find the 19th-century mansion known as Blanchville House. Tim and Monica Phelan, the current owners, have taken great pains (and quite a bit of money!) to restore it to its original splendor. They have been faithful to the original character of the home, and have furnished it with furniture and objet d'art from the period of its original construction.

Quiet grandeur and dignified elegance best describe the atmosphere you'll find at Blanchville House. The drawing room is decorated with – believe it or not – the original wallpaper and features a pleasant fireplace presiding over the room. The high-ceilinged bedrooms are all quite large and tastefully decorated in soft warm colors and exquisite furnishings.

Blanchville House is open from March 1 through the end of October.

NEWPARK HOTEL, *Kilkenny. Tel. (056) 22122, Fax (056) 61111; Website: www.iol.ie/~newparkh. 84 rooms. Rates for singles: £59 to £79 doubles: £43 to £55 per person sharing. Two restaurants, indoor swimming pool, sauna, Jacuzzi, fitness center. All major credit cards accepted. No service charge.*

This older hotel (built in the 1960's) is still a comfortable place to stay, and offers a number of additional amenities, such as pool, sauna, and fitness center. Several years ago 24 rooms were added, and these rooms are of course nicer than the older rooms. They are average size, and furnished comfortably, if not memorably.

MOUNT JULIET, *Thomastown. Tel. (056) 24455, Fax (056) 24522; E-mail: info@mountjuliet.ie; Website: www.mountjuliet.ie. 54 rooms. Rates for singles in the main house and Hunter's Yard: £115 to £190, doubles: £135 to £245, suites: £210 to £432. Rates for singles in the Rose Garden Lodges: £285 to £495. One restaurant, indoor swimming pool, spa, sauna, fitness center, beauty salon, tennis, snooker, golf, shooting, bicycles. All major credit cards are accepted. 12.5% service charge.*

Stunning. There are not enough superlatives in my vocabulary to effectively describe Mt. Juliet to you. (But I'll try, of course!) From the moment you pass through Mt. Juliet's gates you will be in awe of the beauties that await you around every corner. First you drive through acres and acres of the beautifully manicured greens and fairways of Mt. Juliet Golf Club. If you're a golfer, you'll wish you were out there; if you're not, you'll envy those who are. The course was designed by Jack Nicklaus, and was home to the 1993 and 1994 Irish Open Championship tournaments.

As you make your way along the edge of the golf course, you'll come to the spa and leisure center for the estate – soon to be your personal playgrounds. But don't stop yet. Your next views will be of the Hunter's Yard and Rose Garden Lodges. These separate facilities offer different types of accommodations, each exquisite in its own right. As you wend your way through a portion of the 1,500 acre estate, you'll finally come to Mt. Juliet House. Built in the 1750s by the third Earl of Carrick, Mt. Juliet bears the name of the good Earl's lovely wife.

As you enter Mt. Juliet House, you'll have to fight to keep your mouth from gaping open as you view the splendor of this place you will shortly be staying. The rooms in Mt. Juliet House are large and lavishly furnished. Luxurious is the term that will come to mind as you step into your room. The rooms overlooking the River Nore command a premium, although the rooms overlooking the grounds of the estate would be considered premium rooms at most other properties.

If you stay in Mt. Juliet house you'll feel properly pampered by the staff and the surroundings. However, if you opt for a little more privacy, the Rose Garden Lodges and Hunter's Yard offer something more akin to apartment living. Each suite has multiple rooms, and each is decorated individually, expensively, and elegantly. Whether you are in the main house, Hunter's Yard, or one of the Rose Garden Lodges, each room comes with a box of chocolates, a bowl of fruit, plush bathrobes, and full turn-down service in the evenings.

In addition to the gorgeous rooms, Mt. Juliet offers a wide variety of sports activities, including golf, swimming, tennis, croquet, horseback riding, fishing, trap shooting, and archery. If your travel plans include a helicopter, there is a helipad on the estate. This is definitely the way the other half lives. Their award-winning restaurant, Lady Helen McCalmont Dining Room, is elegant; you may read about it in the *Where to Eat* section.

WHERE TO EAT

AN CAISEAN UI CUAIN, *2 High Street, Kilkenny Town. Tel. (056) 65406. £5.95 to £9.95. Open daily 12:30pm to 3:00pm, and 5:30pm to 8:30pm. No credit cards accepted.*

This bar has succeeded in mixing traditional and trendy Irish atmosphere and is very popular with the younger crowd in particular. The food is branded "pub grub," and is tasteful and substantial. Officially, Monday evenings feature traditional Irish music, but with the artsy crowd that frequents An Caisean ui Cuain, impromptu live music can break out spontaneously at any time.

KILKENNY KITCHEN, *Kilkenny Design Centre, Castle Yard, Kilkenny Town. £4.95 to £12.95. Open 9:00am to 5:00pm daily. All major credit cards accepted.*

This sizable restaurant (it seats 165 people) offers a diverse menu for you to choose from. No real specialties other than their breads and pastries, Kilkenny Kitchen is a nice place to stop for a bite to eat. Fish, poultry, and a variety of cheeses are offered.

SHEM'S, *61 John Street, Kilkenny. Tel. (056) 21543. £15.95 to £30. Open daily noon to 9:30pm (only snacks are available on Sundays). All major credit cards accepted.*

Shem's is a delightful country pub with a pleasant ambiance and excellent food. Julie Lawlor presides over the kitchen and serves up soups, salads, sandwiches, and a few pasta dishes.

LANGTON'S, *69 John Street, Kilkenny Town. Tel. (056) 65133. £4.95 to £17.95. Open all day for bar food. All major credit cards accepted.*

Langton's has earned a reputation as sort of a smorgasbord of bars, where you'll find a collection of bars in varying decors and atmospheres. But the reason they are listed here is because of the quality of their pub grub. Salads, chicken, seafood, and beef grace their menu.

LACKEN HOUSE, *Dublin Road, Kilkenny. Tel. (056) 61085. Set dinner menu £23. Open Tuesday through Saturday from 7:00am to 9:00pm. All major credit cards accepted.*

The restaurant housed in this old Victorian home offers a solid Irish menu, a mix of traditional Irish dishes as well as progressive dishes that feature the culinary influences of a variety of European countries. Salmon, trout, and a bevy of seafood dishes including crab grateau and lobster complement a varied meat menu that features Irish beef and lamb as well as several wild meats. Fresh produce from the farms of local farmers guarantees a freshness to all the menu items.

MOUNT JULIET HOTEL RESTAURANT (*also called* **Lady Helen McCalmont Dining Room**). *Tel. (056) 24455, Thomastown. Set dinner menu for £33. Open daily for dinner from 7:00pm to 10:00pm. All major credit cards accepted.*

The dining room at Mount Juliet Hotel is everything you'd expect it to be: elegant, bordering on opulent. Wedgwood china, starched Irish linen, and gleaming silverware punctuate your dining experience. The meal? Equally as exquisite. French with an Irish flair (or is it Irish with a French flair?), the presentation of your fare is as spectacular as it is tasteful. The menu changes, but you might expect the likes of baked escalope of salmon, roast breast of Barbary duck with fruit sauce, or roast rack of spring lamb. Jacket and tie are requested.

SEEING THE SIGHTS

Kilkenny Castle, *The Parade, Kilkenny. Open April and May daily 10:30am to 5:00pm, June through September daily 10:00am until 7:00pm, October through March Tuesday through Saturday from 10:30am to 12:45pm and 2:00pm to 5:00pm, Sunday from 11:00am to 12:45pm and 2:00pm to 5:00pm. Admission is £3.50 for adults, £2.50 for seniors and students, £1.50 for children, and a family ticket is available for £8.00. Tel. (056) 21450.*

In the 12th century, The Earl of Pembroke – Strongbow – built a wooden fortress on a high bank above the River Nore. It held a commanding position, as most fortresses are meant to do. In the 13th century the wooden structure was replaced with a more permanent stone fortress. Over the centuries, the castle has been added to, and it is now a mixture of Gothic and classical architectural styles. In 1391, the powerful Butler family purchased the castle in anticipation of King Richard II's visit to Ireland. They seemed to like the house and the neighborhood – Kilkenny Castle served as the family residence until 1935. The Butlers were known as the Earls and Dukes of Ormonde.

Begin your tour of Kilkenny Castle on the richly landscaped grounds. They are immaculate with hardly a blade of grass or mum out of place. The castle sits along the banks of the River Nore, and is surrounded by acres upon acres of manicured lawns, fountains, and flowers. When you've had your fill of the grounds, venture into the castle. Delightful hosts and hostesses will greet you and see that you have a pleasant visit. The tour includes visits to a number of the castle's rooms, including the drawing and dining rooms, the library, and some of the bedrooms, which are imposing: each has ample numbers of antiques, tremendous tapestries, and plenty of paintings. Many of the furnishings you'll see are original to the castle, and the library has a number of books that have been here for hundreds of years!

By far the most impressive room in the castle is the remarkable Long Gallery, a cavernous room 45 meters long and 9 meters wide, with a ceiling about 60 feet high. Its walls are decked out with the portraits of the Butler family – 500 years' worth! There are over 50 life-size (some are larger-than-life-size) portraits of the former inhabitants of the castle. (At one time over 200 such portraits hung here.) In addition, splendid 17th-century tapestries grace several of the walls. Look closely at those tapestries – they are linen, silk, and wool, and took 65 Parisian artisans three months to weave them! On one wall of the Long Gallery is an impressive Italian marble fireplace, complete with ornate carvings depicting important events in the lives of various Butler family members.

Extensive renovations have been underway for the past few years, and will continue for the next few years. The workers are being meticulous in their efforts to restore the castle to its original splendor.

After you visit Kilkenny Castle, head down the hill to **Kyteler's Inn** on St. Kieran's Street. This old limestone coaching inn is the oldest house in Kilkenny, but the real story here centers around one of the former owners of the house, **Dame Alice Kyteler**. Dame Kyteler was born in 1280, and the attractive lass earned a lucrative living as a "banker" in the small town. By the time she was 44 years old, she had outlived four husbands. Unfortunately, Bishop de Ledrede accused her of witchcraft, and a plentiful stock of herbs, ointments, and other oddities in her home were enough to convict her and her maid of the charge. Dame Kyteler fled the scene, never to be heard of again; Petronella, her maid, wasn't so quick, and she was burned at the stake. Check out the inn. In addition to its fascinating history, it serves a good meal, too.

Shee's Alms House, *Rose Inn Street. Open May through September Monday to Saturday from 9:00am to 6:00pm, Sunday from 10:00am to 5:00pm, and October through April Tuesday through Saturday from 9:00am to 5:15pm. Admission to CityScope is £1 for adults and 50p for children. Tel. (056) 51500.* Next to St. Mary's Hall on Rose Inn Street is the old stone front of Shee's Alms House, a house of charity founded in 1582 by **Sir Richard Shee** as a hospital for the indigent of Kilkenny. It served in that role until 1895. Today, instead of dispensing medicine and compassion, it serves up tourist information – it is home to the Kilkenny Tourist Information Office. They offer a short show called CityScope, which gives the history of 17th-century Kilkenny. If you need a rest, the CityScope presentation isn't too bad; otherwise, pass on it and see the town first-hand.

Rothe House, *Parliament Street, Kilkenny. Open July and August daily from 9:30am to 6:00pm. Open January to June, and September Monday through Saturday from 10:30am to 5:00pm and on Sundays from 3:00pm to 5:00pm. Admission is £2 for adults, £1.50 for students and senior citizens, and £1 for children. Tel. (056) 22893.* In 1594, John Rothe built this home to accommodate his growing family. Little did he realize that he would have to add on several times to make the house large enough for the 12 children that were to eventually bless his life! Mr. Rothe was a wealthy and successful Kilkenny merchant at the turn of the 17th century (good thing!), and his lovely house reflects his affluence. Actually, Rothe House would be better called Rothe *Houses*, as it encompasses three homes that the industrious Mr. Rothe built to house his burgeoning brood. Several years ago, the Kilkenny Archaeological Society purchased Rothe House and they have done a magnificent job of restoring it to its original grandeur. They have a number of fine exhibits that highlight various styles of clothing that was common to Kilkenny citizens of yesteryear, and you'll see plenty of period furnishings.

On Abbey Street in Kilkenny is the 13th-century **Black Abbey**, named after the color of the robes worn by the Dominican Friars who occupied the abbey. In recent years, the Black Abbey was restored and is now in use as a Dominican friary (called Black Friar's Church). All that remains of the original abbey is the nave, south transept, and the tower.

St. Canice's Cathedral, *corner of Dean and Parliament Streets, Kilkenny. Open Easter through September Monday through Saturday 9:00am until 6:00pm, Sunday from 2:00pm until 6:00pm, and October through Easter Monday through Saturday from 10:00am to 1:00pm, and 2:00pm to 4:00pm, and Sunday from 2:00pm until 4:00pm. Admission is £1.00.* St. Canice's Cathedral is an impressive gray granite structure. Modeled after many of the English churches of the period (13th century), St. Canice's stands firm and straight despite the efforts of a number of plunderers, including Cromwell's forces.

St. Canice's Library, *Dean Street, Kilkenny. Open daily from 9:00am until 1:00pm, and from 2:00pm until 6:00pm. Admission is free.* Next to St. Canice's cathedral is St. Canice's Library, the repository of over 3,000 16th and 17th-century manuscripts.

St. Cainneach (anglicized as Canice – pronounced Kenny) founded a monastery on this site in the 6th century, and this cathedral was built in the early 1200s. It is the second largest medieval cathedral in Ireland, next to St. Patrick's Cathedral in Dublin.

THE BLACK DEATH IN IRELAND

Ireland has had its share of tragedies through the centuries. But one of them was not unique to Ireland: the Black Death, a terrible and merciless scourge that spread like wildfire through Europe and Asia in the mid-1300s. Modern medicine believes the culprit was most likely Bubonic Plague.

As Ireland was not immune, neither was tiny Kilkenny, or its Dominican friary, the Black Abbey. Eight of her priests succumbed to the deadly disease as it spread throughout Ireland. One of the inhabitants of the Black Abbey, Friar Clyn, recorded that no household in Kilkenny had lost fewer than two individuals. His last words read, "And I, Friar John Clyn, among the dead expecting death's coming, I have set down these deeds in writing. And lest the writing should perish with the writer, I leave parchment to carry out the work if perchance any man survives or any of the race of Adam may be able to escape this pestilence." The next entry was the record of Friar Clyn's death, written by another scribe.

The Gothic interior is majestic and the view from the back of the chapel to the stained glass windows is memorable. A number of tombs are contained in the cathedral. Many are interesting to study. One of them, that of Viscount Mountgarrett, is in full armor. Be sure and check out the carved black marble of St. Ciaran's chair in the north transept.

Standing next to the cathedral is a 101-foot tall round tower, the only vestige of the original monastic settlement. If you've the desire, 167 steps lead you to the top and a nice view of Kilkenny Town.

Dunmore Cave, *near Kilkenny. Open mid-March through mid-June daily from 10:00am to 5:00pm, mid-June through mid-September it is open daily from 10:00am until 7:00pm, and mid-September through October daily from 10:00am until 5:00pm. From November through mid-March on Saturday and Sunday from 10:00am to 5:00pm. Admission is £2.00 for adults, £1.50 for seniors and students, £1.00 for children and a family ticket is available for £5.00. Tel. (056) 67726.* About seven miles north of Kilkenny on the N78 is Dunmore Cave, a series of natural limestone caves. There are three primary chambers and one mighty 20 foot tall stalagmite (remember – stalagmites attach to the floor) called Market Cross.

Dunmore Cave was once considered the gateway to hell, as most caves were in ancient Irish times. Perhaps the most interesting aspect of Dunmore Cave is the stories of tragedies that occurred here, including stories of Viking massacres. If you've never been in a cave, this might be a good time to go. Like most other caves, this one is damp and clammy. The history of the cave makes it a little more interesting, however.

On the road between Kilkenny and Thomastown (the R700), watch for the signs directing you to Graiguenamanagh Abbey. Turn there, and watch for a weathered signpost directing you to **Coolhill Castle**. After several twists and turns on a very narrow, single lane road, you'll come to this grand castle. This fascinating ruin standing woefully in the middle of a farmer's field is a mere shadow of its former self. But there is enough of its ancient round structure left to help you imagine what a magnificent place it must have been at one time – someone's pride and joy. Long since abandoned, the castle now stands guard over rolling fields, grazing sheep, and landscape that appears to be stitched together by a giant hand. Take your camera – you'll be glad you did.

Jerpoint Abbey, *near Thomastown. Open March through mid-May daily from 10:00am to 5:00pm, June through mid-September daily from 9:30am through 6:30pm, mid-September through mid-November daily from 10:00am through 5:00pm, and mid-November through the end of November from 10:00am to 4:00pm. Admission is £2 for adults and £1.60 for children. A family ticket is available for £5. Tel. (056) 24623.* Jerpoint Cisterian Abbey is two kilometers south of Thomastown on the N9. It is considered one of the best monastic ruins in Ireland. Spend a few minutes walking among the ample ruins, imagining what the life of a monk in the late 12th century would have been like at this monastery. The abbey was built in 1158 for the Benedictine order by Donagh MacGillapatrick, but later passed to the Cisterians in 1180. It functioned under the Cisterians until 1540, when it was abandoned as a result of King Henry VIII's suppression order.

After the abbey was abandoned, the lands were given to the Ormond family, but it was mostly neglected by them and allowed to fall into ruins. The ruin is large – it is nearly the exact length and width of a football field. There are a series of interesting sculptures in the cloister, thought to be the work of the renowned sculptor Rory O'Tunney. Judging from the flowing robes on many of them, they may represent some of the monks who served at Jerpoint Abbey during that time. (O'Tunney is thought to have sculpted them in the first half of the 16th century.) There are several interesting tombs in the church, including one of Bishop Felix O'Dulaney. Bishop O'Dulaney's effigy is interesting: it depicts a snake biting the crosier (a hooked staff, like a shepherd's crooked stick) held by the good bishop.

The small visitor's center provides a history of the monastery. The monastery is a wonderful subject for photographers – amateur as well as professional. It is impressive, and is well worth the small admission fee.

Duiske Abbey, *Graiguenamanagh*. If you can pronounce (correctly) the name of this small town – Graiguenamanagh – you are doing better with your Irish than me. It is an unspoiled little village located on the R703. Its main attraction is Duiske Abbey, currently in use as a Catholic parish church. It's worth a peek inside – while the Gothic arches are the most impressive, the church provides a reverent setting for worship.

The abbey was built in 1204, and the monks quickly endeared themselves to their fellow countrymen by being exceptionally generous and compassionate to the poor and ill. They earned a reputation for kindness in that part of the country. As was often the case in ancient Ireland, a community sprung up near the abbey. The name was a tribute to the goodly monks: *Graigneunmanagh* is the Irish name for "Village of the Monks." The abbey was abandoned in 1540 when Henry VIII ordered the closure of all monasteries in Ireland, and the abbey fell into disrepair. In the early 1980s, the townsfolk began repairing the abbey.

SPORTS & RECREATION
Golf

Mt. Juliet Golf Club, *near Thomastown, County Kilkenny. Tel. (056) 24725, £65/£75.*

I have golfed on many courses, and seen many more golf courses. But I was frankly stunned when I first came upon the course at Mount Juliet. The velvety fairways and silky smooth greens are incredible, and the beauty is breathtaking. The course is renowned for their water hazards, so golfers beware! If you are a golfer, and find yourself in this part of Ireland, please take my advice and play at least one round. It will be one of your most lasting golf memories.

The course was designed by Jack Nicklaus, and was home to the 1993 and 1994 Irish Open Championship tournaments. Visitors are welcome daily. Par 72, 7,172 yards.

Horseback Riding
• **Mt. Juliet Equestrian Center**, *Thomastown, County Kilkenny. Tel. (056) 24455*

PRACTICAL INFORMATION
Laundry Service
• **Brett's Launderette**, *Michael Street, Kilkenny. Tel. (056) 63200*

Post Office
• **Kilkenny Post Office**, *High Street. Tel. (056) 21879*

Tourist Office
• **Kilkenny Tourist Information Office**, *Rose Inn Street, Kilkenny. Tel. (056) 51500*

15. MUNSTER

Munster is the province that comprises the southwestern quarter of Ireland. It consists of six counties, and all but County Tipperary are on the ocean – though County Limerick just barely, by virtue of the River Shannon estuary. The province of Munster has the most developed tourism industry in the country. Part of the reason is that until just a few years ago, all international flights into Ireland from North America were required to land first at Shannon Airport. This provided great strength to the tourist industry in this Irish province.

The major cities in Munster are **Cork**, **Limerick**, and **Killarney**. Rich in history – real as well as embellished or even imagined – all three are delightful places to visit. Using those cities as jumping-off points, you can visit five of Ireland's top 10 tourist attractions. **Bunratty Castle and Folk Park** (on the outskirts of Limerick) hosts over 300,000 tourists every year, and nearly a quarter of a million people annually visit **Blarney Castle** to kiss the magical **Blarney Stone**. The **Fota Wildlife Park** outside Cork City, **Muckross House and Gardens** in Killarney, and the **Rock of Cashel** near Limerick each draw nearly 200,000 people a year.

In addition to these wonderful man-made creations, Munster is rich in natural beauty that goes beyond being merely beautiful and moves into the category of stunning. If you miss the **Cliffs of Moher**, I guarantee you will feel cheated if you ever see photographs of them after you return home. And the **Dingle Peninsula** isn't one iota behind the Cliffs of Moher in majesty and beauty. Killarney has its fair share of natural beauty, with **Killarney National Park**, the **Muckross House estate**, the **Gap of Dunloe**, and **MacGillycuddy's Reeks**.

Munster is where many important events in Irish history have taken place, most of them tragic. For example, the community of Cobh (pronounced *Cove*) on the southern shore near Cork City has seen her fair share of tragedy. It was from Cobh harbor that hundreds of thousands of Irish immigrants fled Ireland from 1845 to 1848, the **Great Potato Famine** snapping mercilessly at their heels. Again it was Cobh harbor that served as the last port-of-call for the **Titanic** on her first – and last – fateful

Clare

Tipperary

Limerick

MUNSTER

Waterford

Kerry

Cork

MUNSTER PROVINCE

cruise in April 1912. Almost exactly three years later in May 1915, nearly 1,200 souls perished in the sinking of the *Lusitania* just 12 short miles down the coast from Cobh.

Oliver Cromwell, the Darth Vader of Irish history, destroyed scores of castles, cathedrals, monasteries, and towns throughout the width and breadth of Munster during his ruthless military campaign that began in 1649. In 1690, **Catholic James** (James II), King of England, fled Ireland forever from Waterford harbor in Munster. He had been the only hope of the tormented Catholic populace for the easing of their oppression. James was never able to return to Ireland and fulfill his promise of Catholic emancipation, as he died three years later while in exile in France.

The new English king, **William of Orange**, was a Protestant, and things got worse for the Catholics in Ireland. In fact, during his reign the infamous "**Penal Laws**" were passed, essentially rendering the Irish people non-entities in their own country. Gone was the ability to vote or be voted for, gone the ability to gain an education, serve in the military, and possess weapons. These appalling laws were not to be repealed for over 125 years, when a brilliant Munster lad named **Daniel O'Connell** fought valiantly for (and won!) the repeal of these vile laws, this ensuring the emancipation of Catholics in Ireland.

MUNSTER'S BEST SIGHTS

ADARE – *Adare is arguably the prettiest town in Ireland.*

BLARNEY CASTLE/BLARNEY STONE – *Everyone who comes to Ireland needs to see the Blarney Stone, which is part of Blarney Castle.*

BUNRATTY CASTLE AND FOLK PARK – *Sure it's touristy, but what a lot of fun! The castle hosts a medieval banquet; the folk park portrays life in ancient Ireland.*

CLIFFS OF MOHER – *The Cliffs of Moher are perhaps the most spectacular scenery in Ireland. Don't miss this incredible sight.*

DINGLE PENINSULA – *The Dingle Peninsula provides incredible seascapes.*

FAMINE GRAVEYARD – *Outside Dungarvan, this over-grown famine graveyard is a solemn reminder of one of the darker chapters in Irish history: the Great Potato Famine.*

GAP OF DUNLOE – *Outside Killarney, the Gap of Dunloe is a wonderful opportunity to take a jaunting car ride through a beautiful work of nature.*

MUCKROSS HOUSE – *Two treats here for the price of one: visit the stately Victorian Mansion called Muckross House and see the lifestyle a former Member of Parliament enjoyed. Then, venture onto the grounds and discover the impressive estate surrounding the home. Walk through the lush gardens, verdant fields and beautiful forest, or take a jaunting car ride through the countryside for a more extensive and relaxing view of a truly remarkable area (bring your camera!).*

ROCK OF CASHEL – *This is perhaps one of the most impressive ruins on the entire Emerald Isle, and is a "photo op" just waiting for you and your camera. The ruins of this medieval cathedral and ancient round tower seem made for Kodak! This is an impressive sight overlooking the Golden Vale of Tipperary, and one you should definitely not miss.*

THE SKELLIGS – *Lying off the southwestern coast of Ireland are the Skelligs, rocky islands that jut dramatically out of the sea. One hosts an enormous colony of birds, and the other is home to a set of monastic ruins that will make you wonder why on earth monks came here, and what they did once they arrived. The Skelligs are well worth the boat trip out to see.*

WATERFORD CRYSTAL FACTORY – *Home of the famous Waterford crystal, the factory includes an hour-long tour that will change the way you look at lead crystal for the rest of your life.*

Munster spawned scores of uprisings throughout the years by patriots seeking to release the shackles so firmly clasped by the English. One of the most notable rebellions in Irish history was the **1798 Uprising**, which had its beginning – and crushing ending – in Munster.

There are numerous ways to see Munster. In my personal travels, I have started in Limerick and fanned out across the province; I have started in north Munster and circled the province in a counter-clockwise fashion; and I have started in Waterford in the southeast corner of the province and worked my way clockwise. It just depends on where you are coming from, I suppose. For the purposes of this travel guide, I'll start with one my favorite Irish cities: Cork. After introducing you to the sights in and around Cork, we'll move on to Killarney, one of the most charming towns in Ireland. From Killarney, we'll head up to the busy city of Limerick and investigate what it has to offer. All along the way, I'll point out day excursions and side trips from each of these cities that will enhance your experience.

CORK CITY

Next to Dublin, **Cork** is probably the most widely recognized Irish city name around the world. I have to be honest – my first impressions of Cork were that compared to Dublin, it was a little more cramped, a bit confusing to get around in, and, well, a big city. However, each time I visit this city I find myself falling more and more in love with it. After exploring its many nooks and crannies over the years, Cork has become one of my favorite cities to visit. As the third-largest city in Ireland, it is rich in history, legend and pride.

Originally granted its city charter over 800 years ago (1185), Cork's importance in Ireland's history has waxed and waned through the years. Cork's Irish name, *Corcaigh*, means "marshy place." Cork City lies between and along the banks of the **River Lee**. As the River Lee flows into the valley where Cork sits, it splits into two channels. Centuries ago, the marshy area between the north and south channels was filled in, and the city grew between those channels. But the River Lee was unable to contain the booming city, and many generations ago the city spread north and south beyond the confines of the river and up the hills that flowed down to the river.

Today, Cork is a busy metropolis with lots of traffic, pedestrians, and one-way streets. But it is a fun city, and one that always seems to be alive with things to do and places to see.

MUNSTER'S BEST PLACES TO STAY

SALLYPORT HOUSE B&B, Kenmare. Tel. (064) 42066, Fax (064) 42067; E-mail: arthur@sallyporthouse.com; Website: www.sallyporthouse.com. 5 rooms. Rates for singles: £65, doubles: £40 to £45 per person sharing. Beautiful views, warm hospitality and wonderful rooms.

EARL'S COURT, Woodlawn Junction, Muckross Road, Killarney. Tel. (064) 34009, Fax (064) 34366; E-mail: earls@eircom.net; Website: www.killarney-earlscourt.ie. 12 rooms. Rates for singles: £50 to £75, doubles: £30 to £55 per person sharing. Earl's Court is the nicest place to stay in Killarney, and has perhaps the most gracious hostess in this part of Ireland.

THE MOORINGS, Scilly, Kinsale. Tel. (021) 772376, Fax (021) 77267[5]; E-mail: moorings.kinsale@indigo.ie; Website: indigo.ie/~moorings5. 8 rooms. Rates for singles: £55, doubles: £50 to £75 per person sharing. This pleasant guesthouse right on the harbor is a nice place to base your exploration of Kinsale.

HOTEL ARD NA SIDHE, Caragh Lake, Killorglin. Tel. (066) 69105, Fax (066) 69282, US toll free 800/221-1074. 20 rooms. Rates for singles: £73, doubles: £115 to £151. This is a very comfortable hotel away from the hustle and bustle of Killarney.

SHEEN FALLS LODGE, Kenmare. Tel. (064) 41600, Fax (064) 41386; E-mail: info@sheenfallslodge.ie; Website: www.sheenfallslodge.ie. 40 rooms. Rates for singles: £168 to £280, doubles: £240 to £350, suites: £300 to £420. The setting for Sheen Falls Lodge is one of the prettiest in the country.

ADARE MANOR, Adare, County Limerick. Tel. (061) 396566, Fax (061) 396124, US toll free 800/462-3273; E-mail: reservations@adaremanor.com; Website: www.slh.com/pages/adeirea.html. 63 rooms. Rates for singles: £110 to £209, doubles: £145 to £285, staterooms: £200 to £285; children under age 12 stay free with their parents. Adare Manor is one of the most beautiful hotels in the country.

DROMOLAND CASTLE, Newmarket-on-Fergus, County Clare. Tel. (061) 368144, Fax (061) 363355, US toll free 800/346-7007; E-mail: dromoland@dromoland.ie; Website: www.commerce.ie/dromoland. 100 rooms. Rates for standard rooms: £140 to £254 per room, deluxe rooms: £216 to £312 per room, state rooms and suites: £231 to £675; children under age 12 stay free with parents. No service charge. This beautiful old castle has been lovingly restored and will be one of your favorite memories if you stay here.

ARRIVALS & DEPARTURES

By Air

The **Cork Airport**, *Tel. (021) 313131*, is located 10 miles south of Cork City. A number of airlines fly into Cork Airport, including Aer Lingus, Air Southwest, British Airways, British Midlands, and Ryanair. Flights arrive directly in Cork from England and other European cities.

As soon as you enter the Arrivals Hall, on your left you'll see a number of car rental agencies. Buses are also available at the airport to take you to Cork City. They are just outside the Arrivals Hall, and the 20-minute ride to the city will cost you about £2.50. Cab stands are also right outside the Arrivals Hall, and a cab ride into Cork will run about £7.

By Bus

The bus depot for Cork is **Parnell Station**, *Parnell Street, Tel. 021 508188.* It is located downtown in a decent neighborhood. There are four buses a day that run between Cork and Dublin, and the fare is £16 for the four and a half hour ride. Buses also arrive from and depart to other areas of Ireland frequently throughout the day.

By Car

Cork is easily accessible via a number of major roadways. The main arteries entering Cork City are the N25 (from the east), the N8 (from the northeast), the N20 (from the north) and the N22 (from the west). All these main roads lead into the heart of Cork City.

If you come to Cork directly from the Shannon Airport, the most direct route is to take the N18 into Limerick (just follow the signs to Limerick), then take the N20 south. Seventy-five miles later you'll find yourself in Cork. If you're coming from Dublin, there are a variety of roads to take. The most direct route is to take the N7 to Portlaoise, then south on the N8. The N8 will take you to the outskirts of Cork. To get to the city center, just follow the signs.

A little more looping trip, but one I prefer, is to take the N11/M11 south out of Dublin (follow the signs for Bray and Wexford). The M11 reverts to the N11 near Bray, and you should follow that to Enniscorthy. From there, pick up the N30 to Waterford, where you'll pick up the N25 and drive right into Cork. This route is a little longer in distance and time, but I like the scenery better.

Sample trip lengths on the main roads:
- Dublin: 4 hours (through Portlaoise) or 5 hours (through Waterford)
- Galway: 3 hours
- Killarney: 1 hour
- Limerick: 1 hour
- Wexford: 3 hours

MUNSTER'S BEST RESTAURANTS

DOYLE'S SEAFOOD BAR, 4 John Street, Dingle, County Kerry. Tel. (066) 51174. Set dinner menu for £13.50. Diners Club, Mastercard, and Visa accepted. 10% service charge. Doyle's gets my vote for the best seafood restaurant in Ireland.

BLUE HAVEN HOTEL RESTAURANT, 3 Pearse Street, Kinsale. Tel. (021) 772209. £12.95 to £21.95. All major credit cards accepted. 10% service charge. Excellent seafood.

FLEMINGS, Silver Grange House, Tivoli. Set lunch menu for £13.50, and set dinner menu for £21. All major credit cards accepted. One of the nicest French restaurants in the country, still relatively unknown.

GABY'S SEAFOOD RESTAURANT, 27 High Street, Killarney. Tel. (064) 32519. £10.95 to £24.95. All major credit cards accepted. Considered by many to be the best seafood restaurant in Killarney.

ARBUTUS LODGE RESTAURANT, Montenotte, Cork City. Tel. (021) 501237. Set dinner menus for £22.95 and £27.75. All major credit cards accepted. Award-winning fare.

ASSOLAS COUNTRY HOUSE RESTAURANT, Kanturk. Tel. (029) 50015. Set dinner menu for £28.00. All major credit cards accepted. No service charge. Elegant and delightful.

LONGUEVILLE HOUSE PRESIDENTS' RESTAURANT, Mallow. Tel. (022) 47156. Set dinner menu for £28. All major credit cards accepted. Great country restaurant.

LA CASCADE RESTAURANT, Kenmare. Tel. (064) 41600. Set lunch menu for £17.50, set dinner menus for £29.50 and £37.50. A la carte menu also available. All major credit cards accepted. Quiet dining enhanced by lovely views of the falls (flood-lit at night).

EARL OF THOMOND ROOM, Newmarket-on-Fergus. Tel. (061) 368144. Set lunch menu for £18, set dinner menu for £35 and £45. All major credit cards accepted. 15% service charge. The restaurant for Dromoland Castle is exquisite in every detail.

By Ferry

Ferry service reaches Cork from the European continent as well as from Britain. Ferries from Swansea, Le Havre, and Roscoff dock at Cork. Check with **Swansea Cork Ferries**, *Tel. 01792 456116 in England*, for schedules and rates.

By Train

For Cork City, the main train depot is **Kent Station**, *located at the edge of the center of town on Lower Glanmire Road, Tel. (021) 506766.* There are

12 trains a day that run between Cork and Dublin, and the fare is £32 for the three and a half-hour ride. Kent Station is in a fairly decent neighborhood, and it should only take you about 10 or 15 minutes to walk into the center of town. Taxis are also available outside the station, and will take you downtown for around £5.

ORIENTATION

Cork City sprawls along, between, and on the hills above the River Lee. The River Lee runs east-west through the valley, and the city was initially built on the island formed in the middle of the river. Many years ago the city grew beyond the island, and now covers the hillsides on either side of the river. The majority of the sights are found in the older part of Cork – on the island, if you will.

GETTING AROUND TOWN

By Bicycle

Cork is a fun city to see astride a bicycle, if you're careful. Some of the sights to see are on pretty steep hills; while the going may be tough going uphill, make sure your brakes are good for going downhill! The Cork City roads are pretty wide, as Irish roads go, but you can anticipate a lot of traffic. Just watch yourself, and you'll be fine. The sights to see in Cork are a little farther apart than in some other Irish cities, so you might like the extra distance a bicycle will give you.

Here are a few places to rent bicycles in Cork City:
- **The Bike Store**, *48 MacCurtain Street. Tel. (021) 505339*
- **Cycle Scene**, *Blarney Street, Cork. Tel. (021) 301183*
- **Rent-a-Bike**, *2 Redclyffe, Western Road. Cork. Tel. (021) 277655*

By Bus

Buses frequently criss-cross this section of the city where the majority of the sights are. Fares run between 50p and £1.10, depending on how far you are going. While I think walking is the best way to see the sights in Cork, if you have had a long day of walking, a bus ride back to the center of town isn't a bad option.

By Car

My best advice to you if you have brought a car to Cork City is to park it! Traffic is heavy, and parking is limited. So, find a parking place and venture out either on foot or on bicycle. Watch for carparks, or just go a couple blocks above the quays and you should find parking along the street. (Don't forget where you parked, though!)

You can get rental cars at the following agencies in Cork:

- **Avis**, *Emmett Place, Tel. (021) 281111, Fax (021) 281122*
- **Avis**, *Cork Airport, Tel. (021) 281169, Fax (021) 281166*
- **Budget**, *Grand Parade, Tel. (021) 274755*
- **Budget**, *Cork Airport, Tel. (021) 314000*
- **Great Island Car Rentals**, *47 MacCurtain Street, Tel. (021) 503536*
- **Hertz**, *Cork Airport, Tel. (021) 965849*

By Foot

The best way to see Cork is to find a carpark and explore the city's sights by foot. Most of the sights are in an area a little over a mile long and a half-mile wide. There always seems to be traffic on Cork's roads, so if you're driving you'll not be doing much sightseeing.

WHERE TO STAY

Cork has a wealth of nice hotels and Bed and Breakfasts to choose from. Some of those I've listed are in the city center, close to all the happenings, and others are outside of Cork in the countryside to offer you an alternative to the activity of the city. Whatever your preference, all the following accommodations should more than meet your lodging expectations.

ISAAC'S HOSTEL, *48 MacCurtain Street, Cork City. Tel. (021) 500011, Fax (021) 506355. 220 beds. Rates for small dormitory (4 to 6 beds): £8.50 to £9.50 per person sharing, large dormitory (9 to 16 beds): £7.00 to £8.00 per person sharing, family room (sleeps 5): £44. Mastercard and Visa accepted.*

Isaac's Hostel is a favorite of many a visitor to Cork. Perhaps it's because of its central location, or perhaps it's because the hostel is one of the nicest in this part of Ireland. Modern and upbeat, its vibrant atmosphere is infectious. The hostel is divided into dormitories of up to 16 beds, with a few family rooms (they sleep five or six). The facilities are clean, bright (some have even called them *sassy*), and comfortable.

There is a self-catering kitchen and a vibrant brasserie-style restaurant directly across the alley from the hostel, as well as a small cafeteria that serves guests. Linens and towels are provided.

This is a popular place, and extremely busy from mid-May through August. Call ahead for reservations, probably as much as several months in advance for the summer weekends. Nice place – you'll like it for budget accommodations. As a bonus, it's located on a street that is lively and fun in the evenings, with hotels, restaurants, pubs and lots of things going on.

BEECHWOOD HOUSE B&B, *Curra, Riverstick, (near Cork City). Tel. (021) 771456. 4 rooms. Rates for singles: £25, rates for doubles: £18 per person sharing. No credit cards accepted. No service charge.*

This attractive B&B on the main Cork to Kinsale road is a pleasant find. Mrs. Brid O'Connor serves as a gracious hostess. Off the street enough to avoid street noises, and situated amid wooded areas and sculpted lawns, Beechwood House B&B offers a relaxing alternative to the hustle and bustle of the other city hotels and hostels.

Beechwood features three ensuite bedrooms and one standard bedroom. While the standard bedroom doesn't have its own in-room bathroom, it has primary access to the one in the hall. The rooms are average size but quite comfortable. Beechwood House features televisions in each of the bedrooms. For those with special needs, Beechwood House is wheelchair accessible. Beechwood House B&B is open from the first of May through the end of August.

BRANDON HOUSE B&B, *South Douglas Road, Hillgrove Lawn. Tel. (021) 893859. 4 rooms. Rates for singles: £16 to £19, rates for doubles: £23 to £25 per person sharing. No credit cards accepted. No service charge.*

Mrs. Barbara Ahern offers warm accommodations and a pleasant Irish welcome to tourists who stay with her at Brandon House B&B. Located in a cul-de-sac just minutes from downtown, this is a nice place to stay for a night or two while you visit Cork City. Brandon House offers four bedrooms, three of which are ensuite. If you want to kick back and enjoy some Irish television shows, you can do so from your own room, as all rooms have TV. Mrs. Ahern respectfully requests that her guests not smoke.

LOTAMORE HOUSE, *Tivoli, near Cork City. Tel. (021) 482-2344, Fax (021) 482-2219. 20 rooms. Rates for singles: £27, doubles: £25 to £48 per person sharing. Rates include breakfast. American Express, Mastercard and Visa accepted. No service charge.*

Wow! Overlooking the River Lee just a few minutes outside Cork City is stately Lotamore House. The first impression you have of this restored Georgian mansion is of the lovely verdant setting and the splendid gardens that accent the house. Your second impression will be just as awe-filled, as you'll marvel at the manner in which the owners have restored it.

Each bedroom is large and spacious, and individually decorated to retain the warmth and character of the home. All come with television, telephone, tea- and coffee-making facilities, and hairdryers. All the rooms offer splendid views of either the River Lee or the verdant Irish countryside.

SILVER GRANGE HOUSE, *Tivoli. Tel. (021) 821621, Fax (021) 821800. 4 rooms. Rates for singles: £55, doubles: £35 per person sharing. Rates include breakfast. Restaurant, gardens. All major credit cards accepted.*

This stately Georgian manor house sits regally amid five acres of gardens. The decor is elegant, the rooms are spacious and inviting, and the welcome is warm and sincere. The Silver Grange House is better known for their restaurant – just another benefit of staying here – but you'll find the accommodations much more than acceptable.

MOORE'S HOTEL, *Morrison's Island, Cork City. Tel. (021) 271291, Fax (021) 272485. 35 rooms. Rates for singles: £35, doubles: £25 to £35 per person sharing. Rates include breakfast. Restaurant. All major credit cards accepted. No service charge.*

In Cork City's business center, Moore's Hotel offers you decent and relatively inexpensive lodging. The hotel overlooks the River Lee, and the rooms at the front offer the best views. They are a little noisy, but not too bad. The rooms are average in size and comfortably furnished. As a family-run hotel, Moore's appreciates what it's like to travel with children. Special rates for children and specially priced meals in their restaurant are examples of their commitment to make your trip with the kids the most pleasant possible. In addition, they offer special rates for seniors (excluding July and August).

FORTE TRAVELODGE, *Cork City. Tel. (021) 310722, Fax (021) 310707. 40 rooms. Rates for room: £40 to £50. All major credit cards accepted.*

Nothing spectacular, but the rooms at the Forte Travelodge are fastidiously clean and comfortable at a rate more closely akin to a B&B than a hotel. The rooms are ample for two, and would serve a family of four or five nicely. In addition to a television and telephone, each room features tea and coffee-making facilities. The two-story Forte Travelodge is located at the Kinsale roundabout several miles from the city center, on your way to the airport. The hotel is wheelchair accessible.

JURY'S CORK INN, *Anderson's Quay, Cork. Tel. (021) 276444, Fax (021) 276144. 133 rooms. Rates for singles: £75, doubles: £80. All major credit cards accepted. No service charge.*

Jury's Inn's are a new idea in Irish accommodations: these inns offer rooms that sleep three adults (or two adults and two children) for one room rate. This relatively new five-story Jury's Inn is located in the center of the city, making it an ideal location from which to base your visit to Cork City and surrounding areas. The rooms are simple, but very pleasantly furnished. In addition to television and telephone, each room offers tea- and coffee-making facilities. The bathrooms are a little small, but they are modern, well lit and adequate. They also offer a number of rooms that are handicap accessible.

MORRISON'S ISLAND HOTEL, *Morrison's Quay, Cork City. Tel. (021) 275858, Fax (021) 275833. 40 rooms. Rates for singles: £80 to £100, doubles: £55 to £110. Restaurant. All major credit cards accepted. No service charge.*

Morrison's Island Hotel is the business person's dream. Located in the main business section of Cork City, the hotel focuses on providing roomy, comfortable suites for business travelers, or for travelers who like a little extra room. As you walk into the small, marbled lobby, you can feel the richness of the experience you'll have during your stay here.

Each room is a suite, and each has an adjoining room that can be used for meetings, quiet work sessions, or just relaxing. All but four of the rooms have kitchenettes, and several are two-bedroom suites. If you have the need for such, baby-sitting services are available through the hotel.

ROCHESTOWN PARK HOTEL, *Rochestown Road, Douglas, Cork City. Tel. (021) 892233, Fax (021) 892178; E-mail: info@rochestownpark.com. 115 rooms. Rates for singles: £70 to £90, doubles: £50 to £65 per person sharing. Rates include breakfast. Restaurant, indoor swimming pool, fitness center, sauna, spa, solarium, gardens. All major credit cards accepted. 12.5% service charge.*

This converted and expanded Georgian home is a nice hotel to stay in while you are in the Cork area. It was originally a home that once housed young men studying for the priesthood, as well as one of the residences of the Lord Mayor of Cork.

The main house is where you'll find the public rooms: reception, sitting rooms, and dining rooms. The bedrooms are in extensions to the main house. The rooms are nice size and include writing desks – they are designed to meet the needs of the business traveler as well as tourists. Additional amenities such as a bowl of fruit, mineral water, and robes give you an extra welcome. The hotel also boasts a fairly extensive fitness center, pool, sauna, steam room and solarium. And if you just want to walk, there are seven acres of gardens that surround the hotel.

IMPERIAL HOTEL, *South Mall, Cork. Tel. (021) 274040, Fax (021) 275375. 99 rooms. Rates for singles: £65, doubles: £85, suites: £170. Restaurant. All major credit cards accepted. 10% service charge.*

If you want to be in the middle of the Cork action, this is the place. Located in the center of the Cork City financial district, the Imperial Hotel is just minutes from many sights in town.

The hotel is not all that impressive though, with its eclectic architectural styles: it seems like they were unsure whether to retain their 19th-century roots or modernize from top to bottom. So they did a little of both. Some of the rooms are graced with antiques, as are a number of locations in the hotel, but most of the rooms are quite modern – to the point of white furnishings and chrome and glass coffee tables.

On the main floor they offer a 1930's style cocktail bar complete with a pianist; they also offer a pub that is frequented by a number of locals as well as tourists. If you are traveling with children, you will benefit from discounts for the young ones on the room rate as well as in the restaurant, where lower-priced children's meals are available. If you want to go out on the town, the hotel will also arrange baby-sitting for you.

There is a bit of a parking problem – parking at the hotel is limited, although there is covered parking a short distance from the hotel.

JURY'S HOTEL, *Western Road, Cork. Tel. (021) 276622, Fax (021) 274477; Website: www.jurys.com/ireland/jury's_hotel_cork.htm. 160 rooms.*

Rates for singles: £115, doubles: £135, suites: £165. Restaurant, gardens, outdoor swimming pool, sauna, spa, squash court. All major credit cards accepted. 12.5% service charge.

If you stay at Jury's Hotel in Cork, you'll find yourself just a few minute's walk from the sights and activities of the downtown area. Many of the rooms face onto a green courtyard, with well-kept lawns and gardens. The rooms, while somewhat small, are brightly decorated in a floral design. They are enhanced with a complimentary bowl of fruit and bottles of mineral water, and the nightly turn-down service is a nice touch.

Jury's Hotel offers a wide variety of leisure activities to help you relax during your stay. You can take advantage of the indoor/outdoor swimming pool, sauna, fitness center, and even a squash court. There's even a playground for youngsters to work their wiggles out. Discounted room rates for the children as well as children's meals in the restaurant help hold down costs if you're here with kids.

Near Cork

BALLYMAKEIGH HOUSE, *Killeagh, County Cork. Tel. (024) 95184, Fax (024) 95370. 5 rooms. Rates for singles: £45, doubles: £35 per person sharing. Restaurant, dinner available for £25. No credit cards accepted. No service charge.*

Margaret Browne is the hostess, a working dairy farm is the setting, wonderful meals complement the lovely home, and the combination seems to work magic for those who stay at Ballymakeigh House. Many who stay here once vow it won't be the last time.

Sitting on a lush green hillside and presiding grandly over the luxurious farmland all around, Ballymakeigh House presents a regal appearance. Inside, you'll find a delightful mixture of hospitality, fresh flowers, and starched linen to complement your stay. If you've brought the kids, you'll really like the discount for children and you can take advantage of their baby-sitting service.

This older house has been renovated to provide a nice set of ensuite bedrooms that are individually decorated and comfortably furnished. But the warm Irish welcome seems to be what brings 'em back. This truly is a special place that you shouldn't miss if it fits your schedule.

Mrs. Browne has gained renown in Ireland as a wonderful cook. After you've savored her meals, you may be tempted to purchase the cookbook she has published, *Through My Kitchen Window*. You'll be able to enjoy her meals in a plant-filled solarium that looks out on the lovely grounds. Her culinary talents, along with the wonderful ambiance found here have made Ballymakeigh House a regular on Ireland-wide travel television shows. Her talents have not gone unnoticed in the industry either. Both she and Ballymakeigh House have won a number of prestigious awards, including *Guesthouse of the Year* (1992) and *Breakfast of the Year* (1994). John McKenna of *The Irish Times*, Ireland's major newspaper, summed it up best when he said, "The secret of Ballymakeigh House is not just the cooking but the alliance of good cooking with great hospitality."

Ballymakeigh House is about 25 miles east of Cork on the N25. When you make your reservations, be sure and ask Mrs. Browne for directions.

BALLYVOLANE HOUSE, *Castlelyons, Tel. (025) 36349, Fax (025) 3678; E-mail: ballyvol@iol.ie; Website: www.ballyvolanehouse.ie. 6 rooms. Rates for singles: £50 to £62, doubles: £38 to £50 per person sharing. Restaurant. All major credit cards accepted. No service charge.*

The renovated Ballyvolane House is located in the countryside southeast of Fermoy between Rathcormac and Castlelyons (about 25 miles north of Cork). Built in 1728, the home has seen a number of renovations and refurbishments throughout the years. The results are splendid indeed, and you're fortunate that Mr. and Mrs. Green share its beauty with guests from all over the world.

Ballyvolane House is situated in an emerald setting of woods and farmland. As you enter the house, you'll be impressed with the entryway: pillared and presided over by a baby grand piano. The sitting rooms are large rooms decorated with rich, dark wood and portraits of ancestors sternly watching Ballyvolane's guests. Your next impressions will be the collection of antiques that are liberally sprinkled throughout the house, including the bedrooms. The bedrooms themselves are a variety of sizes, but are all most comfortable and pleasant. If you're calling ahead to make reservations, ask for one of the rooms with the old claw-footed bathtubs – they're like taking a bath in a small swimming pool!

Ballyvolane House offers wheelchair access; children are welcome and pets allowed.

ASSOLAS COUNTRY HOUSE, *Kanturk, County Cork. Tel. (029) 50015, Fax (029) 50795; E-mail: assolas@tinet.ie; Website: www.assolas.com. 9 rooms. Rates for singles: Standard room with bath from £65 to £70, Superior Room with luxury bathroom from £80 to £90; doubles: Standard room with bath from £55 to £60 per person sharing, Superior room with luxury bath from £70 to £80 per person sharing. Restaurant, tennis, croquet. Dinner available for £28. All major credit cards accepted. No service charge. Open from the end of March through the end of October.*

Stunningly beautiful. Dignified and elegant. That's what I would call Assolas Country House. Just a few minutes outside of Kanturk rests aristocratic, ivy-covered Assolas Country House, the courtly 17th-century country home of the Bourke family. Inside its creeper-clad walls you'll find an impressive collection of antiques, an open fire in the fireplace, and a warm greeting from a member of the Bourke family.

Your hosts are Joe and Hazel Bourke, and they prefer to present

Assolas Country House as their home rather than as a hotel. And they succeed in their efforts – when you stay here you will feel more like an honored guest, perhaps a distant cousin, than a mere tourist who needs a room for the night.

The rooms are large, clean and well maintained, and several have outstanding views of the grounds. Three of the rooms are located out in the courtyard in a restored stone cottage. They are nonetheless nice, and you'll be exceptionally comfortable whether you stay in the rooms in the house or in the stone cottage. Three of the rooms in the main house are very large and have the best views and are categorized as "Superior," and you'll pay just a bit more for them.

The Bourkes have owned and lived at Assolas Country House for generations, and are quite familiar with the surrounding sights to see. They would be pleased to help you plan your exploration of the area, and can even arrange some activities, such as a golf outing compliments of the local 18-hole golf course in Kanturk.

To say that there is a restaurant on-site is somewhat of an understatement – Hazel Bourke presides over the restaurant and directs the efforts of a team of cooks that has garnered international recognition and a number of awards for Assolas Country House Restaurant (see *Where to Eat*).

You'll need a car if you're going to stay at Assolas House. It is located about an hour and 15 minutes north of Cork City. Take the N20 north out of Cork to Mallow, then west on the N72 to the R576 (follow the signs for Kanturk).

BALLYMALOE HOUSE, *Shanagarry, Midleton, County Cork. Tel. (021) 652531, Fax (021) 652021; E-mail: res@ballymaloe.com; Website: www.ballymaloe.com. 33 rooms. Rates for singles: £80 to £105, doubles: £50 to £85 per person sharing. Restaurant, garden, croquet, outdoor swimming pool, tennis, golf. All major credit cards accepted. 10% service charge.*

About 45 minutes east of Cork City sits the handsome, creeper-clad Ballymaloe House. Once a castle, then a farm, and now a hotel, Ballymaloe House seems to have retained the best characteristics of all three. It has the grandeur of the castle, the warmth of a family farm, and the efficiency of a well-run hotel. The Allen family are busy proprietors. In addition to the hotel, they have a highly regarded restaurant on-site, they run the Ballymaloe Cookery School, have a craft and kitchen shop, and run a restaurant in Cork City. Yet they still manage to greet each of their guests with a warmth typical of what you will come to expect in Ireland.

The bedrooms are an eclectic collection ranging from traditional to modern; all are comfortably furnished, and many open out onto lawns and gardens. Perhaps the most intriguing room is one which is housed in the 16th-century gatehouse. It offers a sort of a rustic experience: twin beds, with the bathroom up a steep wooden staircase.

You can relax in the country splendor here, or you can spend some time participating in horseback riding, tennis, a playground for the children, and a swimming pool. In addition, you're only about two miles from the ocean. If you've brought the children along, you'll also appreciate the children's discount available for both the hotel and the restaurant. Several of the rooms have wheelchair access.

AHERNE'S SEAFOOD RESTAURANT AND ACCOMMODATION, *163 North Main Street, Youghal. Tel. (024) 92424, Fax (024) 93633; E-mail: ahernes@tinet.ie. 10 rooms. Rates for singles: £85, doubles: £65 per person sharing. All major credit cards accepted.*

It's difficult to say which aspect of Aherne's is most popular: its award-winning restaurant or its award-winning accommodations. For a review of the restaurant, see *Where to Eat* below. Aherne's has almost a cult following among tourists and the Irish alike. Much of their business is repeat, and new groupies join the ranks every season, having been directed there by the effusive comments of friends and strangers.

The Fitzgibbon family is probably responsible for this following – Kate carries on the tradition of three generations of Fitzgibbon hospitality. And they are small enough – just 10 rooms – to provide attention at an individual level. Open turf fires welcome those who come to Aherne's. The seafood in the restaurant is exquisite, and the rooms are spacious and sumptuous. None of the rooms have memorable views, but the rooms and service are marvelous enough to compensate. This is perhaps the best lodging for the price in County Cork.

You can find Aherne's in the town of Youghal, about an hour's drive from Cork. This would be a nice place to stay if you're headed for or coming from Waterford.

LONGUEVILLE HOUSE, *Mallow. Tel. (022) 47156, US toll-free number 800/223-6510. Fax (022) 47459; E-mail: info@longuevillehouse.ie; Website: www.longuevillehouse.ie. 21 rooms. Rates for singles: £59 to £120, doubles: £60 to £65 per person sharing, suites: £75 to £135. Garden, fishing. Rates include breakfast. All major credit cards accepted. No service charge.*

Talk about an impressive Georgian house! The ancestors of the current owners, Michael and Jane O'Callaghan built Longueville House in 1720. In the 1960's, they converted their large home into a country hotel, and it's obvious they know and love the business they've chosen. Their service is legendary, and those who stay here swear they'll be back.

As you enter the spacious foyer, you'll notice the lavish ornamentation of the house. Gilded portraits of past O'Callaghans greet you with somber expressions, but that will be the only somberness you'll experience at Longueville House. The house is rife with antiques and elegant furnishings, and it is well endowed with quality craftsmanship, from its ornate plaster work to the rich and beautiful woodwork.

To say the bedrooms are spacious would be an understatement; your bedroom at Longueville House may very well be the largest you experience during your stay in Ireland. The furnishings in the bedrooms are all top-of-the line, and most of the bathrooms are marble and offer first-rate facilities. The bedrooms at the front of the house are especially nice: they overlook the Blackwater River Valley, including the ruins of a nearby 16th-century O'Callaghan castle.

Longueville House is located in Mallow, about half an hour north of Cork on the N20.

ARBUTUS LODGE, *Montenotte Cork. Tel. (021) 501237, Fax (021) 502893; Website: www.arbutuslodge.net. 20 rooms. Rates for singles: £55 to £88, doubles: £85 to £125, suites: £140 to £200. Rates include breakfast. Gardens, tennis. All major credit cards accepted. No service charge.*

Formerly the home of the Lord Mayor of Cork, Arbutus Lodge sits grandly above Cork City with commanding views of the sprawling city and the River Lee. Exquisitely furnished with antiques throughout, the hotel also boasts a fine collection of Irish art – new as well as old.

The bedrooms are those befitting the family of the Lord Mayor – large and well furnished. The four most impressive rooms are in a mansion across from the hotel, and are more like mini-apartments. This is a nice place, one of the nicest you'll find in and around Cork City.

WHERE TO EAT

UPTOWN GRILL, *MacCurtain Street, Cork City. Tel. (021) 502120. £3.85 to £8.50. Open Monday through Thursday 10:00am to midnight, Friday and Saturday from 10:00am to 12:30am, and Sundays from 10:00am to 11:30pm. No credit cards accepted. No service charge.*

This small, busy (busy!) café is a great place to pop in for a quick, filling bite to eat. The menu features grilled items, from pork chops to steak, and an assortment of fish dishes. The atmosphere is frankly functional, with small tables covered by red and white checked tablecloths. Don't go here if you are looking for a quiet candlelit dinner; you'll get more of a noisy, vibrant atmosphere here (good food, too!).

FARMGATE CAFE, *Old English Market, Princes Street, Cork City. Tel. (021) 278134. £2.95 to £9.95. Open Monday through Saturday from 8:30am to 5:30pm. Mastercard and Visa accepted. No service charge.*

While you're seeing Cork, stop by the Farmgate Cafe above the Old English Market for a bite to eat. This smallish cafe offers a good selection of snacks, breakfast, lunch, and high tea menu items. Breakfast is served until 11:00am. The freshest ingredients – many of them procured from the Old English Market – are used to enhance the quality and flavor of the simple traditional Irish dishes available. Dress is casual.

BULLY'S, *40 Paul Street, Cork City. Tel. (021) 27355. £7.95 to £10.95. Open Monday through Saturday from noon to 11:30pm, and Sunday from 1:00pm to 11:00pm. No credit cards accepted. No service charge.*

Bully's is sort of a cross between a pizzeria and an Italian fast-food restaurant. The food is good, featuring solid Italian specialties, including pizza, calzone, and a number of homemade pasta and seafood dishes. A few vegetarian dishes are also available.

ISAAC'S RESTAURANT, *48 MacCurtain Street, Cork City. Tel. (021) 503805, £6.95 to £11.95. Open Monday through Saturday for lunch from 12:30pm to 2:30pm, and daily for dinner from 6:30pm to 10:30pm. All major credit cards accepted.*

This brasserie-style restaurant, part of the hotel/hostel of the same name, is light and bright, and belies the building's beginnings as an 18th-century warehouse. Every time I have been here, the diners were enjoying their candlelit tables amidst lots of fun and activity. The furnishings are elegant, yet simple at the same time. The nautical theme portrayed throughout the restaurant reminds you of Cork's history as a harbor town: a large ship's wheel, lobster cages, and colored sails and a mast oversee the festivities at Isaac's.

The menu is trendy, and seems to follow no particular cuisine. The offerings range from such mundane fare as minute steak with onions to more exotic offerings like lamb curry with *poppadums* to grilled prawns in garlic butter. Dress is nice casual.

REIDY'S WINE VAULTS, *Western Road, Lancaster Quay, Cork City. Tel. (021) 275751. £3.95 to £14.95. Open daily from 10:30am to 11:30pm (Sundays from 12:30pm to 2:00pm, and 4:00pm to 11:00pm). All major credit cards accepted.*

Inside Reidy's is an eclectic collection of styles, from country antiques to modern black and white tiles. The impressive and immense mahogany bar presides over the pub's proceedings. Stop by Reidy's for a quick bite of their bar food, which is basic but quite good. Homemade soups and sandwiches join steaks, fresh seafood, and chicken on the menu.

THE GINGERBREAD HOUSE, *Paul Street, Cork City. Tel. (021) 276411. £2.95 to £14.95. Open Monday through Saturday from 8:15am to 10:30pm; they serve dinner from 6:00pm to 10:30pm. No credit cards accepted. No service charge.*

For a quick bite while out shopping or sightseeing, you may want to give Barnaby Blacker's Gingerbread house a try. Open basically all day long, the Gingerbread House has gained some reputation for its excellent pastries and breads (try their homemade carrot cake or French chocolate). They have also developed a decent though limited dinner menu.

CRAWFORD GALLERY CAFE, *Emmet Place, Cork City. Tel. (021) 274415. £3.95 to £19.95. Open from 9:00am to 5:00pm Monday through Saturday. No credit cards accepted.*

The Crawford Gallery is located on the first floor of the Crawford Municipal Art Gallery. It makes a convenient spot to stop for everything from a snack to a full meal before, after, or during your visit to the art gallery. Dress is casual.

THE OYSTER TAVERN, *Market Lane, Cork City. Tel. (021) 272716. £14.95 to £24.95. Open Monday through Saturday from 12:30pm to 2:30pm and 6:30pm to 10:30pm. All major credit cards accepted.*

The Oyster Tavern is a landmark restaurant in Cork City, having served numerous generations of Irish for the past 200 years. As you walk in, you have the unmistakable feeling of walking into the old Victorian period – dark woodwork, red upholstery, a friendly staff, and decent food. The food itself is not extraordinary, but it's good and filling, and the surroundings are a nice complement. Casual dress is fine.

JACQUES, *9 Phoenix Street, Cork City. Tel. (021) 277387. £14.95 to £24.95. Open Monday through Saturday from 11:30pm to 3:00pm and 6:00pm to 10:30pm. All major credit cards accepted.*

This brightly colored cafe is a pleasant place to grab a bite to eat. The Barry's run a nice eating establishment, and have gained a good reputation for their breads and Irish cheeses. Sample menu items might include such treats as warm salad of lamb's kidneys, escalope of fresh salmon on a ginger and spinach bed, and a variety of vegetarian dishes.

MICHAEL'S BISTRO, *4 Mardyke Street, Cork City. Tel. (021) 276887. £12.95 to £24.95. Open Monday through Saturday for lunch from noon to 3:00pm, and for dinner from 6:00pm to 10:30pm. (They are closed on Monday from mid-October through the end of May.) Mastercard and Visa accepted.*

Just around the corner from Cliffords Restaurant, and owned by the same couple, Michael's offers more of an intimate atmosphere than the more formal Cliffords. The menu here is traditional Irish, with some poetic liberties taken. The fare ranges from such offerings as seafood sausage on a bed of leeks to traditional Irish stew. The dessert and cheese selections are surprisingly good.

FLEMINGS, *Silver Grange House, Tivoli, set lunch menu for £13.50, and set dinner menu for £21. Open daily from 12:30pm to 2:30pm for lunch, and from 6:30pm to 10:30pm for dinner. All major credit cards accepted.*

On the outskirts of Cork City on the Dublin road, you'll find this wonderful restaurant. This is one of the nicest French restaurants in the country, and as yet it is still relatively unknown. Michael Fleming, owner and chef of Flemings, cooks up sumptuous offerings, from traditional French to his own delicious concoctions. You might be tempted by baby clams poached in a champagne sauce, pan-fried frog's legs with shallots on an apple and potato gallette, or bran-coated marinated mussels with an orange cream sauce. If your high school French fails to help you decipher the menu (which is written in French), don't despair – English translations are provided.

The wine list aims for quality rather than quantity, and I doubt you'll be disappointed. A jacket is requested.

IVORY TOWER RESTAURANT, *35 Princes Street, Cork City. £12.95 to £25. Open for lunch daily from noon to 4:00pm and 6:30pm to 11:00pm for dinner. Mastercard and Visa accepted.*

The easy-going and relaxed atmosphere at the Ivory Tower Restaurant is one of the things that makes this a popular dining spot for residents of Cork as well as tourists. The menu is sort of "Irish eclectic," and offers a wide range of fare. Entrees range from scallops and prawns to eel and sushi. Vegetarian dishes are plentiful, and they are well-known for their homemade bread and Irish farmhouse cheeses. Dress is casual.

CLIFFORDS, *40 Paul Street, Cork City. Tel. (021) 275333. Set lunch menu for £11.50, and set dinner menu for £27. Open for dinner Tuesday through Saturday from 7:00pm to 10:30pm, and they're open for lunch Tuesday through Friday from 12:30pm to 2:30pm. All major credit cards accepted.*

Located on the west side of the city, this elegant modern restaurant in a converted Georgian townhouse is really a treat. The furnishings are simple and the walls are bedecked with contemporary Irish art. The tables are set with crisp Irish linen and a simple floral center-piece.

The food is traditional Irish with a decidedly continental flair. Typical menu items (most of which change monthly) include fresh brace of quail in a honey and cider vinegar sauce, pan-fried brill with mussels, noisettes of spring lamb with confit of baby onion, and black sole and prawns in a pepper and lime sauce.

ARBUTUS LODGE RESTAURANT, *Montenotte, Cork City. Tel. (021) 501237. Set dinner menus for £22.95 and £27.75. Open Monday through Saturday from 1:00pm to 2:00pm, and from 7:00pm to 9:30pm. All major credit cards accepted.*

The restaurant for Arbutus Lodge is considered one of the 10 finest in Ireland by most food critics. Traditional Irish food prepared with care and presented with an artistic flair all topped by outstanding service are hallmarks of the restaurant. From seafood to steak, lobster to lamb, all the meals are cooked with fresh ingredients, many of them from Arbutus Lodge's own kitchen garden.

Hungry for seafood? Try their pan-fried mussels with a walnut and garlic dip, or perhaps you'd prefer Irish beef. If that's the case, try their spiced beef with chutney or fillet of steak. If it's wild game you'd like, there's always the roast venison with raspberry coulis, or the chartreuse of pigeon and rabbit with fresh chanterelle sauce. As a bonus that you don't get in many upscale restaurants, the portions are large enough to satisfy you.

Near Cork

AHERNE'S SEAFOOD RESTAURANT, *163 North Main Street, Youghal. Tel. (024) 92424. £4.95 to £14.95. All major credit cards accepted.*

Aherne's came to my attention after several tourists I spoke with strongly recommended that I not miss it. Their praise was exuberant. When I showed up at Aherne's, I could see why they were ebullient. As a port city, you'd expect one of the top restaurants in the area to specialize in seafood, and they don't disappoint you. The selection is extensive and varied, and just the sound of the dishes spurs your appetite: prawns in garlic butter or hot creamed oysters, Youghal Bay Lobster, smoked salmon and pasta, grilled black sole, or plaice stuffed with oysters in a red wine sauce are just a few of the choices in this wonderful restaurant.

All in all, you won't go wrong with Aherne's if you like seafood. If not, there are also a few token dishes for meat-eaters.

LOVETT'S, *Churchyard Lane, Douglas. Tel. (021) 94909. Set lunch menu for £14.50, and set dinner menu for £24. Open Monday through Saturday for dinner from 7:00pm to 9:45pm, or for lunch Monday through Friday from 12:30pm until 2:00pm. All major credit cards accepted.*

Lovett's has a loyal following from the residents of Cork, and many tourists as well. And with good reason: it's difficult to know whether its popularity flows from Dermod Lovett's warm Irish welcome or the fine food prepared by his wife Margaret. Probably both contribute to their success. The menu is extensive and features excellent seafood, beef, and vegetarian choices. Typical offerings might include grilled black sole with lemon butter, roast rack of spring Cork lamb, or poached salmon. All the ingredients are fresh, most coming from the local countryside.

Lovett's is about 20 miles northeast of Cork – be sure and get directions when you call for reservations.

LONGUEVILLE HOUSE PRESIDENTS' RESTAURANT, *Mallow. Tel. (022) 47156. Set dinner menu for £28. Open daily for dinner from 7:00pm to 9:00pm. Reservations are needed from June through August. If you'd like to stop by for lunch, Sunday is the only day they serve it, and they are open for lunch from noon until 1:45pm. All major credit cards accepted.*

Try to eat at this elegant country restaurant. On the walls surrounding the dining area are the somber portraits of former Irish Presidents overseeing the service and food in the dining room. They needn't be concerned: the food is exquisite, the service impeccable, and the experience memorable. The freshness, ingenuity, and interesting combinations of delicious edibles all combine to make your dining an event rather than just another meal. Part of the success of the restaurant is Chef William

O'Callaghan's insistence on the freshest ingredients; indeed, many of the vegetables, fruits, herbs, lamb, and salmon come from within a few 100 yards of the house. The others come from nearby farms and waters.

Mr. O'Callaghan tempts his guests with a wide variety of exceptional offerings, including an ever-popular Surprise Taste Menu, which is a seven-course treat. Other tempting specialties include such favorites as roast of Longueville lamb with a gratin of turnips, pan-fried medallions of monkfish, or Kilbrack pork. Desserts will leave you dreaming of those you couldn't order – you may decide to come back another day just for a new dessert! Longueville House is renowned for their pyramid of chocolate with an enchanting orange sauce. All in all, you may not wish to pass this restaurant by. Jacket and tie are requested.

Longueville House Presidents' Restaurant is located in Mallow, about half an hour north of Cork on the N20.

ASSOLAS COUNTRY HOUSE RESTAURANT, *Kanturk. Tel. (029) 50015. Set dinner menu for £28. Open daily from 7:00pm to 8:30pm. All major credit cards accepted. No service charge.*

Simply stated, the restaurant at Assolas Country House is elegant and delightful. The fruits and vegetables you eat, and the herbs that impart such magnificent subtleties of taste to the food, are all grown within the kitchen garden for Assolas Country House. The menu changes daily, but the quality is always the same. Typical offerings may include fillet of brill oven-baked in a basil butter sauce, Kenmare mussels, sautéed oysters with shallots and cream in brioche, and confit of duck. If wild game is your preference, several options are available, including venison, and at times pheasant or quail.

Those in the know say that Hazel Bourke is the genius behind the phenomenal fare offered here. While her husband and parents-in-law run the lodging side of Assolas Country House (see *Where to Stay* section), she has charge of the culinary efforts of the family. Her endeavors have gained international recognition, as the restaurant has been featured in such impressive publications as *Bon Appetit* magazine and the travel section of *The New York Times* (where she was featured on the front page). Her efforts have also garnered a number of awards, including breakfast awards, Cheese Board of Ireland award, and others. Dress is nice casual, although you'll feel more comfortable in a suit and tie or dress.

The Assolas House is located in the tiny town of Kanturk, which is about an hour and 15 minutes' drive northwest of Cork City. It's not difficult to find, as long as you have called ahead for directions. It will take a little effort, but you'll be glad you came.

BALLYMALOE HOUSE RESTAURANT, *Shanagarry. Tel. (021) 652531. Set dinner menu for £30. Open daily for lunch from 12:30pm to 2:00pm, and for dinner from 7:00pm to 9:30pm. All major credit cards accepted.*

The restaurant for Ballymaloe House is open to the public, and that's fortunate for all of us. Chef Rory O'Connell works wonders with a fare that is described as traditional Irish prepared with a continental flair. The menu isn't extensive, but the food is marvelous, relying on only the freshest local produce and meats – much of which comes from Ballymaloe farm itself. Typical fare includes Shanagarry pork with apple sauce and broccoli, grilled sirloin with béarnaise sauce and fried onions, and a rich variety of farmhouse cheeses from throughout County Cork. Following the main course, the dessert trolley will tempt the most prodigious dieter. The set lunch menu is £16.50 and dinner is £30. Dress is nice casual.

SEEING THE SIGHTS

St. Anne's Church, *Church Street, Cork City. Open May through October Monday through Saturday 9:30am to 5:00pm, November to April Monday through Saturday 10:00am to 3:30pm. Admission is £1.50 for adults, 60p for children.* One of Cork's primary landmarks, St. Anne's Church – also called Shandon Church – sits high on the north side of the city. The steeple is 120 feet tall, and has an intriguing design that is fondly referred to as the "pepperpot." Nice views of the city are available from the steeple. The steeple is endowed with eight bells that were cast in 1750 – you can request that they be rung. The church was built in 1722, but has none of the exquisite architectural characteristics of other cathedrals built at that time in Ireland.

St. Mary's Pro-Cathedral, *Cathedral Walk, Cork City. Open daily 9:00am to 6:00pm. Admission is free.* Also presiding over the north side of the city is St. Mary's Pro-Cathedral. The cathedral was built in the early 19th century, and shortly afterward suffered a fire that gutted the interior. The interior was then renovated in Gothic style. The presbytery has an extensive collection of birth and marriage records from 1784.

Merchant's Quay, *Patrick Street.* Back down in the valley, Merchant's Quay is an appropriate site for the large shopping center that resides on Patrick Street between Winthrop Street (a pedestrianized shopping street itself), and Marlborough Street. It was here along Merchants Quay that yesteryear's ships loaded their cargo and slipped down the River Lee and into the Irish Sea, headed for trade on the continent.

Crawford Art Gallery, *Emmett Place, Cork City. Open Monday through Saturday from 10:00am to 5:00pm. Admission is free. Tel. (021) 273377.* This small but impressive gallery is located at the corner of Academy Street and Emmet Place. Inside you'll find a wide range of work primarily by Irish artists, from 18th-century renderings of Cork to much more contemporary works. They also have a nice collection of sculptures.

Cornmarket, *Patrick Street and The Grand Parade.* The open-air market known as "Coal-Quay" was once a lot more thriving than it is now.

Today, you'll find a few used-clothing dealers amid some interesting shops.

English Market, *The Grand Parade*. No preservatives here! The English Market is the place to go in the city to get fresh produce. It's here that the local farmers peddle the fruits of their labors, from herbs to vegetables to chicken, beef, tripe, drisheen, etc. It's a busy place that has changed very little over the centuries.

Bishop Lucey Park, *The Grand Parade*. Bishop Lucey Park is an oasis of green in the city. Among other things, the small park features the statuesque work of local Cork artisans. During the spring and summer months, the park is an especially nice place to escape from the activity and hubbub of the city.

Triskel Arts Center, *Tobin Street. Open Monday through Friday from 11:00am to 6:00pm, and Saturday from 11:00am to 5:00pm. Admission is free. Tel. (021) 272022.* This small arts center is tucked away down an alley (watch for the signpost), and presents small but interesting exhibitions of modern art and crafts. Spend a few minutes here (that's all it will take) admiring the works of various artists, mostly local.

St. Finbarre Cathedral, *Bishop Street. Open daily from 10:00am to 5:00pm. Admission is free.* Three steeples mark the Gothic St. Finbarre's Cathedral, sitting peacefully in the southwest portion of the city. **St. Finbarre** established a monastery on this site over 1,300 years ago, and the Church of Ireland cathedral now bears his name. This cathedral was built in the 19th century. St. Finbarre's is especially striking at night, when it is well lit and glows brightly for all to see, especially if you are up on the north side of the city.

But don't be satisfied with gazing on its beauty from the outside. If you do, you'll miss a stunning treat. As you enter St. Finbarre's, look heavenward, and your gaze will be met with angels and the glorified Lord. The interior of St. Finbarre's is a treasure-trove of masterful mosaics, stunning stained-glass windows, and incredible carvings. So...make your mother happy – don't just loiter outside, but go *inside* the church.

University College Cork, *Donovan's Road. Open Monday through Friday from 9:00am to 5:00pm. Tel. (021) 276871.* The University College Cork sits along the River Lee in scholastic reverence. Most of the University's buildings were built in the 19th century, and sport the Tudor-Gothic style of architecture that was popular at the time.

Walking tours of the college grounds and some of its buildings are available from mid-June through the end of August. During other times of the year, you are free to wander the campus and see the sights for yourself, or you can arrange for a tour by calling the university's main number. Rates for the tours are £2.50 for adults and 75p for children, or £6 for a family ticket.

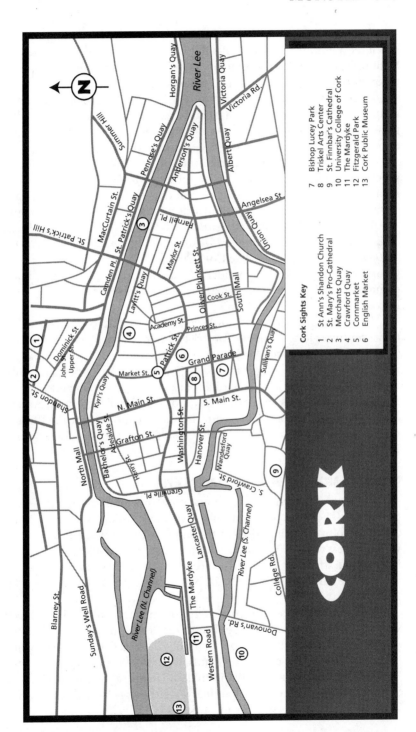

CORK

Cork Sights Key

1 St Ann's Shandon Church
2 St. Mary's Pro-Cathedral
3 Merchants Quay
4 Crawford Quay
5 Cornmarket
6 English Market
7 Bishop Lucey Park
8 Triskel Arts Center
9 St. Finnbar's Cathedral
10 University College of Cork
11 The Mardyke
12 Fitzgerald Park
13 Cork Public Museum

The tour will take you into the main quadrangle building, where you'll see a number of historical exhibits. The tour also incorporates the **Republican Grave Plot**, a cemetery for those rebels who gave their lives through the years struggling for Ireland's independence.

In the western part of the city center lies the green-belt area known simply as **The Mardyke**. It is a favorite place for riverside strolls, frisbee tossing, and people-watching. On the weekends, you may be fortunate enough to catch a game of cricket being played.

Just to the east of The Mardyke and sprawling along the River Lee is spacious **Fitzgerald Park**. This is a popular spot for mothers walking their babies in prams (strollers), young men and women walking hand-in-hand or talking quietly on the grass, and kids running and jumping around.

Cork Public Museum, *Fitzgerald Park. Open Monday through Friday from 11:00am to 1:00pm and 2:15pm to 5:00pm, and Sunday 3:00pm to 5:00pm. Tel. (021) 270679.* The Cork Public Museum is housed in an old Georgian Mansion in Fitzgerald Park. It isn't particularly large, but it contains a nice amount of information and exhibits that chronicle Cork's history.

As you tour the museum, you'll view exhibits that tout Cork's role in their centuries-long struggle for Irish independence. You'll learn of Cork's mayor, Terence MacSwiney, who felt so deeply about the cause that he died after a hunger strike of 75 days in 1920. Another exhibit features Michael Collins, the hard-as-nails Director of Intelligence for the IRA during the years that eventually led to Ireland's freedom. Among other things, Collins is credited with eliminating informers in the IRA and placing his own informers in Dublin Castle, the seat of English power in Ireland.

NIGHTLIFE & ENTERTAINMENT

Cork is a city given to vibrancy and good times, and the nightlife is no exception. There are plenty of pubs for you to explore and enjoy. Some are filled to overflowing with youth, others with tourists, and still others with business people. Whatever your pleasure, you should be able to find it along the streets of Cork. Here are a few of the best places to visit:

AN SPAILPIN FANACH, *28 South Main Street, Cork. Tel. (021) 277949.*

You may not be able to correctly pronounce the name, but take my word for it – this is a place you'll want to visit. Upon entry you'll know you've found one of the most popular pubs in Cork City – it will probably be packed, especially on the weekends. Generally speaking, the clientele here will be more...mature...than you'll find in the other pubs in Cork. An Spailpin Fanach has become a popular watering hole for the businessmen and women as well as tourists in Cork.

The low ceilings and brick walls, coupled with warm earth-tones, give the sense of close friendliness. You'll enjoy a wide range of music from Sunday to Thursday evenings, ranging from traditional Irish to western to blues.

THE LONG VALLEY BAR, *10 Winthrop Street, Cork. Tel. (021) 272144.*

The Long Valley Bar has been entertaining the citizens of Cork for over 150 years (and tourists for somewhat less time than that, I suppose). This pub oozes character and warmth, from the intriguing long bar to the proprietors that are only slightly younger than the pub itself (well, maybe that's stretching things a bit, but Humphrey and Rita Moynihan are 70-something).

The Long Valley Bar is a long, narrow pub with lots of tables and chairs to rest your weary feet after a few hours of seeing Cork's sights. Take a few minutes and notice the old photos on the walls – they tell the story of life in Cork for many decades. The pub has gained quite a reputation in recent years for the "pub grub" they prepare and serve, so you may want to sample some of their fare (but only if you have a hearty appetite – they don't skimp on the servings). The Long Valley Bar is located just around the corner from the General Post Office (*Plunkett Street*).

THE OYSTER TAVERN, *Market Lane, Cork. Tel. (021) 272716.*

If the Long Valley Bar is old, the Oyster Tavern is ancient. When the Long Valley Bar opened its doors, the Oyster Tavern was beginning its sixth decade in operation. It was nearly 10 years old when the 1798 Uprising was put down, and 130 years old when Ireland earned its independence.

Saunter in, pull up a chair in one of the small dining rooms, and sit back and enjoy the warming turf fire or the radiance of the clientele. The Oyster Tavern is haunted by a wide variety of Cork's citizens, from writers and artists, to university students to just plain working folk. There is also a healthy number of tourists sprinkled in. As the name implies, oysters are the specialty of the house.

SPORTS & RECREATION

Golf

Cork Little Island Golf Club, *Cork, County Cork. Tel. (021) 353451, £35.*

If someone were to ask you what Cork Little Island Golf Club and Augusta National Golf Course have in common, you'll be able to smugly reply that they were both designed by golf course architect Alistair MacKenzie. Those who have golfed Ireland's top courses claim this is one of the best. Why not check it out yourself and see if you agree? Visitors are welcome on weekdays, but the weekends are reserved for club members. Par 72. 6,216 yards.

Gaelic Football

You can catch Gaelic Football matches on Saturday, Sunday, or Wednesdays from June to September at Blackrock Stadium. Ticket prices range from free to £15, depending on whether it is a major regional game or just a local one. For information on tickets and game times, call the **Gaelic Athletic Association**, *Tel. (021) 385876.*

Horseback Riding

- **Ballmee Equestrian Center**, *Doneraile, County Cork. Tel. (022) 24135*
- **Knocknamanna Stables**, *Minane Bridge, County Cork. Tel. (021) 887111*
- **Skevanish Riding Center**, *Innishannon, County Cork. Tel. (021) 775476*

Hurling

Hurling matches are also played at Blackrock Stadium, and you can get additional information on time and ticket prices by calling the **Gaelic Athletic Association**, *Tel. (021) 385876.* Ticket prices, like those for Gaelic Football, range from free to £15 depending on the type of game being played (local or regional).

Sailing and Windsurfing

- **Rathcoursey Water Sports Center**, *Earl Ferry, County Cork. Tel. (021) 631634*

Scuba Diving

- **Baltimore Diving and Watersports Center**, *Baltimore, West Cork. Tel. (028) 20300*
- **Cork Sub-Aqua Club**, *Cork, County Cork. Tel. (021) 271224*
- **Kinsale Dive Center**, *Folk House, Guardwell, County Cork. Tel. (021) 772382*

EXCURSIONS & DAY TRIPS

Cork's position in the center of southern Munster makes it an ideal location from which to see southern Munster through day trips and excursions. Driving trips into the countryside, wending along narrow roads amid the ever-present rock walls of County Cork may well be some of your most pleasant memories. But if you want more than memorable country lanes, County Cork can meet those needs also. As one of the largest counties in Ireland, County Cork is also one of the most interesting and varied, providing some fabulous natural and man-made sights. World-famous **Blarney Castle** is just a hop, skip, and a jump from Cork City, and the grand harbor town of **Cobh** on the southern outskirts of Cork City delights the eye, yet simultaneously tugs at your heart-strings. The southwestern part of the county provides rugged peninsulas as well as fine fishing villages like **Kinsale**. The southeastern corner of Munster also provides a treat – **Waterford City** with its famous **Waterford Crystal Factory**.

You can do these destinations as day trips from Cork, or you can plan more extensive visits if you have the time.

PRACTICAL INFORMATION

American Express
- **Heffernan's Travel**, *Pembroke House, Pembroke Street, Cork. Tel. (021) 271081, Fax (021) 271863*

Laundry Service
- **College Launderette**, *Western Road, Cork. Tel. (021) 511133*
- **Cork Launderette**, *14 MacCurtain Street, Cork. Tel. (021) 501421*

Post Office
Cork City Post Office, *Oliver Plunkett Street. Tel. (021) 272000*

Tourist Office
- **Cork City Tourism Information Office**, *Aras Failte, Grand Parade. Tel. (021) 273251, Fax (021) 273504*

BLARNEY

Go ahead, admit it – your trip to Ireland simply won't be complete until you've kissed the **Blarney Stone**! It's okay – you're in good company, since I felt the same way, and judging from the number of visitors annually to the Blarney Stone, I'm sure millions of others feel that way too. The Blarney Stone is to be found at the village and castle of the same name, and all three are about five miles north of Cork City.

ARRIVALS & DEPARTURES

By Bicycle
If you've biked here, you may as well find a place to lock your bicycle up – the town is not very large.

By Bus
Bus Eirann provides frequent service to Blarney Castle with 16 runs a day (10 on Sundays) between Cork's **Parnell Station**, *Parnell Street, Tel. 021 508188,* and downtown Blarney.

By Car

The town of Blarney, along with its famous stone, is located five miles northwest of Cork City. Take the N22 west out of Cork headed for Killarney. Watch for the signs directing you to Blarney (the R579). Once you arrive, park your car and see the castle and stone and then take an hour or so and stroll through town (it's not very big). There is a car park adjacent to the castle that generally has an adequate number of parking spaces.

ORIENTATION

Blarney is a small town overshadowed by the presence of Blarney Castle and Blarney Stone. There are a number of nice shops, and all are within easy walking distance of the entrance to the castle. You can hit just about the entire town within 200 yards of the castle.

GETTING AROUND TOWN

By Bicycle

Bicycling from Cork City to Blarney has been popular for a number of years, and seems to be growing in popularity. It's a nice ride, although be sure of your bearings and the roads you need to be on, unless you want to see more of the Cork countryside than you intended! The Tourist Office on the Grand Parade will be glad to point you in the right direction.

By Car

The same advice I gave for Cork City applies here – if you've driven your car to Blarney, park it and walk.

By Foot

If you want to see more of Blarney than the Castle and Stone, your only real option is on foot. The town is so small that little else makes sense.

WHERE TO STAY

Blarney is a delightful place to spend a little time. I used to suggest that my readers visit Blarney and stay in Cork. But having stayed both places, I believe I would recommend staying in Blarney and driving to Cork for a visit, then retiring back to the peace and quiet of the countryside! There are many B&Bs in the area, and I have listed several of the best below.

LYNVARA B&B, *Killard, Blarney, County Cork. Tel. (021) 438-5429. 3 rooms, 2 ensuite, one standard. Rates for singles: £24 to £26, rates for doubles: £17.50 per person sharing for a standard room and £19.50 per person sharing for an ensuite room. Rates include breakfast. Mastercard and Visa accepted. No service charge.*

Mrs. Philomena Bugler runs Lynvara, a marvelous B&B on the outskirts of Blarney. Philomena has been opening her home to tourists and travelers for nigh onto 20 years, and her gentle, gracious way will make you feel very comfortable and relaxed.

You'll find a wonderful, quiet and well-kept home with ample-sized bedrooms decorated in cream and green pastels with floral accents. Nice tile bathrooms accent the pleasant rooms.

Philomena is a very good cook, and that will be apparent to you as you take your breakfast in the pleasant dining room that overlooks the Irish countryside and the town of Blarney.

You'll feel most comfortable in this large family home that is about one mile from Blarney Castle. Lynvara is open from April through November.

CLARAGH HOUSE, *Waterloo Road, Blarney, County Cork. Tel. (021) 488-6308; E-mail: claraghbandb@eircom.net. 4 rooms, 3 ensuite. Rates for singles: £26.50, rates for doubles: £17 to £19 per person sharing. Visa accepted. No service charge. Breakfast included in the rate. Open from Easter through the end of September.*

It is truly difficult to say which is the loveliest: the Claragh House or your hostess Cecilia Kiely. When two B&B owners in Galway heard I was headed for Cork, they simultaneously insisted I stop and see Cecilia and her B&B. Ever obedient, I did as I was told, and found that they were quite right. Cecilia was as lively and delightful as they assured me she would be, and her B&B was as splendid as they guaranteed me.

Claragh House B&B is relatively new, and the rooms are simply and tastefully decorated in pastels with complementing floral wallpaper. Depending on how far in advance you call, you can choose between a blue, pink, or green room. In addition to having a TV to meditate in front of after your day of touring, the sitting room has a nice large window that looks out onto the green Irish countryside.

If you visit Blarney Castle (you really should!), this would be a wonderful place to stay. It is about a five- or ten-minute drive from downtown Blarney, and is well signposted from the center of town. Claragh House is open from April through October.

GREENWAYS B&B, *Woodside, Kerry Pike, Blarney. Tel. (021) 438-5383. 4 rooms. Rates for singles: £26, rates for doubles: £19.50 per person sharing. Rates include breakfast. Mastercard and Visa accepted. No service charge.*

This lovely B&B tucked into the countryside near Blarney Castle is an ideal place to spend your evenings if you decide to stay in Blarney. Marie McLoughney is rightfully proud of her B&B, and I believe you'll be most pleased you stopped by.

You'll enjoy a wonderful full Irish breakfast in the dining room overlooking the pastoral Irish countryside in this part of County Cork. The breakfast is great, the view is lovely, and the hostess is gracious – what more could you ask for from an Irish B&B?

The home is spotless and the rooms are large and decorated in light pastels. You'll find nice tile baths, television, hairdryer and tea- and coffee-making facilities in each room.

WATERLOO HOUSE, *Waterloo Road, Blarney. Tel. (021) 438-1153. 4 rooms. Rates for singles: £24 to £25, rates for doubles: £15 to £17 per person sharing. Rates include breakfast. No credit cards accepted. No service charge.*

Here's a nice B&B to stay in if you want to begin or end your day in Blarney seeing the famous castle and stone. Built specifically as a B&B, there's an acre of ground with lovely flower gardens that invite a visit. Waterloo House offers four ensuite bedrooms for guests to choose from. The rooms are average size but nicely furnished. They are tastefully decorated in soft, warm colors. The upstairs rooms have gabled windows that allow you views of the Irish countryside.

Baby-sitting service is available should you need it, and you'll enjoy a 15% discount on the room rate if you've brought your children with you.

WHERE TO EAT

MACKEY'S RESTAURANT, *The Square, Blarney. Tel. (021) 538-5261. £4.95 to £13.95. Open daily from 12:00pm to 2:00pm for lunch, and from 6:30pm to 10:00pm for dinner. Mastercard and Visa accepted. No service charge.*

Mackey's is a nice family restaurant on The Square in Blarney. This smallish restaurant offers a variety of fish and beef dinners as well as a nice selection of soups, salads and sandwiches.

The menu changes frequently, but you might find such delicacies as stuffed pork steak served with the chef's special creamy mushroom sauce, or a poached salmon steak.

LEMON TREE RESTAURANT, *The Square, Blarney. Tel. (021) 538-5542. £8.95 to £14.95. Open from 8:00am to noon, 12:30pm to 3:00pm for lunch, and from 7:00pm to 10:30pm for dinner. All major credit cards accepted. No service charge.*

The Lemon Tree is another restaurant on The Square in Blarney. You'll find a dozen or so tables, hardwood floors and a pleasant, chatty atmosphere. If you've come to dine here, you'll also find a lunch menu that features soups, salads, sandwiches and Irish stew. The dinner menu is a bit more substantial, and you will find such meals as oven-baked chicken breast filled with smoked salmon garnished with deep-fried leeks and accompanied by a white wine, cream and chive sauce. You'll also find lamb, pork, fish and beef items.

SEEING THE SIGHTS

Blarney Castle & Blarney Stone, *Blarney. Open in May on Monday through Saturday from 9:00am to 6:30pm, June through August Monday through Saturday from 9:00am to 7:00pm, September Monday through Saturday from 9:00am to 6:30pm, and October through April Monday through Saturday from 9:00am until sundown. They are also open year round on Sunday from 9:30am to 5:30pm. Admission is £3.50 for adults, £2.50 for students and senior citizens and £2.50 for children (children under 8 are free). There is a family ticket available for £7.50 (two adults and two children). Last admission is 30 minutes prior to closing. Tel. (021) 4385252.* Five miles north of Cork City is the town of Blarney and its famous stone. Before my first visit to Ireland, I had no idea the Blarney *Stone* was part of Blarney *Castle*. The famous stone is located atop the ancient keep underneath its battlements.

To kiss the stone – which legend says grants the kisser the gift of *blarney* (flattery) – you lay on your back and slide down and under the battlements. One or two local men are positioned to give you a hand. (May I suggest that you tip them handsomely? After all – they do keep you from falling on your head!) One hundred and twenty-ish steps up a spiral staircase will precede your kiss of the Blarney Stone. The castle and surrounding grounds are delightful. During the summer months, the climb to the top of Blarney Castle can be exasperating at times, as *ascending* tourists battle with *descending* tourists for right-of-way on the same narrow circular staircases. However, the views from the top of the keep, not to mention the smooch of the stone, are well worth the wait and effort. And if you find yourself having to stand in line before you get into the castle, just relax and enjoy the beautiful demesne (estate) the castle is set in. Verdant lawns, lovely trees, and a serene streamlet all add to the majesty of the moment.

Cormac McCarthy, Lord of Blarney Castle, was a renowned negotiator and flatterer. On one occasion, an exasperated Queen Elizabeth I declared of McCarthy's honeyed words and crafty negotiations: "This is nothing but Blarney – what he says, he never means!"

Almost lost in the excitement of kissing the Blarney Stone is Blarney Castle itself. A massive square keep, it stands now as a mere shell of the impressive structure it must have been in its younger days. Its history, like so many other castles in Ireland, is pock-marked with sieges, attacks, and burnings. Cromwell visited here, as did William of Orange after the Battle of the Boyne. (Hint: they didn't come for afternoon tea!)

There is a large home and breathtaking gardens adjacent to Blarney Castle that you can tour for an additional £2.50. These, however, are only open from mid-June through September.

Blarney is small, with a normal population about 2,000, but its ranks swell during the summer months as visitors from all over the world descend upon it. Depending on the time of year you are there, you'll encounter from one to scores of tour buses, each one disgorging tourists of all shapes and sizes who have come to one of the most popular (and obligatory!) sights in Ireland.

PRACTICAL INFORMATION

Tourist Office

· **Blarney Tourist Information Center**, *Town Square. Tel. (021) 381624*

CORK CITY OUTSKIRTS

There are a few sights that are not within the central downtown area of Cork but that you might wish to take a few minutes to see. One of them, the **Fota Demesne and Wildlife Park**, is among the top tourist attractions in Ireland.

I would also heartily recommend a stop in the nearby village of **Cobh**. It may be one of the most poignant experiences you have in Ireland, especially if you had ancestors that left the Emerald Isle during the Potato Famine.

All of the sights listed in this section require a rental car, as it would be cost-prohibitive to take a taxi to them.

WHERE TO STAY

Generally speaking, if you visit these sights while you are in Cork City, I'd suggest you just stay in Cork. However, I stayed at a B&B in Cobh that I found to be quite pleasant, and I recommend it as a nice place to base your exploration of Cobh.

HIGHLAND B&B, *Ballywilliam, Cobh. Tel. (021) 813873, Fax (021) 481-3873. 4 rooms, 2 ensuite. Rates for singles: £25, rates for doubles: £16 to £18 per person sharing. No credit cards accepted. No service charge.*

High above historic Cobh Harbor sits the modern and new Highland B&B. Run by Mrs. Martha Hurley and her husband Pat, this squeaky clean, freshly painted B&B is an exceptionally pleasant place to retire after touring Cork City or Cobh. It is about 30 minutes from Cork City and out of the hustle and bustle of the city.

The rooms are painted in light pastels and three of the rooms offer views of Cobh Harbor. The B&B is at the top of a very tall hill in Cobh. Consequently, rooms at the front of the house have nice views of the harbor below.

Both Pat and Martha are quite familiar with Cork, Cobh, and the surrounding areas, and they are more than willing to help you plan your visits around and about the area. The Highland B&B makes an excellent place to stay while you explore Cobh's offerings, including the Queenstown Project as well as the Fota Wildlife Park.

SEEING THE SIGHTS

Blackrock Castle, *Blackrock, near Cork City*. At the edge of town in the small village of Blackrock stands Blackrock Castle. Sitting on a small jetty that juts into the River Lee just as it widens into Lough Mahon, this 16th-century castle was spruced up in the 19th century and now serves the area as a pub and restaurant.

Fota Demesne and Wildlife Park, *near Cork City. Open from April through the end of September daily from 10:00am to 6:00pm, and Saturday and Sunday from 11:00am to 6:00pm, and weekends in October from 11:00am to 6:00pm. Admission is £4.40 for adults, £3.50 for students, and £2.30 for senior citizens and children. A family ticket is available for £16.50. The car park costs £1, but includes entrance to the arboretum and gardens. Tel. (021) 812678.* Kind of a mini-San Diego Zoo, the Fota Wildlife Park is a 70-acre open-air zoo, where many of the tamer animals roam free. You can see emus and ostriches, zebras, giraffes, monkeys, flamingos and kangaroos. The more dangerous animals, such as the cheetahs, do not have free run of the zoo, for obvious reasons.

In addition to the wildlife park, there is a lovely arboretum, which boasts a wide variety of trees, including a significant number that have been imported from all over the world. There is also a fine collection of Irish landscape paintings.

Cobh Town. Cobh (pronounced "Cove") is unalterably associated with three grand marine catastrophes in Irish history. This small town (current population around 6,200), lived in the memories of a generation of Irish immigrants, for it was from tiny Cobh that hundreds of thousands of starving Irish left farms, families, and certain death during the Great Potato Famine that lasted from 1845 through 1847. Most of them were headed for America and a fresh start. Their last views of Ireland may well have been the majestic steeples of the neo-Gothic St. Colman's Cathedral sitting regally on the hill above Cobh.

A scant 60 years later another maritime tragedy involved Cobh as the *Lusitania* was sunk in 1915 (ostensibly) by German U-boats not far from Cobh's harbor. Every available boat, dory, dingy, curragh and skiff was pressed into service in an effort to rescue survivors of the attack. Hundreds of the victims of the disaster are buried in the Old Church Cemetery in Cobh, and a memorial to them stands on the quay. (Cynics assert that the British government purposely left the Lusitania unguarded, hoping the Germans would sink it and that ensuing American indignation would bring the US into World War I on the side of the Allies.

Worse yet, some even believe the *English* actually torpedoed the *Lusitania*, knowing the Germans would get the blame. Whatever the truth, the *Lusitania* was torpedoed and sunk, hundreds of people died, and US sentiment caused America to enter the war.)

And finally, one last disaster of titanic proportions had roots in Ireland as well as Cobh. The oceanliner *Titanic* was built in the shipyards of Belfast, and Cobh was its last port-of-call before sailing to its watery fate. So if you're the least bit superstitious, you may not want to take the ferry to or from Cobh!

Rochestown Point, *near Cobh*. Five miles away from Cobh, looking out to the Celtic Sea, is Rochestown Point, where a picturesque white-washed lighthouse sits picturesquely along this southwest Ireland coast.

The Queenstown Project, *Cobh railway station. Open daily from 10:00am to 6:00pm. Admission is £3.50 for adults, £2.50 for senior citizens and children. Tel. (021) 481-3591.* This new heritage center in an old building (the old railway station) contains a maritime museum that primarily chronicles the experience Irish immigrants had as they bid the Emerald Isle farewell over the past several hundred years. Two well-done exhibits focus on the sea disasters associated with the *Lusitania* and the *Titanic*, both of which touched the town and lives of the residents of Cobh. The name Queenstown was the name Cobh carried from 1849 until 1922, in commemoration of a visit by **Queen Victoria** in 1849. The name Cobh was reclaimed after independence, and it means "The Haven" in Irish.

Mitchellstown Caves, *near Clogheen. Open daily from 10:00am to 6:00pm. Admission is £3 for adults and £1p for children. Tel. (052) 67246.* If you're into stalactites and stalagmites, Mitchellstown Cave is worth a stop. Head north out of Cork City on the N8. At Mitchellstown, take the R665 east toward Ballyporeen, and watch for the signposts directing you to Mitchellstown Caves. The half-mile tour has some intriguing shapes and sights. For centuries, the caves were used as a hideout for those not wishing to be found by the authorities, including the Earl of Desmond in the 1500s. In Ireland, mystery, awe, and fear have always accompanied caves. In the ancient Druidic religion, caves were considered to be the entrance to the underworld.

SPORTS & RECREATION
Golf
• **Fota Island Golf Club**, *Fota Island, Carrigtwohill, County Cork. Tel. (021) 883700.* Par 72.

Sailing & Windsurfing
• **International Sailing Center,** *East Beach Street, Cobh, County Cork. Tel. (021) 811237*

Scuba Diving
• **Cork Sub-Aqua Club**, *Cork, County Cork. Tel. (021) 271224*

KINSALE

Kinsale is a delightful fishing village about a 30-minute drive from Cork. The Irish name for Kinsale is *Ceann Saile*, which means "Tide Head," and alerts you (if you speak Irish, that is!) that Kinsale is a seaport town. The town is a tidy affair of narrow winding streets, brightly painted Georgian homes, quays, sea breezes, and intriguing ruins. For hundreds of years Kinsale was an important seaport, until the size and draft of ships overcame the ability to use the harbor in the 18th century. At that point, Kinsale was relegated to serving the fishing industry.

One Kinsalean who made good was **William Penn**, founder of the state of Pennsylvania. William's father served as the governor of Kinsale, and William was a clerk of the Admiralty Court prior to seeking his fortune in the New World.

Today, Kinsale has rebounded from the loss of major sea contracts by offering tourists a clean, picturesque harbor town noted for deep-sea fishing trips and fine seafood restaurants. If you're up to an hour-long stroll around town, the Kinsale office of *Bord Failte* offers a booklet for £1 that will direct you to some of the more interesting nooks and crannies in town. Even without the book, there always seems to be lots of things going on in Kinsale for you to busy yourself with.

ARRIVALS & DEPARTURES
By Bus
Bus service runs from Cork to Kinsale daily. Buses depart Cork's **Parnell Station**, *Parnell Street, Tel. 021 508188*, and stops at the Esso Station in Kinsale. The fare is £3.60.

By Car
Take the N27 south out of Cork. Watch for signs directing you to the R600 and Kinsale. The half-hour drive through the County Cork country-side is a pleasant one, so just relax as you wend your way to Kinsale.

ORIENTATION
Kinsale is a wonderful town to explore. The town is centered around a semi-circular harbor, which has served as Kinsale's lifeline to the world all its days. Narrow and winding streets will take you to the harbor or up the hills to get wonderful views of the town and sea.

GETTING AROUND TOWN

By Bicycle

If all you're going to do is stay in the central part of town, you probably won't want a bicycle. The streets are narrow and often choked with cars and tourists. But if you're going to venture into the countryside, or above the town to view the harbor, you will be well advised to rent a bicycle. You can get one at **Deco Cycles**, *18 Main Street, Kinsale, Tel. (021) 774884.*

By Car

Park it!

By Foot

Kinsale was made for walking. Shops and restaurants, harbor views and old forts all offer lots to see while you are in town. So park that car, or lock your bike, and head out to experience Kinsale.

WHERE TO STAY

Kinsale is close enough to Cork that you could stay in Cork and just visit Kinsale for the day. However, there are a few places to stay in Kinsale that are so exceptional that you may wish to stay in one of them. I heartily recommend staying at any of these places (but especially The Old Bank House!).

THE WHITE HOUSE, *Pearse Street and The Glens, Kinsale. Tel. (021) 772125, Fax (021) 772045. 12 rooms. Rates for singles: £45 to £55 , doubles: £45 to £55 per person sharing. Two restaurants. All major credit cards accepted. No service charge.*

If you want to stay in the heart of downtown Kinsale, The White House guesthouse is a great choice. You might say this place is at "action central" in Kinsale, standing as it does at the head of two of the busiest streets in Kinsale. The rooms are nice and large – you'll not be feeling claustrophobic here. Each room is decorated in soft colors – pastels with floral accents. Each room is amply supplied with coffee and tea making equipment, a hairdryer, and trouser press.

Its close proximity to the action might give you some concern about the noise levels at night, but you'll have no worries here – the owners have installed double-glazed windows to hold down the traffic noise.

There are two restaurants on the first floor, so you'll not need to go far for your meals. And even if you don't wish to dine in, there are any number of restaurants within just a few steps of the front door.

THE MOORINGS, *Scilly, Kinsale. Tel. (021) 772376, Fax (021) 77267[5] E-mail: moorings.kinsale@indigo.ie; Website: indigo.ie/~moorings5. 8 rooms. Rates for singles: £55, doubles: £50 to £75 per person sharing. Restaurant, tennis, croquet. Mastercard and Visa accepted.*

The Moorings guesthouse is among the best of the best in this part of Ireland. This marvelous guesthouse is located in downtown Kinsale and overlooks the marina in Kinsale Harbor.

The bedrooms are all ensuite and are spacious and well appointed. Soft colors and modern new furnishings bordering on luxurious make the rooms nice places to spend the night. Most of the rooms have balconies that overlook the harbor. Talk about relaxation! All the rooms have television, telephones, and tea- and coffee-making facilities. The bathrooms are all modern and large, and feature special "power showers" that provide an invigorating shower. (I hope these power showers catch on throughout the Irish B&B industry!)

There is a large lounge for guests that features soft, pleasant colors, comfortable furniture, a piano (if you've brought your children and they need to practice during your vacation!), and lovely views of Kinsale Harbor.

If you are staying in Kinsale, this guesthouse and the next one get my vote as the nicest places to stay in Kinsale. But call ahead. With only eight rooms and gorgeous views, it fills up quickly from late May through August. You'll pay a slight premium (£5 per person) for the rooms that face the sea, but I think the little extra is well worth it. Parking in Kinsale can sometimes be very tough and expensive, especially in the summer months. That makes the private carpark for The Moorings all that much more attractive.

THE OLD BANK HOUSE, *11 Pearse Street, Kinsale, Tel. (021) 774075, Fax (021) 774296; E-mail: oldbank@indigo.ie. 18 rooms. Rates for singles: £80 to £130, doubles: £60 to £90 per person sharing. American Express, Mastercard, Visa. 10% service charge.*

The Old Bank House takes its name from its previous use: it was formerly a branch office for the Munster and Leinster Bank. Much of the quiet dignity old banks have is retained in the guesthouse that now features a plethora of antiques and quality furnishings. The feeling you get is one of refined, old-world elegance.

Since this is an old Georgian home, the rooms are large and spacious. But you may not realize that they, too, are liberally endowed with antiques that provide just the right feel to the rooms. Each room is ensuite, and the bathrooms are modern and well appointed.

To provide a pleasant and enjoyable stay for all, the owners request that their guests not smoke in the public areas of the guesthouse. Children above the age of seven years old are welcome.

THE BLUE HAVEN HOTEL, *3 Pearse Street, Kinsale, Tel. (021) 772209, Fax (021) 774268. 18 rooms. Rates for singles: £75 to £95, doubles: £50 to £90 per person sharing. Restaurant. All major credit cards accepted. 10% service charge.*

The Blue Haven Hotel in downtown Kinsale was recently named Ireland's small hotel of the year by a hotel industry organization. Part of the reason is doubtless the building itself; equally important, however, is the warm country welcome that is part and parcel of the package. Recently refurbished and expanded, the Blue Haven is a slice of peace and tranquillity. From the moment you enter the simple but nice reception area, to the open fire in the pub to the cane-furnished conservatory, you'll find a relaxed and cordial air here.

The rooms are unfortunately on the small size, but simply and comfortably furnished. The recent refurbishment work has gone a long way to making the rooms more comfortable, especially the rooms at the front of the hotel overlooking the street. The Blue Haven is centrally located, but in the past that centrality meant bothersome street noise in the rooms. The rooms have been recently renovated and include double-glazed windows, which cut down on the street noise immensely.

If you'd like to stay the Blue Haven during the summer months, be sure and call ahead for reservations as soon as you know your schedule. The hotel is extremely popular, and tends to fill up quickly.

WHERE TO EAT

There are dozens of little sandwich shops and pubs in Kinsale where you can grab some nourishment without unduly interrupting your exploration of this delightful town. Here are also a few nice restaurants you might want to check out:

RESTAURANT D'ANTIBES, *Pearse Street and the Glens, The White House, Kinsale. Tel. (021) 772125. £11.95 to £21.95. Open for dinner from 6:00pm to 10:00pm daily. All major credit cards accepted. 10% service charge.*

You'll like this restaurant at the intersection of two of the main streets in Kinsale. The last time I was there I had the opportunity to break bread with the owner of Restaurant d'Antibes, Mrs. Rose Frawley. During our conversation, she said, "Our aim is to make each meal that we serve a truly memorable one, and to ensure that all tastes are catered for to the best of our ability."

Judging from the menu (which changes every few months), the Frawley's give more than lip service to ensuring that all tastes are catered for. The menu ranges from your typical seafood (Kinsale *is* a fishing village, after all) and good Irish beef to a surprisingly complete vegetarian selection. While Mrs. Frawley recommended the chef's specialty (Symphony of Seafood), I was also impressed with the Tournedo Casablanca (a generous slice of fillet steak with roast shallots and garlic).

When you enter Restaurant d'Antibes, you'll be greeted by crisp, starched Irish linen and silver settings enhanced by candlelight at each table. Dress is casual, as is the conversation and atmosphere that abounds during dinner.

JIM EDWARDS PUB AND RESTAURANT, *Market Quay, Kinsale. Tel. (021) 772541. £15 to £24.95. Open for dinner from 6:30pm to 9:30pm. All major credit cards accepted. 10% service charge.*

Jim Edwards Pub and Restaurant has successfully bridged the gap between the two enterprises of pub and restaurant. They are noted for excellent seafood as well as fine steaks. The decor is simple, although I found it a little dark, with dark wood tables and greens and reds being the predominant colors. Try the fillet of Irish beef, or any of the local seafood specialties.

BLUE HAVEN HOTEL RESTAURANT, *3 Pearse Street, Kinsale. Tel. (021) 772209. £12.95 to £21.95. Open from 12:30pm to 3:00pm for lunch, and from 7:00pm to 10:30pm for dinner. All major credit cards accepted. 10% service charge.*

The restaurant at the Blue Haven Hotel has earned quite the reputation as an excellent seafood restaurant, which speaks volumes when that restaurant is located in a port town. The atmosphere is elegant – crisply starched Irish linen, china, crystal, and appropriate lighting enhance the flavor and presentation of the meals. The pianist helps continue the tranquil feeling you encounter throughout the hotel. That feeling isn't diminished as you look out the conservatory windows to the flood-lit gardens and fountain.

One of the excellent specialties of the house is Blue Haven thermidor, fish, and miscellaneous seafood cooked in cheese sauce. Other offerings include sole with lemon and parsley butter, or more traditional offerings such as oysters, poached salmon, or sea trout. Even though the specialty is seafood, the chefs do a fine job on other dishes as well, including lamb and beef. Finish off your meal with a selection of fine Irish farmhouse cheeses. Dress is nice casual, although most of the diners will be in suit and tie or dresses.

SEEING THE SIGHTS

Just strolling around this lovely town and drinking in its warmth (maybe by drinking a Guinness, too) may provide some of the most enjoyable experiences you'll have in Kinsale! Stroll down any street and slip into any shop or pub, and you're sure to have a memorable time. However, there are a few specific sights worth hunting up in Kinsale:

Kinsale Museum, *The Old Courthouse, Market Place, Kinsale. Open Monday through Saturday from 11:00am to 5:00pm, and Sunday from 3:00pm to 5:00pm. Admission is £1. Tel. (021) 772144.* The smallish Kinsale Museum has a number of interesting exhibits highlighting the history of Kinsale. Learn of the time the Irish and Spanish joined forces to fight the English who were garrisoned at Kinsale (the English won). There is also an interesting display about the Lusitania, which was sunk nearby.

Desmond Castle, *Cork Street, Kinsale. Tel. (021) 774855. Open mid-April to mid-June Tuesday through Sunday from 10:00am to 6:00pm and mid-June to early October daily from 10:00am to 6:00pm. The last admission is 45 minutes before closing. Admission is £2.00 for adults, £1.50 for seniors and students, £1.00 for children and a family ticket is available for £5.00.* The three-story square keep on Cork Street is Desmond Castle, or as it's also known, the French Prison. Built in 1500 to serve as the residence of the Earl of Desmond, Desmond Castle has served a variety of uses over the centuries.

When the Spanish descended upon Kinsale in 1601, the castle was found to be an excellent location to house soldiers; it was used as a place to hold American prisoners of war during the American Revolution; and it was used as a prison for French seamen during 1754 when it caught fire, killing fifty-four prisoners. During the Great Potato Famine, it was used as a workhouse (like a soup kitchen) to provide relief for the starving population of Kinsale.

Today, you can see a number of exhibits dealing with Kinsale's history and the uses Desmond House saw during its first three centuries.

Charles Fort, *near Summer Cove. Open mid-March through October daily from 10:00am to 6:00pm, and November through mid-March Saturday and Sunday from 10:00am to 5:00pm. Admission is £2.50 for adults, £1.75 for seniors and students, £1.00 for children, and a family ticket is available for £6.00. Tel. (021) 772684.* From Kinsale, get back on the Kinsale-Cork road and watch for the signposts directing you to Charles Fort. This hilltop fort is nearly 400 years old, and covers approximately 12 acres. Guided tours are offered during the summer months.

Old Head, *near Kinsale.* An ancient castle once belonging to the de Courcy family sits atop Old Head outside of Kinsale. The views from here are splendid, and the site is quietly romantic. Farther out on the end of Old Head is a lighthouse.

SPORTS & RECREATION

Angling

If you want to try your hand at deep-sea fishing, try **Kinsale Sea Angling Facilities Center**, *Trident Hotel, Pier Head, County Cork, Tel. (021) 772301.*

Horseback Riding

• **Ballmee Equestrian Center**, *Doneraile, County Cork. Tel. (022) 24135*
• **Knocknamanna Stables**, *Minane Bridge, County Cork. Tel. (021) 887111*
• **Skevanish Riding Center**, *Innishannon, County Cork. Tel. (021) 775476*

Sailing & Windsurfing
- **Kinsale Outdoor Education Center,** *Kinsale, County Cork. Tel. (021) 772896*
- **Oysterhaven Holiday and Activity Center,** *Oysterhaven, County Cork. Tel. (021) 770738*

Scuba Diving
- **Baltimore Diving and Watersports Center,** *Baltimore, West Cork. Tel. (028) 20300*
- **Kinsale Dive Center,** *Folk House, Guardwell, County Cork. Tel. (021) 772382*
- **Cork County Surf Beaches,** *Garrettstown, Courtmacsherry, Barley Cove*

PRACTICAL INFORMATION

Tourist Office
- **Kinsale Tourism Information Office,** *Pier Road, Kinsale. Tel. (021) 772234, Fax (021) 774438. (Open March through November.)*

WATERFORD CITY

Owing to the famous crystal factory of the same name located in this city, you have probably already heard of **Waterford**. Sprawling along the southern bank of the River Suir, Waterford has been and continues to be an important Irish seaport. Reaching the Celtic Sea via Waterford Harbor, it maintains an active trade association with major European ports. The River Suir at this point is quite deep, as it must be to allow modern ships to come to port here.

The Irish name for Waterford is *Port Lairge*, which means "Lairge's Port." You might ask how they got the name Waterford from this? The easy answer is, "They didn't." Waterford is the anglicized version of the *Viking* word *Vadrefjord*, which means "Ford of the Fathers." The town grew from a small gathering of farmers and fishermen in the 9th century into an important port town after the Vikings ran off the native settlers and established yet another stronghold here. They held this advantage for several centuries until Strongbow took the city from them. It quickly became an important city, at times rivaling Dublin in social as well as economic importance.

Shortly after ousting the Danes, Strongbow married the daughter of the Irish chieftain he had come to Ireland to support – Dermot MacMurrough. The wedding was performed in Waterford. Perhaps because of that early union, Waterford generally sided with the British crown over the next five centuries, much to the distaste and displeasure of her neighbors.

But in the mid-17th century when the chips were really down, Catholicism proved to be stronger than political bonds, and Waterford refused to acknowledge the King's supremacy over the Pope in matters of religion. They hoped to walk the tenuous line of supporting the Roman church as well as the London government. But the king didn't appreciate that, and Oliver Cromwell was dispatched to help them understand where their loyalties – their whole loyalties – needed to be placed. Initial efforts at taking the city failed, but in 1650 Cromwell's troops were successful.

Today, with a population in excess of 40,000, Waterford is one of Ireland's largest cities.

ARRIVALS & DEPARTURES

By Air

The **Waterford Airport**, *Tel. (051) 875589*, is about six miles outside of Waterford in Killowen. Flights from England and Glasgow via Dublin land in Waterford. You can rent cars at the airport only if you have pre-booked them (see below for agencies and phone numbers). Otherwise, there are no rental cars available at the airport. There is also no bus service into town, although you can catch a taxi outside the main doors. The short taxi ride into town will cost about £8.

By Bus

The bus depot for Waterford is **Plunkett Station**, *Plunkett Street, Tel. (051) 873401*. The bus ride from Cork takes two hours, and if you're coming from Dublin it will take you about three hours. The cost for the bus trip is £8. The station sits across the River Suir from town, and is just a couple hundred yards' walk into the city's center.

By Car

Waterford is about 80 miles from Cork on the N25. If you're coming from elsewhere in Ireland, look for these roads: the N25 from Wexford, the N9 from Kilkenny, and the N24 from Limerick. All of these are the "express routes" into Waterford. More leisurely routes are available by either following your nose, or by following a good map of the area.

Sample trip lengths on the main roads:
• Dublin: 2 hours
• Galway: 3 hours
• Killarney: 3 hours
• Limerick: 2 hours

By Train

The main train depot in Waterford is **Plunkett Station**, *Plunkett Street, Tel. (051) 873401*. The train ride from Cork City takes about two hours, and if you're coming from Dublin, the train ride is three hours. Located across Bridge Street from downtown, the depot is in a decent section of town and the walk into town is only a couple hundred yards.

ORIENTATION

Waterford City lies primarily along the southern banks of the River Suir as it empties into Waterford Harbor and from thence into the Celtic Sea. It is a combination of wide streets and narrow winding lanes. The main sights to see in town are all clustered about two blocks west of Reginald's Tower.

GETTING AROUND TOWN

By Bicycle

The main sights to see in Waterford City are all within about a two-block area. But if you want to venture a little further afield, a bike rental isn't a bad idea. The Waterford Crystal Factory is about a mile and a half outside of town, a relatively easy bike ride. You can rent bicycles in Waterford City at the following shops:

- **Murphy's Toys and Cycles**, *68 Main Street, Waterford, County Waterford. Tel. (058) 841376*
- **Wright's Cycle Depot**, *Henrietta Street, Waterford, County Waterford. Tel. (058) 874411*

By Bus

City buses run twice hourly out to the Waterford Crystal Factory. You can catch them across the river at Plunkett Station.

By Car

The best way to see Waterford is to have a car. Unless you have rented a bicycle, you'll need a car if you want to see The Waterford Crystal Factory, as it is at the edge of town, and too far to walk to from downtown. Park your car in the downtown area and walk around those sights near the quay and Reginald's Tower. Then hop in your car and head south on the N25 toward Cork to see the crystal factory.

You can rent cars from the following companies:

- **Budget**, *41 The Quay, Tel. (051) 821550*
- **EuropCar**, *Sheridan Garage, Cork Road, Tel. (051) 873144*
- **Hertz**, *Auto Boland, Newrath, Tel. (051) 878737*

By Foot

You can see the few sights downtown Waterford has to offer by walking relatively short distances. But if you want to see Waterford Crystal Factory (the main reason to come down here), then you'll probably need a car or bicycle to get there, as it is about a mile and a half out of town on the N25.

WHERE TO STAY

BLENHEIM HOUSE, *Blenheim Heights, Waterford. Tel. (051) 874115; E-mail: blenheim@tinet.ie. 6 rooms. Rates for singles: £20 to £24, doubles: £20 per person sharing. Rates include breakfast. Credit cards not accepted. No service charge.*

Just outside town, you'll find a beautifully restored Georgian residence that is older than the United States. Built in 1763, it has been furnished throughout with lovely antiques. The rooms are comfortable, tastefully decorated, and well-furnished. Blenheim House is set at the end of a country lane on its own park-like setting with plenty of grass, gardens, and large trees. Across from the house is a fenced area where you are liable to see a herd of deer peacefully feeding.

If you are in Ireland to golf, you may want to stay here while you sample the course at Waterford Castle. World-renowned, the island golf course is about one mile from Blenheim House.

Mrs. Claire Fitzmaurice is your hostess, and she is quite knowledgeable on all there is to see and do in and around Waterford. She will be delighted to help you plan for your day's activities.

KNOCKBOY HOUSE, *Dunmore Road, Waterford. Tel. (051) 873484. 6 rooms. Rates for singles: £24, doubles: £20 per person sharing. Rates include breakfast. Credit cards not accepted. No service charge.*

This is a lovely Georgian residence overlooking the River Suir. There are three ensuite rooms, and three standard rooms. The home is a newer one, and the rooms are all fresh, lively and comfortable. Knockboy House is just 10 minutes or so from the airport, and even closer to downtown Waterford, so it makes an ideal place to hang your hat while touring Waterford and the southern coastal region. Mrs. Jacinta Jackman-Kavanagh is your hostess, and she'll make you feel welcome indeed.

THE PINES, *Knockboy, Dunmore Road, Waterford. Tel. (051) 874452, Fax (051) 841566; E-mail: bjackman@eircom.net; Website: homepage.tinet.ie/ ˜pines. 5 rooms. Rates for singles: £24, doubles: £19 per person sharing. Rates include breakfast. Credit cards not accepted. No service charge.*

The Pines may be one of the best-kept secrets in Munster. This older B&B is set in a veritable garden plot, and it's hard to imagine a more pleasant surrounding for a B&B. This ivy-covered cottage in a rural setting offers you peace and serenity around every corner.

Breakfast itself will be a memorable experience as you sit in the sunlit conservatory looking out on to lovely grounds. After breakfast, or before retiring for the evening, you can find a little additional peace and quiet by strolling in the pleasant garden. When it's time to rest up for another day's sightseeing, you'll find four ensuite rooms or one standard room available to you. Each is simply but comfortably furnished and decorated with a freshness that makes them feel like it's springtime all year long.

FOXMOUNT FARM, *Passage East Road, Waterford. Tel. (051) 874308, Fax (051) 854906; E-mail: foxmount@iol.ie. 6 rooms. Rates for singles: £25, doubles: £25 to £30 per person sharing. Rates include breakfast. Dinner is available for £17.50. Tennis court and Ping-Pong table. Credit cards not accepted. No service charge.*

Foxmount Farm is a farm first, and a B&B second. Not that you'd notice from the reception your hostess, Mrs. Margaret Kent, will give you. While the farm is a going concern that demands the attention of the Kent family, the B&B prospers quite well under Mrs. Kent's watchful eye.

The stately 18th-century home is a delightful place to stay. Ivy-covered and set amid 230 verdant acres, the house sits atop a small swell, assuring its guests marvelous views of lawns, gardens, and meadows. Children will particularly like the attention they can give to several farm animals on-site. The house features numerous antiques and comfortable public rooms, including a drawing room that offers a snug and warm atmosphere. The drawing room is especially nice, bordering on elegant.

As with most of these old Georgian mansions, the rooms are large and high-ceilinged, giving them a feel of even greater spaciousness. The rooms are comfortably if not luxuriously furnished, but each has large windows that offer stunning views of the Irish countryside. Four of the bedrooms are ensuite, and two are standard (they share a common bathroom).

Mrs. Kent has gained international renown for the cuisine she prepares her guests. She was recently the recipient of the *Galtee Best Irish Breakfast* award, a feather in the cap of any B&B or guesthouse owner. The fresh herbs and vegetables from her own garden and the freshest possible meat dishes are the key to her success. (That and a real talent for cooking!) David and Margaret Kent strive hard to provide an atmosphere where their guests feel more like family members rather than mere guests.

BROWN'S TOWNHOUSE, *29 South Parade, Waterford. Tel. (051) 870594, Fax (051) 871953; E-mail: info@brownstownhouse; Website: www.brownstownhouse.com. 6 rooms. Rates for singles: £35 to £45, doubles: £25 to £38 per person sharing, family room: £75 to £85 for family of four. Rates include breakfast. Mastercard and Visa accepted. No service charge.*

Les and Barbara Brown are rightfully proud of their wonderful Victorian Townhouse, and once you visit and stay, you will see why. Located just a short walk from downtown Waterford in a pleasant residential area, this Victorian beauty was lovingly and extensively refurbished in 1996. The results are wonderful, and your stay here will be most enjoyable.

These Victorian townhouses make ideal bed and breakfasts because of the size of their rooms, and each of the Brown's bedrooms is large and spacious. Each is tastefully decorated and furnished with comfortable furnishings. All the bedrooms have cable television, telephone, and tea- and coffee-making facilities. If you are traveling with your children, a family room is available that offers a double, two twin beds and a pull-out bed.

While in Waterford, be sure and plan to stay with the Browns. And while here, take the time to get to know the other owner of Brown's Townhouse, Charlie (the Brown's blonde Labrador retriever).

GRANVILLE HOTEL, *1 Meagher Quay, Waterford. Tel. (051) 305555, Fax (051) 305566; E-mail: info@granville-hotel.ie; Website: www.granville-hotel.ie. 74 rooms. Rates for singles: £70 to £75, doubles: £55 to £70 per person sharing, suite: £80 to £90 per person sharing; children under age 12 stay in parents' room free. Rates include breakfast. All major credit cards accepted. No service charge.*

The Granville Hotel is in the center of Waterford on the quay. An old Georgian Hotel from days gone by, it has been lovingly refurbished and meticulously maintained by owners Liam and Ann Cusack and their crack staff. There is a wide variety of rooms available, but some are a little on the small side. The rooms at the front of the hotel offer views of the river, although they suffer a bit from street noise. Children under 12 years of age stay free in their parents' room.

AHERNE'S SEAFOOD RESTAURANT AND ACCOMMODATION, *163 North Main Street, Youghal. Tel. (024) 92424, Fax (024) 93633. 10 rooms. Rates for singles: £80, doubles: £50 to £60 per person sharing. All major credit cards accepted.*

It's difficult to say which aspect of Aherne's is most popular: its award-winning restaurant or its award-winning accommodations. For a review of the restaurant, see *Where to Eat* below. Aherne's has almost a cult following among tourists and the Irish alike. Much of their business is repeat, and new groupies join the ranks every season, having been directed there by the effusive comments of friends and strangers.

The Fitzgibbon family is probably responsible for this following – Kate carries on the tradition of three generations of Fitzgibbon hospitality. And the B&B is small enough – just 10 rooms – to allow the Fitzgibbons to provide attention on an individual level. Open turf fires welcome those who come to Aherne's. The seafood in the restaurant is exquisite, and the rooms are spacious and sumptuous. None of the rooms have memorable views, but the rooms and service are marvelous enough to compensate. This is perhaps the best lodging for the price in County Cork.

WATERFORD CASTLE, *The Island, Ballinakill, Waterford. Tel. (051) 878203, Fax (051) 879316; E-mail: info@waterfordcastle.com; Website: www.waterfordcastle.com. 19 rooms. Rates for singles: £110 to £215, doubles: £155 to £235 per room, suites: £280 to £375. Gardens, indoor swimming pool, tennis, bicycles, golf. All major credit cards accepted. No service charge.*

Just outside Waterford heading towards Dunmore you'll come across Waterford Castle, an 18th-century castle converted to a five-star luxury hotel. Proudly sitting on its own 310-acre island, Waterford Castle is set amid woods and an 18-hole golf course. The hotel is approached via car ferry that takes you across the water to the hotel. Upon landing, you'll get a close-up look at the impressive carved arch and heavy oak doors that serve as the entrance to the hotel.

Inside, the great hall boasts a huge fireplace, the Fitzgerald coat-of-arms woven into the carpet, and dark paneled walls. There's a liberal sprinkling of antiques throughout the hotel, in the public areas as well as in the rooms, which are lavish and spacious, nicely decorated, and comfortably furnished. Virtually all the rooms have attractive views of the water and grounds surrounding the hotel.

WHERE TO EAT

GATCHELL'S CAFETERIA, *Cork Road, Waterford. Tel. (051) 73311. £1.95 to £4.95. Open daily from 8:30am to 5:00pm. Mastercard and Visa accepted. No service charge.*

Gatchell's is the small cafeteria located on-site at the Waterford Crystal Factory. You'll find an assortment of fruit, sandwiches, coffee, soda, etc., here. Large windows, ample lighting and astounded tourists add to the convivial atmosphere.

THE ESTUARY RESTAURANT, *Dunmore Road, Waterford. Tel. (051) 873082. £10.95 to £15.95. Open for dinner from 12:30pm to 2:30pm and from 6:30pm to 9:30pm daily. All major credit cards accepted. No service charge.*

Pat and Mary Orpen own this family-style restaurant at the edge of Waterford. This pleasant restaurant features a good variety of beef, chicken and sea food dishes – remember, Waterford is a port town!

Inside, you'll find about 18 pine tables, candles and lots of conversation. The soft yellow walls and are bedecked with the artwork of local artists. When the weather is nice, picnic tables on the back lawn are available for your dining pleasure.

THE WINE VAULT RESTAURANT, *High Street, Waterford. Tel. (051) 853444. £12.95 to £18.95. Open Monday through Saturday from 12:30pm to 2:00pm and from 5:00pm to midnight. Visa, American Express, Access, and Diner's Club cards accepted.*

Watch for this little restaurant established in an old Elizabethan townhouse. This energetic bistro has earned a reputation for both fine food and outstanding wine. The restaurant is on the first floor, and the wine vaults from which the restaurant takes its name is located in the basement (an apt location for a wine vault!).

Your dining experience here will be light and pleasant, as the atmosphere is upbeat and busy most of the time. The food isn't bad either – there are a variety of chicken and Irish beef and lamb offerings that are all prepared exceptionally well. They also offer a number of vegetarian dishes that even sound appetizing to non-vegetarians! Finish off your meal with any of a number of fine desserts, or simply choose one of the fresh farmhouse cheeses they offer. Either way, you'll be delighted with your choice.

While you wait for your dinner to be served, you may wish to amble down to the wine vaults to check them out. While there, you may wish to participate in a little wine tasting before you select the fruit of the vine that most interests you.

Dress is nice casual.

DWYER'S RESTAURANT, *Mary Street, Waterford. Tel. (051) 877478. £12.95 to £21.95. Open Monday through Saturday from 6:00pm to 10:00pm. Visa, American Express, Access, and Diner's Club cards accepted.*

After you've visited the Waterford Crystal Factory, continue your Waterford experience by stopping by Dwyer's Restaurant. Former members of the Royal Irish Constabulary never dined as well as you will – Dwyer's is housed in an old set of RIC barracks. The barracks never looked so good either – Martin Dwyer has spruced it up with a mixture of light colors and an eclectic assortment of objets d'art, from an array of antiques to lovely paintings by local artists.

The menu is ever-changing and offers a wide variety of local favorites, from seafood to good Irish beef. Whether its prawns in garlic butter or roast loin of bacon with a mustard and honey crust, you'll be pleased with your selection. Top your dinner off with one of Martin Dwyer's special home-made ice creams, and you'll be glad you stopped here.

WATERFORD CASTLE RESTAURANT, *The Island, Waterford. Tel. (051) 878203. £29.95 to £49.95. Open daily from 12:30pm to 2:00pm and 7:00pm to 10:00pm (9:00pm on Sunday). Visa, American Express, Access, and Diner's Club cards accepted.*

Well, if you want to see how the other half dines, Waterford Castle Restaurant would be a great place to venture a peek. But while you're at it, you might as well stay and dine yourself. Located on the exquisite island that is home to Waterford Castle, it's hard to imagine a more idyllic setting for a restaurant. The ambiance of the restaurant is as exquisite as the meal. The walls are bedecked with fine old oil paintings and old oak paneling. The furnishings are exceptional, and the service will make you feel like a regal guest.

But wait, that's not all. The menu is liberally endowed with entrees that will make your mouth water and your palate yearn for a bite of each. The menu varies, but expect to find such favorites as roast duck with a spectacular honey and mustard glaze, or if seafood is your preference, you might try the poached salmon hollandaise. Vegetarian offerings are also a part of the menu.

Dress is suit and tie or dress, especially at dinner. Like many of the fine restaurants in Ireland, if the price tag for dinner is a little steep for your wallet, stop by for lunch. The same setting and many of the same entrees are available for about half the price of the dinner menu.

SEEING THE SIGHTS

Strongbow was one of the first of the invading Anglo-Normans to attempt to use marriage to cement his grip on Ireland. His wedding to the lovely daughter of Dermot MacMurrough took place shortly after Strongbow's intrusion into Ireland. Tradition sets the venue for the wedding in Waterford City at **Reginald's Tower**, *The Quay, Waterford. Open Easter through May daily from 10:00am to 5:00pm, June through September daily from 9:30am to 6:30am and October daily from 10:00am to 5:00pm. Admission is £1.50 for adults, £1.00 for seniors and students, 60p for children and a family ticket is available for £4.00. Tel. (051) 873501.* Reginald's Tower is a squat, solid structure built by the Vikings in 1003. The walls are 10 feet thick, and 80 feet tall. For centuries it served as the home of a number of Anglo-Norman kings, but it now houses Waterford's Civic Museum. The museum, although small, has an eclectic assortment of Viking and Anglo-Norman items from the city's history. It's easy to find, as it is one of the more prominent sights along the waterfront in downtown Waterford.

Waterford Treasures at the Granary, *The Quay, Waterford. Open June through August daily from 9:30am to 9:00pm, and September through May daily from 10:00am to 5:00pm. Admission is £4.00 for adults, £3.00 for senior citizens and students and £2.00 for children, and a family ticket is available for £12.00. Tel. (051) 871227.* The Waterford Treasures at the Granary was formerly called the Waterford Heritage Center, and is one of the finest and most elaborate museums in the country. In fact, it is so fine that it won the prestigious *Irish Museum of the Year* award for 1999. Over 75,000 artifacts from Waterford's earliest beginnings are owned by the museum, and many of them are on display here. Many of the exhibits focus on the Viking and Anglo-Norman periods, and are quite interesting.

City Hall, *Waterford. Open Monday through Friday from 9:00am to 1:00pm and from 2:00pm to 5:00pm. Admission is free. Tel. (051) 873501.* The home for Waterford's City Hall is a splendid Georgian building built in the late 18th century. Inside are a number of treasures worth seeing. The first is an immense antique Waterford crystal chandelier that's nearly 200 years old. There is also some American Civil War memorabilia including an old American flag as well as the uniform, battle flag, and sword that was carried into the Battle of Fredericksburg by **Thomas Francis Meagher**, a home-town boy who served as a brigadier general in the American Civil War. His birthplace is next door to City Hall in a house that has been converted into the Granville Hotel.

Blackfriar's Abbey, *O'Connell Street, Waterford*. Look for a 13th-century tower at the corner of Bridge and O'Connell Streets. It is all that remains of a Dominican abbey, also referred to as Blackfriars, that ran afoul of Oliver Cromwell's troops in the 17th century.

Victorian Clock Tower, *Merchant's Quay, Waterford*. On Merchant's Quay stands an impressive Victorian Clock Tower. Completed just as the American Civil War was coming to a close (1864), the clock tower still stands tall and serene.

City Walls, *Waterford*. The City Fathers of Waterford claim to have more ancient city walls than any other Irish city, with the exception of Derry in Northern Ireland. Some of the walls were built by the Vikings (9th century), while others are the handiwork of the Normans (13th century). The best places to see the walls are near Mayor's Walk, Castle Street, and near the railway station.

Christ Church Cathedral, *Peter Street, Waterford*. Christ Church Cathedral was built in 1779 and boasts a roomy interior and several fine medieval tombs. Its cavernous interior is richly and ornately decorated, and is definitely worth a visit. While it is not as exquisite as either Christchurch or St. Patrick's Cathedrals in Dublin, it is nonetheless a fine specimen of the religious buildings of Ireland.

French Church, *Greyfriars Street, Waterford*. During the 13th century the Franciscans built an abbey on this site. Centuries of unfriendly visitors and the weather have reduced the French Church to ruins. However, the ruins are extensive, and feature an ornate east window. The ruins take their name from the French Huguenots, who were given the church for their worship in 1695. They worshipped there until early in the 19th century.

Waterford Crystal Factory, *Cork Road, Waterford. Open daily from 8:30am to 5:00pm. The first tour begins around 9:00am. Admission is £3.50 for adults and £2.00 for children. Tel. (051) 873311.* You've seen their crystal works displayed in some of the ritziest stores in the world, and if you're like me, you have probably come to associate the name *Waterford* with excellence, quality, and exquisite beauty. Now you have the opportunity to see first-hand how they earned this reputation for quality. The Waterford Crystal Factory is the main draw to Waterford and southeastern Ireland. It's easy to find, and well worth the visit. You'll never look at a piece of lead crystal the same again! The factory has a nice gallery, and their one-hour tour takes you within a few feet of the master artisans who blow the glass – much as it has been done for several hundred years at this site. Unfortunately, you cannot take photographs or videos while on the tour.

As you wait for your tour to begin, take a few minutes and browse around Waterford's extensive showroom. You'll be absolutely astounded at the perfection and beauty you see (I was!). Several years ago, Waterford Crystal was commissioned to create the trophy for the Super Bowl winners; a replica of the trophy is on display, and it is incredible. (You'll pick it out right away – it looks an awful lot like a crystal football!)

If you go to the Waterford Crystal Factory in hopes of purchasing "seconds" – less than perfect vases, goblets, etc., – forget it. Waterford has one definition of quality – and that is unqualified perfection. Any item that does not meet their exacting specifications is broken, then melted down and the glass is reused. While on the tour, you will doubtless have the opportunity to hear the nerve-chilling sound of crystal shattering as imperfect specimens are destroyed.

County Waterford

The countryside in southeastern Munster is so lovely and the small towns so inviting that you really owe it to yourself to see a few other sights if you've come down to visit Waterford City. This is especially true if you have rented a car and can follow your nose instead of the main roads the buses take. If perchance you did arrive here by bus, don't fear – these sights are still available to you if you rent a car at the Waterford Airport. If you intend to do this, be sure and call ahead. The rental car agencies have a limited inventory at the airport, and they will usually need at least a day's notice to accommodate you. With that in mind, here are a few more lovely – and reflective – places for you to explore while you're down in this part of Munster:

Carrick-on-Suir. The ancient village of Carrick-on-Suir straddles the Tipperary and Waterford County line. Located on the N24 between Clonmel and Waterford, or, if you're coming from Kilkenny, the N76 terminates here. Nestled along the River Suir, its Irish name means "Rock of the Suir" (*Carraig na Suire*). Carrick-on-Suir grew up during the Elizabethan period as English nobles came to Ireland and established themselves. Legend has it that Carrick-on-Suir is the birthplace of Anne Boleyn, although there are several other towns claiming the honor. Anne was the second wife of Henry VIII, and her daughter (Elizabeth I) ascended the throne of England when Henry was unable to produce a male heir. (By the way, did you know that Anne Boleyn had six fingers on her left hand!? I didn't think so!)

Ormonde Castle, *Carrick-on-Suir. Open mid-June through September daily from 9:30am to 6:30pm. Admission is £2.00 for adults, £1.50 for seniors and students, £1.00 for children and a family ticket is available for £5.00. Tel. (051) 40787.* The most interesting attraction in Carrick-on-Suir is this beautiful Tudor mansion formerly owned by the Dukes of Ormonde. Built in 1584, it still stands regally overlooking the River Suir.

About 10 miles south and a little east of Waterford is the beautiful fishing village of **Dunmore East**. Dunmore East continues its centuries-long role as a fishing village, but they have also spruced up a bit to try and catch a few tourists as well. Quiet, clean, and generally good for a few photographs, Dunmore is also worth a stroll if you have a few extra minutes on your itinerary. It sits at the mouth of Waterford Harbor, and the views of the ocean are magnificent from here. The pier that extends into the harbor was built in 1830 at a cost of over £100,000 – quite a sum of money for those days. You can reach Dunmore East by taking the R684 south out of Waterford, and then following the signs.

Famine Graveyard, *near Dungarvan.* Several miles on the Cork side of Dungarvan just off the N25, watch closely for a small signpost entitled **Famine Graveyard**. The Potato Famine, which lasted from 1845 to 1847, is estimated to have been responsible for more than a million deaths and provided the primary motivation for more than a million immigrants to leave the Emerald Isle for America, Australia, and other countries. The graveyard is located about 100 yards off the road, and is marked only by an large lichen-covered stone cross. Access is through a weed-choked drive (walk it, please). The last time I was there, the English signpost was down, and only the Irish sign remained to mark the way. It reads: *Reilig A' TSLE' An Gorta 1847.*

It is not known how many victims of the famine are buried in unmarked graves here, but the shrine is a silent reminder of a terrible period in Irish history. There are countless gravesites such as this throughout the width and breadth of Ireland.

Just a few miles south of the N25 between Dungarvan and Youghal on the R673 is the picturesque village of **Ardmore**. In a country that typifies tidy, Ardmore proudly boasts the title of "Ireland's Tidiest Town." – they actually won a contest to receive the honor. Its Irish name *Ard Mor* means "Great Hill." At the edge of town is a beautiful cliff walk that skirts the sea and offers magnificent views of the Celtic Sea.

Atop a hill overlooking Ardmore is one of the finest examples of a round tower in Ireland. Nearly 100 feet tall, the tower was used as protection by monks from raiders over the years in this tumultuous part of Ireland. As is typical with many round towers, the "front" door is 15 feet off the ground – enabling the monks to get inside, then pull their ladder up with them to keep the invaders at arm's length.

Not far from the round tower sits a diminutive stone church called **St. Declan's Oratory**. Tradition has it that St. Declan's remains were buried there. It is a little sad to consider that while they were once there, they no longer are. The tomb is empty, its contents having been scavenged through the years by the devout seeking St. Declan's intercession in their behalf. Nearby, you'll see the **Cathedral of St. Declan**. Originally built in the 12th century, it has been added to at least three different times since then. In the west gable are carved deep relief figures depicting various biblical scenes. How many can you find? My favorite is one that might be termed *Solomon's Wisdom*.

A short distance from Ardmore, on the N25 about halfway between Dungarvan and Cork, you'll encounter **Youghal** (pronounced *Yawl*), a lovely seaside resort with a fascinating ruin – **Molana Abbey**. Overgrown and mysterious, the ruins invite a personal inspection. If you are a fan of old movies, you may have seen Youghal without realizing it. In the movie *Moby Dick*, Youghal was the setting for Captain Ahab's home town. Its narrow streets and memorable clock tower apparently provided just the setting the director was looking for.

Lismore is northeast of Dungarvan on the N72, and north of Youghal via the R671 (connecting to the N72). This tiny village has a big Irish name: *Lios Mor Mochuda*, which means "Mochuda's Great Enclosure." As with so many other ancient Irish towns, Lismore's beginnings were as a monastic settlement. In the 7th century this quiet spot on the Blackwater River was chosen by St. Carthach as the site for his monastery. And as with so many monastic settlements, its history is marred by plunder and burnings. It was burnt no fewer than four times in the 11th and 12th centuries.

Lismore Castle, *Lismore, gardens open mid-April through mid-October daily from 1:45pm to 4:45pm. Admission is £3 for adults and £1.50 for children. Tel. (058) 54424.* Built in the 12th century at King John's direction, Lismore Castle stands vigil over the Blackwater River from atop its perch on a cliff above the river. Through the centuries, the castle was owned by a variety of individuals, and one of its most noted residents was Robert Boyle. He was born and lived in the castle, and his later work in chemistry resulted in "Boyle's Law."

Unfortunately, the castle is not open to the public, but the gardens are. There are several walking paths through them, and the variety of flowers is astounding. Take a few minutes and visit, and see how many different varieties of flowers you can count. The number may surprise you.

If you travel between Lismore and Clogheen on the R668, you'll go through the pass in the Knockmealdown Mountains called **"The Vee."** As you pass through The Vee, you will be treated to sweeping panoramic views of the **Golden Vale of Tipperary**, the rich agricultural plain in eastern Munster. If you are fortunate enough to take the drive when the heather is in bloom (late summer), you'll have a colorful addition to your views. But if the weather is a little gloomy, (as it is apt to be on occasion!) don't despair – you may have a birds-eye view of a storm (or two!) moving across the valley floor.

Between The Vee and Clogheen, watch for a rock cairn (it looks like a large beehive) on the side of the mountain; it is the final resting place of Colonel Samuel Grubb, who insisted on being interred upright in order to keep an eye on his lands! (Now *that's* a stubborn Irishman!)

On clear days you can see the Rock of Cashel 20 miles to the north. Even on days that aren't so clear, you'll have stirring views of storms moving across the Golden Vale.

SPORTS & RECREATION

Gaelic Football

Gaelic football matches can be seen at the **Waterford Gaelic Athletic Association Grounds**, *Walsh Park, County Waterford. Tel. (056) 77798.*

Golf

• **Faithlegg Golf Course**, *Checkpoint, County Waterford. Tel. (051) 382241. Par 72.*
• **Tramore Golf Club**, *Tramore, County Waterford. Tel. (051) 386170*
• **Waterford Castle Golf Club**, *Waterford, County Waterford. Tel. (051) 71633.* Simply stated, this is a gorgeous course. Waterford Castle is on an island, as is Waterford Castle Golf Course. This park-like course is chock full of velvety fairways and suspenseful greens. The hardest part about this course, however, may be keeping your eye on the ball. Visitors are welcome on weekdays. Call ahead for a tee-time. Par 72.

Horse Racing

• **Tramore Race Track**, *Tramore, County Waterford. Tel. (051) 381574*

Horseback Riding

• **Kilotteran Equestrian Center**, *Kilotteran, County Waterford. (051) 384158*
• **Melody's Horse Riding and Pony Trekking**, *Ballymacarbry, County Waterford. Tel. (052) 36147*

Hurling

Hurling matches can be seen at the **Waterford Gaelic Athletic Association Grounds**, *Walsh Park, County Waterford, Tel. (056) 77798.*

SHOPPING

Dunnes Department Store, *City Square Mall, Waterford. Tel. (051) 853100.* Dunnes carries a large variety of household items, and if you've forgotten, broken or lost anything on your trip, you can probably replace it at Dunnes. (We stopped by to purchase a new curling iron, since my wife's curling iron gave up the ghost while in Waterford.)

Joseph Knox Store, *Barronstrand, Waterford. Tel. (051) 875307.* You'll find a nice selection of Waterford crystal as well as a number of other upscale items of elegance at Joseph Knox's.

Treacy's, *The Quay, Waterford.* Treacy's provides a place to buy a few groceries while on your travels about southeastern Ireland.

Waterford Crystal Factory, *Cork Road, Waterford. Tel. (051) 873311.* In addition to the crystal factory, there is a nice showroom and retail outlet for this most famous crystal. Whether you buy anything or not, it is fun to browse among so much beauty.

PRACTICAL INFORMATION

American Express
• **Harvey Travel**, *4 Gladstone Street, Waterford. (051) 72048*

Post Office
• **Waterford Post Office**, *The Quay, Keyser Street, Waterford. Tel. (051) 74321*

Tourist Offices
• **Ardmore Tourist Information Office**, *Beach Carpark, Ardmore. Tel. (071) 94444*
• **Dungarvan Tourist Information Office**, *The Square, Dungarvan. Tel. (058) 41741*
• **Lismore Tourism Information Office**. *Tel. (058) 54975. (Open April through October.)*
• **Tramore Tourism Information Office**, *Railway Square. Tel. (051) 381572. (Open June through August.)*
• **Waterford Tourist Information Office**, *41 The Quay, Waterford. Tel. (051) 77388*
• **Waterford Crystal Centre Tourism Information Office**. *Tel. (051) 358397. (Open April through October.)*

SOUTHWESTERN COUNTY CORK

Southwestern County Cork offers a potpourri of sights and sounds to delight you in your touring. Touring this part of County Cork is like turning back the calendar several decades. The narrow, wriggly roads will help you take your time as you drive along, and you'll appreciate the scenery you see as you do so.

This part of County Cork has also been designated as a *Gaeltacht*, and area of Ireland where you're likely to hear Irish being spoken in any town where you stop. But not to worry – most of the people you will encounter also speak English. It is fascinating to listen to this language of the ancient Celts. Stop and listen closely to them and see if you can pick up any words that you recognize. (Mostly, the only words you'll recognize will be those that have been added since the Celts used the language – words like *football, United States, President Clinton,* etc.)

ARRIVALS & DEPARTURES

You can reach southwestern County Cork by taking virtually any road heading southwest out of Cork – each has its own personality and offers wonderful scenery.

You can just follow your nose to whatever seems interesting, but at a minimum be sure and wend your way to **Bantry House** and the **1796 French Armada Exhibition Center** in Bantry. This splendid exhibit provides an overview of one of the darker chapters in Ireland's history. Along the way to Bantry, you'll pass through a number of small villages that will beckon you to stop and spend a few minutes with them. Don't resist the temptation. Stop and enjoy the hospitality you'll find in any of these rural, back-roads towns. There are many who feel these small villages represent the "real Ireland," and southwestern County Cork is dotted with many such hamlets.

WHERE TO STAY

BOW HALL, *Castletownshend, Skibbereen. Tel. (028) 36114. 3 rooms. Rates for singles: £50, doubles: £40 per person sharing. Rates include breakfast. Dinner is available for £20. No credit cards accepted. No service charge.*

You'll find Bow Hall in the intriguing medieval town of Castletownshend, sitting proudly and elegantly atop a small rise. Dignified and refined, old and yet somehow youthful at the same time, Bow Hall offers a warmth that will make you want to come back again and again.

Purchased and renovated two decades ago by Dick and Barbara Vickery, this late 17th/early 18th century home has blossomed as a B&B. The Vickery's are part of the reason, and the fact that they have worked hard to preserve the character of the home is testament to their good taste. Once inside, you'll be impressed with the congeniality of the surroundings. Old timber paneling lines many of the walls, and the floors are graced with attractive rugs and the walls are adorned with an assortment of objet d'art.

The bedrooms are large and overlook the extensive flower and vegetable gardens on the property, as well as the sea beyond. Each room is ensuite, furnished with antiques, and all have such extra touches as hand-made quilts (and electric blankets) to add just the right touch to those cool damp days that can occur here on occasion.

Back downstairs, the dining room is a veritable work of art, as are the meals that you'll take here. Barbara has gained quite a reputation in the area as an outstanding cook, and you will be impressed with the variety on the menu and the excellence of her meals. Her comment to me that "Cooking is a passion, and I'm happiest when I'm cooking up a storm for our guests," might well be termed an understatement. Fruits, herbs, and vegetables from Bow Hall's own gardens and greenhouse complement and enhance the flavor of each meal. If you choose fish for your entrée, it will probably be provided by Dick, the fisherman of the family. If it's salmon season, you'll really hope Dick is successful in his endeavors, as fresh, wild Irish salmon is a treat to die for! Be sure and try any of the various jellies, jams, and preserves served during the meals – they are specialties of Barbara's, and of course are made from the fruits in their garden. Before you sit down to dinner, however, the Vickery's will invite you to have a sherry in their exquisite library or living room. You can just sit and enjoy the ambiance of the antique furnishings and roaring fire in the fireplace, or you can even browse through their ample collection of books.

It won't take you long to notice the Vickery's accents are not the typical Irish ones you have been hearing. Three decades ago the Vickery's visited Ireland from America, fell in love with it, and decided to make it their home. And for a night or two, they allow you to make it your home too.

SEEING THE SIGHTS

Ballinspittle's main claim to fame is a grotto containing a statue of the Virgin Mary – nothing extraordinary, especially in this heavily Catholic country. But in 1985, a local lass claimed to have seen the statue rocking back and forth. She ran home and told her family and others, who returned and witnessed the same thing. The incident was reported in the county newspaper, *The Cork Examiner*, and the grotto was suddenly deluged with pilgrims. Thousands of these pilgrims received their hearts' desire: they reported seeing the statue move. Unfortunately, vandals destroyed the statue, and its replacement has been as still as a statue since that time. But many religious faithful still journey here to see it.

West of Kinsale on the R600 lies the small burg of **Timoleague**. The Irish name for Timoleague means the "House of Molaga," and is named after St. Molaga, who founded a monastery here. The ruins located there are of a 14th-century Franciscan friary.

Timoleague Castle Gardens, *Timoleague. Open Easter weekend, then from mid-May through September daily from 11:00am until 5:30pm (Sunday only from 2:00pm to 5:00pm). Admission is £2.50 for adults and £1 for senior citizens and children. Tel. (023) 46116.* While Timoleague Castle is no longer around, visitors can still enjoy the gardens that originally graced its grounds.

Courtmacsherry sits at the edge of Courtmacsherry Bay on the R601 southwest of Kinsale. This quiet little hamlet with the big name offers several nice beaches, boat rides out into the bay, and fishing. If you are continuing southwest in County Cork, cling to the sea and follow the R601 through Butlerstown and on into Clonakilty and you'll be treated to some lovely views.

Clonakilty rests serenely at the confluence of the R588, R601, and the R600 as it comes from Timoleague. The Irish name for this town of 2,400 is *Clanna Chaoilte*, which means "O'Keelty's Clan," so if your name is O'Keelty, you may want to stop and see your ancestral home. Clonakilty caters, as most Irish towns do, to tourists. The image they present is squeaky-clean, and the small market town has a pleasant and energetic feel to it. While it's not as popular as Killarney, it has been discovered by tourists the last few years, and the slightly slower pace (and lighter traffic!) is nice.

Near Clonakilty are several enjoyable beaches if you'd like to get out of the car and walk in the sea breeze. Watch for the signpost directing you south of Clonakilty to **Inchadoney**, where you'll find an inviting sandy beach.

Castletownshend lies southeast of Skibbereen on the R596. If you're coming from Clonakilty, take the R600 to Rosscarbery, then the R597 until it dead-ends into the R596, then turn left for Castletownshend – but it's really easier just to watch for the signpost directing you there.

Castletownshend is renowned as the home of Edith Somerville and Martin Ross, two writers who collaborated on the popular *Tales of an Irish Resident Magistrate*. If that doesn't interest you, then perhaps the town's main street that plunges precipitously toward the sea will. If you're a naval history buff, you might be interested to know that the Castletownshend harbor was the site of a ferocious sea battle between a host of Spanish and English ships in 1602.

Situated south of Skibbereen on a small peninsula (watch for sign-posts south of Skibbereen on the R596) rests the small village of **Baltimore**. The sleepy image that Baltimore portrays belies a turbulent past. Witness the ruins of O'Driscoll Castle on a rocky outcropping above the harbor, or reflect on the 1631 sack of the village by Algerian pirates. Residents were slaughtered, and several hundred villagers were shipped to north Africa to serve as slaves. Today the village is a lot quieter, offering visitors such tranquil activities as sailing, fishing, and strolling.

Just off shore from Baltimore is **Sherkin Island**. Quiet beaches are one of the attractions to this sparsely populated island; there are also the ruins of an ancient Franciscan abbey and an old castle. Ferries run several times a day from Baltimore out to Sherkin Island.

Cape Clear Island has the distinction of being the southernmost point in Ireland. It's also a *Gaeltacht* (Irish speaking area). The ferry ride from Baltimore takes an hour, and offers some splendid scenery on the ride out. The main activity on the island (besides chasing your hat) are the extensive colonies of birds that draw flocks of bird-watchers here. In addition to the omnipresent gulls, cormorants, and puffins, there are a number of rare species of feathered attractions. The facilities on the island are Spartan in the event you choose to stay.

Skibbereen is located on the N71 between Rosscarbery and Bantry. While the name sounds so classically Irish, the town of Skibbereen doesn't have a lot else to draw (or keep) tourists inside its town limits, aside from a few shops.

While Skibbereen may not be a big draw for tourists today, it did produce a number of brave souls who fought valiantly for Ireland's independence during the Elizabethan and Cromwellian periods. Two of the most notable were also two of the least likely: Bishop **Owen MacEgan**, who lost his life against Elizabethan soldiers during a battle in 1602, and Bishop **Boetius MacEgan**, who was hanged in 1650 after an unsuccessful encounter with Cromwell's troops.

Bantry. This small town on the N71 nestled near the head of Bantry Bay is worth a visit, if for no other reason than to see the glittering bay. In the middle of the bay is **Whiddy Island**, and from views above Bantry it is easy to see the old fortifications still in existence on the island. As I looked at those fortifications, I found myself wondering what life must have been like for those manning the fort in days gone by.

Bantry's Irish name is *Beanntraighe*, which means "Descendants of Beann." The primary industry in Bantry for generations upon generations has been fishing. In the center of town on the main square is a statue of **St. Brendan the Navigator**. Many prayers have been directed to this saint for the return of loved ones who were on the waters in search of fish. (Legend says that St. Brendan found America a mere 700 years before Columbus.) Depending on how you drive there, Bantry is about an hour to hour and a half from Cork. But that's how long it takes if you drive straight there without stopping, which few will have the will-power (or inclination) to do.

Bantry House, *Bantry Road, Bantry. Open daily 9:00am to 6:00pm (later during the summer). Admission is £6 for adults, £3.00 for students and senior citizens, and free for children under 14. (027) 50047.* On the southern outskirts of Bantry proudly sits Bantry House, a beautiful mansion sitting amid beautiful gardens looking out to sea. The gardens offer a variety of plant life on their terraced levels. The best views are from the highest terrace. The house itself was built in the early 18th century, and offers lovely period furnishings, statuary, and an impressive collection of ancient tapestries. They also have a small collection of European art.

The Bantry 1796 French Armada Exhibition Center, *Bantry House. Open Aptil through October from 10:00am until 6:00pm daily. Admission is £3.00 for adults, £1.50 for senior citizens and students, and free for children under 14. There is a family ticket available for £5. Joint ticket for the Armada Exhibition and Bantry House at £4.50 for adults and £3 for students. Tel. (027) 50360.* In the courtyard of Bantry House is an exhibit that memorializes the attempted French rescue of Ireland from the British. In 1796, **Wolfe Tone** was successful in persuading the French to send an invasion force of over 15,000 men to assist in rousting British troops from the Emerald Isle. Nearly 50 warships left Brest, France, for Bantry Bay. Unfortunately for the Irish (and the French sailors!), fierce storms arose and sunk almost one-fourth of the ships and the men on them. One of the unfortunate ships was the frigate *Surveillante*, which was no longer seaworthy as a result of the storms. It was scuttled off Whiddy Island. One of the highlights of the exhibit is the cross-sectional scale model of the frigate.

During this period, Wolfe Tone kept a very detailed journal, and it has delighted historians: it sheds light on the sequence of events that took place in the grand scheme gone awry due to the uncertainties of the sea. Excerpts from his journal are on display.

Head north out of Bantry on the N71 and you'll find the town of **Glengariff**, a tiny village (population around 250) situated amid a forest glen. Its Irish name is *Gleann Garbh*, which means "Rugged Glen." A harbor town, Glengariff lies at the head of a long valley that is the River Glengariff's final fling before emptying into Bantry Bay. As you might expect, Glengariff was once a fishing village; nowadays they have found that catching tourists is far more profitable! Pretty much the entire village caters to tourists in one way or another. Shops, restaurants, and hotels are plentiful here.

The warm Gulf Stream makes Glengariff a bit of an oddity here in Ireland – the warm winds foster a very pleasant climate, and the local flora responds well. You can see a number of normally semi-tropical plants here: fuchsia, arbutus, yews, hollies, magnolias, rhododendrons, camellias, and others. There are a number of serene wooded walks available.

Garinish Island, *Glengariff, boat rides cost around £5 (negotiable, depe-ing on the demand, weather, and the boatman's general mood). Open March and October Monday through Saturday from 10:00am to 4:30pm and on Sunday from 1:00pm to 5:00pm, April through June and September Monday through Saturday from 10:00am to 6:30pm and Sunday from 1:00pm to 7:00pm, July and August Monday through Saturday from 9:30am to 6:30pm and Sunday from 11:00am to 8:00pm. Last landing one hour before closing. Admission is £2.50 for adults, £1.75 for seniors and students, £1.00 for children, and a family ticket is available for £6.00.* While you're in Glengariff, see if you can talk a local boatman into taking you out to Garinish Island (I guarantee you'll be able to). The island sits at the mouth of Glengariff Harbor, and is worth a visit to see the formal gardens and other plant life there.

Glengariff is located on the **Beara Peninsula**, and the peninsula gets fewer visitors than some of its more famous neighbors. But it is a lovely, scenic drive, as most of the peninsula is quite mountainous. If you are into rugged beauty, take the R572 out of Glengariff and follow your nose.

SPORTS & RECREATION

Scuba Diving
- **Baltimore Diving and Watersports Center**, *Baltimore, West Cork. Tel. (028) 20300*
- **Cork County Surf Beaches**, *Garrettstown, Courtmacsherry, Barley Cove, County Cork*

PRACTICAL INFORMATION

Laundry Service
- **The Wash Tub**, *Wolfe Tone Square, Bantry. Tel. (027) 51445*

Post Office
- **Bantry Post Office**, *2 William Street, Bantry. (027) 50050*

Rest Rooms
A word to the wise: in the *Gaeltacht* (Irish-speaking) areas of south-western County Cork, many signs, including those on the doors of rest rooms, may only be marked in Irish. If you guess, you'll probably guess wrong: *Mna* is for women, and *Fir* is for men. Take heed, lest you experience more of Ireland than you intend!

Tourism Offices
- **Bantry Tourism Information Office**, *Wolfe Tone Square. Tel. (027) 50229.* Open June through September.
- **Glengariff Tourist Information Office**, *Glengariff. Tel. (27) 63084.* Open July through August.

GUIDE

KILLARNEY

Killarney is probably the most frequently visited town in Ireland by American and Canadian tourists, and the town has been well-tuned to tourism for many years now. In addition to being blessed with great natural beauty, Killarney has honed its image as "the real Ireland" by providing jaunting car (horse and buggy) transportation to and through many of the sights in the city. To some, it's a tad overdone, but for me, I am always enthralled with Killarney each time I visit, and as soon as I leave, I look forward to the next time I'll visit.

You could visit Killarney on a day-trip from Cork or Limerick if you wish, but if you really want to do it justice, I'd suggest you spend a couple of days here. Killarney is an excellent central point from which to explore the Iveragh and Dingle Peninsulas as well as the surrounding countryside. There is simply so much to see and do here that you'll be irritated with yourself if you don't set aside enough time to see what you want to see.

I have included are a multitude of accommodations available in Killarney, from B&Bs to all ranges of hotels, so your lodging needs can be easily fulfilled (be sure call ahead during the summer months though!). After you've seen all there is to see in Killarney itself, I have included several other day trips or excursions you might like to take.

If You Miss These Places, You Haven't Been to Killarney

Some of the most popular sights in Ireland are to be found in and around Killarney. You could easily spend a few days in Killarney and never run out of things to see and do. However, be sure and plan enough time to visit **Muckross House and Gardens**. This beautiful Victorian mansion was built by a British Member of Parliament over 150 years ago. As impressive as the house is, I feel the gardens and estate are the real selling point for this attraction. In the courtyard in front of the house you'll find a number of jaunting car drivers anxious to show you the beauties of the Muckross estate during a leisurely horse-drawn ride.

The countryside immediately around Killarney is as beautiful as any in Ireland. The **Gap of Dunloe** makes for a lovely drive, and nearby **Kate Kearney's Cottage** has nearly a cult following among tourists. **Ross Castle** is also well worth a visit, and a boat ride on **Lough Leanne** will be a memory you carry with you for years to come.

The **Ring of Kerry** is a beautiful drive, although during the summer months you may be distracted by the plentiful traffic, especially at the beginning of the drive. As you begin the Ring of Kerry, take the time to stop and hike up to **Torc Waterfall**. It's not a strenuous hike, and the scenery is well-worth the effort. The Ring of Kerry takes you around the **Iveragh Peninsula**, and there are a number of other fine sights to see here, from **Staigue Fort** (an Iron Age stone Ring Fort) to the incredibly impressive **Skellig Rocks** and their abandoned monastic settlement off the coast.

Finally, if you don't visit the **Dingle Peninsula** while in western Ireland, you should turn in your Claddagh ring and never have a Guinness again in your life! The Dingle Peninsula merely offers some of the most exquisite landscapes on the Emerald Isle. Be sure and have plenty of film before you travel here, because you'll want to use it. Whether a bright sunny day or a day cloaked in mist and mystery, this awesome peninsula deserves your utmost attention!

ARRIVALS & DEPARTURES

By Air

The **Kerry Airport**, *Tel. (066) 64644*, is about eight miles outside Killarney in the small town of Farranfore. Flights from some of England's regional airports land in Kerry Airport. There are a few rental car agencies available at the airport, but no bus service into Killarney. You'll either have to rent a car or take a £14 cab ride into town.

By Bus

For **Killarney**, the bus depot is **Killarney Station**, *Cork Road (N22), Tel. (064) 34777,* where buses from Cork, Dublin, and many other points in Ireland arrive. The ride from Cork takes about two hours, and costs £10, while the six hour trip from (or to) Dublin will cost you £18. The bus station is located across from the Killarney Great Southern Hotel. The neighborhood is fine – quite nice, in fact.

By Car

Killarney is located on the N22 55 miles from Cork. If you're coming from other points in Ireland, there are several main arteries that will carry you to Killarney. If you're coming from Bantry, the N71 enters Killarney from the south. From Galway, you'll take the N18 then connect to the N21 in Limerick, and if you're coming from Limerick, you'll take the N21/N23/N22. If you're coming from Mallow, you'll want to be on the N72.

Sample trip lengths on the main roads:
• Cork: 1 hour
• Dublin: 5 hours

• Galway: 3 hours
• Limerick: 1 hour

By Train

For **Killarney**, the main train depot is **Killarney Station**, *located behind the Killarney Great Southern Hotel just off Cork Road (N22), Tel. (064) 31067.* Train service departs several times daily from Cork. The ride is a pleasant one through the Irish countryside, and only takes about two hours from **Kent Station**, *Lower Glanmire Road* in Cork.

Trains to Killarney from Dublin leaves from **Heuston Station**, *King's Bridge, Tel. (01) 836-6222.* Six trains a day make the four-hour trip between Dublin and Killarney, and the fare is £34. The neighborhood is fine, and within easy walking distance of downtown.

ORIENTATION

Once you arrive in Killarney, you'll find a busy burg full of cars and pedestrians, bicycles and jaunting cars. The main town consists of a handful of streets, in addition to the three main arteries (N22, N71, and N72) that enter town. Main Street is, well, the main street in Killarney, and runs north through town. By the time you reach the north end of town, the name has changed twice, from Main Street to High Street and finally to Rock Street. There are two main east-west streets: Plunkett/College/Fair Hill/Park Road runs east off of Main Street, and New/St. Anne's Road runs east to west almost the width of town as it crosses Main/High/Rock Street. The town's streets are filled with churches, shops, pubs and restaurants, including a few very good ones (see the *Where to Eat* section).

Killarney is one of the hottest tourist destinations in Ireland, especially among American visitors. Before you see any of the many sights in and around Killarney, take the time to explore the town first. Because of its popularity with the Irish as well as tourists, expect a lot of traffic (pedestrian, bicycle, jaunting car, and automobile!) during the summer season. Regardless, it is a delightful town to merely wander the streets and see the sights – popping into this shop and that bakery, this pub or that knit shop. Spend an hour or two of your morning getting acquainted. Leave your car at your B&B, or park in the nearest car park you can.

A word of caution: while driving in and around Killarney, watch for pedestrians, bicycles, and jaunting cars, as they seem to be everywhere.

GETTING AROUND TOWN

By Bicycle

Killarney and the sights around Killarney are made for seeing from a bicycle. From a bike you are right where all the action is, and yet the distances (generally) aren't that far to pose a real problem. Do watch yourself though – there are a lot of Americans driving on the wrong side of the roads around Killarney!

If you want to rent a bicycle, be sure you are up to multiple miles. Most of the sights to see around Killarney are out of town several miles. If you want to see the main sights, such as Muckross Abbey, House, and Estate, Torc Waterfall, Ross Castle, the Gap of Dunloe, etc., you'll be making a day of it.

You can rent bicycles at **Crafts and Curios Rent-a-Bike**, *High Street, Killarney, Tel. (064) 32578.*

By Car

Because the many sights around Killarney are just that – *around* Killarney – you might appreciate having a rental car. There always seems to be a lot of foot, bicycle, jaunting car, and automobile traffic in Killarney and on the road to the major sights, so watch yourself (and others!). If you do rent a car here for the day, prepare to pay handsomely, perhaps two or three times the daily rate in Dublin or Shannon.

You can rent a car at one of the following agencies:

• **Budget**, *International Hotel, Kenmare Place, Tel. (064) 34341.*
• **EuropCar**, *Muckross Road, Tel. (064) 31237.*
• **Hertz**, *28 Plunkett Street, Tel. (064) 34126.*

By Foot

Other than shopping and visiting the restaurants and pubs of Killarney, it isn't very practical to try and see the sights around Killarney on foot. Splurge and either rent a bicycle, a jaunting car, or drive your rental car.

By Jaunting Car

Jaunting Cars are those pony-traps you'll see plenty of while in Killarney. They are a pleasant and leisurely way to see the sights in and around Killarney. If you're in a hurry to see all there is to see in this part of Ireland, don't bother with the jaunting cars – they are very slow, traveling only about walking speed. They'll cost you around £20 to £30 for four individuals (the rates are negotiable with the drivers).

WHERE TO STAY

CARRIGLEA GUESTHOUSE, *Muckross Road, Muckross, Killarney. Tel. (064) 31116, Fax (064) 37693; E-mail: carriglea@oceanfree.net. 9 rooms. Rates for singles: £28, doubles: £21 per person sharing. Mastercard and Visa accepted. No service charge.*

Carriglea is the oldest guesthouse in Killarney and was built over 200 years ago. In 1832, the owners of Carriglea began serving the area as a guesthouse, and continues to this day. Siting on a hill above the Killarney-Muckross Road overlooking the Lakes of Killarney, Carriglea provides a pleasant place to stop for the night.

The original home was a Georgian mansion, and a new addition was added during the Victorian era (over 150 years ago). It has a beautiful sitting room that overlooks the beautiful Irish contryside.

The bedrooms, typical of Georgian and Victorian mansions, are spacious; these are tastefully decorated and generously endowed with antiques, many of them original to the house. Each room has television and a hairdryer. The rooms at the front of the house have exceptional views of the Lakes of Killarney and some of Killarney's most famous mountain peaks: Mangerton, Torque and Eagles Nest.

Carriglea is open from Easter through November 1.

CRYSTAL SPRINGS GUEST HOUSE, *Ballycasheen Cross, Killarney. Tel. (064) 33272, Fax (064) 31188 or 35518; E-mail: crystal@tinet.ie; Website: homepage.eircom.net/!doors. 8 rooms. Rates for singles: £25 to £35, doubles: £19 to £25 per person sharing. Rates include breakfast. Mastercard and Visa accepted. No service charge.*

You'll find Crystal Springs Guest House about one mile from downtown Killarney sitting proudly above the River Flesk. Eileen Brosnan is your hostess, and she will see that your stay in the Killarney area is a pleasant and memorable one. She will greet you with coffee, tea, maps of the area and suggestions of sights to see, restaurants to eat at, etc.

Crystal Springs is exceptionally clean and comfortable throughout. Each of the bedrooms is large and comfortably furnished in bright colors: lemon, pink, green, peach and rust are the predominant colors, highlighted by large windows. All have top quality furnishings.

The dining room is a nice large area that overlooks the ruins of a nearby mill. Light green paint highlighted with dark green and pink carpet accentuates the setting. Linen tablecloths and flowers on the tables add to your breakfast experience.

FRIAR'S GLEN COUNTRY HOUSE, *Mangerton Road, Muckross, Killarney. Tel. (064) 37500, Fax (064) 37388; E-mail: fullerj@indigo.ie; Website: www.indigo.ie/~fullerj. 10 rooms. Rates for singles: £38 to £44, doubles: £26 to £32 per person sharing. Rates include breakfast. Mastercard and Visa accepted. No service charge.*

Nestled comfortably amid 27 acres of some of the prettiest scenery in Killarney, you'll find Friar's Glen Country House. I stumbled on Friar's Glen quite by accident, but you will benefit from my stumbling if you decide to stay here. You'll find a relatively new (1994) country home set in peaceful and serene grounds just a short distance from Muckross House. Mary Fuller is your hostess as well as your breakfast cook, and you will enjoy the attention she gives you in both roles.

Each of the bedrooms is large and well lit thanks to large window look out onto the grounds and Killarney National Park. Each room is tastefully decorated and furnished with new, comfortable furniture. All the rooms have a telephone, television, and hairdryers. Tea- and coffee-making facilities are located in the hallway. The rooms are decorated in the bright summer colors of yellow, green and cream. All the bathrooms are large, well lit and tiled.

There are large windows in the dining room that allow you to look out onto the grounds of Killarney National Park while you feast on the breakfast Mary prepares. You have a nice variety of menu items to choose from, including vegetarian options such as wholewheat pancakes (a favorite of many guests!).

Several hundred years ago, friars from the local abbey would flee to this place for safety when invading armies came calling. It is still a restful place, and one where you will surely feel peace and tranquility.

EARL'S COURT, *Woodlawn Junction, Muckross Road, Killarney. Tel. (064) 34009, Fax (064) 34366; E-mail: earls@eircom.net; Website: www.killarney-earlscourt.ie. 12 rooms. Rates for singles: £50 to £75, doubles: £30 to £55 per person sharing. Rates include breakfast. Mastercard and Visa accepted. No service charge.*

Not only does Earl's Court receive my recommendation as the best place to stay in Killarney, it also ranks as one of the best places to stay in all of Ireland. Since 1995, Ray and Emer Moynihan have run Earl's Court, and it is obvious that they enjoy what they are doing. From the moment you enter the elegance of Earls Court, you will love it. As you walk in the front door, you'll encounter soft music and a lovely antique-laden sitting room. It will be here that you meet your gracious hostess Emer, and she will immediately make you feel at home as she offers you complimentary coffee and tea. As you sign in, take a moment to note the reception desk – it is the desk of one of the former presidents of Ireland.

One of the things you will notice about Earl's Court is the quality that is evident throughout, and that quality extends to each of the bedrooms. Each is large and comfortably furnished, and I guarantee you'll enjoy the power showers that are in each bathroom. Each room has a television, clock radio, modem port and hairdryer, and while the rooms are non-smoking, each has a balcony where that particular activity can be participated in.

Breakfast is taken in a large sunlit dining room. The hardwood floors and pleasant green and yellow décor make for a pleasant place to enjoy your meal. While at Earl's Court, you will most likely have the opportunity to meet Simba, the Moynihan's giant, docile golden retriever. Let his restful repose remind you of the rest and relaxation that awaits you at Earl's Court.

CASTLEROSSE HOTEL, *Killorglin Road, Killarney. Tel. (064) 31144, Fax (064) 31031, US toll free 800/528-1234. 110 rooms. Rates for singles: £65 to £89, doubles: £50 to £72 per person sharing, suites: £165 to £199 per person sharing. Rates include breakfast. One restaurant, tennis courts, indoor pool, sauna, fitness center. All major credit cards accepted. No service charge.*

Castlerosse Hotel sits at the edge of Killarney. This low-rise hotel is a member of the Best Western Hotel group. The hotel is looking a little old, with a need for updated lighting, carpets, and new paint.

The bedrooms are simple and functional, but not very large. Many of the rooms offer fine views of the mountains. All the rooms are ensuite, but the bathrooms in some of them are in need of updating. The biggest draw for the hotel (besides its location in Killarney) is their extensive leisure center. They offer an indoor swimming pool, sauna, and fitness center. They offer children's discounts. The hotel is open from March through the end of October.

HOTEL DUNLOE CASTLE, *Killarney. Tel. (064) 44111, Fax (064) 44583, US toll free 800/221-1074; E-mail: khl@iol.ie. 120 rooms. Rates for singles: £90 to £110, doubles: £110 to £144, suites: £114 to £400. One restaurant, gardens, riding, fishing, swimming pool, sauna, fitness center and tennis court. All major credit cards accepted. No service charge.*

As you turn into the gate of Hotel Dunloe Castle, it's almost like pulling through the gates of a Kentucky horse farm: white rail fences and beautiful horses grazing contentedly in fields of green. Picture that set against a backdrop of the Killarney landscape, and you've got a stunning place to visit.

Hotel Dunloe Castle considers itself a country inn serving families. They succeed in their efforts with a variety of activities that cater to families. Those splendid horses grazing serenely as you enter the grounds are available for horseback riding. In addition, there is a playground and playroom available for the kids to romp in while you check out the indoor swimming pool, sauna, fitness center and tennis court (the kids are welcome at these places, too). The hotel offers room discounts and special meals for children in their restaurant. If your children are younger, the hotel can arrange baby-sitting for you. Pets are also welcome at the hotel.

The rooms are comfortable with modern pine furnishings, and many have outstanding views of the Gap of Dunloe, those grazing horses, or exquisite award-winning gardens in the back of the hotel. The gardens surround the ancient ruins of the 13th-century Dunloe Castle, from which the hotel draws its name. A quiet walk through the gardens also brings you to a point where you overlook the softly flowing Leanne River. The hotel is open from the last week of April though the end of September.

HOTEL EUROPE, *Killarney. Tel. (064) 31900, Fax (064) 32118, US toll free 800/221-1074; E-mail: khl@iol.ie. 200 rooms. Rates for singles: £90 to £110, doubles: £110 to £144, suites: £114 to £400. Two restaurants, indoor swimming pool, gym, sauna, spa, beauty salon, snooker, riding, fishing. All major credit cards accepted. No service charge.*

The Hotel Europe is a lovely five-star hotel sitting on the shores of Lough Leanne. It's a popular site for incentive travel – corporations looking for a place to really treat their top-performing people. The rooms are comfortable, and those in the back of the hotel offer the prettiest views of the lake and the mountains, although they cost an extra £35.

A host of activities and amenities await you when you stay at Hotel Europe. They include a boutique, beauty salon, fishing, boating, cycling, indoor swimming pool, fitness center, and a sauna. In addition, Hotel Europe is within minutes of six championship golf courses. Hotel Europe is open from mid-march through the end of October.

KILLARNEY PARK HOTEL, *Kenmare Place, Killarney. Tel. (064) 35555, Fax (064) 35266; E-mail: info@killarneyparkhotel.ie; Website: www.killareyparkhotel.ie. 66 rooms. Rates for singles: £150 to £220, doubles: £150 to £220, suites: £250 to £500. Breakfast included. One restaurant, bar, indoor swimming pool, fitness center. All major credit cards accepted. No service charge.*

The Killarney Park Hotel is centrally located in Killarney and promises a warm reception and pleasant stay. From the turf fire burning in the entrance hall to the front desk reception to the warm dark furnishings, you'll feel welcome and comfortable. The hotel has been recognized by a number of organizations for their delightful service and top-notch accommodations. The Killarney Park Hotel also has its own set of activities to keep you occupied, including an indoor swimming pool, fitness center, sauna, peaceful gardens to stroll in, and daily entertainment in the lounge.

The rooms are nice and large, some of them bordering on spacious. While not particularly memorable, they are comfortable, clean, and offer a lot of room, especially nice if you are traveling with children. If you have your children with you, you'll be able to take advantage of the special children's rates for the rooms and in their restaurant. In addition, baby-sitting service is available.

KILLARNEY RYAN HOTEL, *Cork Road, Killarney. Tel. (064) 31555, Fax (064) 32438. 168 rooms. Rates for singles: £50, doubles: £35 to £69 per person sharing. One restaurant, two bars, indoor swimming pool, spa, sauna, tennis. All major credit cards accepted. 10% service charge.*

About a mile from the Killarney city center is the Killarney Ryan Hotel. This pleasant low-rise hotel offers a wide variety of activities. Whether you are a serious health fiend or prefer to putter around at miniature golf, you should find something to interest you. Their fitness center includes an indoor swimming pool, Jacuzzi, sauna, and a sports hall, with facilities for basketball, volleyball, soccer, and ping-pong. A miniature golf course (goofy golf) and tennis courts round out their athletic offerings.

The rooms are nothing special but are pleasant and comfortable, clean and close to town. They also include a discount for children. The Killarney Ryan Hotel is closed most of January.

KILLARNEY GREAT SOUTHERN HOTEL. *Tel. (064) 31262, Fax (064) 31642, US toll free 800/448-8355. Rates for singles: £135, doubles: £57 to £73 per person sharing. Breakfast included. Restaurant, garden, indoor swimming pool, sauna, fitness center, spa, beauty salon, boutique. All major credit cards accepted. 12.5% service charge.*

As you walk into this hotel, the lobby speaks of old elegance: a turf fire burning in the fireplace, dark oak floors, crystal chandeliers, plush rugs, and marble pillars. Formerly a railway hotel, it was built in 1854 and has been busy place ever since.

The hotel is set in the midst of 36 acres of gardens; the gardens wend their way around the hotel, and offer nice views from some of the public rooms as well as some of the bedrooms. The rooms are of average size, well-maintained, and nicely furnished. The creeper-clad hotel boasts a fine set of fitness facilities that include an indoor swimming pool, sauna, Jacuzzi, steam room, fitness center, and tennis court. If you have your children along with you, you can take advantage of their discount for children. They are closed from the first of January to mid-February.

HOTEL ARD NA SIDHE, *Caragh Lake, Killorglin. Tel. (66) 69105, Fax (066) 69282, US toll free 800/221-1074. 20 rooms. Rates for singles: £73, doubles: £115 to £151. One restaurant. All major credit cards accepted. No service charge.*

The house was built in 1880 by an English woman who called it the "House of the Fairies." It is approximately 17 miles from Killarney – watch for the signposts on the Killarney-Killorglin Road.

With lots of antique furnishings and an inviting open fireplace, the Hotel Ard na Sidhe feels like you've come home to a regal baronial manor at the end of the day. Beautiful gardens surround the hotel – gardens that have twice won first place in national garden competitions. The rooms are spacious and tastefully furnished with a bevy of antiques. They feel as though you have stumbled on the bedchambers of royalty.

Hotel Ard na Sidhe is owned by the same group that owns Hotel Europe and Hotel Dunloe Castle. You can take advantage of the leisure activities offered by those two larger hotels, including their swimming pools, horseback riding, etc. Ard na Sidhe is open from the last week of April through the end of September.

In Kenmare

Kenmare is on the Ring of Kerry. If you want to get away from Killarney to spend the evening, these would be excellent choices. They are three of the finest places to spend the night in this part of Ireland. I was particularly impressed with Sallyport House and the Park Hotel.

SALLYPORT HOUSE B&B, *Kenmare. Tel. (064) 42066, Fax (064) 42067; E-mail: arthur@sallyporthouse.com; Website: www.sallyporthouse.com. 5 rooms. Rates for singles: £65, doubles: £40 to £45 per person sharing. Rates include breakfast. No credit cards accepted. No service charge.*

The moment you enter Sallyport House, you'll be entranced by its elegance and beauty. From the warmth of the fire in the sitting room to the luxurious furnishings in each of the bedrooms to the dining room overlooking lovely gardens, you'll feel just a little special for having stayed here.

The rooms are tastefully decorated with antiques and reproductions. Each room is a pleasant pastel that makes the generous size of the rooms seem even larger than they are. Depending on your preference (and how far ahead you call!), the bedrooms at Sallyport House offer you views of Kenmare Bay or green orchards and mountains. The Arthurs have established of fine reputation for themselves, and many of their repeat visitors report the main reason for their return to Sallyport House is her proprietors. Why don't you try staying here and see if you agree?

Sallyport House is just a few blocks from downtown Kenmare – close enough to get there walking, but far enough away to make your stay a pleasant and uninterrupted one.

PARK HOTEL KENMARE, *Kenmare. Tel. (064) 41200, Fax (064) 41402; E-mail: phkenmre@iol.ie; Website: www.parkkenmare.com. 50 rooms. Rates for singles: £132 to £152, doubles: £122 to £175 per person sharing, suites: £205 to £242 per person sharing. One restaurant, croquet, tennis. All major credit cards accepted. No service charge. Only open from mid-April through mid-November.*

I must admit, I was probably more curious to meet the owner of the Park Hotel in Kenmare than I was to actually stay at his hotel. It seemed that nearly every hotelier to whom I mentioned my upcoming stay at the Park Hotel indicated a desire for me to say "Hello," to Francis Brennan. Several of them, general managers at some of Ireland's most prestigious hotels, had learned their craft at Francis' hand.

I wasn't disappointed, either in Mr. Brennan or in the hotel. Mr. Brennan is a wonderful host, and those who serve with him are equally enthusiastic. Built in 1897 to serve as the hotel for the railroad that dead-ended there, it has since been renovated and expanded, and the results are marvelous. Many of the rooms are very large, and those in the back are the best, offering views of Kenmare Bay and most of the 11 acres of gardens. The halls are graced with a multitude of antiques and portraits. Some of them are interesting pieces, including a 19th-century wheelchair and an ancient wine press. Amenities include turn-down service, bath-robes, and slippers.

On-site is an award-winning restaurant overlooking Kenmare Bay and providing a delicious repast to augment your experience (see *Where to Eat* section). The simple elegance of the dining room is a fitting complement to the rest of the hotel. Crisp Irish linen and gleaming silverware accent the fine meals prepared by Chef Bruno Schmidt. The ambiance, food, and views all add up to a satisfying and impressive dining experience.

SHEEN FALLS LODGE, *Kenmare. Tel. (064) 41600, Fax (064) 41386; E-mail: info@sheenfallslodge.ie; Website: www.sheenfallslodge.ie. 40 rooms. Rates for singles: £168 to £280, doubles: £240 to £350, suites: £300 to £420. One restaurant, croquet, tennis, gym, sauna, spa, beauty salon, riding, shooting, fishing, golf. All major credit cards accepted. No service charge.*

In the 17th century, William Petty commissioned the building of a luxurious manor house along the banks of Kenmare Bay. Three hundred years later, you can experience the same level of luxury William became accustomed to by staying at Sheen Falls Hotel, which is built around William's original home. The result is a hotel rich in tradition if not actual history. Sitting amid 300 acres of park-like surroundings, the Sheen Falls Lodge is a popular resort spot for the Irish as well as tourists.

The hotel has been expensively and richly decorated, from leather couches to mahogany paneling, from marble to crystal to roaring fire-places. The rooms are of exceptional size, and each has views of Kenmare Bay or the Sheen Falls on the Sheen River. The rooms come with a bowl of fruit, bathrobes, slippers, personal safe, and nightly turn-down service.

If you can pull yourself away from the beautiful bedrooms and public rooms, you'll have other treats awaiting you. If you like woodland walks or horseback rides along sprawling parks, or if you prefer tennis or trap shooting, you can do any or all of these on the grounds of Sheen Falls Lodge. I heartily recommend this very lovely hotel.

WHERE TO EAT

THE LAURELS PUB, *Main Street, Killarney. Tel. (064) 31149, Fax (064) 34389. £2.75 to £12.95. Pub grub served daily from 6:00pm to 10:00pm Monday through Friday. Mastercard and Visa accepted. No service charge.*

This award-winning Irish pub is a popular restaurant on Main Street in Killarney. Inside, you'll find a series of tables and booths, all comfort-ably situated for conversation and dining. You'll also enjoy the open-beam ceilings and a peat-burning fireplace that provide just the right atmosphere for your dining and visiting. The Laurels has earned a good reputation for the quality of their pub grub, and you'll find a variety of soups, salads and sandwiches here. (I found their beef stew to be extraordinary!)

THE FLESK RESTAURANT, *Main Street, Killarney. Tel. (064) 31128. £5.95 to £18. Open daily from 5:30pm to 10:30pm. Mastercard and Visa accepted. No service charge.*

The Flesk was highly recommended by several B&B owners because of the positive comments from numerous of their guests who had dined there. Once I visited there myself, I could see why.

You'll find a pleasant, conversational environment here, along with a varied menu that gives you a good selection to choose from. The choices range from beef to lamb to fish and a even a few vegetarian choices. The menu changes frequently, but you might find such items as large wild Killarney Lake salmon with light hollandaise sauce, or roast half Irish farm chicken with herb stuffing and a delicious red wine and mushroom sauce.

Dermot O'Leary is your host, and he is unique – he an Irish Viet Nam war veteran, and that helps explain the scores of American Legion signs in the restaurant. If you visit with Dermot, you'll find him a pleasant and engaging conversationalist.

BRICÉN RESTAURANT, *26 High Street, Killarney. Tel. (064) 34902. £12.95 to £19. Open daily from 10:00am to 4:30pm and from 6:00pm to 9:300pm. Mastercard and Visa accepted. No service charge.*

The Bricén Restaurant is located above an Irish crafts store on High Street (the continuation of Main Street) in downtown Killarney. This marvelous restaurant oozes class and elegance, and is a most pleasant place to relax, dine, and review your day's activities. Inside, you'll find soft lighting and candle-lit tables set in small private snugs. It provides the feel of a romantic night out. There are separated smoking and no-smoking dining areas, and the tables at the front of the restaurant look out onto High Street, its shops and people.

The menu changes now and again, but you are likely to find darné of salmon poached simply in wine, lemon and butter, of a rack of Kerry lamb roasted with a rosemary and wine sauce.

FOLEY'S TOWN HOUSE, *23 High Street, Killarney. Tel. (064) 31217. £10.50 to £25. Open daily from 5:00pm to 11:00pm. Bar food is available from 12:30pm to 3:00pm. American Express, Mastercard, and Visa accepted. No service charge.*

Foley's has been an institution in the Killarney area for nearly 50 years. By comparison, even though the present owners are new in the business – they've *only* been at it since 1967 – they bring a great deal of knowledge and expertise to the table. While the specialty is seafood, there is also a good selection of beef and lamb dishes. Typical offerings include crab claws in garlic butter, lobster bisque, smoked salmon, fillet of steak, herb-stuffed fillet of pork with creamy apricot sauce, or roast duckling. Add to these dishes an appetizing dessert cart and a surprisingly good wine list, and you have a winner. Dress is casual.

GABY'S SEAFOOD RESTAURANT, *27 High Street, Killarney. Tel. (064) 32519. £10.95 to £24.95. Open for lunch Tuesday through Saturday from 12:30pm to 2:30pm, and for dinner Monday through Saturday from 6:00pm until 10:00pm. All major credit cards accepted.*

Gaby's is considered by many to be the best seafood restaurant in Killarney, although nearby Foley's gives it a run for its money. Geert and Marie Maes have over twenty years experience in the seafood restaurant business, and it shows. Fresh local produce enhances the offerings of the day. The seafood portion of the menu changes daily, depending on the success of the local fishermen. Possible offerings include salmon salad, Kerry seafood platter, and Lobster Gaby in cognac, wine, and cream sauce. They have an extensive wine list. Gaby's has garnered many local and national awards over the years.

In Kenmare

THE LIME TREE, *Kenmare. Tel. (064) 41225. £10.95 to £27.95. Open daily for dinner only, from 6:30pm to 9:30pm. Visa and Access cards only.*

Sitting out front of the Park Hotel, the Lime Tree has found a very comfortable location in an unassuming, converted 1830s parochial schoolhouse. Tony and Alex Daly are your hosts, and they take extra efforts to make sure you have an enjoyable dining experience. The restaurant has been called cozy, but with lots of yellow paint and large mirrors, I found it a little more energetic than cozy. A nice touch to the décor was the addition of a number of paintings done by local artists.

But the real reason for coming here is of course the food, and you'll not be disappointed in your visit. Using only the freshest herbs and seasonings from the surrounding countryside, the fare served here is delightfully delicious. The menu has a wide variety of offerings, including one of the specialties of the house: Kenmare Salmon cooked on an oak plank. Another favorite is the Kenmare seafood potpourri "en papillote." The wine list is certainly respectable, and the dessert offerings are sumptuous. Try the mascarpone covered with sweetened strawberries, raspberries, and blackberries. It is exquisite to say the least.

LA CASCADE RESTAURANT, *Kenmare. Tel. (064) 41600. Set lunch menu for £17.50, set dinner menus for £29.50 and £37.50. A la carte menu also available. Open Monday through Friday from 11:00am to 1:00pm, Sunday from 1:00pm to 2:00pm, and daily for dinner from 7:30pm to 9:30pm. All major credit cards accepted.*

If you've decided to spend the night in Kenmare, the restaurant for Sheen Falls Lodge is a wonderful place to have your dinner. Quiet dining

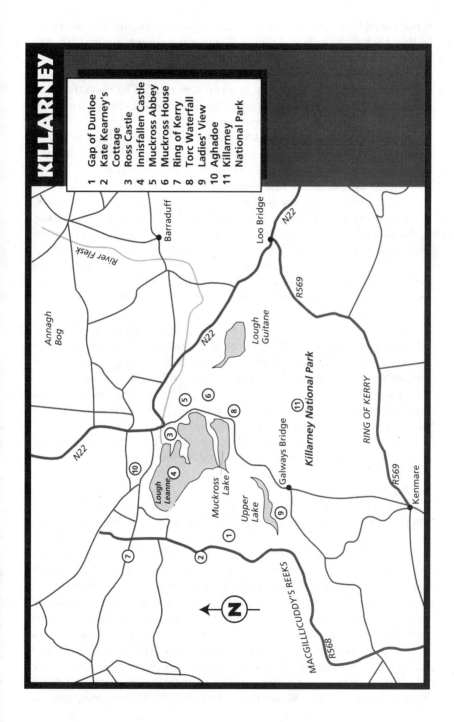

KILLARNEY

1 Gap of Dunloe
2 Kate Kearney's Cottage
3 Ross Castle
4 Innisfallen Castle
5 Muckross Abbey
6 Muckross House
7 Ring of Kerry
8 Torc Waterfall
9 Ladies' View
10 Aghadoe
11 Killarney National Park

is enhanced by lovely views of Sheen Falls (mother nature is helped a bit by flood-lights on the falls at night). The menu is contemporary Irish with a heavy continental influence. You can enjoy a good selection of vegetarian dishes, but the real specialties are salmon, fillet of Irish beef, and some excellent wild dishes, including venison and quail. The restaurant has earned a well-deserved reputation for its fine wine list. Their farmhouse cheeses from the area are also quite good.

PARK HOTEL RESTAURANT, *Kenmare. Tel. (064) 41200. Set dinner menus for £31.80 and £45. Open from 7:00pm to 8:45pm. Reservations are a must from June through August. All major credit cards accepted.*

For an adventure in fine dining, try the restaurant at Park Hotel Kenmare. The dining room is pleasantly situated at the back of the hotel, offering views of the hotel's gardens and grounds, as well as Kenmare Bay in the short distance. The atmosphere is a combination between relaxed and elegant. The tables are set with crisp Irish linen, china, and gleaming silver. While the dining room is not particularly large, its high ceilings and rich furnishings give it a larger, richer feel. Like the rest of the hotel, the room has antiques strategically placed to add just the right amount of class and charm to the ambiance.

But the real treat is the menu. Chef Bruno Schmidt has crafted a series of masterpieces: subtle influences of herbs and sauces complement the natural freshness and presentation of each course. Sample menu items include roast salad of quail with Parma ham, grilled fillet of beef studded with truffles fricassee of wild mushrooms. The dessert menu offers a number of tempting delicacies. The wine list is extensive, and offers a wide range of wines from France, California, Australia and Italy.

Jacket and tie are required for dining. The restaurant, like the hotel, is only open from mid-April through mid-November.

In Dingle

DOYLE'S SEAFOOD BAR, *4 John Street, Dingle, County Kerry. Tel. (066) 51174. Set dinner menu for £13.50. Diners Club, Mastercard, and Visa accepted. 10% service charge.*

While you're out on the Dingle Peninsula you'll surely need something to eat (it's a big peninsula!), and you wouldn't go too far wrong if you choose Doyle's Seafood Bar. Doyle's gets my vote for the best seafood restaurant in Ireland. The setting isn't bad either, amid the splendor of the Dingle Peninsula and the warmth of the village of Dingle. John and Stella Doyle have been cooking seafood for the local populace and tourists since the 1970s. Doyle's combines a homey atmosphere with fresh and exceptionally prepared seafood. One of their specialty dishes is millefeuille of warm oysters with Guinness sauce, a dish that has brought them international attention. Other dishes include baked lemon sole, mussels in herb and garlic sauce, and fried scallops. All in all, if you are a seafood *aficionado*, this is an excellent restaurant for you.

SEEING THE SIGHTS

So much of the beauty of Killarney is natural, and mother nature can be justifiable proud. As with the rest of Ireland, Killarney is stunningly green and it has more than its fair share of loughs and dells, forests and falls. From the rugged Gap of Dunloe to Torc Waterfall and Killarney National Park, to the splendid and expansive Muckross House Estate, you're in for a treat. Throw in the red sandstone mountains (hills, really) of MacGillycuddy's Reeks, and you've got a veritable palate of colors. Add such man-made sights as Muckross House, Ross Castle, and Muckross Abbey and you have all the ingredients for a few days of pure enjoyment.

Gap of Dunloe, *near Killarney, jaunting cars available daily from April through September. Rates vary, but expect to pay around £5 to £7 per person.* Pretty, pretty, pretty! And never so pretty as after a light rain (which happens often around here) has left the Gap a little misty. Drive up to **Kate Kearney's Cottage**, park your car there, and hire a jaunting car to take you up and through the Gap of Dunloe. The round-trip is about eight miles, and takes about an hour and a half in a jaunting car. The trip takes you along an old road that skirts a number of pristine lakes along the way. Sure it's a slow ride, but it gives you a moment or two to watch and reflect.

Ross Castle, *Ross Road, Killarney. Open in March and April daily from 10:00am to 5:00pm, May daily from 10:00am to 6:00pm, June through August daily from 9:00am to 6:30pm, September daily from 10:00am to 6:00pm, and in October Tuesday through Sunday from 10:00am to 5:00pm. Admission is £3.00 for adults, £2.00 for seniors, £1.25 for children and students, and a family ticket is available for £7.50.* Ross Castle, on Ross Road, is about one and a half miles from the town center, and can be walked or driven to easily. As you head out of town towards Muckross House, watch for the signpost directing you to Ross Castle. Turn right and continue a mile or so along a tree-lined street until you reach the castle.

Ross Castle sits along the shores of Lough Leanne, and is one of the finest examples of 14th-century castles in Ireland. It was built in the early 15th-century by the O'Donoghue Clan, and confiscated from them in the 16th-century. Through the intervening centuries it passed through several hands, eventually falling into disrepair and ruin.

A small exhibition centre shows photographs of the castle prior to its restoration in the mid-1970s. As restoration began, Ross Castle was a crumbling, ivy-covered hulk. The restoration work was wonderful, and a 40-minute tour takes you into the rooms that have been restored to their former (austere) beauty. While none of the furnishings are original to the castle, the owners have tried very hard to furnish the castle in period furnishings. You'll be absolutely amazed at the impressive furniture they have found that dates from the 13th to 15th centuries. The tour is well worth the time and the cost of admission.

Innisfallen Island, *Killarney*. If you're still up for a boat ride, rent a rowboat at Ross Castle (£2 per hour) and row out to Innisfallen Island to see some romantic ruins.

Muckross Abbey, *Killarney. Open . Open mid-June to early September daily from 10:00am to 5:00pm. Admission is free. Tel. (064) 31440.* When this Abbey was built in 1448, it must have been one of the most serene abbeys on the entire Emerald Isle. Unfortunately, the abbey didn't always have serene times: it was raided in 1589 by British troops, and burned by Cromwell's troops in 1652.

It remains a grand ruin, however. Its massive center tower contains a number of tombs. Watch for the large yew tree, probably planted by some friar long ago in hopes of gleaning from it wood for carving.

Muckross House, *N71, Killarney. Open daily from 9:00am to 6:00pm, and from 9:00am to 7:00pm in July and August. (The farms are open from March through October). Admission to Muckross House or Muckross Traditional Farms for adults is £3.80 for adults, £2.70 for senior citizens and students, and £1.60 for children, and a family ticket is available for £9.00. A combined ticket is £5.50 for adults, £4.00 for seniors and students, and £2.75 for students and children. A combined family ticket is available for £14.00. Tel. (064) 31440, Fax (064) 33926.* On the outskirts of town on the main road is Muckross House and the intriguing **Muckross Traditional Farms**. The two are side-by-side, and give a view of the way both rich and poor lived in the mid-1800's.

Muckross House was built in 1843 by a former Member of Parliament, Henry Arthur Herbert, and has been beautifully restored. Mr. Herbert didn't spare a dime (10 pence?) in the construction of this lovely Victorian Mansion. Stately and proud, Muckross House now allows tourists to walk where Dukes and Duchesses once strolled. The immense home is filled with period furnishings and artwork that is nearly as exquisite as the house. The self-guided tour lasts as long or as short as your attention span dictates, but I'd suggest at least 30 minutes to stroll through this elegant mansion. Don't forget to visit the lower reaches of the house, where servants toiled to make life pleasant and enjoyable for the mansion's owners in years gone by.

But wait – there's more! Once you leave the home, head for the delightful garden, filled with an amazing variety of azaleas and rhododendrons. After you've had your fill of the gardens, you'll want to explore the vast estate that surrounds Muckross House. You can explore on foot, or if you want to cover a little more ground and have some company and conversation sprinkled with few tall tales, invest the time and money in a ride around the grounds via a "jaunting car." What's that? You don't know what a jaunting car is? Well, it's a two-wheeled horse-drawn cart, and comes complete with a driver who is probably as colorful as the azaleas you just left! (If you saw John Wayne and Maureen O'Hara in *The Quiet Man*, they did their courting in a jaunting car under the watchful eye of Barry Fitzgerald, who served as their driver for the occasion.) The tour travels around the grounds of Muckross House, the ruins of Muckross Abbey, two lakes and a gorgeous waterfall. Two to four people can fit in the jaunting car, and the cost is around £20, depending on how good you are at negotiating.

Across the parking lot are the Muckross Traditional Farms. These three working farms display a representation of the lifestyles of the rural Kerry folk before the advent of electricity. In addition to actors in period dress performing a bevy of old crafts and chores, there are ducks, chickens, and a variety of other farm animals.

SHOPPING

In addition to being located in an area of intense natural beauty, Killarney offers some fine shopping. The primary shopping area is along Main/High/Rock Street. (Remember - Irish streets often change names every block or two.) During the main summer months, this street is choked with tourists. Don't fight it - just go with the flow! Here are a few stores you might stop by:

Blarney Woolen Mills, *10 Main Street, Killarney. Tel. (064) 33222.* Blarney Woolen Mills outlets are located all over Ireland, and feature a wide variety of Irish goods, ranging from woolens and tweeds to Beleek china and Waterford crystal. The prices are a little higher than other places, but the selection is impressive.

Bricén Craft Shop, *26 High Street, Killarney. Tel. (064) 34902.* Located one floor below the outstanding restaurant of the same name, this rather large craft shop features a wide selection of sweaters, tweeds, crystal and Irish art. They have an especially nice selection of Irish art - prints, photographs, etc.

Frank Lewis Gallery, *6 Bridewell Lane, Killarney. Tel. (064) 34843.* If you want to take home a bit of Ireland, the Frank Lewis Gallery offers a wide variety of Irish art and sculptures.

EXCURSIONS & DAY TRIPS

There are a number of wonderful sights to see in the country around Killarney. These side trips will generally require a rental car, although you can get bus service for the Ring of Kerry and Dingle Peninsula from **Killarney Station**, *Tel. (064) 34777.* You can also rent a car at the **Kerry Airport**, *Farranfore Cork Road, Tel. (066) 64644.*

The Ring of Kerry

The Ring of Kerry is one of the most celebrated drives in Ireland. It is a 110-mile scenic drive from Killarney around the Iveragh Peninsula. Traveling 110 miles should take about two hours, right? *Wrong!* Due to narrow winding roads, scores of tour buses, many cars, and an occasional sheep or two, it will easily take you four hours. But don't despair – the Ring of Kerry is filled with beautiful views, striking panoramas, rustic ruins, and lots of brilliant countryside. The views from Killarney to Kenmare are truly beautiful – if you have a clear day you will see some magnificent scenery as you look back down the valley toward Muckross House and the many lakes in the area. Plan to take a lot of pictures.

The first decision you have to make is whether to drive the Ring of Kerry in a clockwise or counter-clockwise manner. I strongly encourage you to choose counter-clockwise for safety reasons. Tour buses are required to drive the Ring of Kerry counter-clockwise. Let me assure you that I am not a big fan of following tour buses, but I am even *less* of a fan of meeting them on the narrow, windy roads you'll find on the Ring of Kerry. However, even if you find yourself behind a tour bus, they stop frequently, and there are also a number of long straight stretches that enable you to get around them. To go counter-clockwise, take the R562 toward Killorglin, then follow the signposts for the Ring of Kerry.

I've highlighted the most interesting, intriguing, and inviting stops for you along the Ring of Kerry below (the stops begin with the Torc Waterfall and end at Killorglin). I usually drive the Ring of Kerry in a clock-wise fashion, so that's the way I've provided the information for you:

As you leave Killarney heading along the Ring of Kerry, watch for the signs indicating the car park for **Torc Waterfall**. Three to four minutes from your car you arrive at a splendid waterfall. The water that comes crashing over the 60-foot cliff comes there innocently enough from a small lake called the Devil's Punchbowl. Admire the waterfall, then take the path that ascends higher up **Mangerton Mountain**. About 15 minutes higher up the mountain and you are treated to stunning panoramic views of the Lakes of Killarney.

Continuing on the N71 toward Kenmare, you come to **Ladies' View**, an area of wonderful views back down Killarney Valley. During the latter part of the nineteenth century, Queen Victoria was a frequent visitor to the Killarney area. This spot on the Ring of Kerry was a point where her Ladies in Waiting often stopped to stretch their legs and see the views on their trips into the countryside.

The lake district around Killarney is beautiful, and much of it lies within the 25,000 acre Killarney National Park. Set in the midst of verdant mountains and shimmering lakes, there are lots of walking paths through the park that lend themselves to getting away from it all.

Kenmare is a comely village whose Irish name (*An Neidin*) means "Little Nest," and is a pleasant place to stop and rest and perhaps have a bite to eat before you continue your tour of the Ring Of Kerry. Founded in 1775, the town is reminiscent of Killarney without the crowds and jaunting cars. The shops, pubs and other buildings are uniform and well kept, and it gives a feel of real orderliness. It also has the distinction of being the only town in Ireland that has more restaurants (36) than pubs (26). (I want to know who did the counting!)

The most notable sights in Kenmare may well be several fine places of lodging. The Park Hotel, Sallyport House, and Sheen Falls Lodge all have well-earned reputations for excellence (See *Where to Stay* entries earlier.) If you're not in a hurry, you might stop into some of the brightly colored shops and see if you can be enticed to buy anything.

Continuing on your tour of the Ring of Kerry along the N71, you'll soon come to another attractive town called **Sneem**. Its Irish name is *An tSnaidhm*, which means "the Knot." (I've not yet been able to find out why it was blessed with such an interesting name!) This sparkling hamlet on the Ring of Kerry route is not unlike a basket of Easter eggs, with its assortment pastel-colored houses, shops, and pubs. Sneem has terrific natural assets: its location on an estuary of the Ardsheelaun River and a bevy of mountain peaks as a panoramic backdrop.

If you're still following the Ring of Kerry, you'll soon come to **Castlecove** and **Westcove**. These quiet little villages sit near a nice sandy beach that is generally not very crowded. Take a few minutes to take your shoes off and sample the sand and sea.

Staigue Fort, *Castlecove. Admission is in the form of a 50p "trespass fee" charged by a local farmer for crossing his property to get to the fort.* Look for the signposts off the N70 near Castlecove directing you to Staigue Fort, an impressive (and largely intact) fort dating from the Iron Age. Archaeologists estimate its age at roughly 2,500 years old. The fort is a massive circular structure whose walls are 13 feet thick at the base and nearly seven feet thick at the top. The undulating walls are of varying height owing to erosion, gravity, and theft, but they are about 17 feet at their highest points and 11 feet at their lowest. All around the inside are steps that lead to the top of each wall. There's one small entrance into the fort on the south side, and the fort has a shallow ditch that runs around the base of the walls.

Derrynane House, *Caherdaniel. Open May through September Monday through Saturday from 9:00am to 6:00pm, and Sunday from 11:00am to 7:00pm, and April and October Tuesday through Sunday from 1:00pm to 5:00pm, and November through March on Saturday and Sunday from 1:00pm to 6:00pm. Admission is £2.00 for adults, £1.50 for seniors and students, £1.00 for children and a family ticket is available for £5.00. Tel. (066) 947-5113.*

Derrynane House was the former house of **Daniel O'Connell**, the man called the "Liberator" by his Irish compatriots for his unceasing efforts to obtain emancipation for Catholics. The house has been perfectly restored with period furnishings, including many of O'Connell's own furniture and appurtenances. A self-guided, script-led tour wends you throughout the house and its sights to see. The house sits amid gardens and greenery – 320 acres worth – that run down to the crashing Atlantic. The whole area is known as **Derrynane National Park**.

Continuing on the Ring of Kerry (N70), you'll come to the village of **Waterville**, which sits quietly along the shores of Ballinskelligs Bay between the ocean and picturesque Lough Currane. Famed as a phenomenal fishing site, Waterville also boasts a fine sandy beach.

Valentia Island off the coast boasts the distinction of being the westernmost terminal of the first intercontinental telegraph cable. The island is reached at its southeast end via a bridge from the town of Portmagee (on the R565). Valentia Island offers its visitors dazzling seascapes, magnificent cliffs, and a bouquet of subtropical flowers throughout the island.

The Skellig Islands

The Skelligs. *The boat trip to the islands is £15 to £20.* Jutting abruptly out of the foaming Atlantic are a small group of islands – rocks, really – called variously The Skelligs, Skellig Islands, and Skellig Rocks. The Irish have a more descriptive term for them: "The Bull, the Cow, and the Calf". Nine miles off the coast, these small islands are fascinating to view from afar, and hold surprises when visited.

If you wish to see the islands up close and personal, tour boats leave from Ballinskelligs, Cahirciveen, Derrynane Pier, Valentia Island, and Waterville. Several local boat operators will take you out, including Dermot Walsh, *Tel. (066) 947-6115,* Des Lavelle, *Tel. (066) 947-6124,* Declan Freehan, *Tel. (066) 947-9182* and Joe Roddy, *Tel. (066) 947-4268.* They'll take you out to Skellig Michael and let you roam around there for about two hours before heading back. It is important to call at least the night before to make your reservations, and several days ahead during the main tourist season. The boats usually leave at 10:00am during the main tourist season, and 11:00am during the off season. If you just want to ride around the Skelligs, but not disembark on any of them, contact the **Skellig Experience Heritage Center**, *Tel. (066) 31633.* Two boats a day go out at 9:30am and 2:30pm. It's a good idea to call ahead and make reservations for this boat trip.

Note: the trips to the Skelligs are only available when the weather is good. Stormy seas and rough rocks don't make for a good combination.

Unbelievably, **Skellig Michael**, the largest of the islands, has the ruins of a 9th-century monastic settlement perched on its craggy ridges. If **St. Finan** was looking for solitude and an inhospitable location, he found both on Skellig Michael. Even during the best of weather, the wind can blow ferociously here. More than 650 stone steps hewn out of the mountain lead to the settlement. When you arrive, you'll marvel at the ruins – six old beehive huts, stone walls, two oratories, two churches and various and sundry remains. It is thought that those who came here were practicing "green martyrdom," which called for the diligent seeker of Christ to voluntarily seek exile in remote (and often inhospitable) places. The Skelligs would certainly fall into that category!

The settlement was abandoned in the 13th century, but for years the faithful continued to make pilgrimages to its site, climbing to the top of the island and kissing a rock inscribed with a cross. There is a lighthouse that silently and solemnly stands vigil on the island. Manned from 1820 to 1987, it must have had its own set of hearty inhabitants.

The boat trip also includes a trip past **Little Skelligs**, a smaller set of sea rocks. They are noted for their vast colonies – over 20,000 by some counts – of various species of birds. The most prevalent birds you'll see are gannets. As you near the island, the cacophony of sound that arises from the screeching birds is incredible, if not unnerving.

Take the time and visit these islands – I guarantee they'll be some of your most vivid memories.

The Skellig Experience, *Valentia Island. Open March through mid-November daily from 9:30am to 7:00pm. Admission is £3 for adults, £2.70 for seniors and students and £1.50 for children. A family ticket is available for £7.00. A combined ticket is available that includes the trip to the islands. It is £20 for adults and £10 for children. Tel. (066) 917-6306.* Just across the bridge to Valentia Island is The Skellig Experience, an exhibit concerned primarily with the Skellig Islands. Interesting information is presented on the monastic settlement on Skellig Michael, the lighthouse and its keepers, the variety of local seabirds who have chosen to roost in this part of the Emerald Isle, and the underwater creatures that inhabit this part of the great Atlantic.

If you don't feel like your sea-legs will handle a boat trip out to the Skelligs, you will probably enjoy the 15-minute audio-visual presentation on the monastic ruins on Skellig Michael.

Back to the Ring of Kerry

Cahirciveen on the N70 is the westernmost point of the Ring of Kerry. The Irish name for Cahirciveen is *Cathair Saidhbhin*, which means "Sabina's Stone Fort." The town has a neat, clean, and tidy feel to it, and there are a number of interesting shops.

The trip from Cahirciveen to Glenbeigh (or vice versa, depending on the direction you are traveling the Ring of Kerry) is one of the most scenic portions of the Ring. Views across Dingle Bay to the peaks of the Dingle Peninsula are wonderful.

Glenbeigh. *Gleann Beithe*, as it is called in Irish, means "The Glen of the Birches." Lots of hikers head for Glenbeigh, as the surrounding mountains offer some wonderful hikes with stunning views of Dingle Bay and Peninsula. Stop and gaze upon the infamous "Wynne's Folly," a mansion that was built at the direction of **Lord Headley Wynne** in 1867. The mansion was built to simulate a castle, but was poorly constructed and not particularly livable – the roof and walls leaked when it rained, which was often. Thankfully, the mansion was destroyed during the destruction that accompanied the troubles in 1922. Lord Wynne did choose a great site for his folly, however; the views are superb.

Killorglin. Killorglin is the northernmost point on the Ring of Kerry (N70) and is either the end of a long 110-mile drive, or near the beginning, depending on which direction you've chosen to travel the Ring of Kerry. In Irish, *Cill Orglan* means "Orgla's Church," and if ever you want to visit, you should do so during the second week of August. Why the second week of August? **Puck Fair**, that's why. This three-day jubilee is looked forward to by the townsfolk and other locals for most of the year.

Locals differ on the origin of the fair; some (the more intellectual types) will tell you it is the remnant of a long-forgotten pagan harvest festival. Others will tell you that it commemorates the time sheep saved the town from Oliver Cromwell's armies. The legend says that hundreds of terrified sheep fled before Cromwell's approaching army, flooding the main street of Killorglin with wool and alarmed bleating. The alerted villagers were aroused and able to defend their village against the approaching army. (Maybe the scores of other towns sacked by Cromwell should have stationed watch sheep?)

The fair features cattle-, horse-, sheep-trading, free concerts, and lots of drinking. The livestock trading is less now than in years past, but the drinking is greater. A wild goat is bedecked with ribbons and doodads and presides over the festivities.

The Dingle Peninsula

Simply put, this is a beautiful part of Ireland! The Dingle Peninsula extends into the Atlantic Ocean, and has the honor of being the most westerly point of Europe. Eons ago, glaciers sculpted a masterpiece on this parcel of real estate. Towering mountains give way to velvety valleys and gleaming lakes. The coastline alternates between sandy beaches and treacherous cliffs that sweep down to the foamy Atlantic.

The Dingle Peninsula is officially a *Gaeltacht* – a district where Irish is the predominant language. But don't worry, English is also spoken and you'll get along just fine. All the signposts are in Irish first with English underneath (well, *most* of the time the English name is given). And I guarantee you'll see more than one sign that has had the English names spray-painted over by those who would prefer to see only Irish on their signposts!

The drive around the peninsula is a mere 100 miles. But don't think you can drive it in two hours. The roads, especially along the coastline, are exceptionally narrow and winding. And with numerous interesting villages to stop in, countless landscapes and seascapes to photograph, and a lot of beauty to take in, you'll want to set aside plenty of time. A full day will allow you the time to see this stunning area without feeling rushed.

There aren't many choices for accessing the Dingle Peninsula. The most common is either the N86 from Tralee or the R561 from Castlemaine. Another way, much less traveled, is from the north side of the peninsula, taking the N86 out of Tralee to the R560 and going through Castlegregory. Just past Castlegregory, at Kilcummin, watch for signposts directing you to Connor Pass to cut across the interior of the Dingle Peninsula. If you take this latter route, you'll come out at the harbor village called Dingle.

Your first stop during your tour of the Dingle Peninsula is little **Dingle** itself – signposted in Irish as *An Daingean* (O'Cush's Fortress). Dingle is located on the southern coast of the Dingle Peninsula on the N86.

If you listen casually, you will hear Irish spoken as the primary language in this part of the country. Tune your car radio to an Irish-speaking station and you'll be amazed – it doesn't sound much like English at all. Get out and explore this old port town. There are a few interesting shops to browse through and spend some of that money you have been anxious to spend.

While in Dingle, take a boat ride out into Dingle Bay and see if Fungi, the Dingle Dolphin, is still around playfully jesting with tourists and fishing boats. Fungi has become a local legend, popular with locals as well as visitors. A ride out into the harbor in search of Fungi with a local fisherman runs about £5 for adults and £2 for children. Most of the fishermen guarantee a "Fungi sighting" or your money back.

Stretch your legs by walking around town (it's not large – the population is about 1,200). Be sure and visit the **Cearolann Craft Village**, where you can purchase silver, leather, knitted goods, and many other Irish crafts.

As you head further out on the Dingle Peninsula, you'll come to **Ventry**, whose fine sandy beaches are the main attraction. **Slea Head** has the honor of being the westernmost edge of Europe. Staggering views of the Atlantic Ocean, with the Blasket Islands in the foreground, await those who stop to gaze, gape, and click their shutters.

The small seaport village of **Dunquin** lies at the northwestern end of Slea Head. During the summer months, you can take a boat ride out to the Blasket Islands. Dunquin Pottery is also located in Dunquin (where else?). Their pottery would make a nice gift for those back home. When in town, stop by the **Blasket Centre**. *Open Easter through October daily from 10:00am to 6:00pm (until 7:00pm in July and August). Admission is £2.00 for adults, £1.75 for seniors and students, £1.00 for children and a family ticket is available for £6.00. Final admission is 45 minutes before closing. Tel. (066) 915-6371.* The Blasket Center (you can't miss it – it's the only modern building around) has a short presentation on the life and times of those who lived on the Blasket Islands.

Off the Dingle Peninsula lie the **Blasket Islands**, and the most obvious one is the largest of those islands, called **The Great Blasket**. These islands were inhabited until 1953 by a particularly hearty folk. Apparently they had a lot of time to think up stories and tell them to the few people they met, as they were renowned as storytellers.

Clogher Strand. This is the spot to get a close-up look at the power of the Atlantic as it pounds the Irish shore. Crashing waves and foaming surf make for great photos. Take a few minutes and step out of your car to get a closer look. But be sure to hold onto your hat – the wind can be fierce here even on the sunniest of days.

Between Ballyferriter and Ballydavid, watch for signposts directing you to **Gallarus Oratory**, and there you'll find an incredibly preserved church – one of the earliest in Irish history. The mortar-free masonry has been watertight for over 1,000 years. It's impressive, but I can't get over the fact that it reminds me of an upside down rowboat. The inside of the church is about 10 feet by 15 feet.

Just a couple miles beyond the Gallarus Oratory is **Kilmakedar Church**, a superb example of a Hiberno-Roman church. In addition, there are a number of examples of Ogham stones and an alphabet stone.

Connor Pass is a thrilling and beautiful mountainous drive. Be sure and stop at the carpark at the apex of the pass and check out the views. Whether you're looking toward Tralee or back toward Dingle, the views are incredible.

NIGHTLIFE & ENTERTAINMENT

Killarney's nightlife is a little more restrained than in the larger cities of Cork and Dublin, but if you are interested in hearing a wee bit of traditional music, or just share a drink with some of the locals, there are a few places you can venture into.

YER MANS, *Plunkett Street, Killarney. Tel. (064) 32688.*

Yer Mans is one of the busiest and most popular pubs in Killarney, and it seems to serve equal numbers of tourists and citizens of Killarney. If you venture here, you'll be able to savor traditional Irish music along with your pint of Guinness.

MUSTANG SALLY'S, *Main Street, Killarney. Tel. (064) 35790.*

The young and the restless are known to gather here for modern rock. This place is definitely for the younger crowd, or for those few who just can't get it out of their systems. You'll not find much in the way of traditional Irish music here.

SPORTS & RECREATION

Angling

To find out where they are biting, or what they are biting, stop and visit **O'Neill's Fishing Tackle**, *6 Plunkett Street, Killarney, County Kerry, Tel. (064) 31970.*

Golf

Ballybunion Golf Club, *Ballybunion, County Kerry. Tel. (068) 27146,* £35/£45.

Ballybunion is considered by many to be one of the finest golf courses in Ireland. There are two courses here, and the massive dunes and tricky greens of either will challenge your skills, and likely destroy your handicap. The new course was redesigned about a decade ago by Robert Trent Jones, and you'll tip your hat to the gentleman's efforts, as the fairways wend their way around and over a multitude of dunes and bunkers en route to smallish, undulating greens.

Ballybunion sits on the western coast of Ireland in County Kerry, and is the epitome of golf in Ireland. If you've not golfed in Ireland, this is a great starting point. A number of the holes parallel or run toward the sea and are superb in their beauty. The 11th hole of the old course, in particular, is one that will probably endure a long time in your golf memory. This 400-yard, par 4 hole is deceptively difficult. Perhaps it's the mile-long beach that stretches just to the right side of the hole, or maybe it's the ever-present wind, but this may be the toughest hole of the day for you. If your drive makes it onto the fairway (a tough proposition on some windy days), you'll have to deal with a pair of sand traps that stand guard over the green. But it can be conquered if you have patience (and keep your slice under control!). Visitors are welcome weekdays. The old course is Par 71 and 6,201 yards. The new course is Par 72 and 6,116 yards.

Beaufort Golf Club, Churchtown, *Beaufort, County Kerry. Tel (064) 34440, £20.*

Visitors are welcome daily. Par 71, 6.096 yards.

Dooks Golf Club, *Glenbeigh, County Kerry. Tel. (066) 68205, £20/£28.*

Dooks is their name, and golf is their game. This ocean-side course is a lovely place to spend a few hours. If your short-irons game is a little rusty, you might have some nasty things to say about Dooks. The greens are small and well protected by traps. Visitors are welcome on weekdays. Par 70, 6,010 yards.

Killarney Golf and Fishing Club, *Killarney, County Kerry. Tel. (064) 31034, £40.*

The Killarney Golf and Fishing Club offers two outstanding courses, Killeen and Mahoney's Point. Killeen hosted the 1991 Irish Open, and is a challenging course. Both courses offer plenty of water, so if you've got a bad slice or a monster hook, bring plenty of golf balls!

The scenery is some of the most spectacular of any course in Ireland. In the distance, beyond Lough Lehane, are the picturesque MacGillycuddy Mountains. Keep your eye on the ball! Killeen is Par 73 and 7,056 yards. Mahoney is Par 72 and 6,705 yards.

Tralee Golf Club, *Tralee, County Kerry. Tel. (066) 713-6379, £45.*

The challenge of this ocean-side links course is enhanced by the omnipresent wind, scores of dunes and traps, and a few nasty cliffs. All in all, these minor aspects will serve to take your eye off the ball and play games with your mind. But it's worth the time and effort to check it out.

So you are pretty confident in your iron's game? No problem then. Check out the 3rd hole. It is short enough – a mere 153 yards. But it is not the distance that's the problem. It is what lies between you and the green that may cause you a few problems. Both the tee and the green teeter precariously atop small atolls above the cliffs and water. The safe way to survive this hole is to lag up to the left of the green, pitch on, then putt out. But the foolhardy and the brave must always try the straight shot. The cliffs and ocean floor testify to the foolishness of this bravado. Which approach will you take!? Visitors are welcome weekdays to this par 71, 6,738-yard course.

Waterville Golf Club, *Waterville, County Kerry. Tel. (066) 947-4102, £35/£60.*

Sea-side views, rolling hills, and classic holes are on the menu for those who choose Waterville to exercise their golf game while in Ireland. Numerous of the holes line the sea, and your concentration will be tried to the limit.

The holes at Waterville seem to get tougher as you go, for the holes begin in gently rolling meadows and get progressively rougher and bespeckled with large dunes and nasty roughs. The 17th hole is perhaps the toughest of the course. It's only 153 yards, but (with any luck) you go directly from the tee to the green – there is no fairway between you and the green, only about 140 yards of rough! Visitors are welcome weekdays. Par 72, 7,184 yards.

Horseback Riding

- **Killarney Riding Stables**, *Ballydowney, County Kerry. Tel. (064) 31686*
- **Hotel Dunloe Castle**, *Killarney. Tel. (064) 44111*
- **Rockfield Riding Stables**, *Rockfield, Tralee, County Kerry. Tel. (064) 32592*

Sailing & Windsurfing

There are two things Ireland has plenty of: water and wind. With such a combination of the two, it is only natural that windsurfing and sailing are popular sports. (Heck, sailing was a popular sport in Ireland before sailing was even considered a sport!) Today, there are a number of sailing and windsurfing centers around the Emerald Isle. Here are a few:

- **Cappanalea Outdoor Education Center**, *Killorglin, County Kerry. Tel. (066) 69244*
- **Derrynane Sea Sports**, *Derrynane, Caherdaniel, County Kerry. Tel. (066) 947-5266*
- **Jamie Knox Windsurfing and Surfing**, *Castlegregory, County Kerry. Tel. (066) 713-9411*
- **Kenmare Bay Sea Sports**, *Dromquinna Manor, Kenmare, County Kerry. Tel. (064) 42255*

Scuba Diving

- **Derrynane Diving School**, *Derrynane Harbor, County Kerry. Tel. (066) 947-5119*
- **Waterworld**, *Tralee, County Kerry. Tel. (066) 713-9557*

PRACTICAL INFORMATION

American Express Office, *Main Street (near the tourist office), Killarney, (064) 35722*. Stop here if you need to replenish your supply of traveler's checks or to report lost traveler's checks.

Laundry Service

- **Gleason's Launderette**, *College Street, Killarney. Tel. (064) 33877*
- **Pantry Launderette**, *Market Street, Kenmare*

Post Office

- **Killarney Post Office**, *New Street, Killarney. Tel. (064) 31288*

Rest rooms

A word to the wise: in the *Gaeltacht* (Irish-speaking) areas of County Kerry (primarily out on the Dingle Peninsula): many signs, including those on the doors of rest rooms, may only be marked in Irish. If you guess, you'll probably guess wrong: *Mna* is for women, and *Fir* is for men. Take heed, lest you experience more of Ireland than you intend!

Tourist Offices
- **Dingle Tourism Information Office**, *Main Street, Dingle. Tel. (066) 915-1188. (Open April through October.)*
- **Killarney Tourism Information Office**, *Town Hall, Killarney. Tel. (064) 31633, Fax (064) 34506.*
- **Tralee Tourism Information Office**, *Ashe Hall, Tralee. Tel. (066) 712-1288*

LIMERICK CITY

Limerick is a great place to begin your tour of the province of Munster if you fly into Shannon Airport. Like so many towns along the Irish coast, Limerick was once a Viking stronghold. And like so many other towns in Ireland its history is stained with violence and death. Originally used as a base for plunder across the countryside, the city's citizens became accustomed to warfare and siege.

Originally founded by the Vikings in the 9th century, Limerick was repeatedly attacked throughout its early years by its Irish neighbors. But it wasn't until **Brian Boru** and his forces made a concerted effort in the 10th century that Limerick was taken and its Viking inhabitants made to leave. In the latter end of the 12th century, Strongbow's men claimed the city for themselves and the British Crown, but were unable to hold it long before it was retaken by the powerful **O'Brien** clan.

The city was visited in 1210 by King John. He recognized the strategic advantage of the city, and he ordered a castle built on the banks of the Shannon. The impressive castle, which still bears his name, was obediently built, and it is one of Limerick's most recognizable landmarks.

The next 400 years saw many battles waged and many lives lost as various armies sought to capture this critical port city. After the Irish forces lost to **William of Orange** at the Battle of the Boyne, they pulled back to Limerick to lick their wounds. But William pursued them and laid siege to the city. William's forces made three unsuccessful attempts to conquer the city before abandoning their siege. A year later, the Irish armies negotiated a truce with another of William's armies, and signed the **Treaty of Limerick** after a two-month siege. The Irish troops were allowed to leave the city peaceably. The treaty, which included a clause granting civil and religious freedom to Catholics, was never ratified by the Protestant congress. (Some say the English never had any intention of keeping the promises made in the treaty.) Over 11,000 of those soldiers left the shores of Ireland to fight for **King Louis** of France rather than join the Protestant forces of King William.

Residents of Limerick are proud of their heritage, and to answer the question that's been burning in your mind: yes, Limerick did lend its name to the humorous poetic ditties that we all learned in junior high school – although some spoilsports disagree!

ARRIVALS & DEPARTURES
By Air

As mentioned earlier, Shannon Airport (airport code SNN) is formerly the only airport in Ireland that accepted transatlantic flights; it now shares that privilege with Dublin International Airport. If you fly into Shannon, you'll find an older but well-maintained airport. If you need to exchange money here, the bank at Shannon Airport is open daily from 6:30am to 5:30pm.

Shannon Airport is about 15 miles from Limerick. To leave Shannon, you can rent a car, take a bus, or hail a taxi.

As soon as you clear Customs, you'll see over a dozen rental car agencies awaiting you with open arms. If it's bus service you prefer, the bus stop is right outside the Arrivals Hall, and for £4, you can take the bus into Limerick. Buses leave every 30 minutes throughout the day, beginning at 10 minutes after the hour (e.g. 7:10 am, 7:40 am, 8:10 am, etc.). Evening bus service isn't quite as frequent, with buses leaving for Limerick at 6:00pm, 7:00pm, 9:00pm, and midnight. If you want a taxi, the taxi stand is right outside the Arrivals Hall, and the ride into Limerick will cost about £16.

By Bus

The bus depot for Limerick is **Colbert Station**, *Parnell Street. Tel. (061) 313333*, where seven buses daily arrive from Dublin, and numerous others arrive from the width and breadth of Ireland. If you're coming from Dublin, the three and a half hour trip costs £13, and most fares from around the country are less than that. The neighborhood the bus terminal is in is marginal, and although it's not a far walk into the center of town, you may want to take an inexpensive (£3 or £4) cab ride if you arrive at night.

By Car

If you are driving, there are a number of ways to get to Limerick. The main road out of Dublin toward Limerick is the N7. If you are coming from Killarney, then the N21/N22 will get you there. If you are coming from the Cork area, then you'll need the N20 to get to Limerick. From Galway, you'll want to be on the N18. Each of these roads will lead you into the heart of Limerick – just keep alert for the signs that indicate "City Center" in the round-abouts on the outskirts of Limerick.

Sample trip lengths on the main roads:
- Cork: 1 hour
- Donegal: 3 hours
- Dublin: 3 hours
- Galway: 1 hour
- Killarney: 1 hour
- Waterford: 2 hours

By Train

The main train depot in Limerick is also **Colbert Station**, *Parnell Street, Tel. (061) 315555*, where you'll disembark if you've chosen to come to Limerick via the train. The trip will cost you £27 from Dublin and generally less than that from other areas of Ireland. Again, the neighborhood is marginal, and although it's not a far walk into the center of town, you may want to take an inexpensive (£3 or £4) cab ride if you arrive at night.

ORIENTATION

You'll find the medieval city of Limerick sprawling along the Shannon River as it moves swiftly along its path to the sea. Limerick is the third largest city in Ireland; the city has grown in recent years into a busy, bustling city of 60,000. The main street is O'Connell/Patrick Street. You'll find it several blocks east of the river running parallel to the river. The most interesting sights and shops in Limerick are centrally located in a part of town called the Heritage Precinct at the north end of O'Connell/Patrick Street. The Tourist Information Office is conveniently located in the heart of this precinct on Patrick Street along Arthur's Quay.

If you are coming into Limerick from Shannon Airport, you will most likely enter the city from the northwest on Ennis Road. As you near the Shannon River, the street changes names and becomes Sarsfield Street, and once in the downtown area it changes its name to William Street. The sights will be on your left as you come into town on Ennis/Sarsfield/William Street. Go to O'Connell Street and turn left, and within just a few blocks you'll come to the Tourist Information Office, King John's Castle, the Hunt Museum, and the other Limerick sights to see.

GETTING AROUND TOWN

By Bicycle

Most of the interesting Limerick sights to see are within a few blocks of the Tourist Information Office on Patrick Street. If you are only going to visit those sights, it's not necessary to get a bicycle. However, if you want

to range a little wider afield, there are several bike rental places in town:
- **Emerald Cycles**, *1 Patrick Street, Limerick. Tel. (061) 416983*
- **McMahon's Cycle World**, *25 Roaches Street, Limerick. Tel. (061) 415202*
- **Rent-a-Bike**, *1 Perry Square, Limerick. Tel. (061) 416622*

By Car

Limerick isn't a bad city to see by car – as long as you park it. I have always found success finding parking spaces around King John's Castle, although during the height of the tourist season (July and August) you'll probably have to park a little farther out. But the sights in Limerick are all located so close to one another, your best bet is to park and walk to them.

The traffic in Limerick is often heavy, although the streets are for the most part wide, and that helps you deal with the traffic. Avoid arriving and departing Limerick during "rush" hours: 7:30am to 9:00am, and 4:00pm to 6:00pm. If you arrive during those times, expect to spend a little time sitting in traffic.

Here are a few rental car agencies in and around Limerick that you might consider if you decide to get a car there for your touring:
- **Budget Rent-a-Car**, *Shannon Airport, County Clare. Tel. (061) 61688*
- **Bunratty Car Rentals Ltd.**, *Coonagh Cross, Caherdavin, Limerick. Tel. (061) 52781, Fax (061) 52516*
- **Tom Mannion Rent-a-Car Ltd.**, *71 O'Connell Street, Ennis, County Clare. Tel. (065) 24211*
- **Treaty Car Rentals**, *37 Williams Street, Limerick. Tel. (061) 46512, Fax (061) 42266*

By Foot

If you haven't gotten the message from the previous two entries, I think that walking is the best way to see Limerick's sights. The sights to see in Limerick are located in about a three-block square area, so it shouldn't be too taxing.

WHERE TO STAY

BUNRATTY WOODS HOUSE B&B, *Bunratty, County Clare. Tel. (061) 369689, Fax (061) 369454. 15 rooms. Rates for single: £22.50 to £27.50, doubles: £22.50 per person sharing. Rate includes breakfast. All major credit cards accepted. No service charge.*

Bunratty Woods House B&B is one of many clustered around Bunratty Castle, but it is one of the best. Maureen and Paddy O'Donovan are your hosts, and they take great pleasure in their business. One of the larger B&Bs in the area, Bunratty Woods has 15 ensuite rooms, two of which are larger mini-suites and one of which serves as the "Honeymoon

Suite." All the rooms are equipped with a television, tea- and coffee-making facilities, telephone, and hairdryer. The rooms are all large and nicely furnished. A sitting room is available for you to put your feet up at the end of the day, or to burn an hour or two as they you wait for the festivities to begin at nearby Bunratty Castle. It is decorated in an "Old World" motif, with furnishings and object d'art from an earlier period.

Maureen O'Donovan was born and raised in Bunratty and is intimately familiar with the things to do and see in this part of Ireland. She is willing and quite capable of assisting you in planning your exploration of the area, making sure that you see all that would be of interest to you. Like other B&Bs in the area, Bunratty Woods House is within 10 minutes of Shannon Airport, so this would make an excellent place to either begin or end your stay on the Emerald Isle.

BUNRATTY LODGE, *Bunratty, County Clare. Tel. (061) 369402, Fax (061) 369363; E-mail: reservations@bunrattylodge.com; Website: www.bunrattylodge.com. 6 rooms. Rates for single: £33, doubles: £18.50 per person sharing. Rate includes breakfast. Visa and Mastercard accepted. No service charge.*

This impressive B&B is the winner of a number of awards in the B&B industry, and is recognized as one of the best around. Mrs. Mary Browne is your hostess, and her two decades of expertise in the industry is evident. The home is a newer, neo-Georgian style home, built specifically to be used as a B&B. Each of the six rooms is ensuite, and is large and nicely decorated with canopy beds, new carpeting, and central heating. Each room has a television, tea- and coffee-making facilities, and hairdryers. The bathrooms are modern and complemented by heated towel racks.

If you've had a long day of driving or sightseeing, or just need to burn a few minutes before attending the medieval banquet at Bunratty Castle, you'll enjoy their luxurious reading room filled with antiques and interesting collectibles. Breakfast is a treat, as it would be for a B&B that has won the prestigious *Galtee Irish Breakfast Award.*

If you are fortunate, your stay may coincide with the stay of actress Maureen O'Hara. Ms. O'Hara has stayed at Bunratty Lodge regularly through the years. Her Irish names and starring role in *The Quiet Man* a few years ago make her a favorite of the Irish folk. Bunratty Lodge is about one and a half miles from Bunratty Castle and five miles from the Shannon Airport. Bunratty Lodge is strictly non-smoking, and is open from March through November.

HEADLEY COURT, *Bunratty, County Clare. Tel. (061) 369768. 5 rooms. Rates for singles: £26, doubles: £19 per person sharing. Rate includes breakfast. Visa and Mastercard accepted. No service charge.*

This is one of the newest B&Bs in the area, and you should give it a try. Kathleen Browne is the proprietor, and she is anxious to have you come and stay and sample both her B&B and her welcome. Built specifically as a B&B just a few years ago, Headley Court has five large ensuite rooms that are comfortably furnished. Each room has tea- and coffee-making facilities and a television. As you would expect, the bathrooms are ultramodern, and very nice indeed.

Headley Court B&B is about one and a half miles from Bunratty Castle and about five miles from Shannon Airport. It would make a nice place to either begin or end your trip to Ireland, as well as to use as a base for exploring this part of the Emerald Isle. It is open year-round.

BUNRATTY CASTLE HOTEL, *Bunratty, County Clare. Tel. (061) 364116, Fax (064) 364891. 61 rooms. Rates for singles: £35, doubles: £25 per person sharing. Restaurant. All major credit cards accepted. No service charge.*

This old Georgian mansion house across the street from Bunratty Castle has been expanded and converted into a hotel. The lobby and pub are in the main house, and most of the rooms are in newer extensions to the house. Unfortunately, the extensions made no effort to continue the feel or quality of the original Georgian mansion, but the rooms are comfortable and clean, albeit a little small. A recent addition added 50 new rooms, and they are the nicest. Several evenings a week, live entertainment is offered in the pub.

BALLYCORMAC HOUSE, *Aglish, (near Borrisokane). Tel. (067) 21129, Fax (067) 21200; E-mail: ballyc@indigo.ie. 5 rooms. Rates for singles: £30 - £40, doubles: £30 - £40 per person sharing. Restaurant. All major credit cards accepted. No service charge.*

In recent years, Ballycormac House has gained some renown as a mini-fishing and hunting lodge. The proprietors, Herb and Christine Quigley, arrange *ghillies* (guides) for guests who would like to fish, ride, or shoot in the nearby countryside. Their guesthouse has five rooms, including one small suite with its own private open fire and a lovely four-poster bed. The other rooms vary in size, several are small and the others are adequate, but all are clean and cheerily decorated. The restaurant here is also considered one of the best in this part of the country.

It's a little difficult to find since Aglish isn't on all maps. A phone call for directions will help immensely. It is north of Borrisokane, which is due north of Nenagh on the N52. (Nenagh is about 30 minutes northeast of Limerick on the N7.) Even though it's tough to find, your efforts will be rewarded with a pleasant lodging experience.

LIMERICK INN, *Ennis Road, Limerick. Tel. (061) 326666, Fax (061) 326281, US Toll-free 800/223-0888; E-mail: limerickinn@limerickinn.ie; Website: www.commerce.ie/cl/limerick-inn. 153 rooms. Rates for singles: £80, doubles: £115 – £126 per room. Rates include breakfast. Restaurant, pub, indoor swimming pool, sauna, spa, tennis, fitness center, snooker. All major credit cards accepted. No service charge.*

At the edge of Limerick City on Ennis Road sits the inconspicuous low-rise Limerick Inn. The hotel offers its guests a wide range of fitness activities including an indoor swimming pool, fitness center, sauna, solarium, snooker room, and tennis courts. The rooms are fairly large and are furnished with comfortable beds and pleasant furnishings. Trouser presses, an iron and ironing board in each room are nice touches.

TWO MILE INN HOTEL, *Ennis Road, Limerick. Tel. (061) 326255, Fax (061) 453783. 123 rooms. Rates for singles: £49 to £63, doubles: £59 to £85. Rates include breakfast. Restaurant. All major credit cards accepted. No service charge.*

This new hotel, located about three miles from the center of Limerick City, offers a bit of a different look from most Irish hotels. One-story units containing bedrooms surround greenbelt areas, giving you the feeling more akin to a country inn than a big city hotel. The rooms are well-proportioned and comfortable. During the summers, the greenbelt is furnished with tables and chairs. The hotel is especially popular with families who are traveling with children, as discounts are offered on room rates and in their restaurant. Baby-sitting service is available if needed.

LIMERICK RYAN HOTEL, *Ennis Road, Limerick. Tel. (061) 453922, Fax (061) 326333. 181 rooms. Rates for singles: £70, doubles: £40 to £53.50 per person sharing. Two restaurants, pub, indoor swimming pool, sauna, spa, tennis, fitness center, snooker. All major credit cards accepted. 10% service charge.*

Another of Limerick's older hotels, this one has a wing that dates to the 1780s. The rooms in this hotel are of average size, but they are quite nicely furnished. The hotel is within a mile of Limerick's city center, and a convenient place to stay while you are exploring the area. The hotel welcomes families with children, and offers discounts on room rates and children's meals in their restaurant. They offer one room that affords wheelchair access.

JURY'S HOTEL, *Ennis Road, Limerick. Tel. (061) 327777, Fax (061) 326400, US toll free 800/843-3311. 95 rooms. Rates for singles: £105 to £125, doubles: £130 to £150. Two restaurants, pub, indoor swimming pool, sauna, spa, tennis, fitness center, snooker. All major credit cards accepted. 10% service charge.*

Just as you enter Limerick on Ennis Road you'll come upon Jury's Hotel. This four-star hotel is set on its own five-acre plot next to the River Shannon, and offers pleasant and tranquil surroundings within a stone's throw of the city. There are two restaurants and a popular pub called Limericks Bar included at the hotel.

There is a mixture of old and new rooms available. Both are about average in size, although they are all comfortably if not elegantly furnished. Nice additions to the rooms include trouser presses and tea- and coffee-making facilities. A fitness center rounds out the package that Jury's Hotel offers its guests. It features an indoor swimming pool, sauna, exercise room, and Jacuzzi. Tennis courts are also available. If you've brought youngsters along with you, Jury's offers discounts on room rates as well as special meals in their restaurants. Baby-sitting service is also available.

CASTLETROY PARK HOTEL, *Dublin Road, Limerick. Tel. (061) 335566, Fax (061) 331117. 107 rooms. Rates for singles: £95, doubles: £120, suites: £160 to £270. Two restaurants, pub, indoor swimming pool, sauna, spa, beauty salon, tennis, fitness center, snooker. All major credit cards accepted. No service charge.*

This hotel is located on the outskirts of Limerick on the main Limerick-Dublin road in an attractive red brick building. The rooms at the Castletroy Park Hotel are large and comfortable. Their focus on business travelers means niceties for tourists as well: plenty of extra space in the rooms, writing desks, two phones, trouser presses, and extra lighting. The hotel offers a slightly upgraded series of rooms called Executive Rooms as well as a number of suites – Junior and Presidential – all of which include nightly turn-down service.

A leisure center available to guests includes an indoor swimming pool, fitness center, sauna, and solarium. There is also a beauty salon on the premises, and there are two rooms available with wheelchair access.

DROMOLAND CASTLE, *Newmarket-on-Fergus, County Clare. Tel. (061) 368144, Fax (061) 363355, US toll free 800/346-7007; E-mail: dromoland@dromoland.ie; Website: www.commerce.ie/dromoland. 100 rooms. Rates for standard rooms: £140 to £254 per room, deluxe rooms: £216 to £312 per room, state rooms and suites: £231 to £675; children under age 12 stay free with parents. One restaurant, indoor swimming pool, spa, sauna, fitness center, beauty salon, tennis, snooker, golf, riding, fishing, shooting, bicycles. All major credit cards accepted. No service charge.*

"A fantasy come true," "A piece of heaven," "Exceeded every expectation I had," – these were the last three entries in the guest book on the morning after a recent stay at Dromoland Castle, and I couldn't agree more. Dromoland Castle is the sister castle to Ashford Castle, and you can certainly see the family resemblance. But if Ashford is the elegant, classic beauty, Dromoland is the sister with the personality. Beautiful in her own right, Dromoland also exudes a quiet grace and charm.

Dromoland Castle was once the estate of the powerful O'Brien Clan, descendants of Brian Boru, High King of Ireland. The original structure was built in 1736 on the site of an older castle. Chock full of antiques and portraits of the previous inhabitants of Dromoland Castle, it retains its regal feeling without being stuffy. Adding to the fairytale feeling, Dromoland Castle is set amid 370 acres of woods, parks, and golf fairways and greens. The rooms are spacious and tastefully decorated; those in the front have lovely views of a small lake and the golf course. Nightly turn-down service, warm robes, and chocolates on your pillow are just some of the amenities here. The Dromoland staff is proud of their new Presidential Suite, a stunning suite overlooking the grounds and filled with amenities and furnishings most kings would be embarrassed by!

On-site is an outstanding restaurant – the Earl of Thomond Room – that provides one of the most delectable dining experiences in the country. (See the *Where to Eat* section.)

All-in-all, this is a dream place to stay if you can afford the rather steep price tag. The owners summarize their property this way: "Dromoland Castle – perfectly combining old world charm with the facilities the new world demands."

WHERE TO EAT

COPPER ROOM, *Ennis Road, Limerick City. Tel. (061) 327777. £9.95 to £16.95. Open from 6:30pm until 10:00pm. All major credit cards accepted. 10% service charge.*

The main restaurant for the Jury's Hotel in Limerick, the Copper Room is a pleasant, bright eatery. Bright colors are a nice contrast to the rich dark wood used on the walls. The food is not particularly memorable, but it's good enough for a quick meal and reasonably priced. Dress is casual but nice.

QUENELLE'S RESTAURANT, *Corner of Henry and Mallow Streets, Limerick. Tel. (061) 400111. Set dinner menu for £21.00. Open Tuesday through Saturday from 7:00pm to 9:45pm. Access and Visa cards accepted.*

The Pollard's are delighted to welcome you to their lovely restaurant. In addition to a pleasant dining experience, they offer exquisite views of the River Shannon from several points in the restaurant. But those views aren't the only beauty you'll encounter during your dining – once your dinner arrives, you'll be astounded at how *pretty* it is – almost too pretty to eat! (Well, *almost* too pretty!) Whether your tastes run to fish, beef, pork, or vegetarian, you will have ample selection to choose from on their menu. One of my favorites is the peppered pork fillet.

Quenelle's is noted for the variety of farmhouse cheeses they offer, and their dessert offerings are simply stupendous. Their desserts have been referred to as imaginative, further evidence that the Pollard's may have missed their calling as artists. (Well, they are certainly *culinary* artists.)

RESTAURANT DE LA FONTAINE, *12 Upper Gerald Griffin Street, Limerick. Tel. (061) 414461. Set lunch menu for £10 and set dinner menu for £23.00. Open for lunch Monday through Friday from 12:30pm to 2:30pm, and for dinner Monday through Saturday from 7:00pm to 10:00pm. American Express, Diners, and Visa accepted.*

If you are looking for fine French cuisine, Restaurant de la Fontaine receives my vote as one of the finest French restaurants in Ireland.

Exquisite surroundings complement the fare, and you'll have to listen to the soft Irish accents around you to be convinced that you have not been transported to a fine dining establishment across the English Channel. The meals are traditional French in origin, with a wonderful use of Irish herbs and spices to give them just the right flavor. Whether you choose rabbit or venison, poultry or Burren lamb, you'll be pleased. And the French wine list you'll be offered may well be the finest in the Emerald Isle. The homemade bread that accompanies your meal is almost overshadowed by the other offerings, but I found it to be marvelous also.

EARL OF THOMOND ROOM, *Newmarket-on-Fergus, Tel. (061) 368144. Set lunch menu for £18, set dinner menu for £35 and £45. Open for lunch from 12:30pm to 2:00pm, and for dinner from 7:30pm to 9:30pm. All major credit cards accepted. 15% service charge.*

I was totally captivated by this restaurant associated with Dromoland Castle. High ceilings, rich dark wood, gorgeous crystal chandeliers, crisp starched linen tablecloths, gleaming china, and Irish harpists, singers, or fiddlers all contribute to the elegance and even opulence of the dining experience in the Earl of Thomond Room. As you dine, the watchful eyes of the former Lords and Ladies of the castle gaze down at you from larger-than-life portraits spread around the room. Doubtless their expectations are as high as yours, as their stern expressions show.

The menu is beyond exquisite, and the food exceeds all expectations. Typical offerings include picatta of milk-fed veal in classic "Nicoise" style, pan-fried fillet of John Dory set upon a nage of leeks and mushrooms, or perhaps even terrine of Dromoland estate venison with fig chutney. All are tastefully presented, the service is impeccable and personalized without being overbearing. Jacket and tie are required to dine here.

SEEING THE SIGHTS

The Limerick city center is a compact area of one-way streets and a few hills, although not steep enough to cause you discomfort in your ramblings. There are a number of interesting sights to see, beginning with King John's Castle. There is a carpark across from the castle where you can park you car and strike out into the city.

King John's Castle, *corner of Castle Street and The Parade, Limerick. Open daily from March through October from 9:30am to 5:30pm, and year-round on Saturday and Sunday from noon to 5:00pm. Admission is £3.80 for adults and £2.10 for children. A family ticket is available for £10.00 (2 adults 4 children). Tel. (061) 411201.* As you enter Limerick from the southwest, one of the most prominent sights you'll see is the 13th century King John's Castle on the Shannon River. Head for it, and enjoy the short but informative slide show about the history of Limerick. Following that is a short tour of the castle. There's not much to go into, mostly just the outside walls remain. Several years ago, while beginning restoration work on one of the walls, workers unearthed a pre-Norman village the castle had been built on top of! Currently archaeologists are working on the find, and tourists are welcome to get some up-close views of the work in progress.

Walk around and investigate the massive walls that encircle the fort and are still standing strong after 700 years. As you look over the walls and experience the commanding views they offer of the river, you'll understand why this point was chosen for fortification.

Before continuing your walking tour of Limerick, walk across the bridge in front of King John's Castle. It's called the **Thomond Bridge**, and it spans the River Shannon. At the far end of the bridge, turn left onto Clancy's Strand and look for the **Treaty Stone** (you'll see it almost immediately). In 1691, the commander of William of Orange's forces signed a treaty at this sight with the Irish rebels who had fled from the previous year's Battle of the Boyne and subsequent skirmishes. Over 10,000 Irish fighters agreed to leave Ireland in exchange for religious and political freedom for the Catholic populace of Ireland. The treaty was signed. The Irish soldiers left Ireland, most of them never to return (this mass departure is known in Irish history as the **Flight of the Wild Geese**). But the English never upheld their part of the bargain. Rather than granting religious and political freedom, the Flight of the Wild Geese opened the door for the issuance of the infamous **Penal Laws**, which basically rendered the Irish people a mere step above chattel in their own country. It was to be another 138 years before they received those freedoms promised in the Treaty of 1691.

Walk back across the bridge and turn right on Nicholas Street. Walk past St. John's Castle and continue for several blocks. On your right you'll come to **St. Mary's Cathedral**, *corner of Nicholas Street and St. Augustine Place, Limerick. Open Monday through Saturday from 9:00am until 1:00pm and from 2:00pm to 5:00pm. Admission is free. Tel. (061) 416238.* In 1168, **Donal Mor O'Brien** gave his palace to the church to be used as they saw fit. They saw fit to convert it into a cathedral. At the western entrance you'll find pillars and a Romanesque entrance. Inside are a number of sights that may catch your eye. Of particular note are the choir stalls with their misericords and their carvings in black oak. They are so incongruous that they have become an attraction in and of themselves. Other interesting sights include stone effigies of the fourth Earl of Thomond and his wife, and an immense stone coffin lid thought to be from the coffin of the cathedral's benefactor, Donal Mor O'Brien.

As you approach the entrance to the cathedral, take particular notice of the gardens. They were meticulously and lovingly nurtured by Katie

Smyth for over 50 years until her death several years ago at the age of 98. A plaque on the garden wall commemorates this conscientious gardener with the following poem:

> *The kiss of Sun for Pardon,*
> *The Song of the bird for Mirth,*
> *One is nearer God's heart in a garden,*
> *Than anywhere else on earth.*

Just down the street and around the corner from St. Mary's is the **Hunt Museum Collection**, *Patrick Street. Open Tuesday through Saturday from 10:00am to 5:00pm and Sunday from 2:00pm to 5:00pm. Admission is £3.90 for adults and £2.50 for students and children. A family ticket is available for £9.00. Tel. (061) 333644.* This wonderful museum offers a unique collection of Irish art and craftsmanship extending from the Neolithic period to contemporary times. Its most impressive exhibit is that of Celtic and medieval treasures, probably the most extensive outside of the National Museum in Dublin. Exhibits include European and Irish religious art, ancient (and exquisite) gold jewelry and Christian brooches, as well as everyday medieval items such as pottery, crucifixes, forks, and spoons.

In addition to the collection of Irish antiquities, the museum has a fine assortment of Stone and Bronze Age implements from Egypt, Germany, England, and Spain. There is also a wonderful selection of early Christian art, including three dozen ancient crucifixes, Bishop's crosiers (hooked staffs), and other religious trappings.

Be sure to check out the silver coin they have on display there – legend has it that this little piece of silver was one of 30 used as payment for betraying a certain Jewish carpenter/preacher about 2,000 years ago.

Hint: if you see drawers beneath the display cases, go ahead and open them. They contain additional items that are of interest to those who do a little extra exploration. (It's okay – the museum staff encourages you to do so!)

The Granary/Limerick Regional Archives, *Michael Street, Limerick. Open Monday through Friday from 9:30am to 5:00pm. Admission is free. Tel. (061) 410777.* On Michael Street you'll find the old Granary, a relatively new building by Limerick standards (1774). The Granary now houses the Limerick Regional Archives, and for a fee will research your Irish ancestors. There is also a library on site.

NIGHTLIFE & ENTERTAINMENT

Limerick has a large student population, and that contributes to the success of pubs in the area. In addition, there are a number of pubs that successfully blend the wide variety of people who seek pub company in Limerick: whether they are attorneys, blue collar workers, tourists, or students.

THE LOCKE PUB, *3 George's Quay, Limerick. Tel. (061) 413733.*

Sitting stoically alongside the banks of the River Shannon, The Locke pub is a pleasant place to stop after a day's sightseeing in Limerick. A number of turf fires throughout the establishment set the atmosphere, and there are a goodly number of snugs, nooks and crannies to get lost in as you enjoy the ambiance or enjoy a conversation or two.

You'll find a wide variety of folks patronizing The Locke, including athletes and former athletes: they feel right at home in Richard Costello's place. Richard played rugby for Ireland's National team a few years ago. Traditional music fills the air on Sunday and Tuesday evenings.

SOUTHS, *O'Connell Street, Limerick. Tel. (061) 410623.*

A black-and-white checker-board floor, a long, tall bar, and all the trappings of an old Victorian Bar is what you'll find at Souths. Snugs scattered throughout the place make it a nice spot for quiet conversation, or the tables here and there allow a more general discussion with those who may interest you.

Souths is a little lower key than a lot of the pubs around town, but it's a nice place to reflect on the sights and sounds of Limerick.

SPORTS & RECREATION

Angling

If you've longed to wet a fly on one of those placid streams you've been seeing on your travels, stop by **Jim Robinson's Angling Center**, *43 Lower Gerald Griffin Street, Limerick, County Clare, Tel. (061) 414900.* You'll find folks there that know fishing and are willing to share their knowledge to help you have a successful outing. Another shop that should be of immense help to you is **Nestor Brothers Sports Store**, *28 O'Connell Street Limerick, County Clare, Tel. (061) 414096.*

Golf

Limerick Golf and Country Club, *Ballyneety, County Limerick. Tel. (061) 44900, £25.*

Picturesque and peaceful, Limerick Golf and Country Club will provide you with a pleasant afternoon of golf. Visitors are welcome daily on this Par 72 course.

Horseback Riding

•**Clarina Riding Center**, *Clarina, County Limerick. Tel. (061) 353087*

EXCURSIONS & DAY TRIPS

From Limerick, you are within an easy drive of a number of impressive and intriguing sights. The adjoining counties of Limerick, Clare, and Tipperary offer some of the most varied and interesting land in Ireland. From the lush green **Golden Vale of Tipperary** to the lunar-like lands of the **Burren**, you'll get to see the two extremes of terrain on the Emerald Isle. Enhance those views with the stunning and precipitous **Cliffs of Moher** in western County Clare, and you'll see some phenomenal sights.

Natural beauties are not the only impressive sights in this part of Ireland. Just down the road a few miles southwest from Limerick is the wonderful town of **Adare**, with its thatch-roofed homes, golf courses, and marvelous ruins. Heading southeast out of Limerick brings you to the rolling farmlands of County Tipperary and the astonishing **Rock of Cashel**, an important religious and secular site during medieval times. Today, it makes for wonderful photo opportunities.

These destinations are detailed in the remaining sections of this chapter.

PRACTICAL INFORMATION

American Express Office, *97 Henry Street, Limerick, Tel. (061) 313066.* Contact the office if you need additional traveler's checks, or need to replace lost ones.

Laundry Service
Speediwash Launderette, *11 Gerard Street, Limerick. Tel. (061) 319380*

Post Office
• **Limerick Post Office**, *Lower Cecil Street, Limerick. Tel. (061) 315777*

Tourist Offices
• **Limerick Tourist Information Office**, *Arthur's Quay, Limerick, Tel. (061) 317522, Fax (061) 317939*
• **Shannon Tourism Information Office**, *Shannon Town Centre. Tel. (061) 361555, Fax (061) 361903*
• **Shannon Airport Tourism Information Office**. *Arrivals Hall. Tel. (061) 471664*

ADARE

Just a few miles south of Limerick City you'll find the village of **Adare**. You will be entranced with this tidy little village, and you should stop for a few minutes and explore some of the ruins you'll find there.

ARRIVALS & DEPARTURES

By Bus

Buses leave six times a day from Limerick's **Colbert Station**, *Parnell Street, Tel. (061) 313333* headed for Adare. The fare will cost you £3.50.

By Car

Take the N20 southwest out of Limerick and you can't miss Adare.

WHERE TO STAY

WOODLANDS HOUSE HOTEL, *Adare, County Limerick. Tel. (061) 396118, Fax (061) 396073. 57 rooms. Rates for singles: £43 to £55, doubles: £34 to £45 per person sharing. Rates include breakfast. Restaurant. All major credit cards accepted. No service charge.*

Located in the tidy town of Adare, the Woodlands House Hotel is run by the Fitzgerald family. This mid-size one-story hotel has been serving visitors to Adare since 1983. In addition to being an excellent place from which to explore Adare and the Limerick area, the hotel is a popular site for weddings, banquets, and other functions. Part of the reason is that the hotel is situated in the midst of over 40 acres of gorgeous gardens and luscious lawns.

Originally a four-bedroom farmhouse, the hotel has been expanded several times over the past decade. Some of the rooms are getting a little outdated, while others are fresh and lively. But all are well maintained, clean, and comfortable. There are also price reductions for children and senior citizens.

DUNRAVEN ARMS HOTEL, *Adare, County Limerick. Tel. (061) 396633, Fax (061) 396541; E-mail: dunraven@iol.ie; Website: www.dunraven@iol.ie. 66 rooms. Rates for singles: £80 to £95, doubles: £100 to £130 per room; suites £130 to £160; children under age 4 stay free with their parents. Restaurant, tennis, riding center. All major credit cards accepted. 12.5% service charge.*

One of the most popular places to stay in Adare is the Dunraven Arms Hotel. The public areas of the hotel are lovely, with their traditional warmth and comfortable furnishings. The hotel was established in 1792, and over the past couple of years it has won a number of industry awards for both its restaurant and hotel. One of the reasons is the excellent service provided by everyone associated with the hotel.

The rooms are splendid, furnished with antiques and comfortable beds and upgraded bathrooms. The rooms provide views of the thatched roofs of Adare's cottages, and some look out onto the meticulous gardens of the hotel. Your room will be complemented with fresh-cut flowers, a bowl of fruit, and mineral water from local springs. The nightly turn-down service is a nice touch, with a wee bit of chocolate candy left on your pillow. There are no tea- or coffee-making facilities in your room, but there's room service available around the clock. A brand new leisure facility offers a variety of activities for guests.

ADARE MANOR, *Adare, County Limerick. Tel. (061) 396566, Fax (061) 396124, US toll free 800/462-3273; E-mail: reservations@adaremanor.com; Website: www.slh.com/pages/adeirea.html. 63 rooms. Rates for singles: £110 to £209, doubles: £145 to £285, staterooms: £200 to £285; children under age 12 stay free with their parents. Rates include breakfast. Restaurant, garden, gym, sauna, snooker, games room, riding, fishing, shooting. All major credit cards accepted. No service charge.*

If you want to see what it was like to live like 18th-century royalty, spend a night or two in Adare Manor. Located in the spotless town of Adare (and I do mean spotless: thatched cottages without a thatch out of place, white-washed walls, and so on), beside the meandering River Maigue, Adare Manor is the former home of the Earls of Dunraven. The hotel features exquisite furnishings, including crystal chandeliers, many antiques, stained-glass, and rich mahogany furniture. Stroll into the gallery, patterned after a room in the Versailles Palace outside of Paris. Sit in the drawing room and look out over magnificent gardens.

The enthusiasm you feel after your initial impressions will carry right on through to the bedrooms. Spacious, individually decorated rooms include many with hand-crafted fireplaces and elegant furnishings. Large, high-quality bathrooms complement the views you'll have out your bedroom windows.

A number of activities are available to Adare Manor's guests, including golf on their Robert Trent Jones-designed golf course, an indoor swimming pool, sauna, fitness center, and a game room. Children are welcome, and kids under 12 years of age stay free in their parents' room. Facilities for pets are also available. Even with all these amenities, perhaps the most pleasant aspect of the hotel is the pampering you'll get from the staff. It really is a pleasant and memorable place to stay.

WHERE TO EAT

THE INN BETWEEN RESTAURANT, *Adare, County Limerick. Tel. £9.95 to £16.95. Open daily 10:30am to 1:30pm and 7:00pm to 10:00pm. All major credit cards accepted.*

One of my favorite places in Adare is The Inn Between Restaurant, a wonderful little restaurant with a thatched roof and great food. Warm and comfortable any time of the year, the Inn Between Restaurant is a nice place to pause for a bite to eat and meet some of Adare's fine citizens. Casual dress is fine.

THE MUSTARD SEED AT ECHO LODGE, *Ballingarry, County Limerick, Tel. (061) 396451. £9.95 to £16.95. Open daily from 7:00pm to 10:00pm. All major credit cards accepted. No service charge.*

Several years ago the owner of the Mustard Seed, Dan Mullane, moved it from downtown Adare to the small village of Ballingarry. The restaurant now occupies the first floor of a lovely Georgian home set in a park-like setting. They share the premises with an 11-room guesthouse, so you might consider staying as well as eating here. The Mustard Seed is a local favorite, and many of the clientele in Adare make the short drive to Ballingarry to continue their dining pleasure, so you might consider making reservations a day or two ahead. Casual dress is fine.

SEEING THE SIGHTS

On your way to Adare, take a short detour and visit a tiny village and an interesting couple of ruins. Six miles west of Limerick on the N69 is the small village of **Ashkeaton**. This tiny burg was a former stronghold of the powerful Fitzgeralds of Desmond. A small rocky island in the River Deel is almost completely submerged by the ruins of a 15th-century castle. Nearby on the banks of the River Deel are the nicely preserved ruins of a 15th-century Franciscan friary. Feel free to wander through this ruin. (You'll need water-wings to wander through the one in the River Deel.)

Take the N20 southwest out of Limerick and soon you'll arrive at the fascinating town of **Adare**. When you reach Adare, slow down. Stop. Adare is without a doubt one of the prettiest towns in Ireland. Somehow, it just looks and feels like an Irish town ought to. Clean. Tidy. Neat. Friendly. Picturesque. Ruins of ancient origin. Thatch-roofed cottages. Its Irish name *Ath Dara* means "The Ford of the Oak Tree."

In the center of town across from the Dunraven Arms Hotel are the large ornamental gates that lead to **Adare Manor**. Built in 1832, this lovely and imposing structure is now a luxury hotel (see *Where to Stay* section for both hotels). Drive through the gates and take in the beauty of the grounds. Adare Manor is open to the public, so spend a few minutes here. Wander about, and try to imagine what life would have been like in such a splendid mansion!

Adare is small enough that you can easily explore it on foot. There are a number of ruins to visit, including several 13th to 15th-century friaries, and portions of an old 12th-century Desmond Castle. As you cross the bridge over the River Maigue at the eastern edge of town, watch for the crumbling and overgrown ruins of an ancient castle at the river's edge, just a few yards from the bridge. It's a great setting for a photograph or two. (However – be careful of the traffic. The bridge is very narrow.)

Lough Gur Interpretive Centre, *near Holycross. Open May through September daily from 10:00am to 6:00pm. Admission for adults is £2.10, and*

£1.20 for children. Tel. (061) 360788. While you're in this part of the county, you should back-track a bit and see Lough Gur. Head back toward Limerick until you hit the N20, and then take that south to Croom. At Croom, pick up the R516 over to Hospital, and then north on the R513 to the R514 and Lough Gur (watch for the signposts directing you there when you get close!)

Lough Gur is the location of an important prehistoric site. Up until the 19th century, this prehistoric settlement was unknown. But when the lough was drained, it yielded a long-hidden treasure: the Neolithic ruins of a community that archaeologists estimate is nearly 4,000 years old. Extensive burial grounds, passage graves, stone forts, and a number of other worthwhile sites are here.

The Interpretive Center provides a glimpse into what life may have been like for these earliest of Irish colonists. From their perspective, this must have been an ideal location, with the nearby lake providing an endless supply of food and water, the low-lying hills provided a semblance of protection from the weather, and nearby forests that yielded timber for their huts, fire, weaponry, and other needs. And of course, the ever-present green hills of Ireland provided ample food for their flocks.

The Interpretive Center provides ample parking and is wheelchair accessible.

SPORTS & RECREATION
Golf
Adare Manor Golf Club, *Adare, County Limerick. Tel. (061) 396566, £30 (resident)/£35 (nonresident).*

Talk about splendor! The golf course at Adare Manor is something else. This course was designed by world-renowned golf course architect Robert Trent Jones. It is a parkland course, and the fairways are exquisitely velvety with greens that are the envy of most of the courses in Ireland.

The first hole is a short, 180-yard par 3. Not too difficult, except that it's hard to keep your eyes off the ruins of the old castle beyond the green and well within your line of sight. My favorite part of the course is the walk from the 14th green to the 15th tee. The short jaunt is taken through the ruins of a 13th-century abbey. Stunning! Visitors are welcome weekdays, and the course is Par 72 and 7,138 yards.

PRACTICAL INFORMATION
Tourist Office
• **Adare Tourist Information Office**, *Heritage Centre, Main Street, Adare. Tel. (061) 396255. (Open March through November.)*

CAHIR

Cahir (pronounced "Care") was once a much more important town than it now is. Formerly the home to several powerful families (the O'Briens and the Butlers), it is now a sleepy little village focused on providing tourists with fascinating tours of an ancient castle.

ARRIVALS & DEPARTURES

By Bus

Buses run between the Cahir Tourist Information Office (located in the carpark of Cahir Castle) and Limerick's **Colbert Station**, *Parnell Street, Tel. (061) 31333* four times a day for a cost of £7.50. You can also catch four buses daily for Dublin for a fare of £10 (or you can come here four times a day from Dublin for the same price).

By Car

Cahir is about 40 miles southeast of Limerick on the N24. It's a hop, skip, and a jump from Limerick, Tipperary, or Cashel, depending on which way you are going to or coming from. If you have hesitated to rent a car while in Ireland because of the narrowness of the roads, you're in good company. However, if you rent only one place in Ireland, this might be a good time to do so. Perhaps it's just my imagination, but it seems the roads in County Tipperary are a little wider and not so curvy as they are in the rest of Ireland.

By Train

Two trains per day run between Limerick's **Colbert Station**, *Parnell Street, Tel. (061) 315555*, and the Cahir **train depot** (off Cashel Street).

WHERE TO STAY

HYLAND B&B, *Ardfinnan Road (R670), Cahir. Tel. (052) 41426, Fax (052) 41426; Website: www.tipp.ie/hyland.htm. 4 Rooms. Rates for singles: £22, doubles: £16 to £19 per person sharing. Rates include breakfast. No credit cards accepted. No service charge.*

The Hyland family runs this delightful B&B that sits at the edge of Cahir near the Swiss Cottage. This immaculate B&B is a treat, and the Hylands will make you feel right at home should you choose to visit them.

Large windows and soft colors make the Hyland B&B a pleasant place to stay. Each of the bedrooms is large, comfortably furnished and tastefully decorated. Breakfast is taken in a lovely floral-print dining room that looks out onto the verdant Irish countryside.

If you are an equestrian at heart, whether amateur or experienced, the Hyland family can also add a bit to your Irish holiday. They have horses available for all skill levels and are more than willing to share their expertise with you. Their rates are most reasonable, and if you take this opportunity, it will simply add another dimension to your Irish holiday! **WISHING WELL B&B**, *Cahir. Tel. (052) 41429, Fax (052) 42937; E-mail: simpsons@iol.ie; Website: www.tipp.ie/wishingw.htm. 6 Rooms. Rates for singles: £20, doubles: £20 per person sharing. Rates include breakfast. No credit cards accepted. No service charge.*

About a half mile from the town center, you'll find Wishing Well B&B, a lovely B&B with a host and hostess that are anxious to welcome you with open arms. Liam and Nancy Simpson are your hosts, and they will do all they can to make your stay at the Wishing Well B&B comfortable.

Each of the bedrooms is decorated with soft colors and floral accents, and the furnishings are quite comfortable. Each room has a nice large window that makes the room bright and cheery.

Breakfast is taken in a multi-windowed conservatory that lets in that brilliant Irish morning sunshine (or shelters you from the whispy Irish rain, as the case may be!)

Ask the Simpsons about *Tobar Iosa*, the wishing well after which the B&B is named. It is nearby and has an interesting history.

CARRIGEEN CASTLE, *Cork Road, Cahir, County Tipperary. Tel. (052) 41370. 7 rooms. Rates for singles: £28, doubles: £18 to £22 per person sharing. Rates include breakfast. All major credit cards accepted. No service charge.*

If it's an honest-to-goodness castle you want to stay in while you're in Ireland but you can't quite fit Dromoland or Ashford Castles into your budget, you might try Carrigeen Castle. This castle, which was built at the beginning of the 17th century, is on the main road into Cahir and offers you just such an opportunity. Stone walls befittingly enclose the castle and make you feel you are entering a fortress for your night's rest.

The rooms in the castle are smallish, and the furnishings are getting a little tired, but the thick walls convince you that you really are staying in a castle. The walls might also remind you of the thickness of prison walls, and that's appropriate since it was used as a prison during the mid 19th century. Today, however, you can come and go as you please. Within a few hundred yards of impressive Cahir Castle in downtown Cahir, Carrigeen Castle makes an excellent place to stay for your exploration of Cahir.

Mrs. Peg Butler is your hostess, and she whips up a pleasant breakfast to start your day out just right.

SEEING THE SIGHTS

On your way to Cahir on the N24 southeast of Limerick you'll come to the town of **Tipperary**. Tipperary's Irish name is *Tiobrad Arann*, which means "The Well of Ara." Tipperary sits amid the lovely **Golden Vale of**

Tipperary, a rich agricultural plain. In the 12th century, King John built a castle here and began the settlement of this area. Today, Tipperary is known primarily for two things: dairy farming and racehorses.

As you continue your trip to Cahir, on the N24, watch for the signpost to the hamlet of Aherlow and the **Glen of Aherlow** (on the R663). Take a short detour and enjoy the drive through the beautiful Glen of Aherlow, or better yet take the time to walk through some of the many wooded walking paths.

As you revel in the beauty of the Glen, you would not suspect that it was the site of many important battles in ancient days. It also served as a refuge for many an Irishman hiding out from his enemies. One of the more notable was **Geoffrey Keating**. Dr. Keating was an early 17th-century preacher who went a bit too far in his remonstrations against the English, earning the severe ire of one of the powerful families of Tipperary. Fearing for his life, he fled to the seclusion of the Glen of Aherlow, where he spent several years quietly writing a history of Ireland.

Cahir Castle. *Cahir Town. Open daily from mid-March through mid-June from 9:30am to 5:30pm, mid-June through mid-September from 9:00am to 7:30pm, mid-September through mid-October from 9:30am to 5:30pm, and mid-October through mid-March from 9:30am to 4:30pm. Admission is £2.00 for adults, £1.50 for seniors and students, £1.00 for children and a family ticket is available for £5.00. A family ticket is available for £5 (2 adults and 2 children). Tel. (052) 41011.* Continue southwest on the N24, and you'll come to the town of Cahir (pronounced "Care") and Cahir Castle, one of the most recognized castles in the world since it has been used as a setting for several medieval movies (the most famous as well as the most recent was *Excalibur*). Built in 1142, the castle sits on a rocky outcropping of the River Suir. The castle features a massive square keep, spacious internal court-yards, and a wonderful "Great Hall."

You can readily see how its picturesque setting and imposing presence must have been awe-inspiring in its day. (Heck, it's awe-inspiring now!) Strong walls and turrets, a protective moat, and trained archers would have made this an impregnable fortress indeed. Today, you can stroll inside the castle and along its battlements in relative safety. I say relative safety, because you'll experience first-hand several architectural schemes that helped make the castle safe for its former inhabitants, but that may trip you up if you are not careful. Watch for the staggered heights of the stairs – while merely inconvenient today, they served to make it difficult for enemies to traverse the stairs quickly. And keep your head down as you enter low doorways that helped impede rapid advancement of enemy troops through the castle.

Cahir Castle was built in 1142 by Conor O'Brien, Prince of Thomond and descendant of the great warrior and Irish High King Brian Boru. In

1375, James Butler, the 3rd Earl of Ormonde, was granted O'Brien's land, including Cahir Castle. Most of what you see today dates from the late 15th century.

The castle is well worth an hour of so of your time to stop and explore. As you do so, ask yourself what life must have been like behind those massive walls. Don't forget to ask yourself why the builders of Cahir Castle built it with such massive walls!

Before you leave Cahir, if you want to stretch your legs with a walk through the Irish woods, I have a suggestion for you. At the back of the Cahir Castle parking lot is a path that takes you to the **Swiss Cottage**, *Cahir, open mid-March to April Tuesday through Sunday from 10:00am to 1:00pm and 2:00pm to 4:30pm, April on Tuesday through Sunday from 10:00am to 1:00pm and 2:00pm through 6:00pm, May through mid-October daily from 10:00am to 6:00pm, mid-October through November Tuesday through Sunday from 10:00am to 1:00pm, and from 2:00pm through 4:30pm. Closed January through mid-March. Admission is £2.00 for adults, £1.50 for seniors and students, £1.00 for children and a family ticket is available for £5.00 (2 adults and 2 children).* This fairy tale cottage was built in the early 1800's by the Lord of Cahir Castle for the Lady of Cahir Castle. But after awhile, she lost interest in it, and legend has it that it became a get-away for the "Mistress of the Castle!"

A 25-minute walk from the castle to the cottage is treat enough, as you wend among the leafy paths and along the peaceful River Suir on your way to the cottage. As you round the last bend and cross the bridge over the river, you see a thatch-roofed cottage that looks for all the world like it was transported here from Switzerland. An underground tunnel serves as the entrance, and once inside the cottage you'll be able to tour parts of the house and see some of the exquisite furnishings that were used to decorate it. Some of them are original to the cottage.

The hike to and from the cottage will take you the better part of an hour, and you'll want to spend at least 30 minutes in the cottage and its grounds, so leave yourself plenty of time. In other words, don't be so rushed that you can't enjoy the myriad beauties of the Irish countryside along the way. If you want to see the cottage but don't want to walk, you'll find the cottage about 2 kilometers south of Cahir off the R670, the Cahir-to-Ardfinnan Road.

SHOPPING

Fleury Antiques, *The Square, Cahir. Tel. (052) 41226.* This antique store in Cahir is an extension of the Dublin Fleury's store. Fleury's is one of the most recognizable names in Irish antiques, since they are one of the nation's largest dealers. I found them to be a little pricey, although it is more than worth a visit just to see the quantity and quality of furnishings and bric-a-brac they offer. Like in the Dublin store, it is sort of like visiting an exquisite museum where you can take pieces home if you are willing to pay the price.

CASHEL

Cashel is a bustling town that has grown up around the mighty Rock of Cashel. In my mind's eye, I can see this town as the places of habitation for the serfs, smithies, coopers, and tanners who served their masters who resided upon the Rock of Cashel hundreds of years ago. The town has truly grown up around the Rock of Cashel, but continues to render obeisance to it, as it now supports the many tourists who come to pay homage at this sight, just as nobles and clerics have done for hundreds of years.

ARRIVALS & DEPARTURES
By Bus
The bus depot for Cashel looks suspiciously like a small restaurant, **Alice's Bistro**, *Main Street.* Four *Bus Eireann* buses a day make the trip between Limerick and Cashel, with a fare of £9. The same number of buses traverse the distance between Cashel and Dublin for the same fare.

By Car
Cashel is about 36 miles southeast of Limerick on the N24, with a change to the N74 in Tipperary. If you detour through Cahir first, then you'll take the N24 to Cahir, and pick up the N8 north out of Cahir to cover the 12 miles to Cashel. Cork is about 60 miles southwest of Cashel on the N8.

ORIENTATION
Cashel is in the middle of the Tipperary plain, also called **The Golden Vale of Tipperary**. This is an incredibly fertile section of Ireland. The Rock of Cashel, the main sight in town, is visible from miles around. The town sprawls in three directions around the ancient secular and spiritual sight.

There is one main road in Cashel, and that is the N8 as it arrives from Cahir. There are several smaller roads that converge on the town (the N74 and the R688), but the N8 is the main road where all the action is.

GETTING AROUND TOWN

By Bicycle

Cashel Town isn't that big, and I'd suggest passing on bike riding. The traffic has a tendency to be rather heavy and the streets narrow, a combination that lobbies against bicycles here. The main thoroughfare in town is also the main Dublin-Cork road.

By Car

You probably got here by car, but as soon as you arrive, park as near to the Rock of Cashel as you can and walk. Even if you have to park on the opposite end of town, you'll only have several hundred yards to walk to get to all the sights in town.

By Foot

Cashel Town is made for walking around, so plan to do so. There are some fascinating shops to investigate as you head between sights.

WHERE TO STAY

CASHEL HOLIDAY HOSTEL, *6 John Street, Cashel, County. Tipperary. Tel. (062) 62330, Fax (062) 62445; E-mail: cashelho@iol.ie. 10 rooms, 40 beds. Rates for singles: £7 to £14, rates for doubles: £7 to £14 per person sharing. Mastercard and Visa accepted. No service charge.*

If you are looking for a nice place to stay in Cashel, try Cashel Holiday Hostel. This very comfortable 200-year-old Georgian townhouse hostel is located about 50 yards off Main Street in Cashel, and just several stones throws from the famous Rock of Cashel (that is — about a four or five minute walk from there).

Salmon-colored walls will greet you in the public areas of this clean and comfortable hostel. Dormitory rooms and four-bed rooms are spacious by hostel standards, and the owners have resisted the temptation to cram one or two more bunk beds in each room. The bathroom facilities are clean and modern.

A self-catering kitchen is available for guests to use along with a large clean dining room. The television room also features a piano and a "digeridoo" (Australian musical instrument), which are available for your entertainment pleasure.

ABBEY HOUSE B&B, *One Dominic Street, Cashel, County Tipperary. Tel. (062) 61104, Fax (062) 61104. 5 rooms, 2 standard, 3 ensuite. Rates for singles: £26 to £27, rates for doubles: £18 to £20 per person sharing. Rates include breakfast. Mastercard and Visa accepted. No service charge.*

Near the foot of the Rock of Cashel you'll find Abbey House B&B, run by Miss Ellen Ryan. This is a very comfortable B&B within just a few moments walk of the Rock of Cashel. Each of the rooms is nice-sized and decorated with pastels and soft colors. One of the rooms has a nice view of the famous Rock.

As you walk throughout the house, note the fine pine woodwork; it was done by Ellen's friend and award-winning joiner Marcus Fogarty. And just so you know, when you are staying here, you are literally staying in Miss Ryan's home – this was the home she was raised in.

ROCKVILLE HOUSE, *Dominick's Place, Cashel, County Tipperary. Tel. (062) 61760. 4 rooms. Rates for singles: £24.50, rates for doubles: £19 per person sharing. Rates include breakfast. Mastercard and Visa accepted. No service charge.*

Patrick Hayes and his mother Anna run this pleasant B&B that stands in the shadow of the Rock of Cashel. (Well, perhaps not in the literal shadow, but it *is* just down the hill from the famous Rock.) You'll find four bedrooms at Rockville House, and each is decorated with simple yet comfortable furnishings. Each of the rooms is large, light and pleasant.

Anna – lovingly referred to by her son as "The Boss," serves up a delicious breakfast for her guests, a treat not to be missed.

Take a moment to check out the pictures along the stairway that leads upstairs – the handsome young man jumping horses is Patrick's younger brother Seamus. The Hayes family hobby is raising and jumping horses.

A carpark out back assures you a place to park when you arrive.

MARYVILLE B&B, *Bank Place, Cashel, County Tipperary. Tel. (062) 61098, Fax (062) 61098; E-mail: maryvill@iol.ie. 8 rooms, 6 ensuite and 2 standard rooms. Rates for singles: £27 to £30, rates for doubles: £19 to £22 per person sharing. Rates include breakfast. Mastercard and Visa accepted. No service charge.*

Not only is Maryville B&B one of my favorite B&Bs in Cashel, it is one of my favorite B&Bs in all of Ireland. Owned and run by Carmel and Pat Lawrence, Maryville is a comfortable and most pleasant place to spend a night or two when you come to visit the Rock of Cashel.

There are eight bedrooms at Maryville B&B, and each is large and tastefully decorated. You'll find new carpet, decorator wallpaper, and warm colors: pinks and yellows. Each room has a hairdryer and tea- and coffee-making facilities. Two of the rooms can be converted into a family room via an adjoining door.

The rooms at the front of the house overlook the busy main street in Cashel, but you needn't worry about the noise being a bother, as these rooms have double-glazed windows that cut out the street noise. Two of the rooms at the back look out onto the Rock of Cashel and are the most popular rooms at Maryville. The deck at the back of the house provides the best view of the Rock of Cashel in town, and countless photographer's tripods have been set here to capture the wonderful sight.

Carmel is a brilliant cook, and your meal will be outstanding. Breakfast is taken in a nice large dining room on the ground floor. The trophies lining the wall belong to the Lawrence's daughter Michelle, who at the time of this writing is a 3-time world champion Irish dancer.

So, whether you decide to stay because of the rooms, the breakfast, the views off the back deck or the chance to meet Michelle, Maryville should be at the top of your places-to-stay-in-Cashel list!

LEGENDS TOWNHOUSE, *The Kiln, Cashel, County Tipperary. Tel. (062) 61292, Fax (062) 62876; E-mail: legendsguesthouse@indigo.ie; Website: www.tipp.ie/legends.htm. 7 rooms. Rates for singles: £35 to £45, rates for doubles: £23 to £33 per person sharing. Rates include breakfast. Mastercard and Visa accepted. No service charge.*

Oh, are you going to like this place! Legends Townhouse, along with Legends Restaurant, nestles at the foot of the Rock of Cashel, and both offer wonderful options for sleeping and dining while in Cashel.

Owners Michael and Rosemary O'Neill are living their dream in owning and running this restaurant and accommodations business. They have done a wonderful job of decorating the seven bedrooms as well as the public rooms. All are invitingly and tastefully decorated. Four of the bedrooms have stunning views of the Rock of Cashel, and these are of course the most popular rooms, so if you want one of them be sure and reserve them ahead of time. All the rooms are non-smoking, and are painted in soft pastels. Each includes a television, large tile bathroom, hairdryer, and tea- and coffee-making facilities.

The dining room is at the back of the house, which means the views of the Rock of Cashel will vie with the food for your attention. What kind of breakfast can you expect? Well, Michael recently arrived in Cashel from his engagement as a teacher at a world-renowned chef's school in Dublin, so your breakfast will be nothing short of wonderful!

WHERE TO EAT

LEGENDS RESTAURANT, *The Kiln, Cashel. Tel. (062) 61292, Fax (062) 62876. £15.95 to £20.95. Open Tuesday through Saturday from 6:30pm to 9:30pm and for Sunday lunch from 12:30pm to 3:30pm. American Express, Mastercard and Visa accepted. No service charge.*

Legends Restaurant is part of the B&B / restaurant combination owned and run by Michael and Rosemary O'Neill. Michael is an internationally trained chef and the B&B and restaurant are the realization of a dream come true for both the O'Neills. Fresh from teaching at a world-renowned chef's school in Dublin, Michael uses his vast skills to whip up meals fit for a king (fit for a queen, too!).

Legends sits at the base of the Rock of Cashel and every table in the restaurant has stunning views of that famous sight. You'll be tempted to ignore your meal, but don't! Michael refers to the fare as classical French and contemporary Irish. The menu changes frequently and depends on the availability of fresh ingredients from the streams, farms and flocks of County Tipperary. You might find such treats as grilled beef medallions with red wine sauce and whole-grain mustard, or grilled lamb cutlets, scallion potatoes and mint sauce. If you have room for dessert, try the warm apple and almond tart with vanilla ice cream sauce, or the roulade of meringue with white chocolate and raspberry puree.

Dress is informal but nice, and you'll want to be sure and make reservation during the tourist season.

SEEING THE SIGHTS

Rock of Cashel. *Cashel. Open mid-March to mid-June daily from 9:00am to 5:30pm, mid-June to mid-September daily from 9:00am to 7:30pm, and mid-September through mid-March daily from 9:00am to 4:30pm. Admission is £3.50 for adults, £2.50 for seniors and students, £1.50 for children, and a family ticket is available for £8.00. Last admission is 45 minutes prior to closing. Tel. (062) 61437.* Save plenty of film for one of the most awe-inspiring sites in Ireland. The setting for this chapel/round tower/cathedral is on a mound towering some 200 feet above the surrounding plains (the peak of the round tower is nearly 300 feet above the surrounding plain). The ruins are amazingly well preserved, and the visitors' center at the foot of the Rock of Cashel is informative. Incredible views of the surrounding Tipperary plains await visitors to the site.

Local legend has it that one day the devil was flying over Ireland. As he approached the Slieve Bloom Mountains, rather than fly over them, he opted to bite a chunk out of them. (Locals will be happy to point out the missing section in the nearby mountains. It's called Devil's Bit.) Displeased with the taste, he spat the earth out here north of Cashel Town.

THE BAPTISM OF KING AENGUS

The Rock of Cashel has hosted many important events, religious as well as secular. One of the most important was St. Patrick's baptism of King Aengus. The story is told that in 450 AD as St. Patrick was preparing to baptize the good king, he tripped and planted his staff rather forcibly into the earth to maintain his balance. After the ceremony, it was discovered that the staff had instead pierced the king's foot, and the grass underneath was moistened by the king's blood. The king hadn't cried out or brought attention to St. Patrick's error, as he thought the pain and suffering were part of the ceremony.

It's this mound of dirt that the structures of the Rock of Cashel have their foundation upon.

The Rock of Cashel (also called St. Patrick's Rock) long held a position of prominence in the history of Ireland. It was used for the coronation of Munster kings from 370 until 1100. The great Brian Boru was crowned here. In 1101, the site was given to the Church by An O'Brien, and it was dedicated "to God, St. Patrick, and St. Ailbhe." A little over two decades later, Bishop Cormac MacCarthy began construction on **Cormac's Chapel**. It can still be seen, and is a fine example of the Romanesque architecture used. Whether you experience bright sunshine, a dull day or a bit of rain while at the Rock of Cashel, is still well worth the visit. Personally, I find that the lowering clouds give the ruins a bit of a mysterious and brooding quality. So regardless of the weather, visit this important and awe-filled site.

St. Patrick's Cathedral is particularly impressive also. Now roofless, it is nonetheless easy to see the grandeur this splendid structure once represented. At the corners of the nave and transepts, spiral staircases run up, up, and up (127 steps) in small round towers up to roof-walks. Connected to the cathedral is the well-preserved **round tower**, which is 92 feet tall. Its door is 12 feet above the ground. The round tower was built in the early 12th century. During the main tourist season (mid-June through September 1), the Rock of Cashel is besieged with tourists, but it is still well worth your time to stop and spend some time here.

Cashel Folk Village, *Moore Lane, Cashel. Open daily 9:30am to 7:30pm. Admission is £2.00 for adults and 50p for children. Tel. (062) 61947.* Watch for the bright yellow, thatched-roof cottage just below the Rock of Cashel. This signals that you have found the Cashel Folk Village, a testament of how much information you can share in a very small area. The Folk Village is a fascinating smattering of items from Ireland's past, and includes half a dozen or so "shops" that represent what you might have seen 100 years ago in a small Irish town. There is a nice collection of surgical tools and medical manuals (thank goodness for advances in science and medicine), as well as a vast supply of farm implements. On a more sober note, look for the "man traps" – large steel leg-hold traps with vicious teeth used to catch men who were stealing food during the potato famine.

There is also a small cottage that houses memorabilia from Ireland's struggle for independence. Old newspaper articles, photographs, firearms, and uniforms help give you the feel for the times and the struggles.

Visitors to the Cashel Folk Village are handed a script that allows them to take a self-guided tour around the exhibits. It's kind of nice to be able to go at your own pace, and still get the information that is of the most interest to you.

GPA Bolton Library, *John Street, Cashel. Open Monday through Saturday 9:30am to 5:30pm, Sunday 2:30pm to 5:30pm. Admission is £1.50 for adults and £1 for children. Tel. (062) 61944.* The GPA Bolton library in Cashel houses an extensive (12,000+) collection of old books and manuscripts, with a few of them dating back to the early days of the printing press. They are especially proud of their first English edition copy of Cervantes' *Don Quixote.* If you are into books as I am, this makes for a fascinating diversion.

The library can be a little difficult to find, but if you like old books and manuscripts, it's worth the effort to find it. From Main Street, watch for the bright yellow building boldly announced as **Cantwell's Pub.** After stopping for a quick pint, turn up the hill there, and watch for the 19th-century Church of Ireland building on your left. The library is on the church's grounds, and shares its parking lot. If you're going to be unable to get to the library during the listed hours, one of the employees from City Hall will let you in if you call them at (062) 62511.

Even if you are not a bibliophile, you may want to head up the hill from Main Street anyway. Behind the library is a fascinating section of the old **City Wall**, which was built between 1319 and 1324. It is augmented now by some intriguing stone coffin lids that were found in the adjacent cemetery during the 19th century and are now a permanent addition to the wall.

Bru Boru Heritage Center, *Cashel. Open June through October daily 9:30am to 11:00pm, November through May daily from 9:30am to 5:30pm. Admission to the Heritage Center is free, and the admission to the cultural evenings is £5 for adults and £2 for children. Tel. (062) 61122.* In the shadow of the Rock of Cashel, (or at least at the bottom of the hill) lies the Bru Boru Heritage Center, a center dedicated to the study of Irish culture, dancing, music and folklore. Exhibits change frequently, so if you've been before, stop in again. There is also a craft shop and genealogy center on-site, as well as a small restaurant. In the evenings from May through September, folk singing, story telling and traditional Irish dancing are demonstrated.

About 10 miles north of Cashel on the R660 is the crossroads town of Thurles, and in Thurles you'll find the **Famine Museum**, *St. Mary's Lane, Thurles, County Tipperary. Open all year on Sunday from 1:30pm to 5:00pm, and June through August on Monday through Saturday from 10:00am to 5:00pm. Admission is £2.50 for adults, £1.25 for seniors and students, £1.00 for children, and a family ticket is available for £5.00. Tel. (0504) 2133.* In 1994, the minutes of the Thurles/Rahelaty Food Committee were uncovered. This important discovery shed light on the way rural congregations attempted to deal with the deadly famine that gripped Ireland in the mid-1840s.

During the 1840s, Archbishop Henry Cotton was the Rector of St. Mary's Church in Thurles. He was so moved by the suffering of his parishioners that he served as the chairman of the local famine food committee. The museum contains a number of interesting documents dealing with the famine period. This isn't a large museum, but rather the efforts of the current parishioners to honor the memory of a million of their countrymen and women who perished in the famine. As such, it's a poignant and heartfelt remembrance.

Kilcooley Abbey, *near Urlingford.* From Cashel, take the N8 northeast toward Urlingford. Once there, take the R689 south to Kilcooley Abbey. A sister abbey to Jerpoint Abbey near Thomastown, the ruins offer an intriguing sight to be prowled through. The original portion of the abbey was built in 1200 by command of Irish High King Donagh O'Brien. In ensuing years, new buildings were added to the abbey.

Today, the abbey is a treasure-trove of sculptural prizes. At the north end is an ancient font with intricate carvings; the wall of the south transept has an abundance of well-preserved reliefs. Above the Gothic doorway is a fine carving of the crucifixion.

PRACTICAL INFORMATION

Post Offices
- **Cashel Post Office,** *Main Street, Cashel. (062) 61418*
- **Tipperary Post Office,** *Davis Street, Tipperary. (062) 51556*

Tourist Offices
- **Cahir Tourist Information Office,** *Cahir Castle Carpark, Cahir. Tel. (052) 41453. (Open May through September.)*
- **Cashel Tourist Information Office,** *Town Hall, Main Street, Cashel, County Tipperary. Tel. (062) 61333. (Open April through September.)*
- **Tipperary Tourist Information Office,** *James Street, Tipperary, County Tipperary. Tel. (062) 51457*

COUNTY CLARE

County Clare has the distinction of playing host to one of the most superb sights in Ireland: the **Cliffs of Moher**. It also boasts the presence of a number of medieval dinners, including those at **Bunratty** and **Knappogue Castles**. Though pretty much touristy, they are a lot of fun, and should be experienced at least once on your trip.

County Clare also has the distinction of being home to **The Burren**, a massive lunar-looking limestone rock garden that has fascinated generations of tourists, geologists, and botanists.

ARRIVALS & DEPARTURES

By Car

As with County Tipperary, I'd suggest you rent a car to see the sights I've listed here. They have a tendency to be a bit out of the way, and even though I've not specifically listed them, there are some lovely sea-side drives along the western coastline of County Clare.

WHERE TO STAY

GREGAN'S CASTLE HOTEL, *Ballyvaughan, County Clare. Tel. (065) 707-7005, Fax (065) 707-7111; E-mail: res@gregans.ie; Website: www.gregans.ie. 22 rooms. Rates for singles: £76 to £140, doubles: £49 to £98 per person sharing, suites £80 to £110. Rates include breakfast. Restaurant. Visa and Mastercard accepted. 15% service charge. Closed from November 1 to early April.*

If you're driving to Gregan's Castle Hotel, especially after a long day, you'll swear you'll never get there. It just seems to be out in the middle of nowhere. But once you get there – whether for dinner at their award-winning restaurant or for a night's lodging – you'll be glad you made the trip. The welcoming turf fire represents the warmth you'll feel from the staff, the decor, and the views that await you here. Situated in a valley at the foot of a road with multiple hairpin curves called Corkscrew Hill, Gregan's Castle – which isn't really a castle at all – has remarkable views of Galway Bay and of the Burren, a limestone rock garden that extends for 100 square miles throughout County Clare.

The rooms are individually decorated to top standards and many have lovely views. However, if you are looking forward to relaxing in front of the TV in your room, you'll be disappointed – to preserve the tranquil atmosphere, the rooms do not have televisions. The hotel is isolated, but offers a wide variety of outdoor activities. You can walk through their lovely gardens, take a stroll or more aggressive trek through the Burren, or stroll along the shores of Galway Bay. If you've brought your children with you, you'll like the discounts they give, and you may want to take advantage of the baby-sitting service they can arrange for you.

WHERE TO EAT

AN FEAR GORTA – THE TEA ROOMS, *Ballyvaughan. Tel. (065) 77023. £4.95 to £9.95. Open Monday through Saturday from 11:00am to 5:30pm, June through the end of September. No credit cards accepted. No service charge.*

The little burg of Ballyvaughan is located about an hour's drive northwest of the Cliffs of Moher on the N67. If you've come to see the famous cliffs and find yourself in Ballyvaughan (perhaps on your way to Galway?), this might be a nice place to stop for a casual bite to eat. This tea room offers an eclectic collection of furniture and snack items for weary travelers. Scones, pastries, Irish cheeses, soups, salads, and a few light seafood lunches are available. The atmosphere is strictly casual, and this is nice place to put your feet up for awhile and enjoy a pleasant lunch. **GREGAN'S CASTLE RESTAURANT**, *Ballyvaughan. Tel. (065) 77005. Set dinner menu for £28. Open daily from 7:00pm to 8:30pm. Like the hotel, the restaurant is closed from mid-October through Easter. All major credit cards accepted. 15% service charge.*

Gregan's Castle restaurant is a dining delight (once you get past the unappetizing mustard-colored walls!). Gregan's touts the fact that they use only the freshest local ingredients for their meals, from local seafood, lamb, and beef to fresh herbs and vegetables. In addition, locally made farmhouse cheeses are available to tempt you.

SEEING THE SIGHTS

If you take the R463 north out of Limerick, you'll come to the shores of **Lough Derg**. Lough Derg forms a portion of the boundary between Counties Clare and Tipperary. This sparkling lake is formed by a widening of the River Shannon over a stretch of several miles. There are several routes around the lake that are noted for their beauty. The R494 on the east and R352 on the west are particularly nice.

If you have problems picking up the R463 in Limerick, you can also take the N7 north toward Nenagh, then catch the R464 at the edge of Birdhill. That will take you over to the lough.

Bunratty Castle, *on the N18. Open daily from 9:30am to 5:30pm. Admission is £4.75 for adults and £2.30 for children. Prices for the banquet are £39.00 for adults, £30.00 for children under 12. Tel. (061) 360788. If you are confident enough in your schedule before you leave the United States, you can call 800/243-8687 to make reservations.* Bunratty Castle and Folk Park is about 10 miles west of Limerick on the Shannon airport road (the N18). Bunratty Castle is a magnificently restored 15th-century castle. Originally the home of the Earls of O'Brien, it was considered one of the most outstanding structures of its day. As you enter the castle, look for the "murder holes" – portals in the roof where various boiling concoctions were dumped on the heads of unsuspecting invaders.

However, if you can fit it into your schedule, your most lasting memories of Bunratty Castle will be of the reception and medieval banquet you'll receive inside. Period costumes, traditional Irish songs, harp music, and lots of fun are in store for you. You'll be greeted in the main reception hall by the Lord of the castle, and all guests are served honey mead – a fruity wine – or a non-alcoholic fruit drink if you prefer. Then off to the banquet hall where you'll be serenaded by lovely Irish colleens while you dine – sans silverware except for a knife – on a meal similar to what the original Lord of the castle would have eaten.

The banquet is held twice nightly throughout the year, at 5:30pm and 8:45pm. From May through October you should make your reservations at least the day before you arrive. On weekdays you may have luck getting a reservation for that evening, but weekends are usually heavily attended, so be sure to call ahead for reservations. The late banquet usually fills up first.

Across the street from Bunratty Castle is a wonderful traditional Irish Shop called Bunratty Cottage. This tax-free shop is fun to browse through whether you buy anything or not.

Bunratty Folk Park, *on the N18. Open September through May from 9:30am to 6:30pm, and June to August from 9:00am to 6:30pm (last tours allowed to begin one hour prior to closing time). Admission is £5.50 for adults and £4.00 for seniors and children. There is a family ticket available for £15.00 (2 adults and 6 children). Tel. (061) 361511.* Adjacent to Bunratty Castle is the Bunratty Folk Park. The Folk Park is a wonderful recreation of 19th-century Ireland complete with artisans replicating the various vocations of that time period: candle makers, blacksmiths, millers, basket weavers, etc. It's a lot of fun and very informative.

Once you've finished your exploration of Limerick and Bunratty, take the N18 north from Limerick toward Ennis. Once in Ennis, take the R489 southeast of Ennis to the diminutive village of Quin and the ruins of **Quin Abbey**, *Quin. Open Monday through Friday from 10:30am to 6:00pm, Saturdays and Sundays from 11:30am to 5:00pm. Admission is free. Tel. (091) 44084.* Quin Abbey, was built in the early 15th century. The religious order that called Quin Abbey home was originally the benefactor of the MacNamara family, and many of the tombs of that family are scattered among the ruins and in the graveyard of the Abbey. The view of the churchyard and surrounding countryside from atop the preserved tower is impressive, and worth the effort to climb the spiral staircase to its apex.

I found Quin Abbey to be particularly intriguing in the mists of morning. It is an impressive, largely intact ruin that beckons you to walk down the narrow footpath for a little exploration. If you are there outside of the hours listed above, there are still plenty of intriguing sights around the Abbey and churchyard; otherwise, you can call the number listed above and the caretaker will gladly open the gate and let you into the inner portions of the ruin.

Knappogue Castle, *near Quin. Open daily from 9:30am to 4:30pm. Admission is £2.55 for adults and £1.55 for children. Prices for the banquet are £32.00 for adults, £24.00 for children under 12. Tel. (061) 368103. If you are confident enough in your schedule before you leave on vacation, you can call 800/ 243-8687 to make reservations.* Knappogue Castle is three miles southeast of Quin on the R469. It's a 15th-century tower house of the warrior-clan MacNamara. It's kind of a romantic setting, out in the middle of the country. A similar program to Bunratty Castle's medieval banquet is held here. A tour of the castle is also available, although the sights are not nearly as impressive or extensive as what you'll see at Bunratty Castle.

Craggaunowen Project, *Quin. Open March through October daily from 9:30am to 6:00pm (last admission 5:00pm). Admission is £4.30 for adults and £2.60 for children, and a family ticket is available for £11. Tel. (061) 360788.* About seven miles east of Quin on the Six-Mile Bridge – Quin Road, you'll discover the ruins of a 16th-century tower house and sitting regally beside a dancing brook in the Munster countryside. The castle was recently part of a historical project whose goal was to restore the old tower house and furnish it with period furnishings, tools, and assorted medieval artifacts. They have succeeded in their goal, and in addition, there are a number of other intriguing items to see and catch your eye at the project. Among them you'll find a replica of the small boat of **St. Brendan the Navigator**, who numerous legends aver discovered America some 700 years *before* Columbus! (Columbus must have had a better PR agent!) In addition to the legends, there are a number of interesting historical and archaeological tidbits that point to the fact that Brendan probably did make the journey to Iceland, as well as North and Central America. (A very *long* trip in a very *little* boat across a very *large* ocean!)

At the project you'll also see a small *crannog* – a fortified island dwelling – that was used by early Irishmen for housing and protection against unwanted visitors. Built on a small island, such medieval structures would have at least slowed the approach of unfriendly neighbors, and made their attacks more difficult to carry out. This is not an original structure, but rather a reproduction to give you a peek into this aspect of Ireland's hazardous past.

You'll also enjoy the *Fulacht Fiadha*, which is the equivalent of an ancient Celtic kitchen. You'll see first-hand what may well be the world's first microwave oven — the ancient Celts used an innovative technique for cooking meat with instant boiling water, and a replica is presented here. It is a testament to the ingenuity of those who went before us.

Craggaunowen is a bit difficult to find amid the winding country roads of this part of Munster. Your best bet is to find Quin (that's easy), then follow the signposts for Craggaunowen Castle.

De Valera Museum and Bruree Heritage Centre, *Bruree, Tuesday through Friday 10:00am to 5:00pm, Saturday and Sunday from 2:00pm until 5:00pm. Admission for adults is £3, and £1 for children. Tel. (063) 91300.* From Quin, head back toward Ennis. At Ennis, watch for signs directing you to Bruree, where you'll find the small but informative De Valera Museum and Bruree Heritage Centre. This recently refurbished museum ife and times of one of Ireland's most influential politicians. served as one of the first Prime Ministers of the rebel Irish It is interesting to learn about the modern history of Ireland and her struggle for independence through the various exhibits here. You'll enjoy an audio-visual presentation that gives you a history of the area as well as a history of Eamon de Valera himself. There are a number of graphic panels and exhibits that feature Mr. de Valera, including articles of his clothing, medals, and other personal effects.

Back in Ennis, watch for signposts to Milltown Malbay (R474). Once you reach Milltown Malbay, follow signposts to **Spanish Point**, where you can contemplate the hapless case of a number of Spanish sailors – a small contingent of the ill-fated Spanish Armada. In 1588 these sailors were fortunate enough to survive both their battle with the English and the wreck of their ship off this point, only to be captured and executed by the inhospitable Turlough O'Brien. Ironically, at the site there is a memorial plaque commemorating the visit of their majesties **King Juan Carlos** and **Queen Sophia** of Spain to this picturesque bay on July 2, 1386, two centuries before their fellow countrymen met their unfortunate fate.

The bay itself is lovely, with about a half mile of white sandy beaches, and nearby changing rooms should you wish to take a dip. Please exercise caution, however: a sign on the beach says, "Bathers are advised to exercise extreme caution at all times at this location." Bathers beware!

Now you're in for a splendid treat. After your visit at Spanish Point, head north along the coast on the N67, and then take the R478 west toward the **Cliffs of Moher**, *Visitors Center is open April through October daily from 10:00am until 6:00pm. Admission is free, although the carpark costs £1.* The dramatic Cliffs of Moher, which run along the coast for about five miles, have awed, intrigued, and astounded visitors and locals alike for centuries with their 700-foot drops to the sea. The Irish name for the cliffs is *Aillte an Mhothair*, which means "Cliffs of Ruin."

Superlatives escape me to adequately describe the breathtaking views that await you at these wonders of nature. You simply must experience them for yourself, and see if you can come up with adjectives that are fitting for these marvelous precipitous cliffs.

Your first stop should be at the visitors' center at the edge of the parking lot. Here you'll learn a little of the history of the area, and they will give you information on the best cliff-side walks available. Take time for them – they will provide some of your favorite memories of the Emerald Isle. In the past, visitors to the cliffs could walk right out to the edge of the Cliffs and peer over the dizzying edge. Large stones along the path now block your ability to do that, and signs ask visitors not to venture too close to the edge. But if you'll walk past O'Brien's Tower, the stone walking path takes you out for additional beautiful views. If the weather cooperates, you can see the Aran Islands.

Buskers (street entertainers) work the crowds in the car park on an ad hoc basis primarily from June through August or September.

O'Brien's Tower, *Cliffs of Moher*. Built originally as a teahouse (really!) in 1835, this tower offers some of the most impressive views in Ireland. If you've seen Irish tourist brochures with a picture of a lonely tower sitting atop monstrous cliffs, this is O'Brien's Tower. During the summers, the tower serves as a small visitor center and gift shop.

Continue north along the coast, or a little more inland, if you prefer. As you drive along, you'll notice changes to the landscape - subtle at first, then gradually more dramatic. The lush green Ireland you have known to this point will slowly give way to a rocky enigma. When this happens, you'll know that you have found the forbidding - and foreboding — wasteland called **The Burren** (from the Irish *Boirinn*, which means "Great Rock"). The Burren is an area of vast limestone slabs with fissures running all through them. The dull gray of the stones is an abrupt change of scenery from all the green you've encountered elsewhere on the Emerald Isle.

The Burren has been described as a vast wasteland and as resembling a lunar landscape. Until you experience it for yourself, you may have a hard time believing that such a place could actually be in Ireland. Oliver Cromwell, the Great Annihilator of Ireland, was not impressed - he complained that there wasn't a tree around to hang any of the Irish, nor was there dirt enough to bury them.

Ancient dolmens with their massive capstones and hundreds of stone "forts" and enclosures speak volumes about the silent peoples that inhabited this fierce and foreboding wasteland during earlier times. These stone structures have been studied exhaustively by archaeologists through the years, and will continue to be studied for years to come.

In addition to being frequented by tourists and archaeologists, the Burren is a hangout of botanists - amateur as well as professional - from all over the world. For some reason this inhospitable section of Ireland hosts a wide variety of plant life, including plants that normally grow only in Arctic regions, alongside other plants more comfortable in the Mediterranean! Take some time to wander around on foot in the Burren. It is really quite fascinating.

While you're in this part of County Clare, you should stop and see **Aillwee Cave**, *near Ballyvaughan. Open March through early November daily from 10:00am to 5:30pm, July and August daily 10:00am to 6:30pm, and January through February there are three tours per day at 11:00am, 1:30pm and 3:00pm, (last tours begin half hour before closing). Admission is £4.75 for adults, £3.75 for senior citizens and students, and £2.75 for children, and a family ticket is available for £13.50. Tel. (065) 707-7036.* You'll find Aillwee Cave about two miles southeast of Ballyvaughan (watch for the signposts). Stop here if you're into caves – otherwise skip it. Aillwee Cave has over 3,400 feet of passages that run underneath the lunar-like terrain of the Burren. Guided tours are well lit – both with lights and Irish mirth.

Just northeast of Ballyvaughan off the N67 you'll find the quiet ruins of **Corcomroe Abbey**. This Cisterian abbey was built in the late 12th century (1180) for Donal O'Brien, King of Munster. While he is not buried there, his grandson is, and his sculptured tomb is still in fairly good condition considering the years that have passed since his departure from mortality in 1267. The ruins of the Abbey are also in excellent condition, and are pleasant to wander through.

SPORTS & RECREATION
Golf

Dromoland Castle Golf Course, *Newmarket-on-Fergus, County Clare. Tel. (061) 368144, £20/£25.*

The fairways and greens at Dromoland Castle Golf Course are exquisite, and the beauty of the course is incredible. You'll encounter rich green grass, water to keep you on your toes, and the occasional rabbit to distract your concentration. Visitors are welcome weekdays. Par 71, 6,876 yards.

Lahinch Golf Club, *Lahinch, County Clare. Tel. (065) 81003, £40.*

Lahinch is a legend in the golf world, and a trip around its hidden holes will have you throw your score card away and just enjoy the challenge. Towering dunes protect well-hidden holes, and your iron game will be tested to the max. Take the fifth hole, for example. It is 476 yards, and a par 5 hole, but unlike any other par 5 hole you've ever played. About 150 yards in front of the green, and directly between the tee and the green you'll encounter a sizable mound. The hill obscures your view of the green, and you must try and put your shot over the hill at precisely the right spot in order to end up on the fairway on the far side. Fortunately, a white stake on the hill shows you the point you should aim for. If you think that hole is tough, don't even go on to the next hole. The pin is again hidden from your view, but this time the long narrow fairway lies sandwiched between two mounds. Your mission, should you choose to accept it, is to hit your tee shot over the first hill, but short of the second hill. Such a shot will plunk your ball smack on the green. A white stone on the first hill marks the location of the pin to help you out. By the way, the green is no picnic either.

If you play Lahinch, relax, don't take your score too seriously, and have a great time. Visitors are welcome daily. Par 72, 6,613 yards. There is a new, kinder, gentler course called the Castle Course that is Par 67 and

5,236 yards. It's not quite as tricky, but won't leave you with as many stories to tell when you're through!

Shannon Golf Club, *Shannon, County Clare. Tel. (061) 471849, £20/ £25.*

Visitors are welcome anytime. Par 73.

Scuba Diving

Kilkee Diving and Underwater Center, *Georges Head, Kilkee, County Clare Tel. (065) 56707*

PRACTICAL INFORMATION

Tourist Offices

- **Ballyvaughan Tourist Information Office**, *Lisdoonvarna Road, Ballyvaughan. Tel. (065) 77105. (Open June to October.)*
- **Cliffs of Moher Tourism Information Office**. *Tel. (065) 81171. (Open April through October.)*
- **Clare Heritage Center**, *Church Street, Corofin. Tel. (065) 37955. (Open June through September.)*
- **Ennis Tourist Information Office**, *Clare Road, Ennis. Tel. (065) 28366*
- **Kilfenora Tourist Information Office**, *next to Burren Display Center, Kilfenora. Tel. (065) 88198. (Open June to October.)*
- **Shannon Airport Tourist Information Office**, *Shannon Airport Arrivals Hall. Tel. (061) 471664*
- **Shannon Town Tourist Information Office**, *Shannon Town Center. Tel. (061) 361555, Fax (061) 361903*

16. CONNACHT

Connacht is the province that covers central and western Ireland. It consists of five counties, all of which are on the sea except County Roscommon. Counties Galway and Mayo are by far the largest counties in Connacht, and two of the largest counties in the country. Connacht – sometimes spelled *Connaught* – is the least populated of Ireland's four provinces. Indeed, large areas of land are relatively unpopulated; driving through portions of County Mayo makes you think you've strayed off the map and are traveling in Wyoming. But in late summer when the heather has changed to purple, the scenes are splendid and you know for sure you're not in the American West.

Connemara is an area of quiet beauty. In western Galway, Connemara is home to the "Twelve Bens," twelve mountains that rise abruptly out of nowhere to dominate the landscape.

CONNACHT PROVINCE

Here and there Connemara is dotted with beautiful loughs, hillocks, and vales.

Galway is the principal city of Connacht, with a population that exceeds 50,000. It's an attractive and active city with a small-town feel. Across from the mouth of Galway harbor are the **Aran Islands**, islands that hearken back to an ancient time. A fun place to visit, the Aran Islands are wind-swept and barren. It's a hearty people that call the Aran Islands home and I think you'll enjoy meeting them.

Connacht is fortunate enough to play host to Ireland's Holy Mountain. **Croagh Patrick** sits impressively along the shores of Clew Bay.

GREAT CONNACHT SIGHTS

ACHILL ISLAND – Achill Island is the largest island off the Irish coast. It is relatively tourist-free, so you might want to venture here for a relaxing and quiet visit.

ARAN ISLANDS – A trip to the Aran Islands is like a journey into Ireland's past. It'll take a day, but it will be well worth the time.

ASHFORD CASTLE – Unfortunately, Ashford Castle is not open to the public unless you are a guest at the luxury hotel now occupying the premises. But its grounds are impressive, and it's worth the time to drive around or stroll through.

CONNEMARA – The Connemara District of Connacht is unlike any other area of Ireland. Lots of wide-open spaces provide serenity and tranquillity.

CREEVYKEEL COURT TOMB – Creevykeel Court Tomb is one of the finest examples of a classic court tomb in existence. Archaeologists estimate it has been here since 3,000 BC.

CROAGH PATRICK – Known as Ireland's Holy Mountain, Croagh Patrick sits regally on the south side of Clew Bay and holds an important position in Irish legend, as it is the site where St. Patrick rid the Emerald Isle of all those nasty snakes.

DRUMCLIFFE – Poets take note: this is the site of the gravestone of W. B. Yeats, inscribed with the epitaph he wrote years before his death.

GALWAY CITY – Galway City is my favorite Irish city. Spend a little time here walking in and out of the shops on Quay/High Street, and take in Eyre Square, Lynch's Memorial Window, and the Salmon Weir Bridge.

KYLEMORE ABBEY – As you are driving through the open expanse of Connemara, you'll have an opportunity to stop and see Kylemore Abbey, an impressive abbey set on the shores of a lake. It has a fairy tale quality about it.

Annually, thousands of devout Catholics make the trek to its summit in a pilgrimage honoring St. Patrick. Further up the coast is the picturesque seaport and shopping haven of **Westport**, where tourism rivals fishing as the number one industry in the city.

My suggestion is that you base your exploration of Connacht in Galway City. It is such a fun and active city, and it's easy to reach the rest of the province from there. So, with that, tighten those safety belts, and here we go!

GALWAY CITY

Galway is one of the nicest towns in Ireland, and one I instantly fell in love with. Galway's name is derived from the Irish word *Gaillimh*, which means "Gailleams's Place." An ancient town, Galway is thought to be the village of *Magnata* identified on a map by Ptolemy in the 2nd century AD. As you might suspect, sitting at the head of Galway Bay, Galway has always been a fishing town.

In 1232, **Richard de Burgh** decided this would be an excellent seat of operations in western Ireland, and he made it so. It remained an Anglo-Norman stronghold for several hundred years. The main families of the settlement formed an important contingent whose descendants would fill leading legal, political, and business positions in the city and region for several hundred years. The names of these prominent families were Blake, Bodkin, Browne, D'Arcy, Dean, Fonts, Ffrench, Kirwan, Joyce, Lynche, Morris, Martin and Skerrit. Watch for those names throughout the town and province – they appear frequently.

The native Irish did not think much of their fellow County Galwegians, and the feeling was mutual. In 1518, a city law was passed that stated "...neither a O' nor Mac shall strutte nor swagger through the streets of Galway." Of course, the Irish didn't take that sitting down, and Galway's history is marred with many battles between the Anglo-Norman families of Galway City and the native Irish of County Galway. The O'Flaherty Clan was a particularly irritating and murderous thorn in the side of these Anglo-Norman interlopers; at one time, the west gate of the city was inscribed with the following prayer: "From the fury of the O'Flahertys, good Lord deliver us."

ARRIVALS & DEPARTURES
By Air

From Britain, you can fly into **Galway Airport**, *about seven miles from Galway City, Tel. (091) 755569*. When you arrive, a number of rental car agencies will be available to you. There is only one bus into town, and that leaves at 1:30 every day. Taxis are available right outside the main doors, and they will whisk you into downtown Galway for about £7.

You can also fly into **Shannon Airport** for your visit to Galway. Many visitors do that, especially once they learn the difference in rental car rates between the two locations. If you do fly into Shannon Airport, as soon as you clear Customs, you'll see over a dozen rental car agencies awaiting you with open arms. The drive from Shannon Airport to Galway takes about an hour or hour and a half.

By Bus

Buses arrive at **Ceannt Station**, *Station Road, Tel. (091) 63555,* in Galway throughout each day from all over Ireland. Nine buses a day arrive from Dublin. The nearly four-hour trip will cost you about £10. The neighborhood the bus station is in is fine, and only a short walk to the hotels and sights to see in Galway.

The bus station is around the corner from the Great Southern Hotel on the east side of Eyre Square.

By Car

Galway City sits at the head of Galway Bay on the west coast of Ireland. The **River Corrib** flows through the center of Galway City on its way to Galway Bay. Galway is reached via the N17 and N59 from the north, and the N16 from the south. The N6 enters Galway from the east and is considered the main road to Dublin.

Sample trip lengths on the main roads:
• Belfast: 5 hours
• Cork: 3 hours
• Donegal: 3 hours
• Dublin: 3 hours
• Killarney: 3 hours
• Limerick: 1 hour
• Wexford: 4 hours

By Train

The bus depot also doubles as the train depot: **Ceannt Station**, *Station Road just off Eyre Square, Tel. (091) 64222.* Ten trains a day arrive from Dublin after their three-hour journey. The fare for the trip is £24. Trains also arrive in Galway from all over Ireland throughout the day.

CONNACHT'S BEST HOTELS

ROCK BARTON LODGE, *Lecanvey, Westport. Tel. (098) 66624. 2 rooms. Rates for singles: £22 to £25, doubles: £18 per person sharing. Rates include breakfast. No credit cards accepted. No service charge. Come and enjoy one of the most gracious hostesses in Ireland!*

Beautiful views of Clew Bay or Croagh Patrick await those who stay here.

LOUGH INAGH LODGE, *Recess, Connemara. Tel. (095) 34706, Fax (095) 34708; E-mail: inagh@iol.ie; Website: ww.commerce.ie/inagh. 20 rooms. Rates for singles: £70 to £92, doubles: £50 to £62 per person sharing, suites: £47 to £60 per person sharing; children under 12 stay free in their parents' room. This former hunting lodge has been restored and is a wonderful place to stay while in Connemara.*

BALLYNAHINCH CASTLE HOTEL, *Recess, Connemara. Tel. (095) 31006, Fax (095) 31085; E-mail: bhinch@iol.ie; Website: www.commerce.ie/ballynahinch. 28 rooms. Rates for singles: £72 to £95, doubles: £52 to £75 per person sharing, suites: £110 to £125 per person sharing. 10% service charge. Ballynahinch Castle has been converted into a four-star hotel with beautiful views of either the mountains or the lake.*

CASHEL HOUSE HOTEL, *Cashel, Connemara. Tel. (095) 31001, (095) 31077, US toll free 800/223-6510; E-mail: info@cashel-house-hotel.com; Website: www.cashel-house-hotel.com. 32 rooms. Rates for singles: £55 to £85, doubles: £54 to £80 per person sharing, suites: £74 to £100 per person sharing. 12.5% service charge. Pound for pound, pence for pence, this is probably the best lodging for the money in western Ireland!*

ROSLEAGUE MANOR, *Letterfrack, Connemara. Tel. (095) 41101, Fax (095) 41168, US toll free 800/323-5463. 18 rooms. Rates for singles: £70 to £95, doubles: £50 to £75 per person sharing, suites: £140. Antiques, large, comfortable rooms, marvelous views, and lovely gardens.*

GLENLO ABBEY, *Bushypark, Galway. Tel. (091) 526666, Fax (091) 527800, US toll free 800/525-4800; E-mail: glenlo@iol.ie; Website: www.glenlo.com. 45 rooms. Rates for singles: £100 to £150, doubles: £140 to £225, suites: £280 to £575. Originally an 18th-century manor house, now a lovely four-star hotel.*

ASHFORD CASTLE, *Cong. Tel. (092) 46003, Fax (092) 46260, US toll free 800/346-1001; E-mail: ashford@ashford.ie; Website: www.commerce.ie/ashford. 83 rooms. Rates for standard rooms: £140 to £254, deluxe rooms: £216 to £312, state rooms: £370 to £467, suites: £545 to £642. I don't believe there is another Irish hotel in the same class as Ashford Castle. Elegance and regal splendor.*

ORIENTATION

Galway lies on the west coast of Ireland, nearly due west of Dublin. It is the principal city of the county that bears its name (or does Galway City bear the name of the county?). As you venture north of Galway, the towns and sights are more rural and ancient, and the beauties tend to be more natural than man-made.

Eyre Square represents the beginning of the town's activity, and it spills over into its very popular shopping avenues southwest of Eyre Square: William/High/Quay Street, Middle Street, and Egglington and Abbeygate Streets. Along the way and intermingled with the shops, there are a number of interesting sights to see, including **Spanish Arch**, **Lynch's Window**, and the **Galway City Museum**.

Galway is a busy town, and is almost always full of tourists. But there's a magic about Galway that makes me not mind all the people that are always on the streets.

The primary shopping and sightseeing area of Galway is in an area about a half mile square. The street that runs along the northwest side of Eyre Square is the beginning of the shopping district. Take it southwest (watch for the crowds) and you'll find some wonderful shops, entertaining pubs, and delicious diners.

Most of the B&Bs are located in the Salthill area, in the southwest corner of Galway City.

GETTING AROUND TOWN

By Bicycle

I wouldn't recommend bicycles in Galway City because of the crowds and traffic. However, if you are using Galway City as a base for riding out into the countryside, then by all means go for it! You can rent bicycles at:

• **Celtic Cycles**, *Queen Street, Victoria Place, Galway. Tel. (091) 566606*
• **Europà Bicycles**, *Hinter's Building, Earl's Island, Galway. Tel. (091) 563355*
• **Mountain Trails Bike Shop**, *The Cornstore, Middle Street, just off Quay Street. Tel. (091) 569888*

By Bus

If you wish, you can catch city buses (fare 60p) to take you to the outlying areas of Galway. The Number 1 bus goes to Salthill, where many B&Bs are located. You can catch the buses at Eyre Square.

By Car

The downtown area of Galway is compact and easy to get around in – if you park your car. If you don't, you may feel as though you are adrift in a sea of tourists and business people as you try to negotiate narrow streets clogged with pedestrians and tour buses! You can cruise the main streets and side streets, but I'd suggest that you head directly for one of several car parks in the downtown area. The closest carpark to the downtown area is about a block northwest of Eyre Square.

You may rent a car at several agencies in Galway, although you will pay a premium to do so. I checked rates here recently and was shocked to discover they were two to three times the cost for rental cars just an hour or so south at the Shannon Airport. But, if you're going to need a car for just a day or so and don't feel like making the trek south to get cheaper rates, here are a few agencies in and around the city:

· **Avis Rent-a-Car**, *Galway Airport, Tel. (091) 568901*
· **Budget Rent-a-Car**, *Eyre Square, Galway, Tel. (091) 566376*
· **Budget Rent-a-Car**, *Galway Airport, Tel. (091) 566376*
· **Budget Rent-a-Car**, *Ballygar, County Galway, Tel. (0903) 24668*
· **Capitol Car Hire**, *Jet Station, Woodquay, Headford Road, Galway, Tel. (091) 65296*
· **Johnson and Perrott Ltd.**, *Higgins Garage, Headford Road, Galway, Tel. (091) 68886*

By Foot
This is the best, quickest, easiest and safest way to see Galway.

CONNACHT'S BEST RESTAURANTS

MCDONAGH'S RESTAURANT, 22 Quay Street, Galway City. Tel. (091) 565001. £5.95 to £10.95. Diner's Club, Mastercard, and Visa accepted. No service charge. Nothing fancy, but very good seafood at reasonable prices.

NEWPORT HOUSE, Newport. Tel. (098) 41222. Set dinner menu for £20. All major credit cards accepted. 12.5% service charge. Many of the ingredients they use in their dishes are homegrown in their own organic kitchen garden.

BALLYNAHINCH CASTLE RESTAURANT, Recess, Ballynahinch. Tel. (095) 31006. Set dinner menu for £23. All major credit cards accepted. 10% service charge. The restaurant for Ballynahinch Castle Hotel is as elegant as a castle dining experience should be, and the food is delicious.

CASHEL HOUSE RESTAURANT, Cashel. Tel. (095) 31001. Set dinner menu for £29. All major credit cards accepted. 12.5% service charge. The menu is simple yet offers plenty of options. The food is splendid. What more could you ask for?

WHERE TO STAY

During your visit to Galway and Connacht, you won't be hard-pressed to find a nice place to stay. If you are here during July or August, you would be best advised to call ahead for reservations, or you may find yourself without having to leave the city to find a night's lodging. There are many wonderful places in and around Galway, as well as throughout Connacht.

Here are the best of the best:

SEA BREEZE B&B, *13 Whitestrand Avenue, Lower Salthill, Galway. Tel. (091) 581530. 4 rooms. Rates for singles: £19 to £21, doubles: £18 to £20 per person sharing. Rates include breakfast. Only open during the summer months. Be sure and call ahead for reservations. No credit cards accepted. No service charge.*

If you want a wonderful place to stay in Galway, you can't go wrong with the Sea Breeze B&B. I first discovered the Sea Breeze B&B through a good friend of mine, a frequent traveler to Ireland. When in Ireland, he and his wife always arrange their schedules so they can stay at the Sea Breeze B&B. Once I stopped by, I could see why they speak so highly of this B&B.

For starters, you'll probably not find a warmer or more genuine greeting than you will receive from Colette and Joe O'Donnell. Next, the Sea Breeze is not a "purpose built" B&B (a home built specifically to serve as a B&B), so it feels more like you are staying in an Irish home than in a B&B. Enhance those qualities with Colette's cooking and Joe's company, and you have a winning combination!

As with many other B&Bs in Ireland, this one has a sitting room for guests. Take a moment and notice the wonderful watercolor paintings on the walls: they were painted by Joe. Scenes of Galway and the Irish countryside are his favorite subjects, and his treatment of them is superb. If you are really persuasive, he might be constrained to sell one or two if you are interested.

Just a block off Galway Bay in a quiet cul-de-sac, the Sea Breeze is within walking distance of downtown Galway, or within a block of public transportation if you'd prefer. There are four rooms, two of which are ensuite, and two of which share a bathroom. Baby-sitting services are available if you've brought your children and wish to have a little time to yourself. The only unfortunate aspect about the Sea Breeze is that they are only open during the summer months. So, be sure and call ahead to make your reservations.

RONCALLI HOUSE, *24 Whitestrand Avenue, Lower Salthill, Galway. Tel. (091) 584159. 6 rooms. Rates for singles: £21, doubles: £19 to £20 per person sharing. Rates include breakfast. Mastercard and Visa accepted. No service charge.*

Carmel and Tim O'Halloran have successfully broken the code for success in the B&B industry in Ireland: provide a pleasant facility warmed by a turf fire and a sincere welcome, situate it in a delightful city, near lovely sea views, and keep it affordable. This modern two-story B&B comes highly recommended by numerous other B&B owners, as well as tourists I spoke with. Right on Galway Bay, you'll enjoy the setting almost as much as the hospitality. And if it's a little cool out, the fireplace will warm you inside and out.

There are six bedrooms, two on the ground floor and four upstairs, and all have their own bathrooms. The two rooms at the front of the house have nice views of Galway Bay. The rooms are pleasant, light, and airy, and feature soft pastels or tasteful floral prints. Don't be concerned about the fact that Roncalli House is on the corner of a busy street – the windows all have double glazing to keep the street noise out. Tea- and coffee-making facilities are available in each of the rooms. You're within a short walk of downtown Galway, as well as Galway Bay.

As impressive as Roncalli House is, the O'Halloran's have another claim to fame: they could hang a sign out that says, "Chelsea Clinton (and her entourage!) slept here." That's right – on her 1997 Irish vacation, Chelsea chose Roncalli House to call home for a few days. If it's good enough for the President's daughter....

ROSS HOUSE, *14 Whitestrand Avenue, Lower Salthill, Galway. Tel. (091) 587431. 4 rooms. Rates for singles: £18, doubles: £19 to £20. Rates include breakfast. No credit cards accepted. No service charge.* Sitting on a quiet cul-de-sac in the Lower Salthill area of Galway is Mrs. Sadie Davy's Ross House B&B. This newer B&B features four ensuite bedrooms that are tastefully (and expensively!) decorated.

The dining room where you'll take your breakfast is elegant yet simple. Sadie is quite proud of the breakfasts she whips up, and you will enjoy them, as many of her return guests have enjoyed them.

Ross House is located about 200 yards from Galway Bay, and many guests enjoy walking along the Galway Bay Esplanade, taking in the scenery and sea breezes that are both plentiful there. It is also convenient to downtown Galway; if you don't mind a 10- or 15-minute walk, you can get downtown on foot. If you prefer to ride, the bus stop is about a block from Ross House.

MARLESS HOUSE, *Threadneedle Road, Salthill, Galway. Tel. (091) 523931, Fax (091) 529810. 6 rooms. Rates for singles: £21, doubles: £17 per person sharing. Rates include breakfast. No credit cards accepted. No service charge.* This delightful two-story red and white neo-Georgian home is a stone's throw from the beach (well, maybe a little farther – about 100 yards). The rooms are large and comfortably furnished, and the pastel colors in each room make it a nice place to relax. All the bedrooms have their own spacious bathrooms with modern fixtures. If a damp day has chilled you a bit, the electric blankets available for all beds will help take care of the chill. Mrs. Geraghty knows how to take care of her guests, and many return to enjoy her hospitality time and again. Tea- and coffee-making facilities are available in each room.

LISCARRA HOUSE, *6 Seamount, Threadneedle Road (N338), Salthill, Galway. Tel. (091) 521299; E-mail: eregan@tinet.ie; Website: homepage.eircom.net/~gerregan. 5 rooms. Rates for singles: £22.50 to £25.00, doubles: £16.50 to £20 per person sharing. Rates include breakfast. Visa and Mastercard accepted. No service charge.*

When you find Liscarra House, you'll have found a pleasant place to stay. This lovely and luxurious new home overlooks Galway Bay and has great views. It is beside the beach, and located near tennis courts, a leisure club, and a number of golf courses.

The rooms are large, bright, and tastefully decorated personally by Mrs. Ethna Regan, your hostess. The rooms include a television, tea- and coffee-making facilities, and electric blankets to help chase the chill away after those dull or damp Irish days that occur every now and then.

You'll take your breakfast in the large dining room that overlooks a lovely landscaped garden. The breakfast menu is varied, and if you have special dietary needs, Mrs. Regan will do all she can to meet them.

Ethna is an expert on all the local sights and sounds to see and hear, and is delighted to help you plan your exploration of Galway and the surrounding areas. This would be an excellent place from which to base your discovery of the Aran Islands, the Burren, the Cliffs of Moher, and Ashford Castle. Ethna can tell you the best ways to get to each of these places, and suggest places to see along the way. Liscarra House is an excellent place to put your feet up at the end of a long day's sightseeing. You'll find a welcome cup of tea and a warm Irish greeting if you do.

JURY'S GALWAY INN, *Quay Street, Galway City. Tel. (091) 566444, Fax (091) 568415, US toll free 800/843-3311. 128 rooms. Rates for singles: £43 to £56, doubles: £43 to £56 per person sharing. Restaurant. All major credit cards accepted. No service charge.*

Jury's Galway Inn is located at the foot of the key shopping street in Galway (Quay/High/Shop/William Street). The idea behind this inn is to provide basic, no-frills accommodations at a reasonable price. The location is an excellent one to base your exploration of Galway.

The hotel lobby is open, pleasant, and modern. Many rooms overlook the River Corrib near the end of its journey to Galway Bay. The rooms themselves are large and plain, but comfortable. You'll find the basics here – telephone and TV – but nothing extra like tea- and coffee-making facilities, flowers, mineral water, etc. Because of its budget focus and nifty location, Jury's Galway Inn fills up quickly during the summer months. If you'd like to stay here, be sure and call well ahead for reservations.

GREAT SOUTHERN HOTEL, *Eyre Square, Galway City. Tel. (091) 564041, Fax (091) 566704. 116 rooms. Rates for singles: £67 to £77, doubles: £50 to £57 per person sharing. Restaurant, indoor swimming pool, sauna, hair salon. All major credit cards accepted. 12.5% service charge.*

Located at the eastern side of Eyre Square in downtown Galway, the Great Southern Hotel has seen Galway City grow up around it. Built in 1845 as a hotel for railroad passengers, the hotel must have been an incredibly grand place for its day. Today, its age is beginning to show, but much of its former grandeur still shines through as you walk into its lobby.

The public rooms have all been renovated, and they retain their old-world feel. O'Flaherty's Pub is a delight, and its decor recalls the hotel's days as the railway hotel for Galway. Guest rooms feature mahogany and brass furnishings, and most are quite large and roomy, although there are a few that are a bit on the small side. The hotel offers a number of fitness activities for its guests, including an exercise room, sauna, and rooftop pool that offers some of the most splendid views of the city.

ARDILAUN HOUSE HOTEL, *Taylor's Hill, Galway City. Tel. (091) 521433, Fax (091) 521546; E-mail: ardilaun@iol.ie; Website: www.commerce.ie/ ardilaun. 90 rooms. Rates for singles: £60 to £70, doubles: £80 to £115, suites: £175 to £375; children under 4 stay free, and 50% reduction for kids under age 10 in their parents' room. Rates include breakfast. Restaurant, pub, gardens, tennis, fitness center, sauna. All major credit cards accepted. 10% service charge.*

This hotel is located amid a quiet residential neighborhood in the Taylor's Hill area of Galway City. Over the years, Ardilaun House has been one of the best places to stay in the Galway City area. Currently, however, it is in need of some attention to things like carpet and wallpaper. The rooms are of varying sizes, decorated in soft colors, and are comfortably furnished. Each room is provided with a trouser press to help you stay unwrinkled. There are a number of fitness activities available to guests at the Ardilaun House, including an exercise room, sauna, and a solarium. There's also a snooker table available.

BRENNANS YARD HOTEL, *Lower Merchants Road, Galway. Tel. (091) 568166, Fax (091) 568262. 24 rooms. Rates for singles: £55, doubles: £70; children under 12 are free in parents' room. Rates include breakfast. Restaurant. All major credit cards accepted. 12.5% service charge.*

Brennan's Yard Hotel is found in Galway's "Left Bank" area, and is a delightful place. From what was once an old warehouse, Brennan's Yard has arisen as a clean and classy place. The bedrooms are each uniquely decorated in a light and airy manner. Antique pine furniture, pottery, and art from local artists grace the somewhat small rooms. Tea- and coffee-making facilities are available in each room.

CORRIB GREAT SOUTHERN, *Dublin Road, Galway City. Tel. (091) 755281, Fax (091) 751390. 180 rooms. Rates for singles: £72, doubles: £104; children under 12 stay free in parents' room. Rates include breakfast. Restaurant, indoor swimming pool, spa, snooker. All major credit cards accepted. No service charge.*

This modern low-rise hotel overlooking Galway Bay has benefited greatly from a recent refurbishment. The rooms are a mix of large, comfortably furnished rooms to smaller but functional rooms. All are well kept and clean and have a trouser press.

The hotel is noted for its animated pub called O'Malleys, and it is popular with both tourists and Galwegians. The views of Galway Bay from O'Malleys are an added bonus. The hotel has a number of amenities available for its guests, including an indoor pool, Jacuzzi, and a steam room. The hotel really caters to families, allowing children under 12 years of age to stay free in their parents' rooms, and offers a discount in their restaurant for children 12 years old and younger. The hotel has a number of rooms that are wheelchair-accessible.

GLENLO ABBEY HOTEL, *Bushypark, Galway. Tel. (091) 526666, Fax (091) 527800, US toll free 800/525-4800; E-mail: glenlo@iol.ie; Website: www.glenlo.com. 45 rooms. Rates for singles: £100 to £150, doubles: £140 to £225, suites: £280 to £575. Rates include breakfast. Restaurant, pub, golf. All major credit cards accepted. No service charge.*

Just four miles outside Galway City, Glenlo Abbey Hotel is a marvelous place to stay. Connected to an 18th-century abbey via a breezeway, this five-star hotel was built in 1993. Originally this was a manor house built in 1740 by and belonging to Lord Ffrench, one of the principal families of Galway. Lady Ffrench felt she needed her own personal chapel if she was to keep up with the Jones's (or the Blakes, Bodkins, Brownes, D'Arcys, etc.). Lord Ffrench was appalled by the hypocrisy and strongly opposed the proposition, but Lady Ffrench prevailed, sort of. The abbey was begun, but Lord Ffrench gave strict instructions that the work was to take a long time. Lady Ffrench died before its completion, and it sat unfinished until the current owners of the Glenlo Abbey Hotel finished it according to the original plans.

They have done a nice job of blending the new sections of the hotel into the existing portions of the original manor house. The rooms are huge and lavishly decorated befitting a five-star hotel. Check out the bars in the Canfield Lounge and the River Room. Both were made from the converted altars of an old Catholic church in Kilkenny.

There is an interesting 9/18-hole golf course associated with the hotel. It's actually nine fairways, each with two greens. On the "front" nine you play one green, and on the "back" nine you play the other green.

ASHFORD CASTLE, *Cong. Tel. (092) 46003, Fax (092) 46260, US toll free 800/346-1001; E-mail: ashford@ashford.ie; Website: www.commerce.ie/ ashford. 83 rooms. Rates for standard rooms: £140 to £254, deluxe rooms: £216 to £312, state rooms: £370 to £467, suites: £545 to £642. Restaurant, gardens, tennis, grounds, fishing, walking trails, golf. All major credit cards accepted. No service charge.*

What an exquisite hotel this is! Resting regally amid 350 acres of lush parkland, this 13th-century Norman castle is a sight to behold. Inside, the amount, quality, and sheer presence of scores of antiques and old portraits combined with rich paneled walls and luxurious carpets gives you the feeling you've stumbled into the private chambers of an ancient monarch. The public rooms are elegant, filled with rich leather chairs, dark paneling, and views of the verdant grounds.

The bedrooms are unique, all well appointed with beautiful furnishings, and are probably the largest you'll find in Ireland for each class of room. Many have antiques aplenty, and all have plush carpets, exquisite furnishings, and marvelous marble bathrooms. Thick robes, slippers, mineral water, and a bowl of fruit greet you upon arrival. Rooms at the front of the hotel overlook the expansive and impressive estate, and those at the back of the hotel look out on fountains and lush lawns that give way to splendid views of Lough Corrib.

If you are romanced by the hotel, you will be positively seduced by the dining experience here. The Connaught Room is a small, intimate restaurant overlooking the grounds of the estate. Rich, dark paneling, an exquisite Waterford crystal chandelier and an open fireplace are the perfect touches to put you in the mood for a wonderful dinner.

But wait – you've only learned about one of the restaurants in Ashford Castle. In addition to the Connaught Room, there is the equally lovely George V Room. With an open fire, gorgeous chandeliers, and beautiful light oak paneling that gives the room less of a regal feel and more of a traditional Irish feel, which is the perfect complement to the traditional Irish cuisine featured here.

There is no question that Ashford Castle is the *créme de la créme* of hotels in Ireland. With such a reputation for excellence, they are able to draw the top talent in the Irish hotel industry, and the service you receive here will be nothing short of remarkable.

Ashford Castle has been featured twice on *Lifestyles of the Rich and Famous*, is repeatedly listed among the top hotels in the world in travel magazines and industry publications, and is quite simply a wonderful place to visit. It has hosted kings and queens, princesses and presidents – so why not you? If you can fit Ashford Castle into your travel plans, I predict it will be one of your most memorable experiences in Ireland.

Ashford Castle is about 25 miles north of Galway on the N84/R234 at the northeastern corner of Lough Corrib.

WHERE TO EAT

MCDONAGH'S RESTAURANT, *22 Quay Street, Galway City. Tel. (091) 565001. £5.95 to £10.95. Open noon to 10:00pm Monday through Saturday, and from 7:00pm to 10:00pm on Sunday. Diner's Club, Mastercard, and Visa accepted. No service charge.*

At the end of High/Quay Street sits the colorful exterior of McDonagh's Restaurant, an award-winning seafood restaurant and a popular eatery with the local folk as well as tourists. Inside, part of the building is a store where you can buy fresh fish, and the other half is an interesting restaurant area. The tables and booths are themselves unremarkable, but there is interesting marine paraphernalia adorning the walls. Lunch and dinner are both inexpensive.

BRIDGE MILLS RESTAURANT, *O'Brien's Bridge, Galway City. Tel. (091) 566231. £2.95 to £9.95. Open daily from 9:00am to 5:30pm, and for dinner during the summer from 6:00pm to 10:30pm. Mastercard and Visa accepted. No service charge.*

Overlooking the Corrib River is the Bridge Mills Restaurant, a casual eatery that is a pleasant diversion from the normal vibrancy of Galway. The restaurant has been divided into a number of small rooms that make you feel as though you are in a much smaller place. The food is primarily snacks: scones, pastries, soups and salads, although dinner is also available in the evenings. Vegetarians in particular will like Bridge Mills Restaurant, as a number of vegetarian dishes are available.

HOUSE OF JAMES, *Castle Street, Galway City. Tel. (091) 565507. £3.95 to £15. Open from 9:00am to 5:30pm. All major credit cards accepted. No service charge.*

Pop into the House of James for a quick sandwich, bowl of soup, or a salad during your shopping. The House of James is noted for its excellent breads and pastries, as well as a number of vegetarian dishes. Dress is very casual.

HOOKER JIMMY'S STEAK & SEAFOOD BAR, *The Fishmarket, Spanish Arch, Galway City. Tel. (091) 568351. £4.95 to £14.95. Open daily from 11:30am to 11:00pm. All major credit cards accepted.*

Hooker Jimmy's relies on the freshest ingredients to ensure that their traditional Irish fare is flavorful. The Glanville family is so intent on this that they own a trawler and much of the fish, mussels, and lobster served in the restaurant are caught off it. The menu is not extensive, but offers standard fare like Irish beef with potato and stir-fried vegetables, and baked oysters with an herb and garlic sauce. Dress is casual.

CASEY'S WESTWOOD RESTAURANT, *Dangan Upper, Newcastle, Galway City. Tel. (091) 521442. Set lunch menu for £12 and set dinner menu for £19.50. Open daily from 12:30pm to 2:15pm for lunch and from 6:30pm to 9:45pm for dinner. American Express, Mastercard, Visa accepted.*

Casey's is a popular eatery, frequented by many Galwegians as well as tourists. The building houses a series of bars and lounge areas, each with its own slightly different atmosphere. The main restaurant offers a variety of modern Irish fare, including such specialties as sausage of duck and wood pigeon on a bed of colcannon with a port and orange *jus*, crab salad with autumn leaves and mango salsa, and a fabulous rack of lamb with a brioche crust and parsnip crumble. Vegetarian dishes are also available, as are excellent desserts. Dress is nice casual.

THE MALT HOUSE RESTAURANT, *High Street, Galway City. Tel. (091) 563993. £9.95 to £16.95. Open daily from noon to 3:00pm and from 6:30pm to 10:30pm daily. All major credit cards accepted. 10% service charge.*

Amid the hustle and bustle of High Street you'll come across the Malt House Restaurant. This small restaurant has a nice atmosphere and is known primarily for its fine fish dishes. Other offerings include duckling a l'orange and escalope of veal Normandy. Dress is casual.

DRIMCONG HOUSE, *N59, Moycullen. Tel. (091) 85115. Set dinner menus from £15.50 to £23. Open daily from 6:30pm to 10:30pm from mid-March through the end of November, when they are closed on Monday and Sunday. All major credit cards accepted. No service charge.*

In many circles, Drimcong House is considered one of the best restaurants in the country. They have garnered many awards over the years. The menu is surprisingly varied and guests will have a number of selections to choose from. Entrees include such tasty offerings as ham-stuffed chicken legs with sweet peppers, honey and onion compote, roast rack of lamb with herb and honey jus, or skate with black butter and capers. There are vegetarian offerings as well.

Drimcong House is just a few miles north of Galway City on the N59. Follow the signs from town directing you to Oughterard, and you'll be on the right road.

THE FFRENCH RESTAURANT, *Bushypark, N59, Galway. Tel. (091) 526666. Set dinner menus for £19 and £27. Open to the public from 6:30pm to 10:30pm daily. All major credit cards accepted. No service charge.*

No, the name is not a misspelling. Glenlo Abbey offers guests more than just rooms and golf. Their dining room, called the Ffrench Room, specializes in modern Irish and international cuisine. The ambiance is quietly elegant; the room is graced with plush maroon carpets that add a regal feeling. The menu is not large, but the selections are varied. Try the roast pork loin, or baked black pudding and spinach wrapped in filo pastry on a white onion sauce. Nice casual dress is fine, although a number of the diners will probably be in jacket and tie.

SEEING THE SIGHTS

Eyre Square is the ideal place to begin your exploration of Galway City. From there, you are within less than a half mile from all the main streets in Galway. The streets are a series of one-way thoroughfares that seem perpetually busy. But since you're going to park your car anyway, that's okay, right? As with most cities in Ireland, Galway's streets change names every block or two. For example, if you are standing at the northeast corner of Eyre Square (near the fountain), the street running along the north side of the square is Eyre Street. If you walk southwest on that street for five blocks, the street will change names from Eyre Street to William Street to Shop Street to High Street, and finally to Quay Street. By the way, this is a great street to stroll down, with many interesting shops and restaurants along the way. In 1999, Galway converted this area into a 'pedestrianized' shopping area, and it rivals Grafton Street in Dublin for entertainment and shopping value. It is a delightful area to stroll, shop, and people-watch.

Eyre Square is the traditional town square that serves as Galway's center point. It's often busy with tourists and business people. It's not a large park, but it is a pleasant one. The gardens in the park are a memorial to John F. Kennedy. The late American president visited Galway on his trip to Ireland less than six months before his assassination in 1963.

On one side of the square you'll find **Browne's Doorway**, the old doorway to the Browne mansion, which has been re-located here. The Browne's were one of the main families that made up the inner circle of Galway's social and political society for centuries. The statue of a little man sitting atop a rock is in honor of Irish-language poet Padraic O'Conaire.

At the corner of Shop Street sits the relatively unimpressive square Allied Irish Bank building, formerly known as **Lynch's Castle**. During the 14th century, members of the Lynch family were wealthy aristocrats in the city of Galway, active in community affairs and politics.

In 1999, Galway changed From Lynch's Castle on Shop Street, turn right on Abbeygate Street, then left on Market Street. Look for the **Lynch Memorial Window**, a black marble skull and cross-bones memorializing the actions of one James Lynch Fitzstephen. It's by the graveyard at St. Nicholas' church. Look up – it's about eight feet off the ground. As mayor of Galway at the time, James Lynch Fitzstephen had the unenviable task of sentencing his own son to death for murdering a Spanish visitor to the city. When no one could be found to carry out the sentence, Mayor Lynch did the unhappy job himself. From these unfortunate circumstances arose the term "lynch law." The marker reads, "This memorial of the stern and unbending justice of the chief magistrate of this City, James Lynch Fitzstephen, elected mayor AD 1493, who condemned and executed his own guilty son, Walter, on this spot." The records indicate that after the tragedy, Mayor Lynch retired from politics and went into seclusion the remainder of his life.

Just below Claddagh Bridge, on the south end of town, you'll find **Spanish Arch**. In former years it served as one of the town gates. Watch for a squat, gray rock structure with two archways permeating it – this is Spanish Arch. This was the point where Spanish ships unloaded their precious cargoes of brandy, wine, and other liquors in days gone by. Originally outside the Galway City walls, you can be sure that many of Galway's citizens found their way here to...assist...with the unloading of such precious cargo.

Galway City Museum, *Galway. Open Easter through September daily from 9:00am to 5:00pm, July through August daily from 9:00am to 8:00pm, and October through Easter on Wednesday and Friday from 10:00am to 5:15pm. Admission is 50p for adults and 30p for children. Tel. (091) 567641.* Located next to the Spanish Arch, the Galway City Museum includes several exhibits on the city's history. It's not a particularly large museum, but it is well done.

An interesting and popular sight is the view from the **Salmon Weir Bridge** in Galway. Bridging the Corrib River at Newtown Smith Street, the stretch of water is often packed with salmon preparing for their journey upstream to Lough Corrib for spawning, stacked like planes waiting in queue at JFK Airport. If you happen to be in Galway the first two months of the year, be sure and check it out – you'll be impressed with the numbers of salmon clearly visible below the bridge.

Near Galway

If you take a short drive north of Galway, you'll come to the small town of **Cong**. In 1951, Cong gained international recognition and interest when it served as the primary setting for the John Ford movie *The Quiet Man*, starring John Wayne, Maureen O'Hara and Barry Fitzgerald. It has not changed much over the ensuing years. The residents are proud of their Hollywood experience and they remember it fondly. On the edge of Cong you'll find the spectacular **Ashford Castle**. Built in the 18th century, this lovely building on the banks of an estuary of Lough Corrib is now a five star luxury hotel.

To get to Cong from Galway, take the N84 north out of Galway to the R334. When you arrive in Cross, watch for signposts for Cong and the R346.

At the edge of Cong are the ruins of **Cong Abbey**, an abbey of the Augustinian order dating from the early 12th century. The abbey and its clerics were the benefactors of **Turlough Mor O'Connor**. He also commissioned the **Cross of Cong**, a beautiful work of religious art. It stood proudly at Cong Abbey for centuries, but has since been moved to the National Museum in Dublin, as it is considered one of Ireland's religious masterpieces. As you walk through the abbey, take the time to look at some of the gravestones. There are some old and interesting ones here – many of which unfortunately serve as flagstones for the paths and are badly worn.

Ashford Castle, *Cong, not open to the public unless you are a guest staying there.* Built in the 13th century, this grand castle, now a five-star luxury hotel, is set in the midst of 350 acres of beautiful park-like lands. This is one of the hotels at which President Ronald Reagan stayed during his 1984 visit to Ireland. But you'll only be able to tour its paneled halls and gaze upon its many antiques if you are a guest of the hotel. (See the entry on Ashford Castle under the *Where to Stay* section.) However, it's worth a slight detour to drive along the long circular entrance lane to take a peek at the castle and marvel at the luxurious estate on which it is situated. To do this, it will cost you £4 per person and £2 per child.

NIGHTLIFE & ENTERTAINMENT
Pubs
Galway offers a host of first-class, enjoyable pubs. Just follow your nose – or a crowd of people you think you'd like to get to know – and you'll be sure to find a pleasant pub.

MCSWIGGAN'S, *3 Eyre Street, Galway. Tel. (091) 568917.*

If you're looking for good traditional music on the weekend, McSwiggan's is one of the better venues in Galway. Saturday and Sunday evenings patrons are treated to fine renditions of traditional Irish music. This is not your ordinary pub; it seems like three or four pubs in one building. There are no fewer than three levels and four bars, so you can imagine the number of individuals they can serve on a busy evening. There are plenty of snugs and open areas as well, and you can have a delightful evening here. McSwiggan's tends to draw a younger crowd most nights, although most evenings seem to have their fair share of tourists.

McSwiggan's has gained a well-deserved reputation for the food they prepare and serve – it's a cut above the run-of-the-mill pub-grub that has become so popular in recent years.

THE SNUGS/GARRAVANS, *William Street, Galway. Tel. (091) 562831.*

If you are a little claustrophobic, you may not want to venture into The Snugs, a cavernous pub that was once a wine cellar in medieval times.

Take notice of the alcove at the rear of The Snugs – it was once a very old and very large fireplace (what on earth did they cook here?). It has been determined that the beam above the hearth is over 700 years old!

The Snugs reminds me of my great-uncle's old root cellar – dark and musky (but not unpleasantly so). The rock walls are whitewashed and give the place a bit of an austere feeling. The walls are decorated with a plethora of photos and paraphernalia from Galway City. Upstairs you'll find a more traditional Irish pub in Garravan's. A turf fire, lots of dark wood and cozy atmosphere abound. Traditional, blues, or jazz music are part of the entertainment Thursday through Sunday evenings.

Theater
TOWN HALL THEATER, *Courthouse Square, Galway. Tel. (091) 569777.*

The Town Hall Theater was originally built in 1820 as the courthouse and town hall. It was renovated in 1995, and today is a 400-seat theater. It plays host to the Galway Thespian community, and has a very active schedule year-in and year-out. Events that have been staged here in the past include performances by the Royal Shakespeare Company, The Abbey Theater, and the Druid Theater. Ticket prices vary, depending on the performance. Contact the theater to find out about their schedule and ticket prices.

SPORTS & RECREATION
Golf
Galway Golf Club, *Salthill, County Galway. Tel. (091) 522033, £25.*

You'll have a hard time trying to decide what to do: golf or sight see. The Galway Golf Course offers fabulous views of the ocean, Aran Islands, and the Burren. Visitors are welcome on weekdays. Par 71.

Galway Bay Golf and Country Club, *Renville, County Galway. Tel. (091) 790500.*

Well, like Galway Golf Club, you'll find it hard to keep your eye on the ball on this lovely course on the shores of Galway Bay. The course was designed by Christy O'Connor, Jr., and takes advantage of the natural terrain around Galway to make for an ideal links course. Visitors are welcome on weekdays. Par 72.

Horseback Riding
• **Ashford Equestrian Center,** *Cong, County Mayo. Tel (092) 46507*
• **Broadfield Stables,** *Turloughmore, County Galway. Tel. (091) 797075*
• **Errislannan Manor,** *Connemara, County Galway. Tel. (095) 21134*

Sailing & Windsurfing
- **Galway Sailing Center**, R*envyle, Oranmore, County Galway. Tel. (091) 794527*
- **Little Killary Adventure Center**, *Salruck, Renvyle, County Galway. Tel. (095) 43411*

Scuba Diving
- **Scubadive West**, *Renvyle, County Galway. Tel. (095) 43922*

SHOPPING

Galway is a wonderful shopping town, with lots of stores to visit. There is probably no larger collection of jewelry stores in Ireland, so if you have been watching and waiting to buy that perfect Claddagh ring, this is the place to do it. There are also a marvelous number of bookstores, woolens and knick-knack stores in Galway. Here are a few:

Claddagh Jewelers, *Eyre Square, Galway. Tel. (091) 562310.* As the name implies, you'll find a nice variety of Claddagh rings, as well as other jewelry at this small store.

Design Concourse Ireland, *Kirwan's Lane, Galway. Tel. (091) 566016.* The Design Concourse features a wide variety of Irish handmade items including wool sweaters, tweeds, linen and crystal.

Faller's Jewelers, *Williamsgate Street, Galway. Tel. (091) 561226.* Faller's features one of the best selections of jewelry in the country. They offer a number of styles and sizes of Claddagh rings, necklaces and brooches. They also have a nice selection of Waterford crystal, Beleek china, and other upscale items.

Kenney's Books, *High Street, Galway. Tel. (091) 562739.* Kenny's is right in the middle of all that is happening on Galway's stylish pedestrianized shopping district. You'll find a wonderful selection of Irish-topic books here. I found a nice selection of Irish coffee table books here, and picked one up myself.

Meadows and Byrne, *Castle Street, Galway. Tel. (091) 567776.* You'll find any household appliances you may need while on holiday in Galway.

O'Maille's, *16 High Street, Galway. Tel. (091) 562296.* O'Maille's is located on Galway's wonderful pedestrianized area, and is a great place to find a wealth of hand-woven sweaters, Donegal and Connemara tweeds, and other upscale clothing.

EXCURSIONS & DAY TRIPS

Galway is an excellent place from which to base your exploration of Connacht. It is easy to reach and there are plentiful accommodations. Trips worth taking include a frothy jaunt out to the **Aran Islands**, a tour of the **Connemara District** of County Galway, and the shopping Mecca of **Westport**. Each is described in full following this section.

PRACTICAL INFORMATION

American Express Office: John Ryan Travel, *1 Williamsgate Street, Galway, Tel. (091) 567375*

Laundry Service
• **The Launderette**, *18 Mary Street, Galway. Tel. (091) 563434*
• **Prospect Hill Launderette**, *Prospect Hill, Galway. Tel. (091) 568343*

Post Office
• **Galway Post Office**, *Eglington Street. Tel. (091) 562052*

Tourist Offices
• **Galway Tourist Information Office**, *Victoria Place, Galway, Tel. (091) 563081*
• **Salthill Tourist Information Office**, *The Promenade, Salthill, Tel. (091) 563081*

THE ARAN ISLANDS

So much of what you see in Ireland is a trip into the past. Now take a day and travel even further back by visiting the **Aran Islands**. Off the western coast of Ireland, these islands open the door into an Irish past like no other place in Ireland. Winding rock walls, ancient ruins, prehistoric forts, and megalithic tombs greet visitors with stony silence. Contrast that silence with the warmth of the thatch-roofed cottages, the friendly island population, and the pubs you'll also find here.

There are three Aran Islands: **Inishmore**, **Inishmaan**, and **Inisheer**, and each juts dramatically out of the Atlantic about 25 miles from Galway City. Inishmore is the largest of the islands, and it receives an abundance of visitors, especially during the summer months.

ARRIVALS & DEPARTURES

There are several ways to get to the Aran Islands – by air, by sea, or a combination of both. The Tourist Information Office in Galway has many brochures of companies that provide service to the islands. Your options will be via ferry from Galway or Rossaveal, or by air from Inverin, 19 miles from Galway. The rates among the companies are similar.

When you get to the islands, you can explore on foot, by bicycle (rented either there or in Galway or Inverin), on small intra-island minibuses, or you can hire a jaunting car. If you are of a mind to spend the evening in the many pubs that feature traditional Irish music and dance, there are also a few B&Bs on the islands that are hospitable and accommodating (see *Where to Stay*). However, the number of B&Bs are limited, so make certain you have lodging before you allow the last flight or ferry to depart for the mainland!

By Air

Aer Arann, *Tel. (091) 93034,* flies to the Aran Islands from the small Connemara Airport in Inverin. The flight takes all of six minutes. A shuttle bus will take you from the Tourist Office in Galway to the airport one hour before flights depart, which are at 9:30am, 11:00am, 4:00pm, and 5:00pm. Return flights from the islands are at 9:45 am, 11:15am, 4:15pm, and 5:15pm.

By Ferry

The ferry is the least expensive means of getting to the Aran Islands: £12 each way for adults, £6 for children. The ferry takes 90 minutes from Galway, and 30 minutes from Inverin. Flying with some of the local air charter companies costs £33 per adult, and £20 for children. The air companies also have several combination packages, including a mix of air and sea transportation, overnight lodging, etc.

Following are the ferry companies that ply the waters to the Aran Islands:
• **Doolin Ferries,** *Tel. (091) 567283*
• **Aran Ferries,** *Tel. (091) 568903*
• **Island Ferries,** *Tel. (091) 561767*

Ferry service runs daily to the Aran Islands, but the frequency varies throughout the year. During the week, ferries generally run from Galway at 9:30am, 10:00am, and 11:00am. Return trips are at 4:00pm and 6:00pm. These are general times; each of the ferry companies has their own times, and they vary throughout the year.

All three ferry companies have offices a half block southwest of Eyre Square on Victoria Place, either next to or across the street from the Tourist Office at the corner of Victoria and Merchant's Streets; all have shuttle service to Rossaveal. The bus costs £3 from Galway to Rossaveal. Buses also leave from the Galway docks, a leisurely five-minute stroll from Eyre Square.

WHERE TO STAY

Note: most of the B&Bs on the Aran Islands are only open from April through October.

RADHARC NA MARA, *Kilronan, Inishmore, Aran Islands. Tel. (099) 61115. 4 rooms. Rates for singles: £18; doubles: £14 per person sharing.*

Radharc na Mara is the ideal name for this pleasant B&B located on the Aran Islands. If you speak Irish, you'll know it means "Sea View." (Of course, even if you don't speak Irish, you now know that's what it means!) A veteran of the B&B industry, Mrs. Anna Beatty is your hostess, and she takes great pride in her home and the welcome she provides her guests.

The views from Radharc na Mara B&B are some of the most wonderful on the island. Looking back to the mainland, you'll have stunning views of the Twelve Bens of Connemara, Galway Bay, the Cliffs of Moher, and the lunar landscape of the Burren in County Clare. If it's local adventure you're looking for, across the street you'll find some rocky cliffs that make for excellent exploration. If you wish, bicycles are readily available for hire to assist in your exploration of the island.

BEACH VIEW HOUSE, *Kilronan, Inishmore, Aran Islands. Tel. (099) 61141, Fax (099) 61141. 6 rooms. Rates for singles: £21.50; doubles: £15 per person sharing.*

Mrs. Bridie Coneely will greet you with a warmth that will thaw the chill you may feel from the winds of Inishmore. Her modern Bed and Breakfast is minutes from a picturesque sandy beach and a short walk from the ancient Celtic fortress of Dun Aengus. All of the rooms are standard, which means there is no in-room bath associated with the rooms. If you've brought young children with you, the McBrides will arrange for baby-sitting services for you if you want to sample the nightlife of Kilronan unencumbered.

AN CRUGAN B&B, *Kilronan, Inishmore, Aran Islands. Tel. (099) 61150, Fax (099) 61468. 6 rooms. Rates for singles: £22 to £25, doubles: £15 to £17 per person sharing. Visa accepted. No service charge.*

On the wind-swept rock known as Inishmore in the Aran Islands, you'll find a haven of peace and comfort in An Crugan B&B. Bridie and Patrick McDonagh have carved their niche in the Aran Islands B&B industry, and their accommodations are some of the most pleasant around. Six bedrooms, five of them ensuite, are featured at An Crugan. Each has been recently upgraded and all are furnished comfortably.

An Crugan is at the edge of the village of Kilronan, about a mile's walk from the ferry port. Its location makes it an ideal place to base your exploration of Inishmore, whether it's the ancient ruins or modern pubs and restaurants that draw your attention. If you've brought children with you, there is a 50% discount for them to stay with you at An Crugan.

If you are going to be staying for a week to really take in the Aran Islands, the McBrides have a two-bedroom chalet at the side of their land that they rent on a flat-rate basis, from £200 to £300 per week, for your accommodations. They do not provide meals with this arrangement, although there is a kitchen in the chalet.

KILMURVEY HOUSE, *Kilronan, Inishmore, Aran Islands. Tel. (099) 61218, Fax (099) 61397. 12 rooms. Rates for singles: £25; doubles: £20 per person sharing. Dinner is available for £13.50. Mastercard and Visa accepted.*

This beautiful large home at the foot of the ancient Dun Aengus fort is a pleasant find indeed. The large, pleasant rooms are exceptional, and the greeting you receive from Bertie and Treasa Joyce will make you feel right at home. If you wish, you can also take your dinner here, and savor Treasa's exceptional cooking skills. If you feel no dinner on the Aran Islands is complete without a nice wine, that's fine too – the Joyce's have a wine license. Both Bertie and Treasa are adept at helping you decide how best to see the Aran Islands. They are willing to share their knowledge of the islands in order to help you see what would be of most interest to you. Like most of the B&Bs on the Aran Islands, Kilmurvey House is open from April through October.

WHERE TO EAT

DUN AONGHASA RESTAURANT, *Kilronan, Inishmore, Aran Islands. Tel. (099) 61104. £7.95 to £14.95. Open from noon to 3:00pm and 6:00pm until 10:00pm. They are closed from November through March. Mastercard and Visa accepted.*

If you come to an island, expect to get good seafood. And if you come to Dun Aonghasa Restaurant on Inishmore, you won't be disappointed. The exceptional seafood is as tasty as the decor is welcoming: the warmth of dark wood and stone, and an open fire will make this a memorable meal for you. Ask for a table near the window and you'll have gorgeous views of Galway Bay.

FISHERMAN'S COTTAGE, *Inisheer, Aran Islands. Tel. (099) 75073, £7.95 to £13.95. Open daily from noon to 5:00pm and from 7:00pm to 8:30pm. They are closed from October through mid-April. All major credit cards accepted.*

Fisherman's Cottage is located on the smallest of the Aran Islands, but the meal they serve is anything but small. Try any number of wonderful seafood dishes, including scallops, lobster, oysters, or mussels. If for some odd reason you don't feel like seafood, succulent Aran lamb is also available here.

SEEING THE SIGHTS

Primarily, the sights to see on the Aran Islands are the ancient windblown rock walls, the few pubs, and the hearty people that live here. An excellent way to do this is to rent bicycles in Galway and ride around to your heart's content.

Inishmore is the largest of the Aran Islands; as such, the greatest number of visitors to the islands land and explore here. The island is approximately five miles long and two miles wide. Visitors will find a hearty population of 900 souls scratching out a living here in this wind-blown limestone wilderness. Minibuses and jaunting cars scour the narrow roads for tourists tired of walking the distances from one sight to another.

Ferries and airplanes arrive on Inishmore at **Kilronan**, the major town on the island.

In Kilronan, you'll find a relatively new exhibit: the **Aran Islands Heritage Center**, *Kilronan, Tel. (099) 61355. Open daily April through October from 10:00am to 7:00pm. Admission is £2 for adults and £1.50 for children.* Many items of local origin are on display here, and give you a flavor for life on Inishmore. Most impressive was the cart used for rescues of individuals who had fallen (or were blown!) off the surrounding cliffs.

Inishmore is home to the most impressive man-made sight on the islands: **Dun Aengus,** *open March through October daily from 10:00am to 6:00pm and November through February daily from 11:30am to 3:30pm. Admission is £1.00 for adults, 70p for seniors and students, 40p for children and a family ticket is available for £3.00.* This semicircular stone-walled fort ends dramatically and abruptly at the edge of a precipitous 300-foot drop to the ocean. Archaeologists estimate the age of Dun Aengus as 4000 years old, but why it was built and who they were protecting themselves against is still a mystery. Massive walls, some 20 feet tall and 18 feet wide, encircle the fort. The structure is 150 feet across, so you can imagine the kind of effort it must have taken to erect this fortress. The fort is located about four miles from Kilronan, so it is a little far to walk. Ride a bicycle or catch a ride on one of the minibuses.

On the way to Dun Aengus, you'll come across the impressive ruins of **The Seven Churches**. These ancient houses of worship conjure up myriad thoughts about who – and how – these ancients worshipped?

Closer to Kilronan you'll find **Black Fort**, an ancient fort estimated to have been built around 3000 BC. As with many of the other ruins on the Aran Islands, Black Fort has also stymied the best efforts of archaeologists trying to determine its purpose.

Inishmaan is the next largest island of the Aran Island chain. Its population of 300-year-round souls brave the wind and the weather to earn a living on the island. As with Inishmore, there are a number of ancient ruins worth poking around in.

Finally, **Inisheer** is the smallest of the Arans at barely two miles square. The most visited sight on this island is the mysterious graveyard and ruins of **St. Kevin's Church**. If you've been paying attention to this book, you might wonder is this St. Kevin also is the St. Kevin who founded

Glendalough south of Dublin. Not so, according to historians. They feel he was a contemporary of that St. Kevin, and some have even suggested that the two were brothers. Whether they were or not is immaterial. I just know that St. Kevin of Glendalough sure picked a lot prettier and more peaceful site for his worship!

Inisheer's St. Kevin's Church is the venue for a special Mass held each year on June 14 in memory of St. Kevin, the patron saint of Inisheer.

PRACTICAL INFORMATION
Post Offices
• **Inishmore Post Office**, *near the pier, Inishmore. Tel. (099) 61101*
• **Inishmaan Post Office**, *Inishmaan. Tel. (099) 73001*

Restrooms
Public restrooms are not prevalent on the Aran Islands; your best bet will be one of the omnipresent pubs. Note: Since the primary spoken language of the Aran Islands is Irish, many of the signs are in Gaelic. Some of the restrooms may only be marked in Irish. If you guess, you'll probably guess wrong: *Mna* is for women, and *Fir* is for men. (So don't guess!)

Tourist Offices
• **Inisheer Tourist Information Office**, *Main Pier, Tel. (099) 75008*. This office is only open during the summer.
• **Inishmaan Tourist Information Office**, *An Cora Restaurant, Tel. (099) 73010*
• **Inishmore Tourist Information Office**, *Main Street, Kilronan, Tel. (099) 61263*

CONNEMARA
Connemara is an area of quiet, rugged beauty. In western Galway, Connemara is home to the **Twelve Bens** (also called the Twelve Pins), twelve mountains that rise abruptly from the Connemara plain to dominate the landscape (see below for more detail). Connemara is dotted with beautiful loughs, hillocks, and vales.

A drive through Connemara gives you time to think and enjoy the country you are driving through. Depending on your mood, and how often you stop, you could easily spend a half day or better in Connemara.

ARRIVALS & DEPARTURES
By Bus
Bus service is limited in the Connemara District of County Galway, so

if you want to see this beautiful part of Ireland, you will need to rent a car (see *Arrivals & Departures* for Galway City).

By Car

Connemara lies between Lake Corrib on the east and the Atlantic Ocean on the west. The best way to see Connemara is to drive from Galway on the N59 to Oughterard, then on to Maam Cross and Recess. From Recess, bear left on the N59 to Clifden, and on around the loop that the N59 makes. If you're not in any particular hurry (you shouldn't be while you're driving through Connemara), you might want to take a few detours. The Cashel Bay area is quite lovely, as are jaunts to Roundstone, Ballyconneely, Cleggen, and Renvyle. Watch for signposts on the N59 directing you to each of these places.

WHERE TO STAY

There are a number of wonderful places to stay in Connemara. Here are a few of the best:

BROOKSIDE YOUTH HOSTEL, *Hulk Street, Clifden, Connemara. Tel. (095) 21812. 36 beds. Rates are £5 to £7 per person. No credit cards accepted. No service charge.*

At the edge of Clifden, you'll find Brookside Youth Hostel. The furnishings, rooms, and about everything else here are basic (some might say Spartan!), but they'll meet your needs if you're looking for a no-frills hostel. Two self-catering kitchens are available for guests. Linens are included.

SUNNYBANK GUESTHOUSE, *Westport Road, Clifden, Connemara Tel. (095) 21437, Fax (095) 21976; E-mail: sunnybank@anu.ie, Website: www.galway-guide.com/pages/sunnybank. 11 rooms. Rates for singles: £22 to £27, doubles: £22 to £27 per person sharing. Rates include breakfast. No credit cards accepted. No service charge.*

The Sunnybank Guesthouse sits proudly and regally atop a hill overlooking Clifden. The converted Georgian house (circa 1814) boasts large, tastefully decorated rooms with high ceilings. All rooms are a little different, and all have been well refurbished. The rooms are quite comfortable. In addition to fine sleeping accommodations, Sunnybank also offers a nice fitness package for their guests. They have an outdoor swimming pool (it's heated), sauna, solarium, and tennis courts.

Sunnybank Guesthouse is the recipient of a number of industry awards, including one for outstanding breakfasts.

THE QUAY HOUSE, *Clifden. Tel. (095) 21369, Fax (095) 21608; E-mail: thequay@iol.ie; Website: www.hidden-ireland.com/thequay. 10 rooms. Rates for singles: £55 to £65, doubles: £40 to £50 per person sharing. Rates* *include breakfast. Restaurant, gardens. American Express, Mastercard and Visa accepted. No service charge.*

The Quay House is most renowned for its excellent restaurant (see *Where to Eat* section), but it also has a few rooms to rent. The rooms are nice sized, and are tastefully decorated. The rooms at the front of the house overlook Clifden Harbor and cost a few pounds more. If you've an extra few minutes, see if you can eat lunch with – or at least chat with – one of the owners, Paddy or Julia Foyle. They are both truly delightful, and are exceptionally pleasant to visit with.

RENVYLE HOUSE, *Renvyle. Tel. (095) 43511, Fax (095) 43515. 65 rooms. Rates for singles: £50 to £90, doubles: £40 to £70 per person sharing. Rates include breakfast. Restaurant, swimming pool, sauna, gardens, tennis, snooker, putting and bowling greens, riding, fishing. All major credit cards accepted. 10% service charge.*

Once considered one of the finest hotels in Ireland, the Renvyle Hotel is still nice but in need of modernization and upgrading. Recent refurbishment of several dozen of their rooms has gone a long way to reclaiming their past glory when, for example, world leaders like Winston Churchill stayed here. Many of the public areas are endowed with photos of past personalities enjoying their stay at Renvyle.

The bedrooms are small for the most part and unremarkably decorated. Several suites have balconies overlooking the pool, but the best views are on the drive to the hotel. Stunning seascapes follow you along the mountain road, but are mostly hidden from view once you reach the hotel.

The hotel has a number of amenities that their guests find enjoyable. They have a swimming pool, tennis court, snooker room, and a playground for the kids. They also offer a discount for families traveling with children, and they'll arrange baby-sitting services for you if you need them. Pets are welcome, and the hotel is wheelchair-accessible.

ABBEYGLEN CASTLE HOTEL, *Clifden, Connemara. Tel. (095) 21201, Fax (095) 21797; E-mail: info@abbeyglen.ie; Website: www.abbeyglen.ie. 36 rooms. Rates for singles: £70 to £85, doubles: £55 to £70 per person sharing, suites: £69 to £85 per person sharing. Rates include breakfast. Restaurant, swimming pool, sauna, gardens, tennis, snooker, pitch and putt golf. All major credit cards accepted. 12.5% service charge.*

Clifden's own *faux-castle*, the Abbeyglen Castle Hotel, offers nice views of Clifden from some of its rooms and from its grounds. Rooms are of fair size, but the furnishings are largely unremarkable. The hotel is set in 12 acres of well-manicured grounds, with gardens, verdant lawns, a swimming pool and tennis courts. But don't expect to stay here if you are traveling with small children; the hotel requests no children under 10 years of age. Seniors, however, are treated with a discount all year except July and August.

THE ARDAGH HOTEL, *Ballyconeely Road, Clifden. Tel. (095) 21384, Fax (095) 21314; E-mail: ardaghhotel@tinet.ie; Website: www.commerce.ie/ ardaghhotel. 21 rooms. Rates for singles: £53 to £63, doubles: £43 to £50 per person sharing. Restaurant. All major credit cards accepted. No service charge. Open from March through October.*

About two miles outside Clifden on the road to Ballyconeely sits the Ardagh Hotel. Overlooking Ardbear Bay, the views are enough to make you want to stay one more night (or two). The rooms are nice sized, and the floral print wallpaper gives them a quiet, homey feeling. The best rooms overlook the Bay, although the views out over the mountains around Clifden are very nice too. Each room has tea- and coffee-making facilities.

CASHEL HOUSE HOTEL, *Cashel, Connemara. Tel. (095) 31001, (095) 31077, US toll free 800/223-6510; E-mail: info@cashel-house-hotel.com; Website: www.cashel-house-hotel.com. 32 rooms. Rates for singles: £55 to £85, doubles: £54 to £80 per person sharing, suites: £74 to £100 per person sharing. Rates include breakfast. Restaurant, gardens, riding, walking trails. All major credit cards accepted. 12.5% service charge.*

Cashel House Hotel is a warm, comfortable, and delightful hotel. It has the feel and personality of a B&B, but the facilities and amenities of a hotel. Built in the 19th century, Cashel House has been magnificently renovated. It's chock full of antiques and old (*old!*) oil paintings. Plush Connemara hand-made rugs grace the floors throughout the hotel.

If that's not enough, their restaurant is considered one of the best in Ireland (see *Where to Eat* section). The restaurant is in a semi-circular conservatory with large windows that overlook the well-manicured lawn and gardens. The food is exceptional, and features the freshest ingredients that add just the right subtle flavorings necessary to make the meals a wonderful dining experience. Whether you prefer fish, beef, or vegetarian meals, there is a tradition of excellence here.

Each hotel room is lavish and unique. Each is tastefully wallpapered and carpeted. Flowers from the extensive gardens are found daily in your room – just the right touch to make you feel that much more welcome.

Riding stables on-site are constantly in use by the guests; in keeping with their thoughtful manner, the owners have provided boots and riding helmets for their guests to ensure they have a safe and enjoyable ride. Luxurious gardens make for a quiet beginning or a romantic end to your day. Pound for pound, pence for pence, this is probably the best lodging for the money in western Ireland! The owners, Dermot and Kay McEvilly, have been in the hotel business since 1968, and the product they offer is full of grace and quiet elegance.

ROSLEAGUE MANOR, *Letterfrack, Connemara. Tel. (095) 41101, Fax (095) 41168, US toll free 800/323-5463. 18 rooms. Rates for singles: £70 to £95, doubles: £50 to £75 per person sharing, suites: £140. Rates include breakfast. Restaurant, gardens, sauna, fishing, boat trips, walking trails, billiards, tennis. American Express, Mastercard, and Visa accepted. No service charge. Closed from November through Easter.*
About nine miles out of Clifden between Clifden and Westport sits courtly Rosleague Manor, an elegant Georgian manor house overlooking Ballinakill Bay. The brother-sister team of Paddy and Anne Foyle jointly owns Rosleague Manor. (Along with his wife, Paddy also owns The Quay House and Destry Rides Again in Clifden.) Together, the Foyles have outserened the serene with Rosleague Manor, which has become a favorite base for those touring Connemara. There are 30 acres of lush lawns and gorgeous gardens available for guests to stroll through.

The house is as exceptional inside as it is outside. Antiques, turf fires, and old portraits set the perfect atmosphere. Spacious bedrooms furnished thoughtfully with antiques and comfortable furniture are complemented by nice bathrooms with modern fixtures. The rooms have wonderful views that make them seem even more tranquil and comfortable.

Resident in the house is an excellent restaurant presided over by Nigel Rush, a Swiss-trained chef. He works his magic with fresh ingredients, imaginative menus, and superb cuisine. A specialty of the house is fish from the nearby Atlantic and many of the inland lakes found scattered throughout Connemara. Beef, lamb, and fowl are also available.

LOUGH INAGH LODGE, *Recess, Connemara. Tel. (095) 34706, Fax (095) 34708; E-mail: inagh@iol.ie; Website: ww.commerce.ie/inagh. 20 rooms. Rates for singles: £70 to £92, doubles: £50 to £62 per person sharing, suites: £47 to £60 per person sharing; children under 12 stay free in their parents' room. Rates include breakfast. Restaurant, gardens, croquet, riding, fishing, walking trails. All major credit cards accepted. 10% service charge.* Once the hunting lodge associated with Ballynahinch Castle, Lough Inagh Lodge is now a fine hotel with a reputation for excellence all its own. Its owners, John and Moira O'Connor, have overseen its refurbishment with a zeal for perfection. The results are outstanding: turf fires, period antiques, and a wonderful, friendly atmosphere.

Like her sibling, Lough Inagh Lodge's rooms are large, tastefully decorated, and all have lovely views of either Lough Inagh or the mountains and countryside. Lough Inagh Lodge caters to families, with a discount available for children. If you've brought a pet, the hotel accepts them also.

BALLYNAHINCH CASTLE HOTEL, *Recess, Connemara. Tel. (095) 31006, Fax (095) 31085; E-mail: bhinch@iol.ie; Website: www.commerce.ie/ ballynahinch. 28 rooms. Rates for singles: £72 to £95, doubles: £52 to £75 per person sharing, suites: £110 to £125 per person sharing. Rates include breakfast. Restaurant, gardens, croquet, riding, shooting, walking trails. All major credit cards accepted. 10% service charge.*

Simply put, Ballynahinch Castle is an entrancing place, from the live red fox that often greets tourists at the front door to the impeccable service. Ancestral home of the Martin Clan of Connemara, Ballynahinch Castle has been converted into a four-star hotel. The rooms – all individually decorated – are spacious and offer beautiful views of either the mountains or the lake.

During the 1930s, the eccentric (and wealthy) Maharajah Ranjitsinji purchased Ballynahinch Castle as a winter get-away to relax and entertain his friends. Pictures of the Maharajah grace some of the walls and help put a name with the face. In recent years, Ballynahinch Castle Hotel has earned the reputation as a shooting center, where sportsmen and sportswomen come from all over the world to participate in five annual woodcock bird hunts sponsored by the hotel. In addition to the exceptional service and the warmth of Ballynahinch Castle, the restaurant is also impressive. Looking out over the Owenmore River as it quietly fills Ballynahinch Lake, the flood-lit shores add a peaceful touch to your dining experience. The food is delicious, the service efficient, and the atmosphere tranquil.

Ballynahinch Castle Hotel is rightfully proud of their designation as *Ireland's Hotel of the Year* in 1994.

WHERE TO EAT

In addition to these two fine restaurants, check out those under *Where to Eat* for Clifden (coming up in a few pages) for more places to address your hunger while touring Connemara.

BALLYNAHINCH CASTLE RESTAURANT, *Recess, Ballynahinch. Tel. (095) 31006. Set dinner menu for £23. Open from 7:00pm until 9:30pm. All major credit cards accepted. 10% service charge.*

The romantic setting of Ballynahinch Castle holds for the dining room as well. The atmosphere is relaxed yet elegant, with service as efficient and attentive as any restaurant in Ireland. Overlooking the Owenmore River as it serenely fills Ballynahinch Lake, it's easy to get distracted from the excellent fare prepared by the chef – until the food arrives, and your attention is diverted back to the task at hand.

Typical offerings include poached breast of guinea fowl with herbs and vegetables, and pan-fried pork fillet with sherry and mushroom sauce. Desserts are terrific; try the three-chocolate mousse with puree of fresh fruit. Jacket and tie are requested.

CASHEL HOUSE RESTAURANT, *Cashel. Tel. (095) 31001. Set dinner menu for £29. Open for dinner daily from 6:30pm to 9:30pm and for lunch from 1:00pm to 2:00pm. All major credit cards accepted. 12.5% service charge.*

Cashel House the restaurant is as impressive as Cashel House the hotel, which is why heads of state dine here on occasion. The dining room overlooks the floral-strewn grounds. The menu is simple yet offers plenty of options. The food is splendid. What more could you ask for? Offerings might include sautéed monkfish with a shrimp sauce, roast rack of spring lamb, filo chicken in a tarragon sauce, or and guinea fowl with grapes and Madeira. Vegetarian dishes are also available.

SEEING THE SIGHTS

To begin your tour of Connemara, take the N59 north from Galway toward **Oughterard**. At Oughterard, head east to the shores of **Lough Corrib**. This splendid lake in the west of Ireland is large – over 30 miles long – and narrow, at some points only about a half-mile wide. Tradition holds that it possesses one island for every day of the year: 365. The lake is reached from several points, but you can receive a tour of parts of the lake in the small village of Oughterard. Local fishermen can be enticed to take small groups out on the lake. A favorite stopping point is Inchagoill, a small island with the ruins of a 5th-century church as well as a 12th-century church. Prices vary and are subject to negotiation, but expect to pay from £5 to £10 per person.

Called the "Gateway to Connemara", Oughterard (pronounced "OOK-ter-ard,") sits proudly on the banks of the River Owenriff, about a mile from the western side of Lough Corrib. Oughterard is a delightful place to stop before continuing on to Connemara. It is also an important angling center in this part of the country.

Aughnanure Castle, *near Oughterard. Open June through mid-September daily from 9:30am to 4:30pm. The rest of the year the caretaker has a key. Admission is £1. Tel. (091) 552214.* Watch for the signposts in Oughterard pointing you to Aughnanure Castle, the former stronghold of the vaunted Irish warriors named O'Flaherty. Members of the O'Flaherty clan were frequent visitors to Galway City during the 15th and 16th centuries. But welcome visitors they were not. In fact, the west gate to Galway City once held the inscription: "From the fury of the O'Flahertys, good Lord deliver us." Another story of the O'Flaherty's fierceness tells of the time they paid the rent on their castle by sending the head of the rent collector to his father.

Their castle is a six-story tower house with several squat round towers. It was recently restored and is now open to the public.

East of Lough Corrib, about a mile north of Headford on the R334, stand the ruins of **Ross Errilly Friary** (follow the signs from the center square of Headford). Built in 1351 by Raymond de Burgo, and enlarged in 1498, Ross Friary was built for the use of the Franciscans. The extensive ruins include the nave, transepts, chapel, choir, cloister, kitchen and bakery. At the end of the 15th century the splendid tower was added.

Ross Friary is wonderfully preserved, and absolutely invites exploration. As you wander through the ruins, you may find yourself contemplating what the lives of the monks who lived here might have been like. You'll find the cloister where the monks meditated, the church where they prayed, and other areas for the more mundane aspects of monkish life. The monks were chased off seven times by unfriendly visitors, including once by the legendary Oliver Cromwell himself. The Franciscans kept returning to the friary until it was abandoned in 1753.

Be sure and check out the wonderful tombstones scattered throughout the church and its grounds. Some are quite old. On a recent visit to Ireland, two of my teenage children claimed this was one of their favorite ruins of all those we visited (and we visited many).

From Oughterard, continue west on the N59. Just outside of Recess, watch for the R340 and signs pointing you to **Cashel Bay**. Along the western coast of Connemara is the splendid secluded cove known as Cashel Bay. In days gone by it served as a haven from the winds that battered ships on the Atlantic, and perhaps provided anchorage for a pirate or two who was seeking peaceful anonymity for awhile. Today it is a popular fishing spot, and provides some wonderful "photo-ops" for tourists. Cashel Bay is actually one of the inland fingers of Bertraghboy Bay.

You can also reach Cashel Bay by a more scenic seaside route if you wish. Take the R336 out of Galway City and follow it along the sea to Screeb. Just past Screeb, take the R340 to Cashel Bay. It will take you a lot longer than the Oughterard route, but it does provide some memorable scenery.

Connemara National Park & Visitor Center. *The park is open daily all year, and the visitor center is open April through September from 10:00am to 6:00pm. Admission is free, although the car park costs £1. Tel. (095) 41054.* This is the starting point for a number of walking trails through Connemara State Park. Walking trails are short or long, depending on your pleasure. There are those who will tell you that the only true way to appreciate the beauty of Connemara is to get out and walk its hills and vales. Try one of the following trekking companies: **Connemara Heritage Walks**, *Clifden, Tel. (095) 21379* or **Western Trekking**, *Galway, Tel. (091) 25806.* They have a number of suggested walks available for walkers of all experience levels, and they'll be glad to help you plan a trip.

As you travel along in Connemara National Park, you'll note the **Twelve Bens** (also called the Twelve Pins), twelve peaks of Connemara. The highest is Benbaun at 2,355 feet in elevation. These mountains are largely devoid of vegetation, except tundra-height plants and low-lying heather. The Twelve Bens are often shrouded in clouds, giving a brooding feeling as they stand guard over the rugged Connemara beauty.

Kylemore Abbey, *near Letterfrack; grounds are open all year daily from 9:30am to 5:30pm; Website: www.kylemoreabbey.ie. Admission is £3.30 for the gardens and £3.30 for the abbey. A combined ticket is available for £6.00. Tel. (095) 41113.* On the N59 between Letterfrack and Leenane, you'll find the impressive Kylemore Abbey. One of the most photographed abbeys in Ireland, it nestles on the shores of Kylemore Lake. Originally built as a residence for a wealthy Member of Parliament in the late 1800's, it now serves as a secondary school for girls. Unfortunately, very little of the Abbey itself is open to the public – one or two rooms in addition to the entry hall. Several hundred yards from the Abbey, around the shores of the lake, is a lovely little Gothic Chapel that's worth walking to and looking at: it reminds me of a dollhouse.

If you come from the direction of Letterfrack, and are headed for Leenane, be sure to look over your shoulder. The best views of Kylemore Abbey are from across the lake, and the diminutive chapel peeking through the treetops almost steals the show from its much larger and more publicized neighbor.

SPORTS & RECREATION
Golf
Connemara Golf Club, *Clifden, County Galway. Tel. (095) 23502, £18/£18.*

Along the shores of the Atlantic Ocean you'll find the Connemara Golf Club. The views are superlative, and the golf isn't too bad either. The fairways snake among small dunes and truly defines links golf. You may find several of the holes unsettling, especially the tough 14th, which has its green set high on the hillside. Visitors are welcome every day except Sunday. Par 72, 7,174 yards.

Horseback Riding
• **Broadfield Stables**, *Turloughmore, County Galway. Tel. (091) 797075*
• **Errislannan Manor**, *Connemara, County Galway. Tel. (095) 21134*
• **Feeney's Equestrian Center**, *Tonabrockey, Bushypark, Galway. Tel. (091) 527579*

PRACTICAL INFORMATION
Post Office
• **Oughterard Post Office**, *Main Street, Oughterard. Tel. (091) 82201*

Restrooms
Public restrooms are not prevalent on the Aran Islands; your best bet to find a restroom will be in one of the omnipresent pubs.

Note: Given the rural nature of Connemara and the wide distances between towns, be on the alert for places of business that might have restrooms (pubs always do!). Irish is frequently spoken in these rural areas, and many of the signs are in Gaelic. Some of the restrooms may only be marked in Irish. If you guess, you'll probably guess wrong: *Mna* is for women, and *Fir* is for men. (So don't guess!)

Tourist Office
• **Oughterard Tourist Information Office**, *Main Street, Oughterard, Tel. (091) 82808*

CLIFDEN
Clifden is an orderly little hamlet at the junction of the R341 and the N59 at the western edge of the Connemara District. It has a serene setting sheltered between the mountains and the Atlantic Ocean. Its Irish name is *An Clochan*, which means "The Stepping Stones."

The steeples of the local Catholic and Protestant churches lift skyward above the town, and beyond them are even higher *natural* steeples – the Twelve Bens – that rise majestically in the distance.

ARRIVALS & DEPARTURES
By Bus
Bus service does reach Clifden. Buses leave Galway from **Ceannt Station**, *Station Road, Tel. (091) 63555* six times a day during the summer, and once a day the rest of the year. Buses arrive and leave from **Cullen's Coffee Shop** on Market Street.

By Car
Clifden is at the western edge of Connemara, County Galway, and Ireland. It is on the N59 about 50 miles west of Oughterard.

ORIENTATION
Clifden is a smallish place with two main streets: Main and Market Streets. They parallel one another, and compete with one another for

your attention. It's a pleasant place to stroll and pop into a shop here or a pub or restaurant there.

GETTING AROUND TOWN

By Bicycle

Unless you arrived here on bicycle and are just passing though, there's no need for a bike here. The town is small enough to traverse on foot in 20 minutes. Some folks catch the bus from Galway, and then rent a bicycle to see the surrounding areas. If that's your idea of fun, stop by **Mannion's Rent-a-Bike**, *Bridge Street, Clifden, Tel. (095) 21160*, and they'll outfit you.

By Car

Park your car. None of the shops has a drive-through window.

By Foot

You guessed it – walking is the way to see Clifden.

WHERE TO STAY

BROOKSIDE YOUTH HOSTEL, *Hulk Street, Clifden, Connemara. Tel. (095) 21812. 36 beds. Rates are £5 to £7 per person. No credit cards accepted. No service charge.*

Located at the edge of Clifden, the furnishings, rooms, and everything else here are basic (some might say spartan). Two self-catering kitchens are available for guests. Linens are included.

SUNNYBANK GUESTHOUSE, *Westport Road, Clifden, Connemara Tel. (095) 21437, Fax (095) 21976; E-mail: sunnybank@anu.ie, Website: www.galway-guide.com/pages/sunnybank. 11 rooms. Rates for singles: £22 to £27, doubles: £22 to £27 per person sharing. Rates include breakfast. No credit cards accepted. No service charge.*

The Sunnybank Guesthouse sits proudly and regally atop a hill overlooking Clifden. The converted Georgian house (circa 1814) boasts large, tastefully decorated rooms with high ceilings. All rooms are a little different, and all have been well refurbished. The rooms are quite comfortable. In addition to fine sleeping accommodations, Sunnybank also offers a nice fitness package for their guests. They have an outdoor swimming pool (it's heated), sauna, solarium, and tennis courts.

Sunnybank Guesthouse is the recipient of a number of industry awards, including one for outstanding breakfasts.

THE QUAY HOUSE, *Clifden. Tel. (095) 21369, Fax (095) 21608. 10 rooms. Rates for singles: £30 to £35, doubles: £30 to £35 per person sharing. Rates include breakfast. Restaurant, gardens. Diner's Club, Mastercard, Visa accepted. No service charge.*

The Quay House is most renowned for its excellent restaurant (see *Where to Eat* section), but it also has a few rooms to rent. The rooms are nice sized, and are tastefully decorated. The rooms at the front of the house overlook Clifden Harbor and cost a few pounds more. If you've an extra few minutes, see if you can eat lunch with – or at least chat with – one of the owners, Paddy or Julia Foyle. They are both truly delightful, and are exceptionally pleasant to visit with.

ABBEYGLEN CASTLE HOTEL, *Clifden, Connemara. Tel. (095) 21201, Fax (095) 21797; E-mail: info@abbeyglen-castle.com; Website: www.abbeyglen-castle.com. 36 rooms. Rates for singles: £64 to £78, doubles: £49 to £65 per person sharing, suites: £69 to £85 per person sharing. Rates include breakfast. Restaurant, swimming pool, sauna, gardens, tennis, snooker, pitch and putt golf. All major credit cards accepted. 12.5% service charge.*

Clifden's own *faux-castle*, the Abbeyglen Castle Hotel, offers nice views of Clifden from some of its rooms and from its grounds. Rooms are of adequate size, but the furnishings are largely unremarkable. The hotel is set in 12 acres of well-manicured grounds, with gardens, verdant lawns, a swimming pool and tennis courts. But don't expect to stay here if you are traveling with small children; the hotel requests no children under 10 years of age. Seniors, however, are treated with a discount all year except July and August.

THE ARDAGH HOTEL, *Ballyconeely Road, Clifden. Tel. (095) 21384, Fax (095) 21314; E-mail: ardaghhotel@tinet.ie; Website: www.commerce.ie/ardaghhotel. 21 rooms. Rates for singles: £53 to £63, doubles: £43 to £50 per person sharing. Restaurant. All major credit cards accepted. No service charge. Open from March through October.*

About two miles outside Clifden on the road to Ballyconeely sits the Ardagh Hotel. Overlooking Ardbear Bay, the views are just enough to make you want to stay one more night (or two). The rooms are nice sized, and the floral print wallpaper gives them a quiet, homey feeling. The best rooms overlook the Bay, although the views out over the mountains around Clifden are very nice too. Each room has tea- and coffee-making facilities.

WHERE TO EAT

O'GRADY'S SEAFOOD RESTAURANT, *Market Street, Clifden. Tel. (095) 21450. £6.95 to £12.95. From June through September O'Grady's is open daily from 12:30pm to 2:30pm, and 6:30pm to 10:00pm. The rest of the year those are their hours, except that they are closed on Sunday. American Express, Mastercard, and Visa accepted. No service charge.*

O'Grady's is a nice quiet restaurant on the main shopping street in Clifden. Known for their excellent seafood menu, you'll be pleased with the entrees you find here. Samples of their menu include fillet of cod, braised monkfish, or grilled fillet of turbot with a compote of rhubarb and champagne butter cream. There are a few non-seafood dishes, but the specialties here are from the depths of the deep blue.

DESTRY RIDES AGAIN, *Main Street, Clifden. Tel. (095) 21722. £3.50 to £11.95. Open Tuesday through Sunday from noon to 3:00pm, and from 6:00pm to 10:00pm. They are closed December through the end of February. Mastercard and Visa accepted. No service charge.*

Destry's is a small sandwich shop cafe in the center of town on Main Street. A pleasant place, the furnishings are simple, the service great, and the food memorable. Destry's is owned by Paddy and Julia Foyle, and if you visit, you will assuredly meet one or the other (if not both) of them.

O'DOWD'S SEAFOOD BAR AND RESTAURANT, *Roundstone. Tel. (095) 35809. £4.95 to £14.95. The bar and the restaurant are open daily from 12:30pm to 9:30pm. (On Sunday the bar is open 12:30pm to 2:00pm, and 4:00pm to 9:30pm.) American Express, Mastercard, and Visa are accepted. No service charge.*

O'Dowd's is a popular seafood bar and traditional Irish pub. The views of the Atlantic are an added bonus. Food is served in both the bar as well as the restaurant area. Seafood is the specialty, and the menu provides a wide selection: lobster, mussels, crab salad, salmon and oysters. They also offer traditional Irish dishes if that's what you're looking for, and a nice wild game menu, including venison, quail, duck, and pheasant.

Roundstone is a little off the beaten track, but well worth the effort to find it. Take the R341 south of Clifden and follow the signposts for Roundstone.

THE QUAY HOUSE, *Clifden. Tel. (095) 21369. Á la carte menu available from £3.50 to £14.95, set dinner menu for £19.50. Open daily for dinner from 7:00pm to 9:30pm, and during the high season (from the end of May through the end of August) they are open for lunch from noon to 4:00pm. Mastercard and Visa accepted. No service charge.*

The Quay House sits quietly overlooking Ardbear Bay, an estuary of the Atlantic Ocean. Paddy and Julia Foyle run the Quay House as well as the cafe Destry Rides Again (see entry above), and while they are quite different as far as atmosphere and ambiance, they have one critical thing in common: the food is of the highest quality and simply delicious. Some of the winners here include warm mussel and bacon salad with anchovy dressing, and the smoked salmon chowder. The dining room is pleasant and bordering on elegant, but not stuffy. A conservatory adjoins the dining room and is a wonderful place to have a spot of afternoon tea.

SEEING THE SIGHTS

The primary things to see and do in Clifden are her shops, and I recommend that you take the time to stroll through those shops. The two-block (side-by-side) shopping district is a pleasant one. Perhaps not as picturesque or extensive as Westport or Galway, there are still some interesting shops and good prices. Take a moment and slip into **O'Hehir's Woolen Shop**, *Market Street, Tel. (095) 21282.* They have a wide selection of sweaters, caps, and other Irish clothing. If you're interested in Irish craftwork, you might also want to stop by the **Celtic Shop**.

If you are interested in art, there are several art shops in Clifden you might enjoy stopping by **Lavelle Art Gallery**, *Main Street, Tel. (095) 21882,* or **Clifden Art Gallery**, *Main Street, (095) 21788.* Both offer marvelous works of art, much of it by local artists. Scenes of the Connemara landscape abound. While you're strolling about, stop by for a sandwich at **Destry's** on Main Street.

Look for the signposts directing you to the **Sky Drive**. This short (10 mile) drive takes you out on the peninsula west of Clifden and offers brilliant ocean views. If you've seen lots of those on your trip, turn your attention inland, and you'll have plenty of wonderful views too.

SPORTS & RECREATION
Golf
Connemara Golf Club, *Clifden, County Galway. Tel. (095) 23502, £18/£18.*

Along the shores of the Atlantic Ocean you'll find Connemara Golf Club. The views are superlative, and the golf isn't too bad either! Visitors are welcome every day except Sunday. Par 72, 7,174 yards.

PRACTICAL INFORMATION
Laundry Service
• **Hillview Launderette**, *Church Hill, Clifden. Tel. (095) 21836*

Tourist Office
• **Clifden Tourist Information Office**, *Market Street, Clifden, Tel. (095) 21163*

WESTPORT
Westport is at the head of Clew Bay, an island-studded estuary on this western edge of Ireland. Its Irish name bears no resemblance to its English name: *Cathair na Mart*, which means, "The Stone Fort of the Beeves." Unlike so many other Irish cities, this one was well planned from the beginning. It was plotted by James Wyatt, a famed architect. Of particular note is The Mall (Westport's main street), which has lines of lime trees on either side of the Carrowbeg River.

Irish and tourists alike head for Westport to savor her shops, and there are many to be visited. I enjoyed the atmosphere, although during the summer months there can be many tourists swarming over Westport and her shops.

ARRIVALS & DEPARTURES

By Air

There is no airport in Westport, however there is one about 35 miles away. Visitors from Britain or elsewhere in Ireland can fly into **Horan International Airport**, *located in the small town of Knock in County Mayo, Tel. (094) 67222*, and known most frequently as Knock Airport. Horan International Airport has about a half dozen rental car desks awaiting you as you enter the small terminal. One of these would be a good choice – there are no other options as far as taxi or bus service to any of the surrounding towns.

By Bus

There is no formal bus station in **Westport**, even though two buses a day arrive from Galway. (Bus service between Westport and Galway is only during the week. There are no weekend routes.) Passengers are dropped off at the Grand Central Hotel on The Octagon in town. The neighborhood is fine, and you'll be right where all the action is.

Bus service runs from Galway to **Ballina** nine times each day (five buses on Sundays). The Bus Station is on Station Road, *Tel. (096) 71800.*

By Car

Westport is nestled in a crook of land at the head of Clew Bay on the western coast of Ireland. It is reached via the N5 coming from the north and by the N59 coming from Galway.

Depending on the route you take and how often you stop, Westport is anywhere from a 90-minute to a three hour drive from Galway. The most direct route is via the N17 north of Galway to Castlebar, then west on the N5 to Westport. The more circuitous route through Connemara affords the opportunity to experience the beauties of that particular area.

By Train

For **Westport**, the train depot is **Westport Station**, *Altamount Street, Tel. (098) 25253*. Three trains a day arrive from Dublin via Athlone (not Galway). The fare for the three and a half-hour ride to Dublin is £24. The station is in a very nice section of town, and a short walk to all of Westport's shops.

The train station in **Ballina** welcomes three trains per weekday from Dublin via Athlone. The station is located at Station Road, *Tel. (096) 71818.*

ORIENTATION

Westport is on the west coat of Ireland, nestled snuggly in the corner of Clew Bay. There are sort of two halves of Westport: one on each side of the softly flowing River Carrowbeg. The Mall is the main thoroughfare in Westport, and is divided by the river. Old bridges (photo-ops for you shutterbugs out there) cross the river at various intervals.

GETTING AROUND TOWN

By Bicycle

Bicycling is a pleasant way to see Westport, although you'll have to watch out for those darned tourists! Actually, there are nice rides along the banks of Clew Bay that are probably some of the most pleasant on the Emerald Isle. You can get a bicycle at **Breheny and Sons**, *Castlebar Street, Westport, Tel. (098) 25020.*

By Car

You'll have lots of traffic to deal with in Westport. That's okay, but you might consider parking for awhile.

By Foot

Again, the best way to see Westport is to hoof it. But there are so many fascinating little shops that you'll want the freedom walking provides to enable you to pop in and out of each of those that interest you most.

WHERE TO STAY

ROCK BARTON LODGE, *Lecanvey, Westport. Tel. (098) 66624. 2 rooms. Rates for singles: £22 to £25, doubles: £18 per person sharing. Rates include breakfast. No credit cards accepted. No service charge.*

One of my personal favorite B&Bs in Ireland, The Rock Barton Lodge, is located on the shores of Clew Bay and at the foot of Croagh Patrick. The rooms are large, pleasantly furnished, and quite comfortable.

Mrs. Ann Colgan is your ever-friendly, capable, and efficient hostess. She has a quality of quiet elegance and the ability to make you feel at home the moment you meet her. Perhaps because of these qualities, she was recently awarded the coveted "Personal Touch" award by Bord Failte (the Irish Tourist Board).

MOHER HOUSE, *Westport-Clifden Road (N59), Liscarney, Westport. Tel. (098) 21360. 4 rooms. Rates for singles: £24, doubles: £16 to £18 per person sharing. Rates include breakfast. Dinner available for £12. No credit cards accepted. No service charge.*

About five miles south of Westport on the N59 you'll find the modern new B&B called Moher House. Upon your arrival at Moher House, you'll be greeted by the owner, Mrs. Marian O'Malley, along with a cup of steaming coffee, scones and jam.

Moher House features four bedrooms, three of which are ensuite with the remaining bedroom having primary access to the bathroom in the hall. The rooms are average in size, but quite comfortable and pleasantly furnished. Large windows look out on the Irish countryside (not to mention Mrs. O'Malley's beautiful gardens) and make for a nice affect. Speaking of Mrs. O'Malley, you'll want to be sure and stay for breakfast in the morning. She has a knack for this aspect of the B&B industry, and her breakfast selections are varied and appetizing.

Moher House is situated near the *Western Way*, a walking trail that has earned somewhat of a cult following among hill-walkers the world over. In addition to being a wonderful B&B, Moher House offers you outstanding views of Ireland's Holy Mountain, Croagh Patrick. People from all over the world have signed Mrs. O'Malley's guest book. Isn't it about time you did also?

CEDAR LODGE, *Kings Hill, Newport Road (N59), Westport. Tel. (098) 25417; E-mail: mflynn@esatclear.ie. 4 rooms. Rates for singles: £24 to £27.50, doubles: £18.50 to £19.50 per person sharing. Rates include breakfast. No credit cards accepted. No service charge.*

This highly recommended inn is a delightful and pleasant B&B within minutes of downtown. Peter and Maureen Flynn are your host and hostess, and they have years of experience in the B&B industry.

Cedar Lodge features four bedrooms, three of which are ensuite. The rooms are ample sized and furnished comfortably. Natural wood throughout the home is a nice touch and gives the B&B a homey quality. Peter and Maureen were both born and raised in the Westport area, and are therefore experts on the sights to see in the area. They are both delighted to assist you in planning your adventures, and they are very helpful in identifying those things you might be most interested in. If golfing is your sport, then Maureen, who describes herself as a "keen golfer," will be especially helpful in pointing you to a course that matches your wishes (not to mention your handicap).

Cedar Lodge is in a quiet secluded area, yet within about five minutes' walk from downtown Westport.

ROSBEG HOUSE, *Westport, (Tel. 098) 25879. 5 rooms. Rates for singles: £40 ensuite, £35 standard, doubles: £25 per person sharing for ensuite and £17.50 for standard. Rates include breakfast. No credit cards accepted. No service charge.*

What a lovely old Georgian home to have a B&B in! As is typical with these old Georgian homes, the rooms are large, with high ceilings that make them seem even more spacious. Three of those spacious rooms overlook Clew Bay and the views are a pure pleasure. Mrs. Kay O'Brien is rightfully proud of her B&B, which is located on a lane just off the R395 on the western edge of town.

THE OLDE RAILWAY HOTEL, *The Mall, Westport. Tel. (098) 25166 Fax (098) 25090; E-mail: railway@anu.ie; Website: www.anu.ie/railwayhotel. 24 rooms. Rates for singles: £40 to £65, doubles: £30 to £60 per person sharing. Rates include breakfast. Restaurant, gardens. All major credit cards accepted. 12.5% service charge.*

The Olde Railway Hotel has been serving guests since 1780, when it was a coaching inn. Today, it stands across from the tree-lined banks of the Carrowbeg River on the Mall in Westport. Classic looking, it is renowned for its generous collection of antiques placed liberally throughout the hotel.

The rooms are tastefully furnished in warm colors and comfortable furniture, and each room has a fine bathroom ensuite. A newly added set of self-catering apartments are an option offered by the hotel. These self-contained units include kitchenettes, and continue the comfortable feeling felt in the rest of the hotel. If you are traveling with children, you can take advantage of the hotel's discount for children.

WESTPORT WOODS HOTEL, *Louisburgh Road, Westport, (098) 25811, (098) 26212 (fax), 95 rooms. Rates for singles: £40, doubles: £35 to £51. Rates include breakfast. Restaurant, tennis, miniature golf. All major credit cards accepted. No service charge.*

This low-rise hotel built in the 1970s is comfortable, but is in need of updating. A recent addition, which added 38 new rooms, was greatly needed. Those rooms are of adequate size, and are decorated tastefully and furnished comfortably. The older rooms are little smaller, and not as nicely furnished, but functional, and include a trouser press. The hotel focuses on families traveling with children, as they offer special discounts, baby-sitting service, both an indoor and outdoor play area, and goofy golf. Special rates are also available for seniors.

THE NEWPORT HOUSE, *Newport. Tel. (098) 41222, Fax (098) 41613. 19 rooms. Rates for singles: £60, doubles: £60 to £75 per person sharing. Rates include breakfast. Restaurant, gardens, fishing, walking trails. All major credit cards accepted. 10% service charge. Open from mid-March through the end of September.*

As you pull up to Newport House, you'll see an attractive ivy-clad old Georgian manor house standing amid beautiful gardens. It oozes character, personality, and a certain mystery. Ancient portraits, a liberal dose of antiques, and exquisite furnishings are found throughout the house. The grand staircase is nearly enough to take your breath away; the carpets are hand-made in Connemara. The bedrooms are large, even spacious, and feature some of the home's fine antiques. Newport House has gained a well-deserved reputation as a base for fishing, and in the mornings you'll run into a number of ghillies (guides) waiting to take their clients out for a spot of fishing. Newport is about a 10-minute drive north of Westport on the N59.

WHERE TO EAT

MCCORMACK'S CAFE, *Bridge Street, Westport. Tel. (098) 25619. £1.50 to £5. Open daily from noon to 2:30pm and from 5:30 to 9:00pm. Mastercard and Visa accepted. No service charge.*

This is a great little cafe for a snack or quick sandwich. Nothing fancy, just convenient to the shopping areas and good, inexpensive food.

JOHN J. O'MALLEY'S, *Bridge Street, Westport. Tel. (098) 27307. £6.95 to £9.95. Open Monday through Friday from 2:00pm to 11:30pm. Mastercard and Visa accepted. No service charge.*

"John J's," as the locals call John J. O'Malley's, is a hot hangout for the younger set who live in or visit the city. Kind of a cross between a cafe and a pub, John J's specializes in burgers, pasta, and some seafood.

THE QUAY COTTAGE, *Westport House Road, Westport, (098) 26412, £8.95 to £15.50. Open Monday through Saturday from 6:00pm to 10:00pm, and Sunday from 1:00pm to 10:00pm. Mastercard and Visa accepted.*

The Quay Cottage has earned an impressive reputation for its wonderful seafood. The restaurant lies just outside the gates to the grounds of the Westport House. Seafood is the specialty here, and they do it well. Fillet of lemon sole, fresh scallops, crab salad cocktail, and monkfish with tagliatelle are just a few of the seafood offerings available. There are other dishes, such as lamb and good Irish beef, but seafood is clearly the main focus.

NEWPORT HOUSE RESTAURANT, *Newport. Tel. (098) 41222. Set dinner menu for £20. Open daily from 7:30pm to 9:30pm. All major credit cards accepted. 12.5% service charge.*

The restaurant for the Newport House relies heavily on fresh produce and herbs to give their gastronomical concoctions just the right flavor. Many of the ingredients they use in their dishes are homegrown in their own organic kitchen garden. Fruits, vegetables, and herbs come from there and add that little extra flavorful touch that separates the great restaurants from the good ones. The Newport House is especially noted for seafood. Typical fare includes escalope of monkfish in a shellfish sauce, salmon cured with whiskey, and grilled turbot with creamed leeks and champagne sauce. There is a nice wine list as well. Dress is nice casual, although many of the diners will have jackets and ties.

ASGARD TAVERN AND RESTAURANT, *The Quay, Westport. Tel. (098) 25319. Set dinner menu £17. Open daily from 6:30pm to 10:30pm. During the off-season, they are only open Tuesday through Saturday. All major credit cards accepted. No service charge.*

Overlooking Clew Bay, Asgard Tavern and Restaurant is another of the find seafood restaurants in Westport, although they do have a fair selection of other dishes to choose from. Typical dishes include poached fillet of salmon hollandaise, lobster in brandy cream, and peppered beef fillet on a warm salad. There are also several vegetarian dishes available, although it's not a wide selection.

THE ARDMORE RESTAURANT, *Quay Street, Westport. Tel. (098) 25994. Set dinner for £18.95. Open daily from 7:00pm to 9:30pm. All major credit cards accepted. 10% service charge.*

The Ardmore Restaurant serenely sits on a small hill overlooking Clew Bay. This is the place for a romantic candlelight dinner. The menu is varied, and offers dishes that range from fresh wild mussels and baked clams to medallions of beef with cognac and cream sauce. Many locals will tell you that this is *the* place to eat in Westport.

SEEING THE SIGHTS

Watch for the signposts in town pointing you toward **The Quay**, which is about a mile outside of Westport. Here you'll find an assortment of pubs and restaurants.

Westport House, *Westport. Open April, May and September daily from 2:00pm to 5:00pm, June Monday through Friday from noon until 5:00pm, Saturday and Sunday from 2:00pm until 6:00pm, July and August Monday through Saturday from 10:30am until 6:00pm, and Sunday from 2:00pm until 6:00pm. Admission is £6.00 for adults and £3.00 for children. A family ticket is available for £17.50 (2 adults and 4 children). Tel. (098) 25430.* Home of the Marquess of Sligo, Westport House is a lovely Georgian Mansion begun in 1730 and completed in 1778. Built on the site of a castle from years gone by, it features an ornate marble staircase and a wide collection of period furnishings. It sits amid nice parklands, although the quest for commercialization overshadows the serenity that would otherwise be here. A caravan (travel trailer) park, arcade games, and campsite on the grounds detract from the otherwise elegant ambiance.

After you've seen Westport House, take a short drive west of Westport on the R335. That large mountain on your left is known as Ireland's "Holy Mountain." **Croagh Patrick** sits regally on the south side of Clew Bay and holds an important position in Irish history and legend. It rises abruptly and majestically over 2,500 feet above the Atlantic waters at its base.

Croagh Patrick is the legendary peak where tradition holds that St. Patrick enticed all the snakes of Ireland to gather. When they were all assembled, St. Patrick rang his bell, and all the snakes cast themselves to their deaths over a cliff. Whether you believe the legend or not (by the way – there are no snakes in Ireland), Croagh Patrick is an impressive mountain, and the site of yearly pilgrimages by many Catholic faithful.

If you are looking for a little exercise, there is a good hiking path up Croagh Patrick that begins in the little town of Murrisk, about five miles west of Westport. The well-worn path ascends to the top of the mountain. The last Sunday of July is the traditional time of the pilgrimage, when worshipers, many of them barefoot, make the two-hour trek to the top. But you can do it any time of the year, and the views from the top are nothing short of stunning.

Resting offshore at the mouth of Clew Bay is the 4,000-acre **Clare Island**. You can arrange for a boat ride out to Clare Island by calling the Bay View Hotel on Clare Island, *Tel. (098) 26307.*

By far its most famous occupant over the centuries was **Grace O'Malley**, the "Uncrowned Queen of the West." Grace was the daughter of Owen O'Malley, chieftain of western Ireland. But she was quite the power in and of herself. She was recognized as a gutsy pirate full of daring and bravado, and more than one ballad has been sung to her feats.

One of her more celebrated exploits involved her second husband. She wed one **MacWilliam Oughter**, another powerful figure of the day. Since both had extensive real estate holdings and financial assets, demure Grace proposed that the marriage begin on somewhat of a trial partnership. If at the end of one year either party wanted out of the relationship, all that was required was for one or the other to say, "I dismiss you." (The original pre-nuptial agreement?)

Over the course of the year, Grace used her wiles to finagle her allies into positions of power in various of Mr. Oughter's strongholds. One year after their marriage when he returned home to **Carrigahooley Castle** on Clare Island, he was dismayed to hear Grace shout from inside the castle, "I dismiss you!" Grace lived and died near the end of the 16th century, and her grave is marked with a plaque in the Clare Island abbey.

Just north of Westport on the N59 10 miles or so is **Newport**, a modern fishing village on the western coast of Connacht. It is a popular haven for Salmon fishermen when the salmon are running.

Achill Island is a large island off the west coast of County Mayo. To get to Achill Island, take the R319 off the N59 in Mulrany. The road takes you across a causeway and deposits you in the town of Achill Sound.

The island is about 15 miles long and 12 miles wide. There's not much in the way of vegetation other than the heather, which is brilliant during the late summer. On the north side of the island are some impressive cliffs, including some that offer spectacular views of the ocean. The island offers shark fishing off its western coast if you're interested.

Owing to the remoteness of the island, tourism hasn't completely taken over. It's more austere than the rest of Ireland, but there are some nice sandy beaches along the coast in between the cliffs. Some of the prettiest beaches are at Keel, Keem Bay, Dugort, and Dooega. There are also lots of walking paths around the island, many of them drawn to the cliffs on the one hand and the mountains that grace the island on the other.

Back on the mainland, follow the N5 northwest from Westport, and you'll come to **Ballina** after about an hour. (Watch the signposts – you actually change to the N58 and the N26 to get there.) **Ballina** sits at the southern end of Killala Bay. It may be small (population around 6,500), but it is the largest town in County Mayo. It has been an important fishing center for generations, and continues to draw interest from the fishing public. Many come to Ballina to fish for salmon and sea trout in nearby River Moy and Lough Conn.

To get to Ballina, you can also take the N59 north to Bangor, where it then turns due east and takes you into Ballina.

Between Ballina and Killala are some ruins you should take the time to see. Two miles from Killala is **Moyne Abbey**, a 15th-century abbey that still retains its tower and cloisters.

Rosserk Friary, *between Killala and Ballina*. About five miles south of Killala on the same coastal road as Moyne Abbey is the 15th century Rosserk Friary, standing grandly next to the River Moy. It is one of the best-preserved ruins of this vintage in Ireland. It still retains its tower and the cloisters are also in good condition.

SPORTS & RECREATION
Golf
Westport Golf Club, *Westport, County Mayo. Tel. (098) 25113, £15/£18.*

Westport Golf Club meanders at the foot of Ireland's Holy Mountain, Croagh Patrick, and in addition to providing a challenging links-style course, it provides lovely views of island-studded Clew Bay. If you come here, you'll find that it is a nice place to spend a few hours (for sightseeing or for golf, you'll enjoy yourself).

Some of the views of Clew Bay may be a little close for your tastes. Take for example the view you have of Clew Bay from the 15th tee. Yes, the view of the inlet is lovely, until you realize that it lies between you and the green. Visitors are welcome daily (call ahead for tee times on the weekends, please). Par 73, 6,667 yards.

Scuba Diving
- **Atlantic Dive Center**, *Georges Street, Killalla, County Mayo. Tel. (096) 32797*

PRACTICAL INFORMATION

Laundry Service
- **The Launderette**, *Cathedral Road, Ballina. Tel. (096) 22358*
- **Westport Washeteria**, *Mill Street, Westport. Tel. (098) 25261*

Post Office
- **Westport Post Office**, *The Mall. Tel. (098) 25475*

Tourist Offices
- **Achill Island Tourist Information Office**, *Achill Sound, Tel. (098) 45384*
- **Ballina Tourist Information Office**, *Cathedral Road, Tel. (096) 70848*
- **Castlebar Tourist Information Office**, *Moy Valley Resources, Lower Main Street, Tel. (096) 43256*
- **Westport Tourist Information Office**, *The Mall. Tel. (098) 25711*

SLIGO TOWN

At the northwestern tip of the province of Connacht lies the very busy town of **Sligo**. Its Irish name *Sligeach* means "The Shelly River." It's a mid-sized town bounded by mountains on three sides. I found it to be very busy and not a little confusing to get around in. But once I parked my car and began my adventures and exploration on foot, I found it to be a delightfully busy, bustling town, with lots of interesting shops to pop in and out of.

Once a strategic town on the Garavogue River, Sligo attracted the attention of just about every group of invaders who hit Ireland: the Vikings, the Anglo-Normans, and of course the infamous Oliver Cromwell, who (twice) didn't want to leave this stone unturned either. Not to be outdone by foreigners, the native Irish tried their hand numerous times also. Today it's a quiet market town, the largest in this section of Ireland.

Some of the most interesting sights around Sligo are the ancient dolmens, cairns, and stone circles that dot the countryside. **Dolmens** are megalithic tombs with three or more stones that serve as pillars or pedestals for a large stone (capstone) that is placed on top of them. Sometimes these capstones weigh up to 100 tons. Head out on about any road into the mountains surrounding Sligo and watch for the signposts, and you're sure to find them. The greatest number of these antiquities are west and south of town.

ARRIVALS & DEPARTURES

By Bus
Four buses a day run between Galway and Sligo Town. Information about schedules and fares can be received by calling the bus station: *Tel. (071) 60006.*

By Car
Sligo is on the N17 about two hours north of Galway. To get there from Galway, take the N17 north until it merges with the N4. Sligo is also about an hour south of Donegal, so you might consider visiting Sligo while using Donegal as your base.

Sample trip lengths on the main roads:
• Belfast: 3 hours
• Cork: 5 hours
• Donegal: 1 hour
• Dublin: 3 hours
• Killarney: 5 hours
• Limerick: 4 hours
• Wexford: 5 hours

GETTING AROUND TOWN

By Bicycle
Sligo is a busy, busy town with lots of traffic and narrow roads – bad combinations for bicyclists. I'd suggest parking your bike and walking around town. However, the countryside around Sligo is tailor-made for bicycling. The roads are of course narrow, but if you're careful you'll be okay. Especially pleasant is the R286 north of town and the R287 south of town. Both skirt Lough Gill, and the views are fabulous.

Two recommended places to rent bikes are:
• **Flanagan's Bikes**, *High Street, Sligo. Tel. (071) 44477*
• **Gary's Cycles**, *Quay Street, Sligo. Tel. (071) 45418*

By Car
Park it as soon as you near the center of town! Otherwise, it will be quite handy to see the sights and scenery around Sligo.

By Foot
Once again, walking is the best way to see downtown Sligo. Unfortu-

nately, there are not a lot of sights to see in downtown Sligo other than shops.

WHERE TO STAY

CROMLEACH LODGE, *Castlebaldwin, near Boyle. Tel. (071) 65155, Fax (071) 65455; E-mail: info@cromleach.com; Website: www.cromleach.com. 10 rooms. Rates for singles: £99 to £105, doubles: £69 to £99 per person sharing. Rates include breakfast. American Express, Mastercard, and Visa accepted. No service charge.*

Don't stay at Cromleach Lodge if you have your heart set on staying in one of those gorgeous Georgian homes or if you have dreamed of staying in a renovated 11th-century Norman castle. But if you're willing to depart a bit from the stereotypical Irish accommodation, you might find yourself pleasantly surprised by this lodge.

Christy and Moira Tighe have a gem atop a hill outside of Castlebaldwin. Splendid views of Lough Arrow complement the fine service Cromleach Lodge has come to be known for. In fact, every room has stunning views of the surrounding countryside. The rooms are large, even spacious by some accounts. They are lavishly furnished, and coupled with the view, are some of the best rooms in the west of Ireland. Each room offers tea- and coffee-making facilities, complimentary fruit bowls, mineral water, and even small bottles of Bailey's Irish Whiskey!

COOPERSHILL HOUSE, *Riverstown. Tel. (071) 65108, Fax (071) 65466; E-mail: ohara@coopershill.com; Website: www.coopershill.com. 7 rooms. Rates for singles: £62 to £69, doubles: £52 to £59 per person sharing. Rates include breakfast. All major credit cards accepted. No service charge. Open April through October.*

Seven generations of O'Hara's have lived at Coopershill House, which was built in 1774. The house itself is regal – sitting in the midst of 500 verdant acres. But don't let this intimidate you. Once inside the doors, you'll feel as comfortable as if you are long-lost and well-loved family coming for a visit.

The bedrooms are large and spacious, and are generously endowed with antiques, old portraits, and four-poster bed in most rooms. Complement those amenities with fresh flowers from the gardens and mineral water and you've all the trappings for a restful stay. (Bring a book – with no television to mar the tranquillity, you may need something besides the late movie to get you ready for sleep.) Lindy O'Hara will be delighted if you choose to stay for dinner, as she serves some of the finest meals in County Sligo. The dining room is grand, and features beautiful antique tables, silver candelabra, and crisp Irish linen. You'll be warmed – physically and emotionally – by a fine log fire.

WHERE TO EAT

TRUFFLES, *The Mall, Sligo Town. Tel. (071) 44226. £5.95 to £14.95. Open Tuesday through Saturday from 5:00pm to 10:30pm. No credit cards accepted. No service charge.*

Truffles specializes in pizza, and we're not talking your basic cheese and pepperoni here. Here's a sampling of the toppings you may find when you arrive: seven different cheeses (okay so far), sausage, grilled leeks, pine nuts, and salmon. And let's not forget cabbage (this is, after all, an Irish restaurant!). Your first impression of the restaurant may be underwhelming, but don't let the unassuming entrance and front façade dissuade you from trying this wonderful restaurant. Once inside, you'll find the atmosphere relaxed and casual, with an eclectic collection of statues and paintings in the dining area. They have become quite popular – maybe even trendy – of late, so during the summer months you may have to wait a bit, but it will be worth it!

BISTRO BIANCONI, *44 O'Connell Street, Sligo Town. Tel. (071) 41744. £11.95 to £16.95. Open daily from 5:30pm until midnight. All major credit cards accepted.*

This nice bistro is stylishly decorated with frescos, plants, and muted lighting. The menu is primarily Italian, with plenty of fresh homemade pastas. Vegetarian dishes are also offered. Once you perch yourself on one of the pine stools at the tall pine tables, you'll be ready to sample some of the delicious menu items. If you're not sure you want to eat here, just pass by the front door and let the marvelous cornucopia of fragrances envelop you; unless your olfactory senses don't work, I believe you'll be drawn immediately into the bistro!

SEEING THE SIGHTS

Sligo County Library and Museum, *Sligo, Steven Street. Open June through September Tuesday through Saturday from 10:30am to 12:30pm, and from 2:30pm to 4:30pm, April, May, and October Tuesday through Friday from 2:30pm to 4:30pm, and November through March on Tuesday and Friday from 2:30pm to 4:30pm. Admission is free. Tel. (071) 22122.* Even though it's billed as the County Library and Museum, the museum features a fine collection belonging to W. B. Yeats memorabilia, a former resident of Sligo. The art gallery also has a number of paintings by Yeats' brother Jack and their father.

Sligo Abbey, *Abbey Street, Sligo. Open early June through the end of September daily from 9:30am to 6:30pm. Admission is £1.50 for adults, £1.00 for seniors and students, 60p for children and a family ticket is available for £4.00. Tel. (071) 46406.* Just a block off Kennedy Parade/Riverside Street on Abbey Street are the ruins of an abbey built by Maurice Fitzgerald for the Dominicans. The ruins are open to the public. They feature a lovely set of lancet windows in the choir. On the south end of the ruins, look for the memorial to the O'Conor, a powerful chieftain among the Celts. The abbey was originally built in 1253, but suffered a fire in 1414. It was rebuilt, but a mere two and a half centuries later it gained the malevolent attention of the Cromwellian minions, who destroyed it.

Strandhill is located a few miles east of Sligo on the R292. It's a picturesque seaport town with soft sandy beaches that are tailor-made for early morning or late evening walks; mid-day isn't bad, either!

Five miles north of Sligo Town on the N15 you'll find the ruins of the monastic settlement of **Drumcliffe**. Its Irish name, *Droim Chliabh,* means "Back of the Baskets." Originally the site of a monastery founded in 574 by St. Columba, the settlement lasted until the early 16th century. The only remaining artifacts are a series of gravestones, the remains of a round tower, and an elaborately carved high cross. The high cross and the round tower sit right next to the road. The high cross was placed here about the year 1000, and is deeply carved with a number of figures. Can you identify the scriptural stories depicted there?

Perhaps the most interesting aspect of your visit here is the grave of revered Irish writer W. B. Yeats in the nearby Protestant graveyard. His simple epitaph reads:

> *Cast a cold eye*
> *On life, on death.*
> *Horseman, pass by!*

Lissadell House, *Drumcliffe, off the N15. Open June through mid-September Monday through Saturday from 10:30am to 12:30pm, and from 2:00pm to 4:30pm (last admission at 12:15pm and 4:15pm). Admission is £3.00 for adults, £2.50 for seniors and £1.50 for children. Tel. (071) 63150, Fax (071) 63906.*

About 10 miles north of Sligo on the N15, watch for signs pointing you to Lissadell or Lissadell House, because here's a short side-trip you'll want to take. Lissadell House is an elegant mansion built in the mid-1830s by Sir Robert Gore-Booth. Square and regal, at once forbidding yet intriguingly inviting at the same time, the mansion is anxiously awaiting your visit. Even though it is as splendid as many of the other mansions around the country, it is not visited as often as some of its better-known cousins because of its location. Travelers usually whisk by this marvelous experience, never knowing they are but minutes from some wonderful scenes.

Once inside the mansion, you'll be awed by the lovely architecture and plentiful *objets d'art*. The two-story hall, complemented by ample marble and Doric columns, is breathtaking. But as much as the architecture, antiques and paintings, you'll enjoy the half-hour tour that spins the history of Lissadell House for you, complete with the tales of some of her most intriguing owners. Among others, you'll hear of Constance Gore-Booth's role in the 1916 Easter Uprising and of her election as the first woman to the *Dail Eirann* (the Irish Parliament).

So...take an hour detour off the N15 and relax amid the splendor, finery, and tales of Lissadell House.

Not far from Lissadell House, also west of the N15, you'll find a poignant memorial that most tourists whisk past without taking the time to investigate. About two miles west of the N15 at Grange, you'll discover the **Spanish Armada Memorial**. The northern and western coasts of Ireland are littered with the wreckage of a score of ships from the Spanish Armada. (To date, 22 wrecks have been discovered off the Irish coastline.) Most history books chronicle the decimation of the Spanish Armada by English guns; few touch on the point that more sailors lost their lives in weather-induced shipwrecks off the coasts of Ireland than perished in the fighting with the English.

The Spanish Armada Memorial sits along one of the bays of the Atlantic Ocean here in western Connacht, within sight of the final resting place of three weather-scuttled ships of the Spanish Armada: the *Juliana*, *La Lavia*, and *Santa Maria de Vision*. All three survived British guns only to be caught in a violent squall just offshore from this point. Although 300 men survived, over 1,200 men lost their lives. The memorial is a rock enclosure and patio around a symbolic mast and the stern of a ship. Take a few minutes and turn off the N15 to visit this sight. I was touched by it, and perhaps you will be too.

Lying just east of the N15 as you travel north from Sligo Town to Bundoran is the large, flat-topped mount called by some as "Table Mountain." Deep ravines ring the edges of the steep slopes of Benbulben.

Next to Croagh Patrick, **Benbulben** is perhaps the next most recognizable mountain in Ireland. As you travel north from Sligo Town toward Bundoran on the N15, watch for a large, flat-topped mountain along the east side of the highway. (It would be difficult to miss!) This impressive mountain that is visible from many miles is called "Table Mountain" by some; it's not difficult to imagine why they call it that.

Benbulben stands out in history as prominently as it does on the landscape. It is a mountain of legends as well as of significant historical events. One such event took place on the slopes of Benbulben: the "Battle of the Books" took place in 561, between the followers of **St. Columba** and **St. Finian**. As the story goes, St. Finian had lent a book to St. Columba, who copied it (by hand, of course). St. Finian claimed not only the original, but also the copy that had been made. The two could come to no agreeable solution, so it was presented to the king of Ireland, who judged in favor of St. Finian. He said, "To every cow its calf, and to every book its copy."

(Early copyright law?). Rather than return the copy, St. Columba decided to fight (not very saintly); over 3,000 men lost their lives in the ensuing battle. St. Columba was reportedly so distraught over the results of his squabble with St. Finian that he vowed to bring as many souls to Christ as were slain in the battle. The records state that he was successful in his penance – more than 3,000 additional souls embraced Christ before the end of St. Columba's life. Unfortunately, the souls he saved were not Irish, but rather Scottish, as he was banished to Scotland for his part in causing the battle.

Recent archaeological discoveries have been made on Benbulben's summit that indicate that some of the earliest of Ireland's inhabitants were drawn to this prominent mountain. Traces of stone-age settlements have been uncovered on the top of Benbulben's tabletop summit. (Once you see the mountain, you'll gain an appreciation for the effort it must have taken for these ancient pioneers to have built their crude huts atop Benbulben!)

Visitors can climb Benbulben, although there are no pre-defined routes. Check with the local tourist information center in Sligo to get an idea of how to attack its steep sides. It is *extremely* dangerous if you don't know what you're doing. Its steep slopes are ringed with deep treacherous ravines. I have seen Benbulben in all kinds of weather and each time I have been impressed. Just when I thought it was the most impressive with its green hillsides bathed in brilliant sunlight, I saw it shrouded in mists that gave it an ethereal, brooding quality. Which was the most impressive? I'm not sure – you'll have to decide for yourself!

Creevykeel Court Tomb, *on the N15 between Cliffony and Castlegal.* Creevykeel Court Tomb is one of the finest examples of a classic court tomb in existence today in Ireland. Archaeologists estimate it has been here since 3,000 BC. Upright stones mark the circular ritual court, and lead to a burial chamber.

HELP, OR SUSTENANCE, AT CREEVYKEEL

If you are so anxious to see the Creevykeel Court Tomb that you lock your keys in your car, there's an obscure pub about 100 meters down the road (on the N15 between Sligo and Ballyshannon) with a comforting turf fire burning, and locals – James and P.D. – willing to help a tourist (and forgetful writer) in need!

Parke's Castle, *near Sligo. Open June through September daily from 9:30am to 6:30pm, and April, May and October Tuesday through Sunday from 10:00am to 5:00pm. Admission is £2.00 for adults, £1.50 for seniors and* *students, £1.00 for children and a family ticket is available for £5.00. Tel. (071) 64149.* Just south of Sligo on the N4, watch for signs directing you to Dromahair and Parke Castle. The drive, along the lovely shores of Lough Gill, is particularly spectacular. The castle sits along the shoreline of the lough, and is particularly impressive at night, when it is basked in bright halogen lights. This 17th-century house was partially built using stones taken from the nearby Breffni Castle. In so doing, the English owner incurred the ire of the native Irish for their thoughtlessness. A short video on the history of the house is also shown.

While an interesting place to visit, it seemed too...*tidy.* It is well kept by the owners, but just seemed a little too neat and clean! It didn't have the charm or romance of some other nearby ruins.

Glencar Lough, *near Manorhamilton.* This little lake lies just off the N16 between Sligo Town and Manorhamilton. Near the north end of the lake are several waterfalls, one of which free-falls about 50 feet over the edge of the mountain.

SPORTS & RECREATION
Horseback Riding
• **Munsboro Riding Holidays**, *Sligo, County Sligo. Tel. (0903) 26449*
• **Sligo Equestrian Center**, *Carramore, County Sligo. Tel. (071) 61353*

Sailing and Windsurfing
• **Sligo Yacht Club**, *Rosses Point, County Sligo. (071) 77168*
• **Sunset Sails and Windsurfing**, *Adelaide Street, Sligo, County Sligo. Tel. (071) 62792*

PRACTICAL INFORMATION
Laundry Service
• **Gurries Launderette**, *High Street, Sligo. Tel. (071) 69238*

Post Office
• **Sligo Post Office**, *Wine Street. Tel. (071) 42593*

Tourist Office
• **Sligo Town Tourist Information Office**, *Temple Street, Tel. (071) 61201*

ROSCOMMON
The county seat of County Roscommon is **Roscommon Town**. Both the town and the county take their name from the Irish name *Ros Comain*, which means "Coman's Wood." **St. Coman** was a goodly cleric who

founded a monastery here shortly after St. Patrick completed his ministry to Ireland. Several fine ruins are to be found in and around Roscommon Town.

ARRIVALS & DEPARTURES

By Car

County Roscommon is the only land-locked county in the province of Connacht. Roscommon Town is at the crossroads of a number of national roads, including the N60, N61, and the N63. It is about 20 miles north of Athlone on the N61, and about 90 minutes northwest of Galway. To get to Roscommon from Galway, take the N6 to Athlone and then the N61 north to Roscommon.

Sample trip lengths on the main roads:

- Belfast: 4 hours
- Cork: 3 hours
- Donegal: 2 hours
- Dublin: 2 hours
- Killarney: 4 hours
- Limerick: 2 hours
- Wexford: 3 hours

SEEING THE SIGHTS

On the south end of Roscommon Town on the N61, you come to **Roscommon Abbey**. This Dominican abbey was built in the 13th century. The tomb of its founder, Felin O'Connor, is found on the north wall, still guarded by the statues of eight *galloglasses* – soldiers of fortune.

At the other end of town from Roscommon Abbey is **Roscommon Castle**. The old ruins are interesting. The castle was built in the 13th century, and was the stronghold of Anglo-Norman rulers who were in the area at the time.

Strokestown Park House, *Strokestown. Open June through September 15, Tuesday through Sunday from noon to 5:00pm. Admission to the house is £3 for adults, £2 for seniors and £1 for children; admission to the museum is in addition to admission to the house, and at the same rate. Tel. (078) 33013.* The tiny town of Strokestown is about 20 miles north of Roscommon. To get there from Roscommon, take the N61 north to Four Mile, then watch for signposts directing you to the R368 and Strokestown. The R368 dead-ends into the N5; turn left, and you'll be in Strokestown in a matter of a few minutes.

Once there, you'll find the palatial home of the Mahon family, which they lived in from 1660 through 1979. The home itself is a not-always-congruent combination of several architectural motifs, owing to several additions over the past 300 years. But it is interesting and is worth a visit, as are their extensive gardens.

A small museum housed in the old stable yards is also worth a visit while at Strokestown. Its topic is the infamous potato famine, and it poignantly and graphically portrays the devastation this area suffered during that time.

Lough Key Forest Park, *near Boyle, Co. Roscommon. Parking in the car park costs £2.* Lovely Lough Key Forest Park lies east of the town of Boyle, and it comprises 800 acres along the shores of a lake. Camping sites, walking paths, boat rentals (the ancient ruins of an abbey to explore are on the island), and bog gardens are a few of the things to do while here. The bog gardens offer you an intriguing setting of heather and small plants that flourish in the moist peat of the bog.

On the northern outskirts of Boyle you'll find the impressive and well-preserved ruins of **Boyle Cisterian Abbey,** *Boyle. Open April through the end of October daily from 9:30am to 6:30pm. Admission is £1.00 for adults, 70p for seniors and students, 40p for children and a family ticket is available for £3.00. Tel. (079) 62604.* Dating from 1161, the nave, choir, and transepts are in good condition and there are a number of interesting carvings. Like so many of their brother and sister friaries and abbeys, Boyle Abbey has a long and peaceful history marred by intermittent violence. Time and again the inhabitants of the abbey were forced to flee from the depredations of unwanted visitors, and time and again they returned to clean and rebuild their abbey and their lives.

PRACTICAL INFORMATION

Laundry Service
• **Athlone Launderette,** *Pearse Street, Athlone. Tel. (0902) 92930*

Post Office
• **Athlone Post Office,** *Barracks Street. Tel. (0902) 83544*

Tourist Offices
• **Athlone Tourist Information Office,** *The Castle, Market Square, Athlone, Tel. (0902) 94630.* This office is open from April through November.
• **Boyle Tourist Information Office,** *Main Street, Boyle, Tel. (079) 62145*
• **Roscommon Tourist Information Office,** *Harrison Hall, Roscommon, Tel. (0903) 26342.* Open only during the summer months.

17. ULSTER

The province of **Ulster** covers the northern quarter of the Emerald Isle. There are nine counties in Ulster, six of which constitute Northern Ireland, a part of the United Kingdom. The counties of Ulster that are not in Northern Ireland are Donegal, Cavan, and Monaghan. I have divided Ulster into two chapters: this chapter covers that portion of Ulster in the Republic, and the next chapter is devoted to Northern Ireland.

There are few major cities in Ulster, and that fact is not lost on tourists – the province of Ulster, particularly County Donegal, is becoming a favorite destination for foreign tourists (it has been popular with the Irish for years). **Donegal** is the town in the Republican section of Ulster that gets the most attention. But much of Ulster's attractiveness lies outside her cities and towns in her mountains, seascapes, parks, and rugged ruins. County Donegal is one of the most secluded areas of the entire Emerald Isle, and it is beautiful. It features little in the way of civilization, but lots in the way of scenic drives, templed hills and wooded vales. Lakes seem to be around every bend and twist of the road, and the lush green of Ireland seems to shine brightest here. Just about any road you choose is going to treat you to bounteous beauties. So have fun exploring!

From County Donegal, I'll transport you to **Counties Cavan** and **Monaghan**, where I'll introduce you to a few sights in these two remaining Republic counties that are part of Ulster. So...fasten your seatbelts, load your cameras, and let's go!

If You Miss These Places, You Haven't Been to Ulster!
For all her romance and loveliness, there are a few Ulster sights you especially won't want to miss. If you do, you can scarcely say you've been to Ulster. **Donegal Town** is an amicable little village that hasn't succumbed to too much "tourist schtick." Sure there are the obligatory sweater and souvenir shops clustered around the town square, but they're able to do it without being too touristy. **Glencolumbkille**, the monastic settlement on the west coast of Donegal, is a reminder of the faith and courage of Ireland's ancient clerics.

Glenveagh National Park is a living picture postcard for the magnificence and natural splendor of Ireland. If you venture to the solid ring fort called Grianan of Ailigh, you'll be treated to some of the most stunning views on the island: Lough Swilly and Lough Foyle, Malin Head, and the expansive Atlantic.

DONEGAL TOWN

This attractive village, home to around 2,500 inhabitants, sits proudly at the head of Donegal Bay on the western shore of Ireland. The Irish name for Donegal, *Dun na nGall*, which means "The Fort of the Foreigners," gives you an inkling of the tenuous and rocky beginnings of Donegal. The town was originally founded in the 9th century by Vikings, who used it as a base of operations for their depredations further into the countryside. The town was eventually taken from the Vikings by the McDonnell clan, and served as their seat of power for centuries.

The town is a lot quieter these days, and its visitors generally do not burn it to the ground nor kill her citizens (thank heavens!).

ULSTER'S TOP LODGING

THE ARCHES COUNTRY HOUSE, Lough Eske, Barnesmore, Donegal. Tel. (073) 22029. 6 rooms. Rates for singles: £27.50, doubles: £20 per person sharing. The Arches wins my Best Irish B&B award.

HARVEY'S POINT COUNTRY HOTEL, Lough Eske, Donegal Town, (073) 22208, (073) 22352, 32 rooms. Rates for singles: £55 to £70, doubles: £45 to £80 per person sharing, suites: £60 to £90 per person sharing. Sitting on the banks of tranquil Lough Eske, Harvey's Point Country Hotel provides a feel of continental Europe mixed with warm Irish hospitality.

ARRIVALS & DEPARTURES

You can reach Donegal by car and bus, but if you're seeing Ireland via train, that particular conveyance isn't available here.

By Bus

Buses stop in front of the Abbey Hotel on The Diamond. Buses leave for and arrive from Dublin six times a day (three times on Sunday). The four-hour trip to Dublin takes a little over four hours and costs £10.

By Car

Donegal Town is located on the N15. It is southwest of Derry, and north of Sligo. Sample trip lengths on the main roads:
• Belfast: 3 hours
• Dublin: 4 hours
• Galway: 3 hours
• Killarney: 6 hours
• Limerick: 5 hours
• Wexford: 6 hours

ORIENTATION

Donegal sits on the northwest coast of Ireland at the head of scenic Donegal Bay. It serves as the gateway to some unspoiled and spectacular scenery. As you enter Donegal from the south, you're treated to some lovely views of island-studded Donegal Bay.

Donegal is a quiet little village with an impressive assortment of interesting shops situated around a picturesque town square called *The Diamond.* Sweater shops, music stores, restaurants, and a host of specialty shops are present on the square for your shopping pleasure. Through the years, Donegal Town has evolved to become the primary marketplace for crafts and goods produced all over County Donegal. From famous Donegal tweeds to hand-crafted knitting, you'll find a large quantity of wonderful goods here.

GETTING AROUND TOWN

By Bicycle

You can rent bicycles in town from **C.J. Doherty's Cycles**, *Main Street, Donegal. Tel. (073) 21119*, or at **The Bike Shop**, *Waterloo Place, Donegal. Tel. (073) 22515.* Donegal the town is small enough to see quite easily on foot, and a bicycle would be a bit of a bother. But a bicycle would be an excellent means of transportation for seeing the picturesque areas north and west of Donegal Town – although you'll find a few more hills in County Donegal than you've become accustomed to in the rest of Ireland.

By Car

If you've arrived in Donegal by car, just find a parking place (you'll probably need to park on one of the side streets). Donegal is far too small to try and see in a car.

By Foot

Like so many other Irish towns in this part of the country, it's easiest to see on foot. The entire downtown section isn't much more than 100 yards square.

WHERE TO STAY

GALLAGHER'S FARM HOSTEL, *Darney. Tel. (073) 37057. 18 beds. Rates are £7 per person, (£6 per person after the first night) for the hostel, or £3.50 per person for campsites. No credit cards accepted – only cash. No service charge.*

This farmhouse hostel is in the converted barn on this Irish farm. The owners have done a nice job in the conversion, and the accommodations are quite comfortable. The dormitory rooms have four, six, and eight beds. There are self-catering kitchen facilities and a washer is available (£2.50 per load). This is a decent place to put up for the night. Linens are included. Gallagher's Farm Hostel is south of Donegal Town on the N15.

THE ARCHES COUNTRY HOUSE, *Lough Eske, Barnesmore, Donegal. Tel. (073) 22029. 6 rooms. Rates for singles: £27.50, doubles: £20 per person sharing. Rates include breakfast. No credit cards accepted. No service charge.*

Nestled snuggly amid the rolling hills of the verdant Blue Stack Mountains, the Arches Country House awaits to welcome you with traditional Irish charm and elegance. Of all the B&Bs I've visited and stayed in, this one earns my vote as the *Best Irish Bed and Breakfast,* and the main reason the Arches gets the nod over many other fine B&Bs is its proprietor, Mrs. Noreen McGinty. She is a lovely and gracious hostess, certain to offer you a positive experience to enhance your Irish holiday. The B&B itself is also wonderful. Its six rooms are all large, and by B&B standards they border on being spacious. They are tastefully decorated with lovely furnishings and light colors. Each of the rooms is individually decorated, all with light floral accents. As a special bonus, each room has large windows, which offer stunning views of peaceful Lough Eske, just down the hill from the Arches Country House. The bathrooms have been recently refurbished with new tile and fixtures. You'll appreciate the quality used in the construction of The Arches – the beautiful dark wood throughout gives the B&B a sense of elegance. The newly added dining room, complete with knotty-pine open-beam ceiling and large windows, offers a marvelous setting in which to enjoy your Irish breakfast. And what a breakfast! Mrs. McGinty offers you a wide variety of breakfast dishes to choose from, and the results are delicious.

The grounds surrounding The Arches provide another bonus to your stay. They include a lovely fountain, walking paths, and chairs and benches for sitting and enjoying the peaceful green Irish countryside. Lots of grassy areas, sculpted trees and an ample car park all attest to the care taken by Mrs. McGinty (and *Mr.* McGinty, too!). About two kilometers down the road from their B&B, the McGintys have purchased some lakefront property. They have a rowboat for their guests to use to explore Lough Eske and enjoy the peaceful beauty of this quiet corner of Ireland. All in all, from top to bottom and from side to side, you can't beat The Arches Country House. If you stay here, I guarantee you'll be glad you did! And when you stay here, please tell Mrs. McGinty "Hello" for me.

The McGinty's ask that you not smoke in any of the bedrooms.

ARDEEVIN, *Lough Eske, Barnesmore, Donegal. Tel. (073) 21790. 6 rooms. Rates for singles: £27.50, doubles: £20 per person sharing. Rates include breakfast. No credit cards accepted. Open April though mid-November. No service charge.*

Next door to The Arches, Ardeevin is another pleasant B&B in the Lough Eske area. The views are great here too. Like the Arches next door, this B&B is managed by Mrs. McGinty. However, this Mrs. McGinty is the wife of Sean McGinty, who owns the sweater shop where you probably bought your sweater today (or will tomorrow)! Together, they have been in the B&B business since 1967, and know their stuff.

Recent and extensive renovations have been made, and their B&B is nicer than ever. Each room is spacious and exquisitely furnished, and all have lovely views of Lough Eske.

Breakfast is nothing short of a treat. It is taken around a large, community table, and Mrs. McGinty is a superb cook. The views of the luscious, landscaped lawns and Lough Eske in the distance are spectacular and a wonderful way to begin your day.

The McGinty's ask that you not smoke in any of the bedrooms.

THE CENTRAL HOTEL, *The Diamond, Donegal Town. Tel. (073) 21027, Fax (073) 22295. 85 rooms. Rates for singles: £43 to £50, doubles: £49 to £68 per person sharing. Rates include breakfast. Restaurant, bistro, pub, gym, Jacuzzi, solarium. All major credit cards accepted. 10% service charge.*

You can't get much more central in Donegal town than the Central Hotel, which sits right on the main square in the downtown area. The rooms are nice sized, although all have essentially the same decor. The hotel is older but clean and functional. The rooms in the front overlook the busy Diamond, but they can be noisy. Opt instead for the rooms in the back that overlook the gardens and an estuary of the sea. Each of the rooms is outfitted with a television, and if you've brought your children along with you, you'll appreciate the reduced rate for children.

ARDNAMONA HOUSE, *Lough Eske, Donegal Town. Tel. (073) 22650, Fax (073) 22819; E-mail: ardnamon@gofree.indigo.ie. 6 rooms, 3 ensuite, 3 standard. Rates for singles: £50 to £57, doubles: £40 to £47 per person sharing. Rates include breakfast. Gardens, forest walks, fishing, boating. American Express, Mastercard and Visa accepted. No service charge.*

Kieran and Amabel Clarke are rightfully proud of lovely Ardnamona, their pleasant B&B that overlooks Lough Eske. While the accommodations are wonderful, the things of most interest in Ardnamona are the gardens. Ardnamona is set in a veritable paradise. The gardens were originally planted in the 1880s, and include cuttings from the Imperial Gardens in Peking and the palace gardens in Katmandu. Radiant Rhododendruns and amazing Azaleas capture most of the attention, but the variety of other plants and trees is impressive.

The house is pretty nice too! A former Victorian shooting lodge, Ardnamona features large and tastefully decorated bedrooms. The rooms in the front of the house offer an extra benefit: splendid views of the lake and surrounding woodlands and gardens. Ardnamona House offers more than mere accommodation: beautiful gardens and acres of woods are available for walks.

HARVEY'S POINT COUNTRY HOTEL, *Lough Eske, Donegal Town, (073) 22208, (073) 22352, 32 rooms. Rates for singles: £55 to £70, doubles: £45 to £80 per person sharing, suites: £60 to £90 per person sharing. Rates include breakfast. Restaurant, walking and bicycle paths, boating. All major credit cards accepted. 10% service charge.*

Sitting along the banks of peaceful Lough Eske, Harvey's Point Country Hotel provides a feel of continental Europe mixed with warm Irish hospitality. The setting is picturesque – in the trees and beside the lake. Lots of nature is available to explore via walking or bicycling (bikes are provided free to guests). Owned by Jody Gysling, Harvey's Point fosters the feel of a Swiss-German resort. Lots of light wood and chalet-style buildings contribute to the feel of a country inn someplace in the Swiss or German Alps. The public areas are light and airy, with lots of windows on the side of the building that faces the lake. An informal brasserie offers delicious meals and a pleasant atmosphere. Another, more formal restaurant features Swiss and French cuisine.

The rooms are spacious and tastefully decorated. If you can afford them, the executive suites are of course the nicest, and most have views of the lake out at least one window. All the rooms feature tea- and coffee-making facilities, and the executive suites offer trouser presses. Although this may sound like a fun place to bring your children, the management requests that you not bring them if they are younger than 10 years old.

ST. ERNAN'S HOUSE HOTEL, *Donegal Town. Tel. (073) 21065, Fax (073) 22098; E-mail: enquiries@sainternans.com; Website: www.sainternans.com. 12 rooms. Rates for singles: £75 to £90, doubles: £60 to £66 per person sharing. Rates include breakfast. Restaurant, gardens, walking paths. All major credit cards accepted. 10% service charge.*

St. Ernan's has an idyllic setting – this stately four-star Victorian hotel sits grandly on its own timbered tidal island, joined to the mainland by a causeway. Serenity is the goal here, and serenity is what the staff helps provide. The rooms are all quite large, decorated individually, and almost all have outstanding views of the sea or the surrounding woodland. Whether you just need a break from charging all over the country, or are just looking for a good night's sleep before charging about again, St. Ernan's is a very pleasant respite.

St. Ernan's is open from April through October.

WHERE TO EAT

THE BLUEBERRY TEA ROOM, *Castle Street, Donegal Town. Tel. (073) 22933. £2.50 to £3.95. Open daily from 9:00am to 9:00pm during the summer, 9:00am to 7:00pm Monday through Saturday the rest of the year. No credit cards accepted.*

Just off the Diamond up a narrow staircase between the Olde Castle Bar and Restaurant and Melody Maker is The Blueberry Tea Room, a popular little sandwich shop. I asked several of the merchants in the area where they took their lunch, and a surprising number indicated this little shop. The decor is unmemorable, but the sandwiches are good and inexpensive. Casual dress – grubbies are acceptable.

HARVEY'S POINT COUNTRY RESTAURANT, *Lough Eske. £12.95 to £22. Open daily from 12:30pm to 2:30pm and 6:30pm to 9:30pm. All major credit cards accepted. 10% service charge.*

Harvey's Point Country Restaurant and Hotel sits on the banks of lovely Lough Eske in County Donegal. The setting is marvelous, and parts of the dining room have views of the lake. Starched linens, crystal, and silver complement the excellent food, like the crepinette of tender farmhouse chicken or the grilled salmon fillet with leek and chive sauce. Or, if beef is your preference, you can't miss with the beef stroganoff and tagliatelle. Casual dress is requested.

ST. ERNAN'S HOUSE RESTAURANT, *St. Ernan's House Hotel, Donegal Town. Tel. (073) 21065. Set dinner £25. Open for dinner daily from 6:30pm until 8:30pm. Mastercard and Visa accepted.*

Associated with St. Ernan's House Hotel, the restaurant is designed primarily for guests of the hotel, but you might luck out and be able to savor the fare here. Call ahead to see how likely it is that you'll get in. If you do, the seafood is the specialty here. Casual dress is requested.

SEEING THE SIGHTS

Donegal Castle, *Donegal, Tirchonaill Street. Open April through September daily from 9:30am to 6:30pm. Last admission 45 minutes prior to closing. Admission is £3.00 for adults, £2.00 for seniors and students, £1.25 for children, and a family ticket is available for £7.50.* In the center of town near The Diamond sits regal-looking Donegal Castle. Originally the home of O'Connell Clan chieftain **Hugh O'Donnell**, the stronghold passed through several hands before being taken by **Sir Basil Brooke**. In 1610, he reworked the structure, adding the mansion and turrets that you see today.

Tours of the castle yield wonderful views of ornate Persian rugs, splendid French tapestries and information panels tell the history of the castle.

At the south edge of town a short stroll from the Tourist Information Office on Quay Street you'll find the ruins of a 15th-century **Franciscan Friary**. Take a few minutes and walk amid their stony silence and wonder what sort of life these stone walls offered to those who lived here.

Speaking of those who lived at the friary, legend has it that some of its most famous inhabitants were the four clerics **Padric O'Cleary, Michael O'Cleerey, Peregrine O'Duignean**, and **Fearfeasa O'Molconry.** The extensive history of Ireland called *The Annals of the Four Masters* is attributed to them. The history begins 40 years before the flood (Noah's flood, that is) and continues until the 17th-century. It is a compilation of the narrative histories that were passed from Irish storyteller to Irish storyteller through the centuries. It is fascinating to read, although modern historians have a hard time separating fact from embellishment in many cases.

About a mile south of town on the N15 is a bevy of craft shops called the **Donegal Craft Village**, where you can shop for knitwear, pottery and china, and assorted other items. The shops are pleasant and the wares are top quality, but the part I most enjoyed was the interaction and conversation with the shop owners.

If you take the N15 north out of Donegal Town just a few miles, you'll see signs directing you to **Lough Eske**. Lough Eske is a serene and tranquil lake nestled amid the Blue Stack Mountains. It offers pleasant views and quite a number of walking and/or bicycle paths for you to enjoy. If you have brought bicycles with you, it would be a very pleasant ride around the lake and some of the surrounding areas. You may rent bicycles at several places in Donegal Town, including **O'Doherty's** on *Main Street, Tel. (073) 21119.*

Just a few miles south of Donegal Town are soft, sandy beaches that you might like to seek out. Take the N15 south out of Donegal Town, and watch for signs directing you to **Rossknowlagh** and Coolmore on the R231. Near Rossknowlagh you'll find some gorgeous beaches that are a lot of fun to walk along.

NIGHTLIFE & ENTERTAINMENT

BIDDY O'BARNES, *on the N15, Barnesmore, County Donegal.*

About six miles northwest of Donegal on the N15 you'll find a pleasant old pub called Biddy O'Barnes, a wonderful country pub that seems to enjoy – nay flourish – on its isolation. Two centuries of County Donegal's residents have made the journey to Biddy O'Barnes, and you should make the trip there too.

The fireplace is the center point of the pub, and it is traditionally surrounded by those from the surrounding countryside that have come to air their gripes, swap their stories and drink their Guinness. Three generations of O'Callaghans have owned Biddy O'Barnes (named after the original Biddy O'Callaghan) and the owners have wisely left well enough alone when it came to decorating the place. Slate floors and much of the woodwork are original. There is a newer addition to Biddy O'Barnes, but the real character (and characters!) is found in the original part of the bar.

If you wish to visit Biddy O'Barnes, it is convenient to The Arches B&B, Ardeevin B&B, and Harvey's Point Country Hotel. But do designate a driver – the road to these places of lodging is fraught with dips and turns, and is quite narrow, of course.

EAS DUN PUB, *The Abbey Hotel, The Diamond, Donegal Town. Tel. (073) 21014.*

The bar at the Abbey Hotel is an enjoyable gathering place for a few of the locals as well as many tourists. Weekday evenings you'll find traditional Irish music going strong, and on the weekends you can join in the dancing. It's a fun place, and there always seems to be a smile on everyone's face.

SPORTS & RECREATION

Golf

Donegal Golf Club, *Murvagh, County Donegal. Tel. (073) 34054, £13/ £16.*

This pretty links golf course is popular with the locals as well as the occasional tourist. Visitors are welcome daily. Par 73, 7,153 yards.

Horseback Riding

• **Ashleigh Riding School**, *Rosslongan, County Donegal. Tel. (073) 22386*
• **Carrigart Riding Stables**, *Carrigart, County Donegal. Tel. (074) 55114*

Sailing & Windsurfing

• **Marble Hill Windsurfing,** *Dunfanaghy, County Donegal. Tel. (074) 36231*

Scuba Diving

• **Donegal Surf Center**, *Donegal, County Donegal. Tel. (073) 21179*

EXCURSIONS & DAY TRIPS

Donegal makes an outstanding place from which to base your exploration of County Donegal. From here, you can reach the farthest extremities of the county within just a couple of hours at the most. Depending on how long you take at each of these sights, you may be able to see all of these in one day. Two days would be better, three would be ideal! The longer you have to spend in Donegal, the better!

Using Donegal Town as a base, you can see the rest of the county relatively easily. And it is such a lovely county that you shouldn't rush through it too quickly.

Lodging

SMUGGLER'S CREEK INN, *Waterville (near Rossknowlagh). Tel. (066) 74330, Fax (066) 74422. 10 rooms. Rates for singles: £30, doubles: £20 to £40£ per person sharing. One restaurant, pub. All major credit cards accepted. No service charge.*

This 100-year old house overlooking the ocean was converted recently into an award-winning restaurant with six bedrooms. Several of the rooms are quite large and have beautiful views of the ocean and an expansive sandy beach. One of those rooms has a balcony. The remaining rooms are smallish, but their distressed pine furnishings give them a homey feeling.

The rooms are actually a side business for Smuggler's Creek Inn. Their real business is a wonderful pub and restaurant (See *Where to Eat* section.) If you are looking to turn in early on Friday and Saturday evenings, this probably isn't a good place to stay – the rooms are above the pub where traditional Irish music is featured from 10:00pm to midnight on the weekend. The Inn is about 15 miles southwest of Donegal Town off the N15. Take the N15 south to the R231, then watch for the signs directing you to Waterville and Rossknowlagh.

CASTLE MURRAY HOTEL, *Dunkineely. Tel. (073) 37022, (073) 37330. 10 rooms. Rates for singles: £30, doubles: £30 per person sharing. Rates include breakfast. Restaurant, pub. All major credit cards accepted. No service charge.*

Castle Murray Hotel is not a castle at all, but a nice new hotel sitting atop a hill and overlooking the scant ruins of its namesake and the ocean beyond. Many of Castle Murray's rooms have gorgeous views of McSweeney Bay and the rugged Donegal coastline. The rooms are large and tastefully decorated with warm pine. There is more of a B&B feel here than at most hotels. The rooms at the front of the hotel offer the best views by far: the Atlantic Ocean crashes onto the shore and the rugged Donegal shoreline is picturesque and photogenic. The owners, Thierry and Clare Delcros, also run a wonderful seafood restaurant on the first floor (see below). In addition to marvelous food, the views are stunning.

CASTLEGROVE COUNTRY HOUSE, *Letterkenny. Tel. (074) 51118, Fax (074) 51384. 7 rooms. Rates for singles: £30 to £45, doubles: £30 to £45 per person sharing. Rates include breakfast. Mastercard and Visa accepted. No service charge.*

It's hard to say which you will enjoy more: the beautifully restored 17th-century house, the splendid views of Lough Swilly, or the warm welcome you'll receive by Mrs. Mary Sweeney. No matter. Every one of them is above expectations, and no matter what you're looking for here, you'll find them at Castlegrove Country House. The pleasant public areas have open fires, the rooms are tastefully decorated, and the service attentive.

KEE'S HOTEL, *Stranorlar, Ballybofey. Tel. (074) 31018, Fax (074) 31917. 54 rooms. Rates for singles: £45 to £55, doubles: £68 to £85, executive rooms: £80 to £99. Restaurant, indoor swimming pool, gym, Jacuzzi, solarium, sauna, spa, steam room. Rate includes breakfast. All major credit cards accepted. 10% service charge.*

Four generations of the Kee family have hosted guests in Kee's Hotel in Ballybofey, and they are very good at their trade. The reception you receive here will be more akin to the personal attention you get at a B&B than what you often find at hotels. Kee's Hotel was built in 1842, and through the years frequent and careful renovations have maintained the Kee's warmth and personality, while keeping it up to date.

The rooms are large and comfortably furnished, including 13 new Executive rooms that offer vistas of the Bluestack Mountains. The rooms in the front of the hotel have been thoughtfully soundproofed to afford a quiet stay to go along with the fine views. All the rooms have tea- and coffee-making facilities and trouser presses. In recent years the hotel has added some wonderful amenities for their guests, and include an indoor swimming pool, sauna, and exercise room. A nice touch is that entrances to these areas have been added with direct access to guests' rooms – no need to walk through public areas to get to any of these facilities.

The hotel is proud of their fine restaurant, and I was impressed with it also (see *Where to Eat*). In fact, I was so impressed with it after my first visit, that I wandered the Donegal roads trying to find it on my last visit. I discovered that my memory hadn't played tricks on me: the food is still incredible. To get here, take the N15 east out of Donegal to Ballybofey.

THE SAND HOUSE HOTEL, *Waterville (near Rossnowlagh). Tel. (073) 51777, Fax (073) 52100, US toll free 800/448-8355; E-mail: info@sandhouse-hotel.ie; Website: www.sandhouse-hotel.ie. 45 rooms. Rates for singles: £63 to £68, doubles: £48 to £53 per person sharing. Rates include breakfast. Restaurant, several pubs, tennis courts, snooker, game room, play-ground, croquet. All major credit cards accepted. 10% service charge. Open from Easter through October.*

A Manor House Hotel, the Sand Hotel sits along one of the most popular surfing beaches in the country. Several pubs are on the premises, including a 1960s-era "surfer's bar." This comfortable bar is home to traditional Irish sessions which are held Wednesday evenings from June through August.

All the rooms are decorated differently, and antiques are sprinkled throughout. The rooms with an ocean view are of course the most popular, and there are no televisions in the rooms to distract you from the beautiful ocean views. The hotel offers a wide variety of activities to its guests, including tennis courts, snooker, a game room, a playground, and even a croquet court. The hotel is delighted to accommodate children, and offers discounts for them. If you've brought a pet with you, it is welcome too.

THE BAY VIEW HOTEL, *Main Street, Killybegs. Tel. (073) 31950, Fax (073) 31856. 38 rooms. Rates for singles: £45 to £55, doubles: £45 to £55 per person sharing, suites: £65 to £85 per person sharing. Rates include breakfast. Restaurant, gym, swimming pool, Jacuzzi, solarium. All major credit cards accepted. 10% service charge.*

This is a nice older hotel in "downtown" Killybegs, overlooking the harbor and its plentiful fishing boats. The rooms are large and the furnishings simple. Ask for a room facing the harbor – the double-pane windows cut down on the noise considerably, and the sights are interest-ing. The hotel has a number of leisure activities to offer their guests, including an indoor swimming pool, exercise room, Jacuzzi, and solarium. In addition, they make it nice for their guests who are traveling with children or pets, as they offer a discount for children and can accommodate pets. Seniors can also benefit from discounts most months of the year (but not in July and August).

Dining

SMUGGLER'S CREEK INN, *Waterville (near Rossknowlagh). Tel. (072) 52366. £9.75 to £12.95. Open daily from 9:00am to 10:00am, 12:30pm to 5:00pm, and 6:30pm to 9:15pm. Mastercard and Visa accepted. No service charge.*

The Smuggler's Creek Inn, a seafood restaurant, has splendid views of Donegal Bay and a long wide sandy beach. They have a number of tables out on the veranda overlooking the ocean, and it is a very popular — and busy — place during the summer months. You probably won't get in without a reservation from June through August. An added bonus is the traditional Irish music played in the bar on Friday and Saturday evenings from 10:00pm until midnight. The menu features a nice selection of seafood entrees with a smattering of beef and vegetarian dishes. Nice casual dress is recommended.

KEE'S RESTAURANT, *Stranorlar, Ballybofey. Tel. (074) 31018. £9 to £20. Open Monday through Friday from 6:30pm to 9:30pm, and Saturdays from 6:30pm to 10:00pm. All major credit cards accepted.*

Years ago I stumbled across the restaurant in Kee's Hotel, and every time I go back to Ireland I try to arrange my schedule to allow me to stop in for dinner. Why? Because the meals I have had here rival any I have had anywhere in the world. The chef who creates the magic is Frederic Souty, and his meals will delight (and fill!) you.

The menu is well represented by beef, seafood, and other wonderful concoctions. Try the roast rack of Donegal spring lamb or the grilled fillet steak with wild mushroom essence. Add one of the finest wine lists in the country, and you have a combination that's difficult to beat. The restaurant has recently been renovated, and the changes only served to enhance the wonderful personality of the room. Dark wood accents the quiet, private atmosphere in the dining room. The framed tapestries decorating the walls are the work of past owners of the hotel and restaurant.

Chef Souty is likely to continue in his role as the head chef at Kee's Restaurant for some time. Several years ago the owners' daughter fell in love with more than the menu, and her marriage to the talented chef assures that you will be able to enjoy his gastronomical handiwork for many years to come! Stop by, and I guarantee you'll feel the same way I do about his expertise. Nice casual dress is fine, although a coat and tie would not be out of place.

CASTLE MURRAY HOUSE RESTAURANT, *St. John's Point, Dunkineely. Tel. (073) 37022. Set menu £13 to £26 or á la carte menu. Open Monday through Saturday from 7:00pm to 9:30pm, and Sunday from 3:00pm to 8:00pm. Mastercard and Visa accepted. No service charge.*

Just outside the drab town of Dunkineely, not far from Donegal Town and overlooking McSweeney Bay, is Castle Murray House Restaurant. This light and airy restaurant offers stunning views of the bay to complement a varied menu. The owners, Thierry and Clare Delcros, are French, and the menu is "French with an Irish flair" according to Clare. You can select a lobster and eat it within site of its home, McSweeney Bay. Or, if you prefer, try the *piece de veau du jour* (the veal of the day). Casual dress is fine.

Sightseeing

Take the N56 west out of Donegal for about 30 miles, and you'll soon come to signposts directing you to the fishing village of **Killybegs** on Road R263. The Irish name for Killybegs is *Na Cealla Beaga*, which means "The Little Churches," referring no doubt to some long-forgotten churches that have faded from memory and history.

Today this busy little harbor town sits abreast a protected cove. The fishing fleet here is big business. Another big business is the hand-tufted carpets produced here. These prized works of art have found their way into the Vatican, the White House, Buckingham Palace, and a number of other important places. (Perhaps your home will be the next important place that features a hand-tufted rug from Donegal!).

Continue west from Killybegs on the R263 to get to the **Slieve League Mountains**. The cliffs of Slieve League Mountains are the highest in Ireland, sloping nearly 2,000 feet into the ocean. They are quite rugged, although for sheer dramatics, I prefer the Cliffs of Moher. Several cliff walks are available in the area. One of them, "One Man's Pass," feels not unlike a high-wire act, and is not for the faint of heart or people suffering from fear of heights.

Further west along the R263 from Killybegs, watch for the signpost directing you to **Glencolumbkille.** This scenic fishing village, scattered as it is on the rocks just out of reach of the Atlantic Ocean, is a pleasant place to stop and visit. To call it a village is almost an overstatement, as it is not very large. Originally it was a monastic settlement of St. Columba and his followers (its Irish name means "Columba's Church of the Glen"). But the settlement of this region is even older than that, as evidenced by the presence of dozens of prehistoric cairns in the vicinity.

St. Columba's House, *Glencolumbkille.* On a crag just north of the village is a small oratory which legend says was used by the good saint himself. Every year at midnight on June 9, worshippers form a processional where they walk barefoot for two miles around a circuit called the "Stations of the Cross."

The Folk Village, *Glencolumbkille, open April, May, and October from Monday through Saturday from 10:00am to 6:00pm and Sunday from noon to 6:00pm, June through September Monday through Saturday from 10:00am to 7:00pm and Sunday from noon to 7:00pm, November they're open Monday through Saturday from 10:00am to 6:00pm and Sunday from noon to 6:00pm. Admission is £2.00 for adults, £1.75 for children. Tel. (073) 30017.* This is an exhibit that depicts three centuries of life in Ireland. The cottages are realistically simple, effectively showing the unadorned lifestyle of past days. Thatched roofs, dirt floors, and simple furnishings are the rule in this folk village. Imagine what your life would have been like had one of these cottages been the place you called home.

From Glencolumbkille, watch for signs directing you to **Glengesh Pass**, and follow those signs to the crossroads town of Ardara. From there, take the N56 north to Dungloe, and watch for signs directing you to **Burtonport**. Burtonport is more commonly known by its Irish name, **Ailt an Chorrain**. This small fishing village on the rocky coastline of the Rosses Headland remains frozen in time, with very little tourist development.

It also serves as the jumping off point for **Aranmore Island**. Aranmore lies four miles offshore from the village of Ailt an Chorrain, and it is the largest island off the Donegal coast. Prehistoric ruins on the island are witnesses that hearty men and women have made this their home for many centuries. Boat trips to the island leave roughly every hour throughout the day. Expect to pay around £2 to £3 per person for a round-trip to the island.

From Burtonport, take the R259 to Dungloe, then north on the N56 to the R257. Follow that to Brinlack, and then watch for signs directing you to **Bloody Foreland Head**, *near Meenlaragh*. As the R257 sweeps along through the back country of Donegal, the vistas just get more and more scenic. One of the high points is Bloody Foreland Head, on the northwestern tip of Ireland. It has earned this name because the rays from the setting sun seem to linger on the granite boulders that line the Atlantic coast, causing them to seemingly "blush" as the day wanes.

Lying nine miles northwest off the northwest coast of Ireland is **Tory Island**. You reach Tory Island via ferry from Meenlaragh. You can reach Meenlaragh by continuing north on the R257. But you'll only have access to the island if the weather is good, and it can be brutal off the coast here. The island itself is a rocky lump sitting amid the crashing surf. If you take the ferry out, be sure to leave early enough in the day to get back, since there are no overnight accommodations available on Tory Island.

In recent years the hearty folk who live on Tory Island have discovered a market for their paintings, to supplement their normal fishing income. There are a number of ruins on the island, mute witnesses to the extent past generations have gone to find their seclusion.

Follow the R257 to the R56, and then north to **Dunfanaghy**. When you arrive, watch for the sign directing you to an oddity of nature: **McSwyne's Gun**. During rough weather, the incoming tide strikes this large natural hole and it sounds as though a cannon has been fired.

Before you leave Dunfanaghy, park your car and take a stroll out to **Horn Head**. County Donegal has many awe-inspiring sights, but this may be the topper of them all. Dramatic drops of 600 feet enable you to see great distances over these cliffs. If you don't feel like walking, you can take a narrow, unnumbered road out on Horn Head to see the sights.

Take the N56 south toward Letterkenny, and watch for signposts directing you to **Glenveagh National Park**, *open mid-March through early November daily from 10:00am to 6:30pm. Admission is £2 for adults, £1.50 for senior citizens, and £1 for children. Tel. (074) 37090.*

In a land of incredible beauty, Glenveagh National Park can hold its own, and then some. Glenveagh Lough is simply gorgeous, as is Glenveagh Castle, and it boasts a set of Castle gardens that are exquisite.

You can't drive through the 24,000-acre park. It is similar to wilderness areas in American parks – no motorized vehicles are allowed in most of the park. You may park at the front gate, and a bus will take you to the castle. Once you arrive, there are walking paths that allow you to see a bit of the park more closely.

It is interesting to note that Americans played an important part in Glenveagh National Park. During the mid-19th century, John Adair began acquiring the land that is now Glenveagh National Park. In 1861 he evicted all the tenants who had been living and working the land. He commissioned the building of Glenveagh Castle in 1870. Immediately upon its completion, he left Ireland for Texas. He never returned. His wife Cornelia left Texas and returned to Glenveagh, where she supervised the care of the land. The gardens you see around the castle are a result of her labors. In 1984, American millionaire Henry McIlhenny graciously donated the estate to Ireland.

Once you finish with Glenveagh National Park, work your way back to the N56 and head south. Follow the signposts toward Ramelton, and then take the R247 north from there to **Rathmullan**, a picturesque little village on the western shores of Lough Swilly. The harbor at Rathmullan witnessed the "**Flight of the Earls**" in September 1607. This was the departure of the Ulster chieftains from Ireland. Most never returned. Their departure opened the way for the **Plantation** – the large-scale settlement of Protestants on the confiscated lands of the departed nobles. To help you understand the troubled history of this part of the Emerald Isle, you'll find a wonderful little museum called **The Flight of the Earls**

Heritage Center, *Rathmullan, open Easter through September Friday from 9:00am to 5:00pm, Saturday from 10:00am to 5:00pm and Sunday from 10:00am to 3:00pm. Admission is £1.50 for adults, £1.00 for senior citizens, and £1.00 for children. Tel. (074) 58229.* The museum is housed in an ancient Martello Tower. A series of these formidable towers were built around the Irish coastline as lookout points for the anticipated approach of Napoleonic troops. The feared invasion never materialized, but the squat, sturdy structures make excellent museums now.

Grianan of Ailigh, *between Letterkenny and Burnfoot.* Head back toward Letterkenny, and follow the N13 southeast out of Letterkenny, and then bend northeast on the N13 until you come to the signpost indicating Grianan of Ailigh. Follow it for about two miles up a winding lane to the top of an 800-foot hill and you're at Grianan of Ailigh – the impressive stone ring fort that was once the stronghold of the O'Neills, former rulers of Ulster.

I have been to the Grianan of Ailigh (also spelled Aileach) during nice weather as well as stormy weather. Regardless of whether it is shrouded in mist or basking in bright sunlight it is an impressive sight indeed. And the views from atop its rocky walls are some of the most spectacular in all of Ireland. From its lofty perch, the land drops away dramatically in all directions, leaving stunning views of the surrounding countryside, all the way to the Atlantic ocean. Off to the north and east you can clearly see two large lakes – Lough Swilly and Lough Foyle. And all around you is the beauty of the patchwork green that is so typically Ireland.

Archaeologists speculate that the fort dates from the Iron Age, making it approximately 3,000 years old! It is a circular structure (77 feet in diameter) with three terraced rings one inside the other. On the inside a series of stone walks bring you to the top of the 17 foot tall walls. Their base is a *mere* 13 feet. The structure you see today was restored from a somewhat disheveled state about 100 years ago.

The origin and ancient history of the fort are a mystery that continues to bedevil archaeologists and scholars alike. It is thought by some that Druidic priests once conducted some sort of religious ceremony inside the circular structure while their followers observed the proceedings from atop the massive walls. Whatever the ancient history was, historians assure us that the O'Neills took it over as their royal residence during their reign over Ulster.

As you stroll along the top of the fort, pause and consider the incredible human effort that must have gone into constructing such an imposing fortress. Consider also what the builders were seeking protection from. The term *Grianan* means the sun, or a sunny place, and the word *Ailigh* means stone, or stone dwelling. Therefore, the ancient name for the Grianan of Ailigh is roughly translated as "The Stone Dwelling in the Sunny Place." Don't miss this sight, it is one of my most enduring memories of the Emerald Isle.

Back down on the N13, at the foot of the hill upon which the Grianan Ailigh presides, is the **Grianan Ailigh Heritage Centre** *near Letterkenny, open daily 10:00am to 10:00pm. Admission for adults is £2, and for children, students and seniors it is £1. A family ticket is available for £5.* The Grianan of Ailigh Heritage Centre is located on the second floor of a converted chapel, above a restaurant/bar. It houses an interpretive center focused on the Grianan of Ailigh. It offers dioramas and a scale model of the fort. As you might imagine, a number of legends swirl around the history and purpose of the ring fort, and several of the more popular ones are presented here.

After visiting the Grianan Ailigh, head back toward Letterkenny on the N13. **Lough Swilly**, a beautiful long narrow lake in the northeast corner of Donegal, is a peaceful and lovely lake to just sit and watch, or to walk along her banks.

From the Grianan of Ailigh, follow the N13 toward Londonderry. As you near Londonderry, watch for the R238, and/or signs directing you toward Buncrana. Proceed through Buncrana following the signs for Malin, beyond which is **Malin Head**. Malin Head is the northernmost point of the Emerald Isle. You've got to go here if for no other reason than to be at Ireland's northernmost point! But there are definitely other reasons to come to Malin Head. The views, especially those along the southern shoreline, are breathtaking, and it's hard to beat the incredible sunsets from this particular vantage point. If the weather cooperates, you'll be able to see the Scottish island of **Islay**, on the northeast horizon. The highest point at Malin Head is 362 feet above sea level, and is topped by the ruins of an old Martello Tower, which was built to provide advance warning of the approach of Napoleonic troops – which thankfully never materialized.

PRACTICAL INFORMATION

Laundry Service
• **Eleanor's Launderette**, *Upper Main Street, Donegal. Tel. (073) 21317*

Post Offices
• **Donegal Post Office**, *Tirconaill Street, Donegal. Tel. (073) 21030*
• **Letterkenny Post Office**, *Main Street, Letterkenny. Tel. (074) 22454*

Tourist Offices
• **Donegal Town Tourist Information Office**, *Quay Street, Donegal, Tel. (073) 21148*

•**Falcarragh Tourist Information Office**, *Falcarragh, Tel. (074) 65070*
•**Flight of the Earls Heritage Center**, *Rathmullan, Tel. (074) 58229*
•**Letterkenny Tourist Information Office**, *Derry Road, Letterkenny, Tel. (074) 21160*

MONAGHAN TOWN

Monaghan Town is the county seat of County Monaghan. *Muineachain*, its Irish name, means "Little Hills" and describes much of the land in this county. The small rounded mounds decorating the countryside are called *drumlins*. A monastery was built on this site in the 9th century, and weathered a series of sieges, sacks, and plunderings until 1161, when it was abandoned. The site was rededicated anew when a Franciscan friary was built here in 1462.

ARRIVALS & DEPARTURES

By Bus

Seven buses a day run between Monaghan and Dublin, and they come and go from the **Bus Depot**, *just off the Diamond. Tel. (047) 82377.*

By Car

Monaghan Town is located northwest of Dublin on the N2, and southwest of Belfast on the M1/A3.

SEEING THE SIGHTS

There are a few interesting sights in and around Monaghan. On the south end of town is **St. Macartan's Cathedral**, a Gothic structure built in the 19th century, topped by a graceful spire. Downtown in the central square called "The Diamond" is an interesting memorial known as **Rossmore Monument**, which looks like a medieval spaceship ready for blast-off! At **St. Patrick's Cathedral** (1836), look for the **Lloyd Monument**, a poignant memorial to a beloved son (Henry Craven Jesse Lloyd) who died while fighting in South Africa during one of the modern wars. It features exquisite sculpting depicting a variety of unique and interesting scenes (native tribesmen, horses, cavalry, an African village, etc.).

Monaghan County Museum, *Monaghan, open year around Tuesday through Saturday from 11:00am to 1:00pm, and from 2:00pm until 5:00pm. Admission is free. Tel. (047) 82928.* Housed in the old Market House, the Monaghan County Museum is a good place to stop and discover the history of the area from ancient times up through the present day. There is an especially intriguing 14th-century cross on display that is called the Cross of Clogher.

While it is a small museum, it is well done, and is the winner of the *European Community Heritage Award* for small museums.

Rossmore Forest Park, *near Monaghan*. Leave Monaghan via the R189 toward Newbliss and you'll come to Rossmore Forest Park, nearly 700 acres of attractive grounds featuring rolling hills, lakelets, and plenty of walking trails. Take a few minutes and stroll through the flora and fauna that will speak volumes by their silence. If you do, it will provide you with some pleasant memories.

Inniskeen Folk Museum, *Inniskeen, open May through August on Sundays from 2:00pm to 5:00pm. They will make appointments for other times if you call ahead. Admission is free, although donations are accepted and appreciated. Tel. (042) 78109.* The hamlet of Inniskeen is about nine miles west of Dundalk on the R178. A small museum here commemorates one of Ireland's great poets, Patrick Kavanaugh. Kavanaugh's body was interred at Inniskeen after his death.

PRACTICAL INFORMATION
Post Offices
• **Monaghan Post Office**, *Mill Street, Monaghan. Tel. (047) 82131*

Tourist Office
• **Monaghan Tourist Information Office**, *Market Street, Monaghan, Tel. (047) 81122*

CAVAN TOWN

The county seat of County Cavan, **Cavan Town** is not large, with about 3,000 residents. Its Irish name is *An Cabhan*, which means "The Hollow Place." Tourists have largely overlooked County Cavan and Cavan Town – neither is on any major roadway. As a result, if you venture here you'll find a slower pace than other places in Ireland.

If the sights are not plentiful, the land is attractive and verdant. Low rolling hills clothed in varying shades of green extend a continuous invitation and temptation to picnic. Lakes dot the countryside and make for quiet, restful views.

ARRIVALS & DEPARTURES
By Car
Cavan is about 70 miles northwest of Dublin on the N3.

SEEING THE SIGHTS
Cavan Folk Museum, *Cavan Town, open mid-June through October.*

Admission is £1.50 for adults and 50p for children. Tel. (049) 37248. Cavan is about 90 minutes northwest of Dublin on the N3. The museum contains a collection of clothing, home, and farm implements from the 1700s to the present. It's actually quite interesting and offers around 3,000 articles to browse through. You might find some of the exhibits interesting.

Cavan Crystal, *Cavan Town, open all year Monday through Friday from 9:30am to 4:30pm. Tel. (049) 31800.* Not nearly as well known as their world-renowned rivals in Waterford, Cavan Crystal nonetheless produces wonderful lead crystal articles that will delight and amaze you. They also offer a short tour of their factory, and it's a fascinating tour. You have the opportunity to be "up-close and personal" with the artisans that blow, cut, and etch the lead crystal. If you love lead crystal and don't require the Waterford brand, Cavan Crystal makes a lovely and less expensive alternative.

PRACTICAL INFORMATION
Tourist Office
• **Cavan Tourist Information Office**, *Farnham Street, Cavan, Tel. (049) 31942*

18♦ NORTHERN IRELAND

Should You Go to Northern Ireland?

The question usually asked by foreigners is: "Isn't travel to **Northern Ireland** dangerous?" I asked that question of a shop owner in the US who was from Northern Ireland. He smiled, and patiently explained that not going to Northern Ireland for that reason was roughly comparable to not visiting the United States because of high crime rates in some cities or the Los Angeles riots of a few years back. He conceded there are areas you don't want to go, but there are those areas in the United States, too.

I took him at his word and ventured north of the border. Here's what I discovered for myself: Northern Ireland is delightful and provides some of the most spectacular and awe-inspiring scenery of the island. Shop owners and B&B proprietors are delighted to greet American tourists. On my first visit to the North, I discussed my concerns with one of the Northern Ireland shop owners. She quipped, "I know we get a lot of bad press in the States, but we haven't lost a tourist yet!"

I have been to Northern Ireland many times, and have simply been delighted each time I visited. Having said that, I'll also tell you that there are a few areas you should definitely steer clear of: **Derry** (Londonderry) and **Armagh**. These are the main hotbeds of dissent and hatred in Northern Ireland. Derry is called *London*derry by those loyal to the British government, and called *Derry* by those who want Ireland united into one country. It was fascinating to notice President Clinton's diplomacy in this matter several years ago. When he visited Ireland in 1996, he called that city "Londonderry" when he was in the North, and referred to it as "Derry" when he was in the South. His diplomacy and sensitivity to the situation wasn't lost on the Irish: he scored points on both sides of the border! It's a shame, because Derry really is a splendid city, and yet I cannot in good conscience recommend that you travel there (sorry, Londonderry Chamber of Commerce!).

A close friend of mine lived in Northern Ireland several years and is intimately familiar with the political climate there. In addition to cautioning against visiting Derry, he reserved his most dire warnings for the city of Armagh. I have been to Armagh (by accident), and have no desire to return. I strongly suggest you skip that troubled city.

Unfortunately, violence occasionally erupts in **Belfast**, and it gets more than its fair share of negative publicity. As the capital of Northern Ireland, it serves as a high-profile target for militant activities. However, I have been to Belfast a number of times, and generally felt very safe there. If you limit your visit to the downtown area I describe (where most of the sights are anyway), you should be just fine.

Certainly the choice is yours whether you travel to Northern Ireland. But don't discount Northern Ireland because of some unpleasantness in a few parts of the country.

History

The history of Ulster is one of conquest, suppression, and **Plantation** (repopulation or resettlement). The idea behind this 16th-century practice was to replace the native (Catholic) population with those who would follow and support the Crown (Protestants). In the north, it proved to be an amazingly effective means of replacing rebels with a population loyal to the Crown. In the south, however, these efforts largely met with failure. For, while Protestant landlords in the south were also given Irish land, the Irish did not leave. The landlords needed their labor, and generally made life (relatively) tolerable for them.

After years of fighting with the English and their mercenaries, the Irish suffered crushing military defeats in Kinsale and Ulster. The leading Irish chieftains in Ulster abandoned the fight, and in 1607, they fled from Ireland to France and Spain, never to return. This was called the **Flight of the Earls**, and many historians feel this was *the* critical turning point in the history of Ulster. After their departure, hundreds of thousands of acres of land that had belonged to the Irish chieftains were confiscated by the Crown and given to Protestants as reward for officials and soldiers who had fought against the Irish.

Because of the mass influx of these Protestants into Ulster, a little over half of the population of Northern Ireland today is Protestant, primarily Anglican, compared to the population in the Republic, which is 93% Catholic. Many of the Protestants who came to this part of Ireland and never left were Scottish *galloglasses* – mercenaries who fought for the English. (Actually, they usually fought for the English, sometimes for the Irish, and often among themselves!) Even today, the accent in rural parts of County Antrim is much more akin to a Scottish brogue than to an Irish lilt.

As the Catholics in the south tried repeatedly to rebel against the English, the Protestants in the north became stronger supporters of the

Crown. In the late 19th century and the early part of the 20th century, when it looked like Ireland might actually have a chance at winning **Home Rule** – independence from England – the Ulster Protestants became militant in their opposition. They felt that "Home Rule" meant "Rome Rule," and they pledged to fight it – in Parliament first, then in the streets if necessary.

In early 1914, it appeared that Ireland was going to win Home Rule and become an independent nation. However, when it became apparent that independence would result in armed conflict in Northern Ireland, a compromise was reluctantly reached. The compromise granted Home Rule to the majority of Ireland, but allowed six counties in the north to remain part of the United Kingdom. It was an unpopular compromise with most, but was agreed to nonetheless. In 1921, Ireland and Britain signed the **Anglo-Irish Treaty**, which gave independence to Ireland, but which kept the six counties – Northern Ireland – part of the United Kingdom.

And there have been troubles ever since. **Republicans** feel that Ireland will never completely be a republic until the entire island is united and independent from Great Britain. **Unionists** or **Loyalists**, mostly the Protestant majority in Ulster, vow that Northern Ireland will remain forever tied to the UK. Many don't care either way – they just want the fighting to stop. Many of the people in the North consider themselves British citizens: they pay British taxes (which are far lower than Irish taxes, by the way), take part in Britain's national health care plan, and 6.3% of them draw their unemployment checks from the British government.

But there is a glimmer of hope! On May 22, 1998, voters flocked to the polls in Northern Ireland. They were expressing their opinion about the **Good Friday Agreement**, a peace accord that had been ironed out on April 10, 1998 by eight warring political factions on the Northern Ireland scene. Over 81% of Northern Ireland's registered voters turned out to vote, and over 71% of those voters approved the peace accord. Nearly 95% of the voters in the Republic of Ireland also approved the accord. (They were voting because the accord required a change in the Irish Constitution.)

The peace accord, crafted under the experienced hand of US negotiator **George Mitchell**, called for the establishment of a 108-member governing body called the **Northern Ireland Assembly**. While Northern Ireland will retain its political allegiance to England, the Northern Ireland Assembly will grant Northern Ireland a significant degree of local autonomy. The accord also called for the disarming of various Northern Ireland paramilitary groups and the release of hundreds of political prisoners currently in British and Irish prisons. (These are issues that still threaten to overturn the apple cart of peace in Northern Ireland, however.)

Will it work? Has peace finally come to this beautiful corner of the world? Even seasoned and cynical political observers are cautiously optimistic about the message sent by the voters. They admit that both the significant voter turnout and the resounding victory of the peace accord at the polls seem to bode well for a peaceful future in Northern Ireland. However, some of the more antagonistic factions in Northern Ireland have bowed their necks and refused to accept the obvious preference of the vast majority of Northern Ireland's citizens. This rebellion – and an associated return to violent means – jeopardizes the incredible progress that has been made.

I am hopeful that this most recent turn of events will indeed mean a peaceful future for the North. It certainly sets the stage for a season or two of peace. Let's hope it continues for many years to come!

TOP NORTHERN IRELAND SIGHTS

BONAMARGY FRIARY – *On the outskirts of Ballycastle you'll find the ruins of Bonamargy Friary. Take a few minutes and prowl through these extensive ruins. Perhaps you'll be fortunate enough to see a forefather (foresister?) of mine, Julia McQuillan, the mysterious (and ghostly) Black Nun of Bonamargy Friary.*

CARRICK-A-REDE ROPE BRIDGE – *Take a walk across a chasm above the Atlantic on a narrow rope bridge, testing your nerve as well as your balance!*

DUNLUCE CASTLE – *Dunluce Castle is perhaps the most photographed set of ruins on the Emerald Isle. These brooding ruins are perched atop a rocky outcropping into the Atlantic Ocean, braving her crashing seas as the McQuillans of old faced the war-like McDonnells! Check out her somber majesty.*

GIANT'S CAUSEWAY – *40,000 symmetric natural basalt columns will amaze and startle you.*

TORR HEAD – *Talk about a sensational seaside drive! You'll snake along the hills of Ulster as they cascade down to the Irish Sea.*

ULSTER FOLK AND TRANSPORT MUSEUM – *If you visit only one folk park in Ireland, choose this one. The extensive displays are impressive.*

ULSTER MUSEUM – *This museum in Belfast isn't particularly large, but it is well done with some interesting exhibits.*

If You Miss These Places, You Haven't Been to Northern Ireland!

If you have the pluck and adventurous spirit to visit those parts of Ulster that comprise Northern Ireland, you'll be delighted with what you find. I may be just a little biased since my ancestors once ruled the majority of what is now Northern Ireland, but I think some of the most magnificent sights on the Emerald Isle are located here.

Closest to my heart (and captured in countless tourist's cameras!) is the impressive **Dunluce Castle**, former ancestral home of my forefathers – the McQuillans. Dunluce Castle is to Northern Ireland what the Leaning Tower is to Pisa, the Coliseum to Rome, Big Ben to London, or Neuschwanstein is to Germany. In a symbolic sort of way, it represents the danger and adventure, the splendor and grace of the North. Candidly stated – don't miss it! Fun and interesting sights include **Giant's Causeway**, thousands of small natural basalt columns gathered together in stair-step fashion on the northern coastline, and **Carrick-A-Rede**, the narrow rope bridge that will test your nerve and balance. On the eastern coast, the **Glens of Antrim** beckon you to their lush greenery.

So...if you're still reading, that means you must have decided to venture into Northern Ireland. Good for you. I predict you'll be glad you did. We'll begin your tour in Belfast, and then we'll extend our trip into County Antrim, where most of Northern Ireland's sights are located. If the thought of going to Belfast still makes you a little queasy, just skip it and go right to the sights in the rest of Northern Ireland.

NORTHERN IRELAND'S TOP LODGING

WHITEPARK HOUSE COUNTRY HOME, 150 Whitepark Road (Coast Road), Ballintoy, Ballycastle, BT54 6NH. Tel. (028) 7073-1482; E-mail: bob.isles@virgin.net; Website: www.whiteparkhouse.com. 6 rooms, 3 ensuite, 3 standard. Rates for singles: UK£30 (standard room) and UK£38 (ensuite room), doubles: UK£24 per person sharing (standard room) and UK£30 to UK£33 per person sharing (ensuite room). Bob and Siobhan Isles run one of the prettiest country homes in the north.

BUSHMILLS INN HOTEL, 25 Main Street, Bushmills, BT57 8QA. Tel. (028) 2073-2339, (028) 2073-2048. 11 rooms. Rates for singles: UK£50, doubles: UK£95. The Bushmills Inn feels like an old stagecoach hotel. Recently inducted into "The Best Loved Hotels of the World."

TEMPLETON HOTEL, 882 Antrim Road, Templepatrick, Ballyclare. Tel. (028) 9443-2984, Fax (028) 9443-3406. 24 rooms. Rates for singles: UK£85, doubles: UK£110, suites: UK£100 to UK£125. The nicest hotel in the Belfast area.

BELFAST

Belfast is the city that is most commonly associated with "the troubles" in the North. As the capital of Northern Ireland, it makes an attractive target for those wishing to make political statements. But it is so much more than that. It is a college town, and it possesses a vibrancy that belies the violence that occasionally erupts here. I found it to be an interesting mixture of old and new, of Catholic and Protestant, and of interesting sights to see.

Earlier in this chapter I detailed my thoughts on visiting Northern Ireland. I honestly feel you can visit both Belfast and Northern Ireland in relative safety, especially if you stay out of those historical flash points of Armagh and Derry.

While Belfast is a great city to visit, there is one time of the year when it should be avoided, and that is the month of July, especially around the middle of the month. Elsewhere in this guide you've read about The Battle **of the Boyne**. On July 1, 1690, the forces of (Protestant) William of Orange defeated the armies of (Catholic) James II, plunging Irish Catholics into years of oppression. While the Republic of Ireland (and much of the rest of the Western world) celebrates St. Patrick's Day on March 17, the Protestants in Northern Ireland choose July 12 to celebrate **Orange Day** in commemoration of William of Orange's victory over James. It is marked by parades and liquor, and the "Wearing o' the Orange." Sounds harmless enough, doesn't it? Unfortunately, the (unwise) parade planners insist on marching through the Catholic neighborhoods of various cities in the North (Armagh, Derry, Belfast, and Portadown specifically).

So, while it is generally safe to travel to Belfast, I'd steer clear during the month of July. Tourist destinations like Dunluce Castle, Carrick-a-Rede, the Antrim Coast, etc., do not have problems during this time.

ARRIVALS & DEPARTURES

There are a number of ways to get to Northern Ireland. Air, car, bus, rail and ferry are all viable options. There is regular bus and train service between the Republic and the North, and recently Aer Lingus expanded their service into Belfast, making it easier to get there by air. Ferry service from England via Wales and Scotland is also available.

Derry has a small regional airport, primarily used by small airlines flying in from some of England's regional airports.

By Air

The main airport for Belfast and Northern Ireland is **Belfast International Airport**, *Tel. (028) 9442-2888*. Formerly called Aldergrove Airport, it is located 20 miles northwest of downtown Belfast out in the country.

Aer Lingus has recently opened transatlantic service to Belfast from the United States. They fly to Belfast from New York City (Kennedy Airport) stopping over in Shannon en route. They also fly to Belfast from Boston, but they stop first in Shannon, then change planes (onto the flight coming from New York) and continue on to Belfast.

In addition to Aer Lingus' flights from the United States, a number of airlines fly to Belfast from a host of English airports, including Heathrow, Gatwick, Luton (London), Birmingham, Bristol, Liverpool, and Manchester. Airlines flying into Belfast International Airport include Aer Lingus, British Airways, British Midland, Manx, Jersey European, and KLM (from Amsterdam).

Getting to Belfast By Bus from the Airport

Buses run from Belfast International Airport to the center of Belfast every half hour (at 10 minutes after the hour and 20 minutes to the hour). The ride will take about 40 minutes, and cost you UK£3.70. The bus stop is right outside the Arrivals Hall.

Getting to Belfast By Taxi from the Airport

Another option for getting into Belfast from the airport is to take a taxi. The taxi stand is right outside the Arrivals Hall, and the ride into town will take about 25 minutes and cost you around UK£20.

By Bus

Ulsterbus, *Tel. (028) 9033-3000*, is the bus service that serves all of Northern Ireland. Its main terminal in Belfast is **Europa Station**, *10 Glengall Street, just around the corner from the Europa Hotel*. The neighborhood is decent enough and should pose no problems for you, especially once you walk the short distance to Great Victoria Street.

Buses run from Europa Station throughout Ulster on a regular basis. In addition, they run between Belfast and **Busaras Station**, *Store Street, Tel. (01) 836-6111*, in Dublin seven times a day Monday through Saturday, and three times on Sunday.

Buses run into Northern Ireland from Belfast's **Laganside Station**, *Chichester Street, Tel. (028) 9023-2356*.

By Car

Once you land at Belfast International Airport, you will be directed into the Arrivals Hall, where you will immediately see a bevy of rental car agency booths clamoring for your business. Here are some agencies where you'll find a rental car:

- **Avis**, *69 Great Victoria Street, Belfast. Tel. (028) 9024-0404*
- **Carriageway Cars**, *21 Hollywood Road. Tel. (028) 9065-2000*

• **Cosmo-Eurodollar**, *181 Airport Road, Tel. (028) 9455-2565*
• **Dan Dooley Kenning**, *175 Airport Road. Tel. (028) 9455-2522*
• **EuropCar Ltd.**, *Belfast Harbour Airport, Sydenham Bypass. Tel. (028) 9045-2017*
• **Hertz**, *Terminal Building, Belfast International Airport. Tel. (028) 9473-2451*
• **McCausland Car Hire**, *171 Airport Road, Tel. (028) 9452-2022*

Sample trip lengths on the main roads:
• Donegal: 3 hours
• Dublin: 4 hours
• Galway: 5 hours
• Killarney: 7 hours
• Limerick: 5 hours
• Wexford: 6 hours

If you are driving to Belfast from Dublin, the trip will take you about four hours. You'll take the M1/N1/A1 north from Dublin. The road is a good one, but it usually carries a lot of traffic, so speeds will average around 40 to 45 mph.

By Ferry

Ferry service from England and Scotland to Northern Ireland is also available. Ferries between Larne (a port town just north of Belfast) and Stranaer, Scotland, are run by **Stena Sealink Ferries** *(toll free in the US and Canada at 800/677-8585 or (01223) 647047 in England)*. The trip takes about 13 hours. There is also a modern new ferry run by **Seacat Ferries**, *Tel. (01304) 240241 in England,* that runs between Stranaer and Belfast and takes about two hours.

Belfast Ferries, *Tel. (01519) 226234 in England,* operates ferry service between Liverpool and Belfast that takes about nine hours.

By Train

Six trains a day run between Belfast and Dublin. The trains at 8:00am and 6:00pm are express trains and take two hours and five minutes; the other four trains are not express and take about 15 minutes longer. Catch the train in Dublin at **Connolly Station**, *Tel. (01) 836-6222 on Amiens Street,* and in Belfast go to **Belfast Central Train Station**, *Tel. (028) 9080-0411 on East Bridge Street.* On Sundays there are only four trains running between the two cities. The ride between these two capital cities will cost you about £23.

Belfast Central Train Station is in an industrial section of Belfast, not the best, but relatively safe. It will take you 10 to 15 minutes to walk to the city center, or you can catch a taxi to take you on your way. The taxi ride to the center of the city should run about UK£5.

NORTHERN IRELAND'S BEST DINING

ESPERANTO CAFE, 89 Dublin Road, Belfast. Tel. (028) 9024-8708. UK£7.95 to UK£13.95, American Express, Mastercard, and Visa accepted. No service charge. Esperanto Cafe is a popular restaurant just off Shaftesbury Square.

MANOR HOUSE CANTONESE CUISINE, 43 Donegall Pass, Belfast. Tel. (028) 9023-8755. UK£7.95 to UK£14.50. All major credit cards accepted. No service charge. This is probably the best Chinese food in Belfast.

THE OLD SCHOOLHOUSE RESTAURANT, 106 Ballyrobin Road, Muckamore. Set dinner menu for UK£19.95. All major credit cards accepted. No service charge. This old schoolhouse is a comfortable and homey country restaurant warmed by open turf fires. The food is really very good, too!

ANTICA ROMA, 67 Botanic Avenue, Belfast. Tel. (028) 9031-0787. Set dinner menus UK£17.95 to UK£21.95, American Express, Mastercard, and Visa accepted. No service charge. Antica Roma is probably my favorite Italian restaurant on the Emerald Isle.

RESTAURANT 44, 44 Belfast Road, Belfast. Tel. (028) 9024-4844, (028) 9023-8755. UK£14.95 to UK£24.95. All major credit cards accepted. No service charge. Great food, intriguing décor.

ORIENTATION

Belfast is a large city, home to 400,000 individuals. It is vast and sprawling, and at times a little confusing. But you needn't see all of it. The principal sights of Belfast are all within a mile or two of City Hall, and that's where you should concentrate your visit.

Belfast is a bouncy, lively, friendly town, especially for a big city. Years of violence have marred her reputation a bit, but her inhabitants are remarkably upbeat. Belfast has significant populations of blue- and white-collar workers, and there is a large youthful population of college students.

Despite her buoyancy, Belfast is a city divided. The city is divided into Catholic and Protestant neighborhoods, there are separate stores for both sects, even separate taxicabs to venture into the respective neighborhoods. Schools are segregated along religious affiliations, and many businesses are similarly divided. Both the Catholic and Protestant neighborhoods are west of downtown Belfast and the M1. The Catholic section is clustered around Falls Road, and the Protestant neighborhood is north of there along Shankill Road. There is a wall, euphemistically called the "Peace Wall," or "Peace Line," that divides the two neighborhoods. This is an area that is not for tourists, so steer clear.

Because of fear of car bombs, much of the downtown area around City Hall is pedestrianized, and vehicles are not allowed. When you're there, you are likely to see military personnel and armored vehicles. It is unlawful to take pictures of the military, so please don't try to include them in your scrapbook. Having said that, I approached an officer during one of my visits to Belfast and asked if I could take a picture of his armored vehicle. He was polite and said, "Certainly," but was not willing to be photographed with it!

GETTING AROUND TOWN

By Bicycle

Belfast is a large, busy city with lots of traffic, but the roads in the downtown area are nice and wide, so bicycling isn't too dangerous. The main sights to see are located within a two-mile by one-mile square area centered on City Hall.

You can rent bicycles at the following places:
- **McConvey Cycles**, *Ormeau Road, Belfast. Tel. (028) 9049-1163*
- **Recycle**, *Albert Square, Belfast. Tel. (028) 9031-3113*

By Bus

Red **Citybuses** run between various points in the city, and are an inexpensive and relatively quick way to get to various points. Depending on your destination, the fare will run between 45p and UK£1.50. There is a discount four-ride ticket available for UK£2.50.

By Car

I have always had good luck finding parking spaces in Belfast, so you should too. The summer months are the toughest. While traffic can be heavy, the roads are generally wide and the traffic flows well. It's not too bad to drive in Belfast, much like most mid-sized cities in North America.

By Foot

This is still my preferred method of transportation while in the downtown area of Belfast. Seldom is anything I want to see much more than a mile from where I am. If I've had a long day and my feet are a little tired, I'll splurge 45p and catch one of the red Citybuses.

By Taxi

Large black British-looking cabs are the main public transport between downtown and West Belfast's working class neighborhoods. For 55p you can visit these neighborhoods, but I'd recommend against it. The Troubles are very serious to those involved in them, and they do not appreciate being gawked at. Taxis are sectarian: Catholic taxis have destination signs reading "Andersontown" or "Shankill," or are written in Irish. Protestant taxis will say, "Falls Road" or have red poppies on them.

For intra-town services, there are a number of different taxi companies. **City Cab**, *Tel. (028) 9024-2000*, and **Diamond Taxis**, *Tel. (028) 9064-6666*, are the two main taxi services in town.

WHERE TO STAY

"The troubles" of recent years have had a serious impact on tourism in general, and on the hotel industry in particular. To be honest, it lags behind its southern cousins in the number and quality of tourist accommodations. For example, in Belfast, the second largest city on the Emerald Isle, it's difficult to find 10 hotels to recommend (literally). Several wouldn't have "made the cut" if the competition had been as stiff as it is in the Republic of Ireland.

The selection of hotels in Belfast are limited at best, especially for a city this size. The nicest hotel in the area is the Templeton Hotel, and it is located some miles outside Belfast on the road to the airport. In town, the Europa, Wellington, and Dukes hotels are probably your best bets.

BELFAST INTERNATIONAL YOUTH HOSTEL, *22 Donegall Road. Tel. (028) 9031-5435, Fax (028) 9043-9699. 120 beds. Rates are UK£9 per person. American Express, Mastercard, and Visa accepted. No service charge.*

As you travel the width and breadth of Ireland, you'll see signs for youth hostels. Some of them are very nice, some not so nice, and many are...well...*adequate*. This hostel falls into the first category, and is a clean and pleasant place to stay. Its central location just off Shaftesbury Square allows you to see many of the main sights in Belfast. The rooms are small but quite clean and in good condition. Each bunk has a small "armoire" for hanging clothes and a deep locking drawer. The hostel is staffed 24 hours a day, so there is no curfew to worry about (some hostels have a curfew and lock the doors at certain hours). It has a nice sitting/TV room and laundry service. Linens are included.

RENSHAWS HOTEL, *75 University Street, Belfast BT7 1HL. Tel. (028) 9033-3366, Fax (028) 9033-3399. 22 rooms. Rates for singles: UK£60, doubles: UK£70. Restaurant, pub. Rates include breakfast. All major credit cards accepted. No service charge.*

This old Victorian schoolhouse has been converted into a homey hotel just around the corner from Queen's University. The rooms, as is typical in these old Victorians, are large and spacious. All are pleasantly furnished, including writing desks for all those postcards you'll be sending. Renshaws is located near Queens University, and is within easy walking distance to Shaftesbury Square, the Botanic Gardens, and the Ulster Museum. The hotel offers discounts for families traveling with children.

ALDERGROVE AIRPORT HOTEL, *Belfast International Airport. Tel. (028) 9442-2033, Fax (028) 9442-3500. 108 rooms. Rates for singles: UK£60 to UK£80, doubles: UK£70 to UK£80; children under 10 stay free in their parents' room. Restaurant, pub, fitness center, sauna, bicycles. Rates include breakfast on the weekends. All major credit cards accepted. No service charge.*

I had planned to write "Except for the noise of the airport..." – but after staying here I realized the entire hotel is incredibly well sound-proofed. This is a nice, newer hotel just a few steps (literally) from Belfast International Airport. The rooms are small, but very clean and comfortably furnished. They are decorated in light and airy colors, which give the rooms a larger feel. From a size and layout standpoint, the rooms reminded me of single dorm rooms at college, although unlike my dorm room, these were spotless and had their own bathroom!

The hotel was built a few years ago as part of the Novotel hotel chain; however, it has since left Novotel and is now under local management. The management has kept Novotel's emphasis on cleanliness and customer service. The hotel offers a pub and an informal restaurant, exercise room, sauna, and bicycles (free of charge) for touring the surrounding countryside. There are also discounts for children, and two children under 10 years old can stay free in their parents' rooms. Several rooms are wheelchair-accessible.

HOLIDAY INN GARDEN COURT, *15 Brunswick Street, BT2 7GE. Tel. (028) 9033-3555, Fax (028) 9023-2999, US toll free 800/465-4329. 76 rooms. Rates for singles: UK£80, doubles: UK£95. Restaurant. All major credit cards accepted. No service charge.*

This 1970s hotel is clean and functional, but that's about it. It is located just off Great Victoria Street not far from the Europa Hotel. The rooms are small and the furnishings a little on the old side. The hotel is located in the heart of Belfast's business and shopping district, and it's within easy walking distance of city hall, the Crown Liquor Salon, Shaftesbury Square, and a number of top-notch restaurants.

DUKES HOTEL, *65 University Street, Belfast. Tel. (028) 9023-7177. 21 rooms. Rates for singles: UK£90, doubles: UK£110; children under age 12 stay in their parents room free. Restaurant, gym, sauna. All major credit cards accepted. No service charge.*

Dukes Hotel was a pleasant find in the university district near Queen's University. The hotel is within walking distance of the university, Ulster

Museum, Botanic Gardens, and Shaftesbury Square. In addition to its convenient location, the hotel features a sauna and exercise room. This modern hotel has a Victorian facade, but the interior is anything but Victorian. The lobby features chrome and leather furnishings, and the staircase follows an intriguing waterfall in clear Lucite troughs. The bedrooms are done in pastels and floral prints. The rooms are large, comfortably furnished, and have double-glazing on the windows to help hold down traffic noise.

TEMPLETON HOTEL, *882 Antrim Road, Templepatrick, Ballyclare. Tel. (028) 9443-2984, Fax (028) 9443-3406. 24 rooms. Rates for singles: UK£90, doubles: UK£120, suites: UK£100 to UK£125. Restaurant, pub, fitness center, sauna, bicycles. Rates include breakfast. All major credit cards accepted. No service charge.*

This is the nicest hotel in the Belfast area, and one of the nicest in all of Northern Ireland. It is a newer hotel about six miles from Belfast International Airport on the main road to the airport, and just a mile or so off the M2. The decor in the public areas is a combination of warm wood and lots of crystal and bright lights – a nice effect that is sort of a cross between modern and rustic, yet not stuffy or stand-offish at all. Furniture and furnishings range from Scandinavian to medieval, depending on which areas of the hotel you are in.

The rooms are spacious, and decorated in soft colors, giving them a restful feeling. All furnishings are new and well-chosen to afford the greatest comfort to guests. There are several family rooms that are very large, furnished in new pine furniture, and exceptionally inviting for families. Combine that with the hotel's discounts for children, and you've got a nice place to stay with your children.

Several executive suites are available in a separate addition. The suites are spacious, and feature Jacuzzis and mini-bars. This would be an ideal location from which to tour Belfast and the surrounding areas of County Antrim.

WELLINGTON PARK HOTEL, *21 Malone Road, Belfast BT9 6RU. Tel. (028) 9038-1111 Fax (028) 9038-5410; E-mail: Wellingtonpark@travel-ireland.com; Website: www.travel-ireland.com/wellpark. 50 rooms. Rates for singles: UK£85, doubles: UK£95; children under 12 stay free in their parents' room. Restaurant, pub. Rates include breakfast. All major credit cards accepted. No service charge.*

Just up the street from Queen's University, the Wellington Park Hotel is an older low-rise hotel that has undergone, and is undergoing, renovation. The public areas suffer a little from the low ceilings and dim lighting, but the staff makes up for any darkness of decor with a brightness and lightness of spirit.

When you are in the public areas of the hotel, take time to notice the paintings and sculptures – they are the works of a number of local artists, and are proudly displayed by the hotel. The rooms are large and comfortable, although none of them have anything approaching a good view. Each room offers tea- and coffee-making facilities. Children's discounts and baby-sitting services are available should you need them.

STORMONT HOTEL, *587 Upper Newtownards Road, Belfast BT4 3LP. Tel. (028) 9065-8621, Fax (028) 9048-0240. 106 rooms. Rates for singles: UK£80, doubles: UK£140. Restaurant. All major credit cards accepted. No service charge.*

This modern new hotel is outside of Belfast on the Newtownards Road across from picturesque Stormont Castle. It is a busy hotel, serving as a business and conference center. The public rooms always seem to be abuzz with activity from the latest conference or exhibition. The pub is a popular spot, and one of the lounges has large windows that look out over the castle grounds. The bedrooms are large and well-lit, providing the opportunity for business people – the hotel's primary clientele – to review proposals, rewrite responses, or catch up on necessary reading. They are furnished comfortably, and the new marble tile baths are spacious.

EUROPA HOTEL, *Great Victoria Street, Belfast BT2 7AP. Tel. (028) 9032-7000, Fax (028) 9032-7800. 184 rooms. Rates for singles: UK£75 to UK£105, doubles: UK£100 to UK£140, suites: UK£130 to UK£195. Two restaurants, pub, beauty salon. All major credit cards accepted. No service charge.*

The Europa has a similar feel to the Gresham Hotel in Dublin: older, but not run down. Built in the 1970s, they have been busy in recent years refurbishing some of their public areas, including the entire front of the hotel. They are proud that President Clinton stayed here when he visited Northern Ireland in 1995 – in fact, they have memorialized the room he stayed in with photographs of the president, and a saxophone hangs on the wall!

The pubic areas of the hotel are an eclectic collection striving to meet the needs and tastes of all their guests. There is an informal brasserie on the ground floor, as well as a pub, and both offer pleasant conversation and ambiance. Upstairs above the lobby is a not-quite-stuffy lounge that provides a bit more of an upscale feel. But at the edge of the lounge is a large open area that overlooks the front lobby entrance and keeps the atmosphere light and conversational. A pianist supplies guests in the lounge with background music most nights. And for the jet-setters (or those that need to work a few kinks out), a disco is also available five nights a week.

The rooms are of average size and with conventional furnishings. The thing that most impressed me about the Europa was their attention to customer service. They seem to go the extra mile to ensure happy and satisfied customers.

Belfast Outskirts

MARINE COURT HOTEL, *18 Quay Street, Bangor BT20 5ED. Tel. (028) 9145-1100, Fax (028) 9145-1200. 51 rooms. Rates for singles: UK£45, doubles: UK£50 per person sharing. Rates include breakfast. Restaurant, garden, tennis, riding, beaches. Visa accepted. No service charge.*

The public areas as well as the service here are underwhelming, but the rooms are the saving grace: large, well furnished, and pleasantly decorated. But as close as they are to the harbor, it's a little disappointing that none of the rooms have views. Each room offers tea- and coffee-making facilities as well as trouser presses. The hotel offers guests an indoor swimming pool, sauna, and fitness center. In addition, discounts for children are offered.

CLANDEBOYE LODGE HOTEL, *10 Estate Road, Clandeboye, Bangor BT19 1UR. Tel. (028) 9185-2500, Fax (028) 9185-2772. 43 rooms. Rates for singles: UK£55, doubles: UK£50 per person sharing; children stay free in their parents' room. Rates include breakfast. Restaurant, pub, bikes, fishing, riding, beaches. American Express, Mastercard, Visa accepted. No service charge.*

Just outside the town of Clandeboye sits the Clandeboye Lodge Hotel. This new brick hotel is already popular with the business community, as it joins an existing business and conference center. The rooms are large, and some of them are even spacious. They are well-equipped and comfortably furnished. Since the hotel caters primarily to the business community, the rooms are well-lit and offer lots of room for writing or reading. They also offer additional phone jacks for modems. Children under 12 stay free in their parents' room.

A traditional Irish pub is located outside of the main building in an old Victorian building, and you will enjoy meeting other tourists as well as some of the local populace there.

WHERE TO EAT

Unlike the dearth of hotels in Belfast, there are quite a number of restaurants in and around the city. Still, on the whole, the quantity and quality of restaurants is nowhere near the level you'll find in Dublin. There are only a few that could go toe-to-toe in competition with Dublin restaurants such as Number 10, The Commons, Restaurant Patrick Guilbaud, or Alexandra's. Many of the following restaurants are found in and around Shaftesbury Square:

BACKPACKER'S CAFE, *22 Donegall Road. Tel. (028) 9031-5435. UK£6.50 to UK£11.95. Open daily from 7:30am to 8:00pm. Breakfast is served from 7:30am to 11:30am. American Express, Mastercard and Visa accepted. No service charge.*

You don't need to stay at the youth hostel at the same address, but the food is decent, filling, and inexpensive. Just off the corner of Shaftesbury

Square, it's a good place to grab an inexpensive sandwich, quick breakfast, or just a cup of coffee.

THE BUTLER, *39 Dublin Street. Tel. (028) 9032-2153. UK£3.80 to UK£5.50. Open Monday through Saturday from 9:30am to 10:00pm. American Express, Mastercard, and Visa accepted. No service charge.*

This quiet little cafe offers unexceptional ambiance, but the food is good and reasonably priced. Dress is very casual – grubbies are fine.

BISHOP'S FISH AND CHIPS, *Bradbury Place. Tel. (028) 9031-1827. UK£2.90 to UK£5.95. Open Monday through Friday from 9:00am to 2:00am, and 9:00am to 3:00am Saturday and Sunday. Mastercard and Visa accepted. No service charge.*

You'll find a little bit o' London at Bishop's Fish and Chips, located close to Shaftesbury Square. Here's where you can go to satisfy your palate for honest-to-goodness fish and chips. This establishment has a cafeteria atmosphere – noisy and chattery, booths lining the walls and down the center. They also have a variety of burgers available, but fish and chips is the main attraction.

THE REVELATIONS INTERNET CAFE, *27 Shaftesbury Square. Tel. (028) 9032-0337. UK£3.50 to UK£7.95. Open Monday through Friday from 10:00am to 10:00pm, Saturday from 10:00am to 8:00pm, and Sunday from noon to 10:00pm. No service charge.*

This small nondescript cafe gives new meaning to Surf and Turf – it is a combination coffee shop/computer lab. Guests can order cappuccino and a sandwich while surfing the net on any of the half dozen computers they have set up for internet access. The sandwiches will run you around UK£4, and connect time is UK£4.50 per hour. They also offer one-on-one tutorials for UK£15 per hour. If you want to contact them, their internet address is www.revelations.co.uk.

THE CELLARS, *Belfast Castle, Antrim Road. Tel. (028) 9077-6925. UK£6.50 to UK£10.95. Open 12:15pm to 2:30pm and 6:30pm to 9:45pm. Mastercard and Visa accepted. No service charge.*

Located in the basement of Belfast Castle, the atmosphere is decidedly cozy and the food is good. Casual dress is fine.

CAFÉ EN SEINE, *3 University Street. Tel. (028) 9032-5137. UK£5.95 to UK£11.95. Open Sunday through Wednesday from 12:30pm to 9:00pm and Thursday through Saturday from noon to 11:00pm. All major credit cards accepted. No service charge.*

Café En Seine is the combination of two former restaurants on this site, Aubergines and Blue Jeans and Saints and Scholars. It maintains the college-age-patron feel and offers a different dining experience. It still has an irresistible appeal to the many students who frequent it. Lots of interesting things on the walls to hold your attention. Keeping with the cafe motif, it has a nice selection of burgers, sandwiches, soups, and salads. Vegetarians will also find a good selection here. Dress is casual. Overall, the food is good and reasonably priced. Casual dress is more than fine here.

DUKES HOTEL RESTAURANT, *65 University Street. Tel. (028) 9023-6666. UK£5.95 to UK£10.50. Open Monday through Saturday from 7:00pm to 9:45pm, and Sunday from 1:00pm to 7:45pm. All major credit cards accepted. No service charge.*

This is a nice chatty restaurant, and the food is good and reasonably priced: try their fried cheese beignet with black currant and cranberry sauce. For more traditional fare, you might try the fillet of cod. Dress is informal.

BELFAST CASTLE RESTAURANT, *Antrim Road. Tel. (028) 9077-6925. UK£4.95, to UK£14.50. Open daily from 6:30pm to 9:30pm. All major credit cards accepted. No service charge.*

Sitting regally on the slopes of Cave Hill overlooking the city, Belfast Castle affords beautiful views of both the city and Belfast Lough. Built in 1870 on the site of several previous castles, the owners chose a beautiful location for their home. One of the former sitting rooms has been transformed into a lovely and elegant restaurant. Beautiful views of the city and lough await diners fortunate enough to be seated near the windows, but even of you don't get those seats, your dining experience will be pleasant. Menu selections include roast chicken with leek and smoked bacon in Dijon mustard sauce, or roast salmon and scallops with oysters and mushrooms. Jacket and tie are requested.

DRAGON PALACE, *16 Botanic Avenue. Tel. (028) 9032-4369. UK£6.50 to UK£11.95. Mastercard and Visa accepted. No service charge.*

This is a nice, quiet Chinese restaurant. Hanging lamps provide each of the tables with muted light, giving the impression of intimacy and privacy. The menu is typical of Chinese restaurants. It's also very busy, so consider calling ahead for reservations. Casual dress.

PONTE VECCHIO, *73 Great Victoria Street. UK£9.85 to UK£12.95. Open Tuesday through Saturday from 5:00pm to 11:30pm and Sunday from 5:00pm to 10:00pm. Mastercard and Visa accepted. No service charge.*

This small Italian cafe gives you the impression of being in a similar cafe on the streets of Rome – except for the New Age music. But the food is good. Try their pollo marsala or tournedos rossini.

ESPERANTO CAFE, *89 Dublin Road. Tel. (028) 9024-8708. UK£7.95 to UK£13.95. Open Monday through Friday from 5:00pm to 11:00pm, Saturday from 4:00pm to 11:00pm, and Sunday from 4:00pm to 10:00pm. American Express, Mastercard, and Visa accepted. No service charge.*

Esperanto Cafe is a popular restaurant just off Shaftesbury Square. The evening I was there it was packed – waiting diners were queued down the stairs out into the entryway. Once you make it to this upstairs restaurant, you'll find checkered table cloths, candles on the table, and a trellis with grape vines hanging down that add a nice touch to your dining experience. Try the chargrilled steak fillet or the frilled salmon fillet. Casual dress is fine here.

MANOR HOUSE CANTONESE CUISINE, *43 Donegall Pass. Tel. (028) 9023-8755. UK£7.95 to UK£14.50. Open daily from noon to 2:30pm and 5:00pm to 11:30pm (Sunday 12:30pm to 11:00pm). All major credit cards accepted. No service charge.*

This is probably the best Chinese restaurant in Belfast. Owned by Joe Wong and his family since 1982, they are very good at what they do. The menu is extensive. Soft colors in the restaurant add a tranquil feeling to the dining experience, even though the place gets busy most of the time. There is a set dinner menu for UK£14.50, and a bargain of a set lunch menu for UK£5.50. Nice casual is the dress.

THE STRAND, *12 Stranmillis Road. Tel. (028) 9068-2266. UK£10 to UK£16.95. Open daily noon to 11:00pm, Sunday from noon to 3:00pm and 5:00pm to 10:00pm. All major credit cards accepted. No service charge.*

Located close to Queen's University, this is an intimate café relying on muted lighting and candlelight to set a quiet atmosphere. The food is good but not exceptional. Numerous vegetarian dishes are available for those who prefer them. Their lunch menu is very reasonable at £4.50.

CAFE SOCIETY, *3 Donegall Square East. Tel. (028) 9043-9525. Set dinner menus from UK£12.50 to UK£17.50. Open Monday from noon to 3:00pm, Tuesday through Saturday noon to 3:00pm and 6:00pm to 10:30pm. Mastercard and Visa accepted. No service charge.*

This modern new cafe near Belfast City Hall offers up excellent fare for sagging shoppers, tired tourists, and busy business people. The menus offer a nice selection, and presentation is an important aspect of the fare. Try their fillet of salmon in herb crust or roasted rack of pork. The dessert menu is great.

VILLA TOSCANA, *Toscana Park West Circular Road, Bangor. UK£11.95 to UK£17.95. Open daily from 5:00pm to 11:30pm, and Sunday lunch from noon to 3:00pm. American Express, Mastercard, and Visa accepted. No service charge.*

Located not far from Belfast City in Bangor. The decor is unmemorable, but they have a recognizable Italian menu with everything you're accustomed to seeing at other Italian restaurants.

GALLERY RESTAURANT, *Great Victoria Street. Tel. (028) 9032-7000. Set dinner menu for UK£21.50. Open daily from 12:30pm to 2:30pm and 6:30pm to 10:00pm (or, as the manager says, "until people quit coming"). Reservations are strongly suggested, especially on the weekends. All major credit cards accepted. No service charge.*

This is a pleasant restaurant. Crystal and starched linens accent the quiet ambiance. The menu is also impressive, with such offerings as pan-fried pheasant with juniper berries and fresh trompettes de la mort and wild mushroom melange, and noisettes of North Down spring lamb sprinkled with red currant cream.

THE OLD SCHOOLHOUSE RESTAURANT, *106 Ballyrobin Road, Muckamore. Set dinner menu for UK£19.95. Open Tuesday through Sunday noon to 2:30pm and 5:00pm to 9:30pm. All major credit cards accepted. No service charge.*

The Old Schoolhouse Restaurant is on the road from Belfast City to the airport, and might just be worth the drive (20 minutes or so) out from the city. Jim Kelly is the owner of this family-run restaurant, which in former times served as the local schoolhouse (from 1850 to 1960). Today it is a comfortable and homey country restaurant warmed by open turf fires. The menu is classical European with French influences. The menu changes monthly, but one of the choices might well be boneless lamb cutlets pan-fried and finished in the oven with herb crust and a Madeira sauce. Casual dress or jacket and tie is fine.

ANTICA ROMA, *67 Botanic Avenue. Tel. (028) 9031-0787. Set dinner menus UK£17.95 to UK£21.95. Open Monday through Saturday for dinner from 6:00pm to 11:30pm, and for lunch Monday through Friday from noon to 3:00pm. American Express, Mastercard, and Visa accepted. No service charge.*

Antica Roma could well be my favorite Italian restaurant on the Emerald Isle. Authentic decor (mosaic floors, columns, murals, etc.) combined with a fine wine list and an extensive and interesting menu add up to an enjoyable Italian meal. The menu items are Italian, but not your standard run-of-the-mill Roman eatery. Examples of the fare include roast guinea fowl with mushrooms, pasta, and rice, or Mediterranean sea bream on a bed of fennel with wild rice and pasta. Dress is nice casual, although you'd not feel out of place with a jacket and tie in the evenings.

SHANKS RESTAURANT, *Blackwood Golf Center, 150 Crawfordsburn Road, Bangor. Set lunch menu for UK£14.95, and set dinner menu for UK£24.95. Open Tuesday through Friday from 12:30pm to 2:30pm, and from 7:00pm to 9:00pm. Saturday they are open for dinner only from 7:00pm to 9:00pm. American Express, Mastercard, Visa accepted. No service charge.*

Shanks is considered one of the best restaurants in the Belfast area. Chef Robbie Millar is gaining quite a reputation for top-notch fare, including marvelous steaks – beef as well as venison – and seafood dishes. Choices for dinner include such tasty treats as roast monkfish with penne, pancetta, and roast garlic; duck with wild mushroom risotto; and an excellent chargrilled Angus steak. The ambiance is bright and airy, with contemporary art, yellow walls, and modern furnishings.

RESTAURANT 44, *44 Belfast Road. Tel. (028) 9024-4844, 238755. UK£14.95 to UK£24.95. Open Monday through Friday 12:30pm to 2:30pm,*

6:30pm to 10:00pm, and Saturday from 6:30pm to 10:00pm. All major credit cards accepted. No service charge

This unlikely restaurant a couple of blocks down the street from City Hall is a pleasant surprise. The look and feel is that of having walked into a bar in India rather than one on the Emerald Isle. Green cane furniture, ceiling fans, and an elephant theme mural graces one wall. A nice selection of traditional Irish dishes cooked with a continental flair are offered. In addition, for those who prefer them, there are a number of vegetarian dishes available. Dress is casual, but no grubbies, please.

ROSCOFF RESTAURANT, *7 Shaftesbury Square. Tel. (028) 9033-1532. Set lunch menu for UK£15.50, and set dinner menu for UK£24.95. Open daily from 12:15pm to 2:15pm for lunch, and from 6:30pm to 10:30pm for dinner. Reservations are recommended on the weekends in particular. All major credit cards accepted. No service charge.*

The owners of this modern restaurant are frequent guests on local cooking shows, and their restaurant is a great showcase for their talent. The set menu changes on a regular basis, and you're never left with too few decisions: often you can choose from five to eight items per course. The main courses consist of such delicacies as confit duck, glazed monkfish, venison with roast shallots, and roast cod with a lobster and tarragon vinaigrette. Combine those offers with an wide variety of fresh appetizers, vegetables, and desserts, and you've got a feast on your hands.

As highly regarded as Roscoff Restaurant is, the interior is decidedly understated. Chrome and cloth chairs and small two-person tables define the ambiance. Coat and tie are suggested.

SEEING THE SIGHTS

Most sights are located in the central downtown area and an area called Shaftesbury Square.

Grand Opera House, *Great Victoria Street, (028) 9024-1919. Tickets range from UK£3 to UK£20.* Across from the Europa and the Crown Liquor Saloon is the Grand Opera House of Belfast. Built in 1895, but allowed to grow seedy over the years, this beautiful Victorian Theater was restored to all its finery in 1980. The restoration was faithful to the original heavy gilding and ornamental plasterwork. Productions range from plays and operas to ballet.

Belfast City Hall, *open Monday through Friday from 9:00am to 5:00pm. Admission is free. Tel. (028) 9032-7000.* The central area of Belfast is Donegall Square, and the central attraction of the square is the City Hall of Belfast. Columned and domed, the building was erected at the turn of the century (1907). The entrance for the general public is located around back. You are free to go in and walk around the open public areas. As you'd suspect, it's marbled and grand. The statue of the woman out front of City Hall is Queen Victoria. On Wednesdays a guided tour takes you into other areas of the structure.

Garden of Remembrance, *Belfast City Hall grounds*. This is an interesting war memorial on the west side of Belfast City Hall. On the eastern side of City Hall is a monument to those who perished in the sinking of the *Titanic*. (Remember – the *Titanic* was built in the Belfast shipyards.)

The Crown Liquor Saloon, *44 Great Victoria Street, open daily 11:30am to 11:30pm, Sunday from 12:30pm to 2:30pm and 7:00pm to 10:00pm. Tel. (028) 9032-5368.* Don't miss the most popular pub in Belfast and Northern Ireland. This marvelous Victorian bar sits proudly across the street from the Europa Hotel. Stepping into the bar is like stepping into a movie set in Victorian times. Gaslights glisten, mosaics on the floor shine, *snugs* (small, semi-private booths with high walls) beckon patrons to share their most intimate secrets, brass fixtures shine brightly, and the ornate mirrors are a sight to behold. The building is so important to Belfast and Northern Ireland that the National Trust of Northern Ireland maintains it. No fear, though – it is a working pub run by an independent company. If you visit only one pub in Northern Ireland, make this be the one.

Shaftesbury Square. Shaftesbury Square is a square formed by the confluence of Great Victoria Street, Dublin Street, Botanic Avenue, Bradbury Place, and Donegall Road – sort of a Times Square of Belfast, complete with a large electronic billboard! There are lots of restaurants, bookies, pubs, movie theaters, the main post office, and a fun place to watch the panorama of Belfast street-life.

Linen Hall Library, *open Monday through Wednesday, and Friday from 9:30am to 6:00pm, Thursday from 9:30am to 8:30pm, and Saturday from 9:30am to 4:00pm. Membership fee runs UK£28 per year.* The Linen Hall Library sits on the north side of Donegall Square. Built in 1788, this fine old library is an architecturally interesting place. They also have a display on the history of linen manufacture.

St. Anne's Cathedral, *Donegall Street*. St. Anne's is the main Anglican church in Northern Ireland. It is suitably austere and imposing. There is an interesting mosaic that depicts St. Patrick's arrival in Ireland. The mosaic is located above the Chapel of the Holy Spirit.

Botanic Gardens, *Stranmillis Road, open daily from sunup to sundown. Admission is free.* This floral spot sits next to Queens's College, and is a nice place to stroll and enjoy the beauty of the flowers, plants, and shrubs. The Ulster Museum is located on the grounds of the gardens. (See entry below.)

Ulster Museum, *Stranmillis Road, open Monday through Friday 10:00am to 5:00pm, Saturday 1:00pm to 5:00pm, Sunday 2:00pm to 5:00pm. Admission is free. Tel. (028) 9038-1251.* Located on the grounds of the Botanic

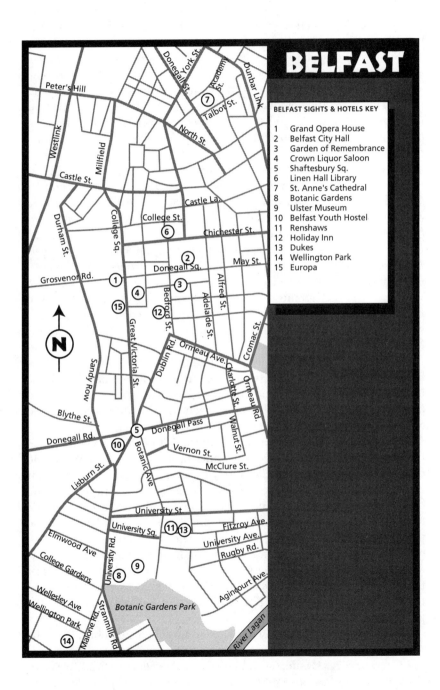

BELFAST

BELFAST SIGHTS & HOTELS KEY

1 Grand Opera House
2 Belfast City Hall
3 Garden of Remembrance
4 Crown Liquor Saloon
5 Shaftesbury Sq.
6 Linen Hall Library
7 St. Anne's Cathedral
8 Botanic Gardens
9 Ulster Museum
10 Belfast Youth Hostel
11 Renshaws
12 Holiday Inn
13 Dukes
14 Wellington Park
15 Europa

Gardens, this museum is Northern Ireland's version of the Smithsonian. It is an eclectic collection of important Irish historical artifacts, natural history, and art.

My favorite exhibit is the paraphernalia recovered from the *Girona*, a Spanish ship that sunk in the cold waters off the Antrim Coast in 1588 after their ill-fated expedition against England. Jewelry, weaponry, articles of clothing, and personal effects are among the collection. The four floors are nicely done, and the exhibits are generally interesting and informative. A third floor cafe serves a reasonable lunch if you find yourself getting hungry.

Ulster Folk and Transport Museum, *near Bangor, open April, May, June and September Monday through Friday from 9:30am to 5:00pm, Saturday from 10:30am to 6:00pm, and Sunday from noon to 6:00pm, and in July and August on Monday through Saturday from 10:30am to 6:00pm and on Sunday from noon to 6:00pm. From October through March, it is open Monday through Friday from 9:30am to 4:00pm, and Saturday and Sunday from noon to 4:30pm. Admission is UK£4 for adults and UK£2.50 for seniors, students and children. A family ticket is available for UK£11.00. Children under five are free. Tel. (028) 9042-8428.* To get to the folk park, take the A2 from Belfast toward Bangor. Just after you go through the town of Hollywood (still on the A2), watch for the signpost directing you to the Ulster Folk Park and Transport Museum.

Perhaps the finest recreation of its kind on the Emerald Isle, the Ulster Folk and Transport Museum features cottages, chapels, schoolhouses, and farms all brought from their original sites and transported here from all over Ulster. They have been painstakingly reconstructed and extensively equipped with period furnishings.

The museum gives you a glimpse of the 18th and 19th century lives of the Ulster folk, from priests to peasants, farmers to fiddlers. What kind of a living could a weaver eke out? How about a tailor? The open-air museum invites you into the very homes of those who practiced these and other professions, so you can more readily visualize their living conditions. The buildings are located over a sprawling 70-acre park-like area, so you get to combine a nature walk with a field trip into Irish history.

A fascinating and informative aspect of the Ulster Folk and Transport Museum is the transportation section. You follow the history of Ulster from horse and buggy days (actually, in Ulster it's *donkey and creel* days) to the mighty ocean liners (the *Titanic* was built in Belfast) and on into the jet age.

It may well take a half day or better to tour all the exhibits. Don't be rushed, as there is plenty to see.

Carrickfergus Castle, *Carrickfergus, open April through October Monday through Saturday from 10:00am to 6:00pm, Sunday from 2:00pm until 6:00pm,* and November through March Monday through Saturday from 10:00am until 4:00pm and Sunday from 1:00pm to 4:00pm. Admission is UK£2.70 for adults and UK£1.35 for children under 16. A family ticket is available for UK£7.30. Tel. (028) 9335-1273. Take the A2 north out of Belfast. As you pass the end of Belfast Harbor, follow the signposts for Carrickfergus. The Castle is at the far edge of town – you won't miss it if you stay on the A2.

Brooding alongside Belfast Lough on a small rocky peninsula, Carrickfergus Castle is a perfect example of the structural excesses the Anglo-Normans went to as they established their footholds on the Emerald Isle. This well-preserved fortification is especially impressive at night as it basks in the light of powerful halogen lamps. It was built in 1180 by one of the earliest Anglo-Norman intruders, **John de Courcy**. Because of its strategic position and ominous firepower, the castle proved a large and desirous target for a host of assailants, from Irish chieftains to the French and even the Scottish. Sometimes the attackers were successful in taking the castle (sometimes not!), but always lost it a short time later to concentrated English efforts to retake it.

Carrickfergus Castle was witness to a number of important historical events in Ireland's history. It was here that William of Orange stopped en route to his momentous victory at the Battle of the Boyne. In fact, a large stone in the harbor marks the spot where he stepped from his boat onto Irish soil. And US naval history was made in the veritable shadow of Carrickfergus Castle; while aboard his ship *Ranger*, the legendary **John Paul Jones** defeated the English warship *HMS Drake* in America's first-ever naval victory just off-shore from Carrickfergus Castle.

The castle itself is magnificent and well worth a visit. Inside the castle is an impressive five-story keep, about 60 feet wide and over 90 feet high, which originally held the well for the castle's drinking water as well as a dungeon. On the third floor is a grand Great Hall. The keep is also home to a Cavalry Regimental Museum, with several fine examples of ancient weaponry. The views from the top of the keep are splendid.

NIGHTLIFE & ENTERTAINMENT

Belfast sports quite a number of pubs, and some of them are as enjoyable as you'll find on the Emerald Isle. But of all the pubs in Northern Ireland, there's one in particular that you shouldn't miss:

THE CROWN LIQUOR SALOON, *44 Great Victoria Street, Belfast. Tel. (028) 9032-5368.*

If you venture into no other pub in Northern Ireland, be sure and stop by The Crown. Located uptown across from the Europa Hotel, this marvelous old Victorian Bar is a splendid place to just stop and stare (see the entry in *Seeing the Sights* above). If you raise only one pint in Belfast, do so in The Crown. Even if you don't drink, you should venture through the doors just to see the place.

SPORTS & RECREATION
Golf
   Malone Golf Club, *Dumnurry, Belfast, County Antrim. Tel. (028) 9061-2758, UK£25/UK£30.*
   Visitors are welcome Monday, Thursday, and Friday. Par 71, 6,642 yards.

Horseback Riding
• **Lagan Valley Equestrian Center**, *172 Upper Malone Road, Belfast. Tel. (028) 9061-4853*

PRACTICAL INFORMATION
American Express
• **American Express Office**, *Kyrenia House, 108 Royal Avenue, Belfast. Tel. (028) 9024-2341.*

Embassies & Consulates
• **American Consulate**, *14 Queen Street, Belfast. Tel. (028) 9032-8239*
• **Canadian Embassy**, *Lesley House, Shaftesbury Square, Belfast 2. Tel. (028) 9033-1532*

Laundry Service
• **Duds and Suds**, *University Road, Belfast. Tel. (028) 9024-3956*
• **Queen's University Launderette**, *Student Union, 17 Donegall Square, Belfast. Tel. (028) 9032-1707*

Post Offices
• **Belfast Main Post Office**, *Donegall Square. Tel. (028) 9032-1532*
• **Botanic Gardens Post Office**, *95 University Road. Tel. (028) 9038-1309*
• **Central Post Office**, *25 Castle Place. Tel. (028) 9032-3740*
• **Shaftesbury Square Post Office**, *Shaftesbury Square. Tel. (028) 9032-6177*

Tourist Offices
• **Bangor Tourist Information Center**, *Tower House, Quay Street, Bangor, Tel. (028) 9127-0069*
• **Belfast Tourist Information Center**, *St. Anne's Court, 59 North Street, Belfast. Tel. (028) 9023-1221*
• **Carrickfergus Tourist Information Center**, *Antrim Street Mall, Carrickfergus, Tel. (028) 9336-6455*

COUNTY ANTRIM

Most of the sights I am recommending for Northern Ireland are located in **County Antrim**. County Antrim is the northeastern-most county of Northern Ireland. It is the closest county to Scotland, and from a sheer natural beauty standpoint, it may well be the most stunning county on the Emerald Isle. From brooding and romantic ruins to lush valleys and expansive sandy beaches, County Antrim has a lot to offer.

ARRIVALS & DEPARTURES

By Air

The major airport in County Antrim is **Belfast International Airport**, *Belfast, Tel. (028) 9442-2888.* There is also an airport in Derry, but as discussed earlier in this chapter, I do not recommend a visit there.

By Bus

Ulsterbus, *Tel. (028) 9033-3000*, is the bus service that serves all of Ulster. It stops throughout the county at various towns and hamlets on the major routes (A2 and A26) in the county. Here are some of the more notable stopping points for buses running into County Antrim:
- **Ballycastle** — Buses stop at **The Diamond** and **The Marine Hotel** *on North Street, Tel. (028) 7076-2222.*
- **Ballygally** – Buses stop in the center of town.
- **Ballymena** – Buses stop at the bus station in town, *Tel. (028) 2565-2214.*
- **Carrickfergus** – Buses stop in the center of town as well as at the **Harbour Carpark**.
- **Giant's Causeway** – Buses go right to the carpark of this sight.
- **Cushendun** – Buses stop at the town grocery store.
- **Larne** – Buses stop at **Larne Harbor**, *Tel. (028) 2827-2345.*
- **Portrush** – Buses stop at the bus station on *Dunluce Street, Tel. (028) 7082-4065.*
- **Waterfoot** – Buses stop in the center of town.

Many of the more popular sights in County Antrim (such as Giant's Causeway, Glens of Antrim, Dunluce Castle) are accessible via bus service from Belfast's **Laganside Station**, *Tel. (028) 9023-2356.*

By Car

The main roads into County Antrim are the A2, which skirts the eastern and northern seaboard of the county, and the A26, which divides the county from north to south. There are also a number of fine roads that run throughout the county.

If you are needing to rent a car, Belfast is probably your best bet. Here are a few local agencies you might try in a pinch, but generally speaking,

you'll find them much more expensive than those you'll find in Belfast.
- **Delta Hire**, *144 Ballymoney Road, Ballymena, Tel. (028) 2565-9136*
- **General Motor Works**, *197 Ballymoney Road, Ballymena, Tel (028) 2566-52171*
- **Model Car Hire**, *Model Road, Ballymoney, Tel. (02656) 63275*
- **Practical Used Car Rental**, *41 Belfast Road, Larne, Tel. (028) 2878-2000*
- **Coastal Self Drive**, *112 Station Road, Portstewart, Tel. (02658) 34088*

By Train

Train service to Northern Ireland is limited. Trains leave for other parts of Northern Ireland from **Belfast Central Train Station**, *East Bridge Street, Tel. (028) 9080-0411,* throughout the day. The trains stop at Larne, Whitehead, Antrim, Ballymena, and Ballymoney in County Antrim.

ORIENTATION

County Antrim lies at the northeastern corner of Northern Ireland. Its county seat is Belfast, but the majority of the county consists of small country towns, lovely loughs, sandy beaches, verdant valleys, and splendid sights.

WHERE TO STAY

The last several years have been banner years for the tourism and hotel industries in the North. As a consequence, several new hotels, B&Bs, and guesthouses have been built, and numerous existing hotels have expansion and renovation plans.

A number of the B&Bs I have recommended in this section are brand new. With the upturn in tourism in the North, B&Bs are springing up like dandelions in spring lawns – they're everywhere. The owners of these new B&Bs are delighted to see American tourists, and quite desirous to see that all needs are met. They are outgoing and anxious to please.

One nice aspect of the hotel industry in Northern Ireland is that most of the hotels don't participate in the odious practice of foisting service charges on their guests.

CASTLE HOSTEL, *62 Quay Road, Ballycastle. Tel. (028) 7076-9822. 42 beds. Rates for singles are UK£7.50 per person sharing in a double room, or UK£6 per person sharing in a dormitory. No credit cards accepted. No service charge.*

The Castle Hostel is located in the heart of Ballycastle just off the round-about at the eastern side of town. Drab from the outside, it's not a castle and never was, but it's a good, relatively clean hostel to hole up for the night. They offer a variety of accommodations, from two double rooms to dormitories that house for, six, or eight occupants. They have two self-catering kitchens, a washing machine, and a place to pitch your tent out back if you prefer.

During the season don't expect to drop in and find a room available for the night – they turn away between 25 and 40 guests per night from June through August. Ballycastle is located on the northeastern edge of Northern Ireland on the A2.

HILLVIEW B&B, *36 Belfast Road, Larne. Tel. (028) 2826-0584. 8 rooms. Rates for singles: UK£15, doubles: UK£15 per person sharing. Rates include breakfast. No credit cards accepted. No service charge.*

Sitting atop a hill above the main Belfast Road into Larne, Hillview B&B gives you fine views of Northern Ireland's templed hills. Mrs. Muriel Rainey runs a nice B&B, with comfortable, nice-sized rooms. Guest rooms are in the main house as well as in a separate adjunct next to the house. The accommodations are modern and comfortable, although not overly large. The dining room is a pleasant sunny area overlooking the country-side. The Rainey's have lived here for many years, and Mr. Rainey can regale you with tales of the activities of allied forces who bivouacked on the lovely Northern Ireland hills across from Hillview B&B. (You didn't realize allied forces were in Ireland, did you?)

SEA VIEW B&B, *12 Shingle Cove, Carnlough, BT44 OEH. Tel. (028) 2888-5033. 2 rooms. Rates for singles: UK£20, doubles: UK£18 per person sharing. Rates include breakfast. No credit cards accepted. No service charge.*

This new B&B just off the main road through Carnlough is clean and comfortable. Mrs. Brenda McAuley is a gracious hostess just beginning in the B&B business, and she is anxious to provide you a pleasant B&B experience. The rooms are tastefully decorated in light colors, and are large and roomy. With only two guest rooms, the Sea View fills up quickly, especially during the summer months. Be sure to call ahead for reservations.

SHINGLE COVE B&B, *6 Shingle Cove, Carnlough, BT44 OEF. Tel. (028) 2888-5593. 3 rooms. Rates for singles: UK£20, doubles: UK£35 for the room. Rates include breakfast. No credit cards accepted. No service charge.*

Situated on a cul-de-sac off the Coast Road, the Shingle Cove B&B has lovely views of the North Channel. This new B&B is comfortable, tastefully decorated, and you'll be greeted with a warm welcome from Mrs. Jennifer McAuley. All the bedrooms are ensuite, and they are large, with large windows that let plenty of sunlight in. Florals and pastels are the predominant motif in the bedrooms. The bathrooms are modern and very clean. Since this B&B is new, all the facilities, furnishings, and linens are new, crisp, and clean.

If you are interested in seeing a bit of the Northern Ireland country-side on bicycle, Mrs. McAuley has bikes available for rent. She also has fishing poles available, and I'm sure she'll be glad to point you to just the spot where you'll be able to land a fish or two! As Shingle Cove B&B is a two-story house, several balconies are available for relaxing at the end of a long day of sightseeing. Be sure and call ahead – with only three rooms and tourism increasing in the North, they fill up quickly.

ROWAN'S B&B, *7 Shingle Cove, Carnlough, BT44 OEH. Tel. (028) 2888-5638. 2 rooms. Rates for singles: UK£20, doubles: UK£18 per person sharing. Rates include breakfast. No credit cards accepted. No service charge.*

Here is another relatively new B&B on the same cul-de-sac as the Sea View and Shingle Cove B&Bs, and Margaret and John Rowan are also new to the B&B business. New they may be, but you can be assured that they are anxious to please you and see that you have a pleasant stay. The rooms at Rowan's B&B are brand new, large, light and airy, and comfortably furnished. I had a feeling more akin to staying in their home rather than lodging in their B&B, and you will too. As with the other two B&Bs in this cul-de-sac, their rooms fill up quickly, so be sure to call ahead for reservations.

(Note: When I visited this B&B it was so new that the Rowans hadn't yet arrived at a name for it. I gave it the name of Rowan's B&B because I felt it was a nice comfortable place to stay and I wanted to include it so you, too, could experience their hospitality. So don't be dismayed if the B&B now has a new name!)

THE MEADOWS B&B, *81 Coast Road, Cushendall BT44 0QW. Tel. (028) 2577-2020. 5 rooms. Rates for singles: UK£18, doubles: UK£15 per person sharing. Rates include breakfast. No credit cards accepted. No service charge.*

Another of the new B&Bs on the Coast Road along the eastern coast of County Antrim, The Meadows is a lovely new facility. Mrs. Anne Carey is proud of this tastefully decorated B&B that looks out on the sea. Rooms at the front of the house have views of the North Channel, and the rooms at the back have views of the countryside. Even though the sea views out the front bedrooms are nice, the B&B sits on a rather busy road, and the traffic noise is noticeable. Try the rooms in the back of the house for the best night's sleep.

CAIREAL MANOR, *90 Glenravel Road, Glens of Antrim, Martinstown, Ballymena, BT43 6QQ. Tel. (028) 2575-8465. 5 rooms. Rates for singles: UK£25, doubles: UK£25 per person sharing. Rates include breakfast. No credit cards accepted. No service charge.*

You'll find this brand new B&B on the A43 between Ballymena and Waterfoot at the edge of Martinstown. The mauve and blue interior is pleasant and warm, and the rooms are tastefully and comfortably furnished. Mr. Pat O'Neill, owner of the Manor Lodge Restaurant, also owns Caireal Manor. The B&B features wheelchair access, one of the few in the country to do so. But Mr. O'Neill knows very well the necessity of that service, as he, too, requires it. A little pricey for a B&B, but a nice place.

WHITEPARK HOUSE COUNTRY HOME, *150 Whitepark Road (Coast Road), Ballintoy, Ballycastle, BT54 6NH. Tel. (028) 7073-1482; E-mail: bob.isles@virgin.net; Website: www.whiteparkhouse.com. 6 rooms, 3 ensuite, 3 standard. Rates for singles: UK£30 (standard room) and UK£38 (ensuite room), doubles: UK£24 per person sharing (standard room) and UK£30 to UK£33 per person sharing (ensuite room). Rates include breakfast. Credit cards not accepted. No service charge.*

Without a doubt, Bob and Siobhan Isles run one of the prettiest country home B&Bs in Northern Ireland. The home is over 250 years old (it was built in 1734), has been lovingly restored, and is richly and tastefully decorated. It has, as they say, a lot of character. It's a classy place, and mirrors its owner's tastes and personalities. Lest you think I am biased in my opinion, others have noticed this wonderful place — it has thrice been named "Guesthouse of the Year" in County Antrim. If plants are your friends, you'll feel right at home here. Whitepark House Country Home might be mistaken for a greenhouse with furniture! Siobhan and Bob combine their domestic capabilities with green thumbs to provide you with a pleasant atmosphere to relax in.

Each of the rooms is individually decorated, and each is large and roomy. Several of the rooms overlook the ocean, and the others overlook the wonderful gardens. This would be a great central point for touring the Antrim coast. Three rooms are standard (no bathroom in the room), and three are ensuite. The ensuite rooms are new, and each has a wonderful view of the sea.

Be sure and call ahead for reservations, because if you don't, there's a good possibility that you won't be spending the evening here. Breakfast is a treat and, as you might suspect, the menu includes vegetarian choices.

DRUMNAGREAGH HOTEL, *Coast Road, Glenarm BT440BD. Tel. (028) 2884-1651. 16 rooms. Rates for singles: UK£40, doubles: UK£60, children under age 12 stay free with their parents. Rates include breakfast. Restaurant and pub. All major credit cards accepted. No service charge.*

This 100-year-old Victorian inn sits atop a hill above the Coast Road, offering stunning views across the Irish Sea to Scotland. It is far enough above the road below that noise from traffic is not an issue. The rooms are all spacious and nicely decorated. Some rooms have views of the Irish Sea, and the others look out on verdant hills and pastoral sheep.

LONDONDERRY ARMS HOTEL, *Glens of Antrim, Carnlough BT44 OEH. Tel. (028) 2888-5255, (028) 2888-5263. 35 rooms. Rates for singles: UK£45, doubles: UK£65. Restaurant and pub. All major credit cards accepted. No service charge.*

Note that while this is called the Londonderry Arms, it is not in Londonderry, but rather in Carnlough among the Glens of Antrim. A lovely old Victorian coaching inn once owned by Winston Churchill, this creeper-clad hotel is a popular base from which to explore the Glens of Antrim and this part of the Antrim coast. The hotel is scattered with antiques throughout, newly refurbished from top to bottom. Across the street from the hotel is their carpark, and beyond that is a series of gardens and patios for guests to enjoy. The views of Carnlough Harbor from here are beautiful.

The public areas are a bit cramped. However, on the first floor there is a delightful sitting room chock full of interesting antique oddities and a warm and aromatic turf fire burning in the fireplace. It's a nice place to relax before or after you investigate the surrounding areas. Two pubs in the hotel are well attended by locals as well as guests. Rooms are large, spacious, and comfortable. Those overlooking the harbor are a little noisy due to the traffic on the street below. The hotel offers discounts for children on room rates as well as in their restaurant. Baby-sitting service is also available.

BUSHMILLS INN HOTEL, *25 Main Street, Bushmills, BT57 8QA. Tel. (028) 2073-2339, (028) 2073-2048. 11 rooms. Rates for singles: UK£50, doubles: UK£95; children under age 12 stay free with parents. Rates include breakfast. Restaurant. American Express, Mastercard, and Visa accepted. No service charge.*

Call ahead and make reservations, because you're going to love this hotel. Located in downtown Bushmills, the Bushmills Inn feels like an old stagecoach hotel. Well-kept and clean, you get an old world feel as you walk into the hotel (the structure dates back to the 1600s). The small reception area is warmed – figuratively as well as literally – by an open turf fire, warm dark wood, gas lights, and a grand staircase leading upstairs. The rooms are large, light, and airy. The rooms facing the main street are a bit noisy, so ask for a room off the street. The Bushmills Inn is proud of their recent induction into the publication entitled, *"The Best Loved Hotels of the World."*

DUNADRY INN, *2 Islandreagh Drive, Dunadry BT41 2HA. Tel. (028) 9443-2474, Fax (028) 9443-3389. 67 rooms. Rates for singles: UK£50, doubles: UK£55 per person sharing; children up to 5 stay free in their parents' room. Rates include breakfast. Restaurant, indoor swimming pool, spa, fitness center, garden, croquet, miniature golf, bicycles, sauna, solarium. All major credit cards accepted. No service charge.*

The Dunadry Inn is a converted 18th-century paper and linen mill, and they have succeeded in providing a nice facility. The hotel is really striving for a country-club feel, and offers an indoor swimming pool, exercise room, sauna, solarium, and even goofy golf. The rooms are large and well furnished. If you've brought your computer along to do a little work, ask for one of the executive rooms, as they offer computer ports. Special discounts for children and seniors are available.

BALLYGALLY CASTLE HOTEL, *Coast Road, Ballygally BT40 2QR. Tel. (028) 2858-3212, Fax (028) 2858-3681. 60 rooms. Rates for singles: UK£49, doubles: UK£74 per person sharing, suites: UK£90 per person sharing. Rates include breakfast. Restaurant and pub. All major credit cards accepted. No service charge.*

Unlike many hotels that call themselves the "Castle Hotel," Ballygally Castle Hotel (or at least parts of it) was once a genuine castle. Built in 1625 (you can still see the date inscribed in one section of the hotel), it was converted into a hotel in the 1970s. The rooms are large and comfortable. A few years ago they recently expanded the hotel, adding 30 new rooms.

The hotel boasts their own friendly, albeit mischievous, ghost. Legend has it the Lady Isabel Shaw had been locked in one of the tower rooms by her cruel husband. To escape her confinement, she cast herself from the window. They say she still visits on occasion, moving softly through the halls, amusing herself by tapping on the doors of guests' rooms. Her room has not been converted to a guest room, and it is furnished much like it might have been during her confinement. You can see the room by ascending a narrow winding staircase up one of the turrets of the original castle.

GALGORM MANOR, *136 Fenaghy Road, Ballymena BT42 1EA. 23 rooms. Rates for singles: UK£65, doubles: UK£65 to UK£90 per person sharing, suites: UK£125 per person sharing. Rates include breakfast. Restaurant, pub, gardens, riding, fishing. All major credit cards accepted. No service charge.*

This converted Georgian "gentlemen's residence" is off by itself near the River Main. The grounds impart a pleasant serenity. The public areas have been recently redecorated, with antiques to set the atmosphere. The best rooms are the Executive bedrooms, as they continue the traditional Irish motif, including a number of antiques. The rest of the rooms, although large and spacious, are more modern and don't give you quite the same feel.

Gillies Pub is a popular venue with both the locals as well as the hotel's guests, and would be a good place for you to rub (and bend!) elbows with a few real characters. The pub, along with the rest of the public areas, carries through the traditional Irish feel and atmosphere. Galgorm Manor sits amid 85 acres, and they have an equestrian center on-site that enables you to see the grounds via horseback if you wish (although there is an extra charge).

WHERE TO EAT

VALERIE'S PANTRY, *125 Main Street, Bushmills. Tel. (028) 7073-2660. UK£1.40 to UK£3.50. Open April through October Monday through Saturday from 9:00am to 6:00pm, and Sunday from 1:00pm to 9:00pm. During* *the winter, the hours are Monday through Saturday from 9:00am to 5:00pm. No credit cards accepted. No service charge.*

Just up the hill on Main Street from the round-about in the center of town is Valerie's Pantry, a delightful little cafe that offers snacks and sandwiches for a quick bite. From scones to roast beef sandwiches, Valerie's offers you good food at fair prices. The furnishings are simple and the food is good.

TEMPLETON HOTEL RESTAURANT, *882 Antrim Road, Templepatrick, Ballyclare. Tel. (028) 9443-2984. UK£7.95 to UK£12.95. Open daily from 7:00pm to 9:45pm. All major credit cards accepted. No service charge.*

The restaurant in the Templeton Hotel is a nice place bordering on elegant. Wedgwood china, crystal, and starched linen tablecloths add accent to the traditional Irish (with French influences) menu. The fare is well presented, tasty, and reasonably priced. Dress is nice casual.

TERRACE RESTAURANT, *Belfast International Airport. Tel. (028) 9442-2033. UK£6.50 to UK£14.50. Open daily from 6:00am to 10:00am, noon to 3:00pm, and 6:00pm to 10:00pm. All major credit cards accepted. No service charge*

You probably won't drive out to Belfast International Airport specifically to eat dinner at the Terrace Restaurant in the Aldergrove Hotel, but if you're staying here or find yourself in the area, it's a decent and reasonably priced restaurant. Try their gammon and pineapple or their roast beef wrapped in bacon. Dress is nice casual.

LONDONDERRY ARMS HOTEL RESTAURANT, *20 Harbor Road, Glens of Antrim, Carnlough. Tel. (028) 2888-5255. Set lunch menu for UK£10.95, and set dinner menu for UK£14.95. Open 8:00am to 10:00am for breakfast, noon to 3:00pm for lunch, and 5:00pm to 9:00pm for dinner. All major credit cards accepted. No service charge.*

The restaurant for the Londonderry Arms Hotel is popular with hotel guests, tourists, and the Irish as well. The atmosphere and decor are unmemorable (although they are planning extensive renovations), but the food is considered a good buy for the money. Try the roast leg of lamb with mint or the grilled fresh cod. They offer set menus as well as á la carte. Dress is casual.

MANOR LODGE RESTAURANT, *120 Glen Road, Glenariff. Tel. (028) 2575-8221. Set lunch menu for UK£11.95, and set dinner menu for UK£15.95. Owner Pat O'Neill says they are open from 11:00am to 9:00pm "or whenever everyone has gone home." American Express, Mastercard, and Visa accepted. No service charge.*

This wonderful restaurant set at the foot of Glenariff Waterfall is a favorite among tourists as well as natives alike. Always busy, the restaurant offers excellent fare for a reasonable price. Try the fresh fillet of Red Bay plaice poached in white wine, or the tenderized Irish beef topped with prawns and sautéed in garlic butter. The dress ranges from casual to jacket. Plenty of patrons here are mid-hike on one of the numerous walking trails at Glenariff National Park.

BUSHMILLS INN RESTAURANT, *25 Main Street, Bushmills. UK£9.45 to UK£17. Open daily from noon to 9:30pm. (They close at 9:00pm on Sunday.) American Express, Mastercard, and Visa accepted. No service charge.*

From the moment you enter, you'll be warmed – first by the open turf fire in the reception area, and then by the service. The restaurant is proud of its membership in the "Taste of Ulster," an elite restaurant society in Northern Ireland. According to the restaurant manager, the secret of their gastronomical success is in the freshness of the local produce, poultry, meat, and seafood they provide. Look for such main courses as roast rack of lamb or braised barony duckling, poached salmon, or smoked sea trout. The menu varies from time to time, and you're sure to find something you'll like. The restaurant itself is a series of booths; old white-washed stone walls and distressed pine gives kind of an old world ambiance. Casual dress is fine.

And don't forget **The Old Schoolhouse Restaurant**, on the road from Belfast City to the airport, and reviewed above in Belfast, *Where to Eat.*

SEEING THE SIGHTS

As you drive on the A2 between Larne and Ballycastle, take in the incredible seascapes. as well as the famous **Glens of Antrim**. Nine of them in all, they are deep, heavily forested glades, some of then with quasi-tropical greenery. The prettiest of these is **Glenariff**, and its Glenariff Forest Park (see below) provides numerous paved walking trails of varying lengths through the lush greenery. Bus service is provided to the Glens by Ulsterbus. *Contact them at Tel. (028) 9033-3000 for times and schedules (they vary throughout the year.*

At Cushendall, watch for signposts for **Glenariff Forest Park** (B14). Known as the "Queen of the Glens," Glenariff Forest Park is billed as an "area of outstanding natural beauty," and it truly is. You have a choice of numerous walking paths, featuring cascading waterfalls, beautiful wild flowers, and dense undergrowth. The beautiful, moist gorges support a wide variety of plant life. Several walking trails are available from a half mile stroll up to a nine mile scenic trek. The three-mile waterfall trail is the most popular and, I think, the prettiest. At the edge of the car park is a sign detailing the various hiking paths available in the park. The various paths range from several hundred yards to 10 miles, with something for everyone, it seems.

In Cushendun, look for signposts directing you to **Torr Head Road**. This ribbon-like road snakes around the northeastern tip of Northern

Ireland, a scarce 12 miles from Scotland at its closest point. It is a very narrow road, but well-maintained. If you get a little queasy on windy roads, follow he signs in Cushendun for Ballycastle, and you'll enjoy a more inland route.

But if you venture out on Torr Head Road, you'll be richly rewarded for your daring. On a clear day the views are stunning, and you might enjoy pulling off the road and listening to the surf crashing against the rocks below you. If you do – hold onto your hat; or better yet, leave it in the car. Otherwise, it may become part of the flotsam below.

Torr Head Road ends about two miles southeast of **Bonamargy Friary**, *Ballycastle*. Lying next to a golf course on the south-eastern edge of Ballycastle on the A2 are the overgrown ruins of Bonamargy Friary. Founded in the 1500s by Rory McQuillan, the friary thrived for several centuries before its destruction by the (dratted) McDonnells, arch-enemies of my kinsmen the McQuillans. Take a few minutes and wander among the ruined walls of this Franciscan friary. See if you can find the small round stone cross of **Julia McQuillan**, the Black Nun (it's easy to find – it's marked). Legend has it that Julia still roams the deserted friary (see sidebar on next page). By the way, watch your head – the entranceways are very low. I have painful first-hand experience.

Look in the corner of the graveyard for a large cross that marks the site of the final resting place of soldiers washed ashore during both world wars.

Ballycastle lies on the northeast coast of Northern Ireland on the A2. Ballycastle is famous for two fun festivals each year. On the last Tuesday and Wednesday of August each year, they hold their *Oul' Lammas* Fair, a festival that has been held here every year since 1606. It is a modern celebration of the Celtic harvest festival called *Lughnasa*. During mid-June, Ballycastle hosts the *Fleadh Amhran agus Rince*, a lively three-day folk festival featuring lots of dancing and traditional music.

Rathlin Island. Lying offshore from Ballycastle is the large, stony Rathlin Island. Its main claim to fame is that it was from Rathlin Island that **Guglielmo Marconi** established the first radio link between the Rathlin Island lighthouse and Ballycastle.

Carrick-a-Rede, *near Ballintoy, open April, May, June and September daily from 10:00am to 6:00pm, and daily in July and August from 10:00am to 8:00pm. Admission is free, although the carpark costs UK£2.50.* West of Ballycastle just off the A2 on the B15 near Ballintoy, watch for the signposts directing you to Carrick-a-Rede rope bridge. The rope bridge is suspended 80 feet above the ocean across a chasm 60 feet wide. Now, neither of those may seem high, until you are in the middle of this swaying rope bridge. Access is via a pleasant half-mile walk up a slight incline. The

THE BLACK NUN OF BALLYCASTLE

Despite the fact that he built Bonamargy Friary – see previous page – the only member of Rory McQuillan's Clan to be buried at Bonamargy Friary is a woman named Julia McQuillan (sometimes spelled McQuillian), known as the **Black Nun.** *Born in the 17th century, Julia, whose Irish name was Thula Dubh Na Uillin, was the Mother Abbess at the friary for a number of years. She was known as a religious recluse and noted far and wide for her humility and piety. In addition, she was considered by many in the country to be a prophetess. She prophesied of the day when carriages would travel the roads of Ballycastle without the use of horses, and that ships would sail the seas without the assistance of sails – clear prophecies of the automobile and steamship.*

As the local prophetess, she was also known for her intolerance of the improprieties of the human creature. Her demands of excessive penance for minor transgressions became legendary, even during her lifetime. But such was the respect bestowed upon her that the local townsfolk supported her enthusiastically.

Even her death is the stuff of legends. One legend is that she died violently during a battle when the McDonnell Clan took the friary from the McQuillans. She is said to have met her death from a McDonnell arrow. As she slumped on the steps of the friary, she reportedly cursed all McDonnells.

Her fame grew after her death when locals learned that Julia had requested to be buried near the steps to the chapel, so that worshipers would tread on her grave as they came to pray – another example of her abject humility.

Her grave marker is a small cross with a round hole in it. Over the centuries since her death, many have reported seeing a shadowy figure dressed in a dark nun's habit, gliding through the friary near the cross. Most claim it's the spirit of Julia McQuillan, doing her own penance for cursing the McDonnell Clan with her dying words.

rope bridge is installed each May and taken down each September by salmon fishermen who need access to the fishery on the small island.

As you walk across the bridge and near the middle, you'll swear there is a prankster behind you jumping up and down on the bridge, causing it to undulate wildly under your feet. A quick glance over your shoulder will prove that it is your own amplified movement on the bridge that is causing the swaying.

Hold tight, move slowly, and you're sure to leave with a pleasant memory and feeling a little bolder for the effort.

Giant's Causeway, *near Bushmills, Causeway Head, open all year. September through June the hours are variable, depending on demand, but generally 10:00am to 5:00pm; July and August it is open daily from 10:00am to 7:00pm. Admission to the audiovisual presentation is UK£2 for adults and UK£1 for children. The car park is UK£3.00, or you can park for free on the road, about 100 yards from the entrance. Tel. (028) 7073-1855.* The Giant's Causeway lies on the B146 just off the A2 between Ballintoy and Bushmills. Watch for the signposts directing you here, whether you are coming from Bushmills or Ballintoy.

Giant's Causeway is one of two things: it is either an incredibly interesting work of nature, or it might be, as the legends say, the handiwork of the giant Finn MacCool who was trying to build a stepping-stone bridge to Scotland to find a wife. Either way, the sight is fascinating.

Geologists tell us that Giant's Causeway is a group of 40,000 symmetric hexagonal stone columns formed millions of years ago by rapidly cooling molten lava. They are absolutely fascinating and probably unlike anything you have ever seen.

Stop first at the Visitors Center. It is well done, and helps you understand the scientific explanation for the geological oddity you're about to see. You'll also learn here about the fate of the *Girona*, a Spanish ship of the ill-fated Spanish Armada that foundered on the rocks not far from the Giant's Causeway at a point now called *Port-na-Spania*. Her cargo of gold and jewelry was recovered in the late 1960s, and some of the more interesting artifacts are on display in the **Ulster Museum** in Belfast.

From the Visitors Center, you have two options to reach the Causeway. The first (my preference) is a cliff-top walk of about a mile and a half to some very steep steps descending to the shore below. You actually overshoot the main attraction by several hundred yards, but the scenery is well worth it. You can come back that way, or do the more direct shot from the rocks up a fairly steep hill back to the Visitors Center. A shuttle bus runs constantly between the two points, and is available for UK£1 each way. The second way is to head straight down the hill by foot or shuttle.

What you find there nearly defies description – you'll almost believe it's not possible that what you are seeing is really the work of mother nature. All these hexagonal basalt pillars stacked next to one another, more than you can possibly count. They're fun to sit on, walk amongst, and get your picture taken on. Don't miss this sight if you're in the area.

Bushmills Distillery, *Bushmills, open June through August Monday through Saturday from 9:00am to 5:30pm, September through May Monday through Thursday from 9:00am until noon, and from 1:30 to 5:00pm, Friday from 9:00am to 1:00pm. Admission is UK£2.50 for adults, UK£1 for seniors and children, and a family ticket is available for UK£6.50. Tel. (028) 7073-1521.*

Bushmills is a quiet village famous for its wild drinks. A distillery on this site has been brewing whiskey since 1608, and by now they have the process down pretty well. It is thought that the Bushmills distillery is the oldest in the world – at least the oldest *legal* distillery! The Bushmills Distillery produces their famous brand of Irish whiskey here on the northern coast of Ulster. Guided tours are conducted to give you a "flavor" for their process, including a wee nip at the end!

As you follow the A2 out of Bushmills toward Portrush, watch for the ancient ruins of **Dunseverick Castle**. Actually, the smallish ruins, between the road and the ocean on a rocky promontory, are really what is left of the gate house of the castle – the castle is long gone. Dunseverick was once the capital of the ancient Irish kingdom of Dalriada. It was from this point that a series of kings ruled this part of Ireland. But alas! Dunseverick fell – not as the victim of war or famine, but rather as the result of treachery, unrequited love, and vengeance. The story surrounding Dunseverick's demise is one of Ireland's oldest love stories (see sidebar below).

A LOST LOVE

*King Conor of Dalriada was a powerful king, as many Irish kings were in the old times. To secure additional power, Conor sought the hand of Deirdre, the daughter of a powerful ally in Scotland. **Deirdre** was agreeable to the arrangement, and made the trip to Dunseverick in preparation for her marriage. However, affairs of the heart interfered with affairs of the kingdom: Deirdre fell head-over-heels in love with **Noisi**, one of King Conor's bodyguards. Before the marriage could take place, Deirdre and Noisi fled to Scotland to unite their love and, I suspect, to avoid the wrath of Conor!*

*King Conor was indeed angry, but he was also filled with guile. He called his trusted captain **Fergus** to his side, and told him that although he loved Deirdre, his greatest desire was for her and Noisi to be happy. He implored Fergus to go to Scotland, assure Noisi and Deirdre that all was well, and bid them return for a celebration of their marriage.*

Fergus found the young couple and convinced them of the king's forgiveness and sincerity. They consented to return to Ireland with Fergus. (Big mistake!) Upon their return, they met reprisal rather than forgiveness. Conor slew Noisi, and took Deirdre as his beloved (if not loving) bride. In her sorrow, Deirdre killed herself by dashing her head against a stone. Fergus was incensed by the duplicity of the king, and in a fit of anger he killed King Conor and razed Dunseverick Castle.

Truth or fiction? We will never know, but the fact remains that only a few rocks resting above the foaming Atlantic are all that remain of the great kingdom of Dunseverick.

Dunluce Castle, *between Portrush and Bushmills, open April 1 through September 30 Monday through Saturday from 10:00am until 7:00pm, Sunday from 2:00pm until 7:00pm; October through March Monday through Saturday from 10:00am to 4:00pm, and Sunday from 2:00pm to 4:00pm. Admission is UK£1.50 for adults and UK75p for children.* Dunluce Castle stands between the A2 and the coast between Portrush and Bushmills, just outside of Portrush. Described variously in tourist brochures as brooding, romantic, somber, and inspiring, Dunluce is perched atop a natural basalt tower that rises abruptly out of the ocean. Surrounded on three sides by the ocean, and on the fourth by a gorge, Dunluce Castle was once considered an impregnable fortress. Its picture graces the cover of almost every tourist brochure for Northern Ireland.

Originally built in the 14th century, Dunluce Castle was the ancestral home of my ancestors — the McQuillans. For many generations, the McQuillans were able to rebuff the attacks of would-be conquerors of Dunluce Castle. Alas, what war could not accomplish, marriage and intrigue did, and the castle finally fell into the hands of the hostile McDonnells in the mid-1500s. (Do I sound bitter? Nah....) Many are the stories and legends that surround Dunluce Castle. Perhaps one of the most startling is the true story about the large banquet that was being hosted within the castle in 1639. The elite guests were gathering, and anticipation was running high when a horrible sound shattered the gaiety. Investigation revealed that the kitchen, along with its complement of cooks, had crashed into the churning sea below! The lady of the castle firmly and adamantly refused to stay one more day at Dunluce!

There is a 20-minute slide and audio show that covers the history of the area, and touches briefly on Dunluce Castle's role in it. The show really could spend more time on the history of the castle, but it is still well done.

SPORTS & RECREATION
Golf
Ballycastle Golf Club, *Ballycastle, County Antrim. Tel. (028) 7076-2536, UK£13/UK£18.*

Watch your wind-blown game here: in addition to the wind, you'll have to battle stunning sea views, a trip around Bonamargy Friary (watch out for the ghostly spirit of Julia McQuillan, the Black Nun!), and a few sand traps to trip you up. Visitors are welcome any time. Par 68, 5,692 yards.

Portstewart Golf Club, *Portstewart, County Derry. Tel. (028) 7083-2015, UK£22/UK£27.*

Portstewart is a venerable course, having hosted a century of golfers. Long fairways, scores of dunes and tricky traps are the menu for golfers who venture onto this links course. There are three courses to try your skills on, each one a little more difficult than the previous. The original course is an 18-hole gem that is perfect for those that are serious about their golf, but perhaps not quite ready for "prime-time." It is a par 64, 4,733 yard course. Next is a short, 9-hole course (par 32 and 2,662 yards). It is a genuinely beautiful course that takes you through the gently rolling hills of the Northern Ireland countryside.

But the real reason people from all over the world venture here is to sample the fairways and greens of the third course, called The Strand. Wending among the dunes and undulating hills in this part of the country, the course seems to get harder with each additional hole. My favorite hole at The Strand is the second. The tee box is elevated, and your drive will (hopefully) carry you between two sizable dunes to the emerald fairway below. But be careful and stay to the left, as the fairway is slanted steeply to the right. If you are even a wee bit too far to the right, you'll have a really tough shot to the green.

The templed hills of Northern Ireland surround the course and make it an especially memorable place to play. Visitors are welcome Monday, Tuesday, and Friday. The Strand is a Par 72, 6,478-yard course.

Royal Portrush Golf Course, *Portrush, County Derry. Tel. (028) 7082-2311, Dunluce Course: UK£37.50/UK£45, Valley Course: UK£15/UK£20.*

As wonderful as many of Ireland's golf courses are, Portrush has one honor that none of the others can claim: Royal Portrush Golf Course is the only Irish golf course to host a British Open. There are two courses here: the Dunluce Course, which hosted the British Open in 1951, and the Valley Course. As you might expect, the Dunluce Course is an intriguing course filled with challenging fairways, deadly roughs, and plenty of sand to navigate. Two of its tougher holes are named *Purgatory* and *Calamity*. The Valley Course is a bit milder and though it provides its fair share of challenges, is a little more amenable to the occasional golfer.

Visitors are welcome weekdays except Wednesday and Friday afternoons. The Dunluce Course is Par 72 and 6,650 yards, and the Valley Course is Par 70 and 6,054 yards. A small 9-hole course called The Skerries is also available for your pleasure.

Horseback Riding

- **Cairnview**, *13 Croft Road, Ballygally, County Antrim. Tel. (028) 2858-3269*
- **Dan Campbell's**, *2 Bridge Street, Larne, County Antrim. Tel. (028) 2827-7222*
- **Grassy Banks**, *5 Cairnbeg Crescent, Larne, County Antrim. Tel. (028) 2827-2438*
- **Te An Teasa**, *4 Coastguard Cottages, Ballygally, County Antrim. Tel. (028) 2858-3591*

Surfing
• **Atlantic Drive and Surf**, *102 Main Street, Portrush. Tel. (028) 7082-3272*

PRACTICAL INFORMATION

Post Offices
• **Ballycastle Post Office**, *Anne Street, Ballycastle. Tel. (028) 7076-2519*
• **Ballygally Post Office**, *Coast Road, Ballygally. Tel. (028) 2858-3229*
• **Cushendall Post Office**, *Mill Street, Cushendall. Tel. (028) 2577-1201*
• **Larne Post Office**, *Main Street, Larne. Tel. (028) 2827-2518*

Tourist Offices
• **Ballycastle Tourist Information Center**, *Sheskburn House, Ballycastle, 7 Mary Street. Tel. (028) 2076-2024*
• **Cushendall Tourist Information Center**, *Mill Street, Cushendall, Tel. (028) 2577-1180*
• **Dunluce Tourist Information Center**, *Portrush, Tel. (028) 7038-2333*

ELSEWHERE IN NORTHERN IRELAND

Because of the "troubles" through the years, and because Northern Ireland is largely rural, Northern Ireland has few developed sights to see, and most of those are in County Antrim. Many of the most impressive sights in the North are natural ones. If you wish to see other parts of Northern Ireland, select a hotel or B&B in County Antrim to use as a base. The **Bushmills Inn Hotel** or **Whitepark House** are two I would heartily recommend. Most of the sights elsewhere in Northern Ireland can be easily reached from either of these places.

If you are going to visit or spend time in western Northern Ireland (near Enniskillen), then I suggest you explore that from the Donegal area, using Mrs. McGinty's **The Arches Country House** as your base.

ARRIVALS & DEPARTURES

By Bus
Bus service is primarily to the major cities and towns of Northern Ireland, including Armagh and Derry (but you're not going to either of those places, remember?!), Omagh, Enniskillen, Newcastle, Portaferry, and Downpatrick. Here is where buses in most of those places stop:
• **Downpatrick** – Buses stop at the bus station at *83 Market Street, (028) 4461-2384.*
• **Enniskillen** – Buses stop at the bus station on *Wellington Road, Tel. (028) 6632-2633.*

- **Newcastle** – Buses stop at the bus station on *Railway Street, Tel. (028) 4472-2296.*
- **Omagh** – Buses stop at the bus station on *Mountjoy Road, Tel. (028) 8224-2711.*
- **Portaferry** – Buses stop at The Square.

By Car

There are many roads that run throughout Northern Ireland. The main arteries to the west are the M1/A4 and M2/A6. The A2 and A24 are the principle roadways into County Down, south of Belfast. Most of the roads are in very good condition, although they share the narrowness attribute with their Republican cousins to the south.

WHERE TO STAY

GLASSDRUMMAN LODGE, *85 Mill Road, Annalong, County Down, BT34 4RH. Tel. (028) 4476-8451, Fax (028) 4476-7041. 10 rooms. Rates for singles: UK£50, doubles: UK£60 per person sharing. Rates include breakfast. Restaurant, garden, tennis, riding, beaches. American Express, Mastercard, Visa accepted. No service charge.*

If it's magnificent views you want, then the Glassdrumman Lodge ought to satisfy you. Along with your room you can either have seascapes or mountain scenes. The rooms of this converted farmhouse are large and comfortable, with little additions such as mineral water, fresh flowers, and warm and friendly Irish hospitality. There is an excellent restaurant associated with this guesthouse also.

Glassdrumman Lodge is located in County Down in the village of Annalong. It is just north of the larger town of Kilkeel on the A2.

SEEING THE SIGHTS

The **Mourne Mountains** make their lofty presence known south of Belfast on the southeastern tip of Northern Ireland. Take either the A1 toward Newry or the A24/A2 toward Newcastle to venture into their rounded presence. **Percy French**, one of Ireland's more famous poet sons, wrote that the Mourne Mountains "sweep down to the sea," and in many cases they certainly do. The highest peaks (these are really very old and rounded granite mountains – not really peaks, *per se*) are 2,800 feet tall. Wind-swept and mostly devoid of trees, the Mournes offer an ominous starkness to the rest of this lush country.

The Mourne Mountains sit serenely on the southeast portion of both County Down and Northern Ireland. They are circumscribed on the west, south and east by the A2 as it glides along the Irish coastline. The B8 between Newry and Newcastle hems them in on the North. While you're in the area, you should definitely stop and see the **St. Patrick Heritage Centre**, *Downpatrick, open Monday through Friday from 11:00am to 5:00pm, Saturday and Sunday from 2:00pm to 5:00pm. Admission is free. Tel. (028) 4461-5218).* An 18th-century jail houses the St. Patrick Heritage Centre as well as the **County Down Museum**. Take a few minutes and tour both (they're not very extensive) for a secular and religious history of the area. Downpatrick is in eastern County Down at the junction of the A7 and the A25. The A7 comes southeast from Belfast directly into Downpatrick, and the A25 comes northwest from the coastal city of Newcastle.

If you venture to the southwestern part of Northern Ireland, you'll doubtless encounter **Lough Erne**. Of all the pretty lakes in Ireland, Lough Erne may well be the prettiest. Deep and blue, long and narrow, punctuated often by green islands, Lough Erne is a favorite with fishermen and families alike.

Lough Erne lies in the northwest corner of County Fermanagh. If you're coming from Belfast, take the M1 southwest from Belfast until it changes into the A4. From there, it will take you directly into Enniskillen, which sits between Lower and Upper Lough Erne. You can also reach it by taking the N15 south from Donegal Town to Ballyshannon, and then east on the R230 into Beleek. From there you can take the A47 to head around the northern and eastern sides of the lake, or you can take the A46 to drive along the southern and western shores of Lough Erne.

Devenish Island, *near Enniskillen, accessible from April through September, daily except for Monday. The fare is UK£2.* About three miles north of Enniskillen on the A32, watch for signposts directing you to Devenish Island. A short ferry ride to the island will introduce you to the ruins of a 12th-century monastery, several Celtic carvings, and a fine high cross.

Royal Inniskilling Fusiliers Regimental Museum. *Enniskillen, open all year Monday through Friday from 10:00am to 5:00pm, and May, through September on Saturday from 2:00pm to 5:00pm. It is also open in July and August on Sunday from 2:00pm to 5:00pm. Tel. (028) 6632-3142.* Enniskillen is a quiet town that sits alongside the River Erne as it flows the short distance between Lower Lough Erne and Upper Lough Erne. Along the banks of the River Erne you'll find **Enniskillen Castle**, home to the Royal Inniskilling Fusiliers Regimental Museum (what a mouthful!). The museum is devoted to soldiers who fought in the Napoleonic Wars. An impressive display of mementos from the war is included in the exhibit, including medals, weaponry, and bright, colorful uniforms.

Belleek Pottery Factory, *Belleek, open March through June Monday through Friday from 9:00am to 6:00pm, Saturday 10:00am to 6:00pm and Sunday 2:00pm to 8:00pm. July through September, Monday through Friday from 9:00am to 8:00pm, Saturday 10:00am to 8:00pm, and Sunday 2:00pm to 8:00pm. October through February Monday through Saturday from 9:00am to*

545 NORTHERN IRELAND 545

5:30pm, closed Saturday and Sunday. Admission is free. Tel. (028) 6865-8501. During your holiday in Ireland, you have doubtless seen many lovely examples of Beleek pottery. This creamy china known throughout the world is produced here along the northern banks of Lough Erne. Half-hour tours of the factory are available during the week. There is also a lovely display area/shop where you can marvel at the elegance Beleek pottery, and of course you can purchase some of their goods if you wish.

The diminutive village of Beleek sits at the junction of the R230, the A46, and the A47. From Enniskillen, take the A46 north along the western shores of the lake, and you can't miss it. If you are coming from Donegal, take the N56 to Ballyshannon, and then take the R230 east to Beleek. If you're coming from elsewhere in Northern Ireland, take the A32 south out of Omagh, and you'll drive right to the center of Lough Erne.

Follow the A47 out of town from Beleek northeast toward Drennan and watch for signposts directing you to **Lough Scolban**. Follow the signs a couple of miles into the countryside and you'll find a real jewel of a lake. This small but picturesque little lough is tucked serenely away in the rolling green hills of Northern Ireland, and you may be one of very few North Americans to see its lovely setting, as it is not mentioned in any other travel guides I am aware of. A nice place to stop, picnic, go for a walk, or skip stones, it could be one of your most pleasant memories of Ireland.

Castle Caldwell, *near Drennan*. Castle Caldwell is just a few miles outside of Beleek, on the A47 as it skirts the northern shores of Lough Erne. Watch for the entrance to the ruins of Castle Caldwell on the right-hand side of the road. The most intriguing artifact here is the tombstone of one Denis McCabe, a fiddler of some ability. While on a pleasure cruise on the lake in 1770, Denis fell overboard and drowned. The epitaph chiseled into his headstone gives us a clue as to the reason for his demise:

"Beware ye fidlers of ye fidlers fate
Nor tempt ye deep least ye repent too late.
Ye ever have been deemed to water
Foes then shun ye lake till it with whiskey flows.
On firm land only exercise your skill,
That you may play and safely drink your fill.
–To the memory of Denis McCabe, Fidler, who fell out of the St. Patrick Barge belonging to Sir James Calldwell Bart and Count of Milan and was drowned off this point August 17, 1770."

Poor Denis!

The headstone and plaque are at the entrance to Castle Caldwell. The headstone is weather-worn and barely legible, but the attached plaque tells the sad tale.

From Drennan, follow the A47 until it dead-ends into the A32. Turn left and follow the signposts to Omagh. About three miles north of Omagh on the A5 you'll come to the **Ulster American Folk Park**, *Camphill, County Tyrone, open Easter through September Monday to Saturday 11:00am to 6:30pm, Sunday from 11:30am to 7:00pm; October through Easter Monday through Friday from 10:30am to 5:00pm. (Last entrance allowed 90 minutes before closing.) Admission is UK£3 for adults and UK£1.50 for children. Tel. (028) 8224-3292.* This particular folk park presents an interesting angle to tourists. They have reconstructed a typical 18th-century County Tyrone village, as well as an American settlement from the same period. Their attempt is to compare and contrast the life Irish emigrants left for the life they found in America.

The main museum in the park is a whitewashed cottage believed to be the home of the ancestors of Andrew Mellon, the famous American millionaire.

The park is interesting, although not nearly as extensive as others of its ilk, like the Ulster Folk and Transport Museum outside Belfast.

SPORTS & RECREATION
Golf
Royal County Down, *Newcastle, County Down. Tel. (028) 4472-2419, UK£50.*

The Emerald Isle has many lovely golf courses, but there are many who contend that Royal County Down is the fairest of them all. As the Mourne Mountains "sweep down to the sea," you'll find Royal County Down nestled between those mountains and the sea they sweep down to. The course is one to try your skill as well as your ego, not to mention your scorecard! Hidden greens (shoot toward the markers!), ghastly dunes, nasty bunkers, and holes that have probably never played the same way twice are what await you at Royal County Down. But there are also lovely sea and mountain views to compensate you for a high score.

Royal County Down has hosted the British Amateur Open as well as the Curtiss Cup. Visitors are welcome Tuesday, Thursday, and Friday. There are two separate championship courses: Par 71, 6,991 yards and Par 71, 6,087 yards.

PRACTICAL INFORMATION
Post Offices
• **Downpatrick Post Office**, *65 Market Street, Downpatrick. Tel. (028) 4461-2061*
• **Newcastle Post Office**, *35 Central Promenade, Newcastle. Tel (028) 4472-2418*

Tourist Offices
- **Downpatrick Tourist Information Office**, *74 Market Street, Downpatrick, Tel. (028) 4461-2233*
- **Fermanagh Tourist Information Office**, *Wellington Road, Enniskillen, Tel. (028) 6632-3110*
- **Newcastle Tourist Information Office**, *10 Central Promenade, Newcastle, (028) 4472-2222.* Open only during the summer months.
- **Omagh Tourist Information Office**, *Market Street, Omagh, Tel. (028) 8224-7831*
- **Portaferry Tourist Information Office**, *Harbor Ferry Dock, Portaferry.* Only open during the summer months.

19. SEARCHING FOR YOUR IRISH ROOTS

Many Americans – an estimated forty million – trace their ancestry to the Emerald Isle. Because of that, many are prompted to return to Ireland and, in many cases, search a bit for their roots. In this chapter, I have included over five hundred and fifty Irish surnames and their traditional ancestral counties. Many Irish surnames originated in Scotland or England (Italy as well!), but since many of them have been in Ireland since the 16th and 17th centuries, they are now considered Irish, so I have included them in this listing.

Indeed, my love affair with Ireland came about as a result of an intense interest in renewing my acquaintance with the country of my forefathers. But my interest didn't end there – I was also interested in seeing if I could connect with any of my long-lost cousins. Never shy, I decided on a bold plan. First of all, it required a letter written to my Irish cousins. This is what I wrote:

Dear McQuillan Family,

Greetings from your long-lost American cousin! Doubtless you were unaware that you had a long-lost American cousin, at least not this one. But you do. In 1619 my tenth-great grandfather Teague McQuillan left County Antrim to see if he could improve his fortunes in the wilds of America. Ten generations later here I am, intensely interested in visiting the part of Ireland he left so long ago.

But that's not all. I am as interested in meeting other members of the McQuillan family as I am in seeing the Emerald Isle. Hence my letter. In May of next year, my wife and I are planning to visit Ireland and would like to be able to visit some of the cousins as well as the part of Ireland Teague was from.

We will be in Northern Ireland from May 3 through May 10, and would love to stop by and meet you. Please let me know if you will be available during that time, and we'll arrange our schedule to meet with you. Please write to us at the address below.

I know this may seem rather presumptuous and just a bit bold, but I really am interested in meeting other members of the McQuillan Clan, however distant along the family tree they may be.

Thanks, and I look forward to meeting with you when we are there.

Daniel McQuillan

After I wrote the letter, I made twenty copies. Then, from a map of Northern Ireland, I selected twenty small towns in County Antrim. (I think something like this will work better with small towns rather than larger cities.) I addressed each envelope with the family name and the name of one of the towns. For example, one of the letters was addressed as follows: *McQuillan Family, Larne, Northern Ireland.*

And then, in the bottom left-hand corner of the front of the envelope I wrote: *POSTMASTER: PLEASE DELIVER THIS LETTER TO ANY McQUILLAN FAMILY IN THE VICINITY.*

I sent the letters six months prior to our trip to Ireland. I was delighted to receive seven responses to my rather unorthodox method of contacting family. But the results were marvelous! We met a number of these Irish families, were entertained in their homes, and they showed us great kindness. We left much richer for our time with them.

The vast majority of Irish-Americans are here because of the mass migration here during the potato famine years of 1845 through 1847. During that dark period, it's estimated that over one million Irish men, women, and children sailed for America. That's almost two hundred and fifty years after my ancestors sailed for America. It is entirely possible that you may find some very near cousins, especially if you know a grandfather's or great-grandfather's name.

So, if you are of Irish extraction, give it a try. If you know nothing of your Irish connection, use the following information on traditional ancestral counties and send letters there. Cousin or not, you're sure to meet some wonderful people, and you'll likely establish some long-lasting friendships.

Another way for you to meet family if you are planning to go to Ireland is to see if your clan holds an annual or semi-annual clan rally (reunion). There is an organization in Ireland called the Clans of Ireland, and they serve as a clearinghouse for information on clan reunions. They are a non-profit organization working under the auspices of the Irish Tourist Board (Bord Failte). To contact the Clans of Ireland office, write or call the following:

Anne Kavanaugh, Clans of Ireland
2 Kildare Street, Dublin 2 Ireland
Tel. (01) 661-8811, extension 410

Below is a partial list of clans who hold rallies. Ms. Kavanaugh can help put you in contact with their representatives.

Allen	Gleeson
Baker	Greene
Barry	Griffin
Bradshaw	Gormley
Brennan	Hanly
Buckley	Hennessy
Butler	Heery
Burke	Heffernan
Callan	Herlihy
Carroll	Hickey
Cassidy	Hogan
Clancy	Horkan
Cleary	Huley
Clune	Jones
Collins	Joyce
Comerford	Kavanagh
Connolly	Keating
Cormican	Kelly
Crawford	Kennedy
Cronin	Kenny
Crowe	Keohane
Crowley	Kiely
Daly	Kilkenny
Dalton	Killoran
Delaney	Kinnane
Devlin	Kissane
Duffy	Lafferty
Dunne	Larkin
Elliott	Lewis
Evans	Long
Ferris	Lynch
Fitzgerald	MacClancy
Fitzgibbon	MacDermot
Gallahue	MacGeoghegan
Geraghty	MacRaith
Gettings	McAnallen

McAteer
McAuliffe
McCabe
McCarthy
McCullagh
McDonagh
McDuffee
McEgan
McGettigan
McGillycuddy
McKenna
McLoughlin
McManus
McNally
Namara
McQuillan
McSweeney
McGennis
Maguire
Maher
Marmion
Managan
Marnane
Moloney
Mooney
Moore
Muireagain
Mulcahy
Mullaney
Nolan
Noonan
O'Brien
O'Byrne
O'Callagan
O'Carragher
O'Cathain
O'Connell
O'Connor
O'Dea
O'Dochartaigh
O'Donnell
O'Donoghue
O'Dowd

O'Driscoll
O'Dubhda
O'Dwyer
O'Farrell
O'Flaherty
O'Flynn
O'Gara
O'Grady
O'Hanlon
O'Higgins
O'Keefe
O'Leary
O'Loughlin
O'Madden
O'Mahony
O'Malley
O'Meara
O'Neill
O'Rahilly
O'Reilly
O'Rourke
O'Shaughnessy
O'Scanlan
O'Shea
O'Sullivan
O'Toole
Patterson
Pierce
Quinlan
Quinn
Rafferty
Riordan
Ronan
Ryan
Shaw
Sheehan
St. John
Sugrue
Tierney
Troy
Turley
Whitty
Wingfield

BIG MAC OR BIG Mc?

Some of the books you read about Irish genealogy will claim that names beginning with "Mc" are Irish, while those beginning with "Mac" are Scottish. In *The Surnames of Ireland*, Edward MacLysaght indicates this is essentially rubbish. He contends that "Mc" is merely an abbreviation for "Mac." "Mc/Mac" means "son of", while "O'" means simply "of" (as in descended of – for example: O'Donnell signified "the descendants of Donnell," or "one who is part of the house of Donnell").

If your name isn't listed below, don't despair (certainly don't be offended!). It is simply not possible to list every Irish name; however, if your name isn't listed here, you can get a more complete listing (along with a history of the names) in several books. The first, *Irish Family Names* (W. W. Norton & Company, Inc., New York, NY 1982) by Brian de Breffny has an excellent listing of many Irish family names and their counties of origin. The other, mentioned above, is *The Surnames of Ireland* (Irish Academic Press Limited, Blackrock, Co. Dublin) by Edward MacLysaght. Both are well-researched and list hundreds of Irish names and the counties the families originated in. Those chosen for this book are the more common names found throughout Ireland and Northern Ireland.

If you can't find your surname, add (or remove) a "Mc" or "O" to (or from) your name. Irish emigrants often anglicized their names by dropping the prefix from their surnames. On the other hand, many Irish families dropped the prefixes while still in the "ould" country, only to have their descendants add the prefix back later.

In the list below, "Co." stands for County.

Acheson - Co. Fermanagh, Wicklow
Adair - Co. Antrim
Ahren - Co. Clare, Cork
Aiken - Co. Antrim
Allison - Co. Antrim, Donegal
Ambrose - Co. Cork, Limerick, Wexford
Anderson - Co. Antrim
Archbold - Co. Wicklow
Arthur - Co. Limerick
Athy - Co. Kilkenny
Aylmer - Co. Kildare

Bagott - Co. Dublin
Bannon - Co. Tipperary
Barnewall - Co. Dublin
Barnwall - Co. Cork, Meath

Barrett - Co. Cork, Mayo
Barron - Co. Waterford
Barry - Co. Cork
Bell - Co. Antrim, Derry, Down
Bellew - Co. Louth, Meath
Bergin - Co. Offaly
Bertagh - Co. Meath
Billry - Co. Limerick
Birmingham - Co. Galway, Kildare
Birn - Co. Mayo
Bissett - Co. Antrim
Blair - Co. Antrim
Blake - Co. Galway
Bodkin - Co. Galway
Bolger - Co. Carlow
Boyd - Co. Antrim, Derry
Boyle - Co. Donegal

Brady - Co. Cavan, Clare
Brehan - Co. Galway
Brehon - Co. Wexford, Tipperary
Brody - Co. Mayo
Brogan - Co. Sligo
Brosnaghan - Co. Kerry
Browne - Co. Galway, Limerick,
  Mayo, Wexford
Bryan - Co. Kilkenny
Buckley - Co. Cork
Burke - Co. Galway, Kildare, Limer-
  ick, Mayo, Sligo, Tipperary
Burnell - Co. Dublin
Butler - Co. Carlow, Kilkenny, Laois,
  Meath, Tipperary, Waterford,
  Wexford, Wicklow
Byrne - Co. Wicklow

Cahaney - Co. Mayo
Cahill - Co. Galway, Tipperary
Campbell - Co. Antrim, Tyrone
Carew - Co. Carlow
Carey - Co. Kerry, Kildare
Carrigan - Co. Cork
Carroll - Co. Kilkenny, Louth
Casey - Co. Cork, Kerry,
Cassidy - Co. Fermanagh
Cavanaugh - Co. Carlow, Wexford
Cheevers - Co. Carlow, Meath,
  Wicklow
Clancy - Co. Leitrim
Cleary - Co. Clare, Galway
Clerkin - Co. Limerick
Clifford - Co. Kerry
Clinton - Co. Louth
Cody - Co. Kilkenny
Cogan - Co. Laois
Colclough - Co. Wexford
Coleman - Co. Louth, Sligo
Coll - Co. Limerick
Comerford - Co. Kilkenny,
  Waterford
Commiskey - Co. Cork

Conaghty - Co. Sligo
Condon - Co. Cork
Connelan - Co. Tyrone
Conran - Co. Waterford
Conroy - Co. Roscommon
Considine - Co. Clare
Conway - Co. Longford
Cooke - Co. Carlow
Cody - Co. Kilkenny
Coghlan - Co. Cork, Offaly
Collins - - Co. Cork, Limerick
Concannon - Co. Galway
Connery - Co. Limerick
Coogan - Co. Galway, Kilkenny
Copeland - Co. Down
Coppinger - Co. Cork
Corcoran - Co. Fermanagh
Corrigan - Co. Fermanagh
Costello - Co. Mayo
Courtney - Co. Kerry
Creagh - Co. Clare
Cronin - Co. Kerry
Crotty - Co. Waterford
Crowley - Co. Roscommon
Cruise - Co. Dublin, Meath
Cullen - Co. Dublin, Kildare,
  Wexford
Culmore - Co. Donegal
Cunningham - Co. Tyrone
Curran - Co. Clare, Galway
Cusack - Co. Clare, Limerick, Meath

Dalton - Co. Meath, Westmeath
Daly - Co. Clare
Danaher - Co. Cork, Limerick,
  Tipperary
Darcy - Co. Galway, Meath
Dardis - Co. Meath
Dargan - Co. Meath
Davis - Co. Antrim, Dublin
Davoren - Co. Clare
Deane - Co. Donegal, Galway, Mayo
Dease - Co. Westmeath

De Bathe - Co. Meath
De Burgo - Co. Antrim, Down, Galway
De Clare - Co. Clare
De Cogan - Co. Cork
d'Exeter - Co. Mayo
De Geneville - Co. Meath
De Gernon - Co. Louth
DeLacy - Co. Antrim, Down
Delahoyde - Co. Dublin
Delamare - Co. Westmeath
Delgany - Co. Wicklow
De Martimer - Co. Meath
De Montmorency - Co. Kilkenny, Wexford
Dempsey-Co. Kildare, Laois, Offaly
Dennehy - Co. Cork, Kerry
De Prendergast - Co. Wexford
De Renzy - Co. Wexford
Dermody - Co. Clare
Desmond - Co. Cork
Devane - Co. Galway, Kerry
Devenish - Co. Fermanagh
De Verdon - Co. Westmeath
Devereux - Co. Wexford
De Vesey - Co. Kildare, Laois
Devine - Co. Fermanagh, Tyrone
Devlin - Co. Derry, Sligo, Tyrone
Dickson - Co. Donegal, Mayo
Dillon - Co. Galway, Mayo, Westmeath
Dineen - Co. Cork
Dobbins - Co. Antrim
Dobbs - Co. Antrim
Doherty - Co. Donegal
Dolan - Co. Cavan, Mayo
Donlevy - Co. Tyrone
Donnegan - Co. Armagh, Tyrone
Donnelly - Co. Donegal, Tyrone
Dowling - Co. Laois, Carlow
Doyle - Co. Dublin
Duffy - Co. Donegal, Monaghan
Duggan - Co. Cork, Galway

Dunluce - Co. Antrim
Dunn(e) - Co. Laois

Egan - Co. Galway, Tipperary
Ennis - Co. Dublin, Offaly
Enright - Co. Limerick, Cork
Eustace - Co. Carlow, Kildare

Fagan - Co. Dublin, Westmeath
Farrell - Co. Longford
Fay - Co. Westmeath
Feeney - Co. Galway, Mayo
Fenton - Co. Cork, Kerry
Ferguson - Co. Antrim
Finnegan - Co. Cavan, Galway
Fitzgerald - Co. Cork, Limerick
Fitzgibbon - Co. Cork, Limerick
Fitzmaurice - Co. Kerry, Mayo
Fitzpatrick - Co. Laois, Cavan
Flanagan - Co. Roscommon
Flannery - Co. Limerick, Mayo
Fleming - Co. Cork, Meath
Flynn - Co. Cork, Mayo
Fogarty - Co. Tipperary
Foley - Co. Kerry, Waterford
Ford - Co. Cork, Leitrim
Fox - Co. Meath
Furlong - Co. Wexford

Gallagher - Co. Donegal
Galligan - Co. Sligo
Garvey - Co. Armagh, Down
Garvin - Co. Mayo, Meath
Gannon - Co. Mayo
Getty - Co. Antrim
Gibbons - Co. Mayo
Gibson - Co. Antrim
Gillen - Co. Sligo, Tyrone
Gillespie - Co. Antrim, Donegal
Gilligan - Co. Derry
Gilmore - Co. Antrim
Gormly - Co. Donegal, Mayo
Gould - Co. Cork

Grace - Co. Kilkenny, Tipperary
Graham - Co. Antrim
Gray - Co. Antrim
Green(e) - Co. Clare, Fermanagh
Greer - Co. Antrim, Down
Griffin - Co. Clare, Kerry
Grimes - Co. Offaly

Hackett - Co. Carlow, Dublin
Hagerty - Co. Derry, Donegal
Hallahan - Co. Cork
Halligan - Co. Armagh
Hamill - Co. Antrim, Tyrone
Hamilton - Co. Antrim
Hanley - Co. Roscommon
Hanrahan - Co. Limerick
Hanratty - Co. Louth
Harrington - Co. Cork, Galway
Harris - Co. Dublin
Harrison - Co. Dublin
Hart - Co. Limerick, Meath
Harty - Co. Kerry, Laois
Healy - Co. Cork, Sligo
Hennessey - Co. Offaly
Henry - Co. Antrim, Donegal
Hickey - Co. Clare, Limerick
Higgins - Co. Sligo, Meath
Hogan - Co. Tipperary
Horan - Co. Galway, Mayo
Houlihan - Co. Clare, Offaly
Hughes - Co. Donegal, Meath
Hurley - Co. Clare, Cork
Hussey - Co. Meath, Kerry

Irwin - Co. Fermanagh
Ivers - Co. Louth, Clare

Jameson - Co. Antrim, Dublin
Jennings - Co. Mayo, Roscommon
Jordan - Co. Mayo
Joyce - Co. Galway, Mayo

Kane - Co. Derry

Kavanaugh - Co. Carlow, Wexford
Keane - Co. Derry, Galway
Kearney - Co. Clare, Mayo
Kearns - Co. Leitrim, Sligo
Keating - Co. Carlow, Wexford
Keegan - Co. Dublin
Keenan - Co. Antrim, Fermanagh
Kelleher - Co. Cork, Kerry
Kelly - Co. Antrim., Galway
Kenneally - Co. Limerick
Kennedy - Co. Clare, Wexford
Kenny - Co. Galway, Tyrone
Keogh - Co. Tipperary, Wicklow
Kerr - Co. Antrim
Kerrigan - Co. Mayo
Keyes - Co. Fermanagh
Kidd - Co. Dublin
Kiernan - Co. Cavan
Kilkelly - Co. Galway
Kilpatrick - Co. Antrim
Kirk - Co. Louth
Kirwin - Co. Galway
Kirkpatrick - Co. Antrim
Kitt - Co. Galway
Knox - Co. Derry, Mayo

Lacy - Co. Limerick
Laffan - Co. Wexford
Lambert - Co. Galway, Wexford
Landers - Co. Kerry
Larkin - Co. Galway, Wexford
Lavelle - Co. Galway, Mayo
Law - Co. Antrim
Lawless - Co. Galway
Lawlor - Co. Laois
Leahan - Co. Galway
Leech - Co. Mayo, Wicklow
Lennon - Co. Cork, Galway
Leonard - Co. Fermanagh
Lindsay - Co. Tyrone
Lockhart - Co. Antrim
Loftus - Co. Galway
Logan - Co. Antrim

Lonergan - Co. Tipperary
Lowry - Co. Tyrone
Lynch - Co. Galway, Tipperary
Lyons - Co. Cork, Galway

Madden - Co. Galway, Offaly
Madigan - Co. Clare, Limerick
Maguire - Co. Fermanagh
Magee - Co. Antrim
Magrath - Co. Fermanagh
Maher - Co. Tipperary
Malone - Co. Offaly, Westmeath
Mannion - Co. Galway
Martin - Co. Tyrone
Mason - Co. Fermanagh
Masterson - Co. Cavan, Wexford
Maxwell - Co. Antrim
Meagher - Co. Tipperary
Meehan - Co. Cork, Leitrim
Molloy - Co. Offaly
Monaghan - Co. Roscommon
Mooney - Co. Dublin, Offaly
Moore - Co. Kerry
Moran - Co. Galway, Kerry
Moriarty - Co. Kerry
Moroney - Co. Clare
Morris - Co. Galway
Morrison - Co. Antrim, Down
Morrissey - Co. Sligo
Moynihan - Co. Cork, Kerry
Mulcahy - Co. Cork, Limerick
Muldoon - Co. Clare, Galway
Mulholland - Co. Derry, Donegal
Mullane - Co. Derry, Tyrone, Kerry
Mulligan - Co. Donegal
Mullins - Co. Clare
Mulrooney - Co. Galway,
  Fermanagh
Mulroy - Co. Mayo
Murdoch - Co. Antrim
Murphy - Co. Cork, Donegal, Mayo
Murray - Co. Roscommon
Murtagh - Co. Meath

McAdam - Co. Cavan, Monaghan
McAllister - Co. Antrim
McAuley - Co. Fermanagh,
  Westmeath
McAuliffe - Co. Cork
McBride - Co. Donegal
McCabe - Co. Cavan, Monaghan
McCafferty - Co. Cavan, Mayo
McCaffrey - Co. Cavan, Fermanagh
McCann - Co. Armagh, Louth
McCarthy - Co. Cork, Tipperary
McCartney - Co. Antrim
McClean - Co. Antrim, Donegal
McClelland - Co. Donegal
McClintock - Co. Donegal
McClure - Co. Antrim
McConnell - Co. Derry, Tyrone
McCormick - Co. Longford,
  Tipperary
McCoy - Co. Galway
McCullough - Co. Antrim
McDermott - Co. Roscommon, Sligo
McDonnell - Co. Antrim, Clare
McDowell - Co. Roscommon
McElhinney - Co. Derry, Donegal
McEvoy - Co. Armagh, Westmeath
McFadden - Co. Donegal
McFarland - Co. Armagh
McGafney - Co. Cavan
McGarry - Co. Antrim, Leitrim
McGill - Co. Antrim, Donegal
McGeraghty - Co. Mayo, Sligo
McGibbon - Co. Mayo
McGilfoyle - Co. Tipperary
McGillicuddy - Co. Kerry
McGilligan - Co. Derry
McGilmore - Co. Monaghan
McGinty - Co. Donegal
McGonigle - Co. Derry, Donegal
McGovern - Co. Cavan
McGowan - Co. Cavan, Donegal
McGrath - Co. Donegal, Fermanagh
McGuiness - Co. Down

McGuire - Co. Fermanagh
McHale - Co. Mayo
McHugh - Co. Cavan, Donegal
McIlroy - Co. Antrim, Tyrone
McInerney - Co. Clare, Limerick
McIntyre - Co. Antrim
McKee - Co. Antrim, Derry
McKenna - Co. Kerry, Monaghan
McKeon - Co. Antrim
McKinley - Co. Antrim
McKnight - Co. Antrim, Derry
McLoughlin - Co. Derry, Donegal
McMahon - Co. Clare, Monaghan
McManus - Co. Fermanagh
McMaster - Co. Antrim
McMillan - Co. Antrim
McMurrough - Co. Carlow
McNally - Co. Antrim, Armagh
McNamara - Co. Clare
McNamee - Co. Derry
McNeill - Co. Antrim, Derry
McNulty - Co. Donegal, Mayo
McQuaid - Co. Antrim, Monaghan
McQuillan - Co. Antrim
McRory - Co. Down
McShane - Co. Antrim, Derry
McSharry - Co. Donegal, Leitrim
McSweeney - Co. Cork, Donegal

Nagle - Co. Cork
Neville - Co. Kildare
Newell - Co. Antrim, Kildare
Newman - Co. Cork
Nolan - Co. Carlow
Noonan - Co. Cork
Noone - Co. Galway, Mayo
Nugent - Co. Meath, Westmeath

O'Bannon - Co. Mayo, Offaly
O'Boyle - Co. Donegal
O'Bradley - Co. Cork
O'Breslin - Co. Donegal
O'Brien - Co. Clare, Limerick

O'Callaghan - Co. Clare, Cork
O'Carey - Co. Kildare
O'Carroll - Co. Kerry, Louth
O'Casey-Co. Limerick, Fermanagh
O'Cassidy - Co. Derry, Fermanagh
O'Coffey - Co. Galway
O'Connell - Co. Kerry
O'Connor - Co. - Kildare
O'Corcoran - Co. Tipperary
O'Cullen - Co. Cork
O'Curran - Co. Donegal
O'Curry - Co. Cavan, Cork
O'Daly - Co. Cavan, Cork
O'Dea - Co. Clare, Cork
O'Dennehy - Co. Waterford
O'Devin - Co. Fermanagh
O'Dell - Co. Limerick
O'Donnell - Co. Donegal, Galway
O'Donnelly - Co. Tipperary
O'Donohoe - Co. Tipperary
O'Donovan - Co. Cork, Limerick
O'Dooley - Co. Westmeath
O'Doolin - Co. Kerry
O'Dowd - Co. Mayo, Sligo
O'Doyle - Co. Carlow, Kilkenny
O'Driscoll - Co. Cork
O'Duffy - Co. Donegal
O'Dugan - Co. Mayo
O'Dunn - Co. Kildare, Meath
O'Dwyer - Co. Tipperary
O'Fallon - Co. Roscommon
O'Feeney - Co. Galway, Sligo
O'Finegan - Co. Roscommon
O'Flaherty - Co. Galway
O'Flanagan - Co. Fermanagh,
  Roscommon
O'Flynn - Co. Antrim, Cork, Kerry
O'Fogarty - Co. Tipperary
O'Gara - Co. Sligo
O'Garvey - Co. Armagh, Wexford
O'Grady - Co. Clare, Kerry,
  Limerick
O'Hagan - Co. Tyrone

O'Hagarty - Co. Derry, Kerry
O'Halahan - Co. Cork
O'Halligan - Co. Meath
O'Halloran - Co. Clare, Galway
O'Hanlon - Co. Armagh
O'Hanrahan - Co. Galway
O'Hara - Co. Antrim, Derry
O'Hare - Co. Armagh, Down
O'Hea - Co. Cork, Limerick
O'Healy - Co.
O'Hurley - Co. Cork
O'Kane - Co. Antrim, Derry
O'Kean - Co. Tipperary
O'Keefe - Co. Cork
O'Keenan - Co. Derry, Fermanagh
O'Kelly - Co. Down, Galway
O'Larkin - Co. Armagh
O'Leary - Co. Cork
O'Looney - Co. Cork
O'Lynch - Co. Cavan, Cork
O'Mahon - Co. Down
O'Mahony - Co. Cork, Kerry
O'Malley - Co. Mayo
O'Meara - Co. Tipperary
O'Moran - Co. Mayo, Sligo
O'Mulcahy - Co. Tipperary
O'Muldoon - Co. Fermanagh
O'Mullen - Co. Derry
O'Mulvey - Co. Leitrim
O'Murray - Co. Derry
O'Neill - Co. Antrim, Carlow
O'Neill - Co. Clare, Donegal
O'Nolan - Co. Carlow
O'Quigley - Co. Derry
O'Quinn - Co. Donegal, Limerick
O'Quinlan -Co. Kerry, Tipperary
O'Quinlevan - Co. Clare
O'Rafferty - Co. Donegal
O'Regan -Co. Cork, Laois, Meath
O'Reilly - Co. Cavan, Meath
O'Riordan - Co. Tipperary
O'Rooney - Co. Down
O'Rourke - Co. Leitrim

O'Ryan - Co. Carlow, Kilkenny
O'Scanlan - Co. Kerry
O'Scully - Co. Tipperary
O'Shanahan - Co. Tipperary
O'Shaughnessy - Co. Galway
O'Shea - Co. Kerry, Tipperary
O'Sheehan - Co. Limerick
O'Sullivan - Co. Cork, Kerry
O'Tierney - Co. Armagh
O'Toole - Co. Kildare, Wicklow
O'Tully - Co. Fermanagh
O'Toumey - Co. Cork

Patton - Co. - Antrim, Donegal
Peppard - Co. Louth
Petit - Co. Mayo, Westmeath
Phelan - Co. Kilkenny, Waterford
Phillips - Co. Kilkenny Mayo
Plunkett-Co. Cavan, Dublin, Louth
Power - Co. Waterford
Prendergrast-Co. Mayo, Waterford
Prunty - Co. Antrim, Derry
Purcell - Co. Kilkenny, Tipperary

Quigley - Co. Derry, Mayo
Quillen - Co. Antrim
Quinlan - Co. Meath, Tipperary
Quinn - Co. Antrim, Clare, Derry
Quirk - Co. Kilkenny, Tipperary

Rafferty - Co. Donegal, Sligo,
  Tyrone
Raftery - Co. Galway
Redmond - Co. Wexford, Wicklow
Reynolds - Co. Leitrim
Riddell - Co. Down
Riordan - Co. Antrim
Roche - Co. Cork, Kilkenny
Rogers - Co. Armagh, Meath
Ross - Co. Donegal, Wexford
Rooney - Co. Down
Rossiter - Co. Wexford
Ryan - Co. Limerick, Tipperary

Sarsfield - Co. Cork, Dublin, Limerick
Savage - Co. Down
Scanlan - Co. Cork, Kerry, Louth
Scott - Co. Laois
Scully - Co. Tipperary, Westmeath
Segrave - Co. Dublin
Sexton - Co. Cavan, Limerick
Shanahan - Co. Clare
Shanley - Co. Leitrim
Shannon - Co. Clare, Fermanagh
Sharkey - Co. Derry, Donegal, Tyrone
Shaw - Co. Cork, Tipperary
Sheehan - Co. Cork, Limerick
Sheehy - Co. Kerry, Limerick
Sheridan - Co. Cavan, Longford
Shields - Co. Donegal
Sherlock - Co. Kildare, Meath
Shortall - Co. Kilkenny
Slattery - Co. Clare, Limerick, Kerry
Spillane - Co. Cork, Kerry, Sligo
Stack - Co. Cork, Kerry
Sutton - Co. Wexford

Taafe - Co. Louth
Taggart - Co. Antrim
Talbot - Co. Waterford, Wicklow
Tierney - Co. Donegal, Mayo
Tobin - Co. Cork, Limerick
Toner - Co. Derry, Donegal
Tracey - Co. Cork, Galway
Troy - Co. Clare, Limerick
Tulley - Co. Cavan, Longford
Tynan - Co. Laois
Tyrell - Co. Dublin, Westmeath

Ventry - Co. Kerry

Wadding - Co. Waterford, Wexford
Wade - Co. Dublin, Longford
Waldron - Co. Cavan, Mayo
Wall - Co. Carlow, Kilkenny
Walsh -Co. Cork, Mayo, Kilkenny
Walsh - Co. Waterford, Wexford
Ward - Co. Donegal, Galway
Warren - Co. Monaghan, Wicklow
Weir - Co. Antrim, Derry
White - Co. Down, Limerick
Wilkinson - Co. Donegal
Woulfe - Co. Cork, Kildare
Wright - Co. Antrim, Derry
Wylie - Co. Antrim

INDEX

For individual castles, all listings are under *"Castles."*

THINGS CHANGE!

Phone numbers, prices, addresses, quality of food, etc, all change. If you come across any new information, we'd appreciate hearing from you. No item is too small! Drop us an email note at: Jopenroad@aol.com, or write us at:

Ireland Guide
Open Road Publishing, P.O. Box 284
Cold Spring Harbor, NY 11724

OPEN O ROAD PUBLISHING